HAVEN CORPORATION

 Frito Lay

RR DONNELLEY & SONS COMPANY

 CURTIS

 ...ANN-ERICKSON

 CNN

Price Waterhouse

 The Mail Order Wizard

WAL★MART

 WB WELBRO CONSTRUCTORS, INC.

 Fidelity Investments

 SPa

WAL★MART

 British Columbia's Children's Hospital

 Levi's

 Mrs. Fields COOKIES

 Architectural Energy Corporation

Coopers &Lybrand

 RAINBOW TECHNOLOGIES

DELL™

 Paramount / Paramount Publishing

Donald H. Kraft & Associates

 Farmland

 AMERICAN EXPRESS TRAVEL RELATED SERVICES An American Express company

 American Red Cross

SARA LEE CORPORATION

 COMPUTERTOTS Computer Fun . . . for little ones

 CHEMICAL

 Pitney Bowes

RR DONNELLEY & SONS COMPANY

 Pitney Bowes

 Peapod

INFORMATION TECHNOLOGY IN
Business

PRINCIPLES, PRACTICES, AND OPPORTUNITIES

James A. Senn

Prentice Hall, *Englewood Cliffs, New Jersey* 07632

Library of Congress Cataloging-in-Publication Data

Senn, James A.
    Information technology in business / James A. Senn
    640 pp.
    Includes index.
    ISBN 0-13-484304-5
    1. Business—Data processing.   2. Information storage and
retrieval systems—Business.   3. Information technology.
4. Local area networks (Computer networks)   I. Title.
HF5548.2.S4366   1995   94-17259
650′ .0285—dc20   CIP

Director of Production & Manufacturing: Grace Walkus
Editor-in-Chief: Richard Wohl
Acquisitions Editor: P.J. Boardman
Development Editor: Steven Rigolosi
Managing Editor: Joyce Turner
Project Manager: Anne Graydon
Design Director: Patricia Wosczyk
Interior Design: Kenny Beck
Production Services Manager: Lorraine Patsco
Electronic Page Make-up: Christy Mahon
Cover Design: Patricia Wosczyk
Cover Illustrator: Syles Graphic Design
Photo Editors: Lori Morris-Nantz, Melinda Reo
Photo Researcher: Teri Stratford
Manufacturing Buyers: Patrice Fraccio, Paul Smolenski
Editorial Assistant: Dolores Kenny
Production Assistant: Renee Pelletier
Marketing Manager: Debbie Emry

©1995 by Prentice-Hall, Inc.
A Paramount Communications Company
Englewood Cliffs, NJ 07632

Printed in the United States of America.
10 9 8 7 6 5 4 3

ISBN 0-13-484304-5

Prentice-Hall International (UK) Limited, *London*
Prentice-Hall of Australia Pty. Limited, *Sydney*
Prentice-Hall Canada Inc., *Toronto*
Prentice-Hall Hispanoamericana, S.A., *Mexico*
Prentice-Hall of India Private Limited, *New Delhi*
Prentice-Hall of Japan, Inc., *Tokyo*
Simon & Schuster Asia Pte. Ltd., *Singapore*
Editora Prentice-Hall do Brasil, Ltda., *Rio de Janeiro*

To Jamie
(The next generation of know-how)
Always exploring; constantly learning;
never too "busy" to laugh…
And always able to get Grand Pa's attention!

Brief Table of Contents

Contents

Preface

A T ONE TIME, PEOPLE EQUATED INFORMATION TECHNOLOGY (IT) WITH computers. In fact, the acronym IT was rarely used because the focus was squarely on computing and data processing (or "DP"). The field, and expectations placed on it over the past decade, have advanced tremendously. Information technology is not just about computers, and it's not just for "computer people." Rather, it's about solving problems and creating opportunities, and it's for anyone who deals with either.

The book's title, *Information Technology in Business: Principles, Practices, and Opportunities*, reflects the basis, realities, and promise of information technology in business, both globally and locally. It also suggests its distinguishing characteristics:

- Focus on **information technology**
- Emphasis on **problem solving**
- Examination of actual **business experiences**
- Application to **professional practice**.

Information technology has three components. The first two are *computers* and *communication systems*. In business, as in all day-to-day activities affected by IT, it's not usually possible (or desirable) to separate one from the other. Capitalizing on the usefulness of one very often depends on the incorporation of the other.

The third component of information technology—the most difficult to describe simply—is *know-how*. In the past, the role of the IT professional was often described by such activities as systems analysis, software engineering and computer programming, database design, and management of data communications. While these roles are still important, they are now seen as part of a much greater design. Simply stated, the primary purpose of IT, and the primary responsibility of those who develop or use IT, is problem solving. Opportunity comes from having the know-how to apply the capabilities of computers and communication systems to solve problems and to help people and organizations reach their potential.

This book includes extensive discussion of the practical uses of IT in business internationally. You'll recognize the many examples of business practice throughout the book, all chosen to show how the world's best-known firms are capitalizing on IT to serve their stakeholders effectively. Because IT is not just for big businesses, many of these examples illustrate the impact of IT in creating opportunities for small business and individual entrepreneurs: artists, athletes, entertainers, inventors, journalists…the list is almost endless.

People look at information technology in many ways. Some focus on the IT capabilities that distinguish the newest action-packed video games.

Others see IT inside automobiles, almost invisible but responsible for their smooth operation. Still others notice IT only occasionally: in the stores, at theaters and concerts, inside the automated teller machine, at the airport, train station, or bus terminal—even at the counters of fast-food restaurants. No matter what focus one takes, one thing is crystal clear: Information technology is a part of our world and our daily life.

This book explores the way information technology is used and applied up and down the street...on main street, on back streets...and on your street. It reflects proven IT theories, frameworks, and principles. But it goes well beyond theory to explore the uses of information technology in the 1990s, always keeping in mind that IT is dynamic and ever-evolving. It examines the way IT is transforming commerce and careers. And like successful business leaders, it sets the stage for business and personal practices beyond 2000.

Organization

This book is organized into five parts. The first module, An Introduction to Information Technology, introduces the principles of information technology and describes the reasons for its extensive use in all types of businesses. Tech Talk, the second part, describes in detail the components of computers, including hardware and programs. A vast array of business uses of these IT components are described through illustration. If you're already familiar with the technical aspects of IT, this part will be useful to review the most recent developments in IT.

Part 3, Single-User Systems, examines the productivity tools people find most useful: spreadsheet programs, database systems, word processing, desktop publishing, presentation systems, and computer graphics. This part also discusses the development of single-user systems, including selection of both computer and communication hardware as well as personal productivity programs.

Multi-User Systems, Part 4, explores the way businesses interconnect many users within departments, across work groups, and throughout an enterprise. End-users also share IT resources that are distributed across miles, countries, or continents. Developing shared databases and shared applications places special requirements on the know-how of IT professionals, as this part also discusses.

Part 5, IT Issues and Opportunities, explores important challenges surrounding the use of information technology, including the issues of ethics, personal privacy, and IT security. The final chapter examines the emerging developments that will take us to the next steps in the Information Age.

Features

Each chapter emphasizes both knowledge and know-how, building a solid foundation of the basics of each topic discussed. The know-how is added through several hundred actual experiences of people in business.

Chapter Outline   Each chapter contains learning tools designed to assist readers in testing their understanding and ability to apply the principles and practices described in the chapter. Included in each chapter are:

- A detailed outline that previews the chapter's contents
- An opening vignette describing a practical use of information technology in business
- Learning objectives that focus readers on understanding key concepts and frameworks
- Practice objectives that ask the reader to consider ways to use the principles and practices in business

- A running marginal glossary of key terms introduced in the chapter
- A chapter summary keyed to learning objectives
- Key terms useful for review
- Review questions that test understanding of the chapter
- Discussion questions that raise thought-provoking, often controversial, issues
- Suggested readings for pursuing topics introduced in the chapter

Business and Professional Illustrations   Because this book focuses on IT practices in business, it emphasizes the actual experiences of real people and businesses as they use IT. All the examples use information drawn from multiple sources, including the companies themselves, to present an accurate, up-to-date description of information technology in action. In all cases, these examples pay particular attention to the guiding principles of IT, the pitfalls to avoid, and emerging opportunities.

For example, you'll recognize the many corporate names, including SONY, Crédit Lyonnais, Toyota, Phillips, Air Products Europe, AT&T, Helene Curtis, Sara Lee, Frito-Lay, Wal-Mart, and many others.

IT Themes   Four themes are highlighted throughout this book, each emphasizing an important aspect of information technology. Each of these themes corresponds to a special featured insert:

- *Global IT*—Explores the unique challenges of using information technology in conducting business around the world
- *People*—Shows how people, the most valuable resource, use and are affected by IT's capabilities
- *Quality and Productivity*—Discusses applications of IT that are making people and organizations more efficient and effective
- *Opportunities*—Visits the new and emerging technologies as they are being implemented in large and small organizations.

For example, you'll find out what it's like to have a word processing system that types in a foreign language, how mail-order companies learn about your purchases, and how ergonomics affects the users of IT daily.

Critical Connections   Critical thinking is an important part of solving problems and capitalizing on opportunities. A special Critical Connection feature emphasizes problem solving. Each chapter introduces a challenge facing an individual or company, drawing on the principles and practices discussed in the chapter. At the end of the chapter, these experiences are revisited and conclusions drawn. Each Critical Connection concludes with a series of discussion questions. Like the other examples throughout the book, Critical Connections focus on a wide variety of businesses from small single-owner start-ups to multinational corporations like McDonald's and Levi Strauss.

Interviews with Leaders   My lecturing, teaching, and research activities enable me to interact regularly, one-on-one, with business and government executives and IT leaders from around the world. To share some of these experiences, I've included in-depth interviews with five very talented professionals. As you read the words of these internationally known CEOs, CIOs, and executives responsible for research and development, you'll have a unique opportunity to share directly their views on, experiences with, and expectations concerning business and information technology. You'll also read about their views on international business and their predictions of what the next decade will bring.

Photo Essays   The "mind's eye" augments written descriptions by allowing us to visualize experience. To further share the experiences of people and companies, I've created a series of photo essays that tell a story through photographs, images, and display screens. Each photo essay tells a step-by-step story in pictures. For example, in Chapter 2 you'll see how Nigel Holmes creates from scratch the infographics used in *Time* magazine. Chapter 7 shows how this book was created on a desktop publishing system. In Chapter 9, you'll see how a company can use Lotus Notes to manage important projects when team members are in different parts of the world.

The History of Information Technology timeline uses a variety of photographs to trace the key events leading up to IT as we know it today. And, if you're buying a PC, whether your first or a new model to replace your current one, be sure to check out the PC Buyer's Guide.

Reality Checks   I often find it useful to step back from what I'm doing, or what I'm reading, to consider the ramifications of what's happening. For this reason I've included a series of Reality Checks in every chapter. Each Reality Check is a personal assessment of a particular principle, practice, or opportunity, and is drawn from a vast array of IT experiences in the worlds of business, government, and research.

Case Studies and Media Cases   Each chapter concludes with a full-length case study of a company, complete with discussion questions. These cases are designed to bring together the information in each chapter by tying it to the experiences of a variety of businesses.

Each part of the book concludes with a media case that is supplemented by a news clip from the ABC News/Prentice Hall Video Library. These timely and topical cases are designed to spur discussion on IT issues in the 1990s and beyond.

The Information Technology Learning System

Instructors using *Information Technology in Business: Principles, Practices, and Opportunities* will be provided with a complete system designed to facilitate education and learning in the dynamic field of IT. Each component of this system has been carefully crafted to ensure that the learning experience is rewarding and effective for instructor and student alike. They are available to instructors who adopt this book for their classes and have their bookstore order from the publisher.

Annotated Instructor's Edition   This four-color edition of *Information Technology in Business: Principles, Practices, and Opportunities* consists of the entire text, augmented by seven different types of marginal annotations:

- Discussion Question
- Teaser
- Misconception
- Insight
- Teaching Tip
- On the Cutting Edge
- Example

Each annotation can be used to highlight lectures, trigger interesting class discussion, and enable the instructor to have maximum impact with students.

Transparency Acetates and Microsoft Powerpoint Electronic Transparencies   A set of 100 four-color transparency acetates with accompanying lecture notes and teaching tips is available. All transparencies are adapted from the four-color art included in the text. In addition, these illustrations are available on diskette for IBM-compatible or Macintosh desktop computers in the format of the Microsoft Powerpoint presentation package. Instructors can customize these color transparency masters, adding information to suit their presentation style and to personalize their lectures.

Instructor's Resource Manual The Instructor's Resource Manual is a complete tool for preparing college lectures. It includes one chapter for each chapter of the text and contains a chapter overview, learning objectives, lecture outlines, additional lectures on special topic areas, and solutions to all questions in the text.

Computerized Test Bank A broad range of test questions, in printed form or suitable for processing on Apple Macintosh or MS-DOS/IBM-compatible computers, is available to adopters of this book. More than 1300 multiple-choice, true/false, and short answer/essay questions are included. The disk version runs on the Prentice Hall Test Manager software, which allows instructors to generate random test forms, edit questions, create multiple versions, and more.

For those wishing outside administrative support, Prentice Hall's Telephone Testing Service allows instructors to order customized tests by calling a toll-free number a few days before the examination is to be administered. Details are available from your Prentice Hall sales representative.

Study Guide The Study Guide is a separate book designed to support the student learning objectives in the text. The summaries, self-tests, and exercises it contains help students assess their level of learning and understanding of the array of IT principles.

ABC News/Prentice Hall Video Library Video cases consisting of interviews, critical analyses, and network news reports drawn from the ABC News library are available to instructors who adopt this book for their classes and have their bookstore order it from the publisher. The cases, chosen for their widespread applicability to business and their usefulness and appeal to students, draw on such ABC News programs as *Nightline, World News Tonight,* and *This Week With David Brinkley.* Several of the video clips accompany the media cases that conclude each part of the text.

A video guide, to assist instructors, is included in the Instructor's Resource Manual.

The *New York Times* "Themes of the Times" Information technology is a constant theme in the news, both because of developments in the IT industry itself and because of the ways business uses it on a day-to-day basis. To enhance access to important news items, the *New York Times* and Prentice Hall are sponsoring "Themes of the Times." Twice a year, Prentice Hall will deliver complimentary copies of a "mini newspaper" containing reprints of selected *Times* articles to instructors who use this book for their classes. "Themes of the Times" is an excellent way of keeping students abreast of the ever-changing world of IT.

Multimedia Toolkit The CD-ROM package that accompanies *Information Technology in Business* is designed to support the text through visuals, sound, and motion. More information is available from your PH sales representative.

Acknowledgments

Somebody once called business a team sport, and rightly so. Success in business requires the capabilities and commitment of many people.

Preparing and delivering a textbook is also a team sport. The author was fortunate to have a skilled and dedicated team participating in the journey from conception to commitment and, finally, to completion of this project.

The Corporate Team   A large number of corporate executives from North America, Europe, and Asia participated in the development of this project by sharing firsthand with the author their business experiences and insights, as well as those of their companies and employees. They were willing to discuss their successes (as well as other experiences that became "significant learning events"). A large number are identified through their company names in this book. I appreciate their support and candor.

I'm also indebted to the many businesses that allowed me to use their logos as well as their stories.

The Research Team   A skilled research team helped conduct research, assemble information, and prepare notes and narratives to bring about the business discussions appearing in the text. I'm indebted to key research assistance from Linda Muterspaugh, Teri Stratford, Cathy Luce, Sherry Fowler, Suzanne Scully, John Blatt, Kristen Knutson, and Harry Knox. Nigel Holmes provided personal documents—sketches, drawings, and final copy—for the photo essay on infographics.

The Learning System Team   Another team worked diligently to deliver the *Information Technology in Business* learning system: Karl Briggs (Indiana University), Lewis Hershey (Hershey Consulting), Sasan Rahmatian (California State University—Fresno), Donald Springer (University of Portland) and Elmer Swartzmeyer (Georgia State University) created tools that will help students and instructors alike to seek and achieve peak performance.

The most important event in creating the vision and concept for this book was a focus group convened early in the process. Members of the group included:

Frank Davis
Bloomsburg University

Adolph Katz
AK Associates and Fairfield University

Donald L. Dawley
Miami University

Robert T. Keim
Arizona State University

Richard Fenzl
Syracuse University

John Pagliarulo
Rockland Community College

Barry Floyd
California Polytechnic State University

John F. Sanford
Philadelphia College of Textiles and Science

The reviewers kept the manuscript's contents on track with their helpful comments and suggestions during the development and delivery of this project:

Gary R. Armstrong
Shippensburg University

Catherine J. Brotherton
Riverside Community College

Anitesh Barua
University of Texas at Austin

Bruce Brown
Salt Lake Community College

Luverne Bierle
Iowa Central Community College

Donald L. Dawley
Miami University

The PH Team   The Prentice Hall team played a pivotal role in this project. The first step toward the launch of this project began in Europe around a discussion of global business IT issues. From then on it was full-speed ahead. The enthusiasm of Valerie Ashton, Joe Heider, Will Ethridge, and P.J. Boardman started high and got higher, interrupted only by the threat of the Pharnsworth Phlu in Phoenix, a conveniently arranged illness brought forth as a threat to the author should he fail to agree to a friendly relationship. From then on, P.J. pulled out all stops to keep every project detail on course and on time.

Steve Rigolosi didn't need a whip. He was armed with something much more effective: an editor's pencil, and a commitment to make sense out of an author's words when even the author didn't know what he was saying. Steve also had Anne Graydon on his side. There was no hiding place which Anne could not find, and so the author was never out of reach, even if he was out of touch.

Dolores Kenny was always ready to make things happen. And she did, too. Working nights and weekends, Christy Mahon created an electronic format for the book that brought all of the elements together in an exceptionally attractive fashion.

Carole Horton stayed in the trenches throughout the project, tending to local details in every way possible. She's got maximum PH points to show it, too. But above all, she's a friend.

Finally, my wife captained the cheerleading section even as she accepted the many hours of my creative, and not so creative, effort while I remained hidden away in one office or another. A constant companion and assistant on the extensive international travel conducted in preparing this book, she played a pivotal role in both its content and completion. But above all…she's my best friend.

—*Jim Senn*
Atlanta, GA

About the Author

J IM SENN IS KNOWN INTERNATIONALLY AS A DYNAMIC SPEAKER on management, corporate strategy, and information technology. He is director of the Information Technology Management Group, a well-known research group that facilitates and promotes research and communication among information systems professionals, executives, researchers, and organization management. The group is international in its focus and interacts with executives around the world on a continuing basis.

Jim Senn is also Professor of Business Administration in the College of Business Administration at Georgia State University in Atlanta, where he recently completed a six-year assignment as Chairman of the Department of Computer Information Systems. Under his direction, the department gained widespread international recognition for its programs and activities. It received an overall national ranking by *Computerworld* as the number two program in the United States (second only to the Massachusetts Institute of Technology), and has been identified as having the top curriculum in the nation.

Senn interacts widely with businesses in many countries. He is the author of several leading books on information systems and systems development that have been translated into multiple languages for use in many countries. He has written numerous articles and papers appearing in leading professional and academic publications. He also writes a regularly appearing column about business strategy for *Network*, a periodical published by the Society for Information Management.

INFORMATION
TECHNOLOGY
IN
Business

PART 1

An Introduction to Information Technology

Talking With Akio Morita
Chairman, Sony Corporation

Akio Morita started Sony with $500 from his family, beginning operations in the basement of a bombed out Tokyo department store. Sony's rise began in 1952 when the company purchased the Japanese rights to Western Electric's newly developed transistor. Using this technology, the company produced the world's first transistor pocket radio. From the beginning, Sony and Morita have used their genius to create products the world's people don't even know they want: the Walkman, the Trinitron television, video watchman, the compact disc (CD), and more.

This interview with Akio Morita is a unique opportunity to examine the thoughts of one of the world's most innovative executives. You'll read Morita's thoughts on four different topics: the relation between hardware and software, and the innovative thinking underlying their use at Sony; the CEO's responsibility to consider a company's stakeholders as well as its shareholders; and the challenges of building a global business.

You refer frequently to the interrelationship between hardware and software, and to the innovations Sony has pioneered to produce the best possible benefits for people. Can you describe what you aspire to in linking hardware and software?

When we came up with the idea of a digital recording on a small disk, with the joint effort of Phillips [a Dutch electronics firm], we were absolutely excited about this invention and the many promising possibilities. We thought it would be a historic innovation in sound recording technique with a similar impact to the invention of Edison's phonographic recording.

If we did not realize the benefit of software as early as we did, I wonder how long it would have taken for CD technology to be appreciated as much as it is now. Sony, by combining CBS Sony audio software to our CD hardware, created a new industry—the CD industry. The music industry as a result has grown with the transition from records to CDs. This success in hardware-software synergy illustrates how hardware alone, no matter how good, is not sufficient for either expediency or enrichment of human

"For companies operating worldwide, true localization is the first step toward becoming a 'global enterprise.' Managers of such global enterprises must consider how to closely knit together or integrate each of their localized operations so that they function as a single corporate entity."

life. Moreover, it supports Sony's belief in how a good relationship between software and hardware can promote the further growth of both industries.

Developing successful business and technology strategies and then carrying them out can take a long period of time. Yet, in some business environments there is a push to demonstrate rapid results from investments. As chief executive of a highly successful world-class company, what are your thoughts about producing rapid results in business?

At times we see some American corporate executives more interested in quick profits. Busily trying to make the bottom line of quarterly reports, their concern is for the amount of profit they can set aside for return to the shareholders. Although this concern should not altogether be criticized, an excessive emphasis on short-term orientation is dangerous. The popularization of this management philosophy has accelerated the establishment of the world financial empire, as well as the service industry, and leaves behind the manufacturing sector, which requires long-term perspectives, as in R&D.

To whom besides employees and investors does a business have responsibility?

[The term] stakeholders literally refers to those who have stake in the company. Or, in a broader perspective, those who share common interests in the business operation, meaning growth and prosperity of the business. This includes a wide range of people with whom corporations are involved in one way or another—

from customers, employees, suppliers, communities, and shareholders.

Corporations need to fulfill the expectations of their stakeholders. However, in trying to apply the stakeholder concept to Japanese firms, we notice that they have for a long time been paying close attention to their own employees, customers and clients, with comparatively less attention to their shareholders. Consideration for their community, whether it be at home or abroad, an essential element in the stakeholder concept, has also been insufficient. This is the reason why Japan's fast growing direct investment in the U.S. sometimes arouses suspicion and in many regions is not always well received.

How difficult is it for Japanese businesspeople, or for that matter any business person, to settle into a new country?

Among Japanese businessmen and their families living in the U.S., the importance of being a part of the community is not widely recognized yet. Of course I understand how difficult it is to become a true member of the community. It is not a simple thing to make the adjustment, because the process is multifaceted. I felt the difficulty myself when my family and I moved to New York back in 1963. But there is always at least one easy way out of problems, and it sometimes happens to be found in the simplest manner. When we were in the U.S., for example, I learned that even strange foreigners like us could easily acquaint ourselves with the American people once we could comfortably sit down with them as friends and neighbors around the backyard barbeque.

What advice do you have for businesspeople about becoming comfortable in an international location—a business or residence outside of their home country?

To be an integral part of the community, Japanese corporations themselves are also required to truly localize in their operations abroad. Localization is the process to formulate and operate a company to serve the local needs and well-being of the local community to its best ability. Making the best use of the talent available locally in management and the work force should be very effective to this end. Only when this true localization has been accomplished will Japanese companies be appreciated and welcomed as good corporate citizens.

Sony has had tremendous success worldwide and is a familiar brand name in many, many countries. Based on your experience, what is the relation between being a global company and being accepted in a local business community? Can a firm be both global and local?

For companies operating worldwide, true localization is the first step toward becoming a "global enterprise." Managers of such global enterprises must consider how to closely knit together or integrate each of their localized operations so that they function as a single corporate entity. What is essential to this end is a universally common management philosophy and technology on how to encourage the work force, and how to develop and market products.

I introduced a slogan—"global localization"—to let Sony people know the importance of these concepts. It is another Sony word, like "Walkman," and who

knows, the phrase may one day appear in a Webster's dictionary either under the word "global" or "local." I believe that I share the same idea with Mr. [Roberto] Goizueta [Chairman of the Coca-Cola Company], who in the past advocated the concept, "Think globally and act locally."

Another similiarity, by the way, between the Coca-Cola Company and Sony is that both of our trademarks were rated as two of the most well-known around the world in a survey conducted by Landor Associates last year.

What do you feel are the most formidable barriers to the globalization of business?

Businesspeople like us, involved in global operations, must cope in a huge market with different cultures, languages, and tastes. This diverse global market is our constituencies, so to speak, as opposed to local constituencies which politicians are most concerned about. In our global constituency, what counts to get votes from our constituents, or customers, is offering attractive products, and not shaking hands nor delivering speeches.

Drawing on your remarkable success, can you suggest a key thought that global managers should remember when introducing products in new countries?

Attractiveness of value-added industrial products measured by factors such as design, quality, reliability, and service capability are critical in the customers' decision to buy.

Thank you for sharing your wisdom, your experience, and your inights so candidly.

Thank you very much.

CHAPTER 1

Information Technology: Principles, Practices, and Opportunities

Learning Objectives

When you have completed this chapter, you should be able to:

1 Describe the five characteristics of the Information Age and discuss the role of information technology as the principal tool of the Information Age.

2 Explain the three primary components of information technology.

3 Identify the six information handling functions and the four benefits of information technology.

4 Discuss the types of opportunities that information technology offers to people.

5 Describe the responsibilities of people who use information technology.

In Practice

After completing this book, you should be able to perform these activities:

1 Watch a business transaction at a store or at an airline ticket counter and identify the roles played by information technology in handling that transaction.

2 Discuss a work process with co-workers, managers, or executives, and understand how information technology has changed or influenced their work activities over the past two decades.

3 Examine a work situation and identify the ways that information technology has influenced or could influence the way the work is carried out.

4 Describe the potential benefits of recently announced advances in computers or communications networks.

5 Identify ways in which information technology can help your career and the limitations you will face if you do not have the same level of IT know-how as your peers.

Added Value
from Embedded Intelligence

T'S THE LEXUS AND ITS STANDARD FEATURES INCLUDE:

- Complete lifetime service history accessible electronically from anywhere in the world
- State-of-the-art entertainment system, complete with cassette tape player, CD-ROM player, and stereo AM/FM tuner
- Programmable, self-adjusting climate control
- Antitheft system designed to thwart the most determined intruder
- Automatic suspension control that ensures a smooth ride over the roughest terrain
- Antilock brakes that sense road conditions and adjust their response for maximum control and safety
- Engine controller that manages resources in an environmentally responsible fashion
- Steering column lock using "smart keys" containing embedded computer chips
- Seat position memory that ensures just the right height and tilt for the driver
- Sensors that release protective airbags on impact.

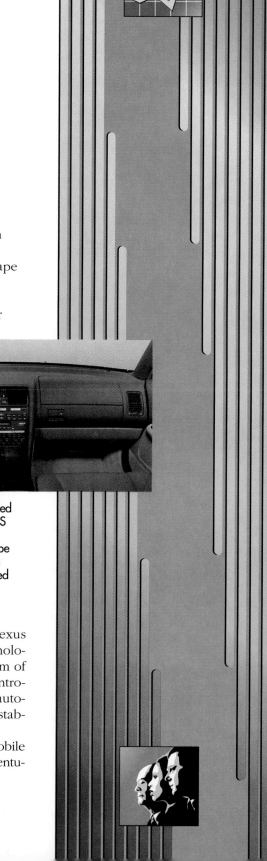

Information technology embedded in the dashboard of the Lexus LS 400 adds value to the luxury automobile. Embedded IT can be a key competitive advantage in the Information Age—*if* it is used to meet customers' needs and wants.

For a product that was designed just a few years ago, the Lexus already has a special place in automobile history. Information technology embedded in the Lexus adds value to the car—value in the form of services and features that drivers want. In the years since it was introduced, the Lexus has expanded the market for high-end, luxury automobiles and at the same time taken market share away from well-established name brands, including Jaguar, BMW, and Mercedes.

The Lexus may be a first, but it certainly will not be the last automobile to include customer-oriented features. As we enter the twenty-first century, even ordinary, run-of-the-mill automobiles can be transformed into smart cars—*if* people believe that doing so will add value to an otherwise ordinary product.   ■

T HIS BOOK EXPLORES THE ROLE OF INFORMATION TECHNOLOGY (IT) IN THE WORLD AROUND us. As we will see, the applications of IT are virtually limitless. Sometimes IT is used to turn ordinary products into smart products, as in the case of the Lexus. But in most cases, IT transforms the way people work and play.

Whether you embark on a career that uses information technology–and today this category includes nearly all professional, manufacturing, and service careers–or enter the IT field in which the technology itself is created, a working knowledge of the principles, practices, and opportunities of IT will help you to be successful.

In the pages that follow, you will encounter many examples that demonstrate how people and companies are developing and using IT today, and planning for its application tomorrow. Although you will see numerous examples of IT in different areas of society, most are drawn from the business world. In the quality-and-productivity conscious, globally competitive environment of the 1990s, business and businesspeople are driving the development of IT, and IT is providing business opportunities that were unheard of only ten years ago. As you read through this book, you'll see a series of boxed features (titled QUALITY AND PRODUCTIVITY, GLOBAL IT, PEOPLE, and OPPORTUNITIES) that emphasize this interconnection between IT and the business world.

Our journey into the world of IT begins with a discussion of what the Information Age is and what it means for each of us.

■ Welcome to the Information Age

We live in a society in which information is an essential resource and where knowledge is valuable. The importance of these resources has come to be recognized gradually. Only in the last 30 to 40 years has knowledge been recognized as a valuable asset to be developed and managed. With this realization the Information Age began. To fully understand the Information Age, you need to know a little more about its evolution.

The Evolution of the Information Age

Before the 1800s, long before the day of the Lexus, people lived in partnership with the land. In most parts of the world, the majority of people were farmers whose lives revolved around agriculture. During the **Agricultural Age,** entire families worked hard to provide enough food for themselves (Table 1.1). This is still the case in many of the world's developing countries.

Gradually, new tools and techniques improved and extended the land that farmers could use for growing crops or grazing their herds. With these new tech-

Agricultural Age   The period before the 1800s when the majority of workers were farmers whose lives revolved around agriculture.

TABLE 1.1   The Evolution of the Information Age

	Agricultural Age	**Industrial Age**	**Information Age**
Time Period	Pre-1800s	1800s to 1957	1957 to present
Majority of Workers	Farmers	Factory workers	Knowledge workers
Partnership	People and land	People and machines	People and people
Principal Tool	Hand tools	Machines	Information technology

nologies, more food could be produced with fewer hours of labor. People began to have surplus food; for the first time, more food was produced than was needed to feed the family. These surpluses led to the barter and sale of food in return for other goods, food, and services.

With the coming of the **Industrial Age,** first to England in the 1800s (and slightly later to other countries), machines began assisting people with their work. These machines extended workers' capabilities, and the partnership became one between people and machines. As the 1800s progressed, machines became the primary tool for the majority of the workers. More and more processes were simplified through mechanization and automation, and the number of people working in manufacturing and industry increased.

Of course, both agriculture and manufacturing are still important today, in the **Information Age.** But the majority of today's workers are involved in the creation, distribution, and application of information. These **knowledge workers** now outnumber those employed in agriculture or manufacturing in the developed world. (In the United States, white-collar workers outnumbered blue-collar workers for the first time in 1957, the date often used to mark the beginning of the Information Age.) In the Information Age, the partnership is one of people with other people, and the principal tool is information technology.

Some knowledge workers are very visible, because they use concrete information daily. Stockbrokers, bankers, accountants, financial planners, and risk managers come to mind immediately. Other types of knowledge workers include telephone communications specialists, physicians, attorneys, systems analysts, computer programmers, journalists, and medical researchers.

Knowledge workers often depend on front-line workers for important data. The counter attendants at McDonald's are not knowledge workers, but they do capture data when entering details of your order into a cash register-like computer terminal. Those data are in turn used by a knowledge worker to manage inventory, order supplies, and schedule workers. Knowledge workers use information generated throughout the organization: on the front line, in the back office, and in the executive suite.

Industrial Age The period that began in the 1800s when work processes were simplified through mechanization and automation.

Information Age The period that began in 1960 in which the majority of workers are involved in the creation, distribution, and application of information.

knowledge workers Workers involved in the creation, distribution, and application of information.

The Characteristics of the Information Age

The Information Age is distinguished from previous ages on the basis of five characteristics:

- The Information Age came about with the rise of an information-based society.
- Businesses in the Information Age depend on information technology to get their work done.
- In the Information Age, work processes are transformed to increase productivity.
- Success in the Information Age is largely determined by the effectiveness with which information technology is used.
- In the Information Age, information technology is embedded in many products and services.

Underlying all of these characteristics is the central importance of data and information processing in the day-to-day activities of most people in the industrialized world.*

Data are facts—details that describe people, places, objects, and events. In and of themselves, they have little value. When a set of facts about an item or issue of interest are gathered and synthesized into a useful form, they become *information*.

information society   A society in which more people work at handling information than at agriculture and manufacturing combined.

An Information Society.   The Information Age came about with the rise of an information society. In an **information society,** more people work at handling information than at agriculture and manufacturing combined. This is true in the United States (Figure 1.1), Great Britain, Australia, and Japan, just to mention a few of the countries that are information societies.

The Information Age is all about working with information technology and allowing people easy access to IT. Person-to-person communications and the links between individuals and businesses are important features of the Information Age. A group of people working together can frequently accomplish more than individuals working alone.

Dependence on Information Technology.   In the Information Age, businesses depend on information technology. As we will see throughout this book, an information society depends on much more than computers alone. Knowing *when* to use computers is as important as knowing *how* to use them. Equally important are the abilities to communicate information using computers and to interconnect people through information technology.

Reality Check.   Too often, people seek magic solutions to problems and challenges. People always seem to be looking for the magic pill that will enable them to eat all the fattening foods they want without gaining weight or affecting their health. Others seek a remedy that will allow them to use all the gasoline they want without creating air pollution or depleting the supply of natural resources.

In the same way, many people have come to expect that their business problems will disappear if they learn how to use a word processing system or how to transmit data electronically. But solutions to real-world problems are never that easy.

Success in the Information Age requires more than knowing how to use a computer. It also means understanding information technology's principles and practices and the opportunities that it can provide, along with its limitations.

Working hard and having the right information are important, but they take a person only so far. The real advantages of IT come when you use the information you have in a way that creates opportunity, produces results, and allows you to move ahead. *The knowledge to do the right thing* can create tremendous advantages for you. Knowledge is much more than knowing.

FIGURE 1.1
U.S. Work Force by Sector
In the U.S. information society of the 1990s, more people work at handling information than at agriculture and manufacturing combined.
Source: United States Department of Labor, 1993.

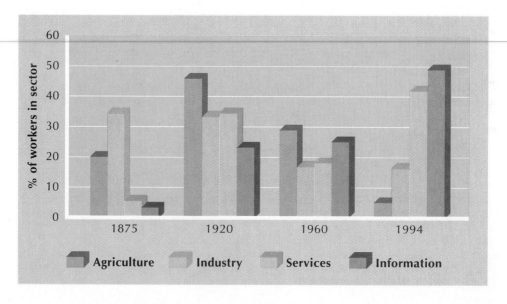

Transformation of Work.   In addition to providing new tools, the Information Age transforms earlier tools and work processes by increasing their productivity and effectiveness. **Work processes** are the activities that workers perform, the way they perform these activities, and the tools they use. **Productivity** is a measure of the amount of work that can be accomplished with a given level of effort. (More formally defined, productivity is the level of output that is produced with a specific amount of input.) **Effectiveness** is the extent to which desirable results are achieved.

Consider, for example, the transformation of agricultural work processes during the Industrial Age. Tractors that pulled plows, cultivators, and harvesters replaced horses as mechanization transformed the work processes of agriculture. Eventually, many of these tools were mechanized themselves, becoming self-propelled so that a tractor was not needed to pull them. As a result of mechanization, productivity improved—more work could be accomplished in the same number of labor hours. In the Agricultural Age, it might have taken two weeks for a family of four to plow a field; with mechanization, the work could be accomplished in no more than a day or two and with fewer people.

Today, in the Information Age, information technology is generating new knowledge about what, when, and where to plant and how to care for the crops once they are planted. Information technology is increasing the productivity of both farmers and the land.

> **work processes**   The combination of activities that workers perform, the way workers perform these activities, and the tools that workers use.
>
> **productivity**   A measure of the amount of work that can be accomplished with a given level of effort. More formally, the level of output that is produced with a specific amount of input.
>
> **effectiveness**   The extent to which desirable results are achieved.

CRITICAL CONNECTION 1
Fidelity Investments of Boston: IT Lets Knowledge Workers Relocate to Lower-Cost Areas

One of the hallmarks of the Industrial Age was urban migration—a mass movement away from the farmland and into the urban centers, where manufacturing, communication, and transportation resources were clustered. Now IT is promising to change both the face and the place of knowledge work.

Consider, for example, the experience of Fidelity Investments of Boston. In 1950, a cross-country telephone call during business hours cost fifteen times more than a local call—a good reason for Fidelity's decision to consolidate all of its operations in an urban area close to the financial markets of New York. Today, though, a phone line linking either computers or employees in Fidelity's Boston office with a branch in Covington, Kentucky, costs less than a cent per minute to operate. What, then, is the logic of maintaining operations in Boston, where all costs are higher? Fidelity's answer is "none"; it is moving a number of jobs to Covington.

Information Technology Influences Success.   The fourth characteristic of the Information Age is closely linked to the third: Information technology is to the Information Age what mechanization was to the Industrial Age.

It was hard to succeed in the Agricultural Age if you didn't understand both the capabilities and the limitations of the horses, land, and farm implements you used. Likewise, it was hard to be effective in the Industrial Age if you didn't know to use and care for your machines. In the Information Age, the most successful are those who know how to make the most of information technology.

Using information technology means much more than just knowing how to key data into a computer or how to print reports. It also means knowing what IT can do to improve your personal performance and how it can enhance a business's products and services in a way that increases their value to the firm's customers.

Embedded Information Technology.   In the Information Age, information technology is embedded in many products and services. Keep in mind, however, that knowledge-based products are desirable only if the knowledge adds extra value to the product. Value may be convenience, quality, reliability, or novelty—any characteristic the consumer feels is useful. The Lexus is more than just an automobile. The information technology embedded in the car redefines the traditional features of the product. So does the integration of information technology into the navigation and guidance system of a giant passenger aircraft or an electronic camera. In all of these cases, we should not lose sight of the fact that information technology is valuable if the recipient *believes* the result to be desirable.

The pervasiveness of knowledge-based products, services, and activities in today's society has so thoroughly changed the way we go about our activities that we often take the technology for granted. Consider, for instance, the introduction of information technology into the personal travel industry (Figure 1.2). Prior to computerized reservation systems, each airline reservation required that a travel agent call the airline directly, providing the passenger's name, address, and telephone number verbally. Tickets were written by hand. Advance seat assignment was not possible. Either you got on the plane and took the first seat available or, in the case of some airlines, a seat was assigned at the gate just prior to boarding.

Today IT not only enables the travel and ticket agents to be more effective but also changes the nature of the services they provide. In addition to placing reservations and accepting payment, agents now can also handle the advance assignment of seats, request special accommodations, and keep track of the number of miles a passenger has flown during the course of a year—all through an information system. In addition, automobile, hotel, and special service information is maintained in the computer network as part of the traveler's personal profile. Personal travel is much easier as a result; the nature of the products and services is transformed because of information technology. Another form of IT that is making life easier is discussed in the Opportunities box titled "Virtual Reality: A New Ally for Business" on page 14.

![] What Is Information Technology?

information technology (IT)
A term used to refer to a wide variety of items and abilities used in the creation, storage, and dispersal of information. Its three main components are computers, communications networks, and know-how.

data   Raw facts, figures, and details.

information   An organized, meaningful, and useful interpretation of data.

knowledge   An awareness and understanding of a set of information and how that information can be put to best use.

The term **information technology** refers to a wide variety of items and abilities used in the creation, storage, and dispersal of information. It is important to distinguish between data, information, and knowledge. **Data** are simply raw facts, figures, and details. **Information** is an organized, meaningful, and useful interpretation of data. **Knowledge** is an awareness and understanding of a set of information and how that information can be put to the best use.

A simple example will clarify these differences. At a retail store, a specific customer's order contains raw *data* identifying the customer, the item(s) and quantity purchased, and the price. At the end of a business period, the details of all orders are assembled, summarized, and compared with expectations. The resulting *information* tells the store's managers that performance is better or worse than expected. This information may be combined with another set of information to create the *knowledge* that some customers are going elsewhere because of a competitor's new low-price program. This knowledge may cause the store's managers to change their pricing strategy. We'll see many examples throughout this book of the role of good information in improving performance.

FIGURE 1.2   Embedded IT in Personal Travel
The travel industry has used IT to increase the number and quality of the services it offers its clients.

AT THE TRAVEL OR TICKET AGENT'S OFFICE
Maintain profile of customers indicating seating and dietary requirements, payment details, and frequent flier number

AT THE HOTEL, RESORT, OR CONVENTION CENTER
Maintain list of traveler's preferences (pillow type, size of bed, smoking/nonsmoking) and payment details; provide automatic baggage handling to and from airport

EMBEDDED INFORMATION TECHNOLOGY

AT THE AIRPORT
Ease passenger check-in and baggage handling, purchase of duty-free goods, and receipt of messages; order on-board services (such as in-flight movies, music and entertainment package); allow self-service check-in

ON THE AIRCRAFT
Use telephone and fax, notebook computers, and information services such as investment databases

AT THE AUTO RENTAL AGENCY
Maintain list of client's preferred automobile size, color, and features; provide routing direct-ions and maps, entertainment, meal and lodging coupons based on destination; allow automatic or self-service check-in

OPPORTUNITIES

Virtual Reality: A New Ally for Business

MANAGERS WHO WAGE A NEVER-ENDING BATTLE TO CUT COSTS, boost revenues, and promote efficiency are finding a new ally in *virtual reality (VR)* technology that lets users interact with computer-generated worlds through sight, sound, and touch. Here are just a few examples.

Architecture.   Any executive who has had to approve an architect's plan for new office construction can tell you it's an exercise in creativity and courage. The creativity? Useful when the executive tries to visualize how the proposed design will "work" for employees. The courage? Essential for signing the approval slip, knowing that a mistake may hamper worker productivity for years. That's why many architectural firms are now using VR to stage "electronic walk-throughs" of "virtual buildings" created by the computer. Such a system helped Hewlett-Packard fine-tune an architect's plan for its new office building in Germany.

VR is also helping architects who design private homes. In the early 1990s, Matsushita Electric Works of Japan opened a "virtual" showroom for people to "walk through" the custom-designed kitchens created by its home construction division. The payoff? Matsushita can custom-design a kitchen and get the customer's approval in about 30 minutes. VR can even increase sales; the showroom's first customer ended up ordering $30,000 worth of appliances.

Product Design.   Caught early, a design error can be fixed for as little as $1; later, the same correction can cost millions. This maxim is spurring interest in VR systems that let design engineers create and test "virtual" models of new products. IBM's Watson Labs, for example, is working with Chrysler to develop a "virtual" car that is letting engineers "test drive" models in the comfort of the lab, long before they order the first clay model. Meanwhile, Northrop Corp. is already using a VR system to redesign the Air Force's F-18 fighter jet.

VR is also cutting the enormous amount of time and money needed to develop new drugs. Some drug designers now wear 3-D goggles (see photo in this box) to view computer-generated graphics showing how drugs lock

The business opportunities for virtual reality are virtually limitless. Some companies have already created teaching programs that help would-be athletes improve their game.

onto disease-causing organisms at the molecular level. This technique helped Agouron Pharmaceuticals in California to design an anticancer drug. And at the University of North Carolina, researchers are using aid from Burroughs Wellcome to design a remote-controlled arm that will let scientists "feel" when molecules lock together.

Manufacturing.   Robots are excellent for performing repetitive tasks flawlessly, but humans are still best when it comes to performing skilled tasks that require judgment. The challenge comes when these skilled workers are in short supply or need to work in hazardous conditions. One of the most promising solutions to this dilemma is "telepresence," a VR tool that lets human operators manipulate heavy or dangerous equipment quickly and accurately from remote locations. Such a VR system lets workers at Fujita Corp. direct a spray-painting robot anywhere in the world. In the near future, telepresence may be used to reduce the hazard of disarming bombs and mines or operating a nuclear plant.

As Figure 1.3 shows, information technology is divided into three primary components: computers, communications networks, and know-how. The ways in which these elements are combined create opportunities for people and organizations to be productive, effective, and generally successful.

computer An electronic system that can be instructed to accept, process, store, and present data and information.

Computers

In simplest terms, a **computer** is any electronic system that can be instructed to accept, process, store, and present data and information. The computer has

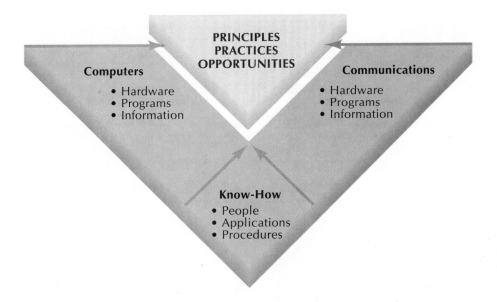

FIGURE 1.3
The Forces of Information Technology
The three components of information technology are inseparable. Computers and communications are of little use without know-how.

become a part of the day-to-day existence of people around the globe. It is difficult to think of any field that does not involve or is not affected by computers.

Computers don't always look the way you might expect them to. Many people use an automated teller system terminal (ATM) to get cash from their bank account. The ATM may not fit your image of a computer, but it is, or is connected to, one. And who can forget those modern marvels, the microwave and the self-focusing camera? Both of these are or use small computers.

Computers come in four different sizes: microcomputers, midrange/minicomputers, mainframes, and supercomputers.

Microcomputers.   **Microcomputers** (often called **personal computers** or **PC**s) are the most frequently used type of computer. They are relatively compact and are often found on a tabletop or desktop. Six common types of microcomputers are illustrated in Figure 1.4 on the next page. You may know them by their brand names: IBM, Apple, Compaq, Dell, Hewlett Packard, Gateway, NEC, Zenith, Group Bull, and Toshiba, to mention just a few sold around the world. Or you may know them by their functions: word processing, account balancing, management of personal or business finances, creation of visuals for use in presentations, sending or receiving messages over an electronic mail system...the list could go on. (Don't be concerned if you are not familiar with some of these uses. We'll explore all of them before the book is over.)

The Apple Macintosh microcomputer occupies a special place in computing. This microcomputer was the first to feature graphical means of interacting with computers. Before "the Mac," people used computers by entering command words. The Mac brought the "point and click" format to the forefront: People use a device called a *mouse* to point to an *icon*, a graphical picture on the computer screen representing the desired command. By clicking the mouse, the user can begin working on the computer.

The Macintosh also introduced the ability to divide the display screen into windows. Each *window* is a section of the display screen that shows a program in use. One or several windows can be open on the screen at one time. The entire computer industry is now adopting both graphical interface and windows capabilities. (Note: The term microcomputer, as used in this book, always refers to both IBM-compatible and Apple Macintosh microcomputers.)

microcomputer (personal computer or **PC)**   A computer that is relatively compact and usually found on a table or desktop.

a) Hewlett-Packard desktop microcomputer with color monitor and printer.

b) IBM Thinkpad notebook computers, models 700C and 700.

c) Apple Macintosh Powerbook 170 laptop computer.

d) Hewlett-Packard 95LX palmtop computer.

e) Grid Systems Corp. pen-based laptop computer.

f) Apple Newton Message Pad.

FIGURE 1.4   Six Types of Microcomputer
At one time, most microcomputers were found on desks or tabletops, but the last decade
has seen an explosion of handheld and portable—and sometimes even wearable—micros.

notebook computer, laptop computer   Smaller versions of microcomputers, designed for portability. All of their components, except a printer, are included in a single unit.

Notebook computers and **laptop computers** are smaller versions of microcomputers (about the size of this textbook), designed for portability. People can easily carry these PCs with them in their car, on airplanes, or when walking from one location to another. Unlike desktop PCs, which may have detachable components, notebooks and laptops include all their components (except a printer) in a single unit.

palmtop computer   The smallest and most portable computer, typically used for a limited number of functions, such as maintaining a personal calendar or address file.

Palmtop computers, among the latest entries into the microcomputer market, are growing in popularity. About the same size as a pocket calculator, palmtops are the smallest and most portable computers. Typically they are used for a limited number of functions, such as maintaining personal calendars, name and address files, or electronic worksheets. PC designers are building more and more power into palmtops and it may not be long before they become an essential tool carried in every knapsack, book bag, or briefcase.

pen-based computer   A tablet-like computer controlled with a special pen.

Pen-based computers are also emerging in the drive to make personal computers ever smaller and more convenient to use. These computers are tablet-like devices that operate more like notebooks than like computers. As their name suggests, they are controlled with a special pen. Touching the pen to a position on the screen is similar to checking a box on a form. In other forms of pen-based computing, handwriting and drawings can be sensed and worked on by the computer.

Pen-based computers are used in many situations in which information must be recorded in a standardized form. For example, law enforcement authorities use them to write electronic tickets for traffic violations. Insurance agents prepare damage claims on the spot by sketching details of the scene on the screen.

personal digital assistant (PDA)   A portable computer generally used as a personal assistant.

Another new type of microcomputer, the **personal digital assistant (PDA),** is small enough to be carried anywhere. Most include a pen-based capability. Even though they weigh less than a pound (454 grams), they are fast and powerful. PDAs allow an individual to sketch ideas on the screen and jot down notes during a meeting. If you want to send a fax to someone, the PDA will retrieve the person's telephone number, dial it, and send the fax over the telephone line to which it is connected.

Like the other types of microcomputers, PDAs are a *personal* assistant. They can provide substantial benefits to individuals by helping them maintain meeting schedules and "to do" lists.

Midrange/Minicomputers and Mainframes. The computers most often associated with business, especially large business, are **midrange computers** (also called **minicomputers**) and **mainframes**. These computers are used to interconnect people and large sets of information. This interconnection may be done on an enterprise level—that is, across the many organizations or departments of an entire organization—or at the department level.

Mainframe computers (Figure 1.5) are generally larger, more expensive, and faster than midrange computers. More individuals can be interconnected with a mainframe than with a minicomputer.

Midrange/Minicomputers (see Figure 1.6 on page 18) are often dedicated to performing specific functions, while mainframe systems are used for several purposes simultaneously. For example, midrange computers are often used to control complex manufacturing processes or to operate the reservation system for a hotel. As computers in general become faster and more powerful, organizations are utilizing a greater number of minicomputers, often using them to perform activities that were previously run on a mainframe.

Supercomputers. The most powerful computers, **supercomputers,** were designed for use in solving problems that require long and difficult calculations (see Figure 1.7 on page 18). Supercomputers can perform millions and millions of calculations per second. Scientists use them to predict weather patterns, to prepare models of chemical and biological systems, to map the surface of planets, and to study the neural network of the brain. Businesses use them for creating and testing new processes, machines, and products. For example, aircraft manufacturers use supercomputers to design a new airplane and to simulate wind and weather conditions. They then "fly" the plane under different simulated weather conditions before it has even been built. All of this happens in the supercomputer. Many automobile manufacturers design new vehicles first on a supercomputer, then test them by simulating different driving conditions (including accidents) to evaluate the structure and safety of their designs.

midrange computer or **minicomputer** A computer used to interconnect people and large sets of information, usually dedicated to performing specific functions. More powerful than a microcomputer.

mainframe A larger, faster, and more expensive computer than a midrange computer, used for several purposes simultaneously.

supercomputer The most powerful of computers, used to solve problems that require millions and millions of long and difficult calculations.

FIGURE 1.5
IBM ES/9000 Mainframe
In a mainframe computer room, cables and cooling lines are mounted below the floor. Operators sit at a workstation with a monitor and a keyboard.

FIGURE 1.6
Digital Equipment Corporation's VAX 8800 Midrange Computer
The terms "midrange computer" and "minicomputer" are used interchangeably. DEC's VAX series is one of the most successful midrange systems.

hardware   The computer and its associated equipment.

program   A set of instructions that directs a computer to perform certain tasks and produce certain results.

software   Instructions that control a computer and manage the hardware.

Hardware, Software, and Business Systems.   Computers and the equipment associated with them—monitors, printers, keyboards, and peripheral devices—are called **hardware**. Each piece of hardware can do nothing on its own. Rather, each must be equipped with a **program** designed to carry out a particular task or set of tasks. **Software,** the instructions that control the computer, manage the hardware. The hardware will not function correctly unless the computers are properly programmed—that is, unless the software is correct.

FIGURE 1.7
Cray 3 Supercomputer
Seymour Cray of Cray Computer Corporation with the Cray 3, one of the most powerful supercomputers in the world. Cray produces more than half the supercomputers sold worldwide. Future generations of the supercomputer may sit on a desktop.

Another important term in IT is *system*. In the broadest sense, a **system** is a set of components—people, computers, other businesses, governmental agencies—that interact to accomplish a purpose. Systems are all around us: the education system, a transportation system, an inventory system. Everyone in the world lives according to an economic system, although not the same economic system.

A business is also a system (Figure 1.8). Its components—marketing, manufacturing, sales, research, shipping, accounting, and human resources—all work together to create a profit or service that benefits the employees and the shareholders of the organization. Each of these components is itself a system.

Businesses also depend on **information systems,** systems by which data and information flow from one person or department to another. Information systems can encompass everything from interoffice mail to telephone links to computer and communications systems that generate periodic reports for various recipients. Information systems serve all the systems of a business, linking the different components together in a way that allows them to work effectively toward the same goal.

system   A set of components that interact to accomplish a purpose.

information systems
Systems by which data and information flow from one person or department to another.

 Reality Check.   Worried about using computers? Don't be. You are already using many of them, knowingly or unknowingly.   ■

FIGURE 1.8   A Typical Business System
A system is a set of components that interact to accomplish a purpose. The business system shown here includes not only people and departments but also procedures for conducting the business efficiently.

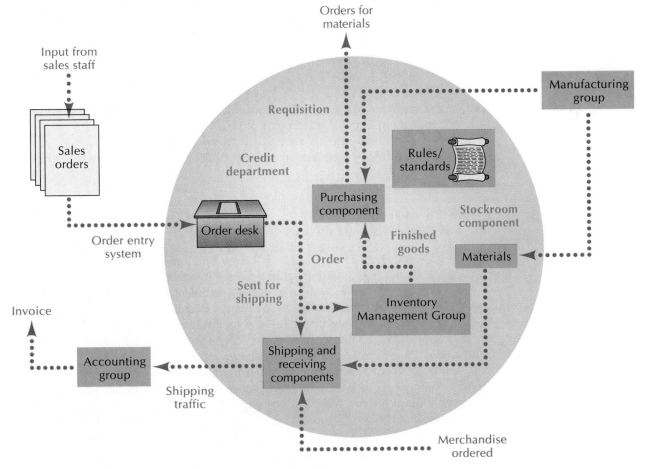

Communications Networks

The invention of the telephone by Alexander Graham Bell in 1876 did a great deal to foster communication between people. Today, you can call someone virtually anywhere in the world. As you speak into the telephone, your voice reaches its destination in less than one second. When the person on the other end of the line talks, you also hear his or her words in a fraction of a second, whether the voice is coming from Britain, continental Europe, Japan, Russia, South Africa, Brazil…virtually any of the 200 countries in the world.

The reason we purchase telephones, and telephones services, is to communicate. A telephone not connected to the public telephone network is not useful at all. (And, increasingly, a computer not connected to a communications network or to other computers will also have limited usefulness.) An integral part of information technology is the ability to **communicate**: to send and receive data and information over a communications network.

A **communications network** is the interconnection of stations at different locations through a medium that enables people to send and receive data and information. Telephone wires and cables are common communications media. **Data communication** is the transmission of data and information over a communications medium.

Communications networks are revolutionizing both personal life and the products and services of business. Airlines use communications networks to connect with each other, sharing information on passenger reservations, meal requirements, and baggage handling. Public networks like Prodigy, Minitel, America Online, and CompuServe, all of which are used by the general public, allow people to correspond with other people electronically and offer a wide variety of shopping services. People connect to these networks using their PCs. We will see many other uses of data communication in the IT practices we'll be examining.

communication The sending and receiving of data and information over a communications network.

communications network The interconnection of different locations through a medium that enables people to send and receive data and information.

data communication The transmission of data and information over a communications medium.

Know-How

Although computers and data communication are very important parts of information technology, an equally critical part of IT is the ability to draw on the power of IT to solve problems and to take advantage of the opportunities it creates. Information technology therefore implies a need for **know-how,** knowing how to do something well.

Know-how includes:

know-how The capability to do something well.

- Familiarity with the tools of IT
- The skills needed to use these tools
- Understanding when to use IT to solve a problem or capitalize on an opportunity.

Let's use an analogy to demonstrate what all this means.

Do you know someone who is a whiz at technical details—whether with cars, sports, electronics, or medicine—but can't put the details into a perspective that other people can appreciate? These people are sometimes too focused on the specifics to see the big picture—the human, day-to-day side of these technical matters.

Imagine, for example, going to a ballgame with "the technician." He knows who holds all of the records; how fast the players run; how often they score; whether they perform better on rainy, sunny, or windy days; and the odds that they will attempt a risky play. But he often seems so caught up in the game that he loses sight of the big picture. There is a time and a place for statistics, but most baseball fans prefer the company of a person who knows the fundamentals but doesn't get caught up in the technical details.

Like those who memorize baseball stats and don't enjoy the game, those who focus too much on the technical details of IT may lose sight of the bigger picture. The excitement in IT lies in what you can do with the technology today while looking forward to what it can do for you tomorrow. It involves knowing when an approach will work *and* when it's likely to be unsuccessful.

Think of IT as you do your automobile. If you're a mechanic, you must know how to diagnose an engine problem and how to tear the engine down, replace parts, and repair existing parts. If you're not a mechanic, you are less interested in knowing how to tear down an engine and more interested in knowing what an automobile will do for you. This could mean providing transportation for yourself, starting a delivery business, or selling car-care products. Users of IT are like the people who are not mechanics. The benefits come from knowing what you can do by *using* IT. The benefits come from know-how.

The Principles of Information Technology

It's always rewarding to have the right answer to a question. In fact, anticipating questions and identifying answers can be quite effective in solving problems. Look at the way people study for examinations: Many attempt to identify the questions that they'll be asked, then master the answers to those questions. But *what happens when the question changes?* The "answer" may no longer apply; it may even be downright wrong. This is precisely the problem with focusing on answers exclusively.

A more effective way of learning is to master the basic facts and to understand the principles underlying those facts. A *principle* is a fundamental rule, guideline, or motivating idea that, when applied, produces a desirable result. Rather than focusing on a particular situation or set of facts, principles prepare you to deal with the wide variety of situations (problems and opportunities) that you will encounter every day.

The most important principle of information technology describes the purpose of IT: ***The purpose of information technology is to solve problems, to unlock creativity, and to make people more effective than they would be if they didn't involve IT in their activities.*** We will see this principle in practice again and again throughout this book.

An equally important principle of information technology is the principle of *high-tech–high-touch*. It says: ***The more you rely on advanced technology, like information technology, the more important it is to consider the "high-touch" aspects of the matter—that is, "the people side."*** A related principle stresses that: ***We should always fit information technology to people, rather than ask people to adjust to information technology.***

These principles suggest that the more we rely on IT, whether in personal activities or in business, the more important it is to be sure that the personal element is not forgotten.

The Functions of Information Technology

What exactly can IT do? As Figure 1.9 on page 22 shows, IT performs six information-handling functions: capture, processing, generation, storage and retrieval, and transmission. The way a person or organization applies these functions determines the impact and results of using IT.

Capture.   It is often useful to compile detailed records of activities. This process, data **capture,** is performed when IT users expect the data to be useful later.

capture   The process of compiling detailed records of activities.

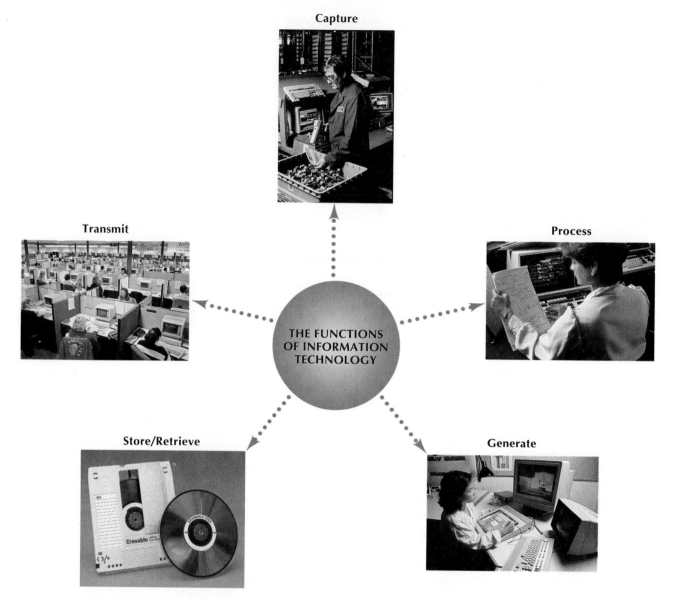

FIGURE 1.9   The Six Functions of Information Technology   The six functions of IT—capturing, processing, generating, storing and retrieving, and transmitting—may take place sequentially. In many cases, however, two or more functions take place simultaneously.

Here are some common examples of data capture:

- When a book is checked out of the library, the name (or identification number) of the borrower and the name (or call number) of the book are captured.
- The theater box office records the assignment of every seat to an attendee as it is sold.
- A monitor records the pulse, heart rate, and white blood cell count of hospital patients.
- When Madonna performs live, people listen. But sometimes her singing is captured and transferred to a cassette tape or compact disc (CD) for listening at a later time.
- The voice and data recorders in aircraft cockpits capture the pilots' conversations and record flight data about the aircraft's location and performance.

Processing.   The activity most often associated with computers, **processing,** is usually the reason that people and organizations purchase computers. The processing function entails converting, analyzing, computing, and synthesizing all forms of data or information.

One of the first business applications of computers, **data processing,** focuses on handling data (raw numbers, symbols, and letters) and transforming them into information. For instance, calculating the balance in a checkbook by taking the starting balance for the month, adding all deposits and subtracting all checks written, and determining the current balance is data processing.

Information processing is a general term for the computer activity that entails processing any type of information and transforming it into a different type of information. Text (reports, correspondence), sound (voice, music, tones) and images (visual information such as charts, graphs, drawings, and animated drawings) can all be processed.

Advances in computer technology have led today to a growing interest in **multimedia systems** (see the Photo Essay on page 40). These systems process multiple types of information simultaneously—for example, an animated presentation displayed on a computer screen using information retrieved from within the computer, perhaps accompanied by music, voice, or other types of sound.

Other types of processing you may have encountered include:

- **Word processing**—The creation of text-based documents, including reports, newsletters, and correspondence. Word processing systems assist people in entering data, text, and images and presenting them in an attractive format. (We discuss word processing in detail in Chapter 7.)
- **Image processing**—Converting visual information (graphics, photos, and so forth) into a format that can be managed within a computer system or transmitted between people and locations. A process called *scanning* converts a print or film image into a form that a computer can use. (We discuss scanners fully in Chapter 4.)
- **Voice processing**—The processing of spoken information. Currently, voice information is most frequently entered through a telephone. Other systems that enable people to "speak" information directly into a computer system are also emerging.

Generation.   Information technology is frequently used to generate information through processing. **Generating** information means organizing data and information into a useful form, whether as numbers, text, sound, or visual image. Sometimes the information is regenerated in its original form. Other times, a new form may be generated, as when recorded musical notes are "played" as sounds with rhythm and pauses—that is, as music.

Storage and Retrieval.   Through information **storage,** computers keep data and information for later use. Stored data and information are placed on a storage medium (for example, a magnetic disk or CD-ROM optical disk—discussed in Chapter 4) that the computer can read. The computer converts the data or information into a form that takes less space than the original source. For example, voice information is not stored as a voice as we know it, but rather as a specially coded form that the computer can manage.

Retrieval entails locating and copying stored data or information for further processing or for transmission to another user. The person using the computer must keep track of the medium on which he or she has stored the data or information and make it available to the computer for processing.

processing   The process of converting, analyzing, computing, and synthesizing all forms of data or information.

data processing   The process of handling data and transforming them into information.

information processing   A general term for the computer activity that entails processing any type of information and transforming it into a different type of information.

multimedia system   A computer system that can process multiple types of information simultaneously.

generation   The process of organizing information into a useful form, whether as text, sound, or visual image.

storage   The process by which a computer keeps data and information for later use.

retrieval   The process by which a computer locates and copies stored data or information for further processing or for transmission to another user.

Transmission.   The sending of data and information from one location to another is called **transmission**. As noted earlier, telephone systems transmit our conversations from a point of origin to a destination. Computer systems do precisely the same thing, often using telephone lines. Computer networks can also send data and information through other media, including satellites and light beams transmitted along plastic or glass optical fibers.

Modern communications networks enable us to send information down the hall or around the world in an instant. PCs, mainframes, and supercomputers can be connected together electronically. People can send data and information to and from one another, using the network to overcome distance barriers.

Two of the most common forms of information transmission are:

- **Electronic mail** (sometimes called **e-mail**)—The acceptance, storage, and transmission of text and image messages between users of a computer system. Messages can be sent between individuals or broadcast to a large number of people simultaneously. Typically, these messages are entered through a computer keyboard and are viewed on the receiving parties' computer monitor (thus eliminating the need for sending paper messages).
- **Voice messaging** (sometimes called **voice mail**)—A form of voice processing in which callers leave spoken messages entered through their telephone receiver. The voice information is transmitted, stored, and retrieved ("played") by the recipients.

The Six IT Functions at Work: The U.S. Export Bureau.   Before a company can sell and ship its products outside of the United States, it must obtain a federal government license and approval to do so. The United States Bureau of Export Administration processes more than 130,000 of these export-license applications annually. Information technology is at the center of the Bureau's operations and rapid approval procedure. Rapid access to the information contained in the application is essential to the timely approval of the request. Quick approval is also important because the requestor is often in a competitive situation. If an exporting firm in another country can obtain approval more quickly, it may be able to acquire a contract, edging out the applicant firm.

The process works like this: The request for authorization, consisting of information identifying the would-be export company, its customer(s), and the nature of the goods designated for export, is submitted to the Bureau either in written form (on paper) or electronically over a communications network. This information is then stored in the Bureau's computer in its Washington, DC office. Within approximately two weeks, one of the 500 export agents in Washington, DC reviews the details of the application on a computer display screen and determines whether to grant export authorization. If all information is complete and correct, and the export is permissible, an authorization is generated. Written correspondence is sent to the applicants who applied in writing. An electronic approval is transmitted to those who applied over the Bureau's communications network. The process does not end there, however. Periodically, export agents select export authorizations at random and perform an audit on the company to determine if all of the statements they made during the application process were accurate and complete.

In this example, we clearly see the six functions of information technology in practice:

- Capture—Incoming documents are accepted either electronically over the Bureau's communications network, or in the form of paper documents, in which case the paper document is captured electronically (that is, scanned) into the computer for storage in the Bureau's computer.

- Processing—Applications are processed so that agents can examine the details of pending applications on a video display screen. During processing, details of these applications are highlighted for review by the staff member. Processing also occurs after applications are approved, when the Bureau audits randomly selected applications.
- Generation—Notices of approval or disapproval, as well as requests to audit company records, are generated by the Bureau's system.
- Storage and retrieval—All applications are stored and can be retrieved for display on an agent's video display screen. After review, details of approval or disapproval are stored with the initial application.
- Transmission—Electronic submission of applications is possible because would-be exporters can transmit their request via a network to the Bureau. After the agent has reviewed the application, a notice of approval or disapproval is sent electronically.

The Benefits of Information Technology

Information technology is used because of the benefits it provides to the people who use it in their personal and business activities. Computers and communications systems collectively offer four major benefits to users: speed, consistency, precision, and reliability (Figure 1.10).

Speed. "Split-second thinking" is something we admire in other people and an ability we would like to have. But what exactly is split-second thinking? Clearly, the term implies *speed*, which means doing something quickly. If a ball bounces in front of the car you're driving, you step on the brake pedal instantly to avoid hitting a child that you suspect might be chasing after the ball. That's split-second thinking: You have a fraction of a second to decide on and take the proper action. You may be remarkably slower at other tasks, however. Most people couldn't write a sentence in a split second, nor could they add a list of 15 deposits and withdrawals from their checking account in a split second.

Unlike people, computers do *everything* in fractions of seconds. They are very fast—much faster than people could ever be. They can perform complex calculations, recall stored information, transmit information from one location to another, and move objects around a computer screen in a matter of seconds.

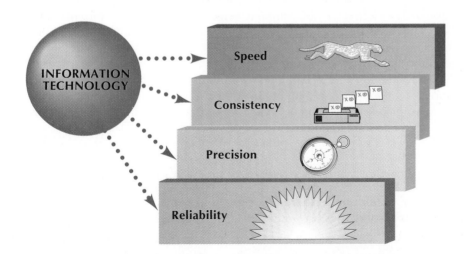

FIGURE 1.10
The Benefits of Information Technology

Consistency.   People often have difficulty repeating their actions exactly. Indeed, doing something once is not nearly as difficult as doing it the same way, and with the same result, repeatedly.

Computers excel at repeating actions *consistently*. Whether running a spell checker built into a word processor or playing multimedia animation for training purposes, a computer will carry out the activity the same way every time.

Precision.   In addition to being fast and accurate, computers are extremely *precise*. They can detect small, even minute, differences that people may not be able to see. In manufacturing an automobile, for example, the precise placement of a part into position may make the difference between long use and early wear. Computers excel in managing the smallest differences...in being precise.

Reliability.   With speed, consistency, and precision comes reliability. When you know that the same procedure will be followed consistently, you can expect *reliability of results*. In other words, you can expect the same result to be achieved again and again. Another kind of reliability, *reliability of use,* means that you can count on computers and communications networks to be available and properly functioning when you need them.

Computers in general are very reliable. Many people have personal computers that have never needed a service call. Communications networks are also very reliable, and are generally available for use whenever needed. Think about how seldom you are unable to use your telephone because the public telephone network is out of service. Usually, phone service is disrupted only when a bad storm has downed a line in your area or when power lines have been damaged by workers.

Reality Check.   You have probably heard some stories about computer failures—maybe even told a few yourself. It's important, though, that you distinguish between inability to get the results you want and a failure of the computer (or the network) itself.

During the early days of computers, the failure rate was high because the components used in the system burned out after only a few hours of use. Today, however, computer designers develop extremely reliable computers and communications networks that continue to operate for years without a hitch. Some systems (called *fail-safe systems* or *nonstop systems*) even include duplicate components. If one component malfunctions, the other takes over to keep the computer running.

Consider this: How often has the National Aeronautics and Space Administration (NASA) failed to bring back a space shuttle because a computer system failed? Despite the many days of flight under the most grueling conditions in outer space, the shuttles almost always return on time.

Nonetheless, computers are not perfect. Computers and networks on some university campuses fail more often than others. Often the cause is excessive use. The systems are overloaded, processing a heavier load than anticipated when the system was designed and implemented.

The Opportunities for Information Technology

IT provides many opportunities to benefit people in general. These opportunities fall into two general categories: opportunities to help people and opportunities to solve problems.

Helping People.   Can I be better than I am now? Can I be more effective, more productive, more creative? These are questions you should ask yourself regularly, for they challenge you to perform at your best and to reach your potential.

Another question focuses your attention outward: How can I help other people? How can I work towards providing affordable health care to all, and jobs to those who want them? How can I help to safeguard the environment, protecting the air, water, and land from pollution and saving endangered species from extinction? How can my business improve the society in which I live? The People box entitled "IT Opens New Doors for People with Disabilities" provides an answer to some of these questions.

These are questions of tremendous importance and challenging complexity. This book cannot solve these problems, but it can shed light on the role IT can

PEOPLE

IT Opens New Doors for People with Disabilities

LIKE OTHER ILLINOIS BELL EMPLOYEES, FINANCIAL STRATEGIST Dorsey Ruley uses a computer workstation to retrieve electronic mail, write and send messages, and order printouts of work. The only difference? Ruley, a quadriplegic, is one of the many workers with disabilities who are using adaptive information technology to lead more productive lives.

In Ruley's case, the information technology takes the form of a voice-recognition system, a combination of hardware and software that lets him direct the computer by speaking into a headset, rather than typing on a keyboard or clicking a mouse. Ruley trained the system to recognize his voice by pronouncing several hundred words into the headset. The system memorized those words and will continue to memorize new words he uses, up to about 35,000 words.

Another type of keyboard replacement uses special switches that respond to eye or tongue movements. A sip-and-puff device, which looks like a wheelchair-mounted straw, is one example. Other types of adaptive technologies include:

- *Monitor enhancements,* such as magnification software that produces large type screen displays for users with limited vision.
- *Voice-output systems,* software and hardware devices that read text and screen displays out loud.
- *Keyboard enhancements,* such as Braille keyboards and overlays that help workers keep their hands centered on the keyboard.
- *Augmented communication technologies,* such as devices that translate screen prompts and other visual displays into audio signals for the visually impaired

Specially equipped personal computer technology has allowed Marilyn Hoggatt to begin work as a part-time facilities administrator at Northeastern State University in Tahlequah, Oklahoma. Hoggatt says: "The [wheel]chair is my legs, the computer is my hands."

and devices that translate audio signals into visual displays for the hearing- and speech-impaired.

Prices for the adaptive technology devices, which range from less than $100 for a specialized keyboard to about $5,000 for Ruley's voice-recognition system, continue to drop in the face of technical advances and increased demand. Without the technology, many people would have much different lifestyles. With the technology, the disabled are working in almost every field, ranging from word processing to computer programming, law, and counseling.

play in improving society. It also describes many opportunities for IT to assist people in their personal lives and in their careers.

problem   The perceived difference between a particular condition and a desired condition.

Solving Problems.   A **problem** is the perceived difference between a particular condition and a desired condition—for example, the study time you need to prepare for an exam and the time you actually have. Problems occur every day. Some are as dramatic as accidents that cause serious harm. Others cause more hassles than they do harm, but all problems can be challenging.

problem solving   The process of recognizing a problem, identifying alternatives for solving the problem, and successfully implementing a solution.

Problem solving is the process of recognizing a problem, identifying alternatives for solving the problem, and successfully implementing a solution. Information technology presents many opportunities for helping people to identify and solve problems. Using a word processing program to prepare term papers and a spreadsheet program to analyze financial cases may help you solve a study time problem, because these programs can enable you to accomplish more in a given amount of time. We will examine the problem solving process in detail in Chapters 5, 6, 8, and 11.

Reality Check.   Problems often cause harm, destruction, and trouble. But there is another side to problems. Problems can create *opportunities*. Out of a difficult situation rises the chance to prove your ability to formulate innovative ways of dealing with the situation. And solving a problem presents an opportunity to create a distinct advantage in a product or service.

Consider, for example, automobile fenders that rust and doors that dent easily. Now those are problems, particularly if they happen to your car. But for the innovators that came up with fiberglass fenders (which do not rust) and high-impact plastic for auto bodies (the kind in which a dent immediately pops back out), rusty fenders were excellent opportunities to create a new product and a new business.

Or take the problem of tire wear on automobiles. Many people are too busy to notice when the tread on their tires is worn down. To combat this problem, tire manufacturers are developing technology in which a microprocessor inserted into a tire senses wear and signals the driver that it is time for a replacement. Thus the problem of worn tires became an opportunity to create a new product: smart tires.

Because we are surrounded by a seemingly endless stream of problems, we are also in the midst of an unending series of opportunities. ∎

Information Technology: All Around Us, Improving Our Lives

Information technology is everywhere. Most people are aware of the many uses of computers where they work, study, and play. But the ways that IT touches on and improves our lives every day go well beyond what we see on a day-to-day basis. Here are a few of the diverse uses of information technology in different industries (Figure 1.11).

Television.   The television networks of the world, including the BBC in England; TF in France; ABC, CBS, and NBC in the United States; and CNN around the world, rely heavily on graphics and animation to illustrate weather patterns, present sports results, and (of course) report the news. Virtually all of these graphics are produced on powerful microcomputers. Whether they are showing the movement of storm clouds across a region or the results of a public opinion poll, the graphics grab our attention in a way that words might not.

Shipping. Couriers and package carriers around the world rely on information technology. DHL, Federal Express, and United Parcel Service use computer systems to keep track of every package they pick up and deliver. Their worldwide communications networks make it possible to determine instantly the origin, location, and destination of the package.

Paperwork. Despite early predictions, we have not yet entered the age of the paperless office. Businesses still send, receive, and store large quantities of paper. However,

FIGURE 1.11   The Uses of Information Technology in Business

a) Stock trading is no longer done only on the trading room floor. The London Stock Market's "Big Bang" system allows stockbrokers to do all their trading electronically, through PCs and computer workstations.

b) Airlines around the world, including American, British Airways, and Lufthansa, use computer-controlled training systems to duplicate the interior of a cockpit and to simulate conditions identical to those that occur during real flights.

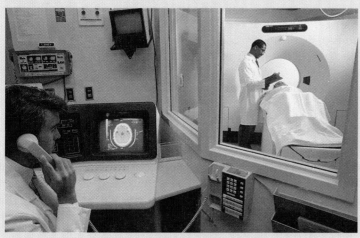

c) CAT scan technology, which allows physicians to look under a patient's skin without performing surgery, has become an important weapon in early cancer detection.

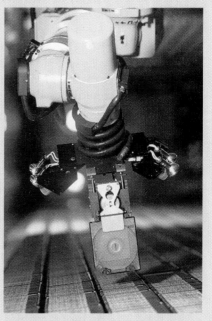

d) Robots used in manufacturing facilities throughout the world perform monotonous tasks tirelessly and precisely.

some companies are taking steps to lighten the paper load. Whenever any correspondence about policies, claims, or premiums arrives at Texas-based USAA Insurance's mailroom, the sheets of paper are entered directly into the company's computer system using a scanner. An electronic image of the correspondence can then be seen on the desktop display screen of any customer service agent (CSA) connected to the company's data communications network. When a customer telephones with an inquiry, the CSA can display the previous correspondence on the workstation simply by punching a few buttons. Several CSAs can display an image of the same correspondence simultaneously. All this means quicker service for the customer and less paper for the company.

Money and Investments.   Stock markets around the world are in transition. On some trading floors, paper is disappearing. In fact, the trading floor itself is disappearing in some places. The London Stock Market launched a system known as "Big Bang" that makes it possible for stockbrokers to do all their trading electronically (Figure 1.11a). Interconnected through a data communications network, brokers submit and receive bids using their PCs and computer workstations. Electronic trading is the wave of the future for investment markets around the world.

Agriculture.   Several chemical and fertilizer companies now offer a planning service that combines their expertise in agriculture with effective use of information technology. Working with company advisors and sophisticated computer programs, farmers can analyze alternative uses for their land. These programs evaluate different planting and fertilizing strategies while estimating crop sensitivity to rain and other environmental conditions. Each strategy can be analyzed to determine the course of action that will bring about the most desirable results in terms of productivity and profits.

Taxation and Accounting.   People don't like to pay taxes, and they don't like filling out forms. In the United States, the Internal Revenue Service (IRS) has installed a system that allows people to file their tax returns electronically using the PC in their home or office. Use of the service has grown substantially every year since its inception in 1989.

Some pioneering public accounting firms have developed the capability to file returns for their customers electronically. H&R Block was one of the first accounting firms to combine the IRS electronic filing process with its own Rapid Refund program. Block's customers can receive a refund on virtually the same day they file their return.

Education.   The ability to read and to do mathematics are prerequisites for success in the modern world. IBM Corp., the largest computer company in the world, distributes multilingual computer packages for use in the countries in which it does business. These packages, called "Write to Read" and "Exploring Measurement, Time, and Money," help young and old to acquire these basic skills. Microcomputers present information in a variety of forms tailored to the user's needs and keep track of his or her progress.

Training.   Some companies are using information technology in employee training programs. For example, insurance adjusters in training at State Farm Insurance can view damage scenes (from automobile accidents or natural disasters) on a computer display screen. Photographs and images of the damage can be "turned" electronically so that all views can be examined for damage and for information about the extent of the repairs needed. Interacting with the computer, the trainees ask questions and retrieve information about the damage. They receive answers only to the questions they ask. At the end of the session, the trainee receives suggestions about other questions to raise and different views of the damage to check for a more complete analysis.

Airlines around the world, including such well-known carriers as Lufthansa, SwissAir, JAL, British Airways, SAS, American, Delta, and United, conduct pilot training in special flight simulators (Figure 1.11b). These computer-controlled training systems duplicate the interior of the cockpit and simulate conditions identical to those that occur during real flights. They also allow pilots to practice corrective actions under simulated emergency conditions that they hope they will never have to face in the air.

The Home.   France Télécom, the French telephone company, stopped giving its customers telephone directories several years ago. Instead, it gave them computer terminals connected to a communications network. Today Minitel, as the network service is called, has become a major vehicle for obtaining a wide variety of goods and services: airline reservations, theater tickets, and of course telephone numbers. Minitel is available to every home in France and is included free with telephone installation. The service is so successful that France Télécom now exports a version of Minitel to Europe and North America.

Health and Medicine.   It will come as no surprise that hospitals and clinics use computers to keep records and generate invoices. But computers also play an important role in medical diagnosis and treatment. For example, the CAT scanner is an imaging device that enables physicians to look beneath the patient's skin (Figure 1.11c). As the scanner passes over the patient, it displays an image of bone and tissue structures on a computer screen. The CAT scanner has become invaluable in identifying cancer and other dangerous conditions that require early treatment.

Manufacturing.   Robots have moved from the realm of science fiction to the manufacturing floors of factories over the last few decades (Figure 1.11d). Virtually all automobiles manufactured around the world, whether made by Daimler-Benz, Peugeot, Ford, GM, Chrysler, Honda, or Toyota, are touched by robots at some point in the manufacturing process. Often they perform the monotonous jobs that people don't want to perform, such as spraying paint or welding seams.

CRITICAL CONNECTION 2
McDonald's Installs Robots in Fast Food Kitchens

McDonald's takes the "fast" in "fast food" seriously. Counter employees serve each customer in less than a minute. In 60 seconds, they enter an order, pull the ordered foods from the bin, pick up one or more bags of McDonald's famous fries, pour a soft drink, assemble the order on a tray or in a recyclable bag, make sure the customer has ketchup, lemon, and other supplies, take the money and make change, and thank the customer.

Now McDonald's is hoping that ARCH will help improve efficiency and product quality. ARCH, short for Automated Restaurant Crew Helper, is the name for McDonald's project to adapt industrial robots to the special demands of fast food preparation. With ARCH Fry, the workers need only to put frozen fries into a hopper and bag them after cooking; the robot does the rest. And with ARCH Drink, all employees need to do is press a button at the cash register; the robot will have a finished drink ready for them by the time they turn around.

Journalism.   Reporters and journalists rely heavily on word processors to prepare news articles and write their columns. Few writers use typewriters any more. The same goes for the graphics people who design the illustrations that accompany the text. At the offices of *USA Today,* the national U.S. newspaper that is sold throughout North America, Europe, and the Middle East, charts and graphs are often produced on a PC using a special illustrator software program. Computer stores make this package (Aldus Freehand) available to anyone for only a few hundred dollars.

Energy.   In countries including France and the United States, a gas pump that accepts credit cards is the wave of the future. Place your credit card in the reader and begin fueling your vehicle. When you are through, the pump's built-in computer notes the cost of the fuel pumped, transmits the details of the transaction over communications lines to your bank or credit card agency, and prints a receipt for you. You never have to go into the station, or move away from your car, or wait for an attendant. Automated gas pumps don't reduce the amount of fuel consumed, but they do reduce the time and energy *you* burn in fueling up.

Large office buildings consume huge quantities of energy in both summer and winter. Thanks to information technology, this energy usage is better managed than ever before. Using a system of thermostats and sensors interconnected through a communications network, a computer monitors temperatures around the clock, controlling heating and cooling devices to maintain the right, prespecified comfort level. At the end of the workday and on weekends, the system automatically adjusts the temperature, thus conserving additional energy. Some systems can also determine whether a room is occupied, shutting off lights when it is empty.

Sports.   Auto racing draws enthusiasts around the world. In all the auto circuits, whether the Formula 1, Indianapolis, or NASCAR, computers are an integral part of race cars and a central element in racing strategy. Today's race cars are fitted with onboard computers and communications capabilities. Data regarding fuel use, engine functions, braking patterns, and speed are monitored, displayed in the driver cockpit, and transmitted from the race car to the crew in the pits. These data provide information that can influence racing strategy and determine whether a team wins or loses.

The Responsibilities in Practice

We use computers and networks almost every day without thinking about them. Those who use information technology (in other words, all of us) have three fundamental responsibilities:

- **To be informed:** To know the capabilities and limitations of IT and how computers and networks can be applied in different situations.

- **To make proper use:** To utilize the inherent capabilities of IT in a desirable and ethical manner that helps people and does not infringe on their privacy, rights, or well-being.
- **To safeguard:** To protect data and information against intentional or accidental damage or loss, and to protect the failure of a process that relies on information technology.

An important principle follows from these responsibilities: ***People who use information technology have the obligation to consider both the benefits and the drawbacks of any use.***

■ The Career Side of Information Technology

Some careers require detailed knowledge of the intricacies of computers and communication systems. Most business careers, however, require only a good understanding of what you can and should do with IT and what you cannot and should not do with IT.

Information Technology as a Career

Careers in the "technical" side of information technology can emphasize many different aspects of the field, from the writing of computer programs to the installation of hardware to the determination of users' needs. We'll examine the roles of these IT professionals in Chapter 2. For now, though, it is enough to be aware of the substantial and growing demand for career specialists in information technology throughout the world. In many areas, there is a shortage of IT professionals. Businesses in the United Kingdom, for example, are very concerned that a continuing shortage of people with IT skills will force companies to relocate outside the country. As one business manager said in a conversation with the author, "Companies can now base themselves wherever in the world the relevant IT skills are, and use international networks to transmit data from there."

As in all other careers, good "people skills" and the ability to communicate ideas effectively are critical ingredients for success in the field of information technology.

Information Technology *as an Aid* to Your Career

Even if you do not plan a career in information technology, IT can help you in the career you decide to pursue. Knowing how IT is used in organizations, acquiring demonstrable skills in IT, and being able to list your IT accomplishments on your résumé can give you an advantage over those with whom you will be competing for a job. Especially important are the abilities to use a PC, to do word processing, to perform problem solving activities, and to communicate electronically. In business as well as in the arts, the sciences, education, medicine, law, and government, information technology—computers, communications networks, and know-how—is an essential tool. Best of all, you don't have to wait until you start your career to begin using information technology. As the Quality and Productivity box on the next page titled "IT Eases the Pain of the Job Hunt" explains, IT can provide major advantages for you as a student while you're still on campus.

QUALITY AND PRODUCTIVITY

IT Eases the Pain of the Job Hunt

IF YOU'VE EVER LOOKED FOR A JOB, YOU KNOW IT CAN BE challenging and exhausting, but you may not realize that the experience is just as hard on employers.

Every year Fortune 500 companies receive thousands of unsolicited résumés, on top of the hundreds of responses generated by classified ads. Even smaller companies sometimes need to hire human resource consultants just to sift through piles of résumés. And consumer giants, like Eastman Kodak, spend thousands of dollars on personalized rejection letters, afraid that not responding will offend potential customers. Add to this the time and money recruiters spend visiting college campuses every year and you are talking about a major investment of company resources.

Information Kinetics Inc. hopes to improve the odds for both employer and applicant. The company's first product is kiNexus, a database containing the résumé information of nearly 200,000 candidates on optical disk.

The idea of a résumé database isn't new. Many were started during the 1980s and almost all failed—mainly because it proved too expensive to sign up candidates and potential employers. Technology was another barrier. Most of the early résumé databases were tricky to access and search.

What sets kiNexus apart, aside from its use of now-affordable technology, is its marketing. The company decided to focus on graduating seniors at the 50 or 60 campuses visited by more than 10,000 companies every year. Students who fill out an electronic information sheet can be entered into the database by their school at no charge. At kiNexus, company-developed software indexes the information on the basis of known hiring criteria. A disk containing the resulting database is sent to employers, who pay $7,500 for an annual subscription and periodic updates. Employers can conduct their own searches by following simple on-screen prompts. Or they can use a toll-free number to reach a search specialist at kiNexus,

who can deliver the results within 24 hours by phone, fax, or Express Mail.

Since kiNexus began, the program has been expanded to include more than 1,800 campuses nationwide, as well as a number of outplacement firms. Other job seekers can buy a kiNexus registration kit at local book and computer stores, and the company is looking for ways to make the service affordable for smaller companies.

Subscribers, such as Dow Chemical, Eastman Kodak, and Johnson & Johnson, like kiNexus because it gives them fast, cost-effective, and anonymous access to candidates who meet specific job requirements.

And what about the job candidates? Just ask Juliana Regan. She filled out a kiNexus form when she was a senior at State University of New York (SUNY) at Buffalo and forgot about it—until American Frozen Foods Inc. called to say they had seen her résumé on kiNexus. Would she like to interview for a job as a sales representative? Regan, who accepted the job, found herself employed without mailing a single printed résumé.

In late 1993, Information Kinetics made another advance in painless job hunting when it announced that it was teaming up with *The New York Times* to offer FasTrak, an interactive way to respond to the paper's classified ads. For a modest fee, job hunters can arrange to have their résumé stored in the *Times*'s FasTrak database for six months. Then, if they see a classified ad that interests them, they can use a touch-tone phone to call the FasTrak number and punch in the FasTrak code shown in the ad. The company will then forward the résumé to the employer via computer. In the future, the company hopes to team up with about 30 other major-market newspapers across the country.

Sources: Adapted from Jim Sulski, "New Database Can Speed Up a Job Hunt," *Chicago Tribune*, November 8, 1992, Sect. 19, p. 7; and Adam Lashinsky, "Help Wanted? Here's Sign of *Times*," *Crain's Chicago Business*, November 8, 1993, p. 20.

SUMMARY OF LEARNING OBJECTIVES

1 Describe the five characteristics of the Information Age and discuss the role of information technology as the principal tool of the Information Age. The five characteristics of the Information Age are (1) the existence of an *information society*, in which more people work at handling information than at agriculture and manufacturing combined, (2) a dependence on *information technology (IT)*, (3) the transformation of earlier tools and *work processes* by increasing their *productivity* and *effectiveness*, (4) the importance of IT in contributing to success, and (5) the embodiment of IT in many products and services.

2 **Explain the three primary components of information technology.** The three components of information technology are (1) *computers,* electronic systems that can be instructed to accept, process, store, and present data and information, (2) *communications networks,* the interconnection of different locations through a medium that enables people to send and receive information, and (3) *know-how,* the familiarity with the tools of IT, the skills needed to use these tools, and the understanding of when to use them.

3 **Identify the six information handling functions and the four benefits of information technology.** The six information handling functions of IT are (1) *capture,* the compilation of detailed records of activities, (2) *processing,* the conversion, analysis, computation, and synthesis of all forms of data or information, (3) *generation,* the organization of information into a useful form, whether as text, sound, or visual image, (4) *storage/retrieval,* and (5) *transmission,* the sending of information from one location to another.

The four benefits of IT are speed, consistency, precision, and reliability.

4 **Discuss the types of opportunities that information technology offers to people.** IT presents users the opportunities both to help people and to solve problems.

5 **Describe the responsibilities of people who use information technology.** Those who use IT have three responsibilities: (1) to be informed—to know the capabilities and limitations of IT, (2) to make proper use—to use IT in a desirable and ethical manner, and (3) to safeguard—to protect data and information against damage or loss.

KEY TERMS

CRITICAL CONNECTIONS

1. Fidelity Investments of Boston: IT Lets Knowledge Workers Relocate to Lower-Cost Areas

Fidelity Investments of Boston is not the only company to realize the opportunity that IT provides to help companies save on costs. First Chicago Corp., for example, has moved its credit card operation to Wilmington, Delaware, where it saw important business advantages. Levi Strauss & Co., meanwhile, uses video conferencing equipment to connect San Francisco designers with Singapore manufacturers. Still others are fleeing locales that have undesirable environmental conditions.

Questions for Discussion:

1. One of the employee benefits of IT is the ability to *telecommute,* or use a computer and telephone line to link a home office with staff headquarters in a distant city or state. Experts estimate that the number of telecommuters doubled in just a five-year period to almost 6 million, and they expect this trend to continue. What do you think this trend means for knowledge workers? For your career? How might telecommuting also benefit employers?

2. Unifi Communications Corp., a small company based in Billerica, Massachusetts, sells a communications system that automatically routes customer

service calls to home-based operators in different locations and time zones. A young mother, for example, could answer calls while the children are in school; by tapping a few keys on a computer terminal, she can call up a customer's record and tell him when the order was shipped and when delivery can be expected. What might this capability mean for the traditional concept of the office?

2. McDonald's Installs Robots in Fast Food Kitchens

McDonald's estimates that the use of the ARCH Fry robot can save eight to twelve seconds per customer—a substantial amount of time, given the number of customers the restaurant serves each day. In addition, quality has been improved; there are fewer broken fries and some managers say the fries have better texture.

Questions for Discussion:

1. Use what you have learned about the benefits of IT to explain why McDonald's believes it might be useful to replace a human fry cook with a computer-controlled robot.

2. Worker safety and robot reliability were high priorities for the McDonald's engineers. To ensure safety, they programmed a feedback system into the robot that shuts it off if a worker accidentally touches the robot's arm. To improve reliability, they developed a simple-to-use system that lets store employees determine why a robot isn't working and, if they couldn't fix it, operate the fry machine manually. What IT principles do these facts illustrate?

REVIEW QUESTIONS

1. Distinguish between the Agricultural, Industrial, and Information Ages. What development brought about the onset of each age following the Agricultural Age?

2. What are knowledge workers? What is their relation to the Information Age?

3. What is meant by the term "information society"?

4. "The Information Age does not replace the activities of earlier ages. It transforms them." Explain this statement.

5. What are the five characteristics of the Information Age?

6. What is information technology? How are information technology and computers related?

7. Distinguish between data, information, and knowledge.

8. Identify the four types of computers.

9. How are hardware and software different? How are they related?

10. What role do communications networks play in an information society?

11. "Know-how" isn't a computer and isn't a data communications network. Why, then, is it is a component of information technology?

12. What is the principle of high-tech—high-touch?

13. What six functions does information technology perform? Briefly describe each function.

14. Describe four benefits of information technology.

15. What is meant by the term "problem"? By "problem solving"?

16. What three responsibilities does the use of information technology create for those who use it?

DISCUSSION QUESTIONS

1. Bell Atlantic Corp. of Philadelphia, one of the "Baby Bells" created by the breakup of AT&T in 1984, recently earmarked $2 billion for Project 2000, a project involving the complete revision of 400 computer applications that support more than 120 business functions. Use what you have already learned about IT and its functions to explain why many IT professionals are now involved with similar projects.

2. "Computers don't make difficult things easier, they make impossible things possible." Do you agree or disagree with this adage? Explain your answer.

3. Procter & Gamble routinely searches databases of public information to discover the names of new parents. The company mails these parents coupons and samples of P&G's disposable diapers in the hope that the offer will win the parents' loyalty for

the next two years. Is this a responsible use of IT? Comment on the ethical or legal issues involved in this form of "micromarketing."

4. How do you think the Information Age will change your personal and work life? What characteristics of the Information Age will have the greatest influence on your career?

SUGGESTED READINGS

Davis, Stan, and Bill Davidson, *2020 Vision: Transform Your Business Today to Succeed in Tomorrow's Economy*. New York: Simon & Schuster, 1991. An excellent discussion of the way computers and data communications networks are reshaping the structure of modern business, allowing firms to improve existing products and services and to create new ones.

Marchand, Donald A., and Forest W. Horton, Jr., *Infotrends: Profiting from Your Information Resources*. New York: Wiley, 1986. A compact discussion of the Information Society and the importance of acquiring and using knowledge in business. The book includes many examples of how companies like Sears, DuPont, General Motors, and Federal Express turned knowledge into a competitive advantage.

Toffler, Alvin, *Powershift*. New York: Bantam Books, 1990. A ground-breaking book in which Toffler, one of today's leading futurists, describes how knowledge is creating tremendous shifts in power at the local and global levels.

Zuboff, Shoshana, *In the Age of the Smart Machine: The Future of Work and Power*. New York: Basic Books, 1988. An in-depth examination of information technology's spread across the business landscape and its transformation of the nature of work. Zuboff demonstrates the benefits of "informating" (empowering working people with overall knowledge) and points out problems that can occur when IT is used merely to automate jobs.

IT: The Secret Ingredient at Mrs. Fields

MILLIONS OF AMERICANS HAVE HAD a chance to sample a gourmet cookie or two from Mrs. Fields Inc. Almost as many know the energetic Debbi Fields, either from her television appearances or from her autobiography, *One Smart Cookie,* which details how she and husband Randy built a cookie empire. What most people don't realize, however, is the support role IT has played in the Mrs. Fields story.

The company's commitment to IT goes back to 1978. That's the year Mrs. Fields opened its second store and began thinking about a third, fourth, and fifth store. It's also the year that Randy realized the company was at a crossroads. Could it continue to grow without selling franchises? A *franchise* is a license granted to someone (a *franchisee*) to use a brand name and a particular system for selling a company's products or services, and it offers company founders (the *franchisors*) both advantages and disadvantages.

On the plus side, franchising provides a steady stream of risk-free revenue for the franchisor. In addition to the initial licensing fees (as much as $150,000 for a nationally known franchise), franchisees pay royalties (based on gross sales receipts) and cooperative advertising fees (to share advertising expenses), and assume full responsibility for daily operating expenses. Another plus for the franchisor is the franchise's selling system, which provides a framework for delegating the management of far-flung outlets to franchisees, who are responsible for motivating employees and maintaining franchise standards.

Franchisors share some control and sales with their franchisees. However, rigid guidelines are often written into the franchise contract, a factor that can make it difficult to react quickly to changing market conditions. This factor worried Debbi and Randy, who could see that competition was heating up in the gourmet cookie market. Equally worrisome was the risk that they would lose the special touch Debbi had brought to managing Mrs. Fields.

For these reasons, franchising posed both opportunities and challenges for Debbi and Randy. They knew they wanted to keep control of every outlet and keep the quality of their product high, but how? For Randy, a former programmer at IBM, the natural answer was IT.

Even before he began to think about specific hardware and software, Randy drew on his IT background to develop a vision of what he wanted IT to do for Mrs. Fields.

The first goal was to control operating expenses. Cookies are a low-price, high-volume product. This means that managers need to keep an eagle eye on costs, to be sure they don't bake too few or too many cookies compared to demand, and to hold to Debbi's dictum that Mrs. Fields will sell no cookie more than two hours old. (After that, the unsold cookies are donated to charity.) A second, related goal was to monitor individual store performance at headquarters and offer suggestions to franchisees for better decision making. Above all, Randy felt, machines that could handle rote tasks and paperwork should do exactly that so that managers would be free to do what only people can do—namely, work with and motivate employees.

Out of this vision grew a system that includes an *expert system,* a computer system that links an in-store PC to a computer at headquarters, which merges store data with Debbi's management techniques to help store managers make more effective decisions. Managers at headquarters can, in turn, monitor store performance. In fact, Debbi often calls store managers personally to congratulate them on meeting or exceeding sales quotas. The expert system, dubbed the PaperLess Management System, is made up of more than twenty software modules, including:

- *Daily Production Planner,* a combination "to-do list" and forecasting system that uses information about past sales, weather, and other conditions to project the amount of ingredients and dough needed on an hourly basis. The Planner monitors actual store traffic throughout the day. If traffic falls below projections, the Planner suggests alternatives, such as cutting back production or dispatching employees to pass out free samples (one of Debbi's favorite marketing techniques).
- *Sales Reporting and Analysis,* which compares the day's total sales to sales projections and other performance norms and suggests corrective actions that will eliminate any shortfalls.
- *Labor Scheduler,* which draws on the company's extensive experience in managing minimum-wage workers, the labor laws of a particular state, employee work preferences, and store characteristics to devise employee

The IT system created by Mrs. Fields, the PaperLess Management System, is now being used at other franchise operations, including Burger King and Fox Photo.

schedules (including work breaks) that optimize service, minimize overtime, and maximize schedule flexibility.

- *Interviewing,* a half-hour computer-aided interview that provides a standardized, unbiased evaluation of a candidate and whether, based on past experience, he or she is likely to be successful at Mrs. Fields.
- *Skills Assessment and Computer-Aided Instruction,* a computer-based system that detects employee weaknesses and provides training, as well as advanced instruction that prepares employees for advancement.

The expert system was so successful for Mrs. Fields that, in 1988, that company created a separate division, the Fields Software Group (now Park City Group), to sell the PaperLess Management System to other retail operations. Fox Photo and Burger King were among the first customers.

Since then, Mrs. Fields has encountered challenging business conditions, as its meteoric growth (more than 700 stores) encountered a recession and reduced demand for gourmet cookies, forcing the company to adopt a recapital-ization plan early in 1993. Throughout the ups and downs, however, Randy Fields's vision of IT has earned nothing but praise throughout the business world.

Questions for Discussion

1. Experts have written that computers will play three roles in the Information Age—that of assistant, adviser, and communicator. Describe how computers are used in these roles at Mrs. Fields.

2. For years many organizations believed that there was a limit to the number of employees that managers could supervise effectively. This belief led to "tall" organizational charts with many levels of middle management. At Mrs. Fields, however, IT lets a headquarters staff of about 130 keep track of more than 5,000 employees at more than 700 stores. Why can Mrs. Fields function with this relatively small number of managers? What do you think this fact means for the organizational chart at Mrs. Fields and other companies in the Information Age?

The Making of the Illuminated Manuscripts Multimedia Series

As a technology, it is called multimedia. As a revolution, it is the sum of many revolutions wrapped into one: "a revolution in communication that combines the audiovisual power of television, the publishing power of the printing press, and the interactive power of the computer."[1] The promise of multimedia in education, as in so many other multimedia applications, is to:

- Enhance the transfer of information.
- Encourage participation and stimulate the senses.
- Enhance information retention.

To be effective, though, multimedia programs must be carefully researched and crafted by experts. This photo essay explores the making of the IBM multimedia series known as *The Illuminated Manuscripts*.[2]

[1]Press release, IBM Corp., August 1991.
[2]IBM publications also refer to the series as *The Illuminated Books and Manuscripts*.

1 All multimedia productions begin with an idea. IBM's idea: to change the way students study great works of literature. To help them achieve this goal, the project team's members chose to use the three key elements of multimedia: (1) natural presentation of information through information technology, (2) nonlinear navigation through information, enabling viewers to choose the sequence they desire, and (3) touch-screen interaction.

Planning for *The Illuminated Manuscripts* series began with meetings to discuss the series concept and to identify the individual manuscripts to be included. After much discussion, planners decided to create a series consisting of five titles: Alfred Tennyson's *Ulysses* (poem), Shakespeare's *Hamlet* (play), the U.S. *Declaration of Independence* (political treatise), Martin Luther King, Jr.'s *Letters from a Birmingham Jail* (political treatise), and John J. Neihardt's *Black Elk Speaks* (oral biography of a Sioux medicine man). The final *Illuminated Manuscripts* series consists of more than 180 hours of interactive information presented intuitively with text, graphics, images, animation, full-motion video, stereo sound, and touch screen.

2 As in any multimedia production, each individual element in *The Illuminated Manuscripts* series was carefully designed. Information in different forms and from a variety of different sources was assembled. The project editors carefully reviewed and selected segments of video tapes, letters, pages from books, photographs, and other documents, then translated them into digital form.

Each segment of the production also includes music. The project planners recorded some musical excerpts using conventional recording methods. They also drew segments from prerecorded sources, including records, tapes, and CDs.

The final multimedia production consists of a set of frames containing images, sounds, and/or text. All of these elements are separately identified and managed within the multimedia program and can be examined on the computer's display screen, one frame at a time. During editing, all the elements are interspersed to play together.

3 All of the productions in *The Illuminated Manuscripts* series rely on touch-screen interaction. Within each manuscript, the viewer can choose subtopics focusing on people, topics, or sections of the document. For example, individuals studying *Ulysses* might choose to focus on Greek mythology. After selecting that topic by touching the screen, they can choose subtopics to investigate such areas as gods, the afterlife, heroes, or the natural world. The processing logic embedded in the system determines when a selection is made and then begins running the chosen program.

4 *The Illuminated Manuscripts* series allows students to choose from five tools displayed on the left side of the screen. Each tool aids in learning more about the manuscript at a different level of inquiry.

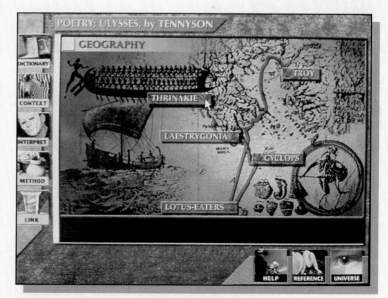

- *Dictionary* helps the student understand the meaning of all the words in the manuscript, including geographical terms. When the student invokes this tool, by touching its icon on the touch-sensitive screen, the system highlights all the words or phrases in the text that might be unfamiliar to the reader. When the student selects a highlighted word, the system responds by presenting a definition in the text, through audio, and with photos and drawn illustrations. It calls up this definition from one of four electronic dictionaries: a traditional dictionary, a rhyming dictionary, a Shakespearean dictionary, and a dictionary of African-American street slang.

- *Context* illustrates the social and historical significance of the literary work by expanding on cultural and historical references in the manuscript. Readers use this tool to invoke stored audio and visual conversations with experts who explain the issues discussed in the text. The system can also show the relevant sections of the text on the computer display. When studying *Black Elk Speaks*, the student can choose among the different contexts of people, events, places, and themes. For the U.S. Declaration of Independence, the system allows the user to choose alternative sections highlighting the multicultural composition of the United States. Included are discussions of Native Americans, Asian-Americans, African-Americans, and Spanish-speaking Americans, as well as a discussion of the important role women played in creating the country.

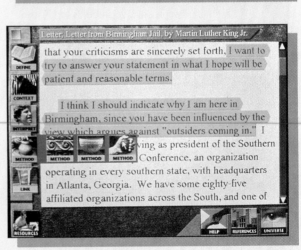

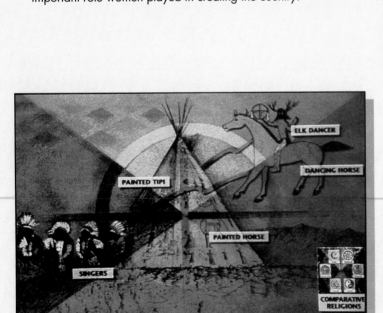

- *Interpret* shows the diversity of interpretations that can be drawn from a particular section of the work under consideration. It offers consideration on recitations and interpretations of the work by a variety of experts. For example, a section within *Black Elk* Speaks provides interpretations of the religious significance of Native-American art.

- *Method* allows examination of the various literary tools used by the work's author, including metaphors, alliteration, and symbolism. For example, Method highlights a section of Dr. King's words to explain both the literary devices he used and the messages he delivered.

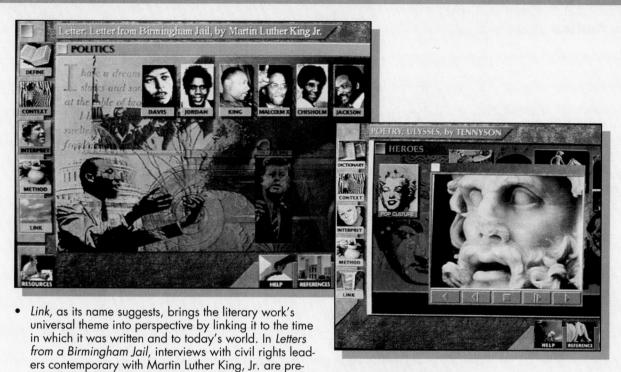

- *Link,* as its name suggests, brings the literary work's universal theme into perspective by linking it to the time in which it was written and to today's world. In *Letters from a Birmingham Jail*, interviews with civil rights leaders contemporary with Martin Luther King, Jr. are presented visually and in audio format, allowing the viewer to hear these leaders' opinions on the U.S. civil rights movement in their own words and voices. In *Ulysses,* experts discuss the relevance of this great work to such topics as pop culture, art, and politics.

5 *The Illuminated Manuscripts* multimedia program is designed to run on a computer display interconnected to a personal computer for viewing by small groups. Alternatively, it can be shown to large audiences over a projection system that displays the images on a movie screen and plays the sound track through theater speakers.

Multimedia's time has come and promises to change the way we learn. Because learning is a lifelong experience, it's likely that you will encounter a growing number of opportunities to learn through the power of multimedia presentations.

CHAPTER 2

A Tour of a Computer System

Learning Objectives

When you have completed this chapter, you should be able to:

1 Identify the five components of a computer system.
2 Explain the four categories of hardware and their functions, and discuss the relationship between hardware and software.
3 Differentiate between an operating system and an application program.
4 Identify eight types of software packages.
5 Explain the four components of information.
6 Distinguish between the users of information technology and IT professionals.
7 Describe the four types of procedures used in computer systems.
8 Explain the difference between single and multi-user systems.
9 List the thirteen information processing activities associated with the six information handling functions of IT.

In Practice

After completing this chapter, you should be able to perform these activities:

1 Observe a business activity and discuss the process with the business's managers or employees to learn how information technology influences their participation in the activity.
2 Examine a business or professional situation in which a software package is utilized and understand why the individual or organization has chosen to use that package.
3 Analyze a business or professional situation and identify the types of information that workers use in that situation.
4 Determine whether or not an information system application has any protection against intrusion or accidental loss of information.
5 Speak with IT professionals and determine whether their work deals primarily with hardware, software, or procedures.
6 Determine whether a particular business transaction that involves information technology makes use of a single- or multi-user system.

Infographics Change *Time*

SOME OF THE TERMS WE ASSOCIATE with the Information Age have been around for hundreds, even thousands, of years. Consider information graphics, which have existed since prehistoric times. The earliest information graphics were done in cave paintings in Lascaux, France around 13,000 B.C. These paintings were created to convey ideas about everyday hunting, social, and religious activities. Leonardo da Vinci, fifteenth- and sixteenth-century Renaissance painter, sculptor, architect, engineer, and scientist, also created information graphics.

A Nigel Holmes infographic showing voting districts in Canada.

Englishman Nigel Holmes is considered the father of contemporary information graphics. Drawing on a strong visual tradition acquired in his homeland, he created a unique pictorial style to convey information, particularly statistical details. Holmes coined the term *infographics* to define his work, which is illustrated above. Infographics combine *information* and *graphics* (that is, pictures or illustrations) in a way that brings ideas to life. In presenting information in visual form, infographics do three things:

- Identify the subject.
- Provide the information.
- Explain the information.

People who read *Time* magazine see Holmes's illustrations frequently, but infographics aren't limited to the pages of *Time*. Indeed, they have become such an important part of the journalistic landscape that it is hard to imagine magazines or newspapers without them.

The value of graphics in conveying information should not be underestimated. When confronted with mountains of data in tabular form, people may not take the time to examine all the details and to extract the full meaning from the numbers. Infographics communicate information visually in a way that people find interesting and useful.

Holmes uses a desktop computer to create his illustrations. He usually begins by putting his ideas on paper as pencil drawings. He then scans the images into his PC and uses illustration software to embellish and refine the drawings, adding lines and shading to create dimensions and perspective.

Once the basic drawing is complete, Holmes adds brief text explanations to the images. He enters these through the computer's keyboard. If he wants to emphasize certain words or phrases, he will style them in a special color. Because he is working with a computer throughout the creative process, Holmes can send and receive sketches, rough drawings, and completed infographics electronically. The Photo Essay at the end of this chapter shows the creation of an infographic step by step.

Best of all, the computer and programs that Holmes uses are available to the general public at retail stores across the nation. And because these tools are easy to use, illustrators can spend their time focusing on the information, the message, and its presentation rather than mastering the intricacies of a difficult piece of technology. ■

A S THE TALE OF NIGEL HOLMES AND HIS INFOGRAPHICS SUGGESTS, INFORMATION TECHNOLO-GY provides us with the chance to accomplish what we need to get done and to become better at what we do best. Holmes doesn't need to know all about the technical side of computers to do his job. What he does need, however, is a general understanding of how computers work and what they can do for him.

As we mentioned in Chapter 1, the goal of this book is to show you what computers can do for you and how they can make you more productive. But before we get started, we need to cover some of the basics. In this chapter, we provide a guided tour of a computer so that you can familiarize yourself with its primary components. This information will be very helpful to you as you use computers, because a working knowledge of the basics will help you avoid problems and so become more effective. (Who wants to spend time on the telephone with hardware or software manufacturers when it's not absolutely necessary?) Remember: An informed user is an effective user.

As Figure 2.1 shows, computer systems are made up of five components: hardware, programs, information, people, and procedures. We'll discuss each of these components—and the know-how you'll need to use them effectively—in turn.

■ Hardware: Computing, Storing, and Communicating

Although the terms "computer" and "computer system" are often used rather loosely, these terms are really too broad for this tour. We need to be more specific. As you learned in Chapter 1, a *computer* is any electronic system that can be instructed to accept, process, store, and present data and information. *Computer system* refers to the computer and all the hardware interconnected with it.

Hardware is the general term for the machines (sometimes called the **devices**) that carry out the activities of computing, storing, and communicating data. As Figure 2.2 shows, computer hardware falls into four categories:

- Input devices
- Processors
- Output devices
- Secondary storage devices

These components are part of most computer systems, regardless of the cost or size of the system. (Some computer systems are designed to store all data and information internally and thus do not include secondary storage devices.)

hardware   The general term for the machines (sometimes called **devices**) that carry out the activities of computing, storing, and communicating data.

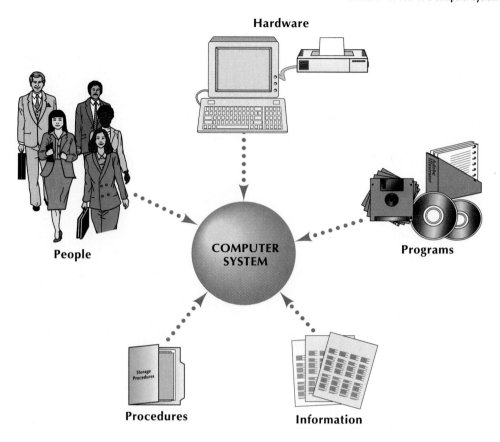

FIGURE 2.1
The Five Components of a
Computer System

Input Devices

Input has two meanings: (1) the data or information entered into a computer, or (2) the process of entering data or information into the computer for processing, storage and retrieval, or transmission. A **cursor**—a blinking box or line on the computer screen—usually indicates the point at which data or information will be input.

Seven different devices are commonly used to input data or information into a computer. These are:

- **Keyboards.** Keyboards (Figure 2.3) containing the letters of the alphabet, numbers, and frequently used symbols (such as $, & and #) are the most common input devices. In some parts of the world, keyboards consist almost exclusively of symbols rather than alphabet letters. In Japan, for example, a popular key-

input   The data or information entered into a computer or the process of entering data or information into the computer for processing, storage and retrieval, or transmission.

cursor   A blinking box or line on a computer screen that indicates the point at which data or information will be input.

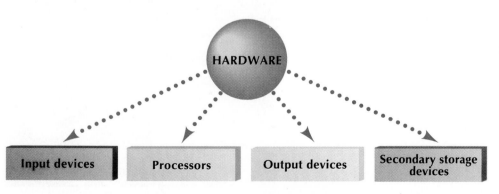

FIGURE 2.2
The Four Categories of
Hardware

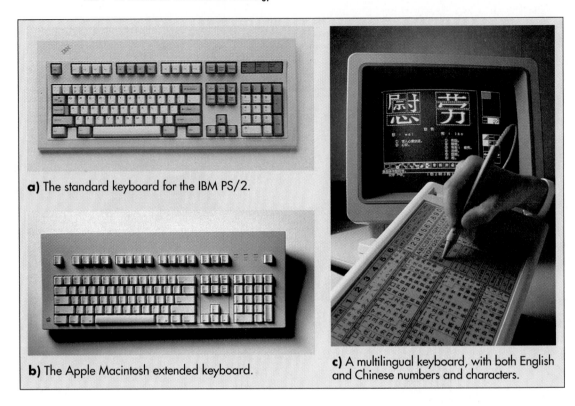

a) The standard keyboard for the IBM PS/2.

b) The Apple Macintosh extended keyboard.

c) A multilingual keyboard, with both English and Chinese numbers and characters.

FIGURE 2.3
Keyboards

board contains the 5,000 letters of the symbolic Kanji alphabet. The Kanji keyboard thus is much larger and contains many more symbols than the keyboards used in North and South America and Europe.

In addition to letters, most keyboards have a numeric keypad. Arranged in a layout similar to that of handheld calculators, numeric keypads are useful for entering data quickly.

- **Point-of-sale terminals.** A variation on the standard business cash register, these terminals typically do not contain alphabet letters. Rather, they consist of a numeric data pad and special purpose function keys, such as for a sale, refund, or void (Figure 2.4). The numeric keypad is used to enter details of the purchase (such as a product or stock number), the cost of the product (if that information is not automatically retrieved from the computer), the amount of money tendered for a cash purchase, or the account number if payment is by a credit or debit card.

FIGURE 2.4
A Point-of-Sale Terminal
in a Supermarket
A variation on the standard cash register, point-of-sale (POS) terminals typically consist of a numeric keypad and special function keys. They are most often used at the point of contact between a business and its customers, hence the name "point of sale."

a) The Microsoft mouse, with its simple and functional design, is now the bestselling mouse in the United States.

b) A variation on the standard mouse, designed by Logitech for children.

FIGURE 2.5
Two Variations on the Mouse

- **Mice.** On the underside of the mouse is a ball that rotates, causing a corresponding movement of a pointer (a large arrow) on the display screen. Two or three buttons (depending on the make) on the top side of the mouse let the user invoke a command or initiate an action (Figure 2.5). Mice offer the advantage of allowing people to control the computer system by pointing to commands rather than entering them through the keyboard.
- **Image scanners.** Image scanners (Figure 2.6) can be used to input both words and images (including drawings, charts, and graphs) directly into a computer. A light illuminates the information one section at a time, with the information under the light being recognized and read into the computer. Image scanners range in size from those that can fit in the palm of your hand to others the size of a newspaper page. Once in memory, the images can be modified or combined with other information.
- **Bar code scanners and wands.** Manual input of data or information takes time and is subject to error. Many retail stores have found that the scanning of *bar code* information is faster and more accurate than entering the same information through a keyboard (Figure 2.7). A **bar code** is a computer-readable code consisting of bars or lines of varying widths or lengths. As the **wand** is waved across the bar code on the package, it recognizes the special letters and symbols in the bar code and inputs this information directly into a PC, midrange computer, or point-of-sale terminal. There the code is translated into product and price information. Sometimes the bar code is passed over a piece of glass, as in a supermarket checkout.

bar code A computer-readable code consisting of bars or lines of varying widths or lengths.

wand An input device used to read a bar code and input this information directly into a computer.

FIGURE 2.6
Image Scanners

a) Hewlett Packard's Deskscan IIC flatbed scanner permts scanning of full-color, large-size documents in just a few seconds.

b) Logitech's ScanMan 256 handheld scanner permits the scanning of smaller documents and is frequently used as an alternative to more expensive flatbed models.

a) Bar code scanning is a fast and efficient way of inputting data. Here, a department manager uses bar codes to replenish inventory in her stock room.

b) Bar code scanning at the grocery store checkout allows clerks to move customers through the line much more quickly than standard cash registers do. It also permits managers to change the price of a product in an instant and to keep track of inventory.

FIGURE 2.7
Bar Code Scanning

- **Microphones.** Often used in multimedia systems, microphones capture the voices or sounds around them for use in computer processing (Figure 2.8). The microphone is attached to a computer by a cable that transmits the sounds.
- **Prerecorded sources.** Tape recorders, cassette decks, record players, and stereo amplifiers can be connected to a computer that captures the sounds as they are played (Figure 2.9). This method of input allows high-quality music and voice reproductions to be merged with text and image information to produce multimedia presentations for education, training, marketing, and many other uses.

Input devices are usually attached to a computer. Sometimes the input device is built directly into the computer. For instance, some PCs and older terminals include the display screen and keyboard in a single case. In contrast, mice, scanners, wands, and microphones are usually separate devices, attached to the computer by a cable. This may be changing, however; recent years have seen the development of wireless input devices (for example, wireless mice).

The Processor

processor or **central processing unit (CPU)**   A set of electronic circuits that perform the computer's processing actions.

microprocessor   A central processor contained on a single computer chip.

The center of action in a computer is the **processor**, also called the **central processing unit (CPU)**. In microcomputers, the processor is a **microprocessor**—a central processor contained on a single computer chip.

A *chip* is a collection of electronic components in a very small, self-contained package. Chips perform the computer's processing actions, including arithmetic

FIGURE 2.8
A Microphone in a Medical Diagnosis System
Microphones are often used in multimedia systems. Here, the computer captures the words spoken by the doctor into the microphone, then processes them to help him determine the best treatment for a patient.

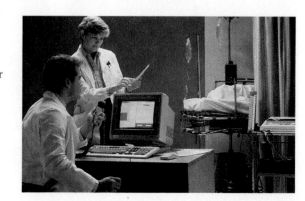

FIGURE 2.9
Prerecorded Sources as Input
Many products that are often considered "consumer electronics" are being used in multimedia systems. Video is provided by videocassette recorders attached to the computer, and stereo sound comes from compact disc players.

calculations and the generation of lines, images, and sounds. Some chips are general purpose and perform all types of actions. Others have a special purpose. Sound chips, for example, do exactly what their name suggests: They generate signals to be output as tones.

System Board.   The processor/CPU can take several forms. Microcomputers contain a specific microprocessor chip as their CPU. This chip is put into a protective package, then mounted onto a board contained within the computer. This board is called a **system board** or **mother board** (Figure 2.10). The system board also contains chips and other circuitry that carry out processing activities.

Larger computer systems may have separate cabinets or freestanding units that contain the chips and circuits that comprise the CPU. At one time, all mainframes and supercomputers had separate units containing the central processor. But today, thanks to the continued miniaturization of chips and circuits, separate units are not always necessary. Even in the most powerful central processors, chips and circuits can be integrated onto a few boards.

Memory.   Both system boards and separate processing units include space for **memory**, sometimes called **primary storage** or **main memory** because it is used by the central processing unit in carrying out all computing activities. Processing does not occur in memory; rather, memory stores data, information, and instructions. When data enter the computer as input, they go into memory/primary storage until they are processed. After processing, the results—information— are retained in memory.

system board or **mother board**   One form of CPU. A board contained within a computer, usually a PC, that carries out the computer's processing activities.

memory, primary storage, or **main memory**   The section of a processor that holds data, information, and instructions before and after processing.

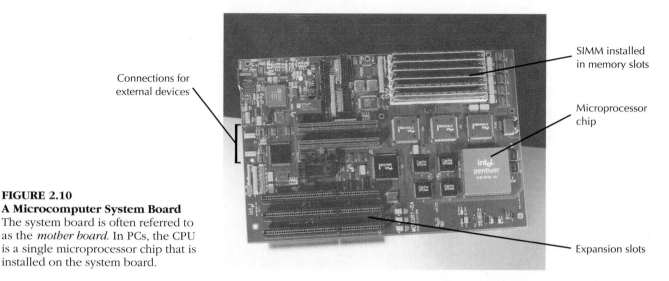

Connections for external devices

SIMM installed in memory slots

Microprocessor chip

Expansion slots

FIGURE 2.10
A Microcomputer System Board
The system board is often referred to as the *mother board*. In PCs, the CPU is a single microprocessor chip that is installed on the system board.

At any given time, a section of memory can hold data and information, or processing instructions. The allocation of memory at the time a program is running will determine whether a particular location will hold an instruction or a unit of data or information.

We discuss the CPU and primary memory fully in Chapter 3.

Output Devices

output   The results of inputting and processing data and information.

People use computers for the **output** they generate—that is, the *results* of inputting and processing data and information. Output falls into two categories: (1) information that is presented to the user of the computer, and (2) information in the form of computer commands that are input to another device.

The most common forms of output geared to the user are reports, schedules, budgets, newsletters, and correspondence. These results can be printed out, displayed on a computer screen, and sometimes played through the speaker built in or attached to a computer (Figure 2.11).

Output from computer processing that is input to another device can perform various functions, including:

- **Controlling a printer.** Output can tell a printer when and what to print, including the location of the data, text, or image on a sheet of paper, film, or transparency. The dimensions of the image and the shades and colors used in the printout (if the printer prints in color) can also be determined.
- **Directing a display.** Computers can display words, graphics, and shapes, either simultaneously or one at a time, on the computer display screen, sometimes called a *video display terminal (VDT)* or *monitor.* Displays can also show **animation**, in which words and shapes move across the display screen. With animation, ideas can be demonstrated, not just described.

animation   The process by which words and shapes move across a display screen.

- **Controlling another device.** Output from computers can direct the actions of other computers and machinery. Computer-controlled manufacturing lathes, automobile ignition systems, and medical CAT scanners (which physicians use to look beneath the skin of a patient to view tissue and bone structures) are all devices that accept computer output as their input—that is, as instructions that guide the actions they perform.
- **Generating sounds.** Output can direct computers to play music, simulate the sound of a jet powering up its engine, or replicate a human voice to announce

INPUT DEVICES   **OUTPUT DEVICES**

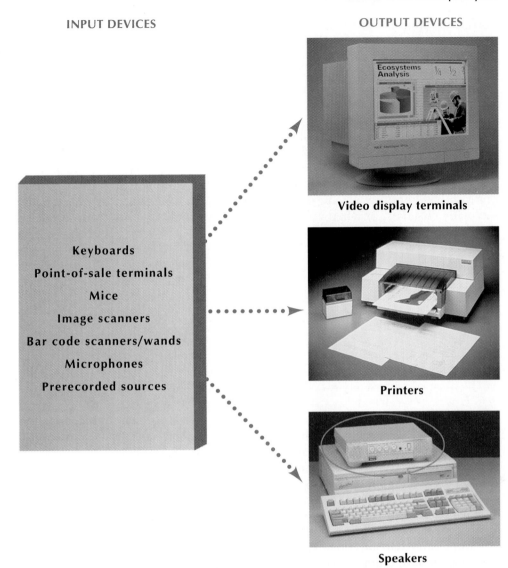

Video display terminals

Printers

Speakers

Keyboards
Point-of-sale terminals
Mice
Image scanners
Bar code scanners/wands
Microphones
Prerecorded sources

Data enter the computer
as input . . .

. . . and are transformed via
processing into output for the user

FIGURE 2.11
The Relationship Between
Input and Output Devices

train stops or telephone numbers. Driven by the need to cut costs and increase responsiveness to callers, many businesses are augmenting telephone switchboards with computer-generated voices to answer information inquiries or instruct callers on how to reach a certain party.

- **Initiating transmission of information.** Because computers are often connected to data communications networks, output is frequently sent over a communications link to another destination, or to multiple destinations simultaneously.

We discuss input and output devices in more detail in Chapter 4.

✓ **Reality Check.**   As you probably know, video games—whether those found in arcades in your local shopping mall or the Super Nintendo Entertainment System in your home, apartment or dorm—are computers. They don't look like the PCs you find on desks and tables, but they do have all the characteristics of computers that we've discussed so far. They use input, do processing, and generate output. (They are not connected to computer networks—at least not yet—and so do not transmit information from one location to another.)

Let's look more closely at these components. The *input* activities are your instructions that control the movement of the characters and vehicles, using joysticks, buttons, steering wheels, or foot pedals. *Processing* takes place before your eyes as the computer translates your actions into the characters' activities. The *output* is shown on the display screen, complete with sound from the speakers. Processing also determines whether you have made good moves, assigning (or subtracting) points accordingly. If the computer chip inside senses that you have not, it will zap, trip, crash, or destroy you. When you have made too many mistakes, or when you have used up your allotted time, the chip ends the game.   ■

Secondary Storage Devices

Computers that run multimedia and other complex programs require great quantities of storage capacity. For this reason, computer systems have several secondary storage options. **Secondary storage** provides the capability to store data, information, or programs outside of the central processor.

The most widely used types of secondary storage, illustrated in Figure 2.12, are:

secondary storage   A form of storage that augments the primary memory of the system board or in the CPU, providing the capability to store data, information, or programs outside of the central processor.

- **Diskettes**—Flexible, flat, oxide-coated disks on which data and information are stored magnetically. For this reason, they are sometimes called **magnetic disks**. Diskettes are either 3 1/2 inches across (the standard size) or 5 1/4 inches across (previously the standard size). Diskettes are removed from the computer when the user is done using the data or information they contain.
- **Hard disks**—Magnetic disks that are not flexible. Ranging from 2 1/2 to 14 inches across, with standard sizes of 3 1/2 and 5 1/2 inches, hard disks can store more data and provide for more rapid storage and retrieval of data and information than diskettes can. Hard disks are usually mounted inside the computer and, unlike diskettes, are not easily removed.

read only   A form of storage from which information can be read but not written onto.

- **Optical disks**—A storage medium similar in design to the compact discs (CDs) played on stereo systems. Many optical disks are **read only**, which means that they can only be played—that is, data, information, and instructions can be read from them but not written onto them. Because of this characteristic, optical disks are sometimes known as **CD-ROM** (compact disk–read only memory). Other types of optical disks allow the writing of information under certain circumstances. (We examine the characteristics of optical disks in detail in Chapter 4.)
- **Magnetic tape**—Used to store large quantities of data and information, often as a second copy of data or information that exists elsewhere. Unlike diskettes, hard disks, and optical disks, which are circular, magnetic tape is linear and comes in reels or cartridges.

drive   The device containing a secondary storage medium's read/write unit.

Information is written to or read from each type of secondary storage medium by a read/write unit contained in a **drive**. The drive rotates the medium during the read/write process. Disk and tape drives read information magnetically, in much the same way that stereo systems read information from cassette tapes. Optical drives use a laser beam to read information.

a) BASF 3.5″ and 5.25″ diskettes.

b) Conner-Pancho 2.5″ hard disk.

c) Optical disk (in protective packaging) with Optimem optical disk drive.

d) 3M 2400-foot magnetic tape reels.

e) BASF EXTRA 2000 magnetic tape cartridges.

FIGURE 2.12   Secondary Storage Media

CRITICAL CONNECTION 1
IT Simplifies Life for Price Waterhouse Auditors

 If you're thinking of becoming a global auditor, be prepared for a challenging career. It will be your job to go over a corporation's financial statements with a fine-tooth comb. Does it follow generally accepted accounting practices? Are its figures accurate? Is there any evidence of fraud? And, because you'll be working on site, are you sure you've packed every tool you might need to do your job completely and accurately? If you're one of the more than 12,000 professionals working for New York–based Price Waterhouse, your tools used to include a suitcase or two for the firm's 40-plus volumes of accounting guidelines.

Now Price Waterhouse is arming its auditors with some of the newest developments in IT. One "weapon" is a high-powered laptop computer, suitable for double-checking the figures on complicated financial statements. The second is a portable CD-ROM drive for the laptop and a CD-ROM disk containing every guideline that used to be issued on paper. Compared to the paper-based volumes, CD-ROM is lighter, more durable, and easier to search; by typing in a keyword, auditors can retrieve relevant data from all 40 volumes in an instant.

Peripheral Equipment

If you listen to computer professionals or systems engineers discussing the components of a computer system, you may hear them refer to "peripherals." **Peripheral equipment** is a general term used for any device that is attached, either physically or nonphysically, to a computer system—whether to a PC, midrange, mainframe, or supercomputer system. Peripherals include input devices, output devices, and secondary storage units. Any device that is ready to communicate with the computer is said to be *online*. A device that is not online is *offline*.

■ Programs: In Charge of the Hardware

Today's general purpose computer systems can perform many different tasks, moving from one to another in an instant. For example, because of the versatility of computers, businesspeople can create drawings and illustrations, write correspondence, prepare detailed financial analyses, do accounts payable, and control inventory on the same system.

The secret to the versatility of computers is programs. By itself, hardware is only a collection of computer apparatus. To be useful, hardware needs software or programs. The two terms are often used interchangeably, but their meaning does vary slightly. **Software** is the general term for a set of instructions that controls a computer or communications network. A **program** is a specific sequence of instructions that tells a computer how to perform a particular action or solve a problem. For example, a communications program instructs the hardware how to send or receive information.

At the center of a computer's activities is the **operating system**, a combination of programs that coordinates the actions of the computer, including its peripheral devices and memory. One of the most common operating systems is **DOS**, a single-user personal computer operating system. (DOS is an acronym for **disk operating system**, which means that the operating system's components reside on a disk and are brought into computer memory as needed.) Gaining in popularity is **Windows**, a single-user PC **graphical user interface (GUI)**, that allows multitasking, in which several programs can be operated concurrently, each in its own **window**, or section of the computer screen. (An **interface** is the means by which a person interacts with a computer.) Using the GUI (pronounced "gooey") to the DOS operating system, individuals direct the computer through the window created by the software. Using a mouse the user can point to icons that activate programs, rather than entering a command word to start processing. Figure 2.13 explains Windows in more detail.

Other popular operating systems are OS/2 for PCs; UNIX for PCs, midrange systems, and mainframes; and MVS and VM, multi-user operating systems for IBM mainframe computers used in business.

Whether used on a PC, midrange, or supercomputer, all operating systems perform the same function: enabling people to interact with the computer and to control the movement, storage, and retrieval of data and information.

Another important type of software is the **application program** (or **application** for short). These programs consist of several programs working together. The illustration program Nigel Holmes uses to create infographics is an application program. Likewise, the programs that a bank uses to process charges, payments, and adjustments to an individual's credit card account are application programs.

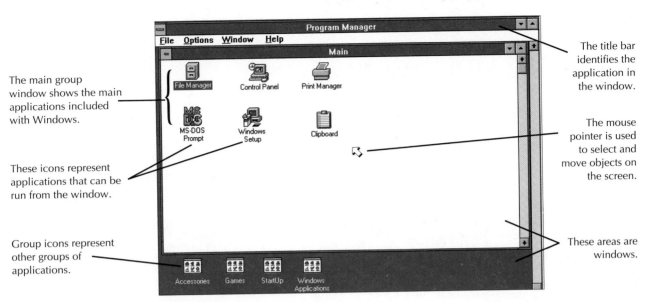

The main group window shows the main applications included with Windows.

These icons represent applications that can be run from the window.

Group icons represent other groups of applications.

The title bar identifies the application in the window.

The mouse pointer is used to select and move objects on the screen.

These areas are windows.

FIGURE 2.13   Sample Windows Interface

Software Packages

Many of the applications used on computers today are purchased as **software packages**, applications that focus on a particular subject and are sold to businesses and the general public. All software packages are accompanied by **documentation**, an instruction manual for the software.* The most frequently used software packages allow users to do spreadsheet analysis, word processing, and desktop publishing; to create illustrations and graphics; to manage databases; to communicate with other computers; and to manage information systems.

Spreadsheet and word processing packages are the most often used types of software. However, as the number of computers in use continues to increase, all of the other types are growing in popularity. Among these other types are packages that teach foreign languages. (See the Global IT box on page 58 titled "¿Habla Usted Español? Multimedia Can Help" for more details.)

Spreadsheet Programs.   The business world—whether large or small, profit or nonprofit organizations—is a world of problem solving. People at all levels of the organization spend a great deal of time reviewing the business's activities, recognizing the occurrence of problems, and identifying alternatives for correcting those problems. As we pointed out in Chapter 1, problems are an everyday occurrence. When they are addressed effectively, these same problems can become opportunities.

Spreadsheet packages are designed to assist in problem solving activities. A **spreadsheet** consists of rows and columns of information. The intersection of each row and column (called a *cell*) can hold data or text, as Figure 2.14 illustrates. New information can be keyed right over old information, so the data in the spreadsheet can be easily updated and recalculated. The software can be easily instructed to add columns, determine percentages, and calculate trends.

Spreadsheet packages make the people using them more effective because they automate time-consuming and error-prone tasks (like adding and subtracting

software package   An application that focuses on a particular subject, such as word processing, and is sold to businesses and the general public.

documentation   An instruction manual that accompanies software. Also, a technical, detailed written description of the specific facts of a program.

spreadsheet   A worksheet consisting of rows and columns of information.

*Note: *Documentation* also refers to a technical, detailed written description of the specific functions of the program.

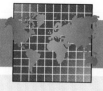

GLOBAL IT

¿Habla Usted Español? Multimedia Can Help

YOU KNOW IT'S BEEN COMING. YOU'VE READ THE WARNINGS IN leading business magazines. You know you should learn at least one foreign language if you're going to work in the global economy. But now the moment of truth has arrived. You've just been offered a great job as a sales rep for a major company. Terrific career opportunity. Good salary, excellent benefits. There's only one catch. Your territory is in Mexico and you know maybe twelve words of Spanish. What will you do?

Help may be as close as your microcomputer and a new batch of software designed to make learning a foreign language fast, easy, and fun—all thanks to multimedia.

Like many other people, you may find you learn best through the total immersion method, in which everything you hear, read, or say will be in the foreign language. That means no communication in English, which forces you to begin absorbing the language fast. This is the method used by the Berlitz Think & Talk Series from HyperGlot Software, which is available for both the IBM PC and the Apple Macintosh. The program, which comes on CD-ROM, teaches you business Spanish, Italian, German, or French by turning your PC into a projector that displays simple stories with plenty of visual hints to help you figure out the correct verbal response. The program can even model the correct pronunciation when it checks your answers.

If you think you'd be more comfortable with the traditional rote drills in grammar, vocabulary, and mock conversations, you're in luck again. HyperGlot also offers the "Learn to Speak" series as well as the Pronunciation Tutor, Tense Tutor, and Word Tutor. Penton Overseas offers the VocabuLearn series (available in three levels of

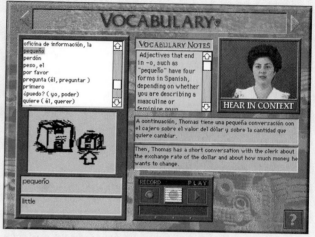

One of HyperGlot's best-selling programs is "Learn to Speak Spanish." The program offers vocabulary notes, reading excercises, and pronunciation practice with a native speaker of Spanish.

difficulty) and Picture It!, a Macintosh program that pairs flash cards simultaneously with a recording of the correct pronunciation.

Don't worry if you can't become fluent overnight. Many of your colleagues and customers will be impressed that you made the effort to learn their language and absorb their culture. And no one will be offended if you turn to a professional translator for help in working out the fine details of your legal or business agreements. It's just good business in the global economy.

---

columns of numbers). People are thus able to spend more time analyzing conditions and opportunities. We discuss spreadsheets in detail in Chapter 5.

Word Processing Programs.   Correspondence (including letters, memoranda, and reports) is an important part of life in both business and personal activities. **Word processing (WP) programs** allow you to enter, change (edit), move, store, and print text information (Figure 2.15). Many programs will also check your spelling, evaluate your grammar, and verify punctuation.

Because word processing programs allow text to be stored and retrieved, they are frequently used to prepare tailor-made versions of correspondence and project proposals. The user can make the necessary changes to a stored document and print a new copy for distribution. Not having to rekey an entire document manually can free an individual's time to perform other, more important activities.

word processing (WP) program   A program that allows the user to enter, change (edit), move, store, and print text information.

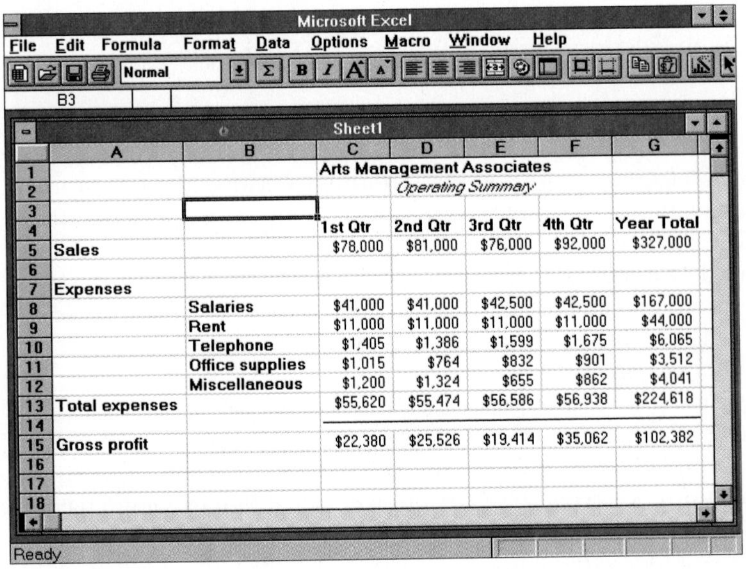

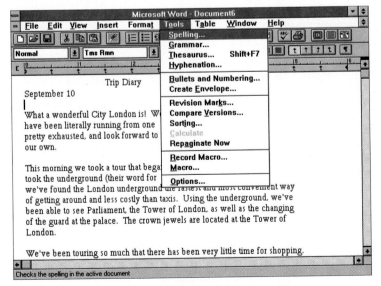

FIGURE 2.14
Worksheet Created with Spreadsheet Software
Spreadsheet software allows a user to change data and perform recalculations easily. For example, if rent were to increase to $12,000 per quarter, the spreadsheet software will automatically adjust both total expenses and gross profit to reflect that change.

Software manufacturers are adding new features to word processing programs all the time. For example, many now let users insert graphics into the body of the text. In many ways, word processing software and desktop publishing software (discussed in the next section) are converging. We discuss these packages fully in Chapter 7.

Desktop Publishing Programs.   **Desktop publishing (DTP) programs** combine text and image handling features with document design capabilities. These programs provide more flexibility in the positioning of text and images (whether drawings or photographs) on a page than word processing programs do. They also allow users to choose from a wide range of type styles and sizes to enhance the appearance of a document.

Desktop publishing came about with the rise of powerful PCs and high-quality software and printers. Many organizations, large and small, rely on this software to

desktop publishing (DTP) program   A program that combines text and image handling features with document design capabilities.

FIGURE 2.15
Sample Word Processing Options
In addition to allowing the user to lay out words in an aesthetically pleasing format, word processing software also checks spelling, grammar, and punctuation. Many newer programs also offer graphics capabilities.

prepare newsletters, brochures, project proposals, advertisements, menus, and theater programs created on a desktop publishing program (Figure 2.16).

Reality Check. At one time, during the early days of information technology, there was a lot of discussion about the "paperless office." The idea was simple: People would enter their ideas through a keyboard and then view them on a computer screen, thus making it unnecessary to print the information. Some people even speculated that the distribution of information would occur by means of magnetic disks, with newspapers, advertisements, and books being read on computer screens.

Well, people *are* putting their thoughts down on computers, but they certainly aren't generating any less paper. In fact, computers have led to a dramatic increase in paper use. We are unwilling to give up the printed word. When preparing a report or document of any kind, we tend to print it repeatedly to view changes and adjustments. Of course, continual printing brings with it the social responsibility to recycle the excess paper generated.

Efforts to reduce the reliance on paper will undoubtedly continue. More organizations are communicating electronically, sending messages and documents over communications networks and allowing the recipients to print out these messages at their discretion. Perhaps one day, more activities will be carried out in this manner. But there is a long way to go.

Graphics Programs. Presenting data that describe trends, chart performance levels, and compare categories often requires charts, graphs, and maps. These **business graphics** can be created using special graphics packages that run on PCs, midrange systems, and mainframes (Figure 2.17). Often included in spreadsheet packages, graphics programs translate tables of data into visual representations. A one-page chart or graph, for example, may summarize many pages of detailed numeric data.

Graphics software programs prepare graphics more quickly and accurately than traditional manual methods. They also help the user to be more precise in drawing

business graphics Charts, graphs, and maps that are created using special graphics packages that translate tables of data into visual representations.

FIGURE 2.16 Desktop Publishing Capabilities
Desktop publishing programs provide a great deal of flexibility in positioning text and images on a page. After the document designer has placed all the items in the desired locations (left), the document can be printed out and used as a master for making copies. Alternatively, the DTP system can be used to create a computer file that is sent on disk to a printer for printing (right). This process is more common with full-color publications.

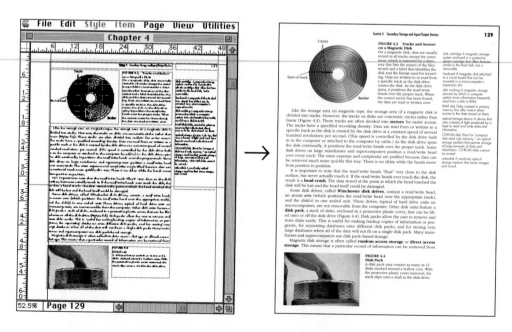

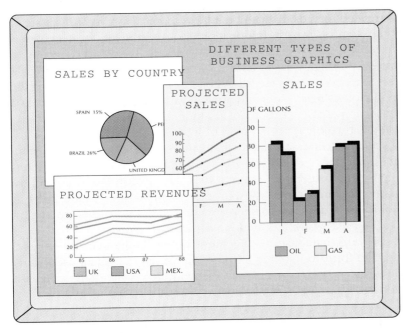

FIGURE 2.17
Sample Graphics Program
Graphics programs translate mountains of data into an easy-to-read, aesthetically pleasing format.

a chart or map and provide for the use of color, shading, and even three dimensions. We examine the uses of graphics software fully in Chapters 5 and 7.

Illustration Programs.   For assistance in drawing images, creating special effects, and translating ideas (rather than data) into visual form, people use **illustration programs**. Using an electronic toolbox that contains brushes, pens, boxes, circles, and other devices, the computer screen becomes a drawing board on which artists bring these ideas to life (Figure 2.18). The finished illustration can then be stored, retrieved, changed, and sent to a printer or similar device.

illustration program   A program in which the computer screen becomes a drawing board on which artists translate ideas into visual form.

No matter what type of illustration the artist wishes to create, an illustration package will enable him or her to do so with greater speed and precision. Yet the artistic ideas and talents originate with the user. The PC is a tool that can increase productivity, but it is not a substitute for creativity and know-how. We discuss illustrator programs in detail in Chapter 7.

database management program   A program that allows users to store information as interrelated records that can be retrieved quickly.

Database Management Programs.   Businesses have a constant need to store and retrieve data and information. **Database management programs** let users store

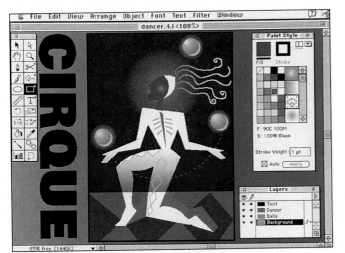

FIGURE 2.18
Illustration Program Capabilities
Illustration programs contain an electronic toolbox containing brushes, pens, boxes, circles, and color palettes.

information as interrelated records that can be retrieved quickly. A *record* is a set of data pertaining to an item of interest. Information about a student, for example, is stored in a student record. Each record is composed of various *fields*, a collection of characters that represent a single type of data. Address, telephone number, and date of birth are all fields in each student's record. A collection of related records (say, the freshman class, or all biology majors, depending on how the database is organized) is called a *file*. The collection of all records about all students comprises the **database**.

With a database information about an item of interest can be retrieved according to a certain specified characteristic of the item. For example, a human resources manager could ask a database system to select the records in an interviewee database and print a list of all interviewees who live in Houston and are experts on international commerce in the European Community (Figure 2.19). A utility company could use a database to keep a record of all the houses, apartment buildings, and businesses to which it provides electricity.

Like all other software, database management programs handle the storage, retrieval, changing, and formatting of the information for the individual user. Many packages are available for use on every size of computer. We discuss database management systems fully in Chapters 6 and 10.

Communications Programs. Data communication is an integral component of information technology and many computing applications. **Communications programs** manage the interaction between a computer system and a communications network and the transmission of data, information, and programs over the network. They provide the versatility needed to link different computers. Communications programs also establish the rules of data transmission and automatically manage the electronic conversation to ensure that the rules are followed. They also control **modems**, the devices that allow computer-to-computer dialogue. In Chapter 9, we examine data communication from several different viewpoints.

Information Systems Programs. Programs to manage business activities comprised the bulk of the software industry prior to the PC boom in the late 1970s and early 1980s. Most businesses acquired their first computers to process data for payroll management, production management, personnel records management, inventory control, and accounting procedures. Today, these applications are still important and account for huge expenditures of business funds in both large and small organizations. Business people often refer to these business management applications as **information systems**, or alternatively as **management information systems (MIS)**.

Information systems differ from spreadsheet packages and the other types of software we've discussed so far in an important way. Information systems focus on business processes (such as the processing of customer orders, the accounting

database A collection of all interrelated records.

communications program A program that manages the interaction between a computer system and a communications network and the transmission of data, programs, and information over the network.

modem A device that allows computer-to-computer dialogue.

information systems or **management information systems (MIS)** Management applications that focus on business processes—for example, processing customer orders, accounting, and inventory management.

FIGURE 2.19
Records of Text and Data in a Job Database
Each individual employee has his or her own individual record that includes three fields: the employee's name, date of hire, and job title. Together, all these records comprise a job database.

NAME	DATE HIRED	JOB TITLE
Sally Thomas	10/2/88	Customer service representative
Morgan Fairfield	5/4/91	Advertising director
Bert Renoso	3/2/76	Customer service manager
James Jones Earl	2/5/78	Quality control supervisor
Ramon Vasquez	6/3/85	Customer service representative
Betty Lin	1/4/65	Operations manager

Record of information

process, the inventory management process, and increasing organizational productivity), while the other types of software focus on solving problems, making personal decisions, and increasing personal productivity. We explore information systems in depth in Chapter 12.

Programming Languages

Computer programs are not written in everyday language or as lines of text. Rather, they are created using a **computer programming language**—a series of commands and codes that the computer can translate into the electronic pulses that underlie all computing activities. A programmer writes the instructions in the programming language, thereby instructing the computer how and when to carry out arithmetic operations, to read data from secondary storage, to store data, and to display or print information.

computer programming language   A series of commands or codes that a computer can translate into the electronic pulses that underlie all computing activities.

Some tasks are performed so frequently during processing that it would be extremely inefficient to code these activities into the program again and again. For this reason, programmers make use of special **utility programs** (sometimes called **utilities**) to perform such functions as sorting records and copying programs from one medium to another. Utilities can either be bundled into an operating system or purchased as software.

utility programs or utilities   Special programs used to perform tasks that occur repeatedly during processing.

Many programming languages have been developed to suit the needs of people tackling different types of problems, with some more popular in business than others. One of the most commonly used business programming languages today is COBOL (COmmon Business-Oriented Language). Other programming languages include C, C++, BASIC, Pascal, and FORTRAN.

All of the computer software packages discussed above are written in a computer programming language. Fortunately for the users of these packages, the programs have already been written. Hence, the user need not know a programming language or how to write a program.

Custom Software

Not all software is prewritten and sold in package form. Much of the software used in businesses is **custom software**, written for a particular firm by systems analysts and programmers (discussed later in this chapter). Applications software is the most common type of software developed by custom programmers (who write the application in a programming language). Custom applications may be developed by *in-house programmers*, who are employed by the company for which the application is developed, or by *contract programmers*, outside experts who are hired by the company to develop a certain program. We discuss the design and development of custom software in Chapter 11.

custom software   The software written specially for a particular business.

■ Information: The Reason for Using Information Technology

The desire to apply information effectively is one of the primary reasons that people use information technology. Computer hardware and software have been developed primarily to process data and generate information.

Recall from Chapter 1 that **information** is an organized, meaningful, and useful interpretation of data. Using information, you determine conditions, assess whether a problem has occurred, evaluate alternative solutions, and select actions. But information is not composed of data only. As Figure 2.20 shows, information may also include text, sound, and images.

information   An organized, meaningful, and useful interpretation of data.

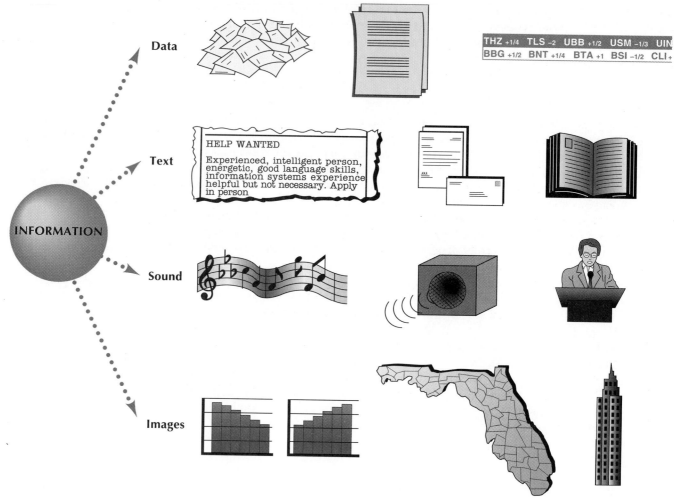

THZ +1/4 TLS −2 UBB +1/2 USM −1/3 UIN
BBG +1/2 BNT +1/4 BTA +1 BSI −1/2 CLI+

HELP WANTED

Experienced, intelligent person, energetic, good language skills, information systems experience helpful but not necessary. Apply in person

FIGURE 2.20   The Four Components of Information
Data do not become information until they are organized logically and usefully. Information may also include text, sound, and images.

Data

data   The raw facts of a situation.

The raw facts of a situation are **data**. Data are abundant in virtually all activities and are described by numbers, letters, symbols, or any combination of the three. Some examples of data are the average points scored by a team's leading player, the number of subscribers to a magazine, the attendance at a rock concert, a mid-day price for a corporate stock, and the number of English majors in the College of Arts and Sciences. Each piece of data describes a fact, a condition, the occurrence of an event, or the results of that event.

Text

text   Written (narrative) information.

Text is written (narrative) information. Whether it is typed, printed, or handwritten does not matter. When you read a newspaper, flip through a magazine, or look at the fine print on a rental agreement, you are using text information. Correspondence includes text information also.

The sports scores and statistics on athletic achievements tell only part of the story. That's why newspapers and magazines always include a narrative description highlighting the most important plays in a game. Without the narrative information, much of the full story would be missing.

Sound

Have you ever called directory assistance to obtain a phone number, only to have the number spoken to you in a human-like (but definitely not human) voice? Then you have heard **spoken information**—information that is conveyed by sound. The same sports statistics that you read in the newspaper may be broadcast to you by an announcer at the game.

Virtually any sound can be captured in a computer system, transmitted over a network, or output through a computer-controlled device. It is now quite common for sound input to originate from people speaking into microphones connected to a computer. In these circumstances, the origin of the sound information is the human voice.

spoken information Information that is conveyed by sound.

Images

An **image** is information in visual form. Images may be used to summarize data, as in charts and graphs. They may take the form of lines, drawings, or photographs. Nigel Holmes's infographics combine data, text, and images. Many multimedia presentations, which use all four of the components of information, use animation to move words and images across the screen.

image Information in visual form.

All of the world's major league sports authorities have begun to establish a "hall of fame" facility to honor outstanding athletes and officials. At the Football Hall of Fame, you will find computer-controlled multimedia displays of the great plays. Sound and image information, stored on optical disk, are retrieved to show the viewer a recreation of the memorable events. The athletes' grunts and groans—and even cheers from the crowd—accompany the action on the display screen. Best of all, the computer-managed displays can be maintained forever, thus providing an important historical record of the sport.

Many people think of using computers to process only data or text. But as you will see throughout this book, sounds and images are as important as, and used almost as frequently as, data and text in computer systems.

People: The Most Important Element

People are the most important element in any computer system. Without them, there would be no need for computers. The people associated with information technology are either users or information technology professionals.

Users

Users are the people who use information technology in their jobs or personal lives. Because they are the ultimate users of a computer system, they are sometimes called **end-users**. There are four types of users (Figure 2.21):

users or end-users The people who use IT in their jobs or personal lives.

- **Hands-on users** use computers or communications systems directly, interacting with them to enter data, do processing, store and retrieve information, transmit details, or produce output.
- **Indirect end-users** do not directly operate a computer but benefit from IT as the recipients of reports, electronic messages, communications, or multimedia presentations.

a) Hands-on users use IT directly, interacting with computers to perform their jobs.

b) Indirect end-users do not operate computers directly, but benefit from IT as the recipients of reports or multimedia presentations.

c) User managers supervise people or activities that involve or are affected by IT.

d) Senior managers incorporate IT's capabilities into their organizations' products, services, and overall competitive stategies.

FIGURE 2.21
The End-Users of
Information Technology

- **User managers** have supervisory responsibility for activities that involve or are affected by information technology. Manufacturing managers, editors, and hospital administrators, for instance, may be in charge of departments or work groups that use IT every day. These managers may not use IT themselves, but they do ensure that their staff members have reliable computer and communication capabilities. It is increasingly rare, however, to find user managers who are not themselves hands-on users.
- **Senior managers** incorporate the capabilities of information technology into an organization's products, services, and overall competitive strategies. They also evaluate the organization's dependence on IT and identify the problems that could arise if the appropriate operating procedures (discussed later in this chapter) are not established or followed. The People box titled "CIO Becomes Key Advisor to CEO" discusses a relatively new senior management position in IT.

CIO Becomes Key Advisor to CEO

IF INFORMATION IS THE LIFEBLOOD OF THE INFORMATION AGE organization, it stands to reason that information managers are pretty important people. That's why hundreds of the world's top corporations have created the position of *Chief Information Officer (CIO)* or senior vice president of IT, a corporate officer who reports directly to the CEO.

CIOs' backgrounds tend to vary. Some have extensive technical backgrounds. Others have MBAs and little or no technical expertise. But they all share a keen awareness of what IT can do for business. What else does it take to be an effective CIO? DuWayne Peterson, a leading IT consultant and former CIO for Merrill Lynch & Co., lists five requirements.

1. *The knowledge that business strategy is the rudder that steers IT planning.* Sometimes a company's IT strategy calls for an entirely new vision of its business. The CIO of Simon & Schuster, for example, is charged with leading the giant publisher into the brave new world of electronic publishing. (See the case study in Chapter 7.) At other companies, the strategic goals are less radical but equally challenging. The CIO at Levi Strauss & Co. is charged with using IT to help the company delegate authority and responsibility to its 32,000 employees around the world. This has meant setting up computer networks that help store managers and suppliers maintain proper inventory levels without intervention from headquarters.

2. *A strong vision of what IT can do to achieve strategic objectives.* In the past, many banks resigned themselves to the idea that customers come and go. As a result, most banks use IT for processing transactions in separate checking, saving, loan, and credit card accounts. Now that competition is heating up, however, Banc One Corp. initiated what has become a banking trend: to win customer loyalty by pursuing a strategy of "relationship banking." At the heart of Banc One's campaign is the Strategic Banking System (SBS), a computer system that integrates 17 systems to create a comprehensive customer profile that can be used to market personalized services. With the help of SBS, for example, the bank's marketing department can identify customers who might need suggestions on financing a college education or preparing for retirement.

3. *The technical ability to develop an IT structure that will provide low-cost, responsive services for all, as well as individualized services for individual business units.* Kmart provides a good example here. One of its CEO's first moves was to ask the senior vice president of information systems for advice on carrying out a new merchandising strategy. At the time, managers of Kmart's 2,400 stores made all buying and restocking decisions, a practice that led to overlapping orders, missed volume discounts, and sometimes empty shelves and lost sales. Five years later, a new satellite-based system lets headquarters track sales at all stores and coordinate the ordering process.

4. *The ability to analyze business processes and make them more efficient before they are automated.* This process, called "re-engineering," is transforming the face of businesses, which need to become more efficient in the face of global competition. At Eastman Kodak, for example, Candy Obourn's title is vice president of information systems and *business processes*; one of her recent projects was the implementation of a software system that would integrate order processing with manufacturing, distribution, and operations.

5. *Effective human resource management programs and skills that produce skilled, well-trained IT workers and end-users.* To train workers CIOs often set up IT training programs for employees at all levels. At Unum Life Insurance Co., for example, the CIO is retraining mainframe programmers to use PC software development tools and training end-users to perform a wider range of "quasi-technical" roles. The CIO at The Chase Manhattan Bank NA oversees several training programs, including Centers of Excellence, in which IT professionals with special expertise act as consultants to their colleagues.

All of this adds up to a big job, one that requires excellent management skills—a fact that is not lost on business analysts. "The IT job used to be a virtual dead end. Now it's a proving ground for future CEOs," says Howard Anderson, president of The Yankee Group, a consulting group.

The retailing industry offers a good example of the ways in which information technology spans all levels of management and influences the company's operations. Wal-Mart, the highly successful ($55 billion) U.S. discount retailer, has become the world's most successful firm of its type through its use of IT. At the store level, cashiers (hands-on end-users) enter sales data into point-of-sale terminals by waving a bar code scanner across a package's bar coded price and stock numbers. The price of the item is then retrieved from the store computer and displayed to the customer on the point-of-sale terminal display. At the same time, the sale of the item is recorded.

Store and department managers who receive reports of store and department sales and inventory levels are indirect end-users. They may not operate a computer directly, but they do rely on the information captured and generated through the company's information system. User managers help to ensure that Wal-Mart maintains remarkably low inventories (approximately 10% of the company's square footage is devoted to inventory, compared to an industry average of 25 percent). The firm's senior managers, including the chief executive officer and corporate vice presidents, use IT to monitor store-by-store sales on a daily basis and to ensure that sales goals are being achieved.

Together, senior and user managers have extended the reach of IT outside of Wal-Mart. The majority of the company's 5,000 vendors now receive point-of-sale information through an electronic linkup. They use this information to determine what is selling and to keep Wal-Mart fully (but not excessively) stocked. Yet the entire process begins with the activities of the hands-on end-user who enters the details about each item sold. (See the case study in Chapter 3 for more on Wal-Mart and its IT activities.)

Information Technology Professionals

information technology professionals   The people responsible for acquiring, developing, maintaining, or operating the hardware and software associated with computers and communications networks.

Information technology professionals are responsible for acquiring, developing, maintaining, or operating the hardware and software associated with computers and communications networks. The following IT professionals have the highest profile:

- **Programmers** use programming languages to create computer and communications network software.
- **Systems analysts** work with users to determine the requirements an application must meet. As part of their job, they may specify the purchase of a software package that gets the job done or order the development of custom software.
- **Systems designers** formulate application specifications and design the features of custom software. In some organizations, the role of programmer, systems analyst, and systems designer may be fulfilled by one person called a **programmer/analyst**.

programmer/analyst   A person who fulfills the role of programmer, systems analyst, and systems designer.

- **Project managers** coordinate the development of a project and manage the team of programmer/analysts.
- **Network specialists** design, operate, and manage computer communications networks.
- **Trainers** work with end-users, helping them to become comfortable and skilled in using hardware or software.

data center or **computer center**   A facility at which large and midrange computer systems are located. These systems are shared by many users who are interconnected with the system through communications links.

- **Computer operators** oversee the operations of computers in **data centers** (sometimes called **computer centers**), facilities at which large and midrange computers systems are located. These systems are shared by many users who are interconnected with the system through communications links. Computer operators also perform support activities, such as starting applications, loading magnetic tape, and anything else that will ensure the smooth operation of computer facilities.

All of the above IT professionals usually work for businesses that use computers or communications technology but that do not design and manufacture the hardware they use. IT professionals in the business of manufacturing computers or computer-related components (such as communication cables and electrical power supplies) generally fall into two categories: **computer engineers**, who design, develop, and oversee the manufacturing of computer equipment, and **systems engineers**, who install and maintain hardware. We discuss other careers in information technology throughout this book.

computer engineers The IT professionals who design, develop, and oversee the manufacturing of computer equipment.

systems engineers The IT professionals who install and maintain hardware.

▉ Procedures: The Way It Goes

Whether an application runs on a PC or a supercomputer, or is used by a single individual or a large number of people, good procedures are essential. A **procedure** is a step-by-step process or a set of instructions for accomplishing specific results. Procedures, combined with people and applications, make up the know-how that is an integral component of IT.

procedure A step-by-step process or a set of instructions for accomplishing specific results.

As Figure 2.22 shows, there are four primary categories of procedures: operations, backup and recovery, security, and development. All of these procedures are for people. They help to avoid problems and provide guidance in dealing with them if they arise.

Operations Procedures

Operations procedures pertain to the execution of an application. Typically, operations procedures describe:

operations procedures Procedures that describe how a computer system or application is used, how often it can be used, who is authorized to use it and where the results of processing should go.

- How a system or application is used.
- Who is authorized to use the system and what each individual is authorized to do.
- How often certain applications are to be used.
- Where results of processing (that is, the output) should go.

For example, at Wal-Mart, the giant discount retailer we discussed earlier, strict procedures govern what information is shared with suppliers and under what circumstances. The guidelines also describe the form in which information is shared,

FIGURE 2.22
The Four Types of Procedures

indicating when raw data should be distributed and when only summary forms should be released.

If you use a PC, you probably follow a set of procedures for starting up and shutting down the computer. Operators of mainframes located in computer centers or midrange computers located in offices must do the same thing. These procedures ensure that information is not lost and that electrical components are not damaged.

Depending on the application, operations procedures can be very simple (for example, "Always make a backup copy of the day's work before shutting down the system") or quite involved (for example, "At the end of every month, make a backup copy of all databases, a copy of all transactions, and reset all account totals to begin the next month").

Backup and Recovery Procedures

backup procedures
Procedures that describe how and when to make extra copies of information or software to protect against losses.

backup copies   Extra copies of information or software made to protect against losses.

recovery procedures
Procedures that describe the actions to be taken when information or software must be recovered.

Nobody wants to spend several days creating a high-impact graphic only to lose it because a power line goes down or because a diskette gets misplaced. As a general rule, you should assume that sooner or later something will happen to cause your work to be lost.

Backup procedures describe when and how to make extra copies (called **backup copies**) of data, information, or software to protect yourself against losses. Should any of these be lost or accidentally changed, the backup copy can be used to restore the original version so that a minimum of work is lost. **Recovery procedures** describe the actions to be taken when data and information or software must be recovered.

Reality Check.   A fundamental "principle" of personal life has been humorously phrased in the form of Murphy's Law, which states simply that *if something can go wrong, it will.* There are corollaries to this principle, including:

Nothing is as easy as it looks.

Everything takes longer than you think.

If you determine that there are exactly four ways in which something can go wrong, a fifth way will suddenly occur.

Nature always takes the side of the hidden flaw.

Murphy's Law applies to information technology too, which means that you should always assume that data, information, and software sooner or later will be accidentally erased, damaged, or lost. Always make backup copies of *everything.* ■

Security Procedures

security procedures
Procedures that are designed to safeguard data centers, communications networks, computers, and other IT components from accidental intrusion or intentional damage.

Security procedures are designed to safeguard data centers, communications networks, computers, and other IT components from accidental intrusion or intentional damage. Backup copies protect against loss; security procedures prevent actions that could lead to that loss.

Security procedures are created because information technology managers must presume that backups are not enough and that explicit protective actions are necessary. Common security procedures entail limiting individual access to certain databases and creating secret passwords that users must input into the computer to perform certain functions.

Security software can play an integral role in protecting systems and data. Such programs allow IT managers to restrict access to files and databases, to disk drives, and even to input/output devices.

Of particular importance is protection against **viruses**—hidden programs that can alter, without an individual's knowledge, the way a computer operates or modify the data and programs stored on the computer. The virus copies itself onto other programs or to diskettes inserted into the system, thereby spreading itself from one computer to another. If undetected for long periods of time, a virus can do a great deal of damage to stored information. The Quality and Productivity box on the next page titled "Computer Viruses Spur the Push for Safe Computing" offers some tips on how to protect your computer from virus damage. We discuss viruses in more detail in Chapter 13.

security software   Software that is designed to protect systems and data.

virus   A hidden program that can alter, without the user's knowledge, the way a computer operates or modify the data and programs stored on the computer.

CRITICAL CONNECTION 2
Rainbow Technologies, Inc.: Sentinel Stymies Software Pirates

It's easy to see why software piracy (the unauthorized copying of software) is so widespread. For the price of a few blank disks, the pirate can make a bootleg copy of a program that sells for hundreds of dollars. However, software piracy is illegal, and it robs software publishers of more than $2 billion every year.

Until recently, software publishers were helpless. One early countermeasure—copy-protection schemes—failed. Legal users detested the awkward ritual of "unlocking" their software, while computer criminals easily wrote—and began selling—the software equivalent of skeleton keys.

Now some software publishers are turning to the Sentinel family of products from Rainbow Technologies, Inc. The Sentinel combines a matchbox-sized device that plugs into the printer connection port with special program codes that are incorporated into the software that is to be protected. When a user issues the command that opens the protected program, these codes trigger a search for mathematical formulas stored in the matchbox. If they aren't found, the program won't run, and therefore cannot be copied.

Development Procedures

Development procedures explain how IT professionals should describe user needs and develop applications to meet those needs. They may also prescribe when and how software should be acquired and put into use. As part of the development process, the IT professional must first examine the business situation, evaluating the alternative methods for improving the situation or capitalizing on an opportunity. In some firms, these findings are recorded according to specific *documentation procedures*.

Good systems development procedures determine whether an application will succeed or fail. Chapter 11 discusses the development of computer and communications applications, showing how application developers work and the decisions they must make to transform a system from an idea into reality.

development procedures   Procedures that explain how IT professionals should describe user needs and develop applications to meet those needs.

QUALITY AND PRODUCTIVITY

Computer Viruses Spur the Push for Safe Computing

ONCE UPON A TIME, MOST PEOPLE ASSOCIATED THE NAME *Michelangelo* with the famous Renaissance artist. That was before computer experts sounded the alarm about a different Michelangelo, a computer virus that was set to "go off" on March 6, the artist's birthday.

As the text discusses, a computer virus is a rogue computer program, a tiny saboteur that sneaks into your computer when you use an infected disk or program. Once inside your machine, the virus copies itself to other files it comes in contact with. Its effects can range from the distressing—the monitor displays "Your computer is now sick"—to the devastating. The system may "crash" as the virus clogs the computer's memory, or all your files may be wiped clean, erasing thousands of hours of work. (Michelangelo has this effect.)

The first known computer virus was created by a University of Southern California student in 1983 to demonstrate that microcomputer security was insufficient. But no one paid much attention until July 1987, when officials at the Hebrew University in Jerusalem learned that a computer virus was poised to erase any computer program executed on Friday the 13th. That virus, dubbed Friday the 13th or Jerusalem B, was the first computer virus to be named.

Today computer viruses are considered one of the most chilling acts of vandalism to hit the computer world. More than 1,500 computer viruses have been identified, and another 50 surface every week. Computer viruses have been discovered in every type of computer and computer network around the world. They have been discovered in shrinkwrapped software and preformatted disks sold by major companies, as well as on the special diagnostic disks used by service technicians.

Microcomputers are most vulnerable to viruses, since they typically aren't protected by the security measures that guard their larger cousins. That's why businesses that depend on micros have issued instructions like these for safe, virus-free computing:

- *Perform regular backups.* Storing a backup of all your disks and your operating system on a write-protected set of disks (disks that can't be written to by another program) won't keep the viruses away, but it can help you restore your system if a virus does attack.
- *Install and use an antivirus package.* These software packages work in one of two ways. Either they scan your computer system for the "signatures" of known viruses or they use artificial intelligence techniques to warn you if the system has obeyed instructions to copy unusual instructions—a potential virus—to program files. Because a few viruses account for almost 80% of all infections, this practice will go a long way toward protecting you and your system.
- *Know the source of your programs.* Many common viruses are spread when users download games and other programs from bulletin board systems (BBSs; see Chapter 9) or share pirated copies of software programs, many of which have been intentionally infected with viruses. Although the major, reputable BBSs and software distributors scan their systems for viruses, most corporations and all prudent end-users scan every program and disk before use. In addition, many corporations forbid employees to share disks or use disks from home.
- *If you think you have a virus, don't panic.* Save what you are working on and turn off your PC. Use your write-protected backup of the operating system to restart the computer and run your antivirus software at least twice. Once you are certain the system is "clean," you can use your backup to restore your hard disk.

Together, these measures should help you stay one step ahead of the virus vandals. In the meantime, the computer industry is working on more permanent cures. The System 7 operating system for Macintosh computers is already immune to two of the most vexing viruses that damage key files, and Microsoft Corporation is releasing a read-only command that will keep viruses from copying themselves from program to program.

An Introduction to Systems

As we noted in Chapter 1, IT can be used by individuals or by groups of people. Let's explore some of the differences between personal systems and multi-user systems. (Recall that a *system* is a set of components that interact to accomplish a purpose.)

Personal/Single-User Systems

Nigel Holmes uses a PC to create his infographics. To him, the PC is a very personal tool, loaded with his favorite software and outfitted with equipment that will enable him to translate his ideas onto paper. Because Holmes is the sole user of his PC, it can truly be considered a *personal* system. It is also a **single-user system**: one that is not connected with other computers or shared by other people.

single-user system   A system that stands alone and is not interconnected with other computers or shared by other people.

The most important benefit of personal systems is their ability to enhance the productivity and effectiveness of those who use them. In Holmes's case, effectiveness means being creative and representing information in an attractive and digestible format. It also means increased productivity, because Holmes can use his personal system to develop illustrations more rapidly than he could by hand.

Multi-User Systems

When people work together or need to exchange information, it is often helpful for their computers to be interconnected. **Multi-user system** is the general term used to describe a system in which more than one user shares one or more systems of hardware, programs, information, people, and procedures. Multi-user systems have three purposes: (1) to increase the productivity and effectiveness of the people using the applications, (2) to increase the productivity and effectiveness of the organizations in which the applications are used, and (3) to improve the services provided to those who rely on others using multi-user applications.

multi-user system   A system in which more than one user shares one or more systems of hardware, programs, information, people, and procedures.

All of the following are reasons to use multi-user systems:

- **To share a computer.**
  Example: American Airlines, Delta Airlines, and TWA interconnect thousands of travel agents by allowing them to share a centralized mainframe system to book reservations for their customers. United Airlines and American Airlines have similar shared computer airline systems.
- **To share hardware.**
  Example: Artists working on separate projects at *The New York Times* share a printer on which they can produce their illustrations. Each artist's computer is connected to the printer through a communications cable.
- **To share software.**
  Example: Rather than requiring students to purchase individual copies of a multimedia biology education program, the University of Minnesota acquired a license from the manufacturer to allow many students to use the software. Students can share the software on a special network set up in the laboratory. The network interconnects separate PCs to a more powerful central PC on which the software is stored and made accessible to the separate student PCs.
- **To share information.**
  Example: Medical personnel at the Stanford Medical Center and at Massachusetts General Hospital can review all of the diagnostic, test, and treatment information on a critically ill patient, including X-rays, because all are stored in a single database maintained at the hospital chosen by the patient.
- **To share communications.**
  Example: Product designers in many companies stay in touch with one another, regardless of their geographic location, by means of an electronic mail system. Both IBM and Digital Equipment Corp. interconnect their employees around the world through their worldwide messaging networks. At Coca-Cola Co., employees use the same network to send and receive messages through their desktop, laptop, or notebook computers.

You can imagine how important multi-user systems are in manufacturing plants. Automobile makers in Japan, South Korea, throughout Europe, and in the United States rely on multi-user systems to interconnect production and assembly equipment, including robots. Networking allows activities to be synchronized so that all actions take place at the right time.

Multi-user systems are neither more nor less valuable than single-user systems. Rather, each offers a particular set of benefits. We discuss single-user systems in detail in Chapters 5 – 8 and multi-user systems in detail in Chapters 9–12.

CRITICAL CONNECTION 3
McKesson Corp: "Wearable" Computers Streamline the Retailer-Distributor Link

When you've got a splitting headache, you won't be pleased to find the drugstore shelf bare of aspirin. This, in a nutshell, summarizes the importance of *distribution*, the wholesale link between manufacturer and retailer. Few companies do distribution better than McKesson Corp., a San Francisco–based distributor of drugs and health care products.

In the pre-IT days, McKesson's customers ordered goods by telephone. Banks of telephone order takers completed order forms and warehouse workers walked about, handpicking items off the shelves. The system was slow, expensive, and error-prone.

McKesson responded in the early 1970s by forging computer network links with manufacturers and retailers. Today, a retailer's employee walks through the store carrying a computer the size of a cellular phone. One swipe of a handheld laser scanner over a bar-coded shelf label and—presto—an order is beamed to a McKesson warehouse. At the warehouse, a central computer radios the order to a revolutionary "wearable" computer strapped to a worker's forearm. The wearable computer combines a portable computer with a two-way radio (for receiving and sending order information), a hand-held laser scanner (for choosing items from warehouse shelves), and a three-inch screen that displays, among other things, the shortest route through the warehouse. When the worker has filled the order, the wearable computer sends a message back to the central computer, which creates an electronic bill for the retailer.

■ Information Technology in Practice at State University: An Example

Now that we've toured the computer and been introduced to its capabilities, it will be useful to put all the pieces together. The example that follows describes the use of PCs, mainframes, and communications networks in the day-to-day activities of a university. You will see how both single-user and multi-user systems play important roles.

Information Technology in the Business Department

The Administrative Coordinator

Linda Savant is Administrative Coordinator for the Department of Business at State University. She is an effective information manager and works well with people. She believes in communicating with students, faculty, administration, and her staff face-to-face, but also finds computers an invaluable tool for doing her job and for helping others.

Linda uses her PC in five ways: to do word processing, to maintain spreadsheets, to maintain departmental databases, to do departmental budgeting, and to communicate electronically.

Word Processing.   Linda prepares many memos, letters, and reports, some of which are sent to people within the university and some of which are sent to the business community. She prepares most of her written documents using word processing software and sends them electronically over a network that interconnects faculty and staff.

Spreadsheets.   Linda routinely prepares and reviews enrollment projections, the staff's travel plans, research budgets, and instructional proposals. To maintain this information, she continually reviews and updates a spreadsheet containing the relevant categories of information.

Particularly important to Linda are "what if" analyses performed using the spreadsheets. What if course enrollments increase by 10% next year? What if faculty member X requests a leave of absence to participate in a program in Tokyo? By entering possible changes into the spreadsheets, Linda is able to determine the likely effects of unexpected changes.

Departmental Databases.   Although the university maintains a great deal of information on students and faculty, Linda's department needs additional information. Linda maintains this information in databases on her PC. For instance, a special database contains personal information for faculty members and adjunct instructors (address and telephone numbers; e-mail address; teaching preferences; research interests; books, articles, and reports published; and research grants applied for or in progress). This database can be used to retrieve the telephone number of a faculty member who is on sabbatical and visiting a university abroad during the current term. It can also be used to prepare a list of all the articles published by department faculty during a recent academic year.

This database resides only on Linda's PC. It is maintained using a personal computer database management software package.

Department Budgeting.   Using an accounting system package running on her PC, Linda maintains the department's financial budget. This application includes information regarding university-provided funds, receipts of funds from outside sources, and contributions by alumni and friends of the department. The university's centralized accounting system does not have this information.

Linda prepares detailed listings periodically to itemize all the department's expenditures. Likewise, she can display or print a summary listing whenever she needs to determine the balance in a specific account. She can even retrieve the details of a specific transaction for review.

Electronic Communication.   A communications network links all of the PCs in Linda's department together. Thus Linda, like every other faculty and staff member in her department, can send and retrieve message or information within the department.

Because the business department's network is also interconnected with the university communications network, Linda can access information that resides on systems at the university's computer center. She can display or print this information, downloading it from the computer center to her PC. Downloading information avoids the necessity of rekeying data or information into the computer.

The Department Administrative Staff

Akio, Mark, Maria, Michelle, Robin, and Ruth are administrative staff members in the business department. Each has a personal computer on his or her desk. Most use IBM-compatible computers equipped with DOS, Windows, and a variety of PC application packages for word processing, desktop publishing, spreadsheets, and graphics. Robin and Akio use Apple Macintosh computers. Their computers are outfitted with the same categories of software created for the Macintosh.

All members of the administrative staff have customized their PCs to meet their needs. All the PCs have a color monitor, keyboard, mouse, diskette drive, and internal hard disk. The PCs used by Michelle and Ruth have been set up to go right into the word processing program when they are turned on. The others are set up so that the staff member must specify the specific application to use after turning the computer on.

All of the personal computers used by the staff members can be operated as stand-alone systems. Each is also interconnected to the department's computer network (Figure 2.23).

The Department Faculty

All business department faculty members have PCs in their offices; some of them are IBM-compatible and some are Apple Macintosh. The department provides each faculty member with the software he or she needs for teaching, research, and public service activities. All faculty use the same word processing package, which the department has chosen as a standard program. In addition, many have spreadsheet, graphics, and desktop publishing packages.

The features and power of the faculty PCs vary with the individual user. Those who do extensive calculations, use databases often, or prepare presentation visuals have faster PCs outfitted with extra memory and storage capacity. Those who use their PCs primarily for word processing (preparing teaching materials, research and instructional improvement proposals, or manuscripts for publication) generally do not ask for the fastest or most powerful PCs.

Because all faculty PCs are interconnected to the department communications network, the members of the department can send messages and information to each other. They can choose to send electronic messages to specific individuals or they can broadcast a message to all members of the department.

The department chair, who is a faculty member with additional administrative responsibilities, routinely disseminates information through the department network. It is easier and more efficient to communicate through the network than to type a memo, duplicate it, and place a copy of it in each faculty member's mailbox.

Faculty's PCs also interconnect with the university's computer network. From their desktop PCs, faculty members can exchange messages and information with other faculty within the university. And because the university's computer is connected to an external communications network, faculty can communicate with their colleagues at institutions around the world.

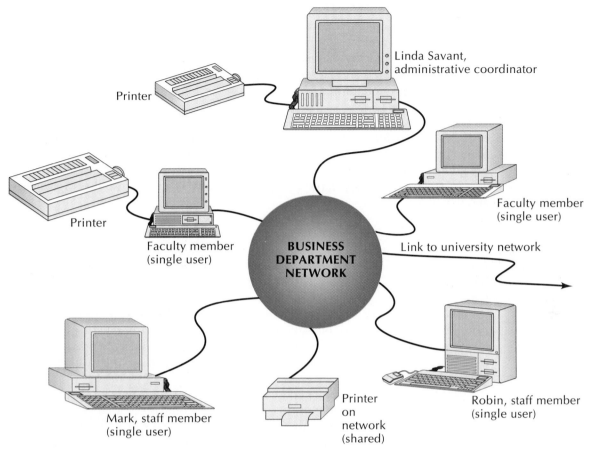

FIGURE 2.23
The Business Department Network at State University

Information Technology at the University

State University operates a large complex of mainframe and midrange computers. These multi-user computers serve several purposes. One midrange computer, for example, is used by all university libraries to maintain the book and periodical collections and to keep track of books checked out and returned. Other computers are general purpose and are shared by members of many academic and administrative departments within the university.

In addition to being the center of the university's communications network, the computers in the computer center contain software that is shared by faculty, students, and staff members. Shared mainframe software is usually expensive and requires computer capabilities that preclude its use on PCs or midrange computers. The administration also maintains centralized databases on students, faculty, facilities (buildings and equipment), and finances. This information is accessible to some department administrators and staff members, who need it to operate their departments and run academic programs.

The research and instructional uses of the university computer center's IT are important, but the system is not limited solely to academic uses. The university administration uses these systems to oversee the school's business processes. The business transacted through the university's computer system includes (but is not limited to):

- University admission transactions
- Course enrollment transactions
- Student tuition and fees payment transactions
- Non-tuition receipt and payment transactions
- Issuance of printed fee statements for payment
- Issuance of printed transcripts

The university-wide applications and databases reside on large systems, rather than PCs, because of the large volume of records that must be maintained. Large-scale applications often require high-speed computing capabilities and large memory and storage capacities. Mainframe computers can provide this capability while also providing access to a large group of people who wish to use the applications and databases.

The University as a Business

Because you register for courses, interact with faculty and staff members, borrow books from the library, and pay fees, the examples above probably seemed quite familiar to you. You may not realize it, but the university is a business. Its products are education, research, and other university services. When you apply for admission, register for a course, or make tuition payments, you are initiating a business transaction that will be processed by computer. At the university, Linda keeps files on faculty members. In a retail business, she would perhaps keep files on customers or suppliers.

All of the uses of computers and communications systems we've seen in use at the university occur routinely in business. Some business computers are used by one person only; others are shared across the departments or divisions of a company. Some are stand-alone and others are interconnected. Each element in our example of IT at State University will serve as a model of the many business uses of IT that are discussed throughout this book.

Information Processing

In Chapter 1, we introduced six information handling functions of IT: capture, processing, generation, storage and retrieval, and transmission. The preceding example of State University includes thirteen information processing activities associated with the six information handling functions of information technology (Figure 2.24). These are:

Capture

INPUT: Entering data into the system for processing. A student registering for a course in person or through use of a touch-tone telephone or a personal computer creates a registration transaction that is treated as *input* to the registration system.

UPLOAD/DOWNLOAD: Many users of the university's computer system receive information from another location within the university network. For example, the Faculty of Arts and Sciences obtains from the central student database the names of individuals who have declared business as their major area of study. Sending information from a PC to a central mainframe system is called **uploading**. The transfer of information from the central system to a desktop computer is called **downloading**.

Processing

COMPUTE: Calculating results through addition, subtraction, and other arithmetic functions. For example, the university's main computer computes the total

uploading   The process by which information is sent from a PC to a mainframe.

downloading   The transfer of information from a central system to a desktop computer.

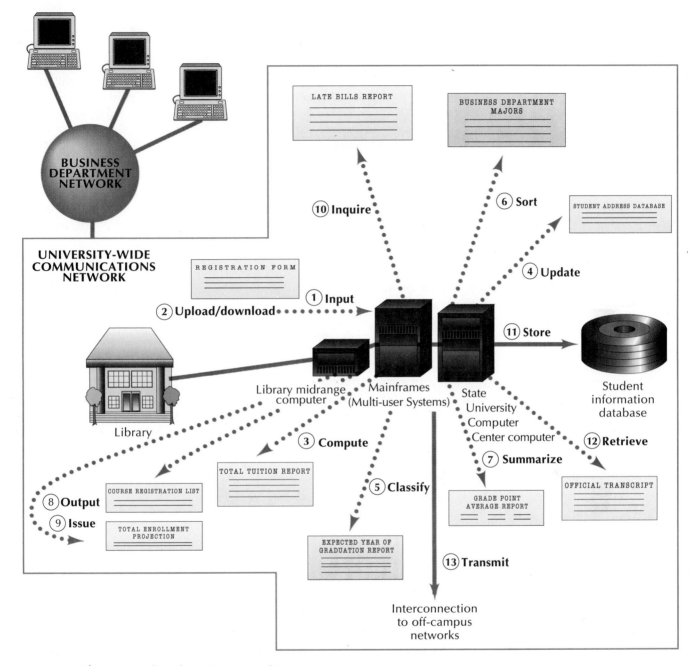

FIGURE 2.24 State University's Computer System
State University's system handles all 13 information processing activities associated with the
six information handling functions of IT.

fees to be paid by accumulating tuition for the term, special fees, and dues for student organizations.

   UPDATE: Adding, deleting, or changing records in a database. There are two
ways that records can be updated. In **batch processing**, all transactions are
grouped and processed at one time. In **real-time processing**, each transaction is
processed as it occurs. For example, if the registrar learns that a student has
changed addresses since last term, the change may be added directly into the database through a terminal, in real-time.

batch processing   The
grouping and processing of all
transactions at one time.

real-time processing   The
processing of each transaction as it
occurs.

CLASSIFY: Categorizing or grouping information according to a particular characteristic. For instance, the Dean's Office groups students by expected year of graduation.

SORT: Arranging information into a useful sequence (for example, alphabetical or numerical order). For example, the Business Department prints out an alphabetical listing of all its majors in order to assign an adviser to each student.

SUMMARIZE: Reducing a large volume of data into a more concise, easily used format that contains sufficient detail to meet the user's need. Grade point averages, for example, are a summary of the grades earned in all courses taken by each student.

Generate

OUTPUT: Preparing a report to be printed or displayed for an intended recipient. For example, each term the administration generates a student course registration list by processing the registration database.

ISSUE: Producing and printing a document. For example, term registration permits are issued by using information in the student database. The same process also generates enrollment projection information for the university and each individual department.

Storage and Retrieval

INQUIRE: Satisfying a request for information through computation or retrieval of stored information. For example, the Bursar's office may ask the system to produce a list of all those students whose bills are in arrears.

STORE: Retaining information for future use by recording the details on disk or diskette (for long-term storage) or in memory (for short-term storage). Student information databases are generally recorded on magnetic disk for long-term retention.

RETRIEVE: Locating and obtaining information specified in an inquiry. For example, a faculty member may retrieve the academic record of a specific individual to fill out a graduate school recommendation.

Transmit

TRANSMIT: Distributing information over a communications network. For example, faculty members regularly transmit information to colleagues in their department, on campus, or across long distances if they are interconnected with a communications network.

SUMMARY OF LEARNING OBJECTIVES

1 **Identify the five components of a computer system.** The five components of a computer system are: (1) *hardware*, the machines (devices) that carry out the activities of computing, storing, and communicating data; (2) *programs*, the specific sequences of instructions that tell computers how to perform specific actions; (3) *information*, organized, meaningful, and useful sets of data; (4) *people*, the end-users of IT or IT professionals; and (5) *procedures*, the step-by-step processes or sets of instructions for accomplishing specific results.

2 **Explain the four categories of hardware and their functions, and discuss the relationship between hardware and software.** The four categories of hardware are: (1) *input devices*, used to enter information or data into a computer; (2) *processors*, sets of electronic circuits used to perform the computer's processing actions, including arithmetic calculations; (3) *output devices*, used to present information to the user or to input information into another device; and (4) *secondary storage devices*, used to augment the computer's primary memory.

By itself, a computer is merely a collection of computer apparatus. To be useful, hardware needs software or programs. *Software* is the general term for a set of instructions that controls a computer or communications network. A *program* is a specific sequence of instructions that tells a computer how to perform a particular action or solve a problem.

3 **Differentiate between an operating system and an application program.** An *operating system* is a combination of programs that coordinates the actions of a computer, including its peripheral devices and memory. It enables people to control the movement, storage, and retrieval of data and information. An *application program* consists of several programs working together.

4 **Identify eight different types of software packages.** Eight different types of software packages are: (1) spreadsheet programs, (2) word processing programs, (3) desktop publishing programs, (4) graphics programs, (5) illustration programs, (6) database management programs, (7) communications programs, and (8) information systems programs.

5 **Explain the four components of information.** The four components of information are: (1) *data*, the raw facts of a situation, (2) *text*, or written (narrative) information, (3) *sound*, or spoken information, and (4) *images*, or visual information.

6 **Distinguish between the users of information technology and IT professionals.** *Users* are people who use information technology in their jobs or personal lives. There are four types of users: hands-on users, indirect end-users, user managers, and senior managers.

IT professionals are responsible for acquiring, developing, maintaining, or operating the hardware and software associated with computers and com-munications networks. Some high-profile IT professionals are programmers, systems analysts, systems designers, project managers, network specialists, trainers, and computer operators.

7 **Describe the four types of procedures used in computer systems.** The four types of procedures used in computer systems are: (1) *operations procedures*, which describe how a computer system or application is used, who is authorized to use it, how often it can be used, and where the results of processing should go; (2) *backup and recovery procedures*, which describe when and how to make extra copies of information and the steps to take when information or software must be recovered; (3) *security procedures*, which are designed to safeguard data centers, communications networks, computers, and other IT components from accidental intrusion or intentional damage; and (4) *development procedures*, which explain how IT professionals should describe user needs and develop applications to meet those needs.

8 **Explain the difference between single and multi-user systems.** A *single-user system* is a system that stands alone and is not interconnected with other computers or shared by other people. A *multi-user system* is the general term used to describe a system in which more than one user shares hardware, programs, information, people, and procedures.

9 **List the thirteen information processing activities associated with the six information handling functions of IT.** The information processing activities performed by IT are: (1) input, (2) upload/download, (3) compute, (4) update, (5) classify, (6) sort, (7) summarize, (8) output, (9) issue, (10) inquire, (11) store, (12) retrieve, and (13) transmit.

KEY TERMS

CRITICAL CONNECTIONS

1. IT Simplifies Life for Price Waterhouse Auditors

The financial statements an auditor examines are important for at least three reasons. First, they present a "snapshot" of the corporation's financial health. Second, they influence investors and competitors. And third, they establish tax liability, which helps determine how much money the government has to work with.

Questions for Discussion

1. Price Waterhouse spent several million dollars on CD-ROM drives, in addition to the expense of creating a database of the accounting guidelines and ordering a "pressing" (copying) of the CD-ROMs (for about $2 a copy). By way of comparison, each paper volume costs less than $2 to print and bind. Why do you think the national director of audit technology for Price Waterhouse estimates that CD-ROM technology has saved the firm a substantial amount of money and actually paid back the investment in one year?

2. The accounting guidelines Price Waterhouse issues for its auditors sometimes need to be updated, and CD-ROM disks cannot be updated. How, then, can the use of CD-ROM be an advantage?

3. Often, clients ask Price Waterhouse questions that can be answered only by consulting more than one volume of guidelines. How might the use of CD-ROM reduce worries that Price Waterhouse will give incomplete answers?

2. Rainbow Technologies, Inc.: Sentinel Stymies Software Pirates

Rainbow Technologies sells most of its Sentinel family of devices to the software publishers of expensive, specialized programs that sell for $500 and up. Another major customer is Microsoft Corp., which has been packing the Sentinel in some software it sells in some countries, where the premium prices charged for foreign-language versions of popular software may lead to more software piracy.

Questions for Discussion

1. Define the concept of "copyright" in your own words and explain why software piracy is a violation of the software publisher's copyright.

2. One explanation for software piracy holds that many users simply don't understand the language of the licensing agreements that forbid "unauthorized" copying. Read three or four of these agreements (see Figure 13.7 for an example) and note any terms or statements that seem unclear or unfair. Do you feel that this explanation is valid or not?

3. Some pirates justify their acts by saying that sample demonstration disks and limited return policies don't give them a fair chance to decide if they like a program before they lay out hundreds of dollars. Does this argument seem valid, given the fact that the pirates' favorite targets include WordPerfect, a word processing program that is standard at many major companies and law firms? How can these pirates make smart buying decisions without resorting to piracy?

3. McKesson Corp: "Wearable" Computers Streamline the Retailer-Distributor Link

McKesson estimates that its wearable computers have increased the productivity of warehouse workers, reduced inventory levels, and cut order errors by 70% — all important considerations in an industry that operates on very narrow profit margins. Moreover, McKesson's investment in IT lets it offer its retail customers such value-added services as improved inventory control, better recordkeeping, and even more accurate profit-and-loss statements.

Questions for Discussion

1. Imagine that you are the CIO at McKesson in the 1970s. How could you convince the CEO to approve a multimillion-dollar investment in a networked computer system?

2. Using what you have learned about personal versus multi-user systems, how would you classify the wearable computers?

3. Major retailers such as Kmart and J.C. Penney are among the 18,000 organizations worldwide that have adopted electronic data interchange (EDI), a standard way of representing and transferring order-related data electronically. The retailers benefit because they can eliminate the paperwork involved in communicating with any manufacturer using EDI; the manufacturers benefit because the giant retailers provide them updated sales and inventory information that is useful in planning production. What does EDI mean for distributors like McKesson? For competition in the retail industry?

REVIEW QUESTIONS

1. What is the hardware in a computer system? List and describe the four categories of hardware.

2. What are the most common types of input devices? Why are there different types?

3. What is the purpose of the central processing unit? By what other names is this hardware component known?

4. What is the purpose of memory? Why is the memory in the central processor sometimes called primary storage?

5. Discuss the different actions that can be triggered by computer output.

6. What is secondary storage? What is its relation to primary storage?

7. Distinguish between the characteristics of four types of secondary storage.

8. Why are some devices called peripheral equipment? What does "peripheral" mean?

9. What are the two types of software? What is the purpose of each?

10. List and briefly describe the eight most popular types of software packages.

11. What is a computer programming language? What is the most commonly used programming language in business?

12. How do custom software and package software differ?

13. What is information? What are the four components of information?

14. What is meant by the term "user"? List and explain the four types of users.

15. What are the categories of information technology professionals? What function does each perform?

16. Discuss the types of procedures needed in managing and using information technology. Why is each needed?

17. How do single user and multi-user systems differ? Is one type better than the other? Explain.

18. Describe each of the following information processing activities: input, upload/download, compute, update, classify, sort, summarize, output, issue, inquire, store, retrieve, and transmit.

DISCUSSION QUESTIONS

1. Make a list of the IT-based systems and applications you encounter in a typical day and discuss how IT affects your activities. Do you agree that people are the most important component of these computer systems? Explain your answer.

2. Look over the list you made for question 1 and list the different types of input devices you encountered. Why do you think there are so many different types of input devices besides the keyboard?

3. Why do you think accounting departments were the first to install mainframe computers back in the early days of computing?

4. At Employers Health Insurance in Green Bay, Wisconsin, IT professionals spend six- to twelve-month "sabbaticals" in user departments interacting with users. The company's next move will be to assign IT managers to each of its business units, where they will present courses on how computer applications are developed. What benefit do these programs offer to Employers Health Insurance?

5. St. Agnes Medical Center of Fresno, California, has created a network that supports both critical patient-care applications and office productivity applications. Users can log on to the network from any PC in the medical center. Why do you think so many organizations, like St. Agnes, are developing computer networks of microcomputers?

CASE STUDY

Weather Looks Fine to SKI Ltd., Thanks to IT

SKI, Ltd.

THE EARLY 1990s WERE BLEAK for some ski resorts. A sluggish economy coupled with meager snowfalls held traffic—and revenues—down during the few short weeks of ski season. But the skies were bluer at SKI Ltd., which had racked up an unprecedented 30 consecutive years of profit growth.

Formed in the late 1950s by CEO Preston Leete Smith, SKI Ltd. now owns the Killington and Mt. Snow resorts in Vermont, as well as the Bear Mountain resort in California. Smith's secret? IT, of course. Each SKI Ltd. resort depends on a quartet of computer systems that are tied into weather-monitoring devices scattered over the resorts' slopes.

Snow-Making. As soon as the PCs in the control room show that weather conditions are right, the system triggers computer-controlled snow guns that can blanket the slopes with four to twenty-five feet of artificial snow. And on the control room's wall, color-coded lights on a three- by four-foot map show the condition of every trail. With the help of the snow-making system, ski season at SKI Ltd.'s Vermont resorts stretches from early October to mid-June.

Staffing. A separate midrange computer system uses data from the weather-monitoring devices to deploy hundreds of full- and part-time workers, ensuring that the supply of workers always matches the anticipated demand for service at parking lots, ski lifts, shops, restaurants, and lounges throughout the day. The workers report their new location by running a bar-coded ID card through a bar code reader on the wall; a separate numeric keypad lets them indicate their next destination. Even out on the trails, employees can radio in their location. With a glance at a computer screen, a manager can see which employees are available to meet unexpected conditions, such as a snowy day that touches off a run on ski goggles in the ski shop. In addition, the system tracks employee hours and handles all payroll tasks.

Marketing. Even before the weather-monitoring devices trigger the snow guns, another of SKI Ltd.'s computer systems is combing the company's database of 2.5 million skiers, targeting past or potential customers who might be swayed by a radio ad or an overnight mailing. To beef up midweek revenues, for example, SKI mailed 90,000 midweek lift ticket discount cards to skiers who lived at least three hours away by car. Midweek skiing now accounts for more than 50% of the company's revenues.

This kind of aggressive database marketing has helped Preston Smith achieve one of his primary goals—transforming the ski facilities into destination resorts, where people spend an entire vacation, rather than a day. To serve them, SKI Ltd. now operates more than 800 condominiums and hotel rooms, 14 lodges with restaurants, 11 rental shops, 14 retail shops, and 3 ski schools, as well as tennis and golf facilities for the warmer months.

Accounting. The monthly financial reports that most companies rely on aren't good enough in an industry that makes its money during the fourteen short weeks between mid-December and the end of March (the traditional ski season, without the help of snow-making guns). That's why SKI Ltd. has created a financial reporting system that lets managers

SUGGESTED READINGS

"Communications, Computers, and Networks," *Scientific American*, September 1991, pp. 62–164. A special issue devoted entirely to network applications of information technology. Contains 12 in-depth articles written by leaders in the IT field.

Penzias, Arno, *Ideas and Information: Managing In A High-Tech World.* New York: Norton, 1989. An excellent source detailing how information technology will shape work in the future, written by the director of research for AT&T Bell Labs.

Poole, Ithiel de Sola, *Technologies Without Boundaries: On Telecommunications in a Global Age.* Cambridge, MA:

Harvard University Press, 1990. An exploration of the dramatic changes brought about by information technology that will affect business and politics and revolutionize culture and society in the twenty-first century.

Vincent, David R., *The Information-Based Corporation.* Chicago: Dow Jones Irwin, 1990. An important work showing how IT can help businesspeople on the front lines make decisions and solve problems, and how firms that have invested in IT can make the most of their investments.

The snow guns on Devil's Fiddle Trail in Killington, Vermont are triggered by a computer system that monitors weather conditions. Snow guns have helped SKI, Ltd. extend the ski season; its resorts now operate almost nine months out of the year.

compare projected and actual revenues and profits on a daily and even hourly basis. Every Thursday, the management staff meets to study the figures and brainstorm explanations and solutions for any problems.

Operating together, the four computer systems make the operation of a complex of ski resorts look as easy as a run down the slope. In fact, Smith spends a lot of time on the slopes and urges his managers to do the same, saying that skiing is not only exhilarating and challenging, but is also a good way to understand the customer's experience.

Despite its success, SKI Ltd. is not resting on its ski poles. In 1991 the company set up two subsidiaries—Resort Technologies and Resort Software Services—to sell SKI-developed computer systems to other resorts and municipalities. An early customer was the state of New Mexico, which bought a $35,000 box office

management system, created at SKI Ltd. to automate the box office for its summer entertainment program.

Other plans for the future include a computer system with touch-screen terminals scattered about the resorts (so that guests can call up information about trail conditions and facilities), as well as an automated reservation system that will use either voice recognition or a touch-tone phone to speed up the process of making and confirming reservations. Another option is a bar-coded "frequent-skier" card that would use a computer to track and reward repeat business.

No one at SKI Ltd. proposes that mere technology is enough to guarantee success, however. Says Chief Financial Officer Martel D. Wilson, Jr., "It's not the technology that provides the advantage, but the way you use it. We've created a culture where people are addicted to information, and that's our real edge."

Questions for Discussion

1. List and describe the five components of the computer system used at SKI Ltd.

2. Why are each of SKI Ltd.'s four computer systems tied to the weather-monitoring devices?

3. Soon after SKI Ltd. bought Bear Mountain in California in 1987, it began a major renovation to upgrade the ski runs, making six of them expert level. The reasoning was that California residents had the time and money for local skiing but preferred to go to Aspen and other resorts, where the slopes were more challenging. Which aspect of IT at SKI Ltd. could have contributed to its decision to upgrade its slopes? Which aspect will determine whether its strategy was successful? What conclusions can you draw about the appropriate use of IT in business?

Nigel Homes' Infographics Inform the World of the Largest Banking Scandal in Modern History

When investigations uncovered the possibility of banking fraud on an international scale in 1991, law enforcement officials and journalists began probing the facts. At *Time* magazine, reporters Jonathan Beaty and S.C. Gwynne, supported by staff researchers, found that the Bank of Credit and Commerce International (BCCI) and its network of alleged crooks and spies had established a worldwide flow of money between well-known people and institutions.

Beaty and Gwynne learned that BCCI was started in 1972 with the mission of becoming an international financial banking powerhouse. Incorporated in Luxembourg and headquartered in London, BCCI's $22 billion empire included more than 400 branches and subsidiaries around the world when bank officials in 62 countries shut it down in July 1991. Spanning Asia, the Middle East, Europe, the United Kingdom, Africa, and North and South America, a network of alleged contacts between bank owners provided the means for paying bribes and buying and selling drugs, weapons, and currency. A secret bank within the BCCI bank served to hide billions of dollars in undocumented funds transfers. This photo essay describes how Nigel Holmes created an infographic to connect all the pieces of BCCI's international network.

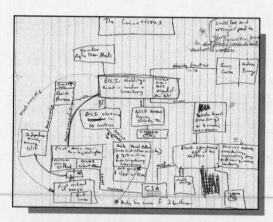

1 As Beaty and Gwynne prepared their story, *Time*'s editor began readying the story's layout. Telling the story would be made easier, the editor decided, by graphics illustrating the many and complicated connections between BCCI's banks and clients. Because BCCI spanned the world, the graphics needed to show the worldwide links. Owners and customers (both known and secret), as well as loans and donations, had to be illustrated to demonstrate the long reach of the bank across countries and continents. Names and dollar amounts had to be shown too. The editor sketched by hand BCCI's worldwide structure, showing operating units, visible and secret ownership, loans, and donations. When Nigel Holmes received the editor's sketch, he redrew the details by hand.

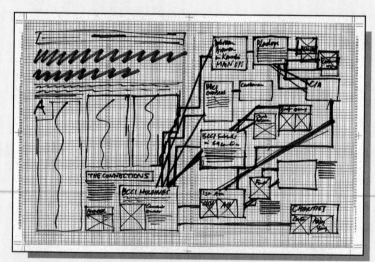

2 Holmes then transferred the data from his earlier sketch to a full-size magazine layout page. He organized the redrawn page to show information in a left-to-right flow corresponding to the movement of money between banks and people.

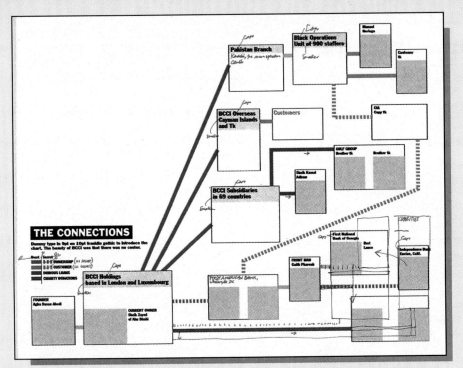

THE CONNECTIONS

Dummy type in 9pt on 10pt franklin gothic to introduce the chart. The beauty of BCCI was that there was no center.

3 Working from his hand-drawn layout, Holmes entered details of the sketch into his computer. He drew boxes to represent bank branches and key people in the BCCI. Holmes chose to use solid lines to represent overt transactions, dotted lines to represent secret transfers of money, and a color scheme of red, green, fuscia, and blue to designate details of information flow. He used a single type style, clean and bold, throughout.

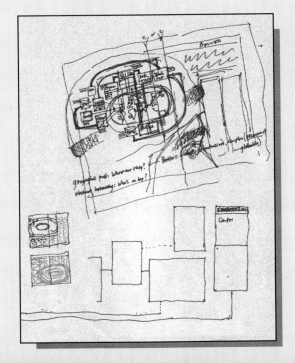

4 After reviewing the printed draft of the computer-drawn infographic, Holmes created a better layout of information. This hand-drawn sketch illustrates the BCCI structure according to the geographic location of people and properties.

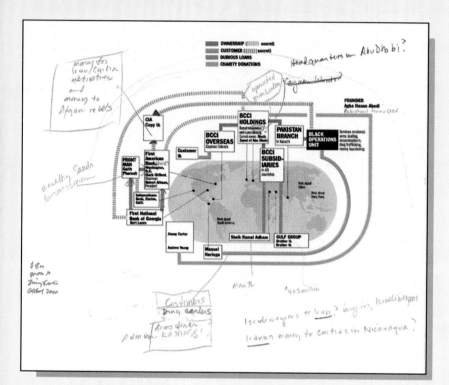

5 Then it was back to the computer to render the drawing electronically. Holmes used the same coding scheme and type style chosen earlier and added a map to emphasize the geographic details. He also added the locations of specific cities, annotated with lines and descriptive information. After printing a color draft of the infographic, Holmes edited the information, adding arrows and additional descriptions.

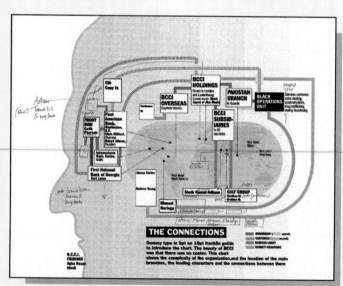

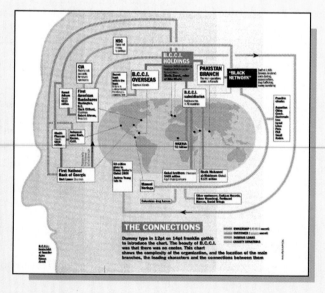

6 Next, Holmes added the head of BCCI founder Agha Hasan Abedi to the infographic to suggest the mastermind behind the bank's structure. He also made additional editing changes both to improve accuracy and to enhance the infographic (left), altering color (such as for the world's continents) and changing type size for some headings to add emphasis (right).

88

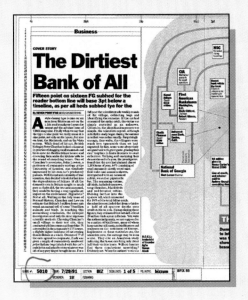

7 Finally, Holmes combined the infographic, text, and headlines for the story on a magazine page. Only the left side of the infographic appears on the first page of the story. Text flows around the image of head, further emphasizing the infographic. Grid marks and line numbers on the top, bottom, and sides of the page are used by editors and staff artists for alignment and reference in reviewing the page layout.

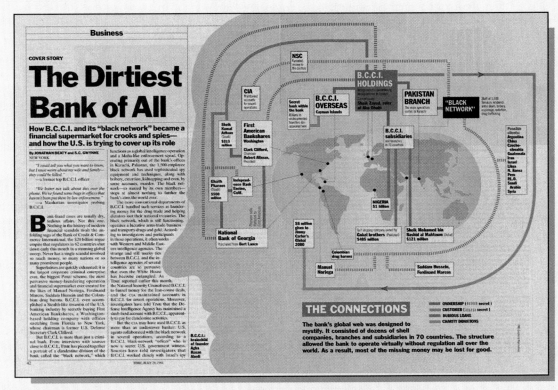

8 When the story appeared in the July 29, 1991, *Time*, the infographic occupied the majority of space on the opening pages. Its skillful design, layout, and color usage convey the central details of the BCCI story. Nigel Holmes's infographic shows and describes the brain map of BCCI's founder and the resulting global network. It both tells the story and draws readers into the narrative.

Illustrations courtesy of Nigel Holmes.

Retailing in the Information Age

As you stroll through a local department store or mall, you may not notice too many changes. Some shoppers are browsing; others are race-walking through the stores with a list; still others are stopping for a snack or a chat with friends. But behind the scenes, retailers are facing some major challenges—challenges they're meeting with the help of information technology. Here are a few examples.

The challenge: The price-conscious consumer. The good news is that the Information Age is creating thousands of new and exciting opportunities in the global economy. The bad news is that economic restructuring tends to make consumers cautious and frugal. The result? A tough new breed of shoppers who are forsaking full-price department stores and boutiques for discount stores such as Toys 'Я' Us and Wal-Mart, warehouse buying clubs, and factory outlets. Often, these discounters offer the same or comparable brands, selection, value, service, and shopping convenience—for less money. According to a recent survey, more than 83% of U.S. shoppers agreed with the statement, "I won't go back to shopping the way I used to."

One solution: Everyday low pricing. To woo price-conscious consumers, many retailers are abandoning sales and promotions for a policy of "everyday low pricing." But they can't do this and still preserve their profit margins if they don't use powerful information technology to minimize inventory costs. Giants such as Wal-Mart, Kmart, J.C. Penney, and Sears kicked off the trend when they began to analyze sales data from point-of-sale terminals. This information determined the size and frequency of reorders, which were transmitted electronically to suppliers. Soon suppliers, such as Levi Strauss and Vanity Fair, were using this constant stream of sales data to plan production, achieving the efficiency they needed to protect their own profit margins.

The challenge: Stocking the goods consumers want to buy. Price is important, but it's not the only consideration. Merchandising—selecting and presenting the goods that capture the buyer's fancy—counts too. Traditional market research sometimes falls short, though, in predicting the most popular items. This is especially true with respect to the demand for grocery items and toiletries. Shoppers might tell a market researcher that they prefer low-fat, healthy foods, even though they still fill their shopping carts with junk food.

One solution: Computer analysis of sales data. With the help of IT, major market research firms such as A.C. Nielsen and Information Resources Inc. collect and analyze data collected at thousands of grocery, drug, and department stores and transform them into valuable information. This information can be used in several ways. Retailers, for example, can use it to be sure they are stocking the most popular items. Suppliers, such as Pepsi-Co. and Procter & Gamble, can use the same information to evaluate sale patterns and the effects of advertising and sales promotions.

The challenge: Giving shoppers a reason to visit the store. Torn between increasing work and family demands, many shoppers are limiting the amount of time they spend shopping. If they visit a mall, they may dash in and out, instead of spending the afternoon. The less time they spend in a store or mall, the less money they spend.

One solution: Use spectacular entertainment options to build traffic. The most successful shopping malls have always used food courts and special events, such as free fashion shows and visits with Santa or the Easter Bunny, to make shopping entertaining. Today, a new generation of retailers is blending traditional shopping with amusement park thrills. At the giant Mall of America, outside of Minneapolis, shoppers can choose between a standard roller coaster or a $1 million, 48 seat Mystery Mine ride-film simulator. These rides, a fixture at major amusement parks, are essentially small movie theaters mounted on computer-controlled flight simulator platforms, which move up and down in sync with the filmed action. Jordan's Furniture, in suburban Boston, is another ride-film fan. In less than a year, the store's ride-film simulator drew 700,000 customers and generated $250,000 in profits (which went to charity). In the same period, the store's sales were up 30 percent.

The challenge: Reaching the time-starved shopper who doesn't go to stores. Some people enjoy shopping, treating it as a treasure hunt and a day out. Others refuse to spend their free time trudging about a vast store filled with noise and confusion. Others work at night or have small children, making it inconvenient to shop during conventional business hours.

One solution: Use information technology to move the store into the customer's home. Catalog shopping has always appealed to busy consumers, who can curl up with

The Home Shopping Club has become the cornerstone of a new age in retailing.

the catalog, make a selection, and then place an order over a toll-free telephone number. Back at catalog headquarters, a computerized telephone system automatically routes the call to the next available operator (who may or may not be at catalog headquarters). The operator then uses a computer terminal to enter the order, confirm inventory and shipping dates, and record the credit card transaction.

This same sort of computerized telephone system is essential to the newest rage in retailing—television's Home Shopping and QVC Networks, the keystones of a new billion-dollar U.S. industry. Their success has excited the designers of interactive TV, which promises to merge the benefits of cable television and information technology. In time, experts predict, subscribers to these new services will use their TVs to cruise an electronic mall with hundreds of shopping options, using their remote controls to order everything from the playing of videos to the delivery of clothing. Traditional retailers such as R.H. Macy, Nordstrom's, and Toys 'Я' Us are already experimenting with home shopping networks, laying the foundation for their forays into the next great age of retailing.

Discussion Questions

1. Entrepreneurs and managers believe that "problems" are just business opportunities in disguise. Identify some of the problems (not identified in this case) that are presenting opportunities to retailers. How can these be transformed into opportunities with the use of IT? What are the international applications of these suggested solutions?

2. Some shoppers are concerned that the new emphasis on everyday low pricing and streamlined product lines is limiting their shopping options. How might this concern be transformed into an opportunity for interactive home shopping networks?

3. Some industry observers predict that interactive TV shopping will eliminate the need for some retailers, like the neighborhood video store, and endanger others, such as the owners and operators of major malls. Do you agree or disagree? Explain.

PART 2

Tech Talk

Talking with Juan Rada

Vice President for Strategic Alliances and New Initiatives
Digital Equipment Corporation International
(Formerly, Director of the Institute for Management
Development—IMD[1])

In this interview, conducted in his office in Geneva, I asked Juan Rada to share his thoughts on the fundamental shifts occurring in the use of information technology in business enterprises, in the IT industry itself, and in virtually all the world's industries.

There's been a lot of discussion about the idea that computing is being reconceptualized. From your vantage point, are you in fact seeing a reconceptualization of computing?

We need a reconceptualization of computing for a number of reasons. If one can look at it from an historical perspective, what we have is one train of development coming from the data processing stream and another train of development coming from the [data] communications stream. In the 80s this was seen as a convergence between communications and computing and it developed in a completely different way than was forecast at the time.

How is this different in the 90s?

What is happening today is basically that in the 90s we are entering an era of the complete digitalization of all forms of signals. And this in itself is creating different conditions for the development of the computing industry. There are two dimensions to this.

One is that the map of the industry is very different. It is no longer the data processing or the information processing industry, but rather we are looking at an industry that is concerned on the one extreme with knowledge representation—highly sophisticated systems—and on the other with products that need to be very comfortable to use by people who are moving from mainframe computers to what some people call "wearable computers." We are going through all of these changes,

---

[1] IMD is one of the top business schools in Europe.

"I always say that the laptop or the palmtop—particularly the laptop and the notebook—is basically a shrunken version of a mainframe. Conceptually we're taking the kitchen to have a picnic. This type of problem is the one the industry must confront in the 90s."

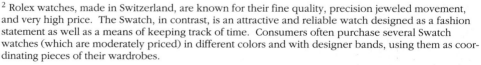

but fundamentally the concept of the computer has not changed. It remains a data processing machine.

Now, the problem is that customers and individuals don't need data processing machines. They need machines that help them do whatever they do. One aspect of it is data processing. I always say that the laptop or the palmtop—particularly the laptop and the notebook—is basically a shrunken version of a mainframe. Conceptually we're taking the kitchen to have a picnic. This type of problem is the one the industry must confront in the 90s. It has to be thought through in a different way. We have to define products in terms of the *context* of the product as opposed to the *nature* of the product itself. I think we're going to see a new wave of development in the computer industry that will be based on this type of consideration.

The context is going to be the driver rather than the product...Can you say a little more about this?

Products are discrete products. Current conventional wisdom is that [the information technology] industry divides itself into value and volume. And this very much reminds me of the Swiss watch industry in the late 1970s and early 1980s where the debate was the same. And people say "Well, the Swiss watch industry should concentrate itself on the value products, namely the Rolex."

Another approach was the one taken by a group who said no, you have to make value out of volume. They created the Swatch.[2] Of course, today the Swatch is an outstanding success and has *de facto* gained market share against [watchmakers in] Japan and Hong Kong. In fact, it has beaten them back when at the time everyone thought it was impossible to win against Seiko and other similar brands. I use that example to

say that... making a distinction between value and volume is a superficial way of looking at the problem.

What does this mean for people who work in business?

We work in offices to perform activities. We don't work in offices to use computers. This is what I mean by the context driving the design of the product, and not the other way around. I think the industry is reaching a degree of maturity now—in terms of the power of the processors, in terms of the economics of memory, and in terms of the value of telecommunications and the economics of telecommunications—in which the design will be from the *customer requirement in*, as opposed to the *technology out*. I think this is what we are going to see happening in the 90s. This will condition the success or failure of the computer companies in the next phase of the industry.

As the industry has developed to this point, the industry's emphasis has been primarily on enterprise and then on individual computing. How do you see that changing in the future?

I think the greatest strategic opportunities for the next decade are in relating individual computing to enterprise computing. It's very interesting, for example, that we do system integration very much within the enterprise and we let the individual go on with a notebook, or whatever. We have not conceived systems that link

---

[2] Rolex watches, made in Switzerland, are known for their fine quality, precision jeweled movement, and very high price. The Swatch, in contrast, is an attractive and reliable watch designed as a fashion statement as well as a means of keeping track of time. Consumers often purchase several Swatch watches (which are moderately priced) in different colors and with designer bands, using them as coordinating pieces of their wardrobes.

up or systems that integrate the individual with the enterprise in a very systematic way.

There's a whole area of strategic opportunity there based on some facts. For example, it is estimated that by 1996, 70% of the hardware will be PCs, of which half of that amount will be the portable type of hardware. This means that you will require wireless communications and so forth. The moment you have half of those machines being portable, you begin to look at a problem of how do you integrate individual workers with the enterprise. Or to put it differently, the integration of the enterprise becomes the problem of orchestrating individuals which on top of that are mobile. So you begin to look at a very different perspective on the process of integrating the enterprise and integrating the individual, and then the individual in the enterprise.

Will there be more complex systems? More complex management problems? How will this play out?

The only way to deal with complexity is a good theory. Everybody knows that Einstein's famous formula is an incredibly complex formula reduced to an incredibly elegant degree of simplicity. When I mean complexity I don't mean *complication*. Rather I mean the complexity where systems will be working together in orchestration. That will be extremely difficult to untangle. But these systems should be modular, they should be scalable...almost like a Lego set.[3] The Lego set is a good example. One can build a whole Lego land with the same building blocks. In fact it's a very simple—elegant, in fact—concept that can lead to extremely complex structures. And I think the same concept applies here.

I don't think the management problems will be different than they are today, which is motivating people, leading people, strategizing, working with people, etc. The only question will be [how] information technology in general will go through a transition in which it will be far more embedded.

Where, then, is industry going?

I think that if one could summarize where the industry is going, it is going from representing information on people's desk or laptops or notebooks to representing knowledge. That will require a significant shift in the nature of software. It will require a significant shift in the capacity of processors and memory. It will require also a different concept of the working environment of individuals.

---

[3] Lego sets consist of plastic building blocks that can easily be snapped together to build models of virtually any type of structure, including houses, warehouses, or skyscrapers. Lego blocks, developed in Denmark, are a favorite toy of children (and parents) the world over because they are simple to use, yet allow the creation of interesting and complicated designs.

Chapter Outline

CHAPTER 3

The Central Processor and Memory

Learning Objectives

When you have completed this chapter, you should be able to:

1 Describe the components and purpose of the central processing unit.

2 Distinguish between primary and secondary storage and between RAM and ROM.

3 Describe the chips and boards that can be used to augment the CPU and main memory.

4 Explain the process by which computers use registers to process data.

5 List and explain the three determinants of processor speed.

6 Describe six ways of increasing processing and computer speed and how these methods can be used in business.

In Practice

After completing this chapter, you should be able to perform these activities:

1 Look inside a desktop computer and identify its memory and processor chips, circuit boards, expansion slots, and add-in boards.

2 Examine a computer, large or small, and point out the external locations of its input/output ports.

3 Identify the adaptor boards in a PC and explain how they change the capabilities and characteristics of a computer.

4 Visit a computer store and ask meaningful questions about the memory capacity of a desktop computer.

5 Evaluate which method of increasing computer speed is best suited to a particular business application.

Off the Front Page

YOU EXPECT THE *REAL* NEWS TO BE on or near page one. Thus, a brief news story appearing on page 46 of the *New York Times* in 1948, announcing still another electronic gadget, drew little attention. Nonetheless, the editors ran the story—a report of the development of a pinhead-sized piece of material called germanium, encased in a sleek metal cylinder one-half inch long.

AT&T Bell Laboratories, the research arm of the giant American telephone company, had assembled a team of three physicists—William Shockley, Walter Brattain, and John Bardeen—to solve a serious problem. The switching devices that made telephone calls possible at the time were slow and prone to failure. In addition to having a negative effect on AT&T's operations, these problems were causing serious difficulties for businesses across the country. After several false starts, more than three years of work, and over $1 million in additional research funds, the group finally achieved success with the germanium transmitting device.

William Shockley, Walter H. Brattain, and John Bardeen (left to right) won the 1956 Nobel Prize in Physics for their research on transistors. The team's accomplishments made the computers of the 1990s possible.

From the 1948 announcement, and the follow-up announcement of a reliable and perfected device three years later, came a new page in electronic theory. By blocking electric current or allowing it to pass (off-on), or by boosting a small voltage around a given threshold (low-high), an electronic circuit could be used to express the two-state language that underlies all modern electronic information processing.

Shockley and his teammates' invention, the *transistor* (an abbreviation of transresistor, the original name of the invention), changed forever the course of electronic technology. Radios, television, high-fidelity stereo systems, and many other consumer electronic devices—in addition to the world's telephone systems—would never be the same. ■

N Chapter 2, we explored the five components of a computer system: hardware, programs, information, people, and procedures. By this point, you should have a good sense of how these elements work together to help people and businesses perform more productively and effectively.

This chapter and the next are geared towards providing you with a closer look at hardware components by building on what you learned in Chapter 2. We begin by taking a tour of the central processor to see what makes computers compute. In the course of our discussion, you'll learn how computers remember information and execute instructions. (The memory components of today's computers are an outgrowth of the research originally done by Shockley and his team.) In the final section of the chapter, we show how and why computers differ in processing speed. We'll conclude our discussion of hardware in Chapter 4, where you'll learn more about input and output devices and secondary storage.

You won't be an expert in electronics or engineering when you've completed these chapters, but you will have a good working knowledge of the way a computer works—an important part of the know-how for productive use of information technology.

■ The Central Processing Unit (CPU)

central processing unit (CPU) or **processor** The computer hardware that executes program instructions and performs the computer's processing actions.

integrated circuit, chip, or **microchip** A collection of thousands or millions of transistors placed on a small silicon chip.

transistor An electrical switch that can be in one of two states, open or closed.

integrating The process of packing more transistors onto a single chip.

Recall from Chapter 1 that a *computer* is any electronic system that can be instructed to accept, process, store, and present data and information. At the heart of the computer's hardware is the **central processing unit (CPU),** sometimes called the **processor,** which executes program instructions and performs the computer's processing actions.

The CPU is a collection of electronic circuits made up of thousands, even millions, of transistors placed onto **integrated circuits**. Integrated circuits are also called **chips** or **microchips** because the transistors are etched onto a small silicon chip. Each **transistor** is an electrical switch that can be in one of two states: open or closed. (Numerically, a closed state is described by the number 0, an open state by the number 1.)

Small transistors allow more transistors to be packed onto one chip. This process, called **integrating**, brought about the "PC revolution" in the 1980s and is the driving force behind many of the advances in today's information technology. Integrating means that more of the CPU's components can be placed onto a single chip, thus eliminating the need for separate chips. Integrating greatly increases the speed of the computer.

Because processing is electronic, you cannot *see* what happens inside the processor. If you open the cover, you will not see moving parts (just as you do not see the electricity moving when you turn on the lights in a room). Processors are designed and constructed in different ways. In PCs the processor is a single microprocessor chip. In larger systems, multiple circuit boards are used. Figure 3.1 shows the two parts of the processor—the control unit and the arithmetic/logic unit.

Control Unit

control unit The part of the CPU that oversees and controls all computer activities according to the instructions it receives.

instructions Detailed descriptions of the actions to be carried out during input, processing, output, storage, and transmission.

Computers "think" by using the on/off pulses of electric current. You might liken the **control unit** to the human brain, which oversees and controls all of our activities, whether we are working, playing, or exercising.

All computer activities occur according to instructions the control unit receives. **Instructions** are the detailed descriptions of the actions to be carried out during input, processing, output, storage, and transmission. Typical instructions may be to add two numbers together, to retrieve information for processing, or to print the results of processing. A wide range of instructions is embedded in such computer

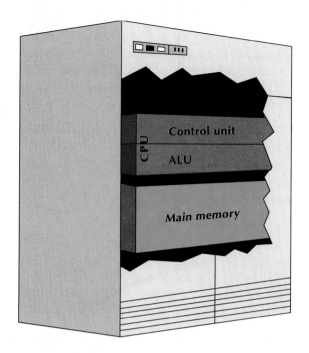

FIGURE 3.1
The Components of the CPU
In microcomputers, the control unit and ALU are found together on a single microprocessor chip (Figure 3.9). In larger systems, the control unit and ALU are usually found on separate boards. Note that main memory is *not* a part of the CPU.

applications as retrieving the details of a specific transaction or transmitting data over a communications network.

The control unit does not actually execute the instructions (just as the brain does not actually do the walking, talking, and gesturing that comprise many of our activities). Rather, it directs other processing elements to do so.

CRITICAL CONNECTION 1
Multimedia Macintosh Plays Angel of Mercy*

Dr. Edna Durbach had a problem. As special advisor for patient and family education at B.C.'s Children's Hospital in Vancouver, British Columbia, she wrote pamphlets and maintained a small but well-stocked resource library. On top of that, the clinical staff spent almost 30% of its time answering questions. Still, anxious parents weren't getting the answers they needed about their sick and injured children.

Part of the problem, Dr. Durbach realized, was that parents simply didn't know enough to ask the right questions. What they needed, she decided, was an angel of mercy and information—a presence that was always calm, cheerful, and collected—to help them gather the knowledge they needed.

But where could the hospital find such an angel? The answer for the 242-bed hospital was a Macintosh, a micro that houses a powerful CPU in a plastic case not much bigger than a child's teddy bear. Twenty-four hours a day, the Mac sits in the resource library offering a variety of specially developed multimedia applications, all available at the click of a computer mouse.

*Donna Barron, "Multimedia in the Hospital," *The World of Macintosh Multimedia* (Vero Beach, FL: Redgate Communications Corp., 1992), p. 30.

Arithmetic/Logic Unit (ALU)

arithmetic/logic unit (ALU)
The part of the CPU that performs arithmetic and logical operations.

The other component of the central processor is the **arithmetic/logic unit (ALU)**. The ALU contains the electronic circuitry that performs the two activities that underlie all computing capabilities, arithmetic and logical operations. *Arithmetic operations* include addition, subtraction, multiplication, and division. When a university's computer tallies the number of credit hours in a student's schedule on a transcript, it's doing arithmetic. So is the Post Office's computer system when it sorts letters by the postal code included in the address.

Logical operations compare one element of information to another. The comparison determines whether one item is greater than, less than, or equal to the other. The outcome of a logical comparison usually determines what type of processing occurs:

- **Greater than (>)**—The ALU compares two values to determine if one is greater than the other. For example, if the number of reservations for a specific flight on an airplane is greater than the number of seats on the plane, the flight is oversold. Actions can then be taken to assist all passengers in reaching their destination, perhaps by scheduling another flight or helping them make reservations at another airline.
- **Less than (<)**—The ALU compares two values to determine if one is less than the other. For example, if the number of students registered for a class is smaller than the number of seats in the auditorium where the class is to be held, then the class is still available for registration.
- **Equal to (=)**—The ALU compares two values to determine if they are equal or not. For example, if the amount of money submitted to a utility company for payment is equal to the amount of money owed, the computer will change the amount owed to show a zero balance.

Arithmetic and logical comparisons are possible because of computers' memory capability. But what exactly is memory?

▦ Memory

When the electronic calculator was first introduced in the 1930s, it was viewed as a breakthrough because of its memory capability. Earlier machines did not have the capacity to store data and information, but calculators—and their descendants, the various kinds of computer—do. The memory, which is composed of computer chips, can be used repeatedly by different applications.

The CPU interacts closely with memory, referring to it both for instructions and data or information. However, memory is separate from the CPU.

primary storage, main memory, or **internal memory**
Storage within the computer itself. Primary memory holds data only temporarily, as the computer executes instructions.

People using information technology refer to computer memory by different names, including **primary storage, main memory,** and **internal memory**. The simple term "memory" is often used to mean primary memory. As Figure 3.2 shows, memory space is used in five different ways:

- To hold the computer's operating system program (for example, DOS, OS/2, VM)—the software that oversees processing and acts as an interface between the hardware and the applications programs.
- To hold application programs—word processing, spreadsheet, order entry, or inventory control programs, for example.

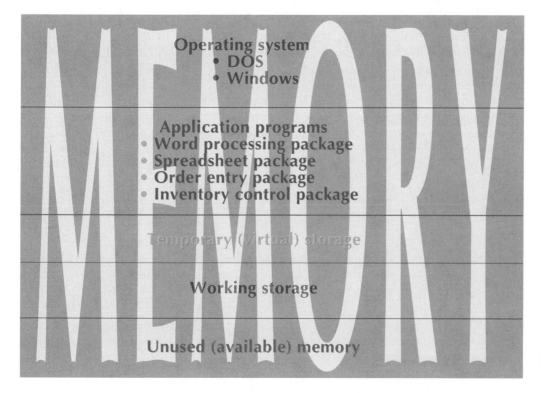

**FIGURE 3.2
Primary Memory
Allocation**

- To hold data and information temporarily (in "virtual memory"), receiving data or information from input devices and sending them to output devices during processing.
- To store other data or information needed in processing in the *working storage* area.
- To provide additional space for programs or data, as needed. If the computer has more memory than is needed for a particular application, the excess memory will go unused but remain available. The amount of memory needed may change during the processing of an application, so it is useful to have excess memory.

It is important that you distinguish between primary storage and secondary storage. *Primary storage* is storage within the computer itself; it holds data only temporarily, as the computer executes instructions. **Secondary storage** is permanent or semi-permanent memory that augments the primary memory and is used to store data long-term. Typically only a portion of the data in use resides in primary memory during processing. The remainder is kept in secondary storage until needed.

secondary storage The permanent or semi-permanent memory that augments the primary memory and is used to store data long-term.

Memory Size

Computers vary widely in the amount of internal (primary) memory they have. The size of memory is measured by the number of storage locations it contains. Each storage location, or **byte**, has a predetermined capacity. In simplest terms, a byte is the amount of memory required to store one digit, letter, or character.

byte A storage location in memory; the amount of memory required to store one digit, letter, or character.

kilobyte, K-byte, KB, or **k**
One thousand bytes.

megabyte, M-byte, MB, or
meg One million bytes.

gigabyte, G-byte, GB, or **gig**
One billion bytes.

terabyte, T-byte, or **TB** One
trillion bytes.

address An identifiable location
in memory where data are kept.

Bytes are generally measured by **kilobyte** (**K-byte, KB,** or **k**)—thousands of bytes[1]; **megabyte** (**M-byte, MB,** or **meg**)—millions of bytes; **gigabyte** (**G-byte, GB,** or **gig**)—billions of bytes; and **terabyte** (**T-byte,** or **TB**)—trillions of bytes. Thus a computer with "6 meg" has 6,000,000 bytes of memory.

Personal computers have memory capacities in the megabyte range. For example, most desktop PCs have a main memory capacity of 2 to 16 megabytes. Midrange, mainframe, and super-computers usually have substantially more.

Each byte is identified by a memory **address** that allows the computer to determine where an element of data or information is stored. (In some cases, a group of bytes may have an address.) As Figure 3.3 shows, memory addresses are similar in principle to the addresses of a house or building—they distinguish one location from another and make each locatable.

Figure 3.4 shows precisely how data are represented electrically using bits and bytes.

RAM and ROM

There are two types of main memory, *random-access memory* and *read-only memory*, with two variations on each type.

**random-access memory
(RAM)** Memory that permits data
or information to be written into or
read from memory only as long as
the computer is turned on.

RAM.   Main memory, the largest area of memory within the computer, is composed of **random-access memory**, or **RAM**, chips. "Random access" means that data or information can be written into or recalled (read) from any memory address at any time. With RAM, there is no need to start at the first location and proceed one step at a time. Information can be written to or read from RAM in less than 100 billionths of a second. However, RAM stores data and information only as long as the computer is turned on. The electrical currents that comprise the data and information cease when the power is turned off.

---

[1]Although users of information technology often equate K with 1,000, doing so is not strictly accurate. A kilobyte of memory is actually 1,024 bytes. If you hear someone describing a computer with 640K memory, a common and acceptable description meaning 640 1K units, the system actually has 655,360 (calculated as 640 x 1024) memory locations.

FIGURE 3.3
Addresses in Computer Memory
In main memory, bytes are identified by a memory address that allows the computer to determine where an element of data or information is stored.

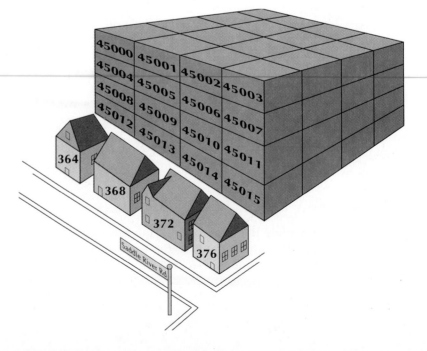

a) Computers use bits and bytes to process and store data. Because they run on electricity, computers know only two things: on and off. This two-state system is called a **binary system**. Using single digits called **bits** (short for *binary digits*), the computer can represent any piece of data. The binary system uses only two digits, 0 and 1. The 0 corresponds to the "off" state, the 1 to the "on" state.

Bit: **0**   o r   **1**

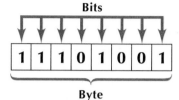

Bits

| 1 | 1 | 1 | 0 | 1 | 0 | 0 | 1 |

Byte

b) Single bits are usually not enough to store all the numbers and characters that need to be processed and stored. For this reason, seven or eight bits are usually grouped together into bytes. Each byte generally represents one character.

When a character is entered through the keyboard, the processor accepts the character into main memory and translates it into coded form. It simultaneously shows the character on the display screen.

Character	EBCDIC	ASCII
A	1100 0001	100 0001
B	1100 0010	100 0010
C	1100 0011	100 0011
D	1100 0100	100 0100
E	1100 0101	100 0101
F	1100 0110	100 0110
G	1100 0111	100 0111
H	1100 1000	100 1000
I	1100 1001	100 1001
J	1101 0001	100 1010
K	1101 0010	100 1011
L	1101 0011	100 1100
M	1101 0100	100 1101
N	1101 0101	100 1110
O	1101 0110	100 1111
P	1101 0111	101 0000
Q	1101 1000	101 0001
R	1101 1001	101 0010
S	1110 0010	101 0011
T	1110 0011	101 0100

Character	EBCDIC	ASCII
U	1110 0100	101 0101
V	1110 0101	101 0110
W	1110 0110	101 0111
X	1110 0111	101 1000
Y	1110 1000	101 1001
Z	1110 1001	101 1010
0	1111 0000	011 0000
1	1111 0001	011 0001
2	1111 0010	011 0010
3	1111 0011	011 0011
4	1111 0100	011 0100
5	1111 0101	011 0101
6	1111 0110	011 0110
7	1111 0111	011 0111
8	1111 1000	011 1000
9	1111 1001	011 1001
!	0101 1010	010 0001
$	0101 1011	010 0100
&	0101 0000	010 0110

c) Two standard systems for representing data have been developed. **EBCDIC** (pronounced "eb-see-dick"), short for Extended Binary Coded Decimal Interchange Code, uses eight-bit bytes to represent a character. In EBCDIC, the capital letter S is represented by 11100010. **ASCII** (pronounced "asskey"), short for American Standard Code for Information Interchange, uses seven-bit bytes to represent a character. In ASCII, the capital letter S is represented by 1010011. All characters—including upper- and lower-case letters—have a unique code in each system. EBCDIC is generally used in mainframes, ASCII in microcomputers.

H = | 1 | 1 | 0 | 0 | 1 | 0 | 0 | 0 | 0 |

↑ Parity bit

d) A special bit called a **parity bit** is sometimes used to detect errors in the transmission of data. The parity bit is an extra bit that is added to the byte before transmission of the data. If a bit is lost during transmission, the total number of bits will be wrong, and the computer will be alerted that there is something wrong with a particular byte.

Decimal	Binary	Hexadecimal
0	0000	0
1	0001	1
2	0010	2
3	0011	3
4	0100	4
5	0101	5
6	0110	6
7	0111	7
8	1000	8
9	1001	9
10	1010	A
11	1011	B
12	1100	C
13	1101	D
14	1110	E
15	1111	F

e) Sometimes computer professionals find it easier to convert binary values to another number system, the **hexadecimal number system**. This system uses the digits 0–9 and the letters A–F. One hexadecimal digit is the equivalent of four bits. For example, hexadecimal B, which represents the number 11, may be easier to deal with than the binary number 1011, which also represents the number 11.

FIGURE 3.4   Bits, Bytes, and Number Systems

Two types of RAM are widely used. *Dynamic RAM (DRAM)* is the major memory component in virtually every computer. DRAM chips hold data and information "dynamically." This means that the computer does not hold data and information indefinitely. Rather, the computer must continually refresh the DRAM cell electronically—several hundred times per second. In contrast, *static RAM* chips retain their contents indefinitely, without constant electronic refreshment. They are faster than DRAM, but are not as compact and use a more complicated design.

RAM chip technology is changing rapidly, both in capacity and packaging. RAM chips are now available in 1M, 4M, and 8M; 16M and 64M versions are emerging.

read-only memory (ROM)
A type of storage that offers random access to memory and can hold data and information after the electric current to the computer has been turned off.

ROM.   Like RAM, **read-only memory (ROM)** offers random access to a memory location. However, ROM chips are able to hold data and information even after the electrical current to the computer is turned off. Unlike the contents of a RAM chip, the contents of a ROM chip cannot be changed. Whatever is inserted into a location during manufacturing of the ROM chip cannot be altered.

Typically, the start-up programs that run automatically when computers are first turned on are written into ROM. These programs, which perform housekeeping checks like ensuring that a keyboard is attached or that memory is functioning, are written into ROM. The instructions can be read again and again, but never changed.

There are several variations on ROM. *Programmable read-only memory (PROM) chips*, first developed as a tool for testing a new ROM design before putting it into mass production, can be modified from its manufactured state only once. These modifications are not reversible. Data or information in *erasable programmable read-only memory (EPROM) chips* can be erased by bathing the chip in ultraviolet light. (This process dissipates the electric charges that created the original data or information values.) *Electrically erasable programmable read-only memory (EEPROM) chips* can be reprogrammed by electronically reversing the voltage used to create the data or information (rather than by using ultraviolet light).

Figure 3.5 summarizes the different types of memory chips.

FIGURE 3.5
Types of Memory Chips

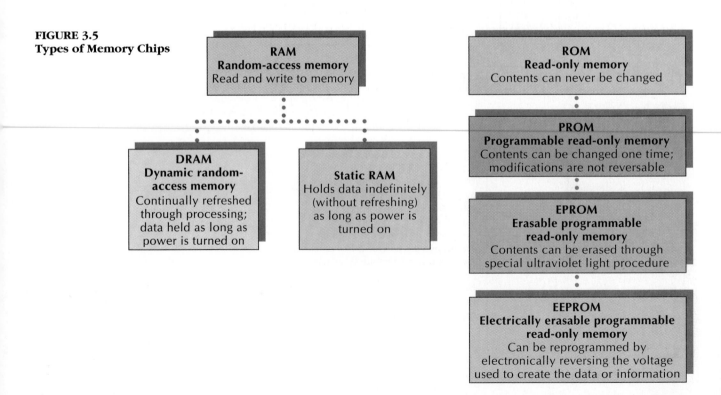

You won't see EPROM or EEPROM chips used in business applications like spreadsheets or course registration systems. Generally, they are used only by engineers and designers who develop devices that contain embedded computers. When Hewlett-Packard develops a laser printer, for instance, its designers write the codes that control the printer's functions, paper handling features, and type styles into EPROM or EEPROM. Using these special forms of ROM, they can rewrite the code without having to remanufacture the chip. When the design is complete and the printer goes into mass production, the EPROM or EEPROM is replaced with a ROM chip containing the final instructions.

▇ Inside the System Unit

Both the CPU and memory units can be augmented by combinations of chips and boards. A **board** is a hardware device onto which chips and their related circuitry are placed. To see how the various hardware components fit together, it will be helpful to literally open up a computer and see what's inside (Figure 3.6).

In all computers the processor is housed inside a hardware unit called the **system unit**. On mainframe or midrange systems, the system unit is typically a cabinet filled with circuit boards (Figure 3.7). On microcomputers a single **system board** is mounted on the bottom of the computer case and attached to an electrical power supply that generates the electrical current needed to operate the computer. The system board of a personal computer contains a processor chip, memory chips, ports, and add-in boards, in addition to the circuitry that

board A hardware device onto which chips and their related circuitry are placed.

system unit The hardware unit that houses a computer's processor, memory chips, ports, and add-in boards.

system board The system unit in a microcomputer, located on a board mounted on the bottom of a computer base.

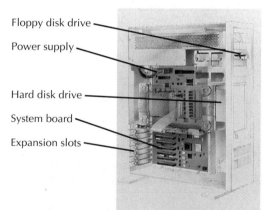

Floppy disk drive
Power supply
Hard disk drive
System board
Expansion slots

FIGURE 3.6
Under the Hood of a Personal Computer
Inside this IBM personal computer are a disk drive, circuit board (with a microprocessor chip), and power supply. The display terminal, keyboard, and printer are all attached by plug-in cables.

FIGURE 3.7
Amdahl 6390 Mainframe System Unit
The system unit of mainframe computers is typically a cabinet filled with circuit boards.

FIGURE 3.8
IBM PS/2 System Board
The system board of most microcomputers contains a processor chip, memory chips, ports, add-in boards, and circuitry that connects all these components. System units in larger computers can also contain all these elements.

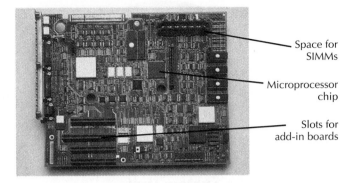

Space for SIMMs

Microprocessor chip

Slots for add-in boards

interconnects all these components (Figure 3.8). Systems units in larger computers can also contain all these elements.

Processor Chips

microprocessor The smallest type of processor, with all of the processing capabilities of the control unit and ALU located on a single chip.

The notion of a "computer on a chip" became reality when all of the processing capabilities of the control unit and ALU could be contained on a single computer chip. The smallest type of processor, a **microprocessor**, is exactly this kind of chip. Sealed in a protective package, the microprocessor is connected to a system board with pins (Figure 3.9). Microprocessors gave rise to microcomputers, which use microprocessors for their CPU.[2]

The most popular processor chips are manufactured by Intel for IBM-compatibles and by Motorola for Apple Macintosh and Commodore Amiga computers (Table 3.1). These chips have evolved over time, with each new chip including more capability and greater speed than its predecessor.

Programs are written to work with a specific microprocessor chip. Thus the software packages written to run on Apple computers, which use Motorola chips, cannot be used with the IBM-compatible computers, which use Intel chips, with-

[2]The terms *microcomputer* and *personal computer* are often used interchangeably. *Microcomputer* is the accurate technical term. The term *personal computer* refers to the way microcomputers are used.

TABLE 3.1   Evolution of Intel and Motorola Microprocessors

Microprocessor	Speed* (MHz)	Computers Using This Chip	Word Size (Bits)[†]	Bus Width[†]
Intel 8088	8	IBM PC	16	8
Intel 8086	8	IBM-compatibles	16	16
Intel 80286 ("286")	8-12	IBM-compatibles	16	16
Motorola 68000	12-20	Apple Macintosh Commodore Amiga	32	16
Motorola 68020	12-33	Apple Macintosh II	32	43
Intel 80386 ("386")	16-33	IBM-compatibles	32	32
Motorola 68030	16-40	Apple Macintosh SE/30 Apple Macintosh IIci, fx	32	32
Motorola 68040	25-33	Apple Macintosh, Quadra Engineering workstations	32	32
Intel 80486 ("486")	25-66	IBM-compatibles	32	32
Intel Pentium	66 and up	IBM-compatibles	32	64

*The higher the megahertz (MHz), the faster the microprocessor.
[†]Discussed later in this chapter.

FIGURE 3.9
The Intel Pentium
Microprocessor Chip
Because of the speed with
which it executes instructions,
the Intel Pentium microprocessor chip is often used in pro-
cessing-intensive applications.

FIGURE 3.10
Single In-Line Memory Modules
Intel's SIMM memory modules are
inserted as a unit into a predesignated
slot on the system boards of selected
IBM, Compaq, Hewlett-Packard, and
Zenith computers.

out substantial changes. However, software developers, ever mindful of people's
desires to use the same software on both IBM-compatibles and Macintoshes, are
finding ways to develop software that will run on both families of chips.

Memory Chips

In the past, memory chips were installed onto the system board eight chips at a
time by connecting the chip to the system board with pins. Memory chips now
often come in modules. A **single in-line memory module**, usually called a
SIMM, is a multiple-chip "card" (Figure 3.10) that is inserted as a unit into a predesignated slot on the system board. SIMM's of 1M, 2M, and 4M are common.

Installed memory is the amount of memory included by the computer's manufacturer on its memory board. **Maximum memory** is the highest amount of
memory that a processor can hold.[3]

**single in-line memory
module (SIMM)** A multiple-chip
memory card inserted as a unit into
a predesigned slot on a computer's
system board.

installed memory The amount
of memory included by a
computer's manufacturer on its
memory board.

maximum memory The most
memory that a processor can hold.

Ports

Any device that is not part of the CPU or the system board must somehow be
attached to the computer. **Ports** are the connectors through which input/output
devices and storage devices can be plugged into the computer (see Figure 3.11
on page 108).

Computers of all sizes are designed to accept additional circuit boards that serve
as ports. When an input/output device needs to be plugged into the system unit
and there is not a built-in part for it, a special add-in board must be added. These
extra boards plug into **expansion slots** on the system board. All systems have a
practical limit to the number of ports that can be added.

port A connector through which
input/output devices can be
plugged into the computer.

expansion slot A slot inside a
computer that allows a user to add
an additional circuit board.

[3]Three memory allocation ranges are found in microcomputers. *Conventional memory* is the memory
managed by the operating system and in which application programs run. Since the creation of the personal computer, this has been limited to 640K, a barrier that will soon be removed. ROM-based instructions, the computer's operating system, and application and communications programs run in conventional memory. A limited number of operating systems use *expanded memory*, the usable memory
beyond the 640K threshold, up to 1 megabyte. Applications software may also use expanded memory.
Extended memory starts at the 1 megabyte boundary and extends upward to 16 or 32 megabytes. This
memory is freely available to application programs. (Note: These three memory allocation ranges pertain to the Intel line of chips, the most frequently used chips in PCs today.)

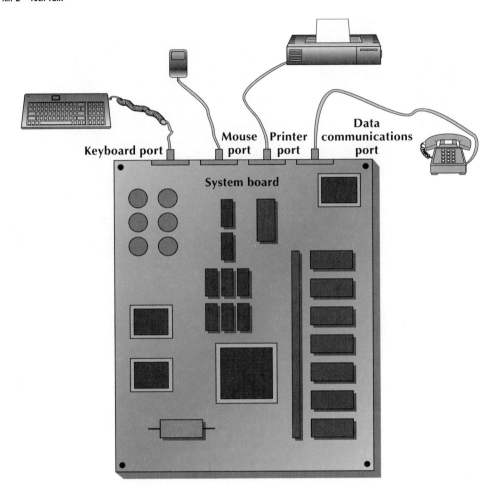

Keyboard port   **Mouse port**   **Printer port**   **Data communications port**

System board

FIGURE 3.11
Ports on a Microcomputer System Board
Most input, output, and storage devices must be plugged into ports on the system board.

Add-In Boards

add-in board A board that can be added to a computer to customize its features and capabilities.

Virtually all micro, midrange, and mainframe computers have an *open architecture*. That is, additional boards called **add-in boards** can be added to the computer, by way of its expansion slots, to customize its features and capabilities. (Computers that do not have this capacity are said to have a *closed architecture*.)

Table 3.2 lists several types of boards that can be added to microcomputers. The variety of add-in boards has continued to expand as people using computers seek more capabilities and as computer manufacturers find ways to meet these demands.

The combination of desktop computers with add-in boards that customize the computers is helping medical schools to change instruction methods in areas previously difficult to incorporate into their classrooms. For example, The American Heart Association, hoping to encourage doctors and medical students to study preventive medicine, now offers medicine schools a computer-based multimedia interactive application focusing on the heart and bloodstream. Medical schools, community health groups, and practicing physicians can load the system onto Apple or IBM-compatible computers outfitted with add-in boards that provide sound and animation capabilities. The system lets users see the effect of high cholesterol levels in the bloodstream, providing an animated view of the heart and how it pumps blood into arteries. Another sys-

TABLE 3.2   Add-In Boards Available for Microcomputers

Board	Function/Description
Accelerator board	Increases the speed of a computer.
Controller board	Allows different printers and storage devices to be attached to a computer.
Coprocessor board	Includes special chips that speed up the system's overall processing capabilities.
Display adaptor board	Permits the use of computer displays by providing interconnection with the processor board.
Emulator board	Allows the computer to act like another type of device, usually a terminal.
Fax modem board	Enables the computer to send and receive facsimile images, data, and information.
Memory expansion board	Extends the computer's memory capacity by adding additional sockets for memory chips.
Modem board	Enables the computer to interconnect with a telephone line to transmit and receive data and information.
Multifunction board	Includes several different functions (such as memory expansion and printer and display connections) on a single add-in board.
Sound board	Contains chips and circuitry that translate data and information into sound output, including music.
Voice board	Produce spoken output.

tem developed by High Techsplanations of Rockville, Maryland, allows surgeons to practice prostate surgery without cutting up cadavers (Figure 3.12).

Marketing professionals are also using add-in boards for market research and target marketing. See the Opportunities box on page 112 titled "Geographic Information Systems Put Marketers on the Map," for more details.

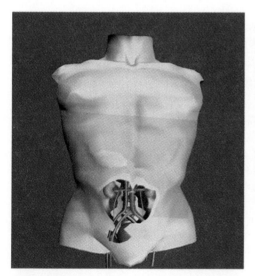

a) Using the program, a medical student can strip away the pelvic bone of a computer-generated torso…

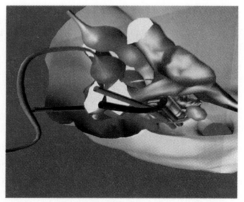

b) …to reveal details of the inner workings of the kidneys, bladder, urethra, and prostate.

FIGURE 3.12
Surgical Simulation Using Add-In Boards
High Techsplanations recently launched a "virtual-reality surgical simulator" to help surgeons learn how to operate on the prostate gland.

CRITICAL CONNECTION 2
Add-In Boards and CADD: The Trump Cards for BSW International

Take an ordinary but high-powered computer, add a stack of add-in boards, and plug in a variety of high-resolution input and output devices and what do you have? The latest tool of the modern architect, the kind that works for BSW International in Tulsa, Oklahoma, where CADD (computer-aided design and drafting) has been the software of choice since the late 1970s.

CADD is important, says BSW General Partner David Broach, because it increases the company's productivity in its specialty—designing hundreds of stores for such retailing chains as Wal-Mart, Pier 1 Imports, and Montgomery Ward. By letting the architects modify an existing design—rather than starting from scratch—CADD can cut the time needed to design a store from a month to as little as twenty-four hours.

One of BSW's more unusual clients was Hallmark, which turned to the CADD-masters at BSW when it embarked on an ambitious program of construction and renovation. Even though Hallmark couldn't reap the greatest benefits from CADD—many of its stores feature different designs—it wanted the convenience and cost savings of dealing with one firm that could handle many projects simultaneously. Without CADD, Hallmark would have had to deal with at least ten firms to meet its goals.

■ The Processing Sequence

By this point you may be wondering exactly how a computer processes data. To understand this process, you need to understand the machine cycle and the role of registers.

The Machine Cycle

All the functions of processing are directed by the control unit, which works with the ALU and memory to perform the following four steps:

- **Fetch**—Obtain the next instruction from memory.
- **Decode**—Translate the instruction into individual commands that the computer can process.
- **Execute**—Perform the actions called for in the instructions.
- **Store**—Write the results of processing to memory.

Collectively, these four steps are known as the **machine cycle**. The first two steps, in which instructions are obtained and translated, are the **instruction cycle (I-cycle)**. The last two steps, which produce processing results, are the **execution cycle (E-cycle)** (Figure 3.13).

machine cycle The four processing steps performed by the control unit: fetch, decode, execute, and store.

instruction cycle (I-cycle) The first two steps of the machine cycle (fetch and decode), in which instructions are obtained and translated.

execution cycle (E-cycle) The last two steps of the machine cycle (execute and store), which produce processing results.

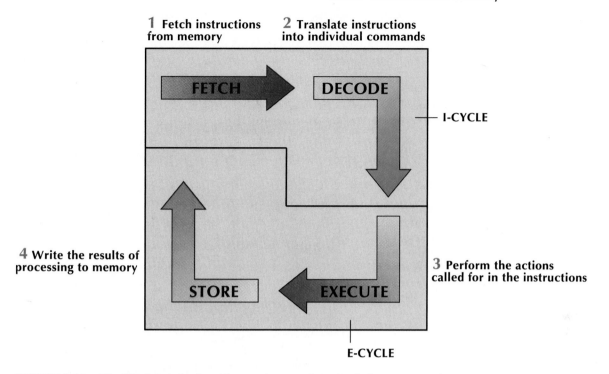

FIGURE 3.13   **The Machine Cycle**   The machine cycle is divided into two cycles. During the instruction cycle (I-cycle), instructions are obtained and translated. During the execution cycle (E-cycle), the results of processing are produced.

Registers

To execute the machine cycle, the control unit depends on **registers**, temporary storage areas in the processor (not in the main memory). Registers, which can move data and instructions more quickly than main memory, momentarily hold the data or instructions used in processing and the results that are generated. They also assist the ALU in carrying out arithmetic and logical operations.

There are four types of registers:

- **Storage registers**—Temporarily store data that have been moved from memory and are awaiting processing or are about to be sent to memory.
- **Address registers**—Contain the address of the data to be used in executing an instruction.
- **Accumulators**—Hold the results of computation as each arithmetic operation occurs. From the accumulator the results are moved into main memory or to another register for additional processing.
- **General purpose registers**—Hold data, addresses, or arithmetic results.

Registers are like staging areas. They are a place in which preparations are made so that an activity, once underway, goes smoothly. Consider, for example, the planning of a parade or group trip. To get every participant organized, the organizer tells people to arrive at a specific location by a particular time. Some people arrive earlier than others, but all should be there by the time the parade or trip is due to begin. This is how registers work also. They assemble all the data instructions so that the computer can perform its next machine cycle quickly and without a hitch.

register A temporary storage area in the processor that can move data and instructions more quickly than main memory and momentarily hold the data or instructions used in processing and the results that are generated.

Geographic Information Systems Put Marketers on the Map

WHAT DO PRESIDENT BILL CLINTON, ARBY'S ROAST BEEF, AND Norwest Bank have in common? They've all profited from the market insights provided by geographic information systems (GISs), a sophisticated type of graphics software that presents the answers to database queries as color-coded maps.

Originally developed in the 1960s to help scientists and government planning departments, GISs required the brute power of mainframes until the late 1980s. That's when two trends converged to make GISs popular with today's savvy marketers. One trend was the emergence of high-powered PCs with the add-in boards needed to operate high-resolution color monitors and high-capacity secondary storage devices—systems that offer the power of a mainframe for a fraction of the cost. The second trend was the increasing availability of computer databases containing demographic and market data with geographic components, such as zip codes and street addresses, which could be plotted on a map showing political or marketing boundaries. The U.S. Census Bureau, for example, sells the TIGER database—an $11,000 collection of 44 CD-ROM disks containing street maps showing economic and population data for the entire United States.

Although the databases and GIS software can be expensive, they're worth it to marketers, because the maps let them *see* and *analyze* patterns in mountains of data—patterns that help them spend their marketing dollars wisely and take advantage of market opportunities.

President Clinton's campaign for the presidency is a good example of a success story in which GIS software played an important role. Janet Handal, a technology strategist at the Clinton campaign headquarters, reported that Atlas Pro (a GIS program selling for around $600) let her team create maps with overlays showing political data. These maps helped the team chart trends in public opinion, recruit volunteers, decide where to send the candidates, and determine the number of television ads to buy in certain markets.

GISs are also great tools for selecting new restaurant sites, reports Hal Reid, Vice President for Development Research at Arby's, Inc. With the help of their GIS, he says, his staff can create color-coded maps that let them compare potential locations on the basis of population characteristics (median age, income, and expenditures for fast food); traffic patterns, and the proximity of competitors.

The GI's power to identify market niches was especially useful to Norwest Bank when it set about remodeling two branches in west St. Paul, Minnesota. With the help of the GIS, Senior Research Manager John Blissenbach saw that many young professionals lived near one branch. To cater to these customers' needs for speed and convenience, the bank

Linda Brown, research analyst for Colorado-based Eagle Marketing Services, Inc., uses mapping software to support the company's database and direct-mail services. The software helps Brown identify the response rate to direct mailings by zip code. "A mapped comparison of good response areas becomes a tool for our salespeople," she says. "They can tell advertisers about the number of potential buyers in any zip code."

installed an automatic teller machine in the vestibule and set up an express counter where clerks can process deposits or loan payments in less than a minute.

GISs can even help the sales reps who work on the front lines. Available for less than $100, a GIS called Automap can produce a detailed map showing the most efficient route between any set of locations in the United States, Canada, and Europe, along with toll-free phone numbers for hotel reservations and suggestions for side trips to national parks and other sites of interest.

Processor Speed

As we noted in Chapter 1, speed is one of the main reasons people use information technology. Computers can perform millions of calculations per second consistently, accurately, and reliably.

Computer speeds are measured in **milliseconds** (thousandths of a second), **microseconds** (millionths of a second), **nanoseconds** (billionths of a second), or **picoseconds** (trillionths of a second). Processors and processor chips tend to operate at microsecond and nanosecond speeds, though new chips are emerging with picosecond capabilities. Secondary storage and input/output devices function at millisecond speeds.

Another common way of describing speeds is by the number of instructions the processor can execute per second. **Millions of instructions per second**, or **MIPS**, ratings range from approximately 1 to 50 MIPS for a typical desktop PC to 200 to 400 MIPS for a mainframe, to even higher speeds for supercomputers. Because computer speeds are always increasing, it is expected that every new computer model will have a higher MIPS capability.

Computing speed is sometimes also measured in **megaflops**, or millions of floating point operations per second. *Floating point operations* is a technical term that refers to the floating of decimal point from calculation to calculation. Megaflops is a measure of how many detailed arithmetic calculations can be performed per second.

millisecond One thousandth of a second.

microsecond One millionth of a second.

nanosecond One billionth of a second.

picosecond One trillionth of a second.

millions of instructions per second (MIPS) A measure of processor speed—the number of instructions the processor can execute per second.

megaflops Millions of floating point operations per second; a measure of how many detailed arithmetic calculations the computer can perform per second.

Reality Check.   It's best to keep in mind that MIPS and megaflops are best used as bases of comparison. Rather than worrying about absolute measures of speed, people need to ask themselves: Will the system I choose do the work I need it to do in an acceptably speedy manner? The answer to this question will depend on the nature of the processing needed and the specific software used. A system used for word processing applications need not be as powerful as one that will process thousands of business transactions per second. The number of people simultaneously using a computer system will also influence decisions about the speed capabilities needed. ■

Determining Processor Speed

What determines processor speed? In automobiles, greater speed comes with more engine power and greater fuel use. Aircraft engines produce higher speeds when they generate more thrust. But engine power, thrust, and fuel use have nothing to do with computers. Three elements determine a computer's speed: the system clock, bus width, and word size.

System Clock.   Because computers work at high speeds, synchronization of tasks is essential to ensure that actions take place in an orderly and precise fashion. All computers have a **system clock**, a circuit that generates electronic pulses at a fixed rate to synchronize processing activities. Each time a pulse is generated, a new instruction cycle begins.

Clock cycles are measured in **megahertz (MHz)**, or millions of electric pulses per second. One megahertz means that one million pulses are generated every second. The megahertz speed built into computers varies. Personal computers typ-

system clock A circuit that generates electronic impulses at a fixed rate to synchronize processing activities.

megahertz (MHz) Millions of electric pulses per second; a measure of a computer's speed.

ically operate in the range of 20 to approximately 132 megahertz.[4] The higher the megahertz, the faster the computer (see Table 3.1).

Bus.   For a computer to process information, the details must be moved internally—that is, within the computer. Data are moved from input devices to memory, from memory to the processor, from the processor to memory, from memory to storage, and from memory to output devices. The path over which data are moved is a **bus**. Like the system clock, the bus is an electronic circuit.

There are two types of bus. An **input/output (I/O) bus** moves data into and out of the processor—that is, between peripheral units (such as input devices) and the central processor. A **data bus** moves data between the central processor and memory (Figure 3.14).

The width of the bus determines the amount of data that can be moved at one time. An eight-bit bus, for example, transmits eight bits of data at a time. Greater bus width means faster movement of data.

Most PCs have 16- or 32-bit buses. Midrange and mainframe systems typically use 32- or 64-bit buses. Three bus standards are in widespread use. The Enhanced Industry Standard Architecture (EISA) is used on many MS-DOS microcomputers and on some IBM PCs. During the late 1980s and early 1990s, IBM also used a proprietary microchannel architecture. The third standard, the NuBus architecture, is used on Apple Macintosh computers.

Word Size.   A **word** is the number of bits a computer can process at one time. Word size is measured in bits. An eight-bit word, for example, consists of eight bits (eight electronic circuits). Alternatively, words are sometimes expressed in bytes. A one-byte word contains eight bits; a two-byte word, 16 bits; and a four-byte word, 32 bits. (Refer to Figure 3.4.)

[4]All computer processing is controlled by the system clock's speed. However, on midrange and mainframe computers, the actual megahertz speeds are much less meaningful. On these systems many tasks are performed simultaneously, and multiple processors are often used. Hence, in business, speed capabilities are usually determined by running a set of processing jobs on different systems and then comparing the results.

bus The path in a computer over which data are moved.

input/output (I/O) bus A bus that moves data into and out of the processor.

data bus A bus that moves data between the central processor and memory.

word The number of bits a computer can process at one time.

FIGURE 3.14
The Two Types of Bus
An input/output bus moves data into and out of the processor. A data bus moves data between units within the central processor.

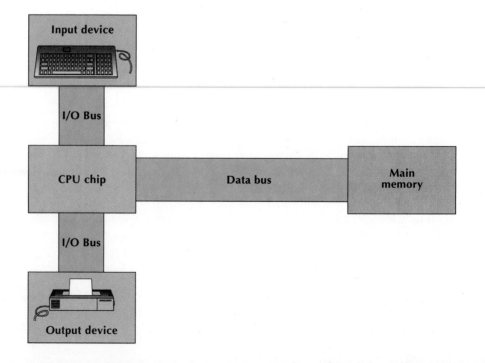

The larger the word size, the faster the computer can process data and perform arithmetic and logic operations. Many micro and most midrange systems use 32-bit words; mainframes and supercomputers are built for 64-bit words. In contrast, most personal computers use 16-bit words (two eight-bit bytes), with the most powerful built around 32-bit word structures.

Increasing Computer Speed

In today's increasingly complex world, the users of information technology are demanding more and more speed from computers. Processing and computer speed may be increased in six ways: through the use of cache memory, coprocessors, accelerator boards, greater chip density, RISC computing, and parallel processing.

Cache Memory.   A special form of high-speed memory called **cache memory** eliminates the need to move data to and from main memory repeatedly. In systems without cache memory, the CPU sends data requests to main memory, where they are read and acted on. Main memory then sends the result back to the CPU. This process can be quite time consuming, depending on the amount of information stored in main memory.

cache memory A form of high-speed memory that acts as a temporary holding/processing cell.

Cache memory acts as a temporary holding/processing cell. As data requests pass between the CPU and main memory, they travel through cache memory and are copied there. Subsequent requests for the same data are recognized and captured by the cache memory cell. The cache cell then fulfills the data request with the CPU. By decreasing the number of data requests to main memory, processing time is cut in half (Figure 3.15).

Coprocessors.   When a certain task is performed again and again, special-purpose chips can be designed to handle it quickly and efficiently. These chips, called **coprocessor chips**, are mounted on the processor board and function simultaneously with the primary processor chip. By taking processing work away from the main processor, they free the central processing unit to focus on general processing needs.

coprocessor chip A special-purpose chip mounted on a processor board; it is designed to handle common functions quickly and efficiently.

FIGURE 3.15
How Cache Memory Works

Central processor   Cache memory   Main memory

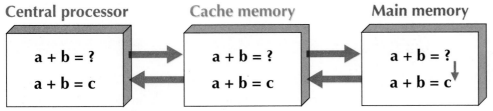
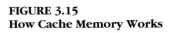

a) The central processor sends a request to main memory, which accepts and acts on the request. When the data travel between the processor and memory, they travel through and are copied into cache memory.

Central processor   Cache memory   Main memory

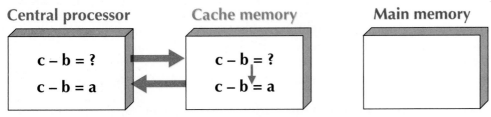

b) Subsequent requests involving the original data are recognized by the cache memory and captured. The cache memory acts on the data requests and provides the response to the central processor. Because the data no longer travel on to the main memory unit, processing time is cut in half.

Math coprocessor chips are used frequently by scientists and engineers who need to do large amounts of intensive calculations. Math coprocessors are also being used in graphics and multimedia applications.

CRITICAL CONNECTION 3
Will the Real Number-Crunching Power Users Please Stand Up?

Here are just a few of the situations in which you may need the number-crunching power of a math coprocessor.

• You might become a loan officer at Chemical Bank, where demographic data are plotted on color-coded, computer-generated maps to make sure the bank is not "redlining," or discriminating against applicants from certain neighborhoods.

• You might become a marketing supervisor at Michigan Bell, where multimedia sales presentations are becoming the norm.

• You might get a job in training at Union Pacific Railroad, where an interactive multimedia training program has boosted company morale and almost doubled on-time package delivery rates.

• You might become a supervisor in the advertising department at Lillian Vernon Corp., where desktop publishing is used to create dozens of colorful mail-order catalogs every year.

The common thread in all these scenarios is computer graphics, most of which are represented inside the computer as series of complex mathematical equations. Click your mouse and the computer will leap into action, performing the millions of floating point operations needed to plot a bigger, smaller, rotated, squeezed, or stretched outline on the computer screen. Multiply this mathematical frenzy by fifteen to thirty frames per second—the speed needed to display the computer animation and video that enliven multimedia applications—and you are talking about an awesome amount of raw mathematical power, the kind math coprocessors are designed to deliver.

accelerator board An add-in circuit board that increases a computer's processing speed.

Accelerator Boards.   An **accelerator board** is an add-in circuit board that increases a computer's processing speed by (1) using a clock speed that is faster than the CPU's, (2) using a faster processor chip, or (3) using an arithmetic/logic unit that speeds up floating point calculations. Any combination of these three is possible.

The characteristics of an accelerator board depend on the nature of the work that it is designed to help accomplish. For example, floating point arithmetic is important to engineering and scientific applications. Thus a PC used in those areas may be outfitted with an accelerator board with a faster ALU. Or the computer may be outfitted with a specialized accelerator board, such as a graphics accelerator board. In most applications, accelerator boards can yield speed increases of 200 to 400 percent.

Increased Chip Density and Integration.   Data and information move through the computer at better than one-third the speed of light (which is 186,000 miles per second). Thus, reducing the distance traveled, even a little, makes a tremendous difference in the computer's speed. This fundamental principle underlies the continual emphasis on miniaturization of circuits and greater **chip density**, the number of circuits on a single chip.

Exactly how many circuits can be packed onto a chip? The Intel 80386 chip (usually called just a "386" chip), first introduced in 1985, holds .25 million transistors. The Intel 80486 (or "486," as it is commonly called), introduced in 1991, operates at speeds of 33 to 66 megahertz; executes at a speed of 54 million instructions per second; holds 1.25 million transistors; and integrates a CPU, input/output controller, high-speed graphics support, a memory cache, and a math coprocessor—all on a chip the size of your fingernail. It is compatible with all of its predecessors and thus can process applications software developed for earlier generations of chips and computers.

The Intel Pentium chip (see Figure 3.9), the successor to the "486," was introduced in early 1993. This chip, which many people expected to be called the "586," has more than three million transistors and operates at a speed of 112 million instructions per second (see Table 3.1).

Experts predict that chips will hold 40 million transistors by the year 2000. Specialized chips will most likely operate at 250 MHz and provide a capability of 1 billion instructions per second, interacting with 1 gigabyte DRAM chips.

The Photo Essay at the end of this chapter shows the steps involved in creating these "marvels of miniaturization."

Reduced Instruction Set Computing (RISC). The quest for greater speed has caused computer designers to rethink the manner in which computers process instructions. One type of processing, **complex instruction set computing (CISC)**, has been used since the first days of computing. CISC moves data to and from main memory so often that it limits the use of registers to store temporary data values. Calling on the memory so frequently means slower overall performance, since a portion of the processor must coordinate the execution of the movement instructions. (The instructions to do so are called the **microcode**.)

Recently, a second type of processing has become popular. **Reduced instruction set computing (RISC)** processes data more simply. With RISC, data for the execution of an instruction are taken *only* from registers. This simplifies (and accelerates) instruction processing greatly because the microcode is not needed. A separate set of instructions moves the data from memory to the registers.

At the University of New Hampshire's Institute for the Study of Earth, Oceans, and Space, scientists use RISC-based workstations to transform data into three-dimensional graphics and animation, an imaging process called *visualization*. The speed of the RISC-system computers is much greater than that of the other computers used in the laboratory, enabling scientists to turn mountains of data into animated pictures relatively quickly.

Through visualization, they can see how the ocean's tidal forces interact with the underwater landscape of the eastern coast of the United States and Canada and simulate tides. These spectacular images are useful for managing fishing and sea life and for managing shipping and commercial fishing activities in the area.

Parallel Processing. Sometimes we do things in sequence, one step after the other. For example, we assemble model cars and airplanes one careful step at a time. Other times, we do things simultaneously. For example, we walk, talk, and gesture when sharing information with a colleague. Computers, too, can be designed to do things sequentially or simultaneously.

Traditionally, computers have been designed for **sequential processing**, in which the execution of one instruction is followed by the execution of another. But

parallel processing Processing in which a computer handles different parts of a problem by executing instructions simultaneously.

single instruction/multiple data (SIMD) method A parallel-processing method that executes the same instruction on many data values simultaneously.

multiple instruction/multiple data (MIMD) method A parallel-processing method that connects a number of processors that run different programs or parts of a program on different sets of data.

in recent years computer designers have been developing **parallel processing**, in which computers handle different parts of a problem by executing instructions simultaneously. In the end, the results of each parallel process are combined to produce a result.

Two types of parallel processing are emerging (Figure 3.16). **Single instruction/multiple data (SIMD) methods** execute the same instruction on many data values simultaneously. **Multiple instruction/multiple data (MIMD) methods** connect a number of processors that run different programs or parts of a program on different sets of data. Communication between the processors is essential to MIMD methods.

In New Haven, Connecticut, a team of scientists and physicians at Yale University is working to incorporate parallel processing into a computer that can monitor the condition of seriously ill patients. Currently, after a patient has surgery, nurses and physicians monitor the patient every few minutes, checking for changes in such vital signs as blood pressure, heart rate, and breathing rate. However, even the most dedicated medical personnel may not be able to detect subtle changes in the patient's condition.

Using parallel processing techniques, separate processors within a computer will be assigned responsibility for monitoring vital signs. Still other processors will be interconnected with medical databases and with the patient's medical history, comparing data from all sources and translating them into meaningful information for the physicians and the medical support staff. Because medicine and the human body are both complex, the system is necessarily very complex, but parallel processing promises to make the complexity manageable by turning over difficult coordination and analysis tasks to the computer.

FIGURE 3.16
The Two Types of Parallel Processing

PARALLEL ARCHITECTURES

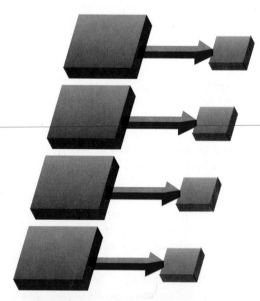

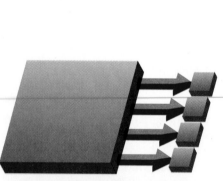

a) Single instruction/multiple data (SIMD) methods. In a SIMD computer, many data items are processed simultaneously by one instruction or by identical instructions on different processors.

b) Multiple instruction/multiple data (MIMD) methods. In a MIMD computer, multiple processors act independently on different data items.

Today, parallel processing is still the exception rather than the rule. In the future, however, it is likely that computer systems of all sizes, from smallest to largest, will have parallel processing capabilities. In fact, massively parallel computers are now beginning to appear. These computers contain hundreds of thousands, even millions, of microprocessors, and will be used in ways that were undreamed of only a few years ago.

SUMMARY OF LEARNING OBJECTIVES

1 **Describe the components and purpose of the central processing unit.** At the heart of the computer is the *central processing unit (CPU)*, or *processor*, which executes program instructions and performs the computer's processing actions. The CPU is a collection of electronic circuits made up of thousands of *transistors* placed onto an *integrated circuit*, also called a *chip* or *microchip*. The two components of the CPU are the *control unit* and the *arithmetic/logic unit (ALU)*.

2 **Distinguish between primary and secondary storage and between RAM and ROM.** *Primary storage* is the storage within the computer itself; it holds data only temporarily, as the computer executes instructions. *Secondary storage* is permanent or semi-permanent and augments primary memory. Secondary storage is used to store data long-term.

Random-access memory (RAM) is memory that permits data or information to be written into or read from any memory address at any time. RAM stores data and information only as long as the computer is turned on. *Read-only memory (ROM)* also offers random access to data, but it can hold data and information after the electric current to the computer has been turned off.

3 **Describe the chips and boards that can be used to augment the CPU and main memory.** Chips and boards can be used to augment the CPU and main memory. *Processor chips* contain all of the processing capabilities of the control unit and ALU on one chip. *Memory chips* can augment primary storage. *Add-in boards* allow users to customize their computers' features and capabilities.

4 **Explain the process by which computers use registers to process data.** The processing sequence is a four-step process called the *machine cycle*. These four steps, all of which are directed by the control unit, are (1) *fetch*, obtain the next instruction from memory; (2) *decode*, translate the instruction into individual commands that the computer can process; (3) *execute*, perform the actions called for in the instructions; and (4) *store*, write the results of processing to memory. To execute the machine cycle, the control unit depends on *registers*, temporary storage areas in the processor.

5 **List and explain the three determinants of processor speed.** Three elements determine processor speed: the system clock, bus width, and word size. All computers have a *system clock*, a circuit that generates electronic pulses at a fixed rate to synchronize processing activities. Clock cycles are measured in *megahertz*; the higher the megahertz, the faster the computer. A *bus* is the path over which data are moved. The width of the bus determines the amount of data that can be moved at one time. Word size is measured in bits. A *word* is the number of bits a computer can process simultaneously. The larger the word size, the faster a computer can process data.

6 **Describe six ways of increasing processing and computer speed and how these methods can be used in business.** Processing and computer speed may be increased in six ways: through the use of cache memory, coprocessors, accelerator boards, greater chip density, RISC computing, and parallel processing.

Cache memory is a form of high-speed memory that acts as a temporary holding/processing cell and eliminates the need to move data to and from the main memory repeatedly.

Coprocessors are special chips designed to handle tasks that are performed often. By taking this processing work away from the main processor, they free the CPU to focus on general processing needs.

Accelerator boards are add-in circuit boards that increase a computer's processing speed. Packing more transistors on a chip—that is, greater *chip density*—also means greater computing speed.

Reduced instruction set computing (RISC) processes data more simply than complex instruction set computing (CISC). With RISC, data for the execution of an instruction are taken only from registers. This both simplifies and accelerates instruction processing.

With *parallel processing*, computers handle different parts of a problem by executing instructions simultaneously. In the end, the results of each parallel process are combined to produce a result.

KEY TERMS

CRITICAL CONNECTIONS

1. Multimedia Macintosh Plays Angel of Mercy

By clicking a mouse on any of a number of colorful computer graphics, parents at B.C.'s Children's Hospital can call up a variety of multimedia applications. Click! The screen displays a guided tour of the hospital, complete with live-action video introducing hospital staff and explaining what they do. Click! The computer takes parents to a hospital "floor" where computer animations and digitized sound recordings explain certain disorders. Click! The Macintosh prints out a reading list of other materials in the resource library. Click! The computer asks parents about their concerns and prints out a list of questions they might want to ask the doctor. The Macintosh can go as fast—or as slow—as the parents want.

Even though the system is still under development, Dr. Durbach reports, parents are already raving about the computer and its marvelous bedside manner.

Questions for Discussion

1. One of the truisms of information technology is that the more powerful the computer's CPU, the more patient and "friendly" it can seem to inexperienced users. Why do you think this is true?

2. One of Dr. Durbach's goals for the hospital's multimedia system is to educate parents—to lead them through the same steps doctors follow when they

make a diagnosis and weigh alternative treatments. Do you think a computer is well-suited to this use? Why or why not?

3. Although the hospital's primary goal is to help sick and injured children, it still must compete with other hospitals for patients. How might the new multimedia system help in this regard?

2. Add-In Boards and CADD: The Trump Cards for BSW International

BSW's points to at least two savings from CADD. First, the powerful software lets the architects spend their time where it counts—on the differences, not the similarities, between stores. Design elements that don't change from store to store, such as distinctive windows or a standard plumbing or electrical layout, can simply be copied from one computer file to another. This allows the architects to spend their time where it counts—on the modifications required by the site, which may have an unusual shape. And second, the computer-created documents are easier to read and modify, which reduces confusion and mistakes at the construction site, where workers are paid by the hour.

Questions for Discussion

1. Many of the add-in boards for architects' computers allow the attachment of input/output devices that feature greater precision than those found on an office worker's computer. Why is this precision important for architects? Is the computer a good tool, in general, for architects? Why?

2. Are stores with basically the same design an advantage for national chains of retail stores? Why or why not? What advantage does CADD contribute here?

3. CADD facilitates continual improvements in the quality of BSW's drawings, because the drawings

for Wal-Mart Store 305 incorporate all the "corrections" made to the drawings for Wal-Mart Stores 1 through 304. Is this an important competitive advantage for BSW? Why?

3. Will the Real Number-Crunching Power Users Please Stand Up?

In the early 1990s, Weitek Corp. of Sunnyvale, California, offered a math coprocessor for $1,000—a reasonable price when you realize that the chip was rated at 40 megaflops, the same as a supercomputer with a $1-million price tag. And within the year, the company's CEO announced, Weitek would offer a math coprocessor rated at a blazing 120 megaflops. Since then, prices for all hardware, including math coprocessors, have dropped sharply; even high-powered sophisticated math coprocessors are now available at steep discounts.

Questions for Discussion

1. Computer experts claim that hardware advances drive advances in software. Why is this fact important to IT professionals and to managers and users of IT?

2. You manage a marketing department that uses a variety of applications software packages. Your staff is asking that math coprocessors be installed in every micro but you know the head of accounting is watching every penny. What arguments could you use to win approval for the purchase?

3. *Dance of the Planets* and *James Gleick's Chaos* are just two multimedia programs that use a math coprocessor to let people explore the wonders of science. What arguments could a local principal use to convince you, a businessperson, to donate such programs to his or her school?

REVIEW QUESTIONS

1. What is the purpose of the central processing unit?

2. What is the difference between data and instructions?

3. Describe the role of the control unit and the two types of activities performed by the arithmetic/ logic unit.

4. What is the role of primary memory in computing? What is the relationship between primary memory

and the central processor? How does primary memory differ from secondary storage?

5. In what five ways is memory space used?

6. What is a memory address?

7. What is the difference between RAM and ROM?

8. How are DRAM and static RAM alike? How are they different?

9. What is a system board? What does the system board of a PC contain?

10. Distinguish between a microcomputer, a microprocessor, and a microprocessor chip.

11. What is SIMM memory?

12. What is a port? An expansion slot? An add-in board?

13. What is the difference between closed and open architectures?

14. What are the four steps of information processing? How are these divided into the machine, instruction, and execution cycles of computing?

15. What is the role of registers in computing? Where are registers found?

16. Describe the purpose of each of the four types of registers.

17. What are MIPS? Megaflops?

18. What three features of a computer determine its processing speed?

19. Distinguish between an input/output bus and a data bus.

20. How do primary memory and cache memory differ?

21. What is a coprocessor?

22. How do accelerator boards increase processing speed?

23. How many transistors are found on Intel's Pentium chip? How many instructions can it execute per second?

24. What does RISC stand for?

25. What is parallel processing? What are its potential benefits? What are the two types of parallel processing?

DISCUSSION QUESTIONS

1. One of the most notable trends in IT today is the availability of affordable micros with powerful processors, large amounts of memory, and the capacity to add boards that control sophisticated input/output devices. What potential business opportunities might this trend create? What difficulties might it create for businesses?

2. The availability of affordable, high-power micros has spurred a trend toward downsizing, or moving business applications from mainframes to mini/midrange computers or PCs. Some companies, such as UPS and BankAmerica Corp., still maintain large data centers built around mainframes. Why do you think this is so?

3. Advertisements for microcomputers often list two amounts of RAM—the amount that comes with the computer and the maximum amount of memory that can be added. Why is this second figure important to a manager who is shopping for a computer?

4. A recent survey compiled by *Computerworld* estimates that graphical user interfaces (GUIs) were used on 1.4 million PCs in 1990; this figure is expected to swell to 25.3 million by the middle of the decade. What does this trend mean for processor speed? For businesses that want to use popular productivity software?

SUGGESTED READINGS

Corcoran, Elizabeth, "Calculating Reality," *Scientific American*, 264, no. 1 (January 1991), pp. 100-109. A lucid discussion of the next generation of high-speed computers and how they will be used to model reality more closely than ever before.

Drexler, K. Eric, *Engines of Creating: The Coming Era of Nanotechnology*. New York: Anchor Press, 1986. An enormously fascinating and innovative book about the consequences of advances in information technology. The author is a pioneering researcher who tells how the "nanotechnology revolution" can be used to achieve social goals like better health, a higher standard of living, and world peace.

Gilder, George, *Microcosm*. New York: Simon & Schuster, 1989. Provides an up-close look at the technological revolution that is creating unprecedented opportunities for business and people in general. Also includes revealing portraits of the leading scientists, engineers, and entrepreneurs, and a comparison of the level of IT usage in different countries.

Pancake, C.M., "Software Support for Parallel Computing: Where Are We Headed," *Communications of the ACM*, 34, no. 11 (November 1991), pp. 52-66. Examines the issues involved in parallel computing and the directions the field is taking.

Pountain, Dick, and John Bryan, "All Systems Go," *Byte*, 17, no. 8 (August 1992), pp. 112-116. A very readable evaluation of the advantages of parallel processing and cache memory.

CASE STUDY

Wal-Mart: Using IT to Change the Face of Retailing

WAL★MART

SAY "WAL-MART" AND YOU MIGHT think of deep discounts (Wal-Mart's claim to fame) or small towns (their usual locations). You might even think of the number 1 U.S. retailer or its status as third-most admired corporation in the United States. But you might not associate Wal-Mart, Inc. with one of the most powerful commercial retail computer systems on the planet.

You can't see the Wal-Mart computer system all in one place. It's a complex system of interconnected computer networks, too big to fit in a single room. But you can see parts of it when you visit any Wal-Mart store.

The first part of the system you might see is a satellite dish outside the store, perhaps on the roof. This is just one part of Wal-Mart's satellite communication system, installed in the late 1980s to speed credit card approvals and ease communication between some of the chain's more remote outlets and company headquarters in Bentonville, Arkansas.

Inside the store, check out the bar codes on the price tags and product packages. Bar codes are useful because they allow the rapid, accurate input of data. Pass the bar code over the scanner in a point-of-sale (POS) terminal and the processor's ALU will match the encoded product maker's ID number and product number with a database of price lists, printing the correct price in an instant. Moreover, because most bar codes are imprinted on the product labels and shipping cartons during the manufacturing process, using them also saves Wal-Mart time and money in the warehouse and the stockroom, where workers use handheld, wireless bar code scanners to update their records.

The use of bar codes also streamlines the daunting task of ordering the thousands of items found in a typical Wal-Mart. Instead of relying on a clerk to notice a reorder card on an empty peg, Wal-Mart set up a computerized "continuous replenishment system" in 1991. Every night, sales data from each store are sent to a satellite dish that beams the data to one of seventeen highly automated distribution centers. There, the system makes arrangements for the delivery of replacement items and prepares an electronic order for replacement stock. The resulting orders are beamed via satellite to headquarters and, in most cases, directly to a supplier as well. Because order quantities are tied to actual sales, Wal-Mart is able to keep inventory costs down. (A typical Wal-Mart store devotes just 10% of its square footage to inventory, compared to an industry average of 28 percent.)

Three major factors underlie Wal-Mart's phenomenal success: a commitment to people, a commitment to low prices, and a commitment to information technology. Wal-Mart's low prices help the chain ring up more sales, which lead to even lower prices, which lead to even more sales.

Once the sales data are at headquarters, a parallel processing system is used to analyze gigabytes of sales data. The sales data are so detailed that Wal-Mart can even determine what sizes and colors are selling best in a particular region or store—something that few other retailers can do. This information helps managers customize the store's product mix and its internal layout to its market. A store that sells more hardware than electronics, for example, will be laid out with a large, well-stocked hardware department and a smaller, less prominent electronics department.

The sales data also give Wal-Mart extra clout with its suppliers. Instead of keeping sales data secret from suppliers, Wal-Mart actually helps them set up electronic links to its database. These sales data help the suppliers estimate demand and plan production runs. The resulting interdependence between Wal-Mart and its suppliers, coupled with the size of Wal-Mart's orders, gives Wal-Mart the power to shape the marketplace. Procter & Gamble, for example, is cutting the number of coupons and grocery-store promotions it offers; Wal-Mart, which accounts for 11% of its U.S. sales, doesn't want them. Aware that Wal-Mart will drop them in an instant if they find a cheaper supplier, even Fortune 500 suppliers feel pressured to keep prices down; many have responded by revamping their operations to increase efficiency. Smaller stores and chains don't have this kind of influence.

Wal-Mart, of course, isn't the only retail giant to use IT to its advantage. It's not even a leader in IT spending. The Boston Consulting Group categorizes Wal-Mart's $600 million investment in information technology and its annual budget as being "more in the midrange," compared to Sears, Roebuck & Co., which "has been in the top bracket in its industry when it comes to spending on new technology."

What sets Wal-Mart apart, it is clear, is its focus on strategy. Every investment in IT is made to support the goal of cutting overhead and keeping customer prices low. In 1992, for example, Wal-Mart upgraded its satellite links so that they could be used for new applications requiring the transmission of gigabytes of data, such as multimedia training (to replace a million-dollar investment in paper manuals). As a result of its IT expertise, Wal-Mart can hold selling and operating expenses to just 15% of sales, versus 28% for Sears, Roebuck & Co.—once the nation's number one retailer.

Questions for Discussion

1. Use your own shopping experiences to list some reasons why Wal-Mart has enjoyed such phenomenal growth in recent years. How many of these reasons can be traced to the company's use of IT? Which aspect of processor performance do you think is most important to shopper satisfaction?

2. Wal-Mart recently announced that it would penalize manufacturers for certain bar-coding errors. Why do you think it took this action?

3. Industry observers have labeled Wal-Mart a "category killer," a chain that meets the market's needs with an efficiency other competitors cannot match. How does Wal-Mart's use of information technology demonstrate the importance of know-how?

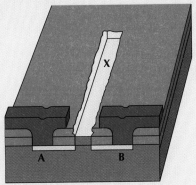

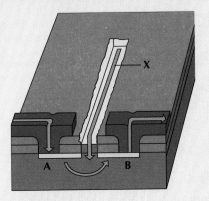

(a) Transistor off

(b) Transistor on

KEY:

- Positively doped silicon substrate
- Silicon dioxide
- Negatively doped silicon
- Pathway X
- Circuit pathway
- ⟹ Direction of electrical charge along pathway X
- ⟹ Direction of electrical charge along circuit pathway

The Making of a Microprocessor

Microprocessors are built from sand and are constructed in layers consisting of circuits and pathways, doped silicon substrate, and silicon dioxide. ("Doping" the silicon allows it to conduct electricity well or not at all. This is important because computing is at heart an electrical process.) This photo essay describes the steps in creating the silicon wafer on which the circuits are created.

Step One: Designing the Microprocessor Chip

1 A microprocessor's design is created using a powerful desktop computer equipped with a design program. Each component of the microprocessor is drawn and positioned using a digitizing tablet that allows the designer to translate images on paper into an electronic format, with the resulting image appearing on a display screen. Today's microprocessors contain millions of transistors and circuits, each microscopic in size.

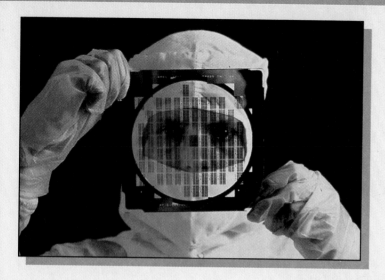

2 The microprocessor's design is transformed into a series of photo masks, one for each layer of the chip. A typical microprocessor design includes 20 or more different photo masks.

Step Two: Manufacturing the Chip

3 The entire process of manufacturing and testing the microprocessor takes place in a *clean room*, a work room that is virtually free of dust—more than 100 times more sterile than a hospital operating room. To avoid contaminating the atmosphere, all engineers and workers are required to don special gowns (called "bunny suits") before they enter the room.

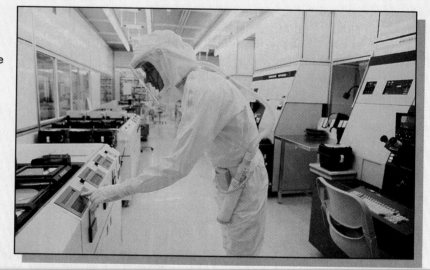

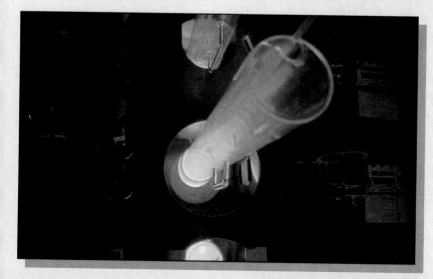

4 The first step in manufacturing is creating cylindrical silicon ingots. Silicon sand (hence the name *silicon* chip) is heated until it melts. The molten silicon, which contains almost no impurities or contaminants, is then grown into a cylindrical crystal that looks like a metal rod.

5 A diamond-tipped saw slices the silicon rod into very thin (3/1000 inch) discs, called wafers. The wafer, which may be 5" to 8" (13cm to 20cm) in diameter, is the base from which the microprocessor chips are built.

6 Wafers are sterilized and their surfaces polished to a shiny, mirror-like finish.

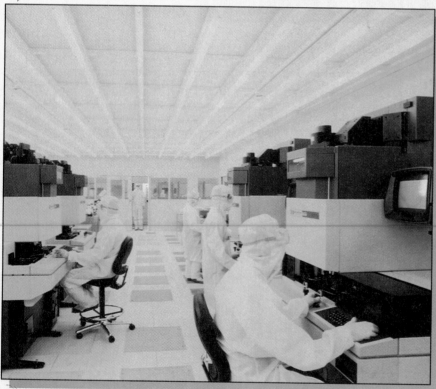

7 During *photolithography*, a gelatin-like substance called *photoresist*, similar to the film used in ordinary photography, is deposited on the wafer's surface. A glass photo mask containing circuit patterns is held over the wafer and ultraviolet light is passed through the glass regions of the photo mask that do not contain the circuit pattern. A portion of the electronic circuit will subsequently be placed everywhere that the light exposes the photoresist on top of the wafer.

8 Wafers are taken into a "yellow room," so called because of the special yellow light used to illuminate the room. Here, after the resist is exposed, it is placed in chemicals to develop it. The exposed resist will remain on the wafer; the unexposed resist will be removed by the chemicals.

Next comes *oxidization*. Silicon heated and exposed to steam or dry oxygen (that is, oxidized silicon) will form silicon dioxide, more commonly known as glass. (An analogy: iron exposed to oxygen forms rust. Silicon "rust" is glass.) Unexposed regions of the wafer can be oxidized to separate the electronic circuits.

Following oxidization, special materials are diffused or implanted into the wafer. These materials change the electrical properties of the silicon so that the electronic circuits (or switches) can be made.

After implantation comes *deposition*, in which liquid metal or other films are "sprayed" on the wafer. These films will later be selectively patterned, following the photolithography steps described in number 7 above.

In the final manufacturing step, called *etching*, chemicals that selectively remove one type of material or another are used to etch away patterned regions on the wafer, leaving only the required circuit patterns.

9 The preceding five-step process is repeated to "build" images and electrical circuits into the wafer. Metals deposited on the wafer are selectively etched to provide thin wires interconnecting the circuits.

10 A wafer contains hundreds of identical chips. The rectangles near the center of the wafer are test circuits for monitoring the quality of the fabrication process.

11 Each wafer contains millions of transistors. The color enhanced close-up photo shown here shows the sections of the chip and the bonding pads along the edges of the chip.

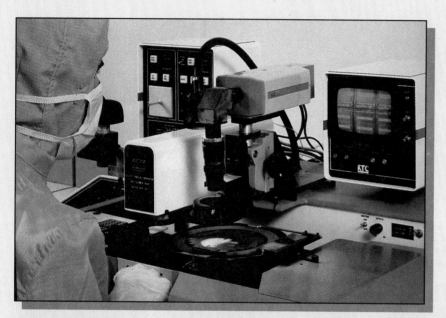

Step Three: Testing the Microprocessor

12 A wafer's *yield* is the number of good chips that result. Testing determines chip quality. During testing, large computer controlled electronic testers determine whether a chip functions as it was designed. The chips that do function as designed are diced out of the wafers using diamond tipped saws. Defective wafers are discarded.

Step Four: Packaging the Microprocessor

13 By itself, the microprocessor chip is too fragile to be handled or used. Hence, it is mounted in a protective package. Each chip is bonded to a plastic base and the chip's wire leads are in turn wired to the electrical gold or aluminum leads on the package. The wire leads of the chip are thinner than a human hair. The microprocessor package is generally shaped in a square as a result of the dicing process.

14 During assembly of system (mother) boards, the leads of the microprocessor package are inserted into holes in the circuit board. Each lead contacts an electrical lead on the board, which is used to transmit to and receive electrical signals from other components mounted on the board.

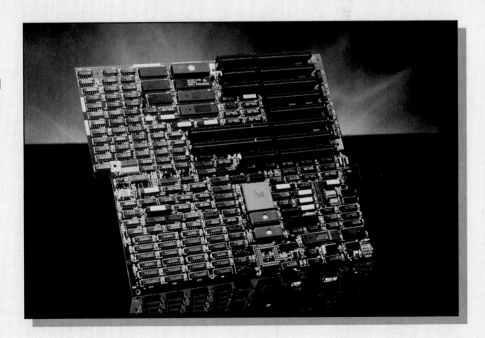

CHAPTER 4

Secondary Storage and Input/Output Devices

Learning Objectives

When you have completed this chapter, you should be able to:

1 Discuss why people use secondary storage, not just the computer's main memory, to store information.

2 Distinguish between the two main types of magnetic storage and identify four newer magnetic storage alternatives.

3 Explain why optical storage is of growing importance in computing, and describe the most commonly used forms of optical storage.

4 Identify the five most widely used input devices and describe how they are used in computing.

5 Discuss the future of voice input and audio output as components of information technology.

6 Describe the four types of output devices and identify their uses in business.

In Practice

After completing this chapter, you should be able to perform these activities:

1 Examine a situation in which information will be stored and determine what type of secondary storage should be used.

2 Discuss data storage with businesspeople who use magnetic disk or tape to back up their programs and information, and understand the risks involved in not performing backup.

3 Evaluate the manner in which information is input to a computer system and determine what alternatives could be used, weighing the advantages and disadvantages of each.

4 Speak with a graphic artist and discuss the methods she uses to create drawings, images, text documents, and visual presentations, including color slides and transparencies.

5 Examine an everyday situation in which information is output from a computer system and assess the feasibility of using alternative forms of output, including voice output.

6 Observe an office setting in which correspondence and documents are printed and determine why a particular printer is used, what other types could be used, and the advantages and disadvantages of each.

Mapping Your Way

I<small>T'S LATE AT NIGHT AND THE FOG IS</small> pouring in from the river. The street lights are flickering and you have the eerie feeling that you are the only person on the road at this hour. You've never been in this part of the state before, and you are completely lost. You drive around aimlessly for an hour before you find an all-night gas station with an attendant who can give you directions to your destination.

There has to be a better way to find your way out of a situation like this, you think. And there is. The marriage of small but powerful computers with low-cost software has resulted in a new automobile technology that allows you to insert a disk into an opening on your dashboard and bring up a map of the area on a display terminal (also located on the dashboard). Most autos don't currently have this capability, but there is a good chance that they will soon.

How does this convenient system work? Let's say you want to begin a trip across a particular region of the country. You put a disk into your dashboard and the first screen appears. This "Overview" screen shows a map of the states in the region. A command at the top of the screen tells you to touch the state on which you want more detail. When you place your finger on the touch-sensitive screen, an inset appears showing the details of the region. Special landmarks, such as bridges, rivers, and important buildings, are all clearly marked.

More than 22,000 drivers in Japan have "personal navigation systems" installed on the dashboard of their cars. The systems combine an antenna, a CD-ROM player, and a computer to display full-color maps that are updated as the car travels. They even direct hungry drivers to the nearest restaurant.

If you need more detailed information about a particular area, simply touch the screen again. Instantly, more detail appears: street names, highway numbers, and directional signs ("One Way," "No Trucks," and so forth). If you want to see a different section of town, touch the screen again, moving your finger up and to the right. A new section of the map scrolls into view. Looking at the local road and interstate motorway interchanges, you spot your destination and see just how you can get there.   ■

W HEN WE THINK OF NEW TECHNOLOGIES, WE SOMETIMES FORGET THAT THERE IS MORE TO a computer system than simply a keyboard and a display monitor. All of the processing work is done "behind the scenes." Computers use data to generate information, but very often information is installed in them through the use of outside storage media. All the maps in the auto guidance system, for example, are contained on secondary storage disks.

We discussed magnetic storage briefly in Chapter 2 in our overview of a computer system. This chapter continues the detailed tour we began in Chapter 3. We begin by discussing secondary storage and its importance to business and personal computing. In the second half of the chapter, we move to a discussion of the many different input and output devices commonly used with computers. As you will see, getting data and information into and out of a computer, whether from primary or secondary storage, depends on having the right equipment.

The same caveat with which we began Chapter 3 applies to this material as well. The purpose of this chapter is not to make you an expert in equipment technology, but rather to make you familiar with the many technological options available to today's businesspeople. Knowing which technology to use can make you both more productive and more successful.

■ Secondary Storage

secondary storage, auxiliary storage A storage medium that is external to the computer, but that can be read by the computer; a way of storing data and information outside the computer itself.

Recall that *primary storage* is the section of the central processing unit that holds data and information and instructions before and after processing. In contrast, **secondary storage**, sometimes called **auxiliary storage**, is a way of storing data and information outside the computer itself. Secondary storage is any storage medium that is external to the computer but that can be read by a computer.

The differences between primary and secondary memory make secondary storage an integral and important part of information technology. This is true for several reasons:

* First, the contents of primary memory can reside there only temporarily (see Chapter 3). Main memory itself is used by many different applications, and between each application the memory is in effect cleared and reassigned to the next application. Hence any information or results obtained from an application must be stored separately from primary memory—that is, in secondary storage.
* Second, primary memory holds data only while the computer is turned on. When the computer is turned off, the contents of primary memory are lost (if ordinary DRAM is used, and it usually is).
* Third, primary memory is seldom large enough to hold the large volumes of data and information associated with typical business applications. For instance, it would be impossible to hold the transcripts of all the students at a large college or university in primary memory.

By doing what primary memory cannot, secondary storage helps the computer process and store large amounts of information. At the same time, it is economical, reliable, and convenient.

There are two main types of secondary storage: magnetic and optical.

Magnetic Storage

Since the earliest days of computing, magnetism has played a central role in storing data and information. The two primary magnetic media are magnetic tape and magnetic disks. The earliest form of secondary storage was magnetic tape. Magnetic disks followed later.

How exactly does magnetism work? Data are stored on the magnetic medium by a **read/write head**, a device that records data by magnetically aligning metallic particles (iron oxide mixed with a binding agent) on the medium. These particles correspond to binary digits (alignment represents a binary one, nonalignment represents a zero). The *write head* records data and the *read head* retrieves them.

Writing, or *recording*, converts the contents of electronic circuits in primary memory into spots on the recording surface of the storage medium. Each spot, or pattern of spots, stores one piece of data. *Reading*, or *retrieving*, is not a reverse of the process, however. Retrieval does not change or move the stored details. Rather, it leaves the stored version intact. The read process senses the coded spots and interprets them as data.

Magnetic Tape.   On larger computers, **magnetic tape** often comes in large reels; on microcomputers, tape cartridges, slightly larger than audio cassettes, are common equipment (see Figure 2.12d). Data are stored, or written, to the magnetic tape by a read/write head on the *tape drive*, a peripheral device that holds and processes the tape. The read/write head alternates the magnetic direction of the metallic particles coating the tape. The *transport mechanism* moves the tape from one reel to the other. Reading and writing occur as the oxide side of the tape passes over the heads (Figure 4.1).

Two recording schemes are common, one using seven-bit bytes per character and the other using nine-bit bytes. This means that the magnetic tape surface is divided into seven or nine **tracks**, narrow areas in which each spot (invisible to

read/write head A device that records data by magnetically aligning metallic particles on the medium. The write head records data and the read head retrieves them.

magnetic tape A magnetic storage medium in which data are stored on large reels of tape.

track The area in which data and information are stored on magnetic tape or disk.

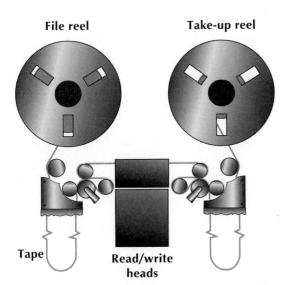

File reel   **Take-up reel**

Tape   **Read/write heads**

FIGURE 4.1
Transport Mechanism for Magnetic Tape Drive Unit
Reading and writing occur as the oxide side of the magnetic tape passes over the unit's read/write heads.

the human eye) is being magnetized or demagnetized (Figure 4.2). (Note: The seven- or nine-bit structure is determined by the manufacturer of the tape drive, and is not something that the person using the drive can decide.)

To read the data, the head reads the magnetic patterns and translates them into electric pulses. The pulses become the 0's and 1's that the computer processes.

The tape drive records onto the magnetic tape in groups or **records**, sets of data about a single transaction (such as the registration for a course or the payment of an invoice). One or more records may be written as a **block**. Because reading and writing occur only while the tape is moving, a space called a **gap** is left before and after the block so that the tape drive can stop without skipping over any data. The drive's **recording density** is the number of characters per inch at which it writes the data. A recording density of 6,250 characters or bytes per inch is most common.

Compared with other forms of secondary storage, reading from and writing to magnetic tape can be very slow. If a very large number of records is stored, a relatively lengthy section of tape will be used to record the data. If you want to recall a particular record, the search for the record must begin at the beginning of the tape and proceed record by record—that is, *sequentially*. The computer may need to scan hundreds of feet of tape to find the desired information.

Despite these disadvantages, magnetic tape storage continues to play an important role today in computers of all sizes because of the advantages it offers. It is relatively inexpensive (approximately $25 for a blank reel) and reliable. Users can store a reel of tape for a long time without worrying about data loss.

Magnetic Disk.   The term **magnetic disk** refers to two types of disk: **flexible disks** (also known as **floppy disks**) which are made of flexible plastic, and **hard disks**, which are made of rigid aluminum.

Data on magnetic disk are stored in the same way they are stored on magnetic tape. Spots are magnetized or nonmagnetized in a coding scheme that corresponds to the on and off states of circuits (bits) in the processor.

Reality Check.   The decision to use aluminum in manufacturing hard disks came about only after a great deal of research. Researchers at IBM (where magnetic disks were invented) tested glass, plastic, brass, and magnesium. However, they discovered that disks made of these substances wobbled when run at high speeds, causing serious data loss and errors. Today, hard disks are made from aluminum laminates clamped together and heated in ovens. ∎

---

record A set of data about a single transaction.

block The writing of one or more records onto a section of magnetic tape.

gap In magnetic storage, a space left before and after a block so that the tape drive can stop without skipping over any data.

recording density The number of characters per inch at which a drive writes data.

magnetic disk A general term referring to two types of disk: flexible/floppy disk and hard disks.

floppy disk, flexible disk A type of magnetic disk made of flexible plastic.

hard disk A type of magnetic disk made of rigid aluminum.

FIGURE 4.2
Data Representation on Seven-Track Magnetic Tape
Representing data on seven-track tape entails magnetizing certain tracks and demagnetizing others. For example, the letter "L" is represented by magnetizing tracks 1, 2, 6, and 7 and demagnetizing tracks 3, 4, and 5. To read the data, the read head translates the magnetic pattern into electric pulses, which the computer then processes, as "L."

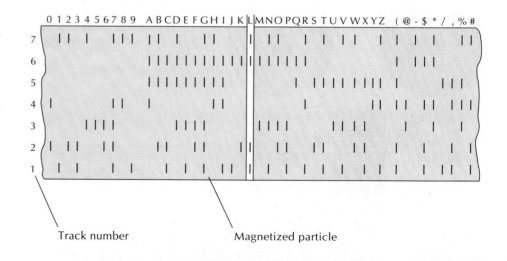

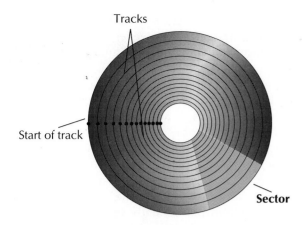

Tracks

Start of track

Sector

FIGURE 4.3   Tracks and Sectors on a Magnetic Disk
On a magnetic disk, data are usually stored in all tracks except the outer-most, which is reserved for a direc-tory that lists the names of the files stored and a label that identifies the disk and the format used for record-ing. Data are written to or read from a specific track as the disk drive rotates the disk. As the disk drive spins, it positions the read/write heads over the proper track. When the correct sector has been found, the data are read or written over.

Like the storage area on magnetic tape, the storage area of a magnetic disk is divided into tracks. However, the tracks on disks are concentric circles rather than linear (Figure 4.3). These tracks are often divided into **sectors** for easier access. The tracks have a specified recording density. Data are read from or written to a specific track as the disk is rotated by the disk drive at a constant speed of several hundred revolutions per second. (This speed is controlled by the disk drive built into the computer or attached to the computer by cable.) As the disk drive spins the disk continually, it positions the read/write heads over the proper track. Some disk drives on large mainframes and supercomputers position a read/write head over every track. The extra expense and complexity are justified because data can be retrieved much more quickly this way. There is no delay while the heads move from position to position.

It is important to note that the read/write heads "float" very close to the disk surface, but never actually touch it. If the read/write heads ever touch the disk, the result is a **head crash**. The data stored at the point at which the head touched the disk will be lost and the head itself could be damaged.

Some disk drives, called **Winchester disk drives**, contain a read/write head, an *access arm* (which positions the read/write head over the appropriate track), and the disk(s) in one sealed unit. These drives, typical of hard drive units on microcomputers, are not removable from the computer. Other disk units feature a **disk pack** a stack of disks, enclosed in a protective plastic cover that can be lifted onto or off the disk drive (Figure 4.4). Disk packs allow the user to remove and store disks easily. This is useful for making backup copies of information or pro-grams, for separating databases onto different disk packs, and for storing very large databases when all of the data will not fit on a single disk pack. Many main-frames and supercomputers use disk pack–based storage.

Magnetic disk storage is often called **random access storage** or **direct access storage**. This means that a particular record of information can be retrieved from

sector A subdivision of a track on a magnetic disk, used to improve access to data or information.

head crash The situation that occurs when the read/write heads that normally float close to a magnetic disk's surface actually touch the surface.

Winchester disk drive A disk drive that contains a read/write head, an access arm, and a disk in one sealed unit.

disk pack A stack of disks, enclosed in a protective plastic cover, that can be lifted onto or off a disk drive.

random access storage, direct access storage The process of retrieving a particular record of information from any track directly.

**FIGURE 4.4
Disk Pack**
A disk pack may contain as many as 12 disks stacked around a hollow core. With the protective plastic cover removed, the stack slips onto a shaft in the disk drive.

FIGURE 4.5   The Fabulous Flexible Diskette   Like most other businesses, today's technology companies realize that packaging is often as important as the product itself. One result: the once-standard black plastic coating for flexible diskettes has been replaced by all the colors of the rainbow.

any track directly. The processor does not have to instruct the drive to start at the beginning of the disk and read each record sequentially. However, systems designers can create a sequential file and perform sequential storage and processing if they desire.

The Fabulous Flexible Diskette.   For the first decade of their existence, all magnetic disks were hard disks. In the early 1970s, however, as transistor chips became the dominant component of computer memories, engineers began seeking a way to preserve data even when the computer's power supply was turned off. (Recall from Chapter 3 that RAM chips are volatile, which means that their contents are lost when the electrical current ceases). Even the computer's operating system had to be reloaded if the computer was powered down for just a moment.

Early attempts to store the operating system permanently in the computer's memory met with no success. Researchers tested all known storage devices, including hard disks, magnetic tape, and even phonograph records, all to no avail.

Then the breakthrough came. One engineer on IBM's research team suggested using a very thin, flexible disk—a disk so thin that it would almost bend in half when held by one edge (hence the origin of the term "floppy disk"). Thinness was extremely important, for the researcher wanted to create a high-storage density on a 6-inch disk (the standard at the time was 14 inches) and to have the disk sit right next to the read/write head without causing damage to disk, data, or head.

The rest is history. Not only did the idea work, but it redefined the way of storing data on computers. Today, the flexible disks, which became known as diskettes, are very inexpensive (less than $1 each) and reusable. Data can be written to and erased from them quickly and easily. They are commonly found in 8-, 5¼-, 3½-, and 2-inch sizes, with the 3½- and 5¼-inch sizes (Figure 4.5) the most popular in business. In all likelihood, diskettes are here to stay.

Reality Check.   The key to the success of the flexible diskette *isn't the disk*. Rather, it's the holder.

The first disks produced by IBM's research team were so flimsy that they required a foam-padded stiffener an eighth of an inch (3.18 millimeters) thick—thicker than the disk itself. After the flexible disk (stiffener and all) began to prove itself, the next question became how to pack the disk. The team custom-designed a flexible plastic jacket to house the disk. Today's flexible disks spin inside their own plastic sleeves. The inside of these sleeves is lined with a special nonwoven fabric that protects the diskette from abrasion, wiping it clean with each revolution. A small rectangular opening allows the read/write heads to write data to or retrieve data from the disk's surface.

The disk and packaging together are what we know as the *flexible diskette*. The term "flexible," however, pertains to the disk inside. Figure 4.6 offers some additional information on the fabulous flexible diskette. ■

Other Magnetic Disk Storage Systems.   Several variations on the disks discussed above have emerged in recent years. Those in widespread use are disk cartridges, hardcards, disk caching, and RAM disks.

- **Disk cartridges** (Figure 4.7) offer most of the features of hard disks. Unlike Winchester disks, disk cartridges are removable. The cartridge—that is, the hard disk sealed in a protective package—is inserted into the disk drive for reading

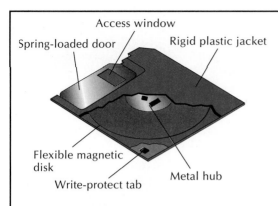
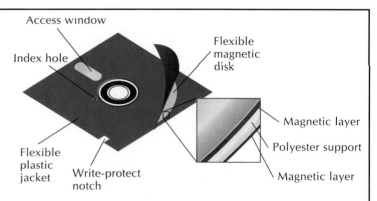

a) 3½-inch floppy disk. A rigid plastic jacket protects the flexible magnetic disk. A spring-loaded door (open in this illustration) covers the jacket's access window. The door remains closed until the floppy is inserted into a disk drive, thus protecting the disk from dust and fingerprints. A metal hub, bonded to the underside of the disk, has one hole that serves to center the disk and another that spins it. Sliding the write-protect tab to open a hole in the corner of the jacket protects the disk from unintentional writing or erasure.

b) 5¼-inch floppy disk. A protective jacket encloses a flexible magnetic disk that has a magnetic coating on both sides of a polyester support *(detail)*. Inside the jacket, liners clean the surface of the disk as it spins. An index hole through both the jacket and disk serves as a reference point for writing and reading data through the access window. A floppy can always be read, but covering the write-protect notch on one side of the jacket with tape prevents data from being written over or erased.

FIGURE 4.6   Inside the Flexible Diskette

and writing data. When one cartridge is full, you replace it with another. Cartridges are a good way of making backup copies of files and databases stored on hard disk.

- **Hardcards** (Figure 4.8) are magnetic disks attached to a circuit board that can be mounted in a microcomputer's expansion slot. The hardcard allows users to extend the life of older microcomputers by increasing their storage capacities.

    Hardcards offer the advantages of easy installation (you just slip the card into an expansion slot), affordability (several hundred dollars), and fast data retrieval. In addition, hardcards do not take up desktop space and do not use a drive slot. (This is beneficial because the drive slot may be needed to add a CD-ROM or magnetic tape drive to the computer.)

- The continuing decline in the price of DRAM (dynamic RAM) has made the use of **RAM disks** a viable alternative to magnetic storage devices. Recall from Chapter 3 that DRAMs are memory chips that offer instant direct access to the

FIGURE 4.7
The Bernoulli Disk Cartridge
Iomega's Bernoulli Box reads Bernoulli MultiDisk disk cartridges. These removable disks are frequently used to make backup copies of files and databases stored on hard disk.

FIGURE 4.8
The Quantum 240 Hardcard
Quantum's hardcard can be mounted in an older microcomputer's expansion slot to increase its storage capacity.

data stored on them. The equivalent of a hard disk can be created in primary memory using DRAM chips. The information stored on this RAM disk is rapidly retrievable. The RAM disk acts like any other disk. Information can be written to and retrieved from the disk as if it were a hard disk. When the power is turned off, however, the contents of this disk will be lost. Any information to be retained must therefore be written to a hard disk before the power goes off.

RAM disks are often used in industrial settings to store the production data used by manufacturing equipment.

- **Disk caching** allows the system to store information frequently read from a disk in RAM. This process speeds up retrieval time because it takes much less time to retrieve data from a disk cache than from a disk.

  Disk caching is used most often to manage large amounts of data. Disk caching also improves retrieval time when used to prepare large documents with desktop publishing software or to perform calculations with spreadsheet software.

There is a tradeoff between storage/retrieval speed and storage capacity. RAM disks offer more speed, but not as much capacity, as hard disks. Optical storage methods, which we discuss in the next section, offer large storage capacity but slower retrieval times.

Optical Storage

The disk technology that made vinyl LPs obsolete by bringing us compact discs (CDs) for recorded music is bringing a similar revolution to information technology. Although optical storage does not make magnetic disk storage obsolete, it does provide an important storage option where high-density data and information storage is needed. Optical storage has been a major element in the emergence of multimedia applications.

optical storage device A device that uses a beam of light produced by a laser to read and write data and information.

Optical storage devices use the principles of light, rather than magnetism, to store information. A beam of light produced by a laser beam is directed through a series of lenses until it is focused on the surface of a metal or plastic spinning disk. The disk's pattern of reflectivity corresponds to the data it carries and is an essential aspect of reading and writing data and information.

Optical disks use the same binary recording scheme that is used in all areas of information technology. During recording, a powerful laser beam makes a pit in the surface of the disk. The presence or absence of these laser pits corresponds to the ones and zeroes of binary code. During reading, a weaker laser beam scans the disk's surface, sensing the pattern of pits. The pattern is reflected back to a reader that interprets the data and sends them to the central processor. Figure 4.9 explains in more detail how data are read from an optical disk.

As in magnetic disks, information on optical disks is stored in circular tracks. However, because the laser beam can be positioned so accurately, the tracks of data on an optical disk can be packed very densely to give immense storage capacities. A floppy disk may have from 25 to 100 tracks per inch, a hard disk several hundred, and a prerecorded optical disk more than 15,000 tracks per inch. Yet any individual track can be identified and read easily.

The most commonly used types of optical storage are CD-ROM and videodisks. In recent years, several newer forms have also been developed.

CD-ROM.   The **CD-ROM** (compact disk–read only memory) **disk**, which we first discussed in Chapter 2 (see Figure 2.12c), was originally adapted from audio disk technology. CD-ROM offers several advantages to users. It is the least expensive way to store large amounts of data and information. CD-ROM disks are also durable and easily handled. Information can be stored on CD-ROM for many years. Because information cannot be erased from a CD-ROM disk, critical material is safe from being accidentally or intentionally destroyed. Finally, CD-ROM disks can hold motion, video, audio, and high-resolution image information—essential features for multimedia applications.

CD-ROM is not without its disadvantages, however. An individual cannot edit what is already written on the disk (a disadvantage if you want to make changes, but an advantage if you want to ensure that changes cannot be made). CD-ROM disks also retrieve data and information three to four times more slowly than magnetic disks.

CD-ROM disk Short for "compact disk–read only memory," an optical storage medium that permits storage of large amounts of data and information. CD-ROM disks cannot be erased.

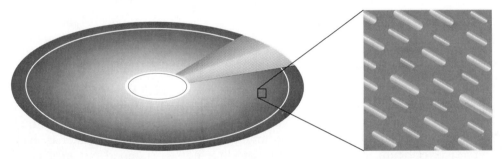

**FIGURE 4.9
Reading Data from an
Optical Disk**

Topography of a disk. The pits on a prerecorded optical disk (detail) resemble parallel lines of regularly spaced ridges. Each of these pits is about .6 micron (.6 millionth of a meter) wide. If 3,000 pits were lined up side by side, they would be about as wide as this letter o.

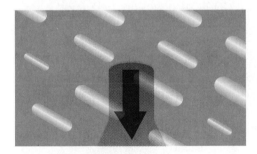

The land. When a focused laser beam hits a flat space between pits—a *land*—much of its light is reflected straight back toward the detector. At the point where the laser strikes the disk, it has been focused to a spot about a micron in diameter. This diameter is only a little larger than the wavelength of the laser light. As a result, the beam, which was originally cone-shaped, assumes a cylindrical shape near its point of focus.

The pit. When the focused laser beam strikes the pit, much of the light is scattered sideways, so that very little is reflected back to the detector. Each time the beam moves from a land to a pit, the reflected light changes in intensity, generating a signal that can be decoded to reproduce the data written on the disk.

FIGURE 4.10
CD-ROM Package
Compton's *Jazz* CD-ROM
package is a complete multi-
media history of jazz in
America.

CD-ROM storage is often used to store large volumes of reference information, such as dictionaries, encyclopedias, and financial reports (see the Quality and Productivity box titled "CD-ROM Publishing Puts Information at Your Fingertips" on page 144 and Figure 4.10). Interior designers and illustrators use CD-ROM storage extensively as a source of predrawn art and prepared photographs. They read drawings stored on CD-ROM into their computer's main memory and then embed them in the documents they are preparing. Similarly, engineers retrieve detailed blueprints from CD-ROM and copy them to main memory for their applications.

The use of CD-ROM is growing in all sectors of society. The Department of Defense, for example, created a program called Computer-aided Acquisition and Logistics Support (CALS) to eliminate paper from all aspects of the documentation needed to operate and maintain complex aircraft systems. Putting all its aircraft manuals on CD-ROM—one of the goals of CALS—will eliminate thousand-page manuals. They will also allow pilots in the cockpit of an aircraft to view the documentation onscreen.

Boeing Aircraft, the largest builder of aircraft in the world, has instituted a similar system to replace all documentation manuals for civilian and military aircraft with CD-ROM versions. CD-ROM offers major benefits to Boeing. When an aircraft is delivered, Boeing must also deliver thousands of pounds of paper documentation. Then it must keep this documentation updated as enhancements and changes are made to the aircraft. Replacing paper with CD-ROM will mean not only less paper but also faster access to information.

Reality Check.   Because the demand for CD-ROM storage and for the delivery of information on this storage medium is growing rapidly, the capability to mass produce CD-ROM disks with volumes of information is essential. Fortunately, CD-ROM disks can be duplicated in a factory by methods similar to those used to duplicate phonograph records. Once a master is made with a laser beam, it can be used to produce copies stamped out in a press. (Duplication of magnetic tapes and disks is not adaptable to mass production stamping. These must be copied individually by recording—a more time consuming and thus costlier process than mass production.) Mass production techniques are both a cause and a result of the fact that CD-ROM drives are becoming a standard component on many computer systems, particularly microcomputers. ■

videodisk A read-only optical storage medium that stores images and sound.

Videodisks.   Like CD-ROM disks, **videodisks** are an optical read-only storage medium. Videodisks (Figure 4.11a) store images and sound, which when sequenced together produce full-motion animated information. Because videodisk players can be attached to computers, they are often an important component of multimedia systems. Organizations use videodisks to deliver marketing information, product demonstrations, and training programs.

For example, just in time for the 500th anniversary of Columbus's discovery of the "new world," IBM introduced a comprehensive multimedia program. Delivered on videodisk, the program included 180 hours of interactive instruction. Developed by Hollywood filmmaker and graphic artist Bob Abel, *Columbus* (Figure 4.11b) includes a rich video collection of manuscripts, artworks, and interviews with 60 of the world's leading authorities on Columbus and his times. The series includes segments on Columbus—the man and his vision, the world in 1492, money and power, changing views of the world, changing views of

a) The use of videodisks in the classroom is increasing. Here, a grammar school teacher uses the *Windows in Science* videodisk package to teach her students about the solar system.

b) A screen from IBM's comprehensive 180-hour *Columbus* Ultimedia multimedia package. Each of the program's ten segments is delivered through a combination of CD-ROM disks and two-sided videodisks.

FIGURE 4.11
Videodisks and Multimedia
Like CD-ROM disks, videodisks are a read-only medium. Because videodisk players can be attached to computers, they are often an important component of multimedia systems.

humankind, and the Renaissance. Each segment is delivered through a combination of CD-ROM disks and two-sided videodisks. The series is designed to run on an IBM personal computer with a CD-ROM drive, videodisk player, and high resolution monitor.

IBM chose to use multimedia technology in *Columbus* (and for several of its other educational titles) because in the company's words, "To make learning fun, you have to make the student not just an observer of the discovery of America, but a participant, a discoverer him or herself."

Newer Optical Disk Formats.   CD-ROM disks and videodisks, which are read-only, were the first commercial applications of optical disk. However, two new types of optical disks that permit computer users to *record* data are emerging: WORM and EOS.

- **Write once, read many (WORM) optical disks** allow users to write information to a disk only once, but to read it many times. People can use WORM disks to store and retrieve archival information or historical data. Because WORM systems do not allow people to alter data once they have been entered, WORM is used where the security of data is essential (in financial and legal documents, for example).
- **Erasable optical storage (EOS) disks** combine the erasability and editing options of magnetic storage devices with the permanence, capacity, and reliability of optical storage. Erasable optical disks tend to be even more reliable than their magnetic counterparts (which themselves are highly reliable). Unlike magnetic disks, EOS disks are immune to the harmful effects of stray magnetic fields that can erase data and information stored on magnetic storage media. And because they rely on light beams instead of mechanical heads to read and write information, they are immune to head crashes.

If banks are required to have one thing besides accuracy, it's the ability to pass an audit. That means being able to show the details of transactions, when they occurred, and the sequence in which they occurred. The audit trail, as the series of documents describing a transaction is called, is a permanent record that serves as a legal document should the need ever arise. Countless banks have moved to the use of WORM optical disks to preserve their auditing activities. Transaction documents

QUALITY AND PRODUCTIVITY

CD-ROM Publishing Puts Information at Your Fingertips

IF YOU'VE EVER WASTED HOURS THUMBING THROUGH A BOOK IN search of an elusive fact or statistic, you're going to love CD-ROM publishing—the distribution of databases, catalogs, manuals, reference works, and even games on CD-ROM disks, which can be searched from beginning to end in minutes. Now that CD-ROM drives are becoming more affordable, this relatively new form of publishing is really taking off. There's already a catalog of *CD-ROMs in Print* (available either on paper or CD-ROM) and a top-ten best-seller list*, compiled by *Fortune* magazine:

1. *Monarch Notes* (Bureau Development)[1]—Study guides for 200 literary classics, combined with excerpts read by professional actors, period music, and high-resolution illustrations.
2. *Microsoft Bookshelf* (Microsoft)[2]—The full text of several highly integrated, fully searchable reference works (including the *Concise Columbia Encyclopedia*), complete with illustrations, animations, and audio; updated yearly.
3. *Mammals: A Multimedia Encyclopedia* (National Geographic Society and IBM)[1]—A complete mammal encyclopedia that combines animated sequences, full-color photos, and video with sound clips for every animal from the aardvark to the zebra; based on National Geographic's acclaimed two-volume work.
4. *Wild Places* (Aris Entertainment)[2]—One part of the "Media Clips" series, a combination of North American nature photography and 50 original New Age music compositions that can be used, royalty free, to dress up multimedia sales and training presentations.
5. *Great Literature* (Bureau Development)[1]—The full text of 1,896 literary classics combined with illustrations, narration, music, and a search-and-browse feature.
6. *The New Grolier Multimedia Encyclopedia* (Grolier Electronic Publishing)[2]—The complete text of the print version's 33,000 articles, supplemented with pictures, maps, sound, and video.

With National Geographic's *Mammals Multimedia Encyclopedia*, viewers can see full-color photos of animals in their habitats, hear their distinctive sounds, and watch brief educational videos.

7. *Reference Library* (The Software Toolworks)[1]—The full text of the seven works contained in the legendary *New York Library Desk Reference*, including *Webster's New World Thesaurus*.
8. *Sherlock Holmes, Consulting Detective* (Icom Simulations)[2]—Ninety minutes of video that let users test their powers of deductive reasoning.
9. *The Oxford English Dictionary, Second Edition* (Oxford University Press)[1]—The world's authoritative 21-volume dictionary offered on a single CD-ROM disk for one-third the price of the printed version.
10. *Street Atlas USA* (DeLorme Mapping)[1]—A map containing every street in the United States; valuable for planning business trips and vacations.

*From FORTUNE, ©1992 Time Inc. All rights reserved.
[1]IBM PC or compatible only.
[2]IBM PC or Apple Macintosh.

are imaged and recorded on WORM disks. Once recorded, this audit trail cannot be altered in any way. At the same time, though, all the details are readily accessible to the banks' personnel and can be retrieved easily through a computer network. WORM technology helps banks fulfill their legal obligations for audit trails, provide good customer service, and maintain records efficiently.

Advances in computer-driven optical recording technology are occurring rapidly. As costs drop and read/write times become speedier, we are certain to see widespread use of read/write optical disks in business.

Computer Interfaces.   To use external storage devices, such as magnetic disk and tape, a computer must have a data controller with its own memory and processor to regulate the flow of data to and from peripherals. This **input/output controller**, which is usually a board, reads data serially from the storage device and translates it into parallel format for input into the central processor or processor chip through the I/O bus. The board is mounted in a slot inside the main computer unit.

input/output controller A data controller with its own memory and processor that regulate the flow of data to and from peripheral devices.

CRITICAL CONNECTION 1
American Express: Optical Storage Creates Country Club Billing

If you've ever been overwhelmed by a flood of monthly bills, consider the three million charge slips that pour into American Express Co. for processing and storage *every day*. With this kind of volume, it's easy to understand why American Express has turned to an image-processing computer system that uses optical storage.

At AmEx, the "images" are digital images of charge slips, which are created when the originals are scanned into the system at regional operations centers in Phoenix and Ft. Lauderdale. The digital images—complete with cardholder signatures—are stored on 12-inch optical disks; the flimsy paper originals are shredded. When cardholders' bills are prepared, the images are sorted by account number and reduced facsimiles are printed eight to a page and enclosed with statements prepared via conventional data processing. The resulting service, called Enhanced Country Club Billing (ECCB), is unique in the industry and is very popular with AmEx's 5.1 million corporate cardholders who need help in documenting expense accounts.

The system also helps American Express. Paper handling is cut by a factor of ten (thus improving productivity and reducing the number of lost or mishandled charge slips) and the optical disks take less storage space than paper records. Moreover, the system shortens the billing cycle and minimizes disputes about charges, which means that AmEx gets paid sooner.

▮ Interaction with Computers: Input Devices

Secondary storage and peripheral devices interact with computers through interfaces and ports. People use input and output devices connected to the ports to interact with the computer. Recall that input is the data or information entered into a computer. Output is the result of inputting and processing returned by the computer, either directly to a person using the system or to secondary storage. **Input devices** are the means by which input is fed into the central processor. **Output devices** make the results of processing available outside of the computer.

The five most commonly used input devices are keyboards, terminals, scanners, digitizers, and voice and sound input devices. Multimedia audiovisual devices are likely to be used more frequently in the future.

input device A device by which input is fed into a computer's central processor.

output device A device that makes the results of processing available outside of the computer.

Keyboards

The most visible and common input device is the computer **keyboard** (see Figure 2.3). All keyboards are used to enter data and text information into a computer of some sort. But computer keyboards differ in four important ways:

keyboard The most common input device, usually consisting of letters of the alphabet, numbers, and frequently used symbols.

- **Characters**—Both alphabetic and symbolic keyboards are available, depending on the country in which the computer is used. In Japan, a symbolic keyboard containing the characters of the Kanji language is widely used. In other countries, an English language keyboard is the norm, with U.S. and international versions available.
- **Key arrangement**—The arrangement of the keyboard's keys may vary. The *QWERTY keyboard* (Figure 4.12) is the most common in English-speaking countries. This keyboard uses the conventional typewriter layout and is so named because the top row of alphabetic keys begins with the letters Q, W, E, R, T, and Y (reading from left to right). A newer design, called the *Dvorak keyboard*, uses an arrangement whereby the most used letters are placed in the most accessible places: The five English-language vowels (A, E, I, O, U) are the home keys of the left hand, while the five most often used consonants (D, H, N, S, T) are the home keys of the right hand. The next most frequently used letters are on the keys one row up, the next easiest position to reach.

    Many countries' languages contain special characters that are not used in English words—for example, à, á, â, ã, ä, å, æ, ç, ñ, ø, ¿, and ¡. Keyboards used in these countries contain the alphabets and characters of the language of the user.
- **Special purpose keys**—Certain keys are designed to assist the individual in entering data or information (for example, the numeric keypad found to the right of the alphabetic keyboard section on many keyboards, as in Figure 4.12) or to control processing (the Ctrl and Alt keys). The uses of these special **function keys** vary from program to program. For example, the F7 key is used in one software package to search a document for specified words or phrases, in another to turn text from bold to italics, and in another to print a report.

function key A key designed to assist the computer's user in entering data and information or to control processing.

- **Detachability**—Most desktop computers have keyboards that can be detached from the rest of the computer system. However, built-in keyboards, the norm for early microcomputers, are also popular and are the norm for notebook and laptop computers.

Choosing a keyboard is often a very personal matter. The right touch, the preferred placement of keys, and the presence or absence of a click when keys are depressed can all be important factors in one's feeling of comfort with a computer. Proper placement of the keyboard can also be an important factor in personal health, as the People box on pages 148–49 titled "What You Need to Know About Ergonomics" explains.

Terminals

A **terminal** is a combination keyboard and video display that accepts input, displays it on the video screen, and displays the output sent by the computer to which it is attached. There are three common types of terminals (Figure 4.13).

terminal A combination keyboard and video display that accepts input, displays it on the video screen, and displays the output sent by the computer to which it is attached.

- **Dumb terminals** do not contain processing capability. (That is, they do not have control units or arithmetic/logic units. If they do, they are called *intelligent terminals.*) Therefore, they can only accept input from the keyboard and display information from the remote computer to which they are attached. Dumb terminals send whatever is entered through the keyboard to the main computer and display whatever they receive from the main computer without doing any processing (not even simple arithmetic).

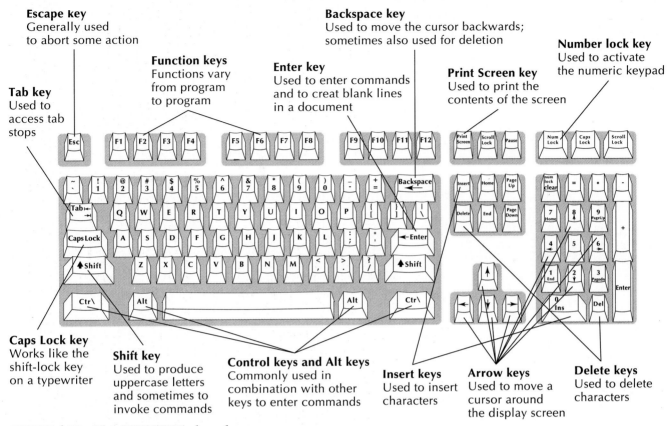

Escape key
Generally used
to abort some action

Tab key
Used to
access tab
stops

Function keys
Functions vary
from program
to program

Enter key
Used to enter commands
and to creat blank lines
in a document

Backspace key
Used to move the cursor backwards;
sometimes also used for deletion

Print Screen key
Used to print the
contents of the screen

Number lock key
Used to activate
the numeric keypad

Caps Lock key
Works like the
shift-lock key
on a typewriter

Shift key
Used to produce
uppercase letters
and sometimes to
invoke commands

Control keys and Alt keys
Commonly used in
combination with other
keys to enter commands

Insert keys
Used to insert
characters

Arrow keys
Used to move a
cursor around
the display screen

Delete keys
Used to delete
characters

FIGURE 4.12   The QWERTY Keyboard

- **Automated teller machines (ATMs)** are limited-function intelligent terminals that usually contain a small video display, a keyboard consisting of only a few keys, and perhaps a sound speaker. ATMs are most often associated with banks, where they are used to dispense cash, accept deposits, and transfer funds between accounts. But the use of ATMs is growing in many other areas as well. Airlines use them to dispense tickets, state motor vehicle offices to issue driver's licenses, and entertainment promoters to sell concert and theater tickets.

FIGURE 4.13   The Three Types of Terminals
The three most common types of terminals are dumb terminals, automatic teller machines, and point-of-sale terminals.

a) The PC attached to IBM's AS/400 is used as a dumb terminal. It only accepts input from the keyboard and displays information from the remote computer (not shown here) to which it is attached.

b) ATMs have revolutionized banking around the world and are now being used in the airline and entertainment industries also.

c) POS terminals are most frequently used in restaurants and in retail, department, and grocery stores.

PEOPLE

What You Need to Know About Ergonomics

Many computer-dependent workers have been disabled by carpal tunnel syndrome, extremely painful damage to nerves and tendons in their wrists. But you can protect yourself and the people you'll be managing if you take a lesson from *ergonomics*, the study of how human bodies interact with equipment in the workplace. Here are a few of the problems to watch for—and some solutions, should you encounter them.

THE PROBLEM	THE HIGH-TECH SOLUTION	THE LOW-TECH SOLUTION
Repetitive stress injuries (RSIs), painful nerve and tissue damage to the wrists and back caused by long hours at poorly designed computer workstations. Accounts for about half of all occupational illnesses; costs employers an estimated $7 billion in lost productivity and medical expenses.	Hire an ergonomics expert to recommend an ergonomically correct chair and computer desk with an adjustable keyboard insert. The chair should allow you to sit with your feet flat on the floor and provide good support for your lower back. The chair cushion should slope down in front, to avoid putting pressure on the backs of your legs. When the chair is properly adjusted, the keyboard should be raised or lowered so that you can type with your wrists and hands parallel to the floor.	Be sure you've adjusted your present chair for optimum support and comfort, using a footrest or cushion if necessary. If the keyboard is too low, prop it up on books; if too high, either adjust the chair height or shorten the table legs. Buy a foam rubber wrist rest and use it during frequent short breaks. Better yet, walk around the room every 30 minutes.
Concern that prolonged exposure to electromagnetic emissions from computer monitors can cause miscarriages, cancer, and other health problems. Research is ongoing.	If your monitor doesn't conform to the stringent Swedish MPR2 guidelines for electromagnetic emissions, buy one that does or switch to a laptop using an LCD (liquid crystal display) screen. As an interim measure, invest in an "anti-radiation" screen. It won't block magnetic emissions, but some brands claim to cut 99% of electric radiation and will reduce overhead glare.	Keep your screen at arm's length or greater, where emissions are only one-sixth to one-eighth the strength found at four inches from the screen. Avoid working closer than four feet to the back or sides of a monitor, where electromagnetic emissions are two times stronger than in front. Turn the monitor off when you aren't using the computer.

- **Point-of-sale (POS) terminals** are in widespread use in department, retail, and grocery stores. Designed to assist salespersons in conducting transactions, POS terminals often feature special keys (such as sale, void, and credit) and a numeric keypad similar to that found on a calculator. They are usually connected to a computer that processes data entered by an employee, perhaps accepting a product or stock number and providing a price in return. Frequently the data entered by employees into the system are also used to update product inventory information maintained on the computer to which the POS is connected.

Scanners

source data automation A method of data entry in which details enter computers directly from their written or printed forms without the intermediate step of keying.

Keying numeric and text data and information into a computer takes time and always includes the possibility of error. As anyone who has ever done any typing knows, it is very easy to strike the wrong key. To avoid errors, many companies use **source data automation**, a method of data entry in which data enter computers directly from their written or printed forms without the intermediate step of keying.

Use a reading lamp for close work, indirect light for general illumination.

2' or more

Top of screen should be no higher than eye level.

Arms should bend down from the shoulders and into angles at the elbow.

Monitor should allow tilt/swivel adjustment.

Chair back and height should be adjustable.

Feet should be flat on floor, with hips and knees bent at right angles.

23-28½" above floor

THE PROBLEM	THE HIGH-TECH SOLUTION	THE LOW-TECH SOLUTION
Eye strain and related vision problems caused by staring at the glare and flicker of a monitor for long periods; affects an estimated 10 million Americans.	If your monitor produces noticeable flicker, replace it or your graphics board with one that creates a more stable image. To help prevent vision-related problems, install an anti-radiation or glare screen, and avoid staring at it. Replace overhead fluorescent lighting with indirect and table-top task lighting using incandescent bulbs.	Minimize glare by positioning the monitor at a right angle to the window and wear an eyeshade to block too-bright overhead lights. To keep eyes from drying out and reduce neck strain, adjust monitor so that the top of the screen is even with your eyes and you're looking down slightly. Take frequent breaks.
"Sick building syndrome"—flu-like symptoms caused when ozone emissions from laser printers and photocopiers, as well as other indoor pollutants, accumulate in work areas.	Seek a consulting engineer to evaluate the ventilation system and make recommendations for configuring the work areas for better air flow. Buy an air purifier for your work area.	Don't work near printers and photocopiers, which also give off electromagnetic emissions. Keep lots of live plants around; they're great at soaking up indoor pollutants.

Scanning, which we first discussed in Chapter 1, transforms written or printed data or information into a digital form that is entered directly into the computer.

Scanners are in widespread use in many industries, including the pharmaceutical industry, where it is extremely important to maintain adequate supplies. Patients do not expect a druggist to be out of stock on a critical drug when they take their prescription to be filled. At the same time, druggists don't want to hold an excess supply. Excess inventories take up room, and have a brief shelf life.

To help druggists maintain the proper inventory balance, San Francisco-based McKesson Corp. has developed a scanner system. (See Critical Connection 3 in Chapter 2.) To place an order, the druggist passes a laser scanner over a shelf ticket in front of the item to be ordered. This single swipe of the scanner captures the product's name and the amount usually ordered. These data are captured in a handheld computer that is later connected to a telephone line to McKesson's order department.

When the orders arrive at McKesson, they are electronically transferred into the company's order processing system. Because none of these entries have to be keyed, mistakes are few. When McKesson's employees fill the orders, IT again plays a piv-

scanning The process of transforming written or printed data or information into a digital form that is entered directly into the computer.

FIGURE 4.14
Source Data Automation at McKesson
Order fillers at McKesson Corp. use AcuMax wrist computers to locate inventory and bill customers' accounts directly.

otal role. Strapped to the wrist of each employee is a combination portable computer, laser scanner, and two-way radio (Figure 4.14). Details of each order are transmitted by radio from the central computer to the wrist computer, telling the employee which items are needed and where they are located in the warehouse. When the order filler reaches the stock location, a quick point of the laser scanner at the shelf ticket confirms that the item is correct. When the worker pulls the stock, McKesson's inventory records are adjusted and the item pulled is added to the customer's bill.

Clearly, both parties benefit. The customer receives much faster service, often receiving stock within 24 to 48 hours. McKesson avoids the cost of errors (a mistake costs five to seven times that of a correctly filled order) and ensures accurate inventory and billing information—not to mention satisfied, repeat customers.

There are two types of scanning: optical character recognition and image scanning.

optical character recognition (OCR) A technology by which devices read information on paper and convert it into computer-processable form.

optical mark reader An OCR device that recognizes the presence and location of dark marks on a special form as the form is scanned.

Optical Character Recognition.   The term **optical character recognition (OCR)** refers to a wide variety of devices that can read information on paper and convert it into computer-processable form. Three types of OCR are widely used: optical mark readers, optical character readers, and optical code readers.

Optical mark readers recognize the presence and location of dark marks on a special form (Figure 4.15) as the form is scanned. Many standardized tests, such as the SAT, are based on this format. Students blacken designated spots on the mark-sense test form. The completed form is then read by an OCR scanner, which sends the student's responses to a processor that determines the number of right and wrong answers and computes the final score. Government and medical offices also use optical mark readers to take large surveys (for example, marketing research surveys and the U.S. Census). The efficiency and reliability of optical mark readers allow these organizations to capture a large volume of information in a consistent format.

Reality Check. You probably remember taking the SAT, the Graduate Record Examination (GRE), or a similar college entrance exam, sitting in a large room with perhaps hundreds of other sweating students. Beside your test booklet was the answer sheet on which you blackened the letter a, b, c, or d using a No. 2 pencil. This process may be obsolete a few years from now.

Students can now take certain standardized multiple-choice exams on a computer. The main advantage of this is convenience. (The tests are not any easier.) Instead of adhering to the normal Saturday test schedule, SAT takers can now call some test centers and make an appointment to take the test on any weekday they wish. And instead of waiting six to eight weeks to find out their results, test takers with enough courage can ask the computer to flash the score as soon as the exam is completed.

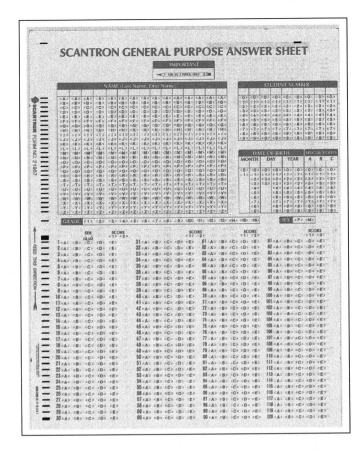

FIGURE 4.15
Sample Optical Mark Test Form
Many standardized tests use optical mark readers to determine score. The test taker blackens a designated spot on the test form, which is then read and graded by an OCR scanner.

Courtesy Scan-Tron Corporation

Optical character readers recognize printed information rather than just dark marks. Optical character readers are often used by retail stores to read the product number of store merchandise, by libraries to read the call number of a library book, and by mail-order companies to read merchandise order numbers (Figure 4.16 on page 152). Bank checks are processed by a special form of optical character reading called **magnetic ink character recognition**. The check, bank number, and customer account number—all of which are preprinted in magnetic ink on the check—are read optically or sensed magnetically (Figure 4.17 on page 152).

Optical code readers are most commonly used by supermarkets. When customers "check out" at the cash register, the items selected for purchase are passed over a piece of glass covering an optical scanner. In this process, the printed **universal product code (UPC)** is read from the package. The UPC is a bar code that identifies the product by a series of vertical lines of varying width representing a unique product number. This number is sent to a store computer, which contains pricing and inventory information. The price is used to ring up the transaction at the register. (Inventory information may also be updated as the price is verified.) Alternatively, the checkout cashier may pass a handheld scanner (a wand or gun) over the UPC code (see Figure 2.7b).

Catalina Marketing of Anaheim, California has turned the supermarket checkout counter and its scanner into an effective marketing tool. The company connects a personal computer to each checkout's scanner, capturing information on what the customer purchases as he or she is making the purchase. Using quick processing, the computer can issue a coupon to promote additional purchases. For example, suppose the buyer purchases cat litter. Knowing the customer probably has a cat, the computer prints out a coupon for a cat food the store or manufacturer wishes to promote. Or perhaps the product is Pepsi; the Coca Cola Company may have

optical character reader An OCR device that recognizes printed information rather than just dark marks.

magnetic ink character recognition A form of optical character reading in which preprinted information written in magnetic ink is read optically or sensed magnetically.

optical code reader An OCR device used to read bar codes.

universal product code (UPC) A bar code that identifies a product by a series of vertical lines of varying widths representing a unique product number.

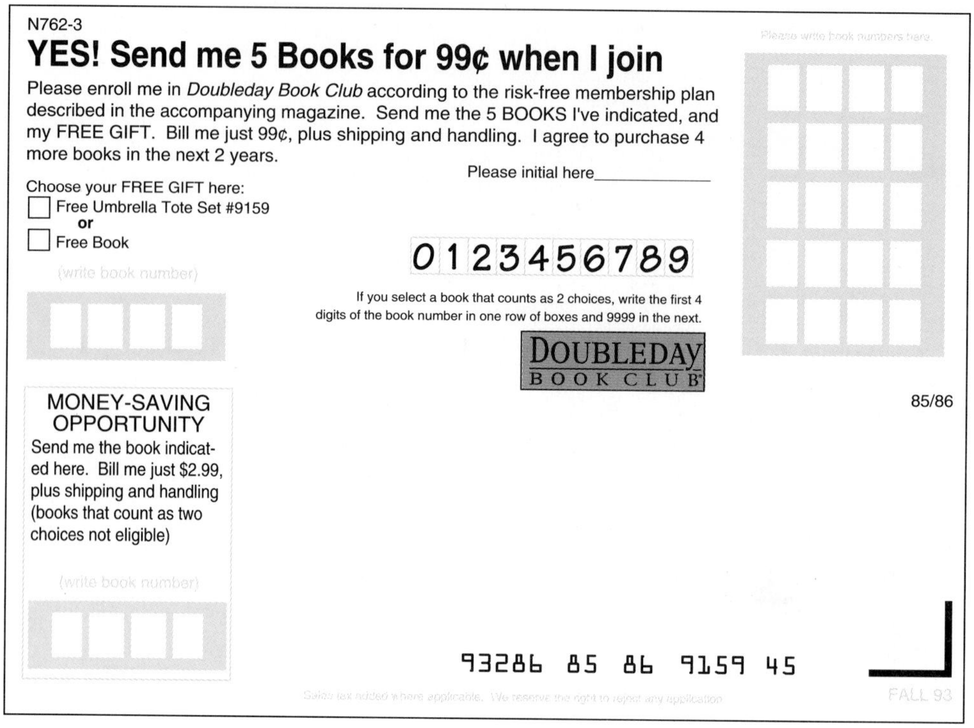
N762-3

YES! Send me 5 Books for 99¢ when I join

Please enroll me in *Doubleday Book Club* according to the risk-free membership plan described in the accompanying magazine. Send me the 5 BOOKS I've indicated, and my FREE GIFT. Bill me just 99¢, plus shipping and handling. I agree to purchase 4 more books in the next 2 years.

Please initial here____________

Choose your FREE GIFT here:

☐ Free Umbrella Tote Set #9159

or

☐ Free Book

(write book number)

0123456789

If you select a book that counts as 2 choices, write the first 4 digits of the book number in one row of boxes and 9999 in the next.

DOUBLEDAY BOOK CLUB

Please write book numbers here.

85/86

MONEY-SAVING OPPORTUNITY

Send me the book indicated here. Bill me just $2.99, plus shipping and handling (books that count as two choices not eligible)

(write book number)

93286 85 86 9159 45

Sales tax added where applicable. We reserve the right to reject any application.

FALL 93

FIGURE 4.16
Optical Character Reading
The Doubleday Book Club, headquartered in Garden City, NY, uses optical character reading on its new member enrollment forms. Members then order books on a different form that is also read with OCR technology.

Reprinted with the permission of Doubleday Book & Music Clubs, Inc.

arranged for Catalina's backroom computer to print a two-for-one coupon for six-packs of Coke. Alternatively, Pepsi may have arranged for a "half-off" coupon for Frito-Lay potato chips to be printed out with a purchase of Pepsi (Frito-Lay is owned by Pepsi).

image scanning The scanning process that translates images into a digital form.

flatbed scanner A large image scanner that works like office photocopiers.

Image Scanning. To scan drawings, entire documents, or photographic images, **image scanning** must be used. The scanner examines the images and translates lines, dots, and marks into a digital form.

Flatbed scanners (see Figure 2.6a) work like office photocopiers. The flatbed scanner is attached to an input/output port on the computer by a cable. The per-

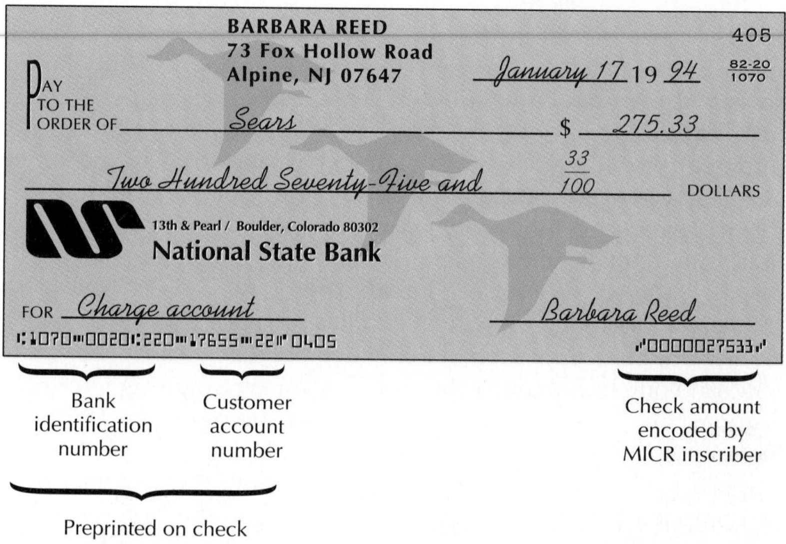

FIGURE 4.17
Magnetic Ink Character Recognition
Magnetic ink characters are located on the bottom line of a check. On the left side are the bank identification number and the customer's account number. On the right side is the check amount, which is imprinted on the check after it has been cashed.

son doing the scanning places the photograph, drawing, or page of text face down on a glass plate on top of the scanner. A bar of light, controlled by software, passes beneath the glass. Light is reflected off the printed image onto a grid of photosensitive cells. The number of light sensors in the scanner determines the quality of the scanner's optical **resolution**—that is, the clarity or sharpness of the image. A scanner with a resolution of 300 dots per inch (DPI), for example, contains 300 sensors in each inch of the scanning mechanism. The more dots per inch, the higher the resolution. The flatbed scanners used with most personal computers range from 300 to 600 DPI. Scanners used by commercial printers range up to 2400 DPI and provide much higher resolution.

> **resolution** The clarity or sharpness of an image.

As the light bar moves down the page, the image data are collected dot by dot. Depending on the type of scanner, the data may be sensed as shades of gray or in 256 or more colors. When the image is transmitted from the scanner to the central processor, gray-scale or color information is included so that the image can be properly recreated for processing, display, or storage.

Flatbed scanners typically cost $1,000 or more. **Handheld scanners** (see Figure 2.6b) offer an inexpensive alternative. Although they are not as powerful or as easy to use as flatbeds, handhelds often sell for less than one-third the price of flatbeds. Like flatbeds, handhelds are attached by a cable to an input/output port on the computer. To be scanned, the original document, drawing, or photograph must first be placed on a flat surface. As the scanner is dragged slowly from one end of the document to the other, the details under the scanner are translated into dot patterns that can be processed by the computer. Handheld scanners are usually only several inches wide and thus cannot scan the entire width of a page as flatbed scanners do.

> **handheld scanner** An inexpensive, handheld alternative to the flatbed image scanner.

The benefits of image scanning are well known to Consolidated Freightways, a nationwide freight carrier. Until recently, it took the company as long as three weeks to respond to a customer's inquiry about an invoice, a damage claim, or a complaint. All this time was needed to locate and assemble the documents required to answer the inquiry. Then, in the early 1990s, the company invested $10 million in an imaging system. All documents and correspondence related to a shipment are now scanned and stored in the company's computer system. Up to three years' of shipping and billing documents—nearly 60 million pieces of paper—are accessible through the centralized system. Now, when a customer makes an inquiry, whether in writing or over the telephone, a customer service rep can locate copies of all pertinent documents in approximately ten minutes.

Digitizers

A **digitizer** is an input device that translates measured distances into digital values that the computer can process. As the digitizing device moves, electric pulses inform the computer of the change in position. The computer responds by shifting an indicator, such as an arrow (⇨) or cross-hair cursor (◆), to the same position as the digitizer. There are five types of digitizers, all of which must be connected to the computer by a communications cable.

> **digitizer** An input device that translates measured distances into digital values that the computer can process.

- The **mouse** (see Figure 2.5) is a familiar input device found with many desktop computers. As the ball on the underside of the mouse moves, the horizontal and vertical coordinates of the corresponding mouse cursor change. By checking the coordinates, the computer knows where the cursor is and displays the indicator in the appropriate place on the display screen.
- The **light pen** (Figure 4.18) looks like a ballpoint pen, except that the light pen's ball is actually a light-sensitive cell. When the tip of the light pen touches

FIGURE 4.18
MicroTouch Light Pen
The MicroTouch light pen works in concert with shipping/billing software and a touch screen developed by Microsoft. After the requisitioner has signed his name with the light pen, he simply touches the "Send" button on the screen to send the order to company headquarters.

a computer's display screen, the computer senses the pen's location on the screen and transmits this information to the processor. Movement by the light pen in any direction is sensed by the processor, which determines the meaning of the movement according to the application program in use. Light pens are used both to draw images and to select options from a menu of choices displayed on the screen.

- Often used to control computer games or simulations, a **joystick** (Figure 4.19) extends vertically from a control box. As the joystick is moved up, down, right, left, or diagonally, it sends a signal to the computer's processor, which senses the distance and direction of the movement. These are incorporated as input data into the program, which then determines action status and steps to take. A visual display of the movement appears on the computer screen.

   Want to fly a jet fighter without hours and hours of training time? Then you may want to get the Falcon 3.0 or the Microsoft Flight Simulator. Each of these computer games provides the operator with a realistic simulation of the inside of a fighter cockpit, complete with moving dials and gauges. Grab the joystick, pull back on it and you will find yourself climbing, gaining altitude quickly. Look to the right or left on the screen and you see the terrain, with trees, buildings, and other objects getting smaller and smaller as you climb higher. Push the joystick to the right and you begin a turn. Push it too far to the right, and you'll be flying upside down.

- A **trackball** (Figure 4.20) is a ball mounted on rollers. As the user rotates the ball in any direction, the computer senses the movement, in much the same way that it does with a joystick. Roll the ball to the left and the cursor moves to the left. Roll the ball to the right and the cursor moves with it.

- Images on paper can be translated to an electronic form by tracing the image using a **digitizing tablet** (Figure 4.21). As a pen-like stylus or cross-hair pointer is passed over the features of the drawing, the computer senses the dots and lines that comprise the drawing and creates an electronic version in memory while displaying the information visually on the screen. Once the drawing is complete, the digitized form can be stored or modified.

Mice, joysticks, and trackballs all recognize movement and position. Light pens and digitizing tablets recognize the presence or absence of information as they move. Digitizing devices are in widespread use on all sizes of computers.

FIGURE 4.19
Logitech Joystick
Although joysticks are often associated with computer games, they are also used in training programs for pilots and astronauts.

FIGURE 4.20
Logitech Trackball
The trackball is gaining in popularity as an input device. Some notebook and laptop computers are now incorporating trackballs directly into their keyboards.

Voice and Sound Input Devices

More and more people are seeking ways to capture the spoken word in digital form. **Voice input devices** provide this capability. A microphone can be attached either to a voice expansion board that fits within an internal slot in the computer or to a special microphone jack on the computer (see Figure 2.8). Special software controls the process of capturing and digitizing the sounds (including human voices) sensed by the microphone. Figure 4.22 explains how this process works.

The United States Transportation Command may use voice input devices to change the way it handles the movement of its aircraft around the world. When the organization's aircraft dispatchers are notified of bad weather or an aircraft running low on fuel, they must divert the plane to an airport that is closest to its current location. But with so many different airports, each with different capabilities for handling large and small aircraft, it is sometimes impossible for the dispatchers to recall instantly all of the information they need to direct the pilot.

For this reason, the organization is considering the creation of a voice input system to assist dispatchers. When the fog rolls in, making it impossible for an incoming aircraft to land at its intended destination in Frankfurt, the dispatcher can speak into a microphone built into the control tower computer: "Give me a list of all airports within one hour of Frankfurt, Germany." Instantly a list appears on the screen. The dispatcher can query the computer by voice again: "Which airport is closest and not closed because of weather?"

voice input device An input device that can be attached to a computer to capture the spoken word in digital form.

FIGURE 4.21
A Digitizing Tablet in Action
Digitizing tablets are often used in combination with graphic design programs. Here, a clothing designer creates a sweater design. Once the original design is created, it can be saved and modified later.

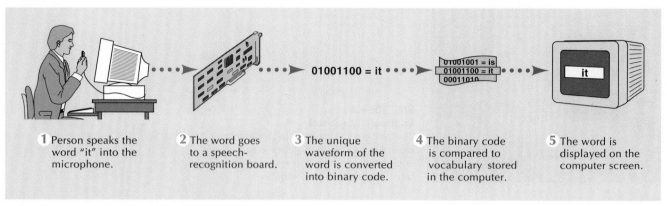

1. Person speaks the word "it" into the microphone.
2. The word goes to a speech-recognition board.
3. The unique waveform of the word is converted into binary code.
4. The binary code is compared to vocabulary stored in the computer.
5. The word is displayed on the computer screen.

FIGURE 4.22   Capturing and Digitizing Sounds

Reality Check. Until recently, research in voice, sound, and speech input advanced slowly because of technological limitations. Most people have a vocabulary of approximately 20,000 words, but the earliest voice input boards could recognize only a limited number of words, usually fewer than 100. Part of the problem was the huge amount of storage needed to store the vocabulary and the time needed to search the list of words.

The massive leaps in storage technology (both for primary memory and for secondary storage) coupled with ever more powerful (that is, faster) processors are changing this situation. Boards that have a vocabulary capacity of over 1,000 words have begun appearing for use on microcomputers. Voice units for newer systems have vocabularies that exceed 10,000 words. It is safe to assume that voice input will soon be a reality, and that the technical barrier will eventually disappear.

But how and where should voice input be used? Certainly there are many situations where voice commands can be helpful. For example, it will undoubtedly be useful for workers in heavy manufacturing to have their hands free to do their work. However, there is little experience to guide us in this area. Will people want to give dictation to their computer and have the system transform it into a polished document (with correct spelling and good grammar)? Will people want their automobiles to have voice-controlled guidance systems, with the dashboard and stick shift levers as we know them becoming mere ornaments? And what about video arcade games? Will voice control create a new dimension of entertainment?

It is not too early for you to start thinking about these matters. Experienced experts have yet to emerge in this area; perhaps you can be one of the first. ■

Multimedia Audiovisual Devices

As microprocessor chips become more sophisticated and memory capacity continues to expand, it is likely that the line between computer input devices and devices currently used only for entertainment will blur. In fact, three common multimedia consumer electronic products are already used as sources of input and output for computer processing (Figure 4.23a).

- **Television**—Partitions (or "windows") of computer display screens can show several television programs simultaneously (Figure 4.23b). Whether the latest news, business reports, or even closed-circuit programs, these programs can be shown, captured, and stored for later viewing. The Global IT box, "Multimedia Lends a Helping Hand to Immigrant Workers," explores the benefits of a very successful multimedia system that uses television.

- **VCRs**—Whatever can be seen and captured on video can also be entered into a computer. An image from a videotape can be transferred into the memory of a computer through a video interface port. The digital form can then be displayed, processed, and stored like any other data.
- **Video cameras**—Both handheld and larger video cameras can be connected to a computer port directly. Individual scenes can be input for display, processing, and storage.

More consumer-oriented input devices will surely follow, as we discuss in Chapter 14.

Texaco uses several multimedia devices in its everyday operations. A good part of the company's profitability depends on getting information needed to determine when to buy and sell crude oil on the world market. Missing a breaking news item by just a few minutes can amount to millions of dollars in lost opportunities. The company's trading room is equipped with high-speed computers that brokers use to create contracts electronically via a worldwide network. In one corner of the display screen is a window showing the live broadcast of Cable News Network (CNN), in color, with full sound—the same broadcast available on an ordinary color television. Such use of IT and multimedia capability not only enables traders to have up-to-date news, but also gives them an advantage over their competitors who rely on delayed news broadcasts.

Audio Response Units

The spoken word is increasingly being sought as a form of output. An **audio response unit**, also called a **speech synthesizer**, transforms data or information into sound. Upon receiving instructions from the central processor, the audio response unit retrieves the prerecorded voice messages and sounds stored in the *voice unit*, wherein they are assembled and sent to a speaker.

audio response unit, speech synthesizer An output device that transforms data or information into sound.

a) The three most common consumer products used as sources of input and output for computer processing are television, VCRs, and video cameras.

b) "Windows" of TV screens can show several programs simultaneously. This feature can be adapted to multimedia uses.

FIGURE 4.23
Multimedia Audiovisual Devices
The line between computer input devices and devices used for entertainment only is blurring.

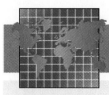

GLOBAL IT

Multimedia Lends a Helping Hand to Immigrant Workers

IN THE RUSH TOWARD THE GLOBAL ECONOMY, U.S. RESIDENTS sometimes forget the valuable contributions made by recent immigrants, especially the migrant workers who labor in the fields and orchards of the United States. Many know little or no English, and many have trouble communicating with the government workers responsible for deciding whether they qualify for government assistance, such as food stamps and Medicare.

The situation is looking a little brighter in Tulare County, California, though. That's because the county has created a multimedia system called "The Tulare Touch" that lets the workers prequalify themselves for aid.

The system is extremely easy to use. Each multimedia station, shown in the photo above, presents a video of a host or hostess who uses one of six languages—English, Spanish, and four Southeast Asian languages—to introduce the system, ask questions, and explain how to answer by pressing a blinking word or animated graphic on the touch screen (no keyboard). The combination of visual and audio cues, stored on a laser disk, allows even illiterate workers to use the system. At the end of the interview, the system prints out a completed application form, which is then reviewed and approved by an eligibility worker.

People particularly like the system's hosts and hostesses. The Latina hostess, for example, is a popular television personality. The eligibility workers like the system too, because it lets them spend more time with applicants and less time with paperwork. And the county likes the system most of all; the $3 million system is expected to save the county $20 million a

The ground-breaking Tulare Touch system offers multimedia instruction in six languages. A combination of audio and visual cues, stored on a laser disk, allows even illiterate workers to use the system.

year and reduce overpayments. Small wonder that government officials from around the country are making the trek to Tulare County to study the Tulare Touch.

Sources: Based on "The Emerging World of Multimedia," *I/S Analyzer,* March 1991, pp. 1–12; and John W. Verity, et al., "Multimedia Computing: PCs That Do Everything but Walk the Dog," *Business Week,* August 12, 1991, pp. 62–63.

Audio response units are in widespread use. Many supermarkets have audio response units attached to their bar code scanners. As products are scanned, the response unit says the name of the product and its price aloud. Because they hear the price charged for an item, customers are assured that they are not overcharged. The directory assistance service of public telephone companies and stock quotation services regularly use audio response units to give callers phone numbers, stock prices, and trading volumes. Both firm and individual benefit from speedier service and ultimately a savings in the costs of providing the service. And many newer airports around the world are using audio response systems to assist passengers. When you move between the concourses connecting the approximately 200 gates at Atlanta's Hartsfield International Airport, you do so by an easily accessible, complimentary shuttle train. A computer-controlled response unit announces the arrival of the vehicle at the gate and gives the traveler instructions on how to proceed. (It also controls the display of the same information in six different languages.)

Interaction with Computers: Output and Information Distribution Devices

Four types of devices are used to display and distribute computer output: monitors, printers, plotters, and film recorders.

Visual Displays (Monitors)

A computer's visual display is probably its most visible component. These visual displays, usually called **video display terminals (VDTs)** or **monitors**, differ in size, color, resolution, bit mapping, and graphic standard.

- **Size**—Monitors come in many different sizes, from the small screen built into palmtops and laptops to extra-large monitors used for special purposes. The standard monitor for personal computers is 13 to 16 inches (32 to 40 cm), measured diagonally, corner to corner. Large screen monitors have been developed for use by engineers and illustrators, who need to examine fine details closely. Large monitors are commonly 16 and 17 inches (40 and 42 cm) wide and provide 45% to 60% more viewing area than standard monitors do.
- **Color**—Many monitors display color, combining shades of red, green, and blue (Figure 4.24). These **RGB displays** can create 256 colors and several thousand variations on them by blending shades of red, green, and blue (hence the term "RGB display"). **Monochrome displays** show information using a single foreground color on a contrasting background color (for example, white on black, black on white, amber on black, or green on black).
- **Resolution**—As we mentioned earlier, all characters and images are made up of dot patterns. The number of dots, or **pixels**, per inch determines resolution, or sharpness of the image. A higher number of pixels means a sharper image. Common resolutions are:

      640 columns x 480 rows of dots (640 x 480 = 307,200 pixels on the screen)
      800 columns x 600 rows (480,000 pixels)
      1,024 columns x 768 rows (786,432 pixels).
- **Bit mapping**—A monitor may or may not have bit mapping capabilities. With **bit mapping**, each dot on the monitor can be controlled individually. Graphics created through bit mapping are sharp and crisp, without unseemly jagged edges. Prior to the evolution of bit mapping, **character addressing** was the norm. This meant that only letters, numbers, and other preformed letters and symbols—no lines or curved images—could be sent to and displayed on the display screen.

video display terminal (VDT), monitor A computer's visual display.

RGB display A video screen display with the ability to create 256 colors and several thousand variations on them by blending shades of red, green, and blue.

monochrome display A video screen display that shows information using a single foreground color on a contrasting background color (for example, black on white).

pixels The dots used to create an image. The higher the number of dots, the better the resolution of the image.

bit mapping A feature of some monitors that allows each dot on the monitor to be addressed or controlled individually. Graphics created through bit mapping are sharp and crisp.

character addressing The precursor to bit mapping that allowed only full characters to be sent to and displayed on a VDT.

a) The Macintosh Quadra 800.

b) The IBM PS/ValuePoint multimedia PC.

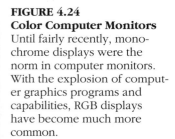

FIGURE 4.24
Color Computer Monitors
Until fairly recently, monochrome displays were the norm in computer monitors. With the explosion of computer graphics programs and capabilities, RGB displays have become much more common.

graphics adapter card An interface board between a computer and monitor used to determine the monitor's resolution and use of color.

multisync/multiscan monitors Monitors designed to work with a variety of graphics standards.

• **Graphics standard**—Related to resolution, *graphics standards* combine resolution and use of color. A computer monitor is used with a **graphics adapter card**, an interface board between computer and monitor that performs according to one of several widely used IBM-compatible standards: *color graphics adapter* (CGA—the oldest and lowest-resolution standard); *enhanced graphics adapter* (EGA); *video graphics array* (VGA); and *super VGA* (SVGA), which has the best resolution of all. Similar standards exist for Macintosh and other computers.

Multisync/multiscan monitors are designed to work with a wide variety of graphics standards, automatically adjusting to provide the best possible resolution for the adapter card and computer configuration in use.

Resolution, color clarity, and graphics capabilities are improving continually, making more sophisticated applications possible. This entire book was designed and laid out using a color monitor. Color and graphic displays on high resolution monitors are changing the business of publishing just as they are influencing the business of commerce and government.

CRITICAL CONNECTION 2
IT: A New Ally in the War Against Disease

Squibb

Scientists who battle cancer, heart disease, AIDS, and other life-threatening diseases have a powerful new ally in the form of computer systems with large, high-resolution color monitors that let them see their opponents "up close and personal."

This use of computers to fight disease is part of a new research technique called rational drug design. Instead of screening thousands of chemicals in the hope of finding one that might work, rational drug designers work backwards. Using what they know about the way the body's immune system "locks" onto invaders, they search for chemicals that mimic or amplify the immune reaction. To do this, they create 3-D computer models of molecules that can be displayed and manipulated on a computer screen. If a potential cure is found, the computer can perform a preliminary evaluation in just minutes, instead of months or years.

The trend to rational drug design was touched off in the late 1970s, when Squibb (a large international pharmaceutical manufacturer) employed the process to create a drug used to treat high blood pressure. Since then, dozens of start-up companies devoted to rational drug design have sprung up. Agouron Pharmaceuticals, for example, now has an anticancer drug in testing. Within a decade, some experts predict, all drug companies will use these tools.

hard copy The paper output from a printer.

impact printing A printing process in which the paper and the character being printed come in contact with one another.

nonimpact printing A printing process in which the paper and the print device do not come in contact with one another.

Printers

Generally speaking, a printer is an output device that produces **hard copy**—that is, paper output. There are two general categories of printers: impact printers and nonimpact printers.

In **impact printing**, the paper and the character being printed come in contact with one another. In **nonimpact printing**, there is no physical contact between the paper and the print device. The characters are produced on the paper through a heat, chemical, or spraying process (Figure 4.25, page 162).

Impact Printers.   Impact printers have existed for many years and have historically been very common in large and small computer configurations. Although they are being supplanted by nonimpact printers, they remain in widespread use. Three important types of impact printers are dot matrix, line, and character printers (Figure 4.26, page 163).

- In **dot matrix printing**, the characters and images are formed by wire rods pushed against a ribbon and paper. A careful examination of the characters shows that each is actually a collection of small dots. Dot matrix printers have been used on systems of all sizes because of their speed, low cost, and simplicity.
- **Character printers** print one character at a time. In contrast to dot matrix and line printers, whose speed is rated at lines per minute, character printers are evaluated at the number of characters they print per second. (The slowest print approximately 30 characters per second, the fastest approximately 200.) Because the characters on a character printer are preformed on the ends of hammers or the petals of a wheel, character printers are not good for printing images. However, they have been widely used in the preparation of manuscripts and correspondence.
- High-speed **line printers** have enjoyed widespread usage on large computers. These units print a full line (up to 144 characters) *at one time* on continuous form paper that can be up to 14 inches wide. Due to their high speed, which ranges up to several thousand lines per minute, they have been used in computer centers that routinely print large volumes of documents or very long reports. Because they are character oriented, they are not suitable for printing images.

Nonimpact Printers.   Laser, ink jet, and thermal printing are the most frequently used kinds of nonimpact printers (see Figure 4.27 on page 164).

- Because of their speed and the capabilities they provide, **laser printers** constitute the fastest growing segment of the printer market. As the laser printer receives information from the central processor, it converts the information into a laser beam (a narrow beam of light) that in turn encodes a photo conductor with the information. This process forms the character or the image to be printed. A *toner,* a black granular dust similar to that used in many photocopiers, is used in the process. The photo conductor attracts toner particles which, when transferred to the paper, produce the full image. Finally, the image is fused to the paper by heat and pressure. The laser printer prints an entire page at a time.

  The process is fast (from four to eight pages per minute on the slowest laser printers) and allows for the printing of both images and text. Black and white laser printers are in widespread use. Color versions are advancing through development and beginning to enter the world market.
- **Ink jet printers** spray tiny streams of ink from holes in the print mechanism onto the paper. The spray makes up a dot pattern that represents the character or image to be printed. Because ink jet printers create characters and images by spraying ink rather than by striking preformed characters against paper, they are often used to create charts and graphs. The application software controls the information to be printed and a controller within the printer oversees the actual printing process.

IMPACT/DOT MATRIX PRINTING

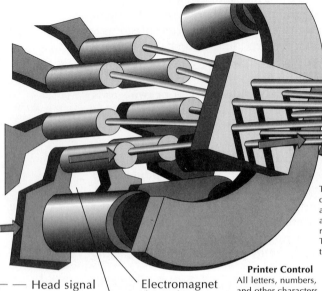

Pin Patterns
The pins strike an inked ribbon that marks the paper with dots. The head signals fire the pins in different combinations so that each character is made up of several vertical dot patterns.

Ribbon

Pins

Paper

Dot Matrix Head
The printer head of a dot matrix printer contains a column of pins. The pins are driven by electromagnets responding to the head signals. These are binary signals that turn the electromagnets on or off.

Quality Printing
Seven pins are shown here for simplicity; good quality printers have 24 pins. To improve quality, the head may pass over the paper again and print dots that overlap with those printed on the first pass.

Head signal

Electromagnet drives hammer

Hammer strikes pin

Printer Control
All letters, numbers, and other characters have standard codes that the computer sends to the printer. A chip in the printer converts these codes into signals that drive the printer head as it moves across the paper and prints the characters. The power drive board amplifies the chip signals. Special motors move the head and paper to the right positions.

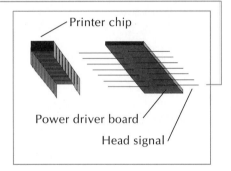

Printer chip

Power driver board

Head signal

FIGURE 4.25
Printing Processes
Source: Redrawn from David Macaulay, *The Way Things Work,* pp. 348–49. Compilation copyright ©1988 by Dorling Kindersley Ltd., London. Illustrations copyright ©1988 by David Macaulay. Reprinted by permission of Houghton Mifflin Company. All rights reserved.

NONIMPACT/LASER PRINTING

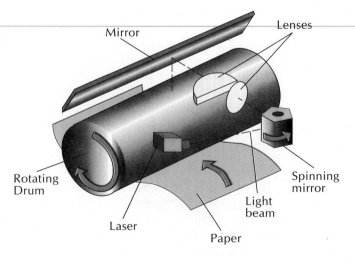

Mirror

Lenses

Rotating Drum

Laser

Light beam

Spinning mirror

Paper

Like a dot-matrix printer, a laser printer builds characters up with dots, but the dots are so small that the printing is very detailed. A laser fires a beam of light at a spinning mirror. Another mirror and lenses then focus the moving beam onto a drum like that in a photocopier. Signals from the computer turn the beam on and off as it scans across the drum, building up an electrical image. The image is transferred onto the paper as in a photocopier.

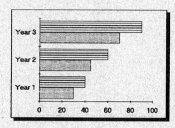

Versatile letter quality printing that's super fast, sharp and quiet

Letter Quality Printing
Sharpest Ultra Letter Quality printing available at 360 dpi with optional film ribbon

Simple, Quiet Operation
A whisper quiet 46.5 dB(A) that's perfect for home or office

Fastest Print Speeds
337 characters per second in Draft and 112 cps in Letter Quality (rated at 15 cpi)

Wide Variety of Fonts
14 easily selectable typefaces, including four scalable from 8 to 32 point sizes

a) Epson LQ-1070+ dot matrix printer and sample printout.

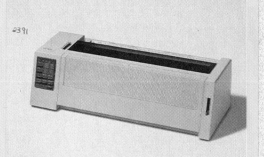

IBM 2391 Printer

IBM 2391 Model Provides Affordable High Speed Impact Printing

The IBM 2391 was designed to be your personal workstation printer; providing sophisticated printing functions yet requiring very limited printer knowledge.

The remarkably affordable IBM 2391 is a great value because it has the features you want--excellent reliable paper handling, superior print quality, an easy-to-use operator panel, multiple fonts and pitches, standard 32K buffer, speeds up to 216 CPS, and all-points-addressable graphics.

The easy-to-use operator panel allows you to conveniently select paper park, as well as other commonly used printer functions. The multiple resident fonts and pitches can be selected with ease. A font/pitch lock selection is available to users desiring additional control of font and pitch.

b) Lexmark 2391 Plus character printer and sample printout.

c) Dataproducts FP 2000 line printer and sample printout.

FIGURE 4.26   Impact Printers and Sample Printouts
In impact printing, the paper and the character being printed come in contact with each other. Although nonimpact printers are becoming the standard, many businesses still use impact printers. The three most common types are dot matrix printers, character printers, and line printers.

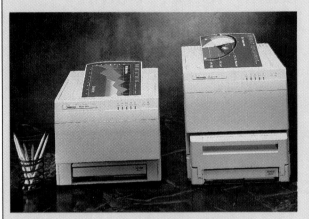
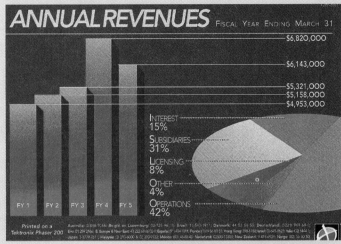

a) Tektronix Phaser 200e and 200i laser printers and sample printout.

b) Hewlett Packard 1200C ink jet printer and sample printout.

c) Elton International's TLP-2044 thermal printer and sample printout.

FIGURE 4.27 Nonimpact Printers and Sample Printouts In nonimpact printing, there is no contact between the paper and the print device. The most frequently used nonimpact printers are laser printers, ink jet printers, and thermal printers.

Frito-Lay driver Bobby R. Wright, who has a route in Texas, checks information on the computer in his delivery truck. The specially-designed printout is geared toward spotting problems and targeting potential sales—two important business activities in an industry where success is determined "bag by bag."

Questions for Discussion

1. Identify the key input and output devices used in Frito-Lay's information system.

2. What steps did the IT professionals at Frito-Lay take to create a system that would be easy to use? If you were a Frito-Lay manager in charge of training, what strategy would you use in introducing employees to the information system?

3. Like many corporations, Frito-Lay wants to create an entrepreneurial atmosphere that allows employees to take charge and react swiftly to changing market conditions. How will Frito-Lay's information system help it achieve this goal?

Gearing Up for Virtual Reality

FOR MOST OF ITS HISTORY, COMPUTING HAS BEEN TIED TO WORDS, numbers, and two-dimensional graphics—data and information we take in with just our eyes. Now virtual reality (VR) promises to let us go beyond sight, to use sound and touch as we interact with three-dimensional computer-generated environments. Long a staple of science fiction, virtual reality is fast moving out of the lab into the world of business, science, medicine, and entertainment. In fact, some predict that VR will become the "ultimate computer interface," a natural and unobtrusive way of interacting with data and information. And, because it lets users share their virtual experiences, many are hailing VR as a potential boon to communication.

These predictions may seem exaggerated if you just look at the relatively crude VR graphics or the bulky gear worn by VR explorers. Users, however, swear their virtual experiences seem real. Consider the first-time experience of newspaper columnist Dale Dauten. Even though he knew he was walking across a solid floor, he couldn't make himself step onto a virtual plank suspended high above a virtual chasm. Creating this kind of computer-generated reality isn't easy, though. Here are just a few of the hardware items you'll need to explore the brave new world of virtual reality.

A head-mounted display unit. If you want to immerse yourself in virtual reality, you may need to forsake your standard computer monitor for a head-mounted display unit, which replaces all real-world sensations with computer-generated images. These units, which range from bulky helmets to lighter goggles and glasses, contain two tiny computer screens—one for each eye. By projecting a slightly different image to each eye, the VR system can create a 3-D effect.

Most of these units use either cathode ray tubes (CRTs) or liquid crystal displays (LCDs). CRTs deliver brighter, higher resolution graphics, but they tend to be heavier than LCDs, fatiguing users. LCDs, while lighter, tend to have lower resolution than CRTs. A compromise is the BOOM, a trademark that stands for Binocular Omni-Orientation Monitor. A BOOM uses a combination of a floor-mounted post, gimbals, and a swiveling frame to suspend heavy but high-quality CRT displays above the floor. To look into a virtual world, you simply pull the BOOM up to your face.

For users who don't need or want to block all real-world sensations, another alternative uses fiber optics to project images onto lightweight, see-through lenses, creating "augmented reality."

Head-mounted audio devices. Providing the right sound effects is important to creating virtual reality. (Imagine watching an action movie without its sound track.) VR uses thousands of sound effects, ranging from thunks and clicks to whooshes and gurgles, to give users feedback about their actions. Sound also helps users locate themselves in space. That's why virtual reality systems use CD-ROMs to store digitized sound effects and sophisticated sound boards and headphones to send two different signals to each ear, creating holographic or 3-D sound.

Tracking devices. The illusion of virtual reality would be shattered if you moved your head but the sounds and images did not. Tracking devices prevent this from happening by monitoring the user's movements, providing the computer the information it needs to shift the user's view. These tracking devices can be mounted on top of VR helmets, on gloves, or even on the ceiling of a room devoted to virtual reality.

Control devices. In a traditional computer system, you can control almost every computer action with a keyboard, a mouse, or a joystick. In a virtual world, you may want a new set of devices. One of the most important is the dataglove, a glove-like device lined with fiber-optic cables and light-emitting diodes that detect when you bend your fingers or wave your hand, issuing commands and handling virtual objects. Some gloves even include tiny air bladders or micropins to provide tactile feedback.

A bodysuit, essentially a dataglove for the body, uses sensors over the body's major joints to monitor body movements, creating an image of the user's body moving within the virtual world. A baseball coach, for example, could use this kind of system to help players evaluate their batting swings. Other applications include physical rehabilitation for injured workers and prevention of repetitive strain injuries.

Navigation devices. The whole idea of virtual reality is to enter into and move about a computer-generated world. Sometimes users can do this by walking about a

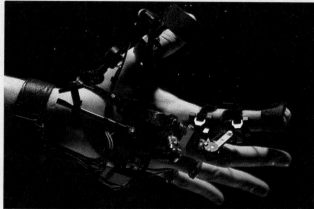

A headset and some sort of handheld input device (left) are necessary for many current virtual reality applications. Exos Inc.'s Dexterous HandMaster (right) allows for extremely fine coordination between hand movements and the virtual reality program.

real room that has been cleared of obstacles. But at other times, they need the sensation of traveling a certain distance at a certain speed. (Taking an electronic "walkthrough" of an architect's virtual building is a good example.) In those cases, the VR system needs to include a navigation device. A treadmill, for instance, might be equipped with a steering device and cables that hook it into the VR system, allowing the user to determine direction, speed, and distance traveled.

A powerful computer. In addition to all these peripherals (and their cables), VR explorers need a powerful computer with huge amounts of secondary storage to store and manipulate an extensive database of graphical, acoustical, and tactile data at a speed that seems "real" to users. (If the speed is too slow, or falls in what VR experts term the "barf zone," users are either baffled or nauseated.) Some VR systems can and do run on desktop computers equipped with powerful graphics cards. But most are built around large processors or graphics workstations. In fact, some VR systems use a network of computers to control and coordinate the various devices. One system, for example, uses two workstations to control the display unit alone—one for each eye.

Discussion Questions

1. Do you agree that VR will become the "ultimate user interface"? Why or why not?

2. Japan's NEC Corp. has designed a prototype VR system that will let up to five people share the same virtual world, even if they are scattered about the globe. Why would a multinational corporation or research institute be interested in buying such a system? How would such a system benefit engineers, executives, or scientific researchers? (Look back at the Opportunities box in Chapter 1 if you need some ideas.)

3. Some descriptions of VR predict that it will sap productivity as users become addicted to acting out their fantasies in role-playing games staged at VR amusement parks or online information systems. Do you agree that this is a danger? Why or why not?

PART 3

Single-User Systems

Talking with Cloene Goldsborough
Director, Information Resource Management, Sprint

Sprint, headquartered in Kansas City, Missouri, is the only U.S. carrier that is in the local, long distance, and cellular telephone businesses. It is the third largest long distance carrier in the United States. I asked Cloene to share her experience and views on the importance of desktop computing and how it is related to end-users, customers, and business opportunities.

With all of the computing and data communications power on the desktop, what's going to happen to larger computing platforms?

I'm not one of these people who thinks mainframe computers are going to go away. I think the mainframe is going to be a big server because there are instances where companies just need to crunch too much data for it to be practical to do this on a desktop or downsized system today. That may change, but it's not the case today. So we see the mainframe becoming part of the distributed processing network as that big server.

Do people clearly want a graphical interface?

Definitely.

Where do you see desktop information technology going? Is it making the management of IT more complex for professionals even as it makes IT simpler for end-users?

[It's doing even] more than that. For people directly in the field interfacing with customers, it is providing a real important connection [to the information they need]. The difference is that people are able to be on the phone, sitting at their desk, talking to a customer and solving their problem interactively, real-time instead of having to say "We'll get back with you

[after we review the data]."

As businesses are able to do that, customers' expectations go up. When they [later] interact with a business that doesn't offer that quality of service, they say, in effect, "I don't have to do this. Other places I call allow me to get a problem solved quickly." What happens is that the leading edge companies that do this raise the expectations for the rest of us. If your company is not there, people walk away. There's not a lot of price differential anymore. So in business it gets down to customer service.

"At Sprint we are now able to bring products to market in about 45 days. That used to be a 9-month process."

Are you saying then that desktop computing and local area networks are changing the way you run the business?

Absolutely.

How is this changing the user's expectations of the IT group?

It's changing their requirements; it's changing what they need. I think in many instances they have come to doubt whether the IT community can live up to their requirements. Their real expectation is when they think you're going to deliver. I think that in a lot of instances they think [the IT group] is not going to be able to deliver. But they know they need it. So this challenges us to step up and change our processes internally so that we can deliver for them. And yes, it does raise their expectations.

When you do deliver, it does raise their expectations that next time you will also be able to deliver. At Sprint we are now able to bring products to market in about 45 days. That used to be a 9-month process.

In what ways do you find user expectations raised?

Speed of delivery and ease of use are probably the two most dramatic ways that we see expectations being raised. And they want it cheaper, too. Faster, better, cheaper. I think it comes from all aspects. It's unacceptable if it's not high quality. Certainly from a quality standpoint they expect it to be of higher quality than ever. Because of the demands of the market it has to be faster and faster and faster to market. And because of the demands of competition, they want you to figure out ways to deliver cheaper. Faster, better, cheaper…That's what they're looking for in order to be more competitive.

Do end-users typically draw as much out of the IT group as they could?

I think it depends on the sophistication of the end-user. Certainly some

end-users are very, very sophisticated. I think they do take real advantage of what IT can provide for them. But you've got others who don't have a vision of what IT can really do until you show it to them. I think that's where prototyping can be so helpful. You can show them a whole new way of doing something—a whole new concept—and then once they understand that, they can really help you improve on that. But sometimes they can't ever bring the original idea to you because they just don't know what's there from the IT standpoint to say that something is even possible.

We're trying to do that with our people right on the front line: bring them a prototype; show them something that begins to really take advantage of IT and how they can utilize it. Then we work with them as they begin to say "If you can do this, then you can do that. If I make this change…If I just had that capability." Get the involvement and iterate through the improvements. That's the approach we're taking. Instead of putting out a 100% perfect solution, we're trying to get something out there quickly and then iteratively improve it as the end-user becomes more sophisticated in using the system. We let them come back and say "Now here's how we can use it even better." I believe where we're the most successful we have that kind of dialog and interaction going.

Can you generalize that into a suggestion for end-users, suggesting how they should work with the IT group?

I think that we do our very best when we get into a situation with end-users where their management team—the end-user group—has picked out a few of their most innovative, creative people and they have been working with the IT people in this prototyping, iterative mode…where as they learn the technology they can take advantage of that and come back with the creative ideas. Then we can give them something that has [those features]. Together we can keep improving.

 *Sprint*

178

What has to happen is that we must be sure the information is there—all the networking capabilities, all the software—because as we do this, they expect us to be able to deliver very quickly. If the infrastructure is not there when we deliver, we run smack dab into that problem where we can't be fast because we don't have the right kind of things in place to allow us to deliver.

We're seeing suites of products, such as Microsoft Office and Lotus Suites, which combine under a single umbrella word processing programs, presentation packages, spreadsheet programs, and data management systems. Each product (or tool) can send data to any of the other programs in the software suite. How do you expect people to use these suites of tools?

I don't see [these programs] becoming one giant tool. What you are going to see is networks that are sophisticated enough to give people access to a lot of different tools.

While the tools will be heterogeneous, the results [of using each one of them] will be carried between them, meaning you'll be able to go from one system to the other. From me in my personal environment sent to you in your personal environment…We're going to have that interoperability. But I can't envision that we're going to have them come together as one single [personal productivity] tool.

Think about the people in your firm who are the most successful in their careers. What stands out among the folks that are most successful? Do they approach business in a different way? Do they approach problems differently?

We're very good at managing the business or engineering part of the business. We're not very good at managing the human side of the business. I think the people who are being successful [are the ones] who are able to lead, facilitate, and motivate others to change…to adapt…to take on these new opportunities. I don't see that being recognized as fast as I think it should be. But clearly, as I look at it, the gulf is going to widen between those who [can and cannot]. It's going to be more important in the future.

Do you find that new people joining your organization tend to rely too much on fact rather than intuition? Too much on analysis rather than interaction with other people who have ideas?

We fight that all the time. We fight the analysis paralysis—wanting to be too perfect, wanting to be absolutely sure of the answer. [Too many people] can't deal with ambiguity. We're working with people on those issues all the time.

You have to have people who are comfortable knowing they can take a risk…It goes into the whole culture of American industry today, particularly in IT. The computer is either on or off. We've grown up with people where the answer is either yes or no. But those kind of people really struggle with ambiguity. There's a lot of ambiguity in the world we have today, even in the technology world we have. They struggle with the hard *people* decisions that must be made, because they can't be so clearly fact-based.

Human beings are hard to figure out. They come in your office and they cry and they're hurt. They're in pain and they struggle. Or they're happy. They take time and they're unpredictable. It's messy stuff. I happen to enjoy that part of it.

Chapter Outline

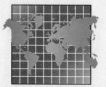

CHAPTER 5

Electronic Spreadsheets: Powerful Problem Solving Tools

Learning Objectives

When you have completed this chapter, you should be able to:

1 Describe the principle functions of spreadsheets and why they are used in business.

2 Identify the elements found on an electronic spreadsheet display.

3 Describe the four types of data created and stored in spreadsheet programs and differentiate between functions and formulas, describing the benefits of each in creating worksheets for problem solving.

4 Summarize the capabilities offered by spreadsheet programs for changing and refining worksheets after data have been entered.

5 Discuss the uses of spreadsheet programs in sensitivity analysis and problem solving.

6 Explain the types of business graphics usually included with spreadsheet programs, when each is used, and how worksheet contents are transformed into business graphics.

7 Discuss the four steps involved in developing a personal spreadsheet application.

In Practice

After completing this chapter, you should be able to perform these activities:

1 Explain why electronic spreadsheet programs are among the most widely used types of computer programs.

2 Visit with an analyst or a salesperson and discuss the manner in which he uses spreadsheet programs in his day-to-day activities.

3 Specify the types of situations in which worksheets should be created using electronic spreadsheet programs.

4 Discuss with a manager how she uses business graphics, prepared from worksheet data, to present information to other mangers or to customers.

5 Evaluate the usefulness of spreadsheets in creating and evaluating a revenue and expense budget, both annually for a department and one time only for a special event at a local arts center or community service organization.

6 Explain how a sales manager may use templates to help his sales force become more effective.

The Spreadsheet of Visible Innovation

AN *ENTREPRENEUR* IS SOMEONE WHO knows where to scratch before there's an itch. An *innovator* seeks a better way to scratch that itch. Both people are essential to progress. They are creating the future today, experimenting with technology that will become commonplace in the future. But how exactly do innovations and advances come about?

Consider the case of Dan Bricklin, a student at the Harvard Business School in 1977. Dan spent most of his evenings working on a seemingly endless series of business cases requiring analysis, decision making, and problem solving skills. For each case, Dan needed to create a worksheet to map out the expenses and other financial concerns of the business he was studying. Each case also required him to consider several alternatives and different assumptions. This meant repeated calculations on the calculator and the construction of worksheet after worksheet to show revenues, expenses, and the effects of competitors' activities. When an arithmetic error occurred—and errors are a normal part of learning—the entire worksheet had to be redone.

Before the electronic spreadsheet…

…and after.

What bothered Dan was not the work or the time devoted to analyzing the cases; such analysis is a critical part of gaining an education and developing expertise. But Dan felt the time he spent keying numbers into the calculator and transferring them to the worksheet was neither exciting nor productive. In fact, it seemed only to get in the way of the learning process. It also left him less time to focus on the important things: analysis and gaining insight into the case solutions.

Dan knew there had to be a better way. During the early months of 1978—when it's cold and snowy in New England—Dan and a friend,

Robert Frankston, stayed indoors, working together to develop a new type of calculator that would ease their "number-crunching" problems. They wondered if they could find a way to use their new Apple II computer as a problem solving tool.

In a few months, Dan and Robert had developed a computer program they called a *visible calculator*. The program performed the spreadsheet arithmetic, allowing the user to enter new data and see how they will affect the final outcome. No longer did Dan need to perform endless calculations by hand every time he had to analyze a case.

After the program's problems were ironed out, Dan's entrepreneurial spirit kicked in. The visible calculator had helped Dan to increase his personal productivity significantly. Surely it could also be of use to other people facing similar problems. But what about the name? Who would buy something called a "visible calculator"? No problem—call it something else. And they did.

VisiCalc, as the program came to be called, ran on the Apple II computer and became a runaway success. In fact, the program is often given credit for selling more Apple computers than any other software product of the day. It literally changed the way people analyze and solve problems throughout the world.

Ultimately, VisiCalc's success led to a long line of new products that improved on its basic concept. When the IBM PC was introduced in 1981, another entrepreneur/innovator, Mitch Kapor (himself an expert in computer software), developed a spreadsheet program that ran only on the IBM PC. As businesses began acquiring more and more PCs, they also purchased thousands of copies of Kapor's spreadsheet program, which became a success as quickly as 1-2-3. In fact, the program was called Lotus 1-2-3 and Kapor's company was known as Lotus Development Co.

VisiCalc and Lotus 1-2-3: Two historic successes created because someone was able to solve a problem—to scratch an itch—in an innovative way.   ■

SIMPLE, YET POWERFUL. THIS IS THE REALITY OF TODAY'S SPREADSHEET. SPREADSHEET PROGRAMS do not provide magical solutions to unsolvable problems, however. Rather, their benefits come from a sound understanding of their capabilities and the principles of effective use. Using spreadsheets for problem solving often involves creating multiple worksheets, each focusing on a different part of the problem.

The first part of this chapter focuses on spreadsheets' problem solving and productivity increasing capabilities. The second part of the chapter explores the uses of business graphics as a problem solving tool. The details entered into a spreadsheet can be used to create a wide variety of business graphics to transform numeric information into visual form, showing the relationships between different components of a problem. The last part of the chapter creates and develops a personal spreadsheet application.

When you have completed this chapter you will have a good understanding of the components of an electronic spreadsheet package. You will also be prepared to design and create a personal spreadsheet application.

■ An Overview of Spreadsheets

spreadsheet or **worksheet** A table of columns and rows used by people responsible for tracking revenues, expenses, profits, and losses.

Spreadsheets—also commonly called **worksheets**—have been used for decades by bookkeepers, accountants, financial analysts, and project planners—the people who plan events and who are responsible for keeping track of revenues, expenses, profits, and losses. You've probably seen spreadsheets often, with their rows and columns of tabular data. But what exactly is a spreadsheet and what is it used for?

What Is a Spreadsheet?

Manual spreadsheets—that is, spreadsheets done by hand with pencil and paper—have served planners and analysts well, helping them organize their work and structure the numeric details of their project. They are also easy to use. Simply read across the horizontal **rows** to see the data for individual categories or items of interest; read down the vertical **columns** to see the relevant data for each time period. Totals are shown at the bottom of each column and sometimes in the far right column.

An **electronic spreadsheet** is an automated version of the manual type, created and maintained by an individual using a software package called an electronic **spreadsheet program**. Because spreadsheets are usually personal applications, not multi-user applications, they are typically run on PCs. Table 5.1 lists popular spreadsheet packages on both IBM-compatible and Macintosh computers. Versions for some mainframes and midrange computers are also available.

row The horizontal elements in a spreadsheet.

column The vertical elements in a spreadsheet.

electronic spreadsheet An automated version of the manual spreadsheet, created and maintained by a spreadsheet program.

spreadsheet program A software package used to create electronic spreadsheets.

Why Use Spreadsheets in Business?

The electronic spreadsheet is often called a "killer app," a type of software that offers so many benefits that even non-computer-owners are persuaded to buy a machine. (Before Bricklin developed the electronic spreadsheet, the business community viewed the PC as a "toy" for hobbyists and game players, not a tool for serious business use.) To understand why businesspeople have embraced the electronic spreadsheet so enthusiastically, consider a few of the ways it can be used to support traditional business functions.

To Automate Record Keeping.   A manager without good business records is operating in the dark and may even be unable to meet financial obligations, collect payments, or plan for the future. The electronic spreadsheet helps here in at least three ways. First, it lets users record and store business data in a clear, legible format reminiscent of an accountant's ledger. Second, the electronic spreadsheet's "search/find" and "sort" functions let users find and reorganize specific data—helping the user prepare, for example, an alphabetical list of all customers with overdue accounts. Third, electronic spreadsheets let users embed mathematical formulas within a spreadsheet. Using these formulas, the computer performs both simple and complex calculations automatically and without errors. The savings in both time and labor are substantial.

TABLE 5.1   Leading Spreadsheet Packages

Software Package	Manufacturer	Computer Versions Available
1-2-3	Lotus Development	Apple Macintosh and IBM-compatible microcomputers, IBM midrange and mainframes
Excel	Microsoft	Apple Macintosh and IBM-compatible
Improv	Lotus Development	IBM-compatible
Quattro Pro	Borland	IBM-compatible

To Summarize Raw Data and Produce Information.   The electronic spreadsheet's ability to total long rows or columns of data is essential to producing the organized, summarized information managers need to understand and analyze the organization's performance. Did the department meet its sales goals? Is the new marketing plan working? What does the latest customer survey say about our service? Often, the best answers can be found in the analyses and summaries produced by using an electronic spreadsheet package. And, if the answers aren't clear enough from the summary data, the manager can use the spreadsheet software to convert them into *business graphics*, charts and graphs that help readers make comparisons and see trends in the data (Figure 5.1).

To Perform Analysis and Improve Planning.   The summary information displayed on a spreadsheet or business graphic is a valuable resource for crafting management goals and plans. But the electronic spreadsheet also lets managers go beyond simple summaries to construct the sort of "what-if" analyses Dan Bricklin struggled with as a student.

Electronic spreadsheets let managers conduct three general types of analyses. In the simplest form of analysis, a user changes one value within the spreadsheet and then lets the computer recalculate all the affected data. This approach gives the user the power to experiment with different alternatives and get instant feedback. What happens to profits if we cut costs by 5 percent? Change the appropriate data in the spreadsheet and you'll get an answer in less than a second.

The second analytical approach incorporates the mathematical tools of management science into the spreadsheet. A good example of this type of analysis is "back-solving" or "goal-seeking." Here, the manager starts with a desired goal or output ("increase profits by 5%") and lets the software work backward, using the spreadsheet data and mathematical formulas to calculate the appropriate values for the various inputs, such as materials, labor, and price. The most sophisticated of these analytical tools, called *optimizers*, let managers seek an optimal balance between minimizing costs and maximizing profits, given certain constraints (such as limited supplies of labor).

The third analytical approach, *scenario planning*, lets the user construct and compare a number of business plans or **models**, which simulate the relationship between events or variables in the business world. Scenario planning is especially useful if the future holds the kinds of uncertainties facing Southern California Edison. That company's managers used scenario planning to create twelve alternate models, ranging from Mideast oil crisis to economic boom. The resulting calculations helped them fine-tune their long-range capacity planning, which governs the number and size of their generating plants.

Together, these analytical powers let managers incorporate many types of data into precise but flexible plans, created with little or no help from the IT staff or financial analysis.

To Simplify the Control Process.   Businesspeople around the world are judged on the basis of the results they produce. Did the organization reach the goals specified in its plans? If there were problems, what were they? What went wrong? The data in a spreadsheet can help answer these questions, which are central to the business control process. Spreadsheets can even be constructed so that the numbers that indicate "exceptions" or potential problems show up in a different color on the computer screen, thus alerting all employees that corrective action is needed.

To Improve Communication and Motivation.   Color-coding data on a computer screen is just one way that a spreadsheet can help businesspeople improve communication. Summarizing data in a spreadsheet or a business graphic is anoth-

model A plan that simulates the relationships between events or variables.

Ray's Lobster Shack- Fourth Quarter Summary	1	2	3	4
	OCT.	NOV.	DEC.	TOTAL
SALES				
Hackensack	12,000	8,500	14,750	35,250
New York	22,000	18,900	26,950	67,850
Philadelphia	16,500	12,000	18,800	47,300
TOTAL SALES	50,500	39,400	60,500	150,400
EXPENSES				
Rent	4,000	4,000	4,000	12,000
Salaries	20,000	20,000	20,000	60,000
Supplies	3,000	2,000	2,000	7,000
Utilities	1,250	1,300	1,400	3,950
TOTAL EXPENSES	28,250	27,300	27,400	82,950
NET BEFORE TAXES	22,250	12,100	33,100	67,450

FIGURE 5.1   The Benefits of Electronic Spreadsheets
In addition to saving time by recalculating data automatically, electronic spreadsheets allow users to create graphics from the data included on the spreadsheet.

MANUAL SPREADSHEET

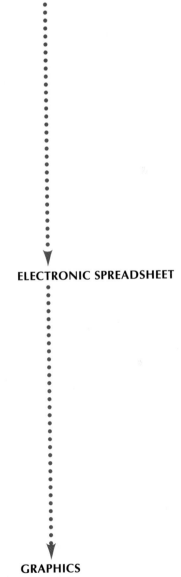

ELECTRONIC SPREADSHEET

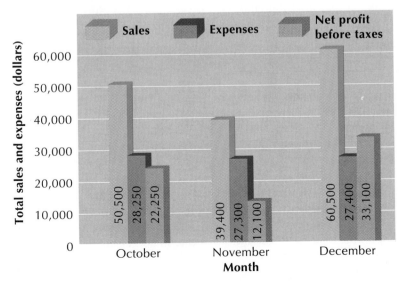

GRAPHICS

er. In fact, many experts suggest that managers begin their reports with a summary graphic, which should later be supplemented with a more detailed table of supporting data. Business graphics that summarize company data can also help a manager lead and motivate employees. (A good example is a chart summarizing sales performance; many spreadsheet packages let users add an annotation, such as "Great work, team!")

To Help Managers Make Decisions.   Although electronic spreadsheets are a powerful and useful aid to business problem solving and decision making, the numbers on the "bottom line" are no substitute for human judgment and common sense. In fact, managers should probably view the numbers on an unfamiliar spreadsheet with a healthy dose of skepticism, since a faulty assumption or formula can throw off the usefulness of many calculations instantly. This is one reason that experienced spreadsheet users follow a clear sequence in setting up and documenting their spreadsheets. We discuss this format later in the chapter, after we discuss what exactly spreadsheets do and how they do it.

CRITICAL CONNECTION 1
Kraft & Associates Create Spreadsheet Magic

Donald H.Kraft & Associates   A spreadsheet is a powerful tool—one that can help any manager work more effectively. The only catch: the typical manager doesn't have time to read through thick manuals, ferreting out the secret keystrokes that create spreadsheet magic. That's why savvy managers turn to consultants like Donald H. Kraft.

Kraft, head of Donald H. Kraft & Associates in Skokie, Illinois, is a specialist in creating automated Lotus 1-2-3 worksheets that he has customized to perform complex tasks with just a few keystrokes or mouse clicks. A typical example is the mortgage-analysis spreadsheet Kraft created for Sears Mortgage Corp., formally a subsidiary of Sears & Roebuck. With the help of Kraft's spreadsheets, tasks that used to take nearly a week are now done in a matter of hours. Kraft's clients range from large corporations and government agencies to small business owners. Although he provides a wide range of services ranging from basic training to general PC consulting, he loves the really challenging projects—the kind that let him use Lotus 1-2-3 to create spreadsheet miracles for his clients.

Reality Check.   Good problem solving tools fit the situation where they are needed, are simple to use, and make you better at what you do. They seem like a natural thing to use when there is a problem to be solved or a solution to be found. The right tool also seems to have the desired characteristics for the problem solving situation.

When you want to pound a nail into a wall, you use a hammer. It suits the situation and gets the job done. You can use other things besides a hammer, but why would you want to? No other item would be as efficient in getting the job done.

Like hammers, spreadsheets help get the job done when used in the proper manner. They are also comfortable to use.

The Functions of Spreadsheet Programs

Spreadsheet programs carry out four principal activities:

- Entering data
- Editing data
- Storing worksheets
- Printing worksheets

Each of these activities includes many options that make it easy for the user to enter and organize data.

Entering Data

Before you can enter data, you need to know your way around the elecrtonic worksheet and some basic spreadsheet terminology.

Dimensions of the Worksheet.   The worksheet is composed of a certain number of cells determined by the user. A **cell** is the intersection of a row and a column. The **cell address**, or **cell reference**, is the intersection of a particular row and column. Much like a memory address, it distinguishes one location from another. For example, the Lotus 1-2-3 spreadsheet software assigns letters to columns (from A to Z, AA through AZ, BA through BZ, and so on to IV) and numbers to rows (from 1 to 8,192). The address of the cell in column 8, row 6 will thus be cell H6.

As we discuss later, multiple worksheets can be created and linked together. Lotus 1-2-3 supports up to 256 worksheets. Each can contain as many as 256 columns and 8,192 rows.

The cell in which the user is currently working is called the **current cell** or **active cell**. It is highlighted with a **cell pointer** to show that data or information can be entered (or are being entered) into the cell. The active cell is also identified at the top left corner of the screen (Figure 5.2 on page 188).

Screen Layout.   The spreadsheet display contains two distinct areas: the window and the control panel.

- **Window.** The largest section of the spreadsheet screen, the *window*, contains the **worksheet area**—the rectangular grid of rows and columns that comprise the worksheet. Along the left side of the window are the row numbers. The column letters or numbers are shown across the top of the worksheet area.

  Because worksheets are often larger than the display screen on which they are viewed, the spreadsheet software will *scroll* the rows and columns onto the screen. On the right side and bottom of the window in Figure 5.2 are the vertical and horizontal **scroll bars**, which allow the user to move around the window (up and down, or to the right or left). As a row or column moves onto the screen on one side, another moves out of view on the opposite side. This scrolling takes place almost instantly and thus does not hinder or distract the user.

- **Control Panel.** The top section of the spreadsheet screen, located above the worksheet area, is the *control panel*. Its contents vary depending on the particular spreadsheet package used. Figure 5.2 shows the control panel for Lotus 1-2-3 for Windows.

cell In an electronic spreadsheet, the intersection of a row and a column.

cell address or **cell reference** The intersection of a particular row and column in an electronic spreadsheet.

current cell or **active cell** In an electronic spreadsheet, the cell in which the user is currently working.

cell pointer The cursor in an electronic spreadsheet.

worksheet area In an electronic spreadsheet, the rectangular grid of rows and columns that comprise the worksheet.

scroll bar A bar located at the right or bottom of the computer screen that allows the user to move around the screen—up, down, left, or right.

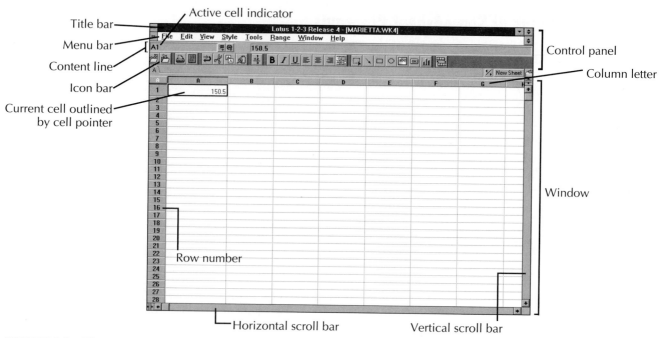

FIGURE 5.2   The Components of an Electronic Worksheet
An electronic spreadsheet display contains two main components: the control panel and the window. In this illustration, the current cell is A1.

title bar The line of an electronic spreadsheet's control panel. It contains the program name and sometimes the name of the file in use.

menu bar The line of an electronic spreadsheet's control panel that contains the commands for working with worksheets, creating graphics, and invoking special data processing actions.

The first line of the Lotus control panel, the **title bar**, contains the program name and sometimes the name of the file in use. The second line, the **menu bar**, contains the spreadsheet commands for creating, storing, retrieving, and editing files and worksheets, creating graphs, invoking special data processing actions, and using other tools that change the appearance of the spreadsheet. Most Windows, OS/2, and Macintosh-based spreadsheet systems also include a "HELP" function to provide assistance. The "HELP" system is *context sensitive*, which means that it provides information about the command you are seeking to use at the time you click on HELP. However, the menu also includes an index of capabilities (a HELP index) so that you can obtain information on any feature of the spreadsheet at any time. Each command includes subcommands that can be invoked by pointing and clicking at the appropriate spot on the command menu. For DOS-based spreadsheet programs, the HELP function (and many other functions) are invoked by pressing the appropriate function key designated by the software.

content line or **edit line** The line of an electronic spreadsheet's control panel indicating the data or information being keyed into the spreadsheet.

icon A small picture that represents a command. Using icons to invoke commands is faster than invoking commands through the menu bar.

icon bar The line of an electronic spreadsheet's control panel that shows the icons used to invoke frequently used commands.

value A number that is entered into a cell of an electronic spreadsheet. It may be an integer, a decimal number, or a number in scientific format.

The third line of Lotus 1-2-3 for Windows, the **content line** (also called the **edit line**), displays the data or information keyed into the active cell of the spreadsheet. The fourth line, the **icon bar**, contains small pictures called **icons** that represent frequently used commands included in the menu bar. The user simply points and clicks on an icon to invoke a command. Some common spreadsheet commands are listed in Table 5.2, and the icons used in the leading spreadsheet packages are shown in Figure 5.3.

Cell Contents.   A cell can hold any of four different pieces of information: values, labels, formulas, or functions.

- A **value** is a number that is entered into a cell. The value may be an integer (500), a decimal number (500.12), or a number in scientific format (5.00 E+2, where "E+2" indicates the number of zeroes to add before the decimal point).

TABLE 5.2   Spreadsheet Commands

Command	Explanation
Sort	Arranges specified data into ascending or descending order
Column width	Sets the width of one or more columns in the worksheet
Delete	Removes one or more columns, rows, or worksheets and closes the space left by the deletion
Exit	Ends the spreadsheet session and returns to the computer's operating system
Graph	Opens a graph window within the worksheet and displays specified graphs
Insert	Inserts blank columns, rows, or worksheets
Move	Transfers data from one section of the worksheet to another
New	Creates a new blank worksheet
Open	Reads a previously created worksheet from secondary storage into main memory, where it can be processed
Print	Prints all or a portion of the worksheet, as specified by the user
Range	Enables user to perform processing on a portion of the worksheet
Save	Saves the worksheet as a file in secondary storage

All values can be used in computation. In Figure 5.4 on page 190, the contents of cells B4 through G4 and B5 through G5 are values.

- A **label** is a piece of descriptive information pertaining to a row or column. Generally they are used as column and row headings or titles. Labels are not used in computation. In Figure 5.4, the contents of cells A1 and B3 through G3 are labels.

label A piece of descriptive information pertaining to a row or column of an electronic spreadsheet.

FIGURE 5.3   Icons Used in Popular Spreadsheet Packages
Source: Lotus User's Guide (left); Excel User's Manual (right). Used by permission.

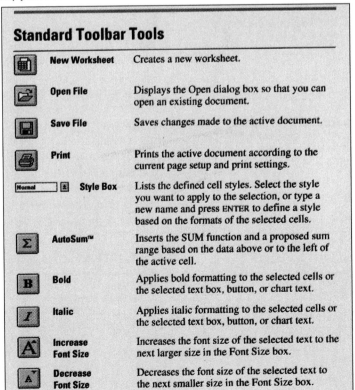

Function

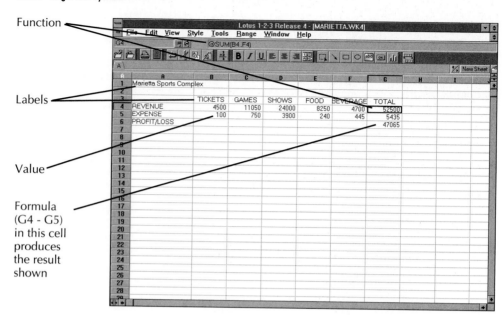

Labels

Value

Formula
(G4 - G5)
in this cell
produces
the result
shown

FIGURE 5.4
Cell Contents
A spreadsheet cell can hold
four types of information: values, labels, formulas, and
functions.

formula An electronic
spreadsheet instruction describing
how a specific computation should
be performed.

- A **formula** is an instruction describing how a specific computation should be performed. The arithmetic symbols used in formulas include a plus sign (+) for addition, a minus sign (-) for subtraction, an asterisk (*) for multiplication, a slash (/) for division, and a caret (∧) for exponentiation. Formulas are used to recalculate results automatically if the values in any cells are changed.

  In Figure 5.4, the formula (G4-G5) embedded in cell G6 tells the software to subtract total revenue from total expense to determine profit. Table 5.3 lists examples of formulas frequently used in spreadsheet programs.

  Depending on the spreadsheet software used, formulas begin with a special symbol that distinguishes them from values. In Lotus 1-2-3, the symbol is an optional + (plus sign); in Excel, it's a mandatory = (equal sign). For example, the formula 3+2 in a Lotus spreadsheet program would be represented by +3+2; in Excel, it would be represented by =3+2. The Quality and Productivity box titled "Electronic Spreadsheets: A Secret Weapon for the Small Business Owner" on page 194 lists some of the questions that small business owners can answer with spreadsheet formulas.

function A formula built into
electronic spreadsheet software that
will automatically perform certain
types of calculation.

- A **function** is a formula built into the spreadsheet software that will automatically perform certain types of calculation. A single function takes the place of several entries that the user would otherwise have to make. (Note: Do not confuse functions with the function keys on computer keyboards.) The symbol @ identifies a command as a predefined function. Among the most commonly used functions are @SUM, which adds the value of a set of cells; @AVG, which calculates the average value of a list of numbers, and @MIN and @MAX, which

TABLE 5.3   Examples of Formulas Used in Spreadsheet Packages

Formula	Explanation
3+2	Add the numbers 3 + 2 and place the result in the current cell.
3 - A1	Subtract the contents of cell A1 from the number 3 and place the result in the current cell.
22*(A1/A2)	Divide the contents of cell A1 by the contents of cell A2. Multiply the number 22 by the result of the division and place the result in the current cell.

determine the minimum and maximum values in a set of cells. Table 5.4 lists some other often-used functions.

In Figure 5.4, the function @SUM(B4..F4) tells the computer to add the values in cells B4 through F4 and to place the result in cell G4.

Figure 5.4, as you may have noticed, shows the labels, values, formulas, and functions used by the Marietta Sports Complex in its revenue/expense/profits spreadsheet. The Complex is a small family entertainment center that takes in revenues from general admission (TICKETS), sports games (GAMES), plays and shows (SHOWS), and concessions (FOOD and BEVERAGE). We will continue to use the Marietta Sports Complex as an example in the pages that follow.

Reality Check.   The functions that accompany a spreadsheet package are extremely useful. However, the list can be overwhelming if you attempt to commit every one to memory immediately. A better approach to learning how to put software to work for you is to first become familiar with the software's general capabilities, then to use its more specialized capabilities.

Some frequently used functions, such as those for summation, determining averages, or identifying minimum and maximum values, are very general and apply to many different areas. Learn how to use these first. Then learn the specific functions that are most applicable to your career field or the responsibilities you hold. After repeated use, they will become second nature to you. You will reach for them automatically as you learn how to apply them to your work. Use, rather than memorization, is the most effective means of learning.   ■

TABLE 5.4   Functions Commonly Used in Spreadsheet Packages

Statistical Functions

@AVG	Averages a list of values.
@COUNT	Counts the nonblank cells in a list of ranges.
@MAX	Finds the maximum value in a list of values.
@MIN	Finds the minimum value in a list of values.
@STD	Calculates the population standard deviation of a list of values.
@STDS	Calculates the sample standard deviation of a list of values.

Date and Time Functions

@NOW	Calculates the value that corresponds to the current date and time on the computer's clock.
@TODAY	Calculates the date number that corresponds to the current date on the computer's clock.

Financial Functions

@IRR	Calculates the internal rate of return for a series of cash flows.
@NPV	Calculates the net present value of a series of cash flows.
@DDB	Calculates the double-declining balance depreciation allowance of an asset.
@SLN	Calculates the straight-line depreciation allowance of an asset for one period.
@SYD	Calculates the sum-of-the-years'-digits depreciation allowance of an asset.
@FV	Calculates the future value of a series of equal payments.
@PMT	Calculates the amount of the periodic payment needed to pay off a loan.
@PV	Calculates the present value of a series of equal payments.
@TERM	Calculates the number of payment periods of an investment.

range A rectangular group of adjacent cells in an electronic spreadsheet. It may be composed of a row, a column, or several rows and columns.

Cell Range. By itself, a single cell is not very meaningful. For this reason, most problem analysts use information from a range of cells. A **range** is a rectangular group of adjacent cells. It may be composed of a row, a column, or several rows and columns. As we saw above, formulas and functions frequently specify ranges for computation. In Figure 5.4, the function used by the Marietta Sports Complex to sum revenues makes use of the cell range B4-F4. Figure 5.5 shows some other cell ranges.

As another example, consider a sales manager who is trying to determine who is the best, average, and worst-performing salesperson on her sales team. To determine this information, she would specify the range of cells in her spreadsheets that contain sales information. She would then use the @MAX, @AVG, and @MIN functions in the specified range of cells to get the information she needs.

importing The ability to read text or numbers from one file into another.

Importing Data. In addition to entering data into a spreadsheet from the keyboard (or some other input device), you can also import data from a file on disk. **Importing** means reading text or numbers into a spreadsheet file from a different spreadsheet file. Alternatively, data may be imported from a file created by a database program, word processing system, or other type of program. In addition to saving keying time, importing also allows data to be shared across several programs.

formatting Software capabilities that allow the user to change the appearance of characters both on the computer screen and when printed.

Formatting Values. Spreadsheet software uses a built-in, prespecified *default* format for data. For example, values are displayed without separators (such as commas) or currency signs (for example, \$, ¥, or £). But spreadsheet programs' **formatting** capabilities allow the user to change the appearance of characters both on the screen and when printed. Among the format adjustments that can be made are:

- Adding characters to the displayed contents of a cell (such as \$, ¥, £, %, or decimal positions).
- Changing the width of columns.
- Specifying the alignment of the contents of a cell so that characters are centered, aligned on the left side of the cell, or aligned on the right side of the cell.
- Changing the style and size of the characters.

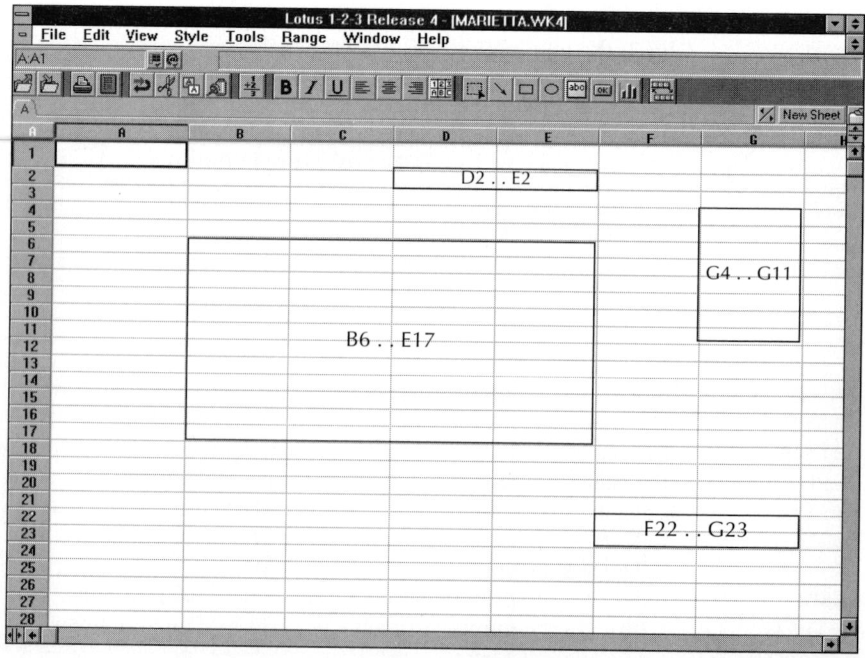

FIGURE 5.5 Cell Ranges
Different spreadsheet programs use different notations for ranges. Some use periods (D2 . . E2); others use one period (D2.E2); others use a colon (D2:E3).

- Adding emphasis by making the characters **bold**, *italic*, or underlined.
- Change the characters from lowercase to UPPERCASE.

Figure 5.6 shows the spreadsheet in Figure 5.4 reformatted to call attention to certain items. The objective of formatting is always to make the information easy to read and to ensure that the most important details of the spreadsheet stand out.

Editing Data

The electronic spreadsheet is a tool for analysis. The details entered when you start to study a problem may change as you study it further. Spreadsheets' powerful editing capabilities are an important feature in helping you analyze the effects of these changes. After you have established your worksheet, spreadsheet programs allow you to:

- **Change, add, and delete data.** Spreadsheet programs allow you to correct or change the contents of a cell quickly and easily. They also allow you to add new data, and to delete the contents of cells, whenever necessary.
- **Insert and delete rows and columns.** As your worksheet grows larger and more complex, you may want to add rows and columns to it. Spreadsheet programs allow you to do so with the click of a button. It is also easy to delete rows and columns when the material they contain is no longer necessary or relevant.
- **Copy, move, find, and sort data and formulas.** Using special commands, spreadsheet programs can copy cells from one part of a spreadsheet to another, and even from spreadsheet to spreadsheet. They can also transfer data and formulas from one part of the spreadsheet to another. Find or search commands allow users to find particular entries quickly, and sort commands allow users to order data numerically or alphabetically.
- **Freeze row and column headings.** When worksheets are large, column and row labels scroll off the screen as you move around the worksheet. To avoid this situation, the software can be instructed to keep the labels in a fixed location on the display screen.

FIGURE 5.6   Reformatting a Worksheet
Electronic spreadsheets offer many options to customize and reformat the standard worksheet.

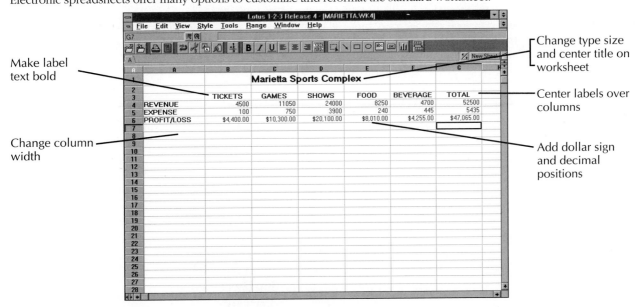

Electronic Spreadsheets: A Secret Weapon for the Small Business Owner

ELECTRONIC SPREADSHEETS ARE ONE OF THE MOST POPULAR types of personal productivity software, mainly because they let even those who are uncomfortable with math use complex formulas. These formulas hold the answers to financial questions that are of vital interest to both individuals and businesses. Some of these questions can be answered by using the spreadsheet's built-in functions. To answer others, you'll have to enter some of the formulas shown in the many handbooks and magazine articles designed to help end-users develop their spreadsheet skills. To understand why a small business owner might use electronic spreadsheets, consider some of the basic business questions they can help model and answer.

- What's my break-even point? How much income do I need to produce each month just to cover my costs?
- Am I over or under budget this month?
- What's my predicted cash flow for the month? Will I have enough cash on hand to pay my bills?
- When should I reorder inventory and supplies and how much should I order?
- My goal is to increase sales by 3% next year. If my costs stay the same, what will happen to profits?
- A lot of businesses seem to increase sales when they discount prices. Would following their example help or hurt my bottom line?
- My business seems to be growing by leaps and bounds. Can I keep growing at this rate without getting a loan?
- I need to take out a loan for my business. Will the bank approve my loan?
- The bank's advertised interest rate sounds too good to be true. What's the actual annual percentage rate, the one that reflects hidden financing costs like loan fees?
- If I get the loan, what will my monthly payments be?

Many sales representatives are installing electronic spreadsheet programs on their portable notebook computers. The programs simplify the customer service process by allowing the reps to perform sophisticated analyses quickly and easily.

- I've been making loan payments for a year. How much do I still owe?
- I'm doing some midyear tax planning. How much can I deduct for interest payments on my business loan?
- I'd like to save some interest charges by paying off the loan a year early. How much more should I pay each month?
- I need a new delivery van for the business. Is it cheaper to buy or lease?
- I'm already setting aside some money for retirement. Can I afford to sell the business and take early retirement when I hit 45?
- I will have accumulated almost $1 million when I retire. Am I rich or will inflation force me to keep working?

- **Adjust column width.** All the cells in a worksheet are prespecified at the same width. When data are longer than the width of the column into which they will be entered, it is a simple matter to enlarge the columns to fit the data. If columns are too wide, it is easy to decrease the column width.

    Most spreadsheet programs spill over data from one column to the next when data values and labels exceed column width, providing adjacent cells are not already in use. This feature is useful if an occasional item is longer than normal. However, when most items exceed the current column width, the width of that column should be adjusted.

- **Undo actions.** If you change your mind after deleting a row of data, removing the contents of a worksheet, or moving data to a different part of the worksheet, all is not lost. Most spreadsheets allow you to reverse your action. The UNDO command restores the affected area to the way it was before you took the action.

UNDO must be performed immediately after an action, before any other step is taken. UNDO does not allow you to reverse printing, storing, or importation activities.

Storing Worksheets

Before ending an electronic spreadsheet session, you must save the worksheet as a file if you want to keep it. To do so, you must give the worksheet a unique name, according to the rules of the computer's operating system (an eight-character name for IBM-compatible computers and a name of up to 32 characters for the Apple Macintosh). The computer will store the worksheet under that name. You can then recall the worksheet at any time by providing the file name. The computer retrieves the file from storage and displays the worksheet on the display screen.

Worksheet templates can also be created as files. A **template** is a worksheet containing row and column labels, and perhaps formulas, but not necessarily any values. The template is distributed to people as a guide for analyzing problems or providing data.

template A worksheet containing row and column labels, and perhaps formulas, but not necessarily any values. It is distributed to people as a guide for analyzing problems or providing data.

The Georgia Research Alliance (GRA), located in Atlanta, is responsible for helping government offices and universities obtain grants and funds to support public-interest programs and to conduct research. One of GRA's goals is to develop cross-organization proposals in which as many as a dozen different program directors join forces to prepare proposals for submission to funding agencies. Coordinating the various directors' proposals is quite a challenge. To facilitate the process, GRA prepares spreadsheet templates for budgets, staffing needs, and equipment and space requirements and distributes them to all the people preparing proposals. By having all parties work from the same templates, GRA ensures that the final proposals have a common appearance and contain all the essential information. Using the templates makes the recipients' jobs easier, too.

Another time-saving capability offered by spreadsheet programs is the macro. A **macro** allows the user to write programs within the worksheet. Each macro is actually a mini-program that is identified by a name and a series of keystrokes. (Some programs also include a built-in macro editor that can perform many of the functions of a software command language.) Creating and using a macro to perform commonly repeated actions (such as boldfacing certain entries, which would normally require three or four steps) can save the user a great deal of time and annoyance.

macro A time-saving mini-program, identified by a name and a series of keystrokes, which is used to perform commonly repeated actions.

Printing Worksheets

When a worksheet is printed, the contents of the entire worksheet or a selected range of cells are transferred to an output medium, usually paper or transparencies. The printing process preserves the format of the worksheet's values and labels. If special type styles or formats have been selected, they also appear on the printed output. Figure 5.7 shows a printout of the spreadsheet in Figure 5.6.

Marietta Sports Complex

	TICKETS	GAMES	SHOWS	FOOD	BEVERAGE	TOTAL
REVENUE	4500	11050	24000	8250	4700	52500
EXPENSE	100	750	3900	240	445	5435
PROFIT/LOSS	$4,400.00	$10,300.00	$20,100.00	$8,010.00	$4,255.00	$47,065.00

FIGURE 5.7
Printed Worksheet
This is the printed report generated by the computer screen shown in Figure 5.6.

◼ Problem Solving Using Spreadsheets

Two integral parts of problem solving are testing alternative solutions and breaking down problems into their component parts. Spreadsheet systems support both these parts of problem solving. (We discuss the problem solving cycle in detail in Chapter 8.)

Recalculation and Sensitivity Analysis

sensitivity analysis The analytical process by which a computer determines what would happen if certain data change.

The benefits of using worksheets with formulas become evident when data change, as they often do. Perhaps the most valuable feature of electronic spreadsheets is their ability to perform **sensitivity analysis**, in which the computer determines what would happen if certain data change. To continue the example we've been using of the Marietta Sports Complex, any adjustment in the complex's revenue and expense categories will result automatically in a recalculation of all totals on the spreadsheet. Spreadsheets thus allow the complex's managers to test the relationship between revenue and cost easily and quickly using many different figures.

Suppose, for example, that the number of tickets sold triples so that ticket revenue is now $13,500 rather than $4,500 (as we've been assuming since Figure 5.4). Figure 5.8 shows the changes in all values in the TOTAL column except for expenses.

FIGURE 5.8   Recalculation to Test Sensitivity
One of the electronic spreadsheets most important features is its ability to recalculate mountains of data automatically when one piece (or many pieces) of data change.

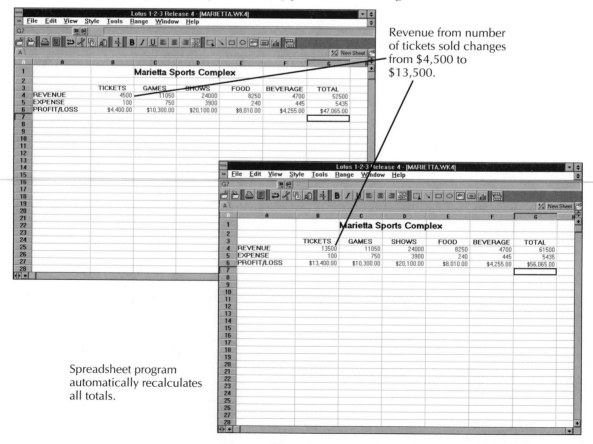

Revenue from number of tickets sold changes from $4,500 to $13,500.

Spreadsheet program automatically recalculates all totals.

Reality Check. In studying behavior in business and everyday life, Nobel Prize winner Herbert Simon found that people who are facing problems and having difficulty finding solutions tend to settle for the first solution that meets their objectives. They accept a solution that is "good enough," even if better solutions are available. Simon coined the term *satisficing* to describe this tendency. When initial solutions are easily identified, however, people continue to seek even better solutions, often finding alternatives that exceed their original objectives by a substantial margin.

Interacting with a spreadsheet system to perform sensitivity analysis can help overcome satisficing. The spreadsheet software's ability to evaluate alternative "what if" ideas quickly and easily leads users to evaluate a greater number of options. For this reason, computer users may have less tendency to satisfice. ■

Linking Spreadsheets

In problem solving activities, each part of the problem must be identified and analyzed independently to assemble information, evaluate strategies, and identify solutions. The parts are then reassembled so that the solution can be managed in its entirety.

All spreadsheet packages allow users to create individual worksheets to deal with each part of a problem. Most also provide a *linkage* capability that allows the user to interconnect the separate worksheets and even to transfer information between them. Often, a *summary worksheet* is designed to accumulate the totals and results of the other worksheets for a particular project.

The sports complex worksheet we've used in this chapter reports the total revenue and expenses for tickets, games, shows, food, and beverages. In our earlier discussions we were concerned only with the accumulated totals of each category. But each of these categories actually consists of several separate categories.

Another way of handling the sports complex information is to establish a separate worksheet for each category, as Figure 5.9 on the next page shows. The food category includes individual revenue and cost estimates for hot dogs, hamburgers, french fries, onion rings, and sausage. The LINKAGE or FILE:COMBINE command interrelates all the worksheets and accumulates the appropriate summary information on the summary worksheet in Figure 5.9.

The financial results shown on each individual worksheet are interrelated. General admission ticket prices determine the number of people who will pay to visit the complex influencing both the expenses incurred and the amount of revenue generated. In turn, the number of people who purchase general admission tickets will influence the revenue and expenses at each game and show, as well as the level of food and beverage sales. The linkage feature of spreadsheet software allows a problem solver to evaluate these interrelationships and the effects of changing admission prices, revenues, and expenses.

CRITICAL CONNECTION 2
Spreadsheets Mimic the Power of Expensive Menu-Costing Programs

Harry's Restaurant Each year thousands of people realize their dream of opening a restaurant. And each year thousands of restaurants go out of business, undone by the cruel realities of narrow profit margins earned on the preparation of perishable foodstuffs with fluctuating prices.

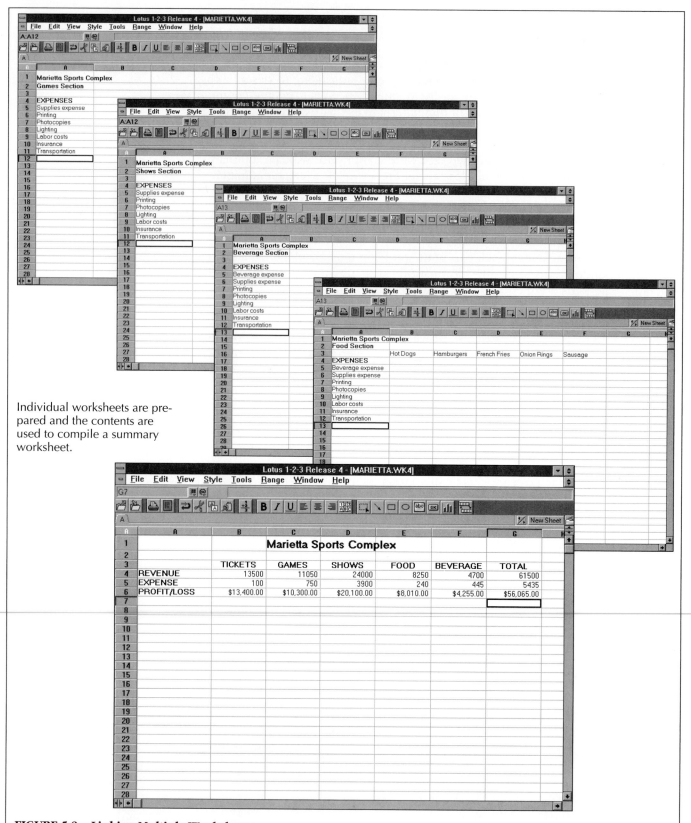

Individual worksheets are pre-pared and the contents are used to compile a summary worksheet.

FIGURE 5.9   Linking Multiple Worksheets
Linking worksheets electronically increases productivity by facilitating the exchange of information between people, departments, and businesses.

That's why large food-service organizations use specialized programs to help them calculate costs and profit margins. But Jon Cohen has shown that the small restaurant owner can harness the power of these expensive software packages— at a fraction of the cost—by using a spreadsheet package. Cohen owns Harry's Restaurant, a popular 55-seat casual-dining operation in Westborough, Massachusetts. He developed his Simplified Menu-Cost Spreadsheet (SMCS) on a Macintosh computer using Excel software, but the system would work on any computer using any spreadsheet package.

The SMCS has two parts. In the first part, the owner enters an alphabetical listing of the meats and seafoods used in preparing entrees, as well as a per-pound cost for each. An embedded formula then calculates the cost per ounce (allowing for a specified amount of waste). This cost is used by the spreadsheet to calculate the cost of the entree alone (for example, an eight-ounce filet mignon) and the total cost of the dinner (including side dishes). The spreadsheet then compares these costs to the selling price to calculate gross profit and other important information.

Reality Check.   The *systems concept* states that components of a system interact with one another to produce a certain result. This concept underlies many business practices and often explains why organizations create departments and units to deal with specific activities. Depending on the extent to which information flows between the different units, people may work independently or they may coordinate their activities to ensure the best possible results.

Spreadsheet packages, which provide the capability for multiple worksheets that are independently created and used yet linked with each other, embody the systems concept. The separate worksheets are individual components of analysis and the entire set of worksheets is an entire system of analysis. Because of the linkage feature, information can flow between the worksheets easily.

The sports complex is an example of a system. The system's components are its main activity centers: games, shows, food service, beverage service, and of course general ticket sales. Each component in turn has subcomponents. The food group consists of the five different foods discussed above.

These groups are linked together so that a change in one event affects the overall outcome. If attendance is higher than expected at the minor league baseball game, revenue for the game and sports complex will also be higher. So will food sales, beverage sales, and profits.   ■

■ Creating Business Graphics

As noted earlier in this chapter, an important feature of spreadsheets is their ability to produce high-quality business graphics from the data included in them. The numeric information that is created and analyzed through a spreadsheet provides powerful support to problem solvers. When translated into graphic form, this information can be even more effective.

The Benefits of Business Graphics

Business graphics present information visually through charts, graphics, and symbols. Generally, they are used to illustrate the relationships between items included in the spreadsheet (for example, revenue and expenses). Because they are visual, they usually convey information about the relationships more quickly than do numbers in tabular form. They are also more exciting to look at.

Graphics do not replace the need for accurate and reliable information. Nor do they substitute for tabular presentation of numeric detail. Rather, they are an effective supplement that can be used to illustrate trends, proportions, highs and lows, and relationships. Figure 5.10 shows several popular forms of business graphics.

Spreadsheets and Business Graphics

Five types of business graphics are usually included in spreadsheet software:

- *Bar charts* consist of a series of bars, each representing a particular element in the worksheet. The length of a bar represents the value of the data: the longer the bar, the higher the value of the data it is presenting. Bars can be "stacked" to show different values of an element at different times.
- *Pie charts* show the proportion or percentage of the whole represented by each element. The proportions are shown as a part of a circular graphic—that is, a pie.

FIGURE 5.10
Popular Forms of Business Graphics
Business graphics present data in a visually appealing summary form.

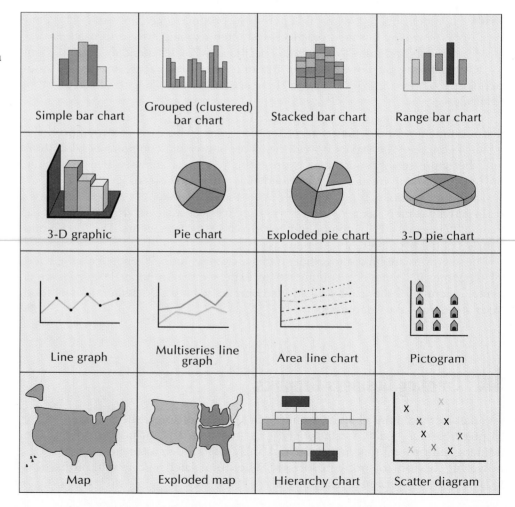

- **Area line charts** use lines that are "stacked" or combined to show the total in each category. Each lines' values are added to those of the line below.
- **Line charts** plot changes in data values over time and connect these points by a line. Each line in the graph represents the fluctuation of a single element.
- **Pictograms** depict data using icons or symbols that represent the magnitude of the data values. Usually the image is symbolic of the element it represents. For example, a pictogram showing real estate sales might use houses as icons, with one icon representing 100 houses sold.

Figure 5.11 offers some tips for choosing the best type of graphic to use in different business situations.

FIGURE 5.11 Choosing the Best Type of Business Graphic
Choosing the right type of business graphic can help you summarize your data and grab your readers' interest, motivating them to look for the detailed information contained in a spreadsheet like this one for The Runner's Foot chain of shoe stores.

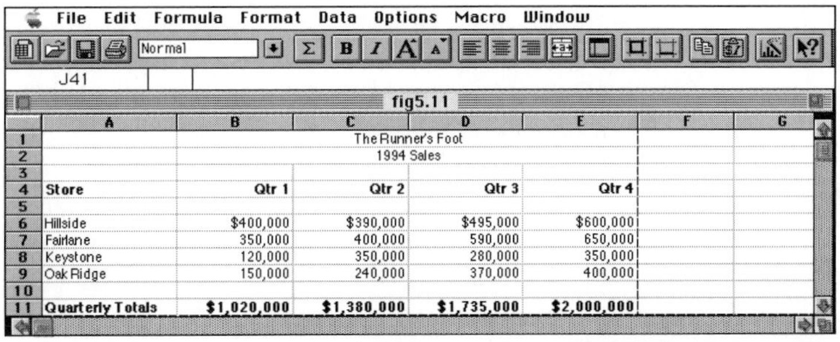

When You Need to...	Choose a...		Description
Compare data values associated with a specific time period, such as regional sales per quarter.	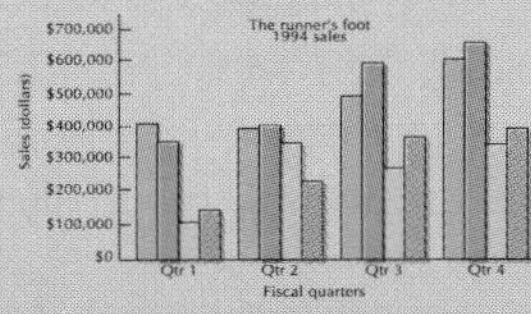	Bar Chart	Transforms each row or column of spreadsheet numbers into a set of bars with the same pattern or color; resulting bars are then grouped by time and/or location.
Compare the change in totals at specific time periods or compare several groups of data in a clear, concise way.	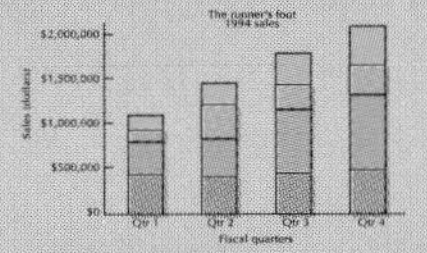	Stacked Bar Chart	Same as a bar chart except the colored or shaded bars are stacked on top of each other, showing a total for each time and/or location.
Show the magnitude and significance of data totals and/or increase corporate identity or motivation.		Pictogram	Replaces bars of bar chart with a number of icons or symbols; each icon or symbol represents a specific unit of measurement.
Provide a quick overview of budgets, market share, or any other data that can be divided into a limited number of categories.	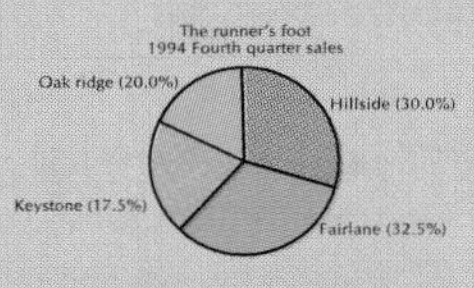	Pie Chart	Shows the relationship between a total and its components, usually expressed as percentages. Each "slice" represents a data value within a spreadsheet row or column.
Show trends or changes over time.	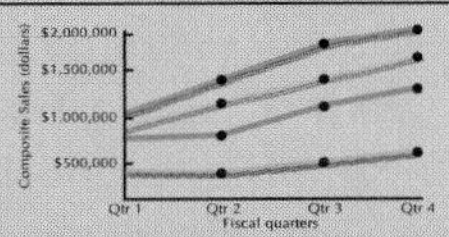	Line Chart	Uses a line (or "curve") to link data points that represent the numbers within a spreadsheet row or column.
Emphasize general trends, rather than differences between regions or product lines.	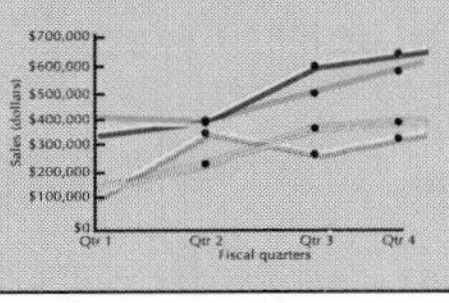	Area Line Chart	Uses the sum of two adjacent cells to create a "stacked" line chart; the area beneath the uppermost curve represents a total for all divisions or product lines.

Always keep in mind that well-prepared graphics do not automatically improve the effectiveness of data presentation. Business graphics are most effective for:

- Detecting patterns in data.
- Detecting trends or changes in trends.
- Identifying relationships.

They are least effective for:

- Determining the values of specific data points.
- Determining the absolute change in numeric values represented in trends.
- Representing a small amount of data (that is, a few data values).

Also keep in mind that the graphic chosen should be appropriate to the data it is illustrating. An unfamiliar form will confuse and irritate. For example, a business income statement, an income tax statement (in the United States), or a value-added tax statement (in Europe) in graphic form would be unfamiliar and probably unacceptable.

A picture (or a graph) is worth a thousand words, as the saying goes—but only if it has an immediate and positive impact. Lotus Corp. found this out the hard way when it introduced a program with only moderate graphics capabilities in Japan. For more details, see the Global IT box titled "Lotus 1-2-3: Meeting the Japanese Challenge" on page 205.

Generating Graphic Information with Spreadsheets

Users can generate graphic information with spreadsheet software quickly and easily because the software uses the values in the worksheet's rows and columns to generate the graphs. To create a graph, the user follows six steps:

1. Select the values to be graphed from the worksheet.
2. Activate the spreadsheet's graphing commands.
3. Select the type of graph desired.
4. Generate the graph.
5. Add descriptive information to the graph.
6. Store or print the graph.

Suppose that the Marietta Sports Complex's managers are interested in preparing a graphic to show the complex's proportion of revenues relative to expenses. In this case, a bar chart comparing revenue and expenses for each category (tickets, games, shows, food, and beverage) seems appropriate. To create the graphics the manager highlights the revenue and expense rows and the column headings for each category. She then selects a side-by-side bar chart from the list of graphics options. Finally, she adds the headings and annotations after the computer has drawn the graph. The result is shown in Figure 5.12.

A pie chart may also be a useful graphic for illustrating the proportion of profit to expense. The values in column G, rows 5 and 6 of Figure 5.4 describe total expenses and profits respectively. The resulting pie chart drawn from these data is shown in Figure 5.13.

Figure 5.14 on page 204 offers some tips for preparing a spreadsheet report with business graphics.

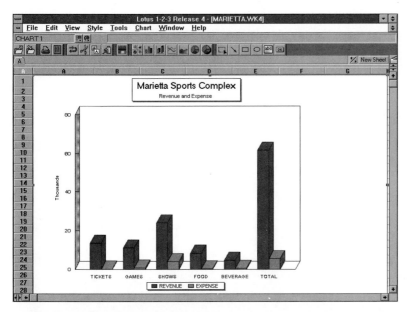

FIGURE 5.12
Bar Chart Generated from Worksheet Data
The spreadsheet program created this bar chart automatically from the data in Figure 5.4.

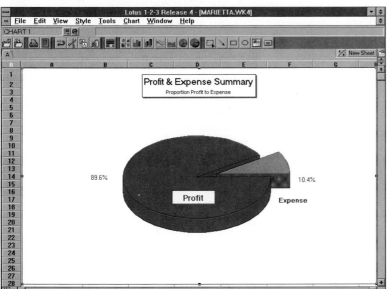

FIGURE 5.13
Pie Chart Generated from Worksheet Data
The spreadsheet program created this summary pie chart automatically from the data in Figure 5.4.

Developing a Personal Spreadsheet Application

If you're setting up a spreadsheet to do a few quick calculations or some preliminary planning, you can be fairly casual in the way you label rows and columns and enter formulas. But the value of spreadsheet software is that it helps you solve recurring problems. That's why the businesspeople who build, use, and share spreadsheets on a daily basis follow a more formal process in setting up and documenting their spreadsheets. This problem solving process has several advantages:

• It helps you think through a problem and identify the inputs, outputs, assumptions, and formulas needed to devise a solution.

GLOBAL IT

Lotus 1-2-3: Meeting the Japanese Challenge

FOR SEVERAL YEARS, LOTUS 1-2-3 WAS THE MOST POPULAR spreadsheet for IBM-compatible PCs in the United States. So it's not surprising that, by 1984, Lotus was looking to conquer the rest of the world. Gaining a foothold in Europe was relatively easy. But Lotus faced both technical and cultural barriers in Japan. The challenges it faced—and the solutions it found—offer valuable lessons for any business that wants to be a player in the global economy.

Challenge: *Understanding the Japanese business market and its expectations for software.*

Solution: *Form a lasting relationship with local experts.* Lotus realized fairly early that it needed some insight into the Japanese software market. One of the company's advantages here was its president, Jim Manzi, who had spent two years in Japan as a management consultant. Another advantage was the two years the Lotus development team spent working with SoftBank, Japan's largest software distributor. SoftBank taught Lotus that it had to make 1-2-3 much easier to use and improve the business graphics dramatically if it wanted success in Japan.

Challenge: *Making Lotus user-friendly when your users aren't accustomed to using a keyboard.* The standard QWERTY keyboard is a fixture in U.S. offices, and most high-school graduates have mastered it. Not so in Japan. The main problem here stems from trying to fit almost 2,000 Japanese *kanji* and *kana* characters—as well as Latin, Greek, and Cyrillic characters—onto a keyboard with a limited number of keys.

Solution: *Delegate the challenge to local experts.* Lotus formed a technical partnership with Kanri Kogaku Kenkyusho (K3), a Japanese software house. K3 wrote a pop-up program that can transform phonetic phrases, typed in the Latin alphabet, into the proper *kanji-kana* characters onscreen. K3 also helped create Japanese-language menus, help screens, and manuals; a Japanese learn mode; an electronic tutorial in Japanese; and built-in formulas and chart types customized to Japanese needs.

Challenge: *Meeting Japanese standards for graphics.* Japanese consumers, accustomed to the sophisticated graphics of Japanese computer games, were decidedly unimpressed by the crude graphics created by early versions of Lotus 1-2-3.

Solution: *Jump-start your product development to meet local standards.* The Japanese version of Lotus impressed potential customers by offering eight types of grid lines in its graphs, user-selectable onscreen colors, and other high-quality graphing functions. Many of these same fea-

Lotus 1-2-3 rose to the Japanese challenge by customizing its electronic spreadsheet to the needs of its Japanese customers. Within a month of its release, the program was number one on the Japanese software best sellers list.

tures were later incorporated in the next update of Lotus 1-2-3 for the United States.

Challenge: *Winning acceptance in a market that is attuned to buying Japanese products.*

Solution: *Ask consumers and local experts how buying decisions are made.* When the Lotus team asked about the consumer decision making process, it learned that Japanese consumers often base their buying decisions on the number of how-to books that are available for a particular package. Lotus responded by hiring eight authors to write Japanese-language books on Lotus 1-2-3. The books were printed and stocked in bookstores before the software began shipping.

Lotus also mounted an advertising campaign on Japan's crowded subways, a tactic no other software company had tried. As a result, millions of consumers were exposed to the Lotus name.

The happy ending: Within a month of its release, the Japanese version of 1-2-3 was at the top of the sales chart and stayed there for the rest of the year. At year's end, it received the Software of the Year award from *Nikkei PC* magazine. To celebrate its success, Lotus bought a full-page advertisement in *Nihon Keizai Shimbun*, the Japanese equivalent of *The Wall Street Journal*. Its subject? A very humble and Japanese thank-you and salute to the consumers who had made Lotus 1-2-3 Japan's favorite spreadsheet software.

Source: Carol Ellison, "Why Japan Can't Write Software" and "Selling 1-2-3 in Japan," *PC Computing*, December 1988, pp. 110–122. Copyright ©1988, Ziff-Davis Publishing Company, L.P.

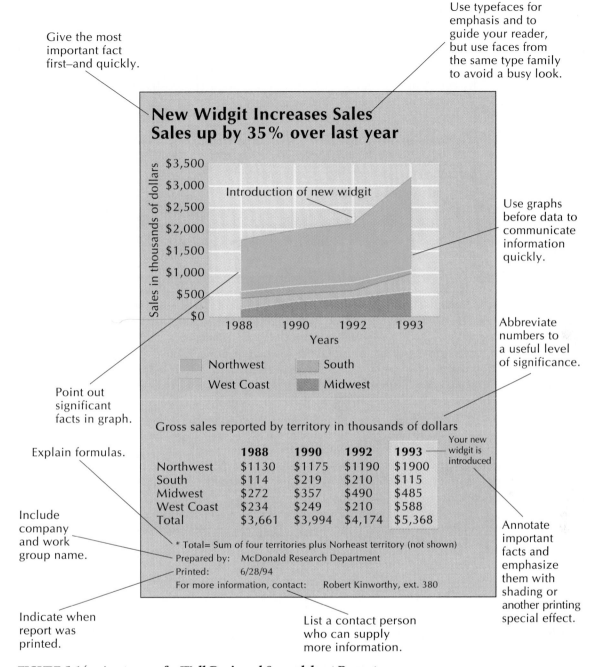

Give the most important fact first–and quickly.

Use typefaces for emphasis and to guide your reader, but use faces from the same type family to avoid a busy look.

Point out significant facts in graph.

Use graphs before data to communicate information quickly.

Abbreviate numbers to a useful level of significance.

Explain formulas.

Include company and work group name.

Annotate important facts and emphasize them with shading or another printing special effect.

Indicate when report was printed.

List a contact person who can supply more information.

**New Widgit Increases Sales
Sales up by 35% over last year**

Introduction of new widgit

Sales in thousands of dollars

$3,500
$3,000
$2,500
$2,000
$1,500
$1,000
$500
$0

1988   1990   1992   1993

Years

Northwest   South
West Coast   Midwest

Gross sales reported by territory in thousands of dollars

Your new widgit is introduced

	1988	1990	1992	1993
Northwest	$1130	$1175	$1190	$1900
South	$114	$219	$210	$115
Midwest	$272	$357	$490	$485
West Coast	$234	$249	$210	$588
Total	$3,661	$3,994	$4,174	$5,368

* Total= Sum of four territories plus Norheast territory (not shown)
Prepared by: McDonald Research Department
Printed: 6/28/94
For more information, contact: Robert Kinworthy, ext. 380

FIGURE 5.14   Anatomy of a Well-Designed Spreadsheet Report
A well-designed spreadsheet report should be informative and easy to read.
Source: Daniel Gasteiger, "The Outs of Spreadsheet Power," *PC/Computing*, June 1990, p. 110.
Copyright © 1990, Ziff-Davis Publishing Company, L.P.

- It helps you remember the assumptions and formulas you used in building the spreadsheet.
- It helps you find your way around a large spreadsheet with many rows, columns, and links to other spreadsheets.
- It lets you create instructions and documentation that will help others use your spreadsheet for their own work.
- It gives you—and others—an opportunity to evaluate your logic and to test your spreadsheet with simple data before you begin to use it or share it with others.

- It creates a more flexible spreadsheet that is easy to revise and adapt to different circumstances.

The problem solving process of developing a spreadsheet application can be divided into four basic steps (Figure 5.15):

1. Define the problem.
2. Plan the spreadsheet's layout.
3. Enter the spreadsheet into your computer.
4. Test and use the spreadsheet.

To give you a better idea of how this process works in practice, let's look at how you might use it to solve a problem in your own business, The ShirtWorks.

The ShirtWorks Problem

You created The ShirtWorks almost by accident, after some volunteer committee work made you an expert on working with the wholesalers, artists, and printers needed to produce T-shirts imprinted with the names and slogans of campus groups. Now, after reading that the average American buys about eight printed T-shirts a year,[1] you've decided to widen the scope of your business.

Your current system is as follows. After speaking to a potential customer about the group's T-shirt needs, you draw up an estimate that reflects the cost of the blank shirts, shipping, and printing; a markup (or profit); and, in some cases, the cost of artwork you've commissioned from a graphic artist. If the customer likes your ideas and your price, you ask for a 50% deposit, which gives you the money to order the T-shirts and begin the manufacturing process. You work directly with the suppliers and the printer and collect the balance due when you deliver the finished shirts to your customer.

Like many small business owners, you've been running the business out of a spare bedroom on a part-time basis, figuring your prices by using a calculator and

[1]Zorn, Eric, "Just What We All Need: New T-Shirt," *The Chicago Tribune*, June 8, 1993.

FIGURE 5.15
Developing a Spreadsheet Application, Step by Step
Each phase of spreadsheet application development requires the designer to answer several key questions.

Step	Key Questions to Answer
1. Define the problem.	What is the spreadsheet's purpose? What are the desired outputs? What inputs can be changed? What assumptions will be used in your calculations? What formulas will be used to calculate the desired outputs?
2. Plan the spreadsheet's layout.	How will you organize labels, data, formulas, and other instructions for maximum efficiency, clarity, and flexibility?
3. Enter the spreadsheet layout into your computer.	What commands are needed to enter, edit, and store values, labels, formulas and functions in the desired layout?
4. Test and use the spreadsheet.	Does the spreadsheet produce accurate results when sample data are entered?

handwritten notes on a scratchpad. You think you have been doing fairly well. Now, you are receiving a growing number of inquiries from the representatives of local businesses, sports teams, theater groups, and music groups who like to use custom-printed T-shirts for promotions and advertising.

Clearly, it is time to take The ShirtWorks more seriously. You attend a seminar on price setting, only to come away with a sinking feeling. It turns out that your prices are the lowest around; too low, in fact, to cover your expenses and leave an adequate profit. Your worries are confirmed when you go to the library and find an article, "Starting a T-Shirt Business," by Spider, who runs a T-shirt business called Spider & Co. with his wife from their home in Mesa, Arizona.[2] An artist, printer, lecturer, and consultant with 35 years' experience in the T-shirt business, Spider warns that "improper pricing can drive newcomers out of business before they really get going." Now you'd like to use your Macintosh computer and Microsoft Excel software to develop a spreadsheet application that will incorporate all the professional advice you've been gathering. Before you turn on your computer, though, you need to do some preliminary planning.

Step 1: Define the Problem

Before you can set up a spreadsheet, you need to define the problem you are trying to solve and your requirements. To do this, you need to decide on the spreadsheet's purpose, its desired outputs, and the inputs, assumptions, and formulas needed to produce these outputs. If you were developing a spreadsheet for other people, you would need to spend some time talking to them, helping them to define their problem.

Because you have lived with The ShirtWorks' pricing problem for a while, though, you find it fairly easy to define the problem and the spreadsheet's purpose. The problem: Your prices are too low and you are not making sufficient profit.

The Spreadsheet's Purpose.   It is not hard for you to decide on the spreadsheet's purpose. After some thought, you decide your goal is to automate the process of setting customer prices, calculating the deposit required with an order, and preparing an order form.

The Desired Outputs.   You want the spreadsheet to produce four outputs:

1. A *wholesale cost* that reflects your cost of goods (the price you pay for blank T-shirts, shipping, and printing) and a markup (to represent your profit).
2. A *wholesale price* that reflects your wholesale cost plus overhead costs (the money you spend on business-related rent, utilities, telephone, and automobile expenses).
3. A *total order price* that includes the wholesale price of the printed T-shirts plus any charges and commissions on original artwork.
4. The *deposit* required before you will accept the order.

The Necessary Inputs.   The inputs into the spreadsheet are the values that can vary from time to time and affect the outputs produced by the spreadsheet. These include:

1. The cost of the blank T-shirts.
2. The shipping cost charged by the blank T-shirt supplier.
3. The cost for printing.

[2]Spider, "Running a T-Shirt Business," *Home Office Computing*, November 1992, pp. 46–47.

4. The markup, expressed as a percentage of the T-shirt's wholesale cost.
5. Monthly overhead costs.
6. The fee charged by a graphic artist.
7. The commission you charge on artwork, expressed as a percentage of the price of the artwork.

The Basic Assumptions.   A few basic assumptions will simplify your calculations and affect the figures you show your customers.

1. The minimum order size allowed by both T-shirt suppliers and printers is one gross (12 dozen, or 144) shirts; orders must be placed in multiples of one gross. You will pass this requirement onto your customers.
2. To simplify calculations and presentations to customers, printed T-shirt prices will be expressed per unit, or shirt.
3. The cost of blank T-shirts and shipping costs will come from the supplier's latest catalog.
4. Overhead costs per shirt will be based on the assumption that only one order of 144 shirts will be processed per week.
5. The cost of original artwork will vary; it will be billed along with your commission directly to the customer.

The Formulas Used.   The formulas you embed in your spreadsheet will determine the accuracy of all the spreadsheet's calculations. That's why you need to state them, using business terms like "markup," in a mathematical format that you will convert into spreadsheet formulas. These statements allow you to evaluate your reasoning and find any errors in logic. As you think through the problem, you realize you'll need a number of formulas for your spreadsheet. The key formulas for the ShirtWorks' spreadsheet are listed in Table 5.5.

This kind of painstaking analysis may seem like a waste of energy for such a relatively simple problem. But you will appreciate it six months from now, when you need to consider the effect of a rent increase on overhead costs or reexamine the assumptions you used to set a minimum order size. Think, too, about the number of assumptions and input values you needed to solve this relatively simple problem. Then imagine the number of assumptions, data values, and formulas you would need to handle a larger, more complex spreadsheet. Could you or your coworkers remember them from week to week without some sort of memory aid?

TABLE 5.5   Formulas Used in The ShirtWorks Pricing Worksheet

Unit Cost	= Cost per Gross
Unit Cost of Goods	= Unit Cost of Shirt + Unit Cost of Shipping + Unit Cost of Printing
Markup per Unit	= Unit Cost of Goods × Markup Percentage
Wholesale Unit Cost	= Unit Cost of Goods + Markup
Wholesale Unit Price	= Unit Cost of Goods + Unit Cost of Overhead
Monthly Overhead Costs	= (One Year's Business-Related Rent + Business-Related Utilities + Business-Related Telephone Expenses + Business-Related Car Expenses) ÷ 12
Artwork	= Artist's Fees × (1 + Your Commission)
Total Order Price	= (Wholesale Unit Price × Quantity Ordered) + Artwork
Deposit Required	= Total Order Price × .5

Important: All formulas to be used in the spreadsheet should be checked for accuracy before they are embedded in the spreadsheet. The formulas here use × for multiplication and ÷ for division; these will need to be converted to "*" and "/" when the formulas are embedded in the worksheet.

Step 2: Plan the Spreadsheet's Layout

After you've defined the problem, you need to plan your spreadsheet's layout in a way that will be clear to you and others. Although there is no right or wrong way to lay out your spreadsheet, it is helpful to follow some general guidelines. One guideline mandated by all the experts: Don't be afraid to underestimate your own memory or the knowledge of others who will be using your spreadsheet. Another guideline: Divide your spreadsheet into six sections: a title page, user instructions, the input information area, the calculations area, a scratch area, and a summary. These can be six sections of a large spreadsheet, or six linked spreadsheets (Figure 5.16).

The Title Page.   Like the title page of a book, the title page of a spreadsheet includes important information. This information, shown in Figure 5.16, includes:

- The computer file name and an expanded spreadsheet name. If you were working on an IBM-compatible PC, your file name would be limited to eight characters. This restriction sometimes leads to creative but cryptic file names. You are working on the Macintosh, though, and the Macintosh operating system lets file names be as long as 32 characters. As a result, there is no difference between your Macintosh file name and the application name, so the title page shows only the file name.
- A statement of the spreadsheet's purpose. (You can pick this up from the problem definition.)
- The name, title, and affiliation of the person preparing the spreadsheet. This may seem like overkill for a one-person business like The ShirtWorks, but it is

FIGURE 5.16   A Guide to the Well-Designed Spreadsheet
Well-designed spreadsheet applications have six district areas: a title page, user instructions, an input information area, a calculation area, a scratch area, and a summary.

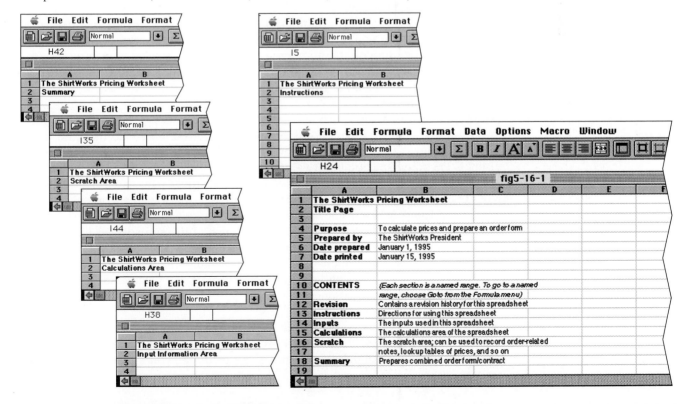

vital in larger businesses, where people routinely share spreadsheet applications developed by others. Entering the application developer's name here gives other users a person to call with their questions or comments.

- The date this application is developed.
- The date this report is printed.
- A table of contents, or *map*, showing the file's major divisions. This feature helps readers move around the spreadsheet quickly and easily. You can key the map to specific ranges of cells (B22:H22, for example), or you can assign the range a descriptive and easy-to-remember name, such as January Sales. The map shown on the title page in Figure 5.16 uses range names. To move around the spreadsheet, users simply call up the Goto command and type in the range name.

Note that the first entry in the map refers the user to a *revision history*, a table of who revised the spreadsheet, what was revised, and when. As the ShirtWorks grows, for example, you might decide to hire salespeople to work on commission. This decision would force you to revise the spreadsheet to include this cost in your calculations.

User Instructions.   This section of the spreadsheet includes step-by-step guidelines for entering data and using the results of calculations. Often, the instructions section will end with directions for using a macro to print the instructions on paper. Having the instructions on paper is a comfort to inexperienced users. It also saves time for users who have moved on to other sections and need to review the instructions from time to time.

The Input Information Area.   This section incorporates the input information you generated in Step 1 into your spreadsheet file. Including this information here has one major benefit: It identifies the inputs that will be used in the formulas in the calculations area. The data values for these inputs can be changed at will, allowing you to perform what-if analyses (for example, "What happens if I increase markup to 50 percent?").

If your spreadsheet uses a number of macros, you should group an explanation of them somewhere within the spreadsheet, showing the keystrokes used to activate each. Depending on the number and type of macros used, you can place this explanation in this section or at the top of the calculations section. Both locations will make the macros easy to find and revise.

The Calculations Area.   This section of the spreadsheet is reserved for a table of formulas that will produce the answers you need. You'll want to use care in the way you enter your formulas. A common mistake made by beginning spreadsheet users is encoding specific input values into the formulas contained in the calculations area. This shortcut hides some of your input values—for example, the size of your commission—when the spreadsheet is printed. It also defeats one of the main benefits of using an electronic spreadsheet—the power to change one number and let the spreadsheet calculate the effect on the rest of the spreadsheet numbers. To see the drawbacks of this shortcut, look at Figure 5.17, where the markup is entered as 50%. What happens if you want to change the markup? You will need to go into the spreadsheet and change several formulas by hand—a time-consuming and potentially error-producing task.

Scratch Area.   Just as you use scratch paper when you are working with paper and pencil, you can use the spreadsheet's scratch area for any intermediate calculations or notes you might want to make. For example, you might use this area to

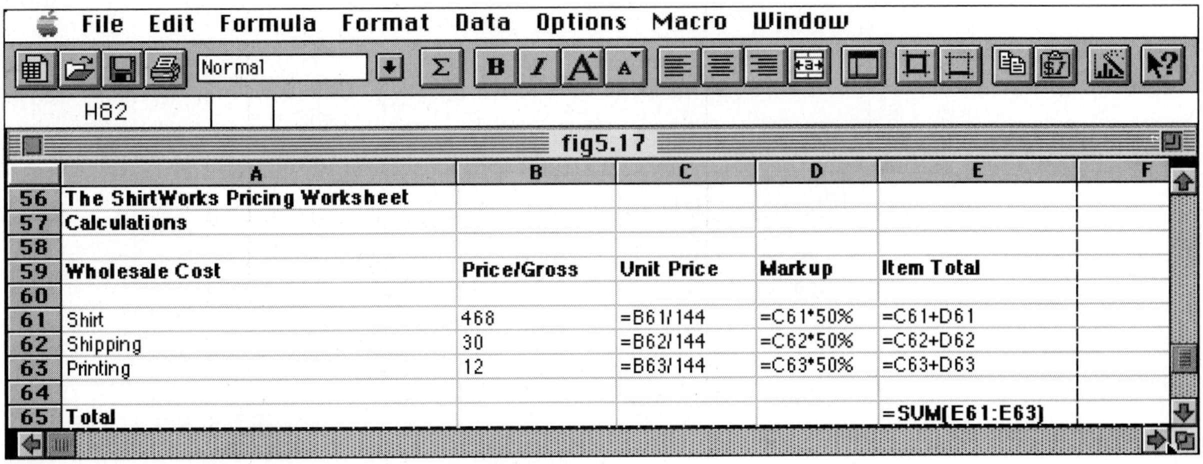

```
 🍎  File  Edit  Formula  Format  Data  Options  Macro  Window
┌────────────────────────────────────────────────────────────────────────────┐
│ [▦][🖿][🖫][🖶] │Normal        │[▼] │Σ│[B][I][A][A]│[≡][≡][≡][⊞]│[▢][▢][▢]│[🖻][💲][📊][▶?]│
├────────────────────────────────────────────────────────────────────────────┤
│   H82  │              │                                                      │
└────────────────────────────────────────────────────────────────────────────┘
```

	A	B	C	D	E	F
56	The ShirtWorks Pricing Worksheet					
57	Calculations					
58						
59	Wholesale Cost	Price/Gross	Unit Price	Markup	Item Total	
60						
61	Shirt	468	=B61/144	=C61*50%	=C61+D61	
62	Shipping	30	=B62/144	=C62*50%	=C62+D62	
63	Printing	12	=B63/144	=C63*50%	=C63+D63	
64						
65	Total				=SUM(E61:E63)	

FIGURE 5.17   Improper Calculations Area Design
The calculations area should include formulas only, not specific input values like "50%".

record details of orders (color, size, and quantities ordered, say). Or you might calculate your estimated profit on the order as part of a quick tax-planning session. Or you might create a table of shirt or shipping costs so that you don't have to stop your work at the computer to search through a paper catalog.

You can also use the scratch area to create summary tables that group selected rows or columns from the calculations area. This capability is useful for spreadsheet packages that can create spreadsheet graphics only from rows and columns that are next to each other.

Summary.   The summary section of the spreadsheet is generally used to create a summary table or business graphic illustrating the solution created by the spreadsheet. But you can also use this section to create an entirely different table, form, or report for your business. Consider your problem at The ShirtWorks. Calculating a price for your shirts is just one issue. You also need to summarize the price estimate and present it to your customers, along with the details of their order and the deposit they need to give you before you accept their order. Figure 5.18 on the next page shows how you could use the summary section to create an order form summarizing the order, the price, and the terms of a contract you will ask your customers to sign. Data from your spreadsheets can be automatically entered into this form.

Step 3: Enter the Spreadsheet Into Your Computer

It may seem natural to plan some of the spreadsheet's layout as you sit at the computer. After all, it is often hard to estimate how much you can fit on a computer screen when you are working with paper and pencil. If you haven't entered your layout or if you've begun the process but need to finish it, you need to do so. When you have completed entering the spreadsheet layout, you should save it as a template or blank form ready for the entry of particular data values.

Step 4: Test and Use the Spreadsheet

The final step in developing a spreadsheet application is creating or collecting test data, then loading the data into your spreadsheet to see if it calculates the correct

THE

SHIRT 👕 **WORKS**

ORDER FORM

Date			
Customer Name		**Address**	**Telephone**
Organization		Street	Day
Contact		City/State/Zip	Evening

Description of Order

Shirt Type	Size	Quantity (Dozens) (Minimum Total Order: 12 Dozen)
Color 1	Small Medium Large X-Large	
Color 2	Small Medium Large X-Large	
Color 3	Small Medium Large X-Large	
Printing color(s) and location		
Source of artwork (attach sketch)		

Pricing Summary

Quantity Shirts Ordered x Unit Price (Minimum Order: 12 dozen or 144 shirts)	Customer Pays
Artwork	
TOTAL	
DEPOSIT REQUIRED (Balance due on delivery)	

Customer Signature _____ Date _____

FIGURE 5.18   Order Form Created for Summary Area
The summary area of the spreadsheet may contain a special form designed to summarize the details of a transaction.

answers. You might draw your data from examples given in the pricing seminar or the magazine article written by the T-shirt expert, or you might collect simple representative data from your own files. At the minimum, you should construct three sets of data. Because you will be trusting this spreadsheet with your business's lifeblood—its prices—you may want to test more than three samples, looking for formulas that produce inaccurate answers.

As you complete each test, print a copy of the spreadsheet that shows the input values and results. These results will become an important part of your records. Having paper-based proof that the spreadsheet worked at one time will help you find errors introduced during future revisions.

When you have completed testing to your satisfaction, you may begin entering real data into the spreadsheet.

CRITICAL CONNECTION 3
Compilers at First Mutual Multiply Spreadsheet Power at a Fraction of the Cost

First Mutual of Boston

How do you let all your employees use a spreadsheet without buying them their own copies of a package like Lotus 1-2-3? How can you be sure they know how to use a certain spreadsheet, unless you send them to training classes? And once you get the software installed and the employees trained, how can you be sure they are all using the same format, as well as the same assumptions and formulas, in creating their spreadsheets?

These were the questions facing First Mutual of Boston, which needed to find a way to let department heads prepare annual entries for a general ledger based on Lotus 1-2-3 spreadsheets. The solution was to buy a compiler. A *compiler* is a special type of computer program that transforms one type of computer input, such as a Lotus 1-2-3 template or spreadsheet, into a stand-alone program called a *run-time program*. Most spreadsheet compilers also include special macros and commands for changing the screen's color scheme, adding context-sensitive help screens, and preparing business graphics.

The run-time version of the program can be distributed and used by persons who do not have the spreadsheet program. Users cannot change the run-time program or perform any action not embedded in the run-time version. First Mutual estimates that the compiler saved the bank thousands of dollars in direct costs, simply because it eliminated the need to buy multiple copies of the software. More importantly, First Mutual can be sure that all department heads are using the same format, formulas, and assumptions to prepare their annual budget figures.

◼ A Final Word

We should close on a cautionary note. The integration of calculating, charting, and editing features in spreadsheet software has changed the way people solve problems. The spreadsheets' potential for improving people's productivity and effectiveness is substantial. However, like all aspects of information technology, the benefits provided by these tools are only as good as the people who use them. Productivity tools will never replace people—they can only help make them better.

SUMMARY OF LEARNING OBJECTIVES

1 **Describe the principle function of spreadsheets and why they are used in business.** Spreadsheets help planners and analysts organize their work and structure the numeric details of their projects. Spreadsheets are used in business to automate record keeping, to summarize raw data and to perform analysis and improve planning, to simplify the control process, to improve communication and motivation, and to help managers make decisions.

2 **Identify the elements found on an electronic spreadsheet display.** The spreadsheet display contains two distinct areas: the *window* and the *control panel*.

The window contains the *worksheet area*—the rectangular grid of *rows* and *columns* that comprise the worksheet. The intersection of a row and a column is called a *cell*.

The control panel, located at the top section of the spreadsheet screen, consists of: (1) the *title bar*, which includes the program name and sometimes the file name; the *menu bar*, which contains spreadsheet commands for creating, storing, retrieving, and editing files and worksheets; the *content line*, which contains the cell address and data or information entered into the active cell; and the *icon bar*, which contains small pictures (icons) used to represent frequently used commands in the menu bar.

3 **Describe the four types of data created and stored in spreadsheet programs and differentiate between functions and formulas, describing the benefits of each in creating worksheets for problem solving.** A spreadsheet cell can hold any of four different pieces of information: values, labels, formulas, or functions. A *value* is a number that is entered into a cell. It may be an integer, a decimal number, or a number in scientific format. A *label* is a piece of descriptive information pertaining to a row or column. A *formula* is an instruction describing how a specific computation should be performed. A *function* is a formula built into the spreadsheet software that will automatically perform certain types of calculation. Formulas and functions are often used to create worksheets to solve problems.

4 **Summarize the capabilities offered by spreadsheet programs for changing and refining worksheets after data have been entered.** A spreadsheet's editing capabilities allow the user to change, add, and delete data; insert and delete rows and columns; copy, move, find, and sort data; freeze row and column headings; adjust column width; and undo actions. The spreadsheet program will automatically recalculate or adjust all data that have been affected by these changes.

5 **Discuss the uses of spreadsheet programs in sensitivity analysis and data linkage.** Perhaps the most valuable feature of electronic spreadsheets is their ability to perform *sensitivity analysis*, in which the computer determines what would happen if certain data change. All spreadsheet packages allow users to create individual worksheets to deal with each part of a problem. Most also provide a linkage capability that allows the user to interconnect the separate worksheets and even to transfer information between them. The linkage feature allows the problem solver to evaluate relationships and the effects of changing data.

6 **Explain the types of business graphics usually included with spreadsheet programs, when each is used, and how worksheet contents are transformed into business graphics.** *Business graphics* present information visually through charts, graphics, and symbols. They are an effective supplement for tables of numeric details. Five types of business graphics are usually included in spreadsheet software: *Bar charts* consist of a series of bars, each representing a particular element in the worksheet. The length of a bar represents the value of the data. *Pie charts* show the proportion or percentage of the whole represented by each element. *Area line graphs* use lines that arre "stacked" or combined to show the total in each category. *Line charts* plot changes in data values over time and connect these points by a line. *Pictograms* depict data using icons or symbols that represent the magnitude of the data values.

Six steps are involved in creating business graphics from a spreadsheet program: (1) select the value to be graphed from the worksheet; (2) activate the spreadsheet's graphing commands; (3) select the type of graph desired; (4) generate the graph; (5) add descriptive information; and (6) store or print the graph.

7 **Discuss the four steps involved in developing a personal spreadsheet application.** The four steps involved in developing a spreadsheet are: (1) define the problem; (2) plan the spreadsheet layout; (3) enter the spreadsheet into the computer; and (4) test and use the spreadsheet.

KEY TERMS

CRITICAL CONNECTIONS

Donald H.Kraft & Associates

1.   Kraft & Associates Create Spreadsheet Magic*

On a typical project, Donald Kraft begins by meeting with clients and asking many, many questions. What do they need to do? How much do the end users already know about spreadsheets? What is their deadline? "Often, I don't know what I don't know about a job until I am alone in front of my computer and I start designing a spreadsheet," says Kraft. "I usually make another list of the questions and go back to the client a second time."

Once the project's goal and scope are clear, Kraft settles into his office and starts to work. Drawing on his 23 years' experience with IBM, he uses professional programming techniques to plan and structure his work. Then he begins to write macros to perform certain procedures or tasks. On one of his projects, a data analysis worksheet for a major pharmaceutical company, Kraft says, it took exactly 999 lines to record the macros.

To make the macros easy to find and use, Kraft may show them as new entries on the standard pull-down menus of Lotus 1-2-3 for Windows. Or he may create an entirely new menu that groups all the macros in one place. He can even replace the standard menu bar with one that has been customized for his client. Kraft can also create customized dialog boxes, information boxes, and on-screen color-coded annotations to guide users. As a finishing touch, Kraft uses his flatbed scanner to capture the client's logo, displaying it on the opening screen and on printed reports. Once he has tested and debugged the spreadsheet using sample data, he finalizes the spreadsheet's documentation, providing training and ongoing support as needed.

"Most of the people I've worked with have been incredibly sharp," says Kraft. "But in almost every case I found that they were doing too many tasks by hand, instead of letting the spreadsheet work for them."

Questions for Discussion

1. Why do you think Kraft spends so much time talking to his clients before he begins to create the spreadsheet?

2. It's Kraft's business to make spreadsheets that let people perform complex tasks easily and quickly. Nevertheless, he still feels that even casual end-users need to understand spreadsheet software and how it works. Why do you think he believes this?

3. Kraft says that his most challenging assignments occur when he is hired to revise a spreadsheet application that has been created and modified by individuals who are not familiar with the practices used by IT professionals. What types of challenges might arise as a result?

*Source: Personal interview with Kraft.

Harry's Restaurant

2.   Spreadsheets Mimic the Power of Expensive Menu-Costing Programs

Calculating the gross profit generated by each entree in a restaurant is an enormous help to the restaurant owner. But the real beauty of the SMCS is the way it helps the owner take control of the business's financial future.

Take, for instance, the industry's basic rule of thumb: Food costs (including the cost of beverages and desserts) should be no more than 32% of total costs (including staff and other overhead costs). If the restaurant's food costs are falling outside this guideline, it would be a simple matter to look at the column showing total entree costs as a percentage of selling price. Cells with high values here might indicate a problem—either food costs are too high or the selling price is too low. To fix the problem, all the owner has to do is change either costs or selling price and let the spreadsheet recalculate the results. With this kind of power, it is easy to explore the effect of increased costs and make sure costs and profit margins are on target.

Questions for Discussion

1. Explain how you could use the SMCS to set the selling price of a daily special created to take advantage of a seasonal bargain on scallops.

2. Restaurants are often said to "make their money" on beverages and desserts. How could you use a spreadsheet to calculate the profit on these menu items? How would this information help a restaurant owner evaluate the results produced by the SMCS for entrees?

3. What special management challenges face the small restaurant owner? How could the SMCS help the small restaurant owner meet these challenges? Explain your answer.

First Mutual of Boston

3. Compilers at First Mutual Multiply Spreadsheet Power at a Fraction of the Cost

Saving money isn't the only advantage of using a spreadsheet compiler. The compiler also freezes and hides the formulas used within the spreadsheet. This has two advantages. First, it protects the spreadsheet from accidental changes that would throw off the calculations. Second, it hides the formulas and other information that help to create a unique application. The international accounting firm Arthur Andersen & Company, for example, used a compiler to hide the formulas and calculations used in a personal tax-planning template sold by the company.

Questions for Discussion

1. Managers often supervise employees with widely different computer skills. Some may know only one spreadsheet program; others will know little or nothing about using a computer. How could a spreadsheet compiler be of use in this situation, given a company-wide goal of computerizing most financial operations?

2. How does a spreadsheet compiler blur the line between IT user and programmer? What might this say about the future of the IT department?

3. John Finnan, the microcomputer resource consultant for the state of Washington's Department of Licensing, is also an amateur astronomer. As part of his hobby, he has developed a spreadsheet application that includes a database of eyepieces that can be purchased for telescopes. With the help of a compiler, Finnan intends to transform this spreadsheet application into a program he can sell to other amateur astronomers. What does his experience say about the benefits of learning to use a compiler?

REVIEW QUESTIONS

1. Describe the purpose of a spreadsheet. Does the purpose differ depending on whether the spreadsheet is created manually or through computer software?

2. What is an electronic spreadsheet program?

3. For what reasons do people use electronic spreadsheets in business?

4. What is the difference between a row, a column, and a cell?

5. What two areas comprise an electronic spreadsheet display?

6. Describe the contents of each line of the control panel.

7. What four types of information can a worksheet cell contain? Explain each type.

8. What does "data importing" mean?

9. Describe six data editing activities.

10. Describe the characteristics of a template. What benefits do templates provide to their users?

11. What is sensitivity analysis? What benefits does it offer?

12. Why is the capability to link spreadsheets useful in problem solving?

13. What benefits do business graphics offer?

14. What five types of business graphics are usually included with spreadsheet packages?

15. What four steps are involved in developing a spreadsheet application?

16. Define "model".

17. What six sections should a spreadsheet include?

18. What is the value of testing a spreadsheet before entering "real data" into it?

DISCUSSION QUESTIONS

1. Because their contracts call for payments that are tied to specific milestones, contractors who handle highway and other heavy construction often need help forecasting cash flow. How might such contractors use spreadsheets in their business?

2. In his book *The Education of David Stockton*, William Greider describes the way David Stockton, the director of U.S. President Reagan's Office of Management and Budget, used a spreadsheet to analyze the effects of the President's tax cuts. When the first try showed that the cuts would produce huge budget deficits (a politically undesirable answer), Stockton worked with the spreadsheet until it showed the "right" answer—a move that may have contributed to the large budget deficits of the 1980s. What ethical question does this example raise about the use of spreadsheets in business?

3. Leading financial consultants suggest that small business owners who want to computerize their finances use either a spreadsheet or a personal finance manager. (A personal finance manager, such as Quicken or Managing Your Money, is designed to handle routine financial matters, such as balancing a checkbook or tracking expenses for software.) Under what circumstances could a spreadsheet package be the better choice?

4. A leading consultant suggests that the "perfect" spreadsheet report begins with a business graphic. Why do you think he makes this recommendation? Do you agree or disagree?

SUGGESTED READINGS

Paller, A. T., "Improving Management Productivity with Computer Graphics," *IEEE Computer Graphics and Applications*, 1, no. 4 (October 1981), pp. 9–16. This article discusses the impact of graphics presentations on individual performance and emphasizes the difference that good business graphics can make on individual productivity.

Person, Ron, *Using Excel 4*. Indianapolis, IN: Que, 1992. This how-to book teaches the beginner the ins and outs of Microsoft's Excel spreadsheet package.

Robinson, Phillip, "Variations on a Screen," *Byte*, 14, no. 4 (April 1989), pp. 249–288. This article is one of a series in a special supplement on computer graphics. The supplement emphasizes the impact of computer hardware and software on the display of graphic information.

Using Lotus 1-2-3. Indianapolis, IN: Que, 1993. A good introduction to both the basic and advanced features of the Lotus 1-2-3 program. The book includes excellent illustrations of both personal and business uses of spreadsheet programs.

CASE STUDY

Start-Up Ad Agency Works by the Numbers

Horton Ahern Bousquet

IT SOUNDS LIKE AN AMERICAN fairy tale come true: Horton Ahern Bousquet, a small start-up ad agency in Providence, Rhode Island, brings in almost a quarter of a million dollars in its first year. Add the fact that the three founding partners (and only employees) fled the corporate world, though, and the tale takes on a decidedly modern twist. Another modern twist is the central role played by Macintosh computers and spreadsheet software in the firm's success. To understand the role of IT at HAB, let's go back to the agency's beginning.

First, there was John Horton, who left another ad agency shortly before it went bankrupt. Despite his fifteen years in marketing, public relations, and client management, Horton rejected the idea of going it alone as a consultant. "I knew my own strengths and knew I needed two other legs on the stool," says Horton, who founded HAB in 1990.

He found the other two legs in Tom Ahern and Lisa Bousquet, both of whom had strong backgrounds—and numerous contacts—in the health, education, and high-tech fields. An award-winning expert with a personal computer and Pagemaker desktop publishing software, Ahern had extensive experience in advertising and marketing. (In his most recent staff position, he had been manager of marketing promotion at GTECH, a company that runs state lotteries.) "I was in business for myself," he says, "but had reached my limit. I didn't know how to make a business grow." Ahern became the agency's creative director. Bousquet, meanwhile, had worked in both sales (for a pharmaceutical firm) and marketing (for a health-assessment facility) before leaving to have her first child. She became the agency's operations manager.

The agency's success is even more impressive when you realize how close it came to failing. After just two months, the partners got a rude surprise: they were all caught up on their work and didn't have any new business coming in. That's when the agency began to work by the rules on numbers.

- **Remember the 80/20 rule.** A common rule in sales holds that 20% of a business's customers will bring in 80% of its income. HAB used this rule to work backward from its basic goal: If it wanted to make $300,000 its first year, 20% of its clients would provide $240,000, while the other 80% of its customers would bring in $60,000.

Using price estimate based on their previous work experience, the partners translated this rule into new-business requirements. On average, they needed to develop one major new client every 1.5 months and pick up 2.6 minor new clients every month.

- **Spend 40% to 60% of your time looking for new business.** "At the basic level, getting new business is a numbers game. Everyone told us that and now we know it," says Ahern. Horton shoulders the heaviest burden here; he has a goal of making 40 sales calls each week. However, each partner is responsible for making five new contacts each week, and the agency has a goal of sending out at least one sales letter or promotional piece per day.

To help them meet these quotas, the partners loaded spreadsheet software onto their personal computers. Horton uses Excel to print out daily action lists, while Bousquet uses FileMaker Pro (a database package—discussed in the next chapter) and Excel to create time-management sheets summarizing the amount of time each partner spent on getting new business (as opposed to client-service or administrative tasks). Just one month after the new system was in place, new-business efforts averaged 31 percent. The next month, the agency hit its goal of 40 percent.

- **Focus your marketing energies on high-profit jobs.** The partners also used spreadsheet software to perform a monthly billing analysis for each job, showing the amount billed for marketing, public relations, and production services, as well as the direct costs billed to clients for printing and mailing direct-mail pieces and newsletters. Because these direct costs don't contribute to agency profits, the partners decided to focus on jobs with higher creative charges—and bigger profit margins.

Of course, making contacts would not help the agency win and keep clients if HAB didn't offer outstanding service. Just like the big ad agencies, HAB focuses on "relationship marketing," ensuring its staff listens to their clients' problems and presents clear but powerful solutions. A case in point: The first issue of the agency's promotional newsletter, *2nd Thoughts (300 seconds of reading to help you market better [Really!])*, netted them a new client who wanted "a newsletter just like that for myself." In fact, the agency uses everything from its stationery to follow-up sales letters to emphasize the benefits it offers. As one promotional piece reads, "Because our overhead is low, since we use computers for

When John Horton, Tom Ahern, and Lisa Bousquet started HAB, they thought of their agency as a fairly traditional one that would create and place ads. Now, because the market they've entered is made up primarily of companies that don't use traditional ad agencies, they think of themselves as problem solvers with a specialty in direct mail. "We solve problems with communications," says Ahern. "And direct response is the communications product of the moment."

much of our work, our rates are lower than those of comparable agencies—at least a third lower. Our standards are unreasonably lofty—our prices are not."

The partners also maintain and upgrade their skills continuously. The agency budgets $100 a month for business-related books, and the partners routinely attend small-business conferences and workshops on sales, marketing, and management. Ahern, the chief copywriter (and a professor of marketing and public relations at Brown University and the Rhode Island School of Design), even uses Grammatik, a grammar-checking program, to analyze his copy. If it has

too many sentences compared to prize-winning direct-mail pieces, he sits down at the computer and goes over the copy again—until the analysis produces acceptable results.

Questions for Discussion

1. Discuss the ways the partners at HAB are using spreadsheet software to manage their business.

2. How might the information provided by spreadsheets improve the services HAB offers?

Source: Based on Nick Sullivan, "From $0 to $200,000 in One Year Flat," *Home Office Computing,* February 1992, pp. 62–66.

Chapter Outline

CHAPTER 6

Database Applications for Personal Productivity

Learning Objectives

When you have completed this chapter, you should be able to:

1 Explain why businesses use databases.

2 Describe the main components of a database.

3 List and describe five objectives of database management systems.

4 Identify when a business should use a spreadsheet and when it should use a database.

5 Identify the seven-step sequence for developing database applications.

In Practice

After completing this chapter, you should be able to perform these activities:

1 Discuss with a systems analyst the way he develops a database application for an existing database.

2 Discuss with a database user the way she interacts with the database system or application.

3 Examine a situation in which data are collected and stored and determine the entities, data items, and groupings of data into records that would be most appropriate for the situation.

4 Specify the types of data items likely to be included in records of data for various business transactions.

5 Explain how problem solving and database design are interrelated.

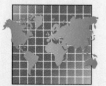

A Personal Problem

The solution to this problem may be a personal database customized to your needs.

Y OU CAN'T HAVE A SOCIAL OR BUSI-ness life without a personal telephone directory—a listing of the people you know or don't dare forget (they're not necessarily the same thing). But there's one problem. Few people, it seems, have just one directory.

If you're like most people, you probably have multiple telephone lists—the one you carry in your book bag or briefcase, another file (or pile) of business cards on your desk, and perhaps another that a spouse or assistant keeps. Then there's probably a telephone list you keep near the phone at home or at work. Are they all important? Yes. Do they contain the same information? Perhaps there is some overlap, but not always. Are they useful? Apparently so, or you wouldn't keep them around.

Just how did you end up with multiple phone lists? You probably started each one at a different time. One time you decided to get organized and created your personal telephone directory—the one you carry with you. But gradually another list sprang up as you jotted down frequently dialed numbers on a sheet of paper near the phone. (After all, you can't always have your master directory with you.) As you visited stores or talked with salespeople, job recruiters, or friends in business, you accumulated business cards containing names, addresses, telephone numbers, and fax numbers. You could have written all the cards' information into your directory and then tossed the cards, but you never did. Instead, the cards have piled up in your wallet or on your desk.

A quick check will probably reveal some information common to your multiple directories. The same names and telephone numbers often appear both in your personal directory and on your handwritten phone list. But there are likely to be some discrepancies also. A business card contains a telephone number different from the one in your personal directory. And then there's the telephone number of a close friend. You have called it so often that you remembered it easily and never wrote it down. But now it's been weeks since you and your friend have chatted...and your head is full of other important information. In other words, you've forgotten the telephone number. What do you do now? ◾

THIS CHAPTER WILL NOT SOLVE YOUR PERSONAL PHONE DIRECTORY PROBLEM—AT LEAST NOT directly. But it will provide a great deal of insight into the greater challenge of making important information available to you when you need it. Having this information available or on hand will help you capitalize on opportunities and solve problems. We begin by exploring the characteristics of personal database systems (first introduced in Chapter 2) and how they can be used to structure and organize data and information. We'll also discuss the steps involved in developing and using a database system.

◼ An Overview of Personal Database Systems

database A collection of data and information describing items of interest.

A **database** is a collection of data and information describing items of interest. Traditionally, the contents of the database have included text and numbers—hence the name *data*base. Increasingly, however, people and organizations are broadening their view of databases to include image, graphic, and voice information. For example:

- California's Division of Motor Vehicles maintains a computerized driver's license database that includes drivers' names, addresses, and personal attributes (height, weight, birth date, and so forth) along with a photograph of the person and an image of his or her signature. (For more on this database, see Critical Connection 1 in Chapter 10.)
- Many hospitals and medical centers, including Massachusetts General Hospital, the Mayo Clinic, and the Harvard Community Health Plan, have begun to maintain patient records in databases that include personal information, insurance and financial data, medical history, and medical images (such as x-rays and electrocardiograms).
- Manufacturing and service companies, such as IBM, Wal-Mart, and General Motors, are installing multimedia training systems that feature databases containing video clips, color slides, narrative (text) screens of information and instructions, self-test questions, and voice narrations. The training systems use all of the trainee's senses (with the possible exception of smell, and they're working on that too).

The point is clear. People collect data and information because they expect it to be useful later—whether to identify drivers, to diagnose and treat medical problems, or to train business associates. In other words, the subtle but important assumption underlying database creation is that data and information should be stored when they are expected to be useful in problem solving.

At one time, people focused primarily on storing data—numbers and text. However, with the advances in computers' storage capabilities, the contents of personal and organization databases have broadened. As a result, the terminology is gradually changing too. The term **information repository**, or simply **repository**, may soon replace database as the name of this information resource. (We'll stick with *database* in this chapter because it is still the most widely used. But *repository* is the term of the future.)

information repository or **repository** A synonym for database.

The Benefits of Databases in Business

Most of the databases you'll encounter in organizations will be large, multi-user systems developed and maintained by IT professionals. But a growing number of managers and staff members, as well as small business owners, are turning to smaller personal database systems as a way to boost their productivity. To understand this trend—and to get an idea of how a personal database might help you in business—consider some of these benefits.

Identifying and Structuring Data Needed to Solve Business Problems. Marketers need to analyze customer likes and dislikes; salespeople need to track sales calls and results; and accountants need to record key details about all business transactions. To meet these needs, managers must be familiar with the relationship between business events and their business goals. Then, they need to identify the resources that are necessary for people to be effective and efficient in reaching those goals.

Along with people, a business's most important resources are data and information. Developing a database system can help a business collect and structure these data. As you'll see later in this chapter, studying a business problem and identifying the users' data information requirements are the first two steps to developing any database.

During these steps, managers may even identify better ways to solve business problems. Perhaps certain procedures can be improved through IT, saving time and effort. Some process steps may be eliminated entirely. Many large corporations are overhauling their business procedures to weed out unnecessary steps. (We discuss this process, called *re-engineering*, in detail in Chapter 11.)

Collecting, Storing, Editing, and Updating Data.   Data and information are useless unless there is an effective system for collecting, storing, and retrieving them. These capabilities are especially important for businesses, which may need to manage a huge database of their customers, suppliers, or a mailing list for the quarterly catalog.

Database systems can help here in a number of ways. First, the database software used to create and maintain databases can be used to display a blank form on the computer screen. If users fill in all the blanks, they will have collected the "right" data. And, if users follow good procedures for saving and backing up their data, they can be reasonably sure the data are stored safely. Second, database software is especially designed to help users *manage* data. As you'll see a little later, database software functions include routines for editing, updating, and integrating databases; ensuring their accuracy; and protecting them from unauthorized users.

Retrieving and Sharing Data.   One of the most important benefits of a database is the ability to retrieve and share data. Data collected on sales, for example, can be organized and summarized into information useful for planning a marketing campaign or determining inventory levels.

In some cases, users or IT professionals will use the database software to create **database applications**, routines for collecting, retrieving, or manipulating data to meet recurring needs. A quarterly sales report, broken down by division or salesperson, is a typical result of a database application. Collecting new visitor information at a hotel or inn is another. The People box titled "Databases Support a Global Alliance" describes how a husband-and-wife team uses database software to manage their businesses on two continents.

database application A computerized database routine for collecting, retrieving, or manipulating data to meet recurring needs.

query A question to be answered by accessing the data in a database.

In other cases, individuals meet short-term or pressing needs by posing **queries**, questions to be answered by accessing the data in a database. There are three general techniques for querying a database system.

- *Menus.* The simplest, but least flexible, technique displays menus that guide users through the query process.
- *QBE.* Short for **query by example, QBE** shows users a blank table that reflects the database's underlying structure. To form a query, users fill in the appropriate blanks with either simple commands or conditions. (Look ahead to Figure 6.13 if you'd like to see an example.) QBE is easy to learn and use.
- *Query Languages.* A **query language** is a specialized computer language that forms database queries from a limited number of words (such as SELECT, FROM, and WHERE) that are combined according to specific rules. The languages themselves are fairly simple and can be used to create flexible and powerful queries. The most widely used query language is **SQL**, short for **structured query language**.

query by example (QBE) A query format in which the user fills in the blanks with simple commands or conditions.

query language A computer language that forms database queries from a limited number of words.

structured query language (SQL) The most widely used query language.

PEOPLE

Databases Support a Global Alliance

Odile Rousseau, shown here with her daughter Sophie, spends her summers running a guest house in the ruins of a medieval French abbey (background). Rousseau's husband, Brian Wood, is a New York City-based painter. Information technology allows the couple to lead a seasonal lifestyle— New York in the winter, France in the summer.

BRIAN WOOD AND ODILE ROUSSEAU ARE LIVING A GLOBAL alliance. During the winter, they and their four-year-old daughter Sophie share a loft in New York City's Chelsea neighborhood, where he sells his paintings to fashionable art galleries. Come spring, the family jets off to France's Loire Valley, where he paints and she runs an exclusive guest house built into the ruins of a medieval abbey. And they owe it all to shared goals and personal databases.

His database contains all the records he needs to treat his art as a business—a mailing list of collectors, galleries, and museums, as well as a schedule of his exhibitions. Her database contains a list of past and potential clients, as well as reservation records for the abbey—maintained with the help of an assistant in France, who stays in touch by phone and fax.

Although Rousseau mails out brochures and advertises in *The New York Times*, much of her business comes through word of mouth. Wood says, "It's a wonderful place, people love it, and she's a great hostess." Rousseau agrees: "What makes this business a success is my welcome, of course," she says. "But the technology makes it so much easier to run the whole thing. It's perfect." As for the future, Wood says, "I'll always do business in New York—that's where the art world is." But he's also looking into more sophisticated computers that will make it easier for him to "shift the global balance" any time he wants.

Source: Based on Michael Rubner, "Dear Abbey," *Home Office Computing*, December 1992, pp. 60–62. Used by permission of Scholastic, Inc.

Empowering Knowledge Workers. If you read the business magazines and journals, you've probably read about "empowered" knowledge workers who have the information, skills, and authority to make effective decisions and act independently. A database system can help to empower workers. First, the database system lets users collect, store, and retrieve the company data and information they need to act, independent of a supervisor or file clerk. Second, experience with one database system can give users the skills and confidence needed to work with other database systems, such as the growing number of databases that can be accessed by modem. By tapping into these online databases, users can retrieve timely data and information that can help them make key decisions. Third, understanding and using database systems can aid any staff member, manager, or small business owner who needs to interact with an IT professional in developing a database system.

CRITICAL CONNECTION 1

Contact Manager Helps Farmland Boost Sales

When most people think of a farm in the United States, they picture a solitary tractor tilling the earth from dawn to dusk. But the modern farmer is also a major consumer, one who spends thousands of dollars on feed, fuel, and chemicals at the local farm cooperative. The co-op, in turn, buys its wares from distributors, such as Farmland Industries, which has thousands of salespeople criss-crossing the Midwestern portion of the United States.

Because Farmland's salespeople tend to specialize in certain product lines, several might visit the same co-op—with mixed results. One problem, the company found, was this duplication of effort. Another, more serious, problem: Salespeople didn't know what their colleagues had already sold, meaning missed opportunities for the company to sell other, related farm supplies.

The firm decided to turn to IT for help. Most of the company's salespeople already had laptop computers with modems, which enabled them to access a database of products and prices. The next, logical step was to install a contact manager on the network. A *contact manager* is a data management system designed to help salespeople manage their work. With the recently installed network-based contact manager, the Farmland salespeople can use their modems to tap into a centralized database and extract a complete account history for each customer, including a record of what colleagues may have sold on their last sales calls.

Database Terminology

Database users rely on precise terminology to describe the structure and the details of a database. These terms make it possible to generalize across many different situations without getting bogged down in the jargon of a particular industry, company, or problem setting. Five of the most commonly used database terms are entity, attribute, data item, record, and relation.

Entities and Attributes. An **entity** is a person, place, thing, event, or condition about which data and information are collected. For example, universities and col-

entity A person, place, thing, event, or condition about which data and information are collected.

leges collect information about several entities, including students, faculty members, courses, and degree programs. Information in a hospital database typically focuses on such entities as patients, physicians, nurses, and rooms. In business, entities may include customers, suppliers, and orders.

Choosing entities is an important part of understanding a problem and devising its solution. The right entity must be agreed upon before a problem can be addressed effectively. For instance, to institute a new security system, a university needs information about each of its students, including:

Entity	Data and information needed (Attributes)
Student	Name of student
	Street address
	City
	State
	Postal code
	Student ID number
	Telephone
	Date of birth
	Residency status
	Contact person in case of emergency
	Fingerprint
	Picture

attribute A category of data or information that describes an entity. Each attribute holds a fact about the entity.

Each category of data or information describing the entity is called an **attribute**. Each is a *fact* about a student. The last two attributes of the student entity, fingerprint and picture, may surprise you, because they suggest a different form of information from the other items, all of which can be recorded in text or numeric format. But, remember that information can be composed of several different components, including data, text, graphics, sound, and images (Figure 6.1). In the future, other details may be added: voice prints, spoken phrases, and video segments.

data item The specific details of an individual entity stored in a database.

record A grouping of data items that consists of a set of data or information that describes an entity's specific occurrence.

Data Items and Records.   When the specific facts of an individual entity are stored in a database, they are known as **data items**. Hence the university's name data items may include entries such as Thomas O'Rafferty and François La Fleur. A **record** is a grouping of data items and consists of the set of data and information

FIGURE 6.1
The Components of Information in a Database
In addition to data and text information, a database can contain graphic, sound, and image information.

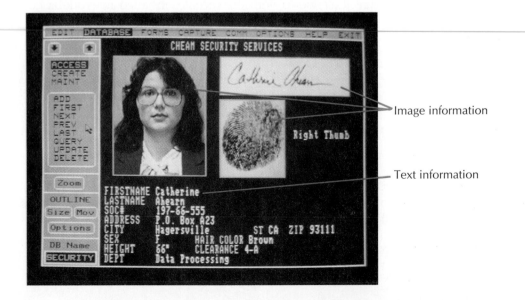

(data, text, sound, or image) that describe an entity's specific *occurrence* (or *instance*). Each record in a database describes one specific occurrence of an entity. For example, as Figure 6.2 shows, the record for the student Thomas O'Rafferty includes the data items describing one occurrence of the "student" entity.

Reality Check. Knowledge entails more than just collecting facts and details. Indeed, collecting data is not nearly as important as arranging those data in a useful way. A good database organizes all the data relevant to an entity and gives you the ability to assess a situation and determine what course of action to take.

For example, a university's database may contain data on students: their name, their dates of birth, where they live, the courses they have taken, their grade point averages, and when they plan to graduate. *Knowledge* comes from assembling and synthesizing these details in a way that allows a person to assess a situation or answer a question, such as

- Is the individual someone you want to recommend to a prospective employer?
- Do you think this person will graduate on time?
- Is the individual highly creative and innovative?

The answers to these questions are not contained as facts in the database. Rather, they come from analyzing facts contained in the database. Knowledge comes from making use of data and information, but only when they are relevant to the situation at hand. ■

Records hold the information about each instance, one record per instance. If the university used a paper-based system, it would probably create a paper record: a form or an index card for each student. Records stored in a computer database are usually maintained on magnetic storage.

Relations. The most common type of database is a **relational database**.[1] In this type of database, information is structured in a table format consisting of horizontal rows and vertical columns.

relational database A database in which information is structured in table format.

[1]Other types of databases common in the past include hierarchical and network database structures (see Chapter 10), which are sometimes found on mainframe and midrange computer applications today. However, because relational databases are today the predominant type across all classes of computers, large and small, we will not discuss the other types here.

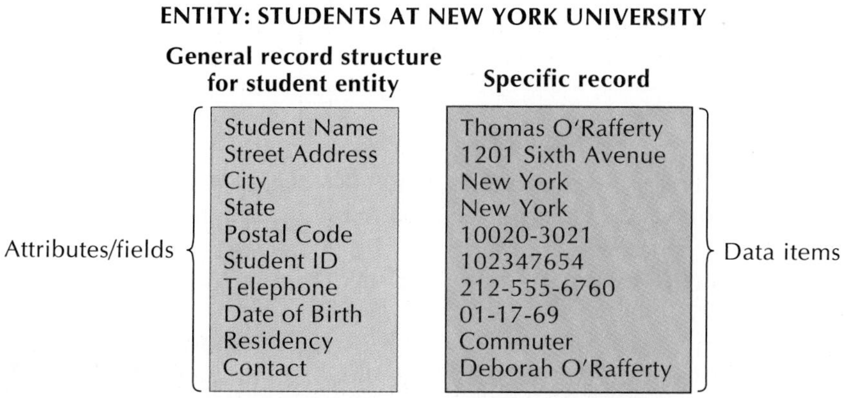

ENTITY: STUDENTS AT NEW YORK UNIVERSITY

General record structure for student entity / **Specific record**

Attributes/fields:
Student Name — Thomas O'Rafferty
Street Address — 1201 Sixth Avenue
City — New York
State — New York
Postal Code — 10020-3021
Student ID — 102347654
Telephone — 212-555-6760
Date of Birth — 01-17-69
Residency — Commuter
Contact — Deborah O'Rafferty

Data items

FIGURE 6.2
Database Terminology
Each record in a database specifies one instance of an entity. Here, the specific instance of the student entity is Thomas O'Rafferty.

STUDENT RELATION

Name	Student ID Number	Street Address	City	State	Postal Code
Gorzynski, John	253054720	71 West Washington	Chicago	Illinois	60602-1634
Markus, Lewis	762027721	22 Ocean Blvd	Atlantic City	New Jersey	08103
Martin, Carol	934841834	33 Hightower Lane	Montgomery	Alabama	36116
O'Rafferty, Thomas	102347654	1201 Sixth Avenue	New York	New York	10020-3021
Patterson, Jane	376358722	440 Holcomb Lane	Atlanta	Georgia	30338-1538

Attributes or Fields (heading at right); *Records or Tuples* (label at left)

FIGURE 6.3 The Elements of a Relation

relation or **file** The table in a database that describes an entity.

tuples The rows of a relation. Also called records.

fields The columns of a relation. Also called attributes.

The table itself, called a **relation** or **file**, describes an entity. The rows of the relation are its **records**, or **tuples**, representing instances of interest. The relation's columns are its attributes or **fields**.

Relations have four general characteristics:

1. Each column contains a single value about the same attribute.
2. The order of columns in the relation does not matter.
3. The order of rows in the relation does not matter.
4. Each row is unique—one row cannot duplicate another.

As Figure 6.3 shows, all the records in a relation contain the same number of data items. However, there can be any number of records in the relation and they can be entered in any order. (Processing will retrieve information in a particular sequence if the application requires that.)

A word of advice: Don't let the different terms confuse you. People often alternate between the formal and common names for database components:

Formal name	Common names
attribute	field
tuple	record
relation	databa.se or file

We'll use the more common names throughout this book. However, you should be familiar with the formal terms, particularly if you interact with systems analysts or other information technology professionals.

The Objectives of Database Management Systems

The personal phone directory example that opens this chapter makes it clear that it is much better to *manage* data and information than to allow them to just accumulate. Managing data is precisely the objective of the various personal **database management system (DBMS)** packages now on the market. The most popular of these packages are listed in Table 6.1.

database management system (DBMS) A software package that allows the user to manage data and increase productivity.

data definition language (DDL) A tool that allows users to define a database.

Database management systems provide users with three tools. First, they include a **data definition language (DDL)** that allows users to define the data-

TABLE 6.1   Popular Personal Database Management Systems

Software Package	Manufacturer	Computer Versions Available
Access	Microsoft	IBM-compatible
dBASE IV	Borland	IBM-compatible
FilePro	Claris	Apple Macintosh
Foxpro	Microsoft	IBM-compatible
Paradox	Borland	IBM-compatible

base. Second, they include a **data manipulation language (DML)** that allows users to store, retrieve, and edit data in the database. (A query language is a type of data manipulation language.) Third, they include a variety of other capabilities that help users increase their productivity. (We discuss these capabilities later in this chapter.)

Managing data means taking deliberate actions guided by specific objectives. Database management systems are designed to achieve five objectives. You might think of these as both problem *solving* and problem *avoiding* objectives:

- Integrating databases
- Reducing redundancy
- Sharing information
- Maintaining integrity
- Enabling database evolution

Integrating Databases.   Because the data and information needed in problem solving often reside in several databases, people need to integrate databases. Database management systems allow separate files, created at varying times or by different people, to be merged.

Integration is often done to process an inquiry or to create a report. Suppose the university discussed earlier wants to generate a report listing all courses, instructors, and office numbers and office hours of each instructor. As Figure 6.4 on the next page shows, the DBMS prepares this report by integrating information retrieved from separate databases. Integrating databases means that specialized databases (for example, a course database and an instructor database) can be maintained while achieving the benefits of processing them together.

Reducing Redundancy.   *Redundancy* is duplication of information between databases. Some information may be repeated in databases when files are developed independently. Unfortunately, multiple copies of data and information sometimes become inconsistent with one another. Because the data and information in databases are updated or changed at varying times, often by people who are not aware that other databases with the same information exist, only one copy may be changed. The others will be out of date and therefore inaccurate.

In well-managed databases, most data items are not duplicated. Rather, the DBMS extracts copies of the information from the appropriate databases to produce the necessary report.

Not all redundancy is bad. For instance, in the student/course/instructor example, several data items are included in all the databases (see again Figure 6.4). Information that is common to different databases makes possible the integration of descriptions and the preparation of reports. Figure 6.5 on page 231 identifies areas in a database where redundancy is and is not appropriate.

data manipulation language (DML) A tool that allows users to store, retrieve, and edit data in a database.

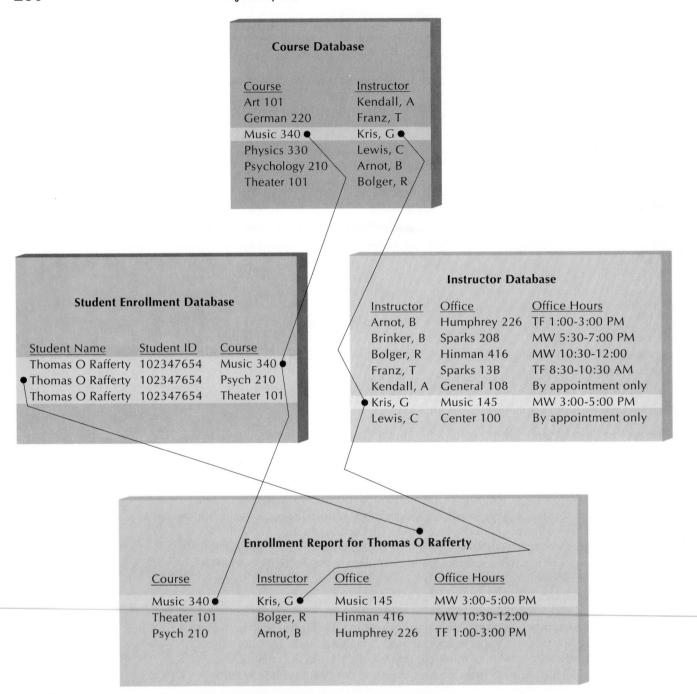

FIGURE 6.4   Integrating Databases to Produce a Report
Database management systems frequently integrate information from separate databases
into a special report.

Sharing Information.   An important advantage of databases is their ability to
share information among multiple persons in various locations. The *information
sharing* capabilities of database management software allow information to be
stored once and then retrieved by any authorized user. This capability both
reduces overall storage needs and helps to ensure consistency.

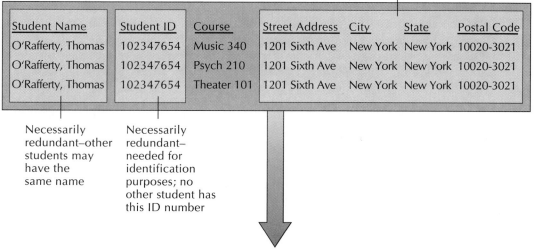
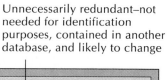

FIGURE 6.5   Database Redundancy—Necessary or Unnecessary
The student's street address, city, state, and postal code are not needed in the student enrollment database. Each student's ID number is unique and is enough to ensure that two students with the same name are not confused.

Information sharing also means that the same information can be shared by different applications. The alternative is to have a different set of information for each application. This means redundancy and, most likely, inconsistency between the different sets.

Maintaining Integrity.   Database management systems play an important role in database security. When a database is *secure*, access to its information is controlled so that only authorized people are able to retrieve or process it. The security of data and information is important, especially when personal information (such as salary history and telephone numbers) is involved.

A DBMS also helps to ensure database reliability. *Reliability* means that the information in the database is accurate and available when needed. A DBMS forces users to take precautions to ensure that information entering the database is correct. It also makes users take steps to maintain backup copies of the database in case of loss or damage.

Database integrity results from providing database security and reliability.

Enabling Database Evolution.   Databases are not stagnant. They evolve because the environment in which they are used is continually changing, whether at home, on campus, or at the office.

Databases change in two ways:

- Changes in contents—The data items in current records change, new records are added, and existing records are deleted.
- Change in structure—The data items that make up a record change the database's logical structure, either because fields are added or deleted, because data items' characteristics change (for example, more space may be needed for a data item than is currently allocated), or because the way the database is stored physically changes.

Database changes happen everyday. This is not a problem, provided provisions for the evolution of the database are made. Problems occur only when people find that they cannot adjust the database to fit the new circumstances. Database management systems provide the capability to modify the database and to avoid inflexibility.

Database or Spreadsheet—What's the Difference?

Lotus 1-2-3, the spreadsheet that swept the business world in the early 1980s, actually integrated three basic functions: an electronic spreadsheet, database management, and business graphics. Since then, many users have tried to use Lotus 1-2-3 and similar spreadsheet packages to build personal databases, only to find they really needed a database management system.

Three Basic Questions.   How can you decide whether you should use a spreadsheet or a database management system in your work? Simply ask yourself three basic questions.

1. **What do I need to do with the data?** Much of the power of a spreadsheet comes from its embedded formulas, which let you explore the numerical relationship between business variables, such as costs, price, and profit. Thus, the spreadsheet is an ideal tool for performing "what-if" financial analyses and forecasts. The database, in contrast, is designed to collect, store, and retrieve data items that are structured in a particular way. Although database management systems can perform mathematical functions (such as sums and averages), their main strength is their ability to maintain the *relationships* between data items.

2. **How much data do I need to store?** Spreadsheets provide "find" and "search" functions that help users retrieve specific records, but the process can be slow and cumbersome if the spreadsheet is very large. (And some spreadsheets can become very large.) Thus, a small store owner might find it practical to record accounts payable in a spreadsheet; a major credit card company, in contrast, would find it more practical to use a database.

3. **How important are the data?** Data and information are often described as the lifeblood of the modern organization. With them, managers can monitor the organization's performance and plan for the future. Data and information can even have life-and-death consequences; a record of patient drug allergies or side effects is a good example of this. Other data, such as sales forecasts or employee salaries, may be sensitive and confidential; in the wrong hands, these data could harm the organization or individuals. Hence, it is important that data be accurate and protected from unauthorized users.

A spreadsheet does not offer much help here. Anyone who can access the spreadsheet file can also read—or change—the data it contains. A database management system, in contrast, contains many functions a spreadsheet cannot perform, including (but not limited to) those that are designed to eliminate common data entry errors and protect the data from unauthorized users. (You'll read more about these functions a little later in this chapter.)

Spreadsheets and DBMSs: A Team for the Future.   Spreadsheets and databases both have a valuable role to play in the modern organization. At many firms, for example, corporate data are warehoused in a multi-user database system and safeguarded by a database management system. Authorized users, however, can use queries to download a copy of specific data into their desktop computers, where they can use a spreadsheet to perform what-if analyses. Or, as an alternative, they can use a PC and a spreadsheet to collect raw data, which are then transferred into the multi-user database system. (Au Bon Pain, an international chain of French-style cafés, uses this arrangement.) Clearly, effective knowledge workers of the future will need to be able to use both spreadsheet and database software.

Developing Database Applications

Like the process of developing a spreadsheet application, the process of developing a database application is a form of problem solving. It proceeds in a deliberate fashion, with one action leading to the next in the most efficient and effective manner possible. Database application development can be viewed as a 7-step sequence (Figure 6.6 on page 234):

- Study the problem
- Determine the requirements
- Design the database
- Create the database
- Design the application
- Create the application
- Test the application

In the sections that follow, we will use a problem commonly faced by student association offices on university campuses to illustrate each phase of the development process.

Study the Problem

Studying the problem at hand involves determining its characteristics and how database creation and processing can assist in solving it.

The problem is as follows: The Student Association Office (SAO) at the University of Wyckoff is responsible for keeping all the members of all student clubs informed of membership requirements and special events. In the past, the director's office has maintained a file of index cards on which names, addresses, telephone numbers, and other personal information have been recorded. Now there are nearly 50 organizations on campus, with 25 to 50 members each, and the director wants to develop a better system.

After studying the problem, the director and staff members decide to develop a database for the SAO. Using the student database in the university's student records office would make their job much easier, but university policy dictates that this database can be used only for official university business. It is not available to social and service organizations.

Because the director's office already uses personal computers, the director and staff decide the database would ideally be created and maintained on a PC. Before getting started, they check to ensure two important conditions are met:

- The designated PC on which the database will be established has adequate storage capacity for the database and for the computer-based procedures that will be needed to use the database.
- The database management software they seek to use will run on the designated IBM computer and the system's main memory and disk storage capacity are sufficient.

With these conditions met, they can set out to determine the application's requirements.

Determine the Requirements

The database's *requirements* are the capabilities the system must have for capturing, storing, processing, and generating data and information. These include input/data-entry requirements, query requirements, and output requirements. Determining requirements begins with the formation of a project committee to oversee the effort. This committee includes both managers and informed staff members, as well as students. Bringing these people together ensures that all meaningful ideas will be considered.

The project committee sits down to evaluate the manual system of index cards currently in use, determining which features work well and which are less efficient. Because database applications have a way of generating additional uses after they are developed, committee members also try to identify possible future uses of

FIGURE 6.6
Database Application Development Sequence
The seven steps in database application development are common to all database development projects, whether large or small.

Step	Description
Study the problem	Describe the system's data entry (input) requirements, inquiry requirements, and output requirements.
Determine the requirements	Determine the problem's characteristics and how database creation and processing can assist in solving the problem.
Design the database	Identify entities of interest, determine the data or information that describes them, and determine which data items will be used to distinguish one entity from another.
Create the database	Name the database; establish the database structure (field names, types, widths, and decimal positions; field indexation).
Design the application	Develop data entry, report generation, and query processing methods.
Create the application	Write the programs to perform data processing tasks.
Test the application	Evaluate the application's processes and procedures to ensure they are performing as expected.

the data and information that will be included in the database. For example, the committee may decide that a likely new use of the database will be to keep track of the location of student club alumni after graduation.

After much discussion, the committee formulates the following characteristics. People using the new system must be able to:

- Enter and maintain records in the database.
- Prepare reports listing all members of student clubs

    In alphabetical order.
    In postal code order.
    In alphabetical order by name of student club.

- Prepare mailing labels.
- Process queries to display or print information on a particular club member who is identified by name or by student ID number.
- Make copies of the database for backup purposes.
- Protect the database from unauthorized use.

Committee members believe that all of these requirements can be met in the design of the new application.

Design the Database

With the requirements set, the project leader can turn to the design process. Database design consists of three activities:

- Identifying the entities of interest
- Determining the attributes that describe the entity of interest
- Determining which data items will be used to distinguish one entity from another (for retrieval purposes)

For the student club database, the primary entity is the student member. The most important attributes describing the members are:

- NAME.

    LAST NAME
    FIRST NAME
    MIDDLE INITIAL

- STUDENT ID NUMBER.
- STUDENT CLUB/SOCIETY NAME.
- ROOM NUMBER (in student club facilities).
- YEAR OF GRADUATION.
- OFFICE HELD IN STUDENT CLUB (if any).

Each office staff member wants to be able to retrieve information from the database using the individual's name (last name and then first name). But they expect that in some instances it will be necessary to rely on the individual's student ID number also. As was the case in Figure 6.5, each student will have a unique ID number even though some students will have the same last, and even first, name. These three data items—last name, first name, and student ID number—are all used as **index keys** or **search keys**. When the user specifies a search key, the database management software searches through the database to locate the record containing the specified data item.

index key or **search key**
A data item used by database management software to locate a specific record.

Create the Database

After the database has been designed, its structure must be created. Creation of the database entails naming the database and defining the *database structure*, which consists of five elements (Figure 6.7):

- Names of the individual fields (attributes)
- Type of information stored in each field
- Maximum width of information stored in each field
- Number of decimal positions allowed in each field (when appropriate)
- Whether or not each field will be indexed.

Field names.   Field names distinguish one field from another. The guidelines for naming the fields depend on the data management software used. For example, in the popular dBASE IV data management system, field names can be up to 10 characters long. The first character must be a letter. The other characters may be letters, numbers, or the underline (_). Blank spaces within a field name are not permissible. (For example, the 10-character field name DAY OF WK ("day of week") is not permissible because it contains blank spaces. However, DAY_OF_WK is allowed. The underline is not considered a blank.)

The SAO has decided to use dBASE IV to create its database. The student club database will contain eight fields with the following names: LASTNAME, FIRSTNAME, INITIAL, STUDENT_ID, SOCIETY, ROOM_NUM, OFFICER, and YEAR_GRAD.

Field types.   In addition to naming each field, database creators must specify the *type* of data that the field will hold. The most popular database systems permit six different types of data (Figure 6.8):

- **Character.** The letters A-Z, the numbers 0-9, and any other characters on the keyboard (such as & and #). Most fields contain character information. The terms "character" and "alphanumeric" are used interchangeably. Numbers treated as character data cannot be used in arithmetic or computation, but are for identification purposes only (for example, student ID numbers).
- **Numeric.** Any integer (that is, any whole number, such as 1, 2, 50, or 100) or any number with a decimal point or a minus sign (-). Unlike alphanumeric data, numeric data can be used in arithmetic processes.

FIGURE 6.7
Database Structure for Student Club Database (using dBASE IV)
The database structure contains five elements: field name, field type, field width, decimal positions, and field indexation.

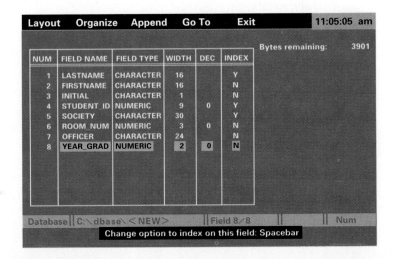

NUM	FIELD NAME	FIELD TYPE	WIDTH	DEC	INDEX
1	LASTNAME	CHARACTER	16		Y
2	FIRSTNAME	CHARACTER	16		N
3	INITIAL	CHARACTER	1		N
4	STUDENT_ID	NUMERIC	9	0	Y
5	SOCIETY	CHARACTER	30		Y
6	ROOM_NUM	NUMERIC	3	0	N
7	OFFICER	CHARACTER	24		N
8	YEAR_GRAD	NUMERIC	2	0	N

Layout   Organize   Append   Go To   Exit   11:05:05 am

Bytes remaining: 3901

Database | C:\dbase\ <NEW> | Field 8/8 | Num
Change option to index on this field: Spacebar

Field type	Description	Example
Character or alphanumeric	Alphabetic or special characters and numbers (cannot be used in arithmetic processes)	O'Rafferty 12001 Sixth Avenue
Numeric	Any integer or any number with a decimal point or minus sign (can be used in arithmetic processes)	540 -12 4.7
Floating point	Decimal numbers (typically used in applications involving frequent multiplication and division)	128.6
Logical	One space used to indicate True or False, or Yes or No.	Tt Ff Yy Nn
Memo	Text data used to explain or annotate other details contained in the record, frequently at length.	"Details captured by Jerri Olenburg during interview with student on April 14."
Date	Calendar date in the format mm/dd/yy (month, day, year)	07/15/96

FIGURE 6.8
Field Types
The six most common field types are listed here. In the near future, database management systems are likely to include image and graphic field types also.

- **Floating point.** Decimal numbers (for example, 1.5, 2.33, 50.84, and 100.992). Floating point numbers are used when greater precision is needed. Floating point numbers can speed arithmetic processing when the numbers are very large.
- **Logical.** Only a single character: Y or y (yes), T or t (true), N or n (no), or F or f (false). Some systems allow entry of yes or no values and convert them to true or false when storing the data in the database.
- **Memo.** Text information consisting of alphanumeric characters. Memo fields are designed to hold long blocks of text, often several thousand characters in length.
- **Date.** A date in the form mm/dd/yy (month/day/year). For example, January 3, 1996 can be described as 01/03/96. The data management system inserts the slash (/) character.

In the not-too-distant future, we can expect to see database management systems including image and graphic data types as well.

Field Width.   The width of the field specified in the database structure determines how long, in characters, each field can be. Some fields, like the logical, date, and memo fields, have a length predetermined by the database management system. Other field lengths are specified by the database designer. For instance, the chosen length of the STUDENT_ID field will depend on the number of characters the university includes in all student identification numbers. Wyckoff University uses social security numbers as student ID numbers, so the width of the STUDENT_ID field is 9 characters (see again Figure 6.7).

Decimal Positions.   When decimal data will be included in the database, the designer specifies the number of positions to allow after the decimal point. If a field will describe money, two decimal positions is customary (for example, the monetary figure $34.78 has two decimal positions). The SAO at Wyckoff University does not need to use decimal numbers in its database, so the relevant fields have decimal positions of zero.

indexing A database system's capability to find fields and records in the database.

Indexation.   **Indexing** permits the database system to find fields and records in the database. The designer must specify which fields will be used for retrieval so the database management system can create the index of key fields and storage locations. The database management system does all the work once the designer chooses the respective fields. Figure 6.7 shows that the SAO has chosen to index LASTNAME, STUDENT_ID, and SOCIETY. The "Y" means that the field will be indexed. An "N" means that it will not.

Design the Application

Database processing includes a variety of features that make the data and information accessible to people and that help safeguard the existence of the database. During *application design*, these features are determined. The most important of these are the methods for data entry, report generation, and query processing.

data entry The process of populating a database with data and information.

Data Entry.   Database creation, as we just saw, is the process of establishing the database's structure by defining the database's different fields and their characteristics. **Data entry** is the process of *populating* the database with data and information. During data entry, new records are added to the database by providing the details for each field in the record. At the University of Wyckoff, data entry methods will determine how all the student club details, such as LASTNAME, FIRST-NAME, and STUDENT_ID, will be entered into the database.

data entry form A custom-developed video display used to enter and change data in a database.

Data entry forms are custom-developed video displays used to enter and change data in a database. Forms can be very basic, or they can be designed to look like the paper forms and reports that the database will generate. Figure 6.9 shows two different data entry forms. The form at the top asks the user to enter data directly using field names as a prompt. The form at the bottom has been specially designed and formatted for ease of use and aesthetic appeal.

The data entry portion of application design involves determining the method and sequence in which the data are entered. Typically, data are entered through the keyboard. Scanners, microphones, and light pens are also being used more frequently.

Report Generation.   A *report* is a printed or onscreen display of data or information in the database. Some reports are simply a list of the records in the database, one record after the other; others contain only certain elements of the database (Figure 6.10). Most of the time, however, the report is more than just a list. A good report organizes data into a form that is meaningful and helpful.

Reports are most useful when they:

- Contain the records that meet the recipients' needs.
- Contain *only* the information that is needed from the records.
- Present information arranged in a sequence that fits the users' needs (perhaps in alphabetical order or grouped by category according to the contents of particular fields).
- Have the date of preparation, titles that identify the purpose of the report, and headings that identify the contents of the rows and columns of information.
- Have numbered pages, with the title repeated on each page when reports are lengthy.

In a well-designed report, such as that shown in Figure 6.11 on page 240, information appears where users expect it while headings and titles are clear and useful. In other words, the design itself is hardly noticed. The focus is on the information rather than the design.

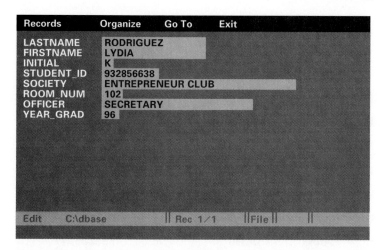

a) Direct data entry using field name as prompt

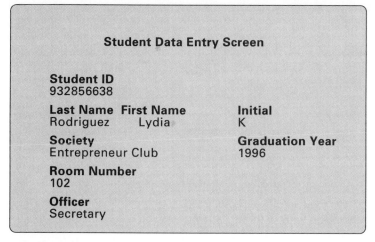

b) Data entry using specially designed and formatted data entry screen

FIGURE 6.9
Data Entry Forms
In some database systems, data are entered through a keyboard onto a standard form listing field names. In other applications, a more visually appealing form is used.

LASTNAME	FIRSTNAME	INITIAL	STUDENT_ID	SOCIETY
JAMISON	JULIETTE	R	535460299	ENTREPRENEUR
HUNT	MARTHA	L	325937742	ENTREPRENEUR
RODRIGUEZ	LYDIA	K	932856638	ENTREPRENEUR
LING	MAI	T	535257812	ENTREPRENEUR
GONZALEZ	RAMON		285339934	STUDY ABROAD
MARKS	DAVID	M	883226077	STUDY ABROAD
CHO	JOHN	D	488249931	STUDY ABROAD

FIGURE 6.10
Unformatted Database Printout
This report is simply a printout of certain elements of the student club database. It contains information from the database but is not organized usefully.

CLUB MEMBERSHIP

SOCIETY	LASTNAME	FIRSTNAME	INITIAL	STUDENT_ID
Page No. 1				
08/08/94				
ENTREPRENEUR	HUNT	MARTHA	L	325937742
ENTREPRENEUR	JAMISON	JULIETTE	R	535460299
ENTREPRENEUR	LING	MAI	T	535257812
ENTREPRENEUR	RODRIGUEZ	LYDIA	K	932856638
STUDY ABROAD	CHO	JOHN	D	488249931
STUDY ABROAD	GONZALEZ	RAMON		285339934
STUDY ABROAD	MARKS	DAVID	M	883226077

FIGURE 6.11
Formatted Database Report
This report contains the same data as the printout in Figure 6.10, but is organized alphabetically by club and student's last name.

Database systems also can generate output in the form of labels. At the Universtiy of Wyckoff, items from the database are printed on mailing labels or on labels for file folders and reports (Figure 6.12).

Query Processing.   Recall that a *query* (also called an *inquiry*) is a question that guides the retrieval of specific records in a database. In solving problems, it is common to pose "who are" or "how many" queries. In the student club example, for instance, the SAO may ask:

–Who are the members of the Entrepreneur Club?
–How many students expect to graduate this year?
–Who are the members of the Entrepreneur Club who expect to graduate this year?

An important part of designing a database application entails establishing the form of the queries. Figure 6.13 shows how a database management system processes the query "Who are the club members who graduate before 1998?" The fields at the bottom of the screen in Figure 6.13 are the **view**, the fields that the

view A grouping of the fields that a database will use to retrieve data.

FIGURE 6.12
Mailing Labels Generated as Database Output
Database management systems allow users to custom-design mailing labels with data items from the database.

```
HUNT  MARTHA L
325937742 ENTREPRENEUR
- - - - - - - - - - - - - - - -
JAMISON  JULIETTE R
535460299 ENTREPRENEUR
- - - - - - - - - - - - - - - -
LING  MAI T
535257812 ENTREPRENEUR
- - - - - - - - - - - - - - - -
RODRIGUEZ LYDIA K
932856638 ENTREPRENEUR
- - - - - - - - - - - - - - - -
CHO JOHN D
488249931 STUDY ABROAD
- - - - - - - - - - - - - - - -
GONZALEZ  RAMON
285339934 STUDY ABROAD
- - - - - - - - - - - - - - - -
MARKS DAVID M
883226077 STUDY ABROAD
```

Query: Who are the club members who graduate before 1998?

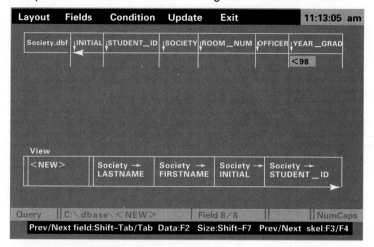

Query form uses the Society database and requests the database system to display LASTNAME, FIRSTNAME, INITIAL, and STUDENT_ID of club members who graduate before 1998.

FIGURE 6.13
Query for Retrieval of Selected Data

database will use to retrieve the necessary data. The "<" symbol in the YEAR_GRAD field is called a **relational operator**. Relational operators tell the database system to make a comparison to call up the requested data. The most commonly used relational operators are listed in Table 6.2.

Of course, you could review each record in the database, one by one. But this is not an efficient use of time. Well-designed database systems, like the Everlink system used in the entertainment industry, allow users to search them quickly and accurately. For more details on Everlink, see the Opportunities box on page 242 titled "Database Plays Matchmaker for Show Biz Professionals."

relational operator A symbol that tells a database system to make a comparison to call up the requested data.

Create the Application

Most microcomputer-based database systems contain a set of commands that can be combined to carry out the desired processing activities. Database applications contain procedures for the following processing actions:

- Add records
- Delete records
- Edit records
- Process queries

TABLE 6.2   Commonly Used Relational Operators

Relational Operator	Comparison
<	Less than
>	Greater than
=	Equal to
< > or #	Not equal to
<=	Less than or equal to
>=	Greater than or equal to

OPPORTUNITIES

Database Plays Matchmaker for Show Biz Professionals

As a former producer for *Saturday Night Live*, John Kelly knows that a producer's life is not always a bed of roses. Like all business managers, producers face all the usual challenges of financing, budgeting, and scheduling. They also spend countless hours in preproduction, a grueling treasure hunt for the locations, actors, and behind-the-scene artisans needed to create magic on the silver screen. Worldwide, about 145,000 commercial productions—ranging from television commercials to industrial films—go through preproduction every year. Sensing a major problem (and an appealing business opportunity), Kelly teamed up with Howard Gollomp to create Everlink, an online multimedia database network for the entertainment industry.

For a small fee, actors and behind-the-scene specialists can list their résumés and credits in the database. Meanwhile, anyone who pays a one-time fee of about $200 can access the database for $1 a minute, using either an IBM-compatible or Macintosh computer. The system features a simple query language that lets producers search for specific needs, such as blond actors who speak French or a list of all sound stages in Arizona. Everlink also offers a graphic user interface that lets users call up actors' photos and even manipulate their hair color onscreen.

The database made its debut in late 1992, following testing by some of Hollywood's hottest production companies—Ron Howard's Imagine, Francis Ford Coppola's American Zoetrope, and Rob Reiner's Castle Rock. Within months, it seemed, the entire industry was talking about how the database can help producers save time and money. "Everlink seems to save so much lost time in tracking down people such as cinematographers by just giving you their phone numbers," says Clarisse Perritte of Sharona Productions, a smaller, independent production firm.

Sources: Based on Matthew Mandell, "Network Makes Movie Debut," *Computerworld*, April 19, 1993, p. 45; Steve Morgenstern, "The Best Software for Tracking Contacts," *Home Office Computing*, May 1992, pp. 66–72.

- Prepare reports
- Make copies of the database (for backup purposes)
- Process information: carry out calculations
- Process information: sort information into a particular sequence

Figure 6.14 shows the processing menu on the SAO's Student Club database.

During application creation the actual programs to perform these database processing tasks are created.[2] Two common methods are used to create database processing applications on microcomputers. In **custom programming**, individuals write detailed procedures using the commands and functions built into the database management software. Every step of each application must be specified in detail. In **application generation**, programmers use menus and simple commands to describe the application to an *application generator*, a system program that creates the set of detailed commands to perform the procedures as they have been defined. The trend is toward developing increasingly powerful application generators so that users can concentrate on the problem to be solved rather than on the detailed programming procedures needed to produce the information. Figure 6.15 details the steps involved in using an application generator.

custom programming In a database system, the writing of detailed procedures using the commands and functions built into the database management software.

application generation In a database system, the use of menus and simple commands to describe the application to a system program that creates the set of detailed commands.

[2]Database processing on mainframe and midrange computer applications often use general purpose programming languages, such as COBOL, Focus, or Natural.

DATE: 04/18/9X

DATABASE PROCESSING MENU
SOCIETY DATABASE

1   Add student records

2   Edit student records

3   Delete student records

4   Retrieve student record

5   Prepare reports

6   Backup the database

X   Exit from system

FIGURE 6.14
Database Menu for Selection of Processing Actions
Using the main menu of the student club database system, the user can add, edit, delete, or retrieve student records; prepare reports; backup the database; or exit the system.

FIGURE 6.15
Creating Applications Using an Application Generator
Application generators save time and in some cases can eliminate the need for a technically trained programmer.

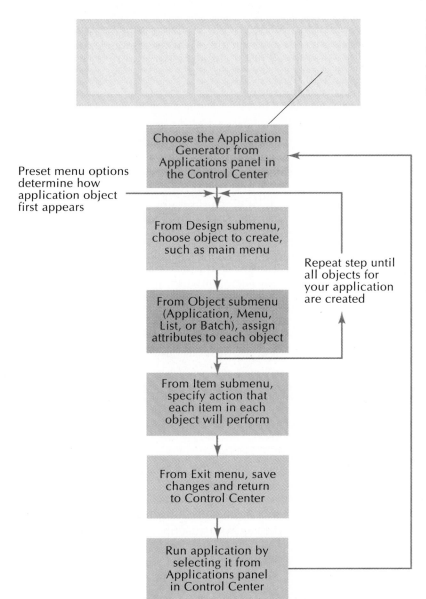

Preset menu options determine how application object first appears

Choose the Application Generator from Applications panel in the Control Center

From Design submenu, choose object to create, such as main menu

From Object submenu (Application, Menu, List, or Batch), assign attributes to each object

Repeat step until all objects for your application are created

From Item submenu, specify action that each item in each object will perform

From Exit menu, save changes and return to Control Center

Run application by selecting it from Applications panel in Control Center

Test the Application

No application design, and no problem solving process, is complete until the solution is used and evaluated. *Testing* entails using the application to ensure that it performs in the expected manner. Tests are performed by using sample data to verify that the results come out as expected. Testing will reveal mistaken assumptions, incorrect procedures, or errors in completing a particular stage of design and development. Failure to test an application can create new problems.

CRITICAL CONNECTION 2
Database Revs Up Torque Travel, Inc.*

Torque Travel As a driver and official on the International Motor Sports Association (IMSA) circuit, Donald Douglass knew all the headaches of making travel arrangements and finding hotel rooms, especially in rural areas like Sebring, Florida and Watkins Glen, New York. "Travel was an awful mess," he recalls. "So after a couple of years, I decided to make a business of it by bringing some order to it." Working from a home office in western Massachusetts, he created Torque Travel.

Within months, Douglass accumulated an enormous amount of data. In addition to collecting the names of potential clients—the hundreds of owners, drivers, mechanics, officials, reporters, and suppliers who worked the IMSA circuit—he began using SABRE, the American Airlines reservation system used by travel agents to book airline reservations and rental cars. He also compiled a list of smaller hotels and inns that would give him a discount if he reserved a block of rooms. (In return for this discount, Douglass would handle all reservations and billing.) The challenge was to match clients and travel arrangements.

Even though Douglass didn't know much about computers, he knew he needed to develop a database. Along the way, he discovered a principle used by IT professionals: Divide the data on customers and inventory (hotel rooms and so on) into separate files, which can be combined in a third file to create travel orders, customer invoices, and so on. After successfully setting up his database, Douglass generated substantial revenue in his first year of business.

*Based on Lisa Kleinholz, "Make Your Business Succeed by Taking Control of Data," *Home Office Computing*, July 1991, pp. 32–33.

▰ A Final Word

Our main example in this chapter has focused on the creation of a fairly simple database. But whether the application is a student club directory or a business database used to manage day-to-day contact with customers and suppliers or the processing of important transactions, the steps in creating the database are the same. The capabilities of database management systems can make the individual more effective—provided the appropriate steps are taken in creating and using the database.

SUMMARY OF LEARNING OBJECTIVES

1 Explain why businesses use databases. In addition to people, a business's most important resources are data and information. Databases can help businesses identify, structure, collect, store, edit, and update these data. Databases are also useful because of their ability to retrieve and share data and to empower knowledge workers.

2 Describe the main components of a database. The five most common terms used to identify the components of a database are entities, attributes, data items, records, and relations. An *entity* is a person, place, thing, event, or condition about which data and information are collected. Each category of interest in an entity is an *attribute*, of that entity. A *data item* is a specific piece of data or information about an entity's attributes entered into the database. A *record* is a grouping of data items. A *relation* is the table (consisting of rows and columns) in a database that describes an entity.

3 List and describe the five objectives of database management systems. Database management systems have five objectives: (1) integrating databases, (2) reducing redundancy, (3) sharing information, (4) maintaining integrity, and (5) enabling database evolution.

4 Identify when a business should use a spreadsheet and when it should use a database. If a business has only a small number of variables to record or needs an application that will examine the numerical relationships between business variables, such as costs and profits, it should use a spreadsheet. If a business has many records structured in a particular way or needs to put security measures in place to protect the data, it should use a database.

5 Identify the seven-step sequence for developing database applications. There are seven steps to developing a database application: (1) study the problem, (2) determine the requirements, (3) design the database, (4) create the database, (5) design the application, (6) create the application, and (7) test the application.

KEY TERMS

CRITICAL CONNECTIONS

1. Contact Manager Helps Farmland Boost Sales

In addition to helping Farmland's salespeople share valuable account histories, the contact manager can help them maintain a customer address book, schedule sales calls, create to-do lists, track expenses, and create a special "tickler" file to remind them of important dates and appointments. The contact manager also lets salespeople create extra displays of demographic information to support their sales presentations. Says the firm's network manager, "Our goal is to turn our salespeople into consultants. If a salesperson can have the account's information, then the salesperson can know the needs of the co-op rather than just selling one product."

When a new release of the contact manager software added some tracking and analysis features, Farmland's salespeople capitalized on the new capabilities. Now, as they make their calls, they can use the built-in scheduling feature to record the time spent with each customer and make comments. At the end of the week, summary reports are sent to regional managers, who can track their staff's performance and then work closely with people who are not top performers.

Questions for Discussion

1. How can Farmland's sales staff use the contact manager to meet its needs for up-to-date pricing data?

2. How can the contact manager make Farmland's sales staff more efficient? How can the contact manager make the staff more responsive to the needs of Farmland's customers?

2.   Database Revs Up Torque Travel, Inc.

Torque Travel

In setting up Torque Travel's database, Donald Douglass divided the agency's data into nine separate relations or files. In the Races file, he logs the year's race schedule, including the race track name and location, his contact at the track, and the types of cars that will be entered. In the Client file, he records client names and addresses, as well as fax, phone, and credit card numbers. In the Hotel file, he enters basic data about the hotels—the address, fax, and phone numbers; the contact person; average rates; and comments about the rooms (distance from the track and so on). These three files are then combined to create the remaining six files.

In the Bookings file, Douglass tracks data about the blocks of rooms he has reserved at each hotel. By combining these data with data from the Schedule and Hotel files, he can tell exactly how many rooms he has available at each hotel for any night of a racing event.

Douglass uses this information to advise clients when they call to make reservations, which are recorded in the Orders file. Order details and agency charges are then summarized in the Confirmation file, which in turn is used to create the contents of the Invoice file. Both a confirmation and an invoice are faxed to customers and these records are maintained in the Fax file.

In his second year of business, Douglass' gross receipts increased twentyfold, from $50,000 to $1 million. The agency is still going strong.

Questions for Discussion

1. Use what you have learned about the functions of DBMSs to explain why IT professionals follow the principle of creating smaller files that can be combined to produce information stored in a third file.

2. How does Douglass' use of database technology give him a competitive advantage in the hotel booking business?

REVIEW QUESTIONS

1. What is a database?

2. Discuss the meaning of the term "information repository" as it relates to a database.

3. Name four benefits of using databases in business.

4. What is a query? What purpose does it serve?

5. Describe entities, data items, records, and relations.

6. What are the formal terms for fields, records, and databases?

7. Describe the three tools included with a database management system.

8. Identify and describe the five objectives of database management systems.

9. Why is the ability to integrate databases valuable in problem solving?

10. Why should redundancy in databases be managed? Should redundancy be eliminated from databases entirely?

11. What two components comprise database integrity?

12. In what two ways can databases change?

13. To decide whether you should use a spreadsheet or a database, what three questions should you ask yourself?

14. What seven steps are involved in database application development?

15. What three activities take place during database design?

16. List the five elements of a database structure.

17. What six types of data can a database field hold?

18. What is the difference between database creation and data entry?

19. What data or information must a database report contain to be useful?

20. Distinguish between custom programming and application generation.

DISCUSSION QUESTIONS

1. When Mary Ann Morley was hired as human resources assistant at the American Pharmaceutical Association in Washington, DC, one of her first assignments was to collect the data needed by managers to reschedule all salary reviews for January and prorate each employee's new salary. (At the time, salaries were reviewed at 75 different dates throughout the year, based on each employee's starting date.) Morley accomplished the task with a relational database for human resources departments. What data items or fields do you think Morley included in each row or tuple of her database? Explain your answer.

2. How does Morley's use of the database illustrate the benefits of using a database in business?

3. Levi Strauss & Co. maintains a PC-based interactive computer network called OLIVER (On-Line Interactive Visual Employee Resource), which allows employees to tap into a mainframe database and review their total compensation packages. Which function of a DBMS would be most important in creating this type of application, in your opinion?

4. OLIVER uses a series of easy-to-use menus to help employees learn about their benefits, including health care, disability, and pension earnings. Why do you think the system's designers chose this access method?

SUGGESTED READINGS

Grehen, Rick, Ben Smith, and Jon Udell, "Database Building Blocks," *Byte*, 17, no. 1 (January 1992), pp. 204–224. Part of a special section on databases and microcomputers. Explores the development of database applications, with special emphasis on assembling libraries of procedures to avoid developing applications from scratch. Other articles in the section evaluate different personal databases, feature by feature.

Johnson, Elizabeth Swoope, *Paradox: A Short Course.* Englewood Cliffs, NJ: Prentice Hall, 1991. A concise and effective presentation of the central features of the Paradox data management system. Includes good discussion of creating forms, reports, and on-line queries.

Senn, James A., *dBASE IV: The Student Edition.* Reading, MA: Addison Wesley, 1990. A comprehensive examination of the features of the dBASE IV system. Each chapter includes both a concepts and tutorial section. Case examples demonstrate the practical use of each dBASE IV capability.

Townsend, James J., *Introduction to Databases.* Indianapolis, IN: Que, 1992. An excellent discussion of the characteristics of personal database systems, describing features and uses in a variety of different application settings.

Haven Corporation: Do-It-Yourself Attitude Spawns a Million-Dollar Business

Bruce Holmes has given a new meaning to "do-it-yourself." When the former fitness guru couldn't find a good, affordable software package to help him manage his mail-order business, he wrote his own. Today, almost a decade later, the mail-order business is gone and Holmes is the CEO and president of Haven Corp., a software company based in Evanston, Illinois.

The company's leading product is Mail Order Wizard, the program Holmes created in the mid-1980s. The cost of a single-user version runs from $695 to $995; multi-user versions range from $2,995 to $6,995. But the program's users think it is well worth the money.

Peggy Glenn, for example, uses Mail Order Wizard to manage a mailing list of more than 10,000 names for the Firefighters Bookstore, the catalog she uses to sell special-interest books by mail and by phone. She has since learned that she might have been able to duplicate the Wizard's features with a less expensive, general-purpose relational

(clockwise from upper left) Haven Corp. founder Bruce Holmes coaches a local school's chess team. Peggy Glenn uses the Mail Order Wizard package created by Holmes to manage a mailing list of more than 10,000 names for the Firefighters Bookstore and the catalog she uses to sell books for firefighters. Glenn says, "I'm convinced that it's because of the program that I've been able to grow so effortlessly and so quickly. I'm not working any more hours than when I first started, I'm able to get a lot more done—and make a lot more money—in the same amount of time."

DBMS. But she's the first to admit she didn't (and still doesn't) have the know-how to do it herself. Moreover, Holmes's package includes many useful features she might not have thought of. "I'm convinced that it's because of the program that I've been able to grow so effortlessly so quickly. I'm not working any more hours than when I first started, I'm just able to get a whole lot more done—and make a lot more money—in the same amount of time."

She especially likes the software's conversational onscreen messages that help her learn the system. But the software's "user-friendly" style hides a number of sophisticated and powerful database features, including:

- *The ability to recognize names.* Enter a name and the software will search the database. If it finds a match, it will display a message asking if this is the same customer who lives at such-and-such an address.
- *The ability to fill in customer information.* If the database has found the right record, a user taps a function key and the software fills in the address and billing information, as well as such comments as "slow pay; accept only COD orders."
- *The ability to track inventory.* If an item is out of stock, the software beeps and initiates a back-order transaction. (A *back order* is an item that is shipped to the customer after the stock has been replenished.) The software also prints an inventory list, sorted by supplier, to simplify the restocking process.
- *The ability to track customer buying habits and analyze ad responses.* The software lets users enter special codes that can help them analyze the cost-effectiveness of ads and special promotional pieces.
- *The ability to create and print invoices, mailing labels, charge-card slips, bank-deposit forms, past-due notices, packing slips, mailing labels, and so on.* This feature alone saves entrepreneurs like Peggy Glenn countless hours. In addition, the software can create reports showing overdue accounts, quarterly revenues, and the amount of sales tax owed to the government.

But even the most sophisticated features can't ensure the kind of customer loyalty enjoyed by Haven Corp. Bruce Holmes traces that to customer service, his obsession. This service includes a year of toll-free technical support, a quarterly newsletter, regular customer-satisfaction surveys, and annual get-togethers for "family of software users" in party towns like New Orleans. Every new feature suggested by a user goes on an electronic wish list; if enough customers request it, Holmes tries to include it in the Wizard's next upgrade. As one user wrote, "We really bought more than software. We got a support team we feel is on our side."

Although referrals accounted for about 20% of Haven Corp.'s business in 1992, the company recently launched a direct-mail campaign using specially designed postcards and brochures and an ad campaign in computer and direct-marketing magazines. In 1993, after 1992 revenues approached $1 million, Holmes finally had to move his business out of his three-story Victorian home to a more formal office building. "Progress caught up with us," Holmes admitted. "I never looked far enough into the future to imagine 18 people working out of my home."

Questions for Discussion

1. Describe the database functions contained in Mail Order Wizard.

2. In addition to Mail Order Wizard, Haven Corp. sells a variety of other mail- and list-management programs, including WizKid, a scaled-down Wizard program for smaller, start-up businesses. Looking to the future, Holmes plans to expand into software for retail, contact management, telemarketing, and shipping. Do you think this is a smart marketing move? Explain your answer.

Sources: Lisa Kleinholz, "How One Mail-Order Company Makes Business Grow," *Home Office Computing*, April 1991, pp. 32–33; Rosalind Resnick, "Best Businesses Contest Winners: Creating a Customer Haven," *Home Office Computing*, July 1993, pp. 42–43.

CHAPTER 7

Word Processing, Publishing, and Graphics Systems: The Tools of Words and Images

Learning Objectives

When you have completed this chapter, you should be able to:

1 Describe why people use word processing systems and the five functions of word processing systems.

2 Explain the time-saving and productivity-enhancing features of a word processing system.

3 Differentiate between the purpose of a word processing program and the purpose of a desktop publishing system.

4 Describe the four operations common to all desktop publishing systems and the three steps involved in preparing a desktop published document.

5 Explain the five types of graphics used in business documents and presentations.

In Practice

After completing this chapter, you should be able to perform these activities:

1 Describe the advantages a word processing program offers to anyone who prepares correspondence, reports, or other documents.

2 Explain why there are so many different word processing and desktop publishing programs in use.

3 Visit with a word processing specialist and discuss the ways he uses his system to prepare various types of documents encountered in his everyday activities.

4 Evaluate the impact of different type styles on the appearance of a document.

5 Speak with someone in the publishing industry and discuss the ways that word processing, desktop publishing, and graphics programs have changed her job.

6 Discuss with a graphics designer the way he manages the development of documents and the manner in which he uses clip art.

7 Speak with a commercial printer and discuss the advantages and disadvantages of camera ready documents.

250

The Professional Toolbox

A PROFESSIONAL TOOLBOX IS A COLLECtion of tools that help get the job done. The best toolboxes have the right assortment of tools collected in one place, with none more than a short reach away.

No two professions have exactly the same toolbox. Carpenters work with nails, screws, hammers, and saws. Architects work with drafting tables, protractors, and compasses. Doctors carry thermometers, stethoscopes, and tongue depressors. Accountants use spreadsheet programs, worksheets, and calculators.

A *word processing system* is a toolbox for people who work with words, something most people do in one form or another. Carpenters may send out newsletters to the community to drum up some business. Architects need to correspond with contractors, suppliers, and clients. Doctors frequently write columns for local newspapers or submit articles to the *American Medical Journal.* Accountants need to prepare reports of their findings for managers and stockholders.

The tools of word processing, desktop publishing, and graphics programs can help people improve their communication skills. These skills are perhaps the most important skills in the business world today.

Word processing programs help users in two ways. First, like spreadsheet and database programs, they make users more efficient by decreasing the amount of time they spend on the mechanical aspects of their work. Rather than centering and typing a page number at the bottom of each page of a report, for example, you can instruct a word processing program to place the page number in brackets in the upper right-hand corner of each page. Rather than using White Out to patch together a hastily typed term paper, you can use a word processor and a laser printer to make your papers look perfect and professional every time.

Second, word processing programs allow users to concentrate on what they do best by helping them compensate for some of their weaknesses. Working with words contains many traps for the unwary: Words can be misspelled, sentence structure can be awkward, punctuation may be confusing, and paragraphs may ramble. Word processing systems allow you to correct your spelling and punctuation, clarify your writing style, and add some variety to your writing—all at the touch of a few keys. Improved writing leads to improved communication skills, perhaps the most important assets in the business world today.

Word processing is just one part of document preparation, however. In this age of visuals, images and photographs are just as important as—and sometimes more important than—the words that accompany them. (Recall Nigel Holmes and his infographics from Chapter 2.) As many businesspeople have discovered, the effectiveness of their words can be improved by a snazzy layout or by other visual aids. Brochures, newsletters, and posters all look the way they do for a reason. They are designed so that important information stands out, with photographs and drawings complementing the information on the page.

Today's *desktop publishing* and *graphics* systems allow for easy manipulation of words and images. Graphic specialists and artists can use color monitors, special software, and color printers to design advertising, create magazine layouts, and rearrange images on a page in a fraction of the time it would take to do these tasks manually. As many companies are finding, the savings in both money and time are considerable.

I N THIS CHAPTER, WE PROVIDE AN OVERVIEW OF THE CAPABILITIES OF WORD PROCESSING, desktop publishing, and graphics systems. Advances in information technology promise to make typing a thing of the past sometime in the future, but right now you must be able to type to use computers and other information technology effectively. This is especially true with word processing programs.

An Overview of Word Processing

word processing (WP) The creation and management of text documents, and the tailoring of the physical presentation of those documents, using a word processing program.

text document Any document that can be created on a computer.

Word processing (WP) entails creating and managing text documents and tailoring the physical presentation of the information contained in those documents. A **text document** is any document, such as a letter, report, or term paper, that can be created on a computer. Text documents may include words, symbols, figures, and tables. When you glance at a text document, you see mainly lines of text information, with some pages or sections containing illustrations or tables of information interspersed between lines of text.

TABLE 7.1   Leading Word Processing Programs

Software Package	Manufacturer	Computer Versions Available
AmiPro	Lotus Development	IBM-compatible
MacWrite	Claris Software	Apple Macintosh
Professional Write	SPC Publishing	IBM-compatible
Right Writer	Que	IBM-compatible
Word	Microsoft	Apple Macintosh and IBM-compatible
WordPerfect	WordPerfect Corp.	Apple Macintosh and IBM-compatible
WordStar	WordStar Corp.	IBM-compatible
WriteNow	T/Maker	Apple Macintosh

The Functions of Word Processing Programs

Some of the most frequently used word processing systems are listed in Table 7.1. These word processing programs carry out five main activities:

- Entry of information
- Display of information
- Editing of information
- Storage and retrieval of information
- Printing of information.

Entering Information.   Information can be entered into a word processing system in a number of ways. In the most traditional (and common) method, information is entered by typing on a keyboard. Alternatively, information may be scanned into memory and then added to the document. Scanning text avoids the need for retyping and is an extremely efficient way of entering previously printed information. On the horizon is the ability to enter information verbally. In the future, people who use dictation equipment to "write" letters and reports may "speak" to their computer instead.

A feature called **wordwrap** allows the user to enter text in a continuous stream, without concern for the document's left or right margin. At the end of each line the software automatically continues the text on the next line. Wordwrap makes entry of information easier and enables the person to work faster. The **justification** feature allows the user to align both the left- and right-hand margins, as in this textbook.

Word processing systems allow the user to set margins—the distance between the edge of the page and the text information—before beginning information entry (and to adjust these margins at any time). The **default**, or preset, margins on many systems are 1 inch (2.6 cm) from the top and bottom of any page and 1.25 inches (3 cm) from the left and right edges of the page.

People may choose to override the default margins because their organization uses stationery that requires different margin settings or because they want to allow room for binding or for holes in documents to be inserted into loose-leaf binders. Margins may also be adjusted to improve readability (shorter lines are easier to read than longer ones) or to change document length (smaller margins leave more room for information on the page and can therefore reduce the page length of a document).

An important part of information entry entails preparing the document's format. A document's **format** defines its appearance and determines its position on the page, the position and highlighting of its text, the use of blank lines and space, the indentation of lines, and the number of columns over which the text is displayed.

As a general guideline, it is advisable to avoid crowding information when formatting a document. The information on the résumé in Figure 7.1 is grouped together, almost as though it were typed one line right after the other. The only blank space is at the end of the page—and that's because the information ended before the end of the page. The document in Figure 7.2 looks much better. It's more attractive and much easier to read. Here are the formatting changes that have been made:

- **Vertical centering**—Information is centered from top to bottom (vertically) on the page.
- **Page centering**—The body of text is centered so that margins are equal on both sides of the page. Once the margins are set for a document—a very simple task— the word processing software takes care of the rest. If the margins are adjusted, the software will automatically reformat the text to adjust it to the new margins.
- **Line centering**—The most important information on a résumé is the individual's name, address, and telephone number. These lines of information are cen-

wordwrap A word processing feature that allows the user to enter text in a continuous stream, without concern for the document's left or right margins.

justification A word processing feature that allows the alignment of right and left margins.

default The preset value that is assumed by a program, unless it is changed by the user.

format A document's physical appearance.

Robert T. Stemper   43 Lakeview Drive, Chicago, Illinois 60625
(312) 555-1212

Career Objective: To be a member of a management team in an innovative, forward looking company, in a position offering personal growth,
challenge, and responsibility.
Strengths: Highly motivated and goal-oriented. Excellent analytical
and organization skills. Skilled in public relations and customer communications.
Experience:
1993–1995 Administrative Assistant, Waterford College: Responsible
for assisting Alumni Fund Director in fundraising projects. Maintained
daily and monthly reports of fundraising activities. Organized and coor-
dinated meetings and luncheons.
1992–1993 Operations Supervisor, Pizza Time Theater: Responsible
for managing customer service and food preparation.
1991–1992 Stockperson, Acme Foods: Responsible for pricing and
stocking grocery items and for assisting in ordering replenishment merchandise.
1990–1991 Harper Lawn Service: Responsibilities included general
upkeep of customer properties, including maintenance of grounds and
landscaping.
Education:
B.B.A. (Business Administration), Waterford College, 1995
Professional Associations:
American Marketing Association
References:
Available on request

FIGURE 7.1   Improperly Formatted Document

Robert T. Stemper
43 Lakeview Drive
Chicago, Illinois 60625
(312) 555-1212

Career Objective: To be a member of a management team in an innovative, forward looking company, in a position offer-
ing personal growth, challenge, and responsibility.

Strengths: Highly motivated and goal-oriented. Excellent analytical and organization skills. Skilled in public rela-
tions and customer communications.

Experience:
1993–1995   Administrative Assistant, Waterford College:
Responsible for assisting Alumni Fund Director in
fundraising projects. Maintained daily and monthly
reports of fundraising activities. Organized and coor-
dinated meetings and luncheons.
1992–1993   Operations Supervisor, Pizza Time Theater:
Responsible for managing customer service and food
preparation.
1991–1992   Stockperson, Acme Foods: Responsible for pricing
and stocking grocery items and for assisting in
ordering replenishment merchandise.
1990–1991   Harper Lawn Service: Responsibilities included general upkeep of customer properties, including main-
tenance of grounds and landscaping.
Education: B.B.A. (Business Administration), Waterford
College, 1995
**Professional
Associations:**   American Marketing Association
References: Available on request

FIGURE 7.2   Properly Formatted Document
Here, the document in Figure 7.2 has been reformatted to
improve its appearance and emphasize important information. This résumé is now ready to be printed and mailed to
prospective employers.

---

tered at the top of the page. Line centering is easily accomplished, either by
clicking on a centering button or icon or by entering a simple command.

- **Blank lines**—Space—blank lines—separate major sections of the document
(for example, career objective and education). The blank lines make the text
easier to read and serve to emphasize the importance of each section.

Important text can also be highlighted through five other methods:

- **Bullets**—Markers that set off and call attention to lists of information can be
added. (Examples of bullets are: ● ○ ■ □ ◆ ★).
- **Type style and size:** A larger, contrasting type size can be used to separate
headings from text.
- **Boldface**—Makes text darker and heavier (regular text; **bold text**), as in Robert
Stemper's name in Figure 7.2.
- **Italics**—Makes text slant to the right (*italic text*).
- **Underline**—Underscores text (underlined text).

Overuse or inconsistent use of highlighting features will detract from rather than
enhance a document's appearance. Notice in Figure 7.2 that only the writer's name
and the six major sections of the résumé are boldfaced. No other information is boldfaced. Figure 7.3 summarizes some of the features available in document formatting.

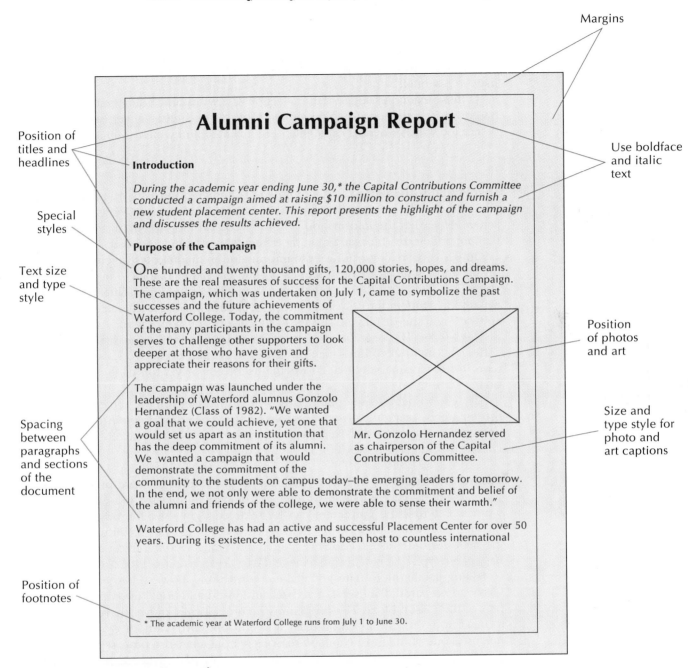

FIGURE 7.3   Document Formatting

✓ **Reality Check.**   Not all word processors offer the same capabilities in choosing type style and size. Some may allow a choice between only two type sizes, comparable to elite and pica type on typewriters.

In addition, some word processing programs have a limited ability to handle highlighted text. For example, some packages provide the capability to mark the text to print in boldface, italics, or underline, but do not show the information in the designated format on the screen. The highlighting is visible only when the document is printed.

The importance of having these features depends on the individual's needs. If the system will be used primarily for preparing correspondence, highlighting features may be less important. But when the system will be used frequently to prepare reports, project proposals, or important business documents, these features may be essential.

As these examples suggest, the selection of a word processing system should be based on its intended use. You should look beyond glitzy advertised features to determine which essential capabilities are included and which are missing.   ■

Displaying Information.   As information is entered into a word processing system (whether by keyboard, scanner, or voice), it comes into view on a display screen. Note that the information is not entered *on* the screen, but rather into the computer memory. It is shown on the screen almost simultaneously.

Only a very small portion of the information in a computer's memory is visible on the display at any given time. (A 24-line computer display, for example, will show only 0.0024% of the contents of a 4-megabyte memory.) Thus the display is actually a *window* into the manuscript. Depending on the characteristics of the software and the display screen itself, the size of the window may vary. Full-size displays typically show 24 lines of information in normal type size. If type size varies, the number of lines may be fewer or greater. Some word processing systems include a capability that allows the user to display a full page of information on the screen.

Those who need to see other parts of the document on the screen can display those parts by using the arrow keys to scroll (move) up or down through the document. The Page-Up and Page-Down keys can be used to move through larger chunks of texts more quickly.

Editing Information.   One of the most useful features of word processing programs is their ability to make text changes quickly and easily. If a wrong letter or word is entered, the correction can be rekeyed right over the original entry. A missing letter can simply be inserted. Word processing systems virtually eliminate the need for the erasers, correction tape, and White Out so often used with ordinary office typewriters. They also make it easy to copy entire blocks of text.

Editing entails more than just making corrections, however. After a document has been prepared, the user can go back and insert additional information into any part of the existing text. The program will automatically move the rest of the text to make room for the insertion. Easy and efficient correction, or *editing*, of information is one of the most common reasons people use word processing systems.

Editing can also include deleting characters, words, or blocks of information completely or moving entire sections of information from one part of the document to another. This is similar to the manual process of cutting a section of a document with scissors and pasting that section into another location. In word processing, this *cut and paste* is performed electronically—no scissors and no tape. Some systems allow the user to move text by highlighting it with the cursor and then *dragging* the text to the new location.

Storing and Retrieving Information.   Document storage entails saving documents on a disk—either an internal hard disk, an external diskette, or magnetic tape (see Chapter 4 for a review of secondary storage). Any information that is entered into a word processing system can be retained indefinitely by storing it on disk or tape.

When the word processing software writes a document to storage, it includes not only the text itself, but also its formatting information. When the document is retrieved from storage, whether for editing, copying, or printing, it will appear in the original format.

Printing Information.   When documents are printed, information from either computer memory, disk, or magnetic tape is transferred to an output medium—usually to paper by way of a printer. Other WP output options are mailing labels, transparencies, and 35mm film (Figure 7.4).

The printing process preserves the format, layout, and highlighting of information created during the entry and editing stages. Margins, special characters, and images (for example, clip art—which we discuss later in this chapter) appear on the output in the same form and at the same location as specified by the person using the WP system. (Behind the scenes, the program and the printer are communicating to transfer format and content information to produce the printed images.)

Features of Word Processing Systems

WP software developers are continually adding new features to help individuals be more productive and more effective. Most packages now contain a variety of special tools. Among the most frequently used are spelling and grammar checkers, thesauruses, macros, and sorting capabilities. In addition, WP packages used in different countries offer different character sets; see the Global IT box on page 258 titled "Word Processing in the Global Economy" for more details.

Spell Checker and Grammar Checker.   Using a **spell checker**, a person can scan the contents of a document for misspelled words, the occurrence of two words in a row, and improper abbreviations. A dictionary stored on disk, which can be customized to include names and frequently occurring special terms, is used to verify the correct spelling of each word in the document. The spelling dictionaries used in the most popular word processing packages include more than 100,000 words.

spell checker A word processing feature that scans the contents of a document for misspelled words, the occurrence of two words in a row, and improper abbreviations.

FIGURE 7.4
Word Processing Output Options
In addition to printed reports, word processing programs can output mailing labels, transparencies, and 35 mm film.

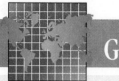

GLOBAL IT

Word Processing in the Global Economy

PICK UP ANY OF THE HIGH-TECH THRILLERS ON THE BEST-SELLER list and you'll be immersed in a heady world where a few clicks of a computer keyboard can zap a secret message across international borders. But fact is rarely as easy as fiction. Just ask the word processors at multinational corporations who face the mission of preparing and exchanging computer files with foreign subsidiaries.

One obstacle is the number of symbols and characters used in the world's languages. French, German, and Spanish, for example, extend the English alphabet by adding special characters and punctuation marks, such as the ñ and ¿ of Spanish, the ç of French, and the ö of German. Other languages, such as Russian, Japanese, and Arabic, use entirely different alphabets.

To further complicate matters, some languages, such as Hebrew and Arabic, are written from right to left, not left to right. Chinese and Japanese can be written vertically, as well as horizontally. In addition, 8 1/2″ x 11″ paper isn't standard around the world, and some countries follow different conventions for displaying dates and currency. All of these differences must be taken into account by a word processing program.

Computer users who need to write in a language other than English have two basic options today. One is to buy a WP program, such as WordPerfect or Microsoft Word, that has been customized for a specific language. This means that the manuals, screen prompts, and spell checkers have all been translated into the proper language. The second option is to buy a multilingual word processor—one that has been designed to handle many languages at the same time. One of the leading multilingual word processors is MultiLingual Scholar; its basic package supports more than 25 languages.

Does this mean that a user of MultiLingual Scholar can use a computer file prepared with the Norwegian version of Microsoft Word? Probably not. To understand why, we need to look at ASCII's extended character set (see Chapter 3), the 128 "slots" or numeric values that can be used to represent nonstandard characters and symbols, such as ä and ¥, within the computer. Unlike ASCII's standard character set, used to represent the English language, the extended character set varies. On an IBM PC, for example, ASCII code 128 represents the letter Ç; on an Apple Macintosh the same code produces the letter Ä.

Another problem is that ASCII's standard character set provides only 256 "slots" or numeric values. This is not enough to represent the complex alphabets of Arabic or Russian, or the thousands of ideographs that make up Chinese and Japanese. This size limitation forces programmers to devise different "workaround" schemes for representing foreign characters and ideographs. Multilingual Scholar, for example, may use one system to represent the

Norwegian alphabet, while Microsoft Word uses another. This inconsistency blocks the exchange of files between the two programs.

Help is on the way, however, thanks to Unicode, a new coding system being developed by an international consortium of hardware and software developers. Many computer professionals describe Unicode as an extended ASCII that will expand the standard character set to 65,536 slots. Under the Unicode standard, every character, symbol, or ideograph used in each of the world's major languages can be assigned a specific numeric value. When Unicode becomes the standard coding system, exchanging text files will be almost as simple as it is in the thrillers.

The major word processing software companies, including Microsoft and WordPerfect, have customized their WP programs for languages other than English. The screens shown here are taken from WordPerfect's Russian version.

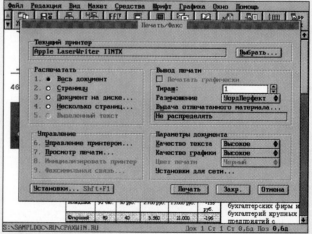

Spell checkers can be used to check a word, page, section, or entire document. They also suggest alternate spellings and abbreviations (Figure 7.5), and can replace all occurrences of a word with another word throughout the entire document.

Grammar checkers work in a similar fashion, scanning documents to identify sentences with grammatical errors or poor phrasing (Figure 7.6). Inconsistency in noun and verb forms, use of split infinitives, duplicate words, and incorrect prepositional phrases are among the most important errors spotted by grammar checkers. Many grammar checkers also evaluate how easily the document's writing can be understood by the average reader.

Thesauruses.   A **thesaurus** searches for and displays synonyms (words having identical or similar meanings) and antonyms (words with opposite meanings) for a particular word chosen by the user (Figure 7.7 on the next page). The thesaurus feature helps writers choose words and vary their phrasing.

Macros.   When identical tasks are performed repeatedly, it is often useful to create a **macro**, a mini-program that is identified by a name and a series of keystrokes. Frequently, employees will establish a WP macro to create mailing labels,

grammar checker A word processing feature that scans the contents of a document to identify grammatical errors and poor phrasing.

thesaurus A word processing feature that searches for and displays synonyms and antonyms for a particular word chosen by the user.

macro A mini-program that is identified by a name and a series of keystrokes.

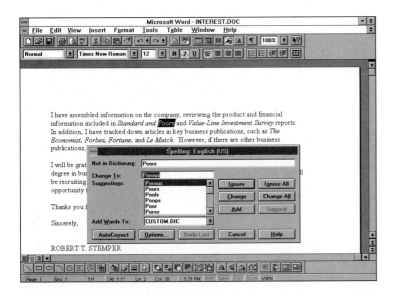

FIGURE 7.5
Spell Checking Feature of a Word Processing System
In addition to suggesting alternative spellings for words not found in its dictionary, a spell checker can be customized to include names and often-used special terms. Businesspeople who refer to *Standard and Poor's* frequently would want to add this term to their spell checker's dictionary.
Reprinted with permission of Microsoft Corp.

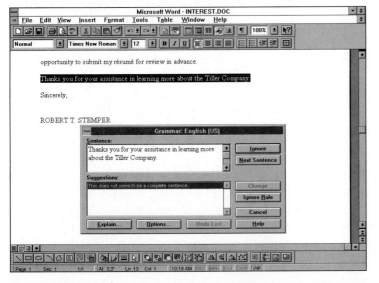

FIGURE 7.6   Grammar Checking Feature of a Word Processing System Grammar checkers can identify sentence fragments, improper subject-verb agreement, split infinitives, and incorrect punctuation.
Reprinted with permission of Microsoft Corp.

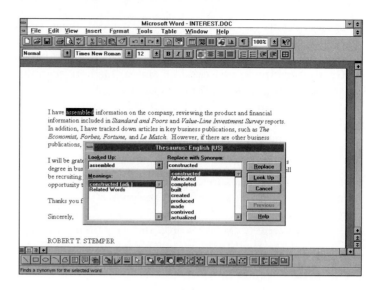

FIGURE 7.7   Thesaurus Feature of a Word Processing System   The thesaurus feature helps writers choose their words and vary their style. Reprinted with permission of Microsoft Corp.

an often-performed task in many offices. When the user tells the system to perform the LABEL macro (or whatever the name assigned to the macro), the system will prompt the user for information needed, including the size of labels, whether to prepare a single label or a series of labels, which printer to use, and what files will be used to generate the labels. Using this information, the macro carries out the various steps involved in preparing and printing the labels. The user benefits by saving time while knowing that the steps will be carried out consistently and reliably each time.

sorting A word processing feature that allows the user to arrange lines and paragraphs of text alphabetically or numerically, or sets of information by date.

Sorting.   The **sorting** feature of WP programs lets you arrange lines and paragraphs of text alphabetically or numerically, or sets of information by date. You can choose either ascending order (from a to Z and 0 to 9) or descending order (from Z to a and 9 to 0) (Figure 7.8).

Sorting is useful when information must be organized to correspond to particular actions. For example, when preparing mailing labels, it is useful to sort the names and addresses by postal code before printing the labels. (Companies can receive a discount on postage if they do so.) If personalized letters including a person's name and address are prepared for a direct mail campaign, the sequence of names can be sorted to correspond with the mailing label sequence, making matching of letter and envelope easy and efficient.

Other Word Processing Activities.   Other word processing activities supported by many, but not all, word processing programs include:

redlining A word processing feature that makes editing changes visible in a document.

- **Redlining (editing).** Using the **redlining** feature makes editing changes visible in a document. Eliminated words are shown with a line through them almost as if they had been manually crossed out on the display screen. A single command can make the redlined words visible or invisible, onscreen and/or on the printed output.

search and replace A word processing feature that allows the user to scan a document for a particular word or phrase and replace it with a different word or phrase.

- **Search and replace.** When you need to find and change all occurrences of a word or phrase throughout a document, the **search and replace** function is the quickest and easiest way to do so. The user simply tells the system to scan the document for a specific word or phrase and to replace it with a substitute word or phrase. The search can match or ignore capitalization of words, and can make all changes at one time or prompt the user for instructions at each occurrence.

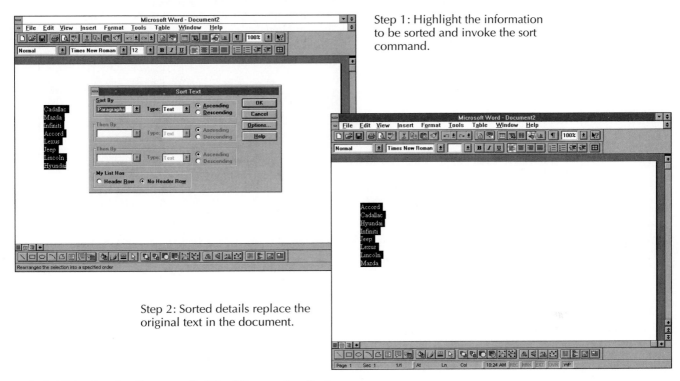

Step 1: Highlight the information to be sorted and invoke the sort command.

Step 2: Sorted details replace the original text in the document.

FIGURE 7.8   Sorting Feature of a Word Processing System
Sorting data and information is particularly useful when information must be organized to correspond to particular actions.
Reprinted with permission of Microsoft Corp.

- **Mail merge.** The **mail merge** facility allows you to create and personalize multiple copies of a document. The word processor inserts—that is, merges—personalized information (such as name, address, and personalized greeting) from a mailing list into a document contained in a different file (Figure 7.9 on the next page). The results may be sent directly to a printer or captured and stored in a third file. Mail merge processing does flawlessly and in a few seconds what could take someone hours to do manually.
- **Headers and footers.** Sometimes it is desirable to have descriptive text printed on the top or bottom of each page. **Headers** and **footers** may include the name of the document, the date, author, or other information that should be repeated on each page. The text for headers and footers is typed only one time; the word processing software automatically inserts it on each page when the document is printed.
- **Footnotes.** A footnote is a number, symbol, or mark in the text calling attention to additional text at the bottom of the page. When the user needs to add a footnote to a document, the word processing program inserts a footnote number or symbol at the designated location and opens a window into which the footnote text is typed. The program automatically reserves space at the bottom of the page for each footnote, adjusting the amount of text on the page so that the footnote will fit in its entirety at the bottom.
- **Math functions.** Math functions allow users to perform a limited number of calculations, including simple arithmetic, percentages, and square roots, during the course of word processing. Numbers and symbols are stated as an equation (such as 12*$583) and processed using the built-in math function. The calculated result ($6996.00) is inserted directly into the document.

mail merge A word processing facility that allows the user to create and personalize multiple copies of a document.

header The descriptive text printed at the top of each page of a document.

footer The descriptive text printed at the bottom of each page of a document.

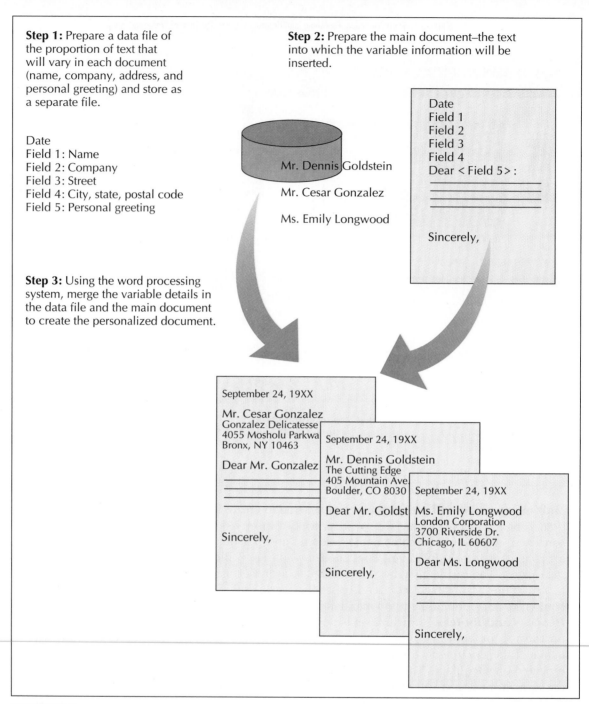

Step 1: Prepare a data file of the proportion of text that will vary in each document (name, company, address, and personal greeting) and store as a separate file.

Date
Field 1: Name
Field 2: Company
Field 3: Street
Field 4: City, state, postal code
Field 5: Personal greeting

Step 2: Prepare the main document—the text into which the variable information will be inserted.

Date
Field 1
Field 2
Field 3
Field 4
Dear < Field 5 > :
_____
_____
_____

Sincerely,

Mr. Dennis Goldstein

Mr. Cesar Gonzalez

Ms. Emily Longwood

Step 3: Using the word processing system, merge the variable details in the data file and the main document to create the personalized document.

September 24, 19XX

Mr. Cesar Gonzalez
Gonzalez Delicatesse
4055 Mosholu Parkwa
Bronx, NY 10463

Dear Mr. Gonzalez

Sincerely,

September 24, 19XX

Mr. Dennis Goldstein
The Cutting Edge
405 Mountain Ave.
Boulder, CO 8030

Dear Mr. Goldst

Sincerely,

September 24, 19XX

Ms. Emily Longwood
London Corporation
3700 Riverside Dr.
Chicago, IL 60607

Dear Ms. Longwood

Sincerely,

FIGURE 7.9
Mail Merge Feature of a Word Processing System
In only a few seconds, mail merge processing performs tasks that would take hours to perform manually.

- **Index and table of contents generation.** Word processing programs can create an index of a document's key terms, listing the terms and the page on which they occur. They can also create an entire table of contents, listing the document's section headings and the page on which each begins. As each term is entered, the user marks it (usually with a nonprinting symbol) for inclusion in the index or table of contents. Later, a macro is executed to prepare and print the index or table of contents.

- **Orphan and widow elimination.** A **widow** is the last line of a paragraph at the top of a page and an **orphan** is the first line of a paragraph at the bottom of a page. Most word processing programs include an option to eliminate widows and orphans by establishing the minimum number of lines that can be separated by a page break. When the program detects a widow or orphan, it adjusts the number of lines on the page to avoid widowed or orphaned lines.

- **Reading level check.** Reading level functions scan a document and compile *readability* statistics describing the content and reading level. Common readability statistics used in leading WP packages are the Flesch-Kincaid method, which identifies the school grade level needed to read the document easily, and the Gunning Fog Index, which measures the overall sentence length and number of multisyllable words in the document.

- **Importing and exporting files.** Many WP systems allow document files created in one system to be used in another. **Importing** reads an external file into a word processing document, converting its contents into the proper format. **Exporting** writes a document to storage in a format needed by another application. Both text and graphics files are commonly imported and exported between different programs. Gaining in popularity is the importing of **clip art**, prestored files of graphic images (Figure 7.10). Files of clip art containing drawings, logos, photographs, and symbols can be purchased for a modest cost and imported into virtually any document to enhance its appearance and/or message.

As word processing systems become more sophisticated, we can expect this list to continue growing.

widow The last line of a paragraph at the top of a page.

orphan The first line of a paragraph at the bottom of a page.

importing The process of bringing an external file into a chosen format by converting its contents into the proper format.

exporting The process of writing a document to storage in a format needed by another application.

clip art Prestored files of graphic images.

FIGURE 7.10
The Uses of Clip Art
The pieces of clip art shown at left can be easily imported into a wide variety of business documents (right).
Courtesy Clipper Creative Art Service.

Team Sets Up Shop with WP Software

> **Comprehensive Support Systems**
>
> In 1986 Mary Workman was ready for a change. That's when she left her job as a personnel director in the health care field to start Comprehensive Support Services in Silver Spring, Maryland. The company's goal: to provide word processing and related services to area businesses and individuals.
>
> At first, Workman's only piece of office equipment was a rented typewriter. Within a year, business was so brisk that her husband Patrick quit his job as a truck salesman to work full-time alongside his wife. By 1992 the couple was using four computers, four printers, and WordPerfect software in their 1,000-square-foot home office. Gross annual receipts topped $50,000, based on a rate of $2 to $4 per page and $20 per hour for such special projects as assembling and managing a mailing list or stuffing envelopes.

▓ An Overview of Desktop Publishing

desktop publishing (DTP) The arrangement of textual information and images into a format that is easily understandable and visually appealing using a desktop publishing program.

Unlike word processing, which is concerned mostly with the placement of words (and the occasional graphic image or piece of clip art) on the printed page, **desktop publishing (DTP)** concentrates on arranging both textual information and images (photographs, drawings, charts, and graphs) into a format that is easily understandable and visually appealing. This final product includes not only the information that is to be conveyed to the reader, but also special design features like icons, spacing variations, lines and boxes, and different type styles.

Some desktop publishing software can perform all the functions of word processing software: entry, display, editing, storage and retrieval, and printing of information. Other publishing software has layout and editing capacity only; the original documents must be imported into the publishing program from a word processing program. Some of the leading desktop publishing programs are listed in Table 7.2.

Because desktop publishing was designed to move several steps beyond word processing, it includes several important features that are not found in WP software. The most important of these are *document design* and *content positioning features.*

TABLE 7.2   Leading Desktop Publishing Programs

Software Package	Manufacturer	Computer Versions Available
QuarkXPress	Quark	Apple Macintosh and IBM-compatible
Aldus PageMaker	Aldus	Apple Macintosh and IBM-compatible
Publisher	Microsoft	IBM-compatible
Ventura Publisher	Xerox	IBM-compatible
Ready Set Go	Letraset	Apple Macintosh

In desktop publishing lingo, the **design** of a document—whether it is a newsletter, an annual report, a magazine, or a newspaper—is the arrangement of the document's information and a specification of its features. A design consists of several elements:

- A grid with margin and column guides.
- Text, including headers and footers.
- Graphics, such as symbols and icons, that will appear in the document.
- Type specifications, including the type style(s) and size(s) used and the spacing between words, letters, and lines.

design The arrangement of a DTP document's information and a specification of its features.

Depending on the nature of the document and the capabilities of the software, a design may be specified for an entire document or for a single page.

In addition to creating the design specifications for a document, desktop publishing software positions the design elements within the document. That is, the software handles the insertion of information into a specific location, as well as the cutting and pasting of text and images. When performed manually, these activities are very time consuming and prone to errors. An image positioned by a desktop publishing system will rarely be pasted into place upside down or in a crooked position.

Reality Check.   Although people often draw a distinction between word processing and desktop publishing, the line is becoming increasingly blurry. More and more desktop publishing capabilities are being added to word processing software. Many of today's WP systems incorporate the capability to use multiple type sizes and styles, insert photos and drawings in the middle of the text, arrange text in multiple columns, and insert lines and boxes. Some even feature WYSIWYG ("what you see is what you get") capabilities that allow you to see an image of the printed document on the screen.

Nonetheless, word processing and desktop publishing have fundamentally different missions. Word processing programs continue to focus on the entry of lines of information, while DTP programs focus on the design of document pages and the positioning of information.

Desktop Publishing Operations

Although different DTP software packages offer different capabilities, all programs share certain elements. These include:

- Preparation of previously established text information for use in the desktop system
- Selection of typeface, point size, and fonts
- Control of kerning and leading
- Ability to incorporate graphic information.

Preparation of Text Information.   The text of a document is frequently prepared using a word processing program. Using a special capability, this information can then be imported into the DTP program, where it will be formatted according to the design set up by the publishing program. You can also type information into the document using the publishing software, or edit information that has been imported, then store the changes you've made.

typeface (type style) A family of characters that have the same basic design.

point size A measure of a character's height. One point equals 1/72 of an inch or .35 cm.

font A complete set of characters in a particular typeface.

kerning The spacing between the characters in a word.

leading The vertical spacing between the lines of text on a page.

Selection of Typeface, Point Size, and Fonts. A **typeface** (also called a **type style**) is a family of characters (letters, numbers, and symbols) that have the same basic design. Within the family, the characters may vary in weight—they may be regular "lightface" type or heavy **boldface** type. Typefaces may also vary in style; most typefaces have an *italic* form that is used for emphasis in documents. Some common typefaces are illustrated in Figure 7.11.

A type's **point size** is a measure of its height. One point equals 1/72 of an inch or .35 cm. Ordinary office typewriters have traditionally used 10 point Pica or Courier type and 12 point Elite type. This book uses 16 point type for its main headings and 10 point type for the running text. Clearly, point size influences readability—the larger the type, the easier it is to read. Point size can also be used to emphasize important information. Figure 7.12 shows assorted point sizes in the Helvetica typeface.

A **font** is a complete set of characters in a particular typeface, including all weights, styles, and point sizes. It includes all upper and lowercase letters, numbers, common symbols (for example, &, $, and #), and punctuation marks. Fonts are of two types. Serif fonts have *serifs*, small projections stemming from the upper and lower ends of the strokes used to form the character. *Sans serif* fonts have no projections (Figure 7.13 identifies parts of a character). The Quality and Productivity box on page 271 titled "Some Dos and Don'ts of Desktop Publishing" offers some pointers on when and how to use fonts and typefaces.

Control of Kerning and Leading. **Kerning** is the spacing between the characters in a word. In most programs the kerning is set automatically to a default kerning. However, to improve the appearance of a document or to create a desired effect, designers may choose to adjust the kerning.

Leading (pronounced "ledding") is the vertical spacing between the lines of text on a page. Again, default leading is often used, but designers may adjust leading to create an effect or enhance readability. Generally, the more space between lines, the easier a document is to read. Figure 7.14 on page 268 illustrates different types of kerning and leading.

Incorporating Graphic Information. Graphic information consists of line drawings and halftones. Typically, each is prepared by another computer tool (for example, a drawing program or graphics package) and imported into the desktop publishing document.

Lines and rules of varying lengths, widths, and styles can be used to emphasize, set off, or separate portions of a document. Lines should not be confused with

FIGURE 7.11
Common Typefaces

Avant Garde	ABCD abcdefghij
Helvetica	ABCD abcdefghij
New Century Schoolbook	ABCD abcdefghij
Script	ABCD abcdefghij
Times	ABCD abcdefghij

Eight point 1234567890
Nine point 1234567890
Ten point 1234567890
Twelve point 1234567890
Fourteen point 1234567890
Eighteen point 1234567890
Twenty-four point 1234567890
Thirty-six point 1234567
Forty-eight point 12
Sixty point 123
Seventy-two

FIGURE 7.12   Point Sizes in Helvetica Type

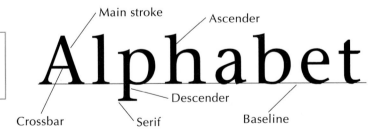

Serif fonts:
Times Roman
MS Serif
Courier

Main stroke   Ascender

Alphabet

Crossbar   Serif   Descender   Baseline

FIGURE 7.13
Serif and Sans Serif Typefaces
Interestingly, textbooks are
rarely set in sans serif faces
because serif faces are generally
considered easier to read.

Sans Serif fonts:
Helvetica
MS SansSerif
Avant Garde

Main stroke

Alphabet

Baseline

KERNING

loose
normal
tight
verytight

A *Un-kerned Letter Pairs*
B *Kerned Letter*

WALTER
WALTER

Without
With

LEADING

Leading is the vertical spacing between lines of text on
a page. Default leading is often used, but designers may
adjust leading to create an effect or enhance readability.
Generally, the more space between lines, the easier
a document is to read.

a) 10/12 leading

Leading is the vertical spacing between lines of text on a
page. Default leading is often used, but designers may adjust
leading to create an effect or enhance readability. Generally,
the more space between lines, the easier a document is
to read.

a) 10/9 leading

Leading is the vertical spacing between lines of text on

a page. Default leading is often used, but designers may

adjust leading to create an effect or enhance readability.

Generally, the more space between lines, the easier

a document is to read.

a) 10/18 leading

FIGURE 7.14
Examples of Kerning and
Leading

line drawing or **line art** A
graphic that consists of only simple
lines and areas of black, white, or
color.

line drawings (also called **line art**), which are graphics that consist of only simple lines and areas of black, white, or color (Figure 7.15). The lines in line drawings may be straight, crooked, or curved, and several inches long or as short as a
single dot. Designers working for a sailing magazine, for example, might create a
sailboat icon for the magazine by drawing the sailboat's features one line at a time,
then importing the finished line art into the publishing software.

halftone A collection of minuscule
dots that collectively portray a
subject.

Halftones resemble photographs. But unlike photographs, they are actually a
collection of minuscule dots (not visible to the naked eye) that collectively portray
the subject (Figure 7.16). The smaller the dots that make up the halftone, the clearer the resolution. Dot size is a function of the capabilities of the software and the
printer (or other output device) on which the halftones appear (see Chapter 4). A
halftone of a sailboat would appear similar to a photograph taken with a camera,
but without the glossy surface.

FIGURE 7.15
Example of Line Art

Preparing a Desktop Publishing Document

Generally, preparing a desktop publishing document entails three steps:

- Design and layout specification
- Placement of information
- Printing

You can see this process in action in the photo essay at the end of this chapter.

FIGURE 7.16
Examples of Halftones
The black-and-white and color halftones shown here have been enlarged to show the collection of tiny dots that collectively portray the photo's subject.

Design and Layout Specification.   Before the various components of a document are put together, the document must be designed. One of the most important aspects of a design is the **layout**, or the arrangement of the elements that make up the document. Layouts determine the overall composition of a page (Figure 7.17).

Text on a page is contained within a **text block**, a portion of a document that contains only text (no drawings or halftones). There may be more than one text block on a page. For example, the page headings and footers may be in separate blocks from the narrative that comprises the bulk of the page. Text blocks can be moved around from place to place with no effect on the rest of the document's components. Type styles and sizes may vary within text blocks.

layout The arrangement of the elements that comprise a DTP document.

text block A portion of a document that contains only text.

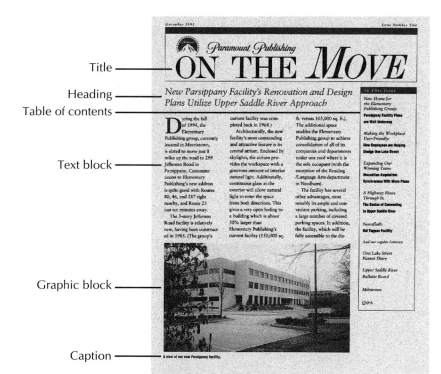

Title

Heading

Table of contents

Text block

Graphic block

Caption

FIGURE 7.17
Sample Page Layout
A document's layout specifies the arrangement of its elements.

graphic block A portion of a document containing any type of image information.

grid The guide used in DTP systems to aid in the structuring of information on a page.

Graphic blocks contain any type of image information. Like text blocks, several graphic blocks may be used independently of one another on a page. Each can be moved and resized (that is, made larger or smaller) to suit the designer's objective.

Grids are used as guides to aid in the structuring of information on a page (Figure 7.18). The horizontal and vertical lines that comprise a grid appear on the screen as guidelines, but do not show when the final document is printed. The number and complexity of grids used in a document varies according to the document's purpose.

Placement of Information.   Using the layout grid as a guide, the user places the various forms of information into the document, specifying which information should go in which location. The DTP program places text information into text blocks and graphics into graphic blocks and prevents the different kinds of information from being intermingled.

When text information is imported from another program—say, from a word processing file—the publishing software acts on the user's instructions to read the information from the disk file and place it into the specified text block. The program will divide sentences into lines that will fit within the allocated space. If necessary, the information will flow from one page to the next, always following the layout guidelines.

Most publishing software contains an option that directs the program either to break lines between words or to break words if necessary. A *hyphenation dictionary* included with the software contains the correct spelling and syllabication of words so that the program will break the word at the right spot and insert a hyphen correctly.

Image placement is carried out in much the same way as text placement. The software copies the image into the designated section on the page. If necessary, the software can automatically increase or reduce the size of the image so that it fits perfectly into the allotted space.

Printing.   Printing a desktop publishing document is easily accomplished by a simple command or the click of a button. But behind the scenes, a great deal of processing is occurring within both the computer and the printer. The publishing program must not only tell the printer the text and graphic information to be printed, but also describe its appearance and its placement on a page.

**FIGURE 7.18
Sample Page Layout Grids**

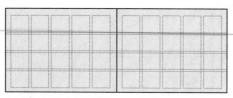

5 column, 4 row

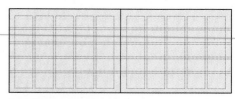

5 column, 5 row

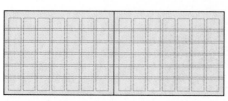

7 column, 6 row

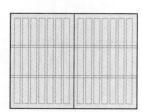

7 column, 3 row

QUALITY AND PRODUCTIVITY

Some Dos and Don'ts of Desktop Publishing

IF YOU'RE A NOVICE AT USING LAYOUT, TYPE, AND GRAPHICS, here are a few tips to help you look like a real pro.

- **DO** match your layout, type, and graphics to your message. Some typefaces (for example, Gothic) are great for holiday party invitations but not so good for résumés.
- **DO** use heads and generous amounts of white space to signal your organization, break the text into manageable chunks, and make the page look inviting.
- **DO** avoid the "Ransom Note School of Design." Even though you have access to 60 typefaces, limit yourself to one serif face for all body type (or text) and a complementary sans serif face for heads, captions, and other short blocks of type.
- **DO** consider readability, the ease with which our eyes find the beginnings of lines and scan them for word shapes. Some rules of thumb: body type should be between 9 and 12 points in size; lines should be 7 to 14 words long; and you should allow at least two points leading, between lines.
- **DO** look for opportunities to convert tables to line graphs or bar charts that communicate quickly and add visual interest.

- **DON'T** clutter your layouts with too much type or too many pieces of clip art. Remember: Every element on the page should be there for a reason, and its importance should be indicated by its size and position.
- **DON'T** forget readability when you consider type alignment. If you use justified type (aligned at both the left and right margins) or flush left type (aligned at the left margin only), use hyphenation to avoid unsightly gaps or short lines.
- **DON'T** get so wrapped up in playing designer that you forget to proofread. Better yet, ask a friend or colleague to help.
- **DON'T** be afraid to experiment. It takes a while to develop a designer's eye, but you can speed the process by reading some of the many excellent books on desktop design. Two outstanding ones are Roger C. Parker's *Looking Good in Print: A Guide to Basic Design for Desktop Publishing* (second edition, 1990, Ventana Press) and Daniel Will-Harris's *TypeStyle: How to Choose and Use Type on a Personal Computer* (1990, Peachpit Press).

Special **page description languages** are used for this purpose. The languages, which are embedded in a chip in the printer and integrated with software commands in the publishing program, permit specification of the printed information's fonts, type sizes, and type styles. They translate the rules, lines, and graphics into the dots that the printer prints. They also specify where every element of a page should be printed, character by character and dot by dot. (All of this is handled automatically by the software, so you do not need to work with page description language yourself.)

The *PostScript* description language is very widely used on many Apple and IBM-compatible computers and printers, and on high-resolution typesetting machines used by commercial printers. Hewlett-Packard also uses its own language, *Printer Command Language (PCL)*, on its popular family of LaserJet printers. (Some less expensive brands of dot matrix printers have a very limited capability to print published documents because they do not accept any page description language.)

Printed pages are often treated as **camera ready copy**, high-quality printouts that can be used as masters in printing. A commercial printer will make a printing plate from camera ready copy, mount it on the press, and begin printing. Camera ready copy lowers the cost of printed documents substantially, because the printer need not prepare the lines of type or paste up drawings and images on the page layout forms.

page description language
The language, embedded in a printer chip and integrated with software commands in a publishing program, that permits specification of the printed information's fonts, type sizes, and type styles.

camera ready copy High-quality printouts that can be used as masters in printing.

Desktop Publishing Options

Like word processing programs, DTP programs offer a wide variety of options that can be customized by the user.

- **Page size and master pages.** Typically, word processing documents are a standard office paper dimension, such as 8 1/2 x 11 inches or 8 1/2 x 14 inches, or A4 size. Desktop publishing, in contrast, may feature many different paper sizes, both standard and custom. Often an 11 x 17 inch size is specified for reports, because when folded it provides four standard-size pages. Books, brochures, booklets, newsletters, and posters may be created in different sizes—some larger and some smaller.

  The design of a desktop document is included in **master pages**, which contain the format and any information that is repeated on each page of the document (for example, headers and footers). Often a master right page will be separate from a master left page.

- **Column formatting and document magnification.** An essential element of a document's layout is its column formatting. The best column design is determined by the type of document. A sales brochure or report may, for example, be best designed in a single-column format. For newsletters, a single column of text may be difficult to read. Two- and three-column formats are easier on the eyes. It is easy to change the design for a layout; the user need only select a new layout and the publishing software creates the instructions for the master pages (Figure 7.19).

- **Border creation.** Borders around text and images set off the information and enhance the document's appearance. DTP systems allow you to create many kinds of borders in many different weights. Following your artistic inclinations, you can add double lines, dashed lines, or shaded lines for borders. The software makes certain that every border on every page is identical, if you desire—or completely different, if you prefer.

- **Use of clip art.** As we mentioned earlier, clip art makes an array of professionally prepared images available at the click of a button. These images can be imported into the document and positioned within a graphic box included in the layout. If necessary, the software can adjust the size and shading of the image. When documents are created in color, the software can even alter the colors used in the clip art to produce an illustration that conveys the message you have in mind.

master page In desktop publishing, a page containing the format and any information to be repeated on each page of the document.

FIGURE 7.19 Single- and Double-Column Layouts on Display Screen
Courtesy of Aldus Corp.

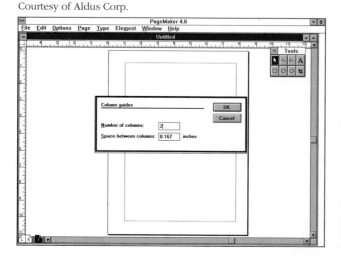
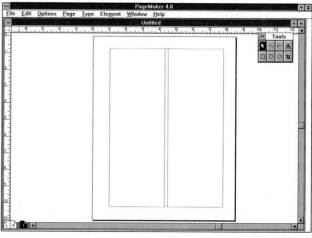

CRITICAL CONNECTION 2
WP and DTP Help AT&T Meet Proposal Deadlines

AT&T   Many of us associate AT&T with long-distance telephone service, but a big part of its business is based on submitting—and winning—bids to provide goods and services to the U.S. government. These bids are the responsibility of the Proposal Development Engineering Department and can be worth millions of dollars. There's just one catch: The proposals have to follow strict guidelines and, if they're even a minute late, government staff members by law must ignore them.

Deadline pressure at AT&T is compounded by the challenge of creating many complex documents with overlapping teams of technical writers, illustrators, and designers. Add the inevitable last-minute changes that need to be incorporated flawlessly into both text and graphics and you have the potential to miss deadlines that are carved in stone.

To avoid missed deadlines, AT&T has created a publishing resource center. The heart of the center is a network of computers, managed by a network administrator, and the Change Management System (CMS). CMS is a document management software system created to track the components of a proposal as they move across the network from writers using WP software, to illustrators using graphics software, to page layout artists using DTP software. If an illustrator needs to change an illustration, for example, he or she simply checks it out of the system, much like you would check a book out of the library. This feature lets every team member determine the location and status of proposal components at any time.

And how is AT&T doing since it created the publishing resource center? It hasn't missed a single deadline, and has won several large and lucrative contracts.

■ Graphics in Business Documents and Presentations

Five types of graphics are commonly used in business documents and presentations: decorative graphics, business graphics, presentation graphics, illustration graphics, and animation graphics.

Decorative Graphics

Decorative graphics (Figure 7.20) are primarily ornamental. They appear as borders (more intricate than those created through desktop publishing programs) on documents or as special symbols separating portions of documents. Unlike the other types of graphics, their purpose is not to convey information but to enhance the appearance of a document. The computer user can draw decorative graphics as combinations of lines and curves, or import clip art images into a document and paste them into the desired location.

Business Graphics

Business graphics, which we described in Chapter 5 as a means of illustrating data from spreadsheets, display information visually through charts, graphics, and symbols. They represent visually the data that describe an event or a process.

decorative graphics Graphics that are primarily ornamental.

business graphics Visual presentations of information through charts, graphics, and symbols.

FIGURE 7.20   Decorative Graphics   Decorative graphics, like the border on the award certificate shown here, is primarilily ornamental.

Business graphics are most useful for illustrating trends, proportions, highs and lows, and relationships between items.

The five principal types of business graphics—bar charts, pie charts, area line charts, line graphs, and pictograms (see Figure 5.11)—help us to compare data and spot trends and differences more quickly than tables of numbers. Notice in Figure 7.21 how apparent the line graph makes the differences between regions.

Presentation Graphics

In business, people sharing ideas to solve problems often make presentations. Thus far, this chapter has emphasized the presentation of ideas on the printed page. But many business presentations are done in front of an audience, usually with the use of visual aids. Good presentations often begin with the creation of good graphics created from graphics programs (Table 7.3).

TABLE 7.3   Leading Graphics Programs

Software Package	Manufacturer	Type	Computer Versions Available
Action	Macromedia	Animation	IBM-compatible and Macintosh
Animator Pro	Autodesk	Animation	IBM-compatible and Macintosh
Director	Macromedia	Animation	IBM-compatible
Premier	Adobe	Animation	IBM-compatible and Macintosh
Canvas	Deneba Software	Drawing	IBM-compatible and Macintosh
CorelDraw!	Corel Systems	Drawing	IBM-compatible
Harvard Graphics	Software Publishing	Drawing	IBM-compatible
Illustrator	Adobe	Drawing	IBM-compatible and Macintosh
Freehand	Aldus	Drawing	IBM-compatible and Macintosh
Digital Darkroom	Aldus	Imaging	Macintosh
Photoshop	Adobe	Imaging	IBM-compatible and Macintosh
Photostyler	Aldus	Imaging	IBM-compatible and Macintosh
Paint	Claris	Paint	Macintosh
Superpaint	Aldus	Paint	Macintosh
Photoshop	Adobe	Paint	IBM-compatible
Fractal Painter	Fractal Design	Paint	IBM-compatible
Powerpoint	Microsoft	Presentation	IBM-compatible and Macintosh
Freelance	Lotus Development	Presentation	IBM-compatible
WordPerfect Presentations	WordPerfect	Presentation	IBM-compatible
Persuasion	Aldus	Presentation	IBM-compatible and Macintosh

FIGURE 7.21
Business Graphic Created Through Spreadsheet Software

Presentation graphics are visual aids used to support verbal presentations of comments and ideas. Presentation media are typically color slides, transparencies, or handouts on paper. The graphics themselves may include any or all of the following:

presentation graphics Graphics used as visual aids to support verbal presentations of comments and ideas.

- **Text**—Words and phrases that outline an agenda, explain key ideas and concepts, or describe other graphics included in the presentation
- **Tables**—Data and information in rows and columns
- **Line art** or **clip art**—Drawings that illustrate activities, models, and processes
- **Photographs**—Color or black and white photos
- **Business graphics**—Imported from a spreadsheet or business graphics program.

Presentation graphics programs provide capabilities for planning, composing, and displaying entire presentations. Most of these provide the capability to create four different types of output:

- **Slides**—Single 35 mm slides consisting of any combination of the presentation graphic components (Figure 7.22); contents may be presented in color or black and white

FIGURE 7.22 Business Graphic from Spreadsheet Embedded in Presentation Slide

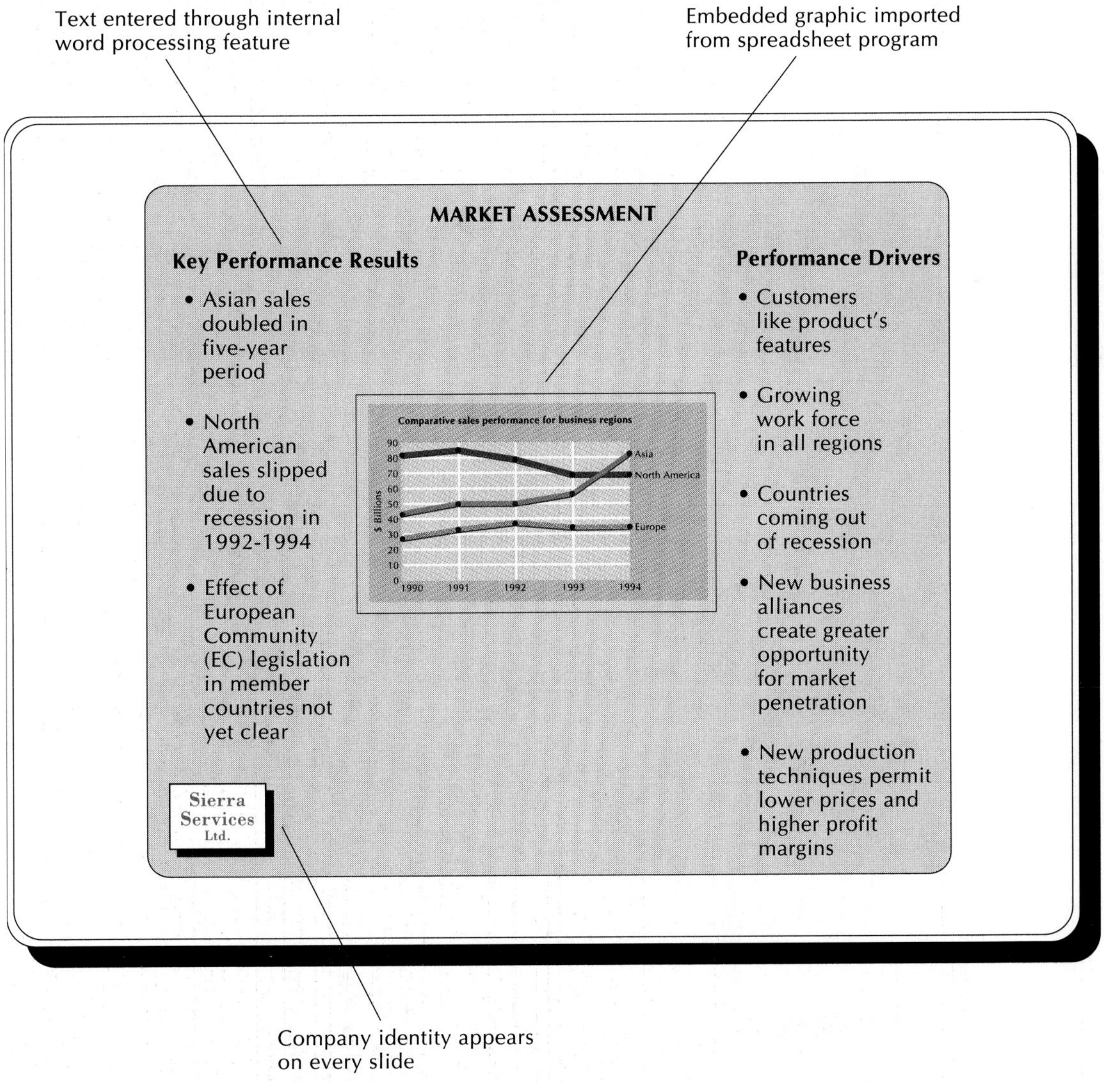
Text entered through internal word processing feature
Embedded graphic imported from spreadsheet program
MARKET ASSESSMENT
Key Performance Results
• Asian sales doubled in five-year period
• North American sales slipped due to recession in 1992-1994
• Effect of European Community (EC) legislation in member countries not yet clear
Comparative sales performance for business regions
$ Billions
90
80
70
60
50
40
30
20
10
0
1990
1991
1992
1993
1994
Asia
North America
Europe
Performance Drivers
• Customers like product's features
• Growing work force in all regions
• Countries coming out of recession
• New business alliances create greater opportunity for market penetration
• New production techniques permit lower prices and higher profit margins
Sierra Services Ltd.
Company identity appears on every slide

- **Note pages**—Single pages containing a reduced image of an entire slide or components of a slide as well as additional comments and text prepared with the word processing capability included in the presentation software or on an external word processing program and imported into the presentation software (Figure 7.23)
- **Audience handouts**—Pages containing reduced copies of slides, created by the software for distribution to the audience (Figure 7.24).
- **Outlines**—Listings of a sequence of topics and details, with each main entry on the outline corresponding to the topic of a specific slide (Figure 7.25 on page 278).

FIGURE 7.23
Note Page Containing Presentation Slide and Comments

Questions to raise:

1. What other features and services should we provide to our customers?

2. What advantages do we have in services that our competitors cannot duplicate?

3. What are the most successful salespersons in our firm doing?

4. What are our competitors doing?

Sierra
Services
Ltd.

FIGURE 7.24 Audience Handout Page

Annual Customer Meeting, Monte Carlo, June 18–24

Notes

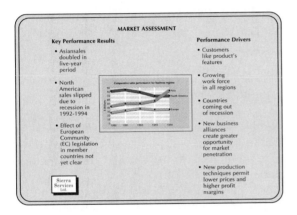

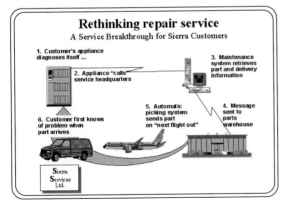

Outline entries correspond to presentation slides

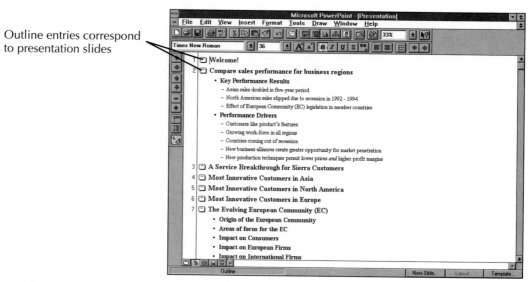

FIGURE 7.25
Presentation Outline Created Using Presentation Program
Reprinted with permission of Microsoft Corp.

Like DTP software, presentation software packages let the preparer choose a wide variety of text fonts, styles, and sizes. They also:

- Provide many different line widths, spacing alternatives, textures and patterns, and palettes for mixing and blending colors.
- Allow the creation of templates containing information that will be incorporated on each slide (such as the name of the presentation, a company logo, or the presenter's name or organization). The template specifies the location of graphics or text blocks, as well as details of the presentation's color scheme.
- Include an extensive set of drawing tools that make it relatively quick and easy to illustrate a presentation. The user simply selects the drawing tool needed to enter text, draw a line or circle, or surround text in a box, and then draws the image (Figure 7.26).

After the presentation is created, it is stored on disk and identified by a name chosen by the preparer. The presentation can then be printed, displayed, or edited at any time. Slides created in presentation programs can also be inserted into word processing or desktop publishing documents.

Illustration Graphics

illustration graphics A collection of graphics tools used by professional illustrators to create three-dimensional drawings with depth, complex curves, shading effects, and thousands of different color combinations.

Although presentation programs contain drawing tools, their principal purpose is creating slides to accompany presentations. **Illustration graphics**, in contrast, are used primarily by professional illustrators. They provide their users with many more options for preparing line drawings, allowing illustrators to create three-dimensional drawings with depth, complex curves, shading effects, and thousands of different color combinations. The programs respond to a pointing device, such as a mouse, which the illustrator uses to display on the screen the result corresponding to the drawing motions.

Text and drawing tools

Contents of slide

Work surface
(drawing board)

Clip art imported to
illustrate the slide

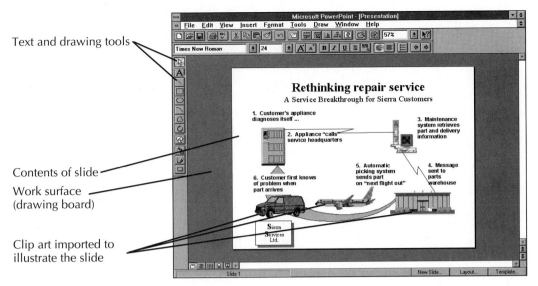

FIGURE 7.26
Tools and Work Surface of Presentation Program

There are three principal types of illustration software: drawing, painting, and image editing programs.

- **Drawing programs**, as their name suggests, provide many different capabilities for creating line drawings. Each element created in the drawing program can be increased or reduced in size, rotated, or reshaped in countless ways.
- **Paint programs** allow the illustrator to control the color and density of individual dots (pixels) that collectively create a colorful image on the screen or printout (Figure 7.27). The toolbox of a paint program contains an assortment of paintbrushes of varying widths, a magnifying glass for examining an image close up, paint buckets for filling sections of an image with a specified color, a lasso for selecting and copying a portion of an image, and an eraser to remove parts of the image.

drawing program A program designed to create line drawings.

paint program A program that allows the illustrator to control the color and density of individual dots that collectively create an image.

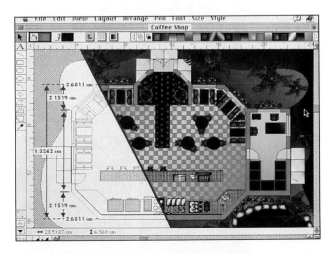

FIGURE 7.27
Sample Screen from a Paint Program
Paint programs allow the illustrator to control the color and density of the individual dots that collectively create a colorful image. In the screen shown here, an architect is using a paint program to design a coffee shop.

- **Image editing programs** have evolved from paint programs. These programs have the capability to scan color or black and white photographs, pictures in magazines, or virtually any other type of image. Once these images are in memory, the user can retouch them, changing colors, brightening or softening shades and hues, and correcting imperfect areas to create a continuous flow of color (Figure 7.28). Image editors also allow the user to make *color separations*, displaying the blue, yellow, black, and magenta components of a full-color image separately. Creating color separations is an essential step for printing documents in full color.

The *San Francisco Examiner*, a daily newspaper, cranks out five different editions every day, each containing color photos. Preparing color documents of any type takes longer than preparing black and white documents because of the extra production steps—such as preparing color separations—involved. Yet in the newspaper business, short deadlines (often less than one hour) are the norm. The combination of word processing, document layout, and graphics software tools has been a boon to the newspaper publishing industry.

When photographers for the *San Francisco Examiner* go out to cover a story, they load their camera with color film. After the photos are taken, the film is developed and imaged into a desktop system. Editors then review the images right on the display screen, making size and color adjustments almost instantly. With the system, the newspaper can get a color photo from the photographer's camera, into the newspaper, and on the printing presses in only 40 minutes.

FIGURE 7.28
The Output of an Image Editing Program
Computer Associates used image editing programs to "play with" Leonardo DaVinci's original Mona Lisa. The images are being used in advertisements for the company's CA-Cricket line of illustration graphics programs.

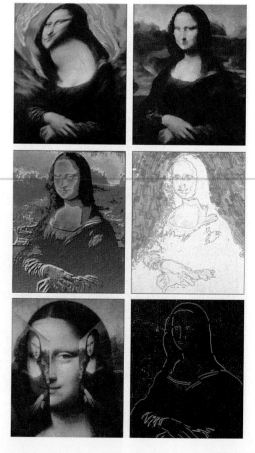

Animation Graphics

Animation programs make it possible to add motion to images and drawings (Figure 7.29). Using a mouse, the illustrator can trace a path on the display screen along which an image should move. Music and sound from almost any band or orchestral instrument can be linked to the image. Even the speed and rhythm of the music can be controlled and put in sync with the moving images.

A growing number of businesses are looking at ways to incorporate multimedia information, complete with animation, in their online product catalogs for customers and in their training programs for employees. Accompanying the text portion of each document is a graphic box that, when clicked, displays a product or service technique complete with sound and animated explanation. The text is created with word processing software, the remainder with various graphics and presentation tools. This capability is developing very rapidly and is likely to influence business practices in many ways.

animation program A graphics program that makes it possible to add motion to images and drawings.

CRITICAL CONNECTION 3
Presentation Graphics Help Dun & Bradstreet Economist Bring Numbers to Life

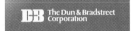

The graphics used in economics—tables and graphs—are sometimes inadequate for economists, who often need to show how social change and economic trends converge to create business opportunities. That's why Joseph Duncan chose to become an expert in computer-generated graphics and animation.

Duncan, chief economist at Dun & Bradstreet in New York, has the job of analyzing the global economy and presenting his views to audiences around the world through weekly presentations.

Today Duncan's toolbox includes a PC with a CD-ROM drive and sound board, as well as Microsoft Excel and Harvard Graphics, a powerful software package that can combine static graphics with video and animated graphics. With this system, Duncan can create multimedia presentations that bring his numbers to life. At a presentation to the D&B board of directors, for example, Duncan used vivid graphics to illustrate a report on a joint venture in the former Soviet Union.

FIGURE 7.29
Animation Graphics
Animation programs make it possible to add motion to images and drawings. Many companies have reported great success with computerized training programs that make use of animation graphics.

SUMMARY OF LEARNING OBJECTIVES

1 **Describe why people use word processing systems and list the five functions of word processing systems.** People use word processing systems to create and manage text documents, and to tailor the physical presentation of the information contained in those documents. The five functions of word processing programs are entering information, displaying information, editing information, storing and retrieving of information, and printing information.

2 **Explain the time-saving and productivity-enhancing features of a word processing system.** Word processing programs make people more efficient by decreasing the amount of time they spend on the mechanical aspects of their work. In addition, word processing programs allow users to concentrate on what they do best by helping them compensate for some of their weaknesses. The WP tools particularly useful here are spelling and grammar checkers, thesauruses, macros, and sorting capabilities.

3 **Differentiate between the purpose of a word processing program and the purpose of a desktop publishing system.** Word processing systems are concerned with the placement of words—and the occasional graphic image or piece of clip art—on the printed page. Desktop publishing (DTP) programs concentrate on arranging both textual information and images—photographs, drawings, charts, and graphs—into a format that is easily understandable and visually appealing.

4 **Describe the four operations common to all desktop publishing systems and the three steps involved in preparing a desktop published document.** The four operations common to all desktop publishing systems are: (1) preparation of previously established text information for use in the desktop system, (2) selection of typeface, point size, and fonts; (3) choice of kerning and leading; and (4) the incorporation of graphic information into the DTP document.

Three steps are involved in preparing a DTP document: (1) design and layout specification, (2) placement of information, and (3) printing.

5 **Explain the five types of graphics used in business documents and presentations.** There are five types of graphics used in business documents and presentations.

Decorative graphics are primarily ornamental. They appear as borders on documents or as special symbols separating portions of documents. *Business graphics* display information visually through charts, graphics, and symbols. *Presentation graphics* are visual aids used to support verbal presentations of comments and ideas. *Illustration graphics* are used by professional illustrators to create three-dimensional drawings with depth, complex curves, shading effects, and thousands of different color combinations. *Animation programs* make it possible to add motion to images and drawings.

KEY TERMS

CRITICAL CONNECTIONS

Comprehensive Support Systems

1.   Team Sets Up Shop with WP Software

Aside from their equipment, the biggest ongoing expense for Mary and Tom Workman at Comprehensive Support Services is advertising. The Workmans place daily ads in the *Washington Post* and advertise regularly with an association of local writers, who often give them meaty assignments typing book manuscripts or screen plays.

A large part of the Workmans' success has come as a result of a recent trend in corporate America to job clerical projects out to independent contractors, like the Workmans. Many believe that this trend offers several benefits: Small businesses thrive, while large corporations do not need to keep clerical help on staff or pay their benefits. The Workmans expect this trend to continue.

Questions for Discussion

1. Many people like the idea of starting a word processing service because it requires a relatively modest investment in computer hardware and software. As a result, the field is becoming increasingly competitive. What special services can word processing companies, like Comprehensive Support Services, offer to win and keep clients?

2. During times of peak demand, many small businesses have to add part-time staff or "outsource" certain projects to independent contractors, such as students who have the necessary skills. Keeping this fact in mind, what types of business decisions might the Workmans need to anticipate if they decide to expand their business to include desktop publishing services?

AT&T

2.   WP and DTP Help AT&T Meet Proposal Deadlines

In making plans for the publishing resource center, the supervisor of AT&T's Proposal Development Engineering Department was determined to avoid some of the problems associated with the old system. That's why the system was put in place one step at a time. The first job that needed changing was that of the illustrators, who are responsible for the most frequent and most labor-intensive changes in the production process.

Questions for Discussion

1. At first, the illustrators resisted the new system, mainly because CMS requires more clerical steps

than the previous system had. Then they had to revise a proposal that had been created just before CMS went into effect. By the end of the revision process, many had become supporters of the new system. Why do you think this is so?

2. In addition to letting users check the status of proposal components, CMS is helping AT&T develop a catalog of "best" proposals. Given the department's time pressures and the fact that few proposals are created from scratch, why might this proposal catalog be an advantage for AT&T's staff of technical writers?

 The Dun & Bradstreet Corporation

3.   Presentation Graphics Help Dun & Bradstreet Economist Bring Numbers to Life*

Joseph Duncan sees three key benefits of the presentation graphics system he uses. First, his presentations are easy to update. As new economic data become available, he simply enters them into the Microsoft Excel spreadsheets that feed into Harvard Graphics. (Previously, he had to turn to a commercial film lab and wait for it to update the slides for him.) Second, the system helps Dun & Bradstreet save money. When Duncan used the outside lab to produce his slides, he spent $400 to $500 every time he updated the presentation.

Most important, the presentation graphics system helps Duncan communicate more effectively. Instead of presenting his slides in a single, fixed order, for example, Duncan can build in "hyperlinks" to link him into the projection unit. These links let him jump to more detailed presentations or related topics and are especially useful during question-and-answer sessions.

Questions for Discussion

1. How might Duncan's use of presentation graphics create a competitive advantage for Dun & Bradstreet?

2. Can you think of any drawbacks or risks in using presentation graphics to present economic analyses? Explain your answer.

3. A multimedia consultant works on contract with Dun & Bradstreet, helping Duncan and others evaluate and choose hardware and software. Why might Dun & Bradstreet have hired a consultant for this purpose?

*Source: Robert M. Knight, "Sound, Vision Add Presentation Punch," *Computerworld*, January 25, 1993; p. 69.

REVIEW QUESTIONS

1. What is word processing?
2. What is a text document?
3. Identify and describe the five functions of word processing programs.
4. What is wordwrap? How does it work, and what benefit does it provide to someone using a word processing system?
5. Which features of a WP system can be useful to people who are unsure of their syntax and spelling?
6. Of what use is mail merge to a business?
7. Distinguish between exporting files from and importing files into a WP document.
8. How are desktop publishing and word processing software different?
9. Describe the four elements of a document's design.
10. What capabilities are offered by all DTP systems?
11. What three steps are involved in preparing a desktop published document?
12. Why do desktop publishers use clip art?
13. Name the five types of graphics commonly used in business documents and presentations.
14. What elements may presentation graphics contain?
15. List four types of output generated by presentation graphics programs.
16. Explain the three types of illustration software. Which includes the most capabilities?
17. Of what use can animation graphics be to business?

DISCUSSION QUESTIONS

1. Every morning, head chef and co-owner Greg Morton uses a Macintosh and word processing and desktop publishing software to revise the menu for the Bridge Street Café in the Buzzards Bay resort area of Massachusetts. In addition to adding detailed descriptions of the daily specials, Morton experiments with creating specialty menus. Twice a year (during the heavy summer season and the slow winter season), he uses the same system to create *Café Communiqué,* a newsletter that publicizes upcoming specials and the café's catering service. Besides the obvious savings in time and money, what other advantages might WP and DTP technology offer Morton? Can you think of any possible disadvantages of using this technology?

2. Paper Direct is one of many companies that sell printed brochure templates, envelopes, postcards, business cards, transparencies, and other presentation materials that have been preprinted with full-color borders and graphic elements. These products can be personalized by anyone who has word processing software and a laser printer. Why do you think that even large companies, like Chase Manhattan Bank, have been buying and using these supplies to create and test promotions?

3. The training center media department of Boise Cascade's Deridder, Louisiana, paper mill uses a combination of presentation graphics, video, and animation software to produce a variety of programs. These include a slide show designed to educate local students and civic groups about the prevention of wildfires that destroy local forests (the mill's primary resource), training programs that use animated cartoons, and a monthly management report that uses video and color graphics. How might the use of multimedia in these programs make them more effective?

SUGGESTED READINGS

Dynamic Graphics, *Step-by-Step Electronic Design*. Peoria, IL: Dynamic Graphics, Inc., 1988. Helpful tips for making any document created through word processing or desktop publishing effective. Emphasizes efficient design and layout procedures.

Gallo, Guy, *Take Word For Windows to the Edge*. Emeryville, CA: Ziff-Davis Publishing, 1993. How to use Microsoft's Word program in innovative and highly effective ways. Many of the methods described apply to other word processing programs also.

Parker, Roger C., *Newsletters from the Desktop*. Ventana Press, 1990. A discussion of how to use desktop publishing software to produce high-quality, effective newsletters.

Scarpichio, Mark, et al., *Winning Forms*. New York: Random House, 1992. Discusses the use of word processing systems to create business documents. Includes dozens of forms for personal and business productivity.

Sources of computer clip art: DiskArt, PO Box 354, San Ramon,CA 94583; Dover Publications, 180 Varick St., New York, NY 10014; Dynamic Graphics, Inc., 6000 North Forest Park Dr., Peoria, IL 61614-3592; T/Maker Co., 1290 Villa St., Mountain View, CA 94041

Graphically Speaking. Elk Ridge Publishing, 1993. Defines, explains, and illustrates approximately 3,000 commonly used terms pertaining to the design, review, and presentation of graphics in presentations and publications.

CASE STUDY

Simon & Schuster Sets Sail for the Electronic Age

To many computer users, word processing is simply a way to simplify the process of revising and proofreading a document. But to a major publisher like Simon & Schuster, word processing is the gateway to a new world of electronic publishing.

The publishing industry is using the term "electronic publishing" to mean three different things. Some people use it simply as a synonym for desktop publishing. Others use it to describe the concerted efforts corporations are making to use DTP to save time and labor, which translate into lower costs and more profit on the bottom line.

The third—and most forward-looking—use of "electronic publishing" encompasses all the computer-based products that can be produced once words and images are captured in digital form. The text, photos, and illustrations of an encyclopedia, for example, can be printed on paper, transferred to a computer disk, loaded onto an online information service, or used as the basis of a multimedia presentation that includes high-resolution color graphics and animation, as well as music and spoken passages. Unlike their paper-based counterparts, the electronic formats are lightweight, portable, and can be organized as a database, which makes a search for and retrieval of specific information quick and easy.

By the early 1990s, R.R. Donnelley, the nation's largest printer, had made a strong commitment to serve traditional publishers who wanted to produce material in electronic form. Sony, meanwhile, has started to produce "electronic books" on CD-ROM, and Microsoft Corp. has joined the growing list of publishers who are converting reference works and even novels to electronic formats.

To maintain its strong position in the publishing industry, Simon & Schuster has launched an ambitious four-year drive to move the company into the electronic age.

To appreciate the magnitude of the task, consider the challenges facing the company. First, Simon & schuster and its subsidiaries produce thousands of new titles every year. Second, the company uses the talents of thousands of skilled professionals—authors, editors, illustrators, and designers—who are trained in traditional, paper-based methods. Some of them had used computers only rarely.

Third, the company faced a major investment in computer hardware, software, and training to move its products into electronic formats.

Some Simon & Schuster subsidiaries are already ahead of the game. The Business, Technical, and Professional Group, for example, has a strong foothold in providing online information services to the tax, law, accounting, insurance, real estate, legal, and financial communities. And Simon & Schuster's Computer Curriculum Corp. develops integrated, computer-based learning systems for schools as well as corporations, which often need to provide basic skills training for employees. This is estimated to be a $100-million-a-year market.

The other division managers are pursuing a slow phase-in strategy similar to that of Marilyn Williams, vice president of product development at the Prentice Hall School Division, a Simon & Schuster subsidiary that publishes textbooks for the elementary and high school markets. When Williams took the job in the late 1980s, she found the editors using IBM PCs, but the production managers (the people responsible for every stage from typesetting to printing) using traditional methods. Her first goal was to make the staff comfortable with DTP processes. She then created some small projects with the help of outside vendors who were using DTP. The next step was to get computers for everyone in the design and production departments. Within a year, the division had produced its first full-color text with electronic publishing. Looking back, Williams admits that the computers were scary at first. "But now," she says, "if I took their Macs away, people would find it very hard to function."

Questions for Discussion

1. What factors does a publishing CEO need to consider in deciding to make the major investment required to move into electronic publishing?

2. Although new technology, like electronic publishing, can streamline the work process, it can also disrupt traditional work roles, relationships, and procedures. What would you do to try to simplify the transition?

Creating a Textbook with DTP

Just a few years ago, desktop publishing was used primarily to produce black-and-white newsletters, flyers, and newspaper advertisements. Today, sophisticated programs, color monitors, and color printers make it possible to produce any publication electronically. This book was 100% designed and produced at Prentice Hall's New Jersey facility.

Traditional methods of college textbook production require approximately twelve to fifteen months to turn a manuscript into a bound book. Using DTP software, the same four-color textbook can be produced in under ten months. The processes are the same; the time (and money) are saved by eliminating middlemen like typesetters and page layout houses.

Of course, DTP is never a substitute for the creativity of the author and publishing team. Here's how Prentice Hall and the author worked together to conceive and create this textbook.

1 As the author prepares the manuscript, the production, art, and editorial teams go to work to design the book. Working with a list of the book's elements (for example, text, boxes, case studies, footnotes, and so forth), a designer creates a color palette and type specifications. This book was designed by Kenny Beck, a freelance designer based in New York City. The design process (which includes cover design) was managed by Pat Wosczyk, art director for Business and Economics at Prentice Hall.

Once the design is complete, a meeting is called to solicit comments and feedback. Each team member has a specific function in completing the project *(seated, left to right):* Anne Graydon, production editor, oversees the production of the entire text, from manuscript through printed book. Steven Rigolosi, development editor, edits the manuscript and art program, ensuring that the book is meeting the requirements of its intended audience. Renée Pelletier, production assistant, supports the production staff in a variety of ways, including proofreading and manuscript trafficking. P.J. Boardman, acquisitions editor, contracts with the author to write the book and has the lead role in marketing and selling the book. Joseph Heider, editor-in-chief, manages the entire publishing process.

(Standing, left to right): Dolores Kenny, editorial assistant, commissions reviews of the text to ensure its currentness and accuracy. Joyce Turner, senior managing editor of production, oversees the pre-press production of all Business and Economics textbooks at Prentice Hall. David Shea, assistant editor, compiles all the ancillary materials that accompany the text (for example, transparencies and the study guide). Not pictured is Patrice Fraccio, manufacturing buyer, who buys paper and contracts with a printer to print and bind each job.

2 Working from a list of specifications provided by the author, the Image Resource Center researches and secures permission to reproduce all the photos that will ultimately appear in the book. This is a major undertaking; this book contains more than 350 photos. Here, the photo team chooses the photos for Chapter 2. Pictured left to right are: Steve Rigolosi; Lori Morris-Nantz, manager of the Image Resource Center; Melinda Reo, photo research coordinator; and Anne Graydon. Not pictured is Teri Stratford, who conducted the photo research and submitted the final images for approval.

3 After the manuscript has been edited and keyboarded, the art drafted, and the photos chosen, the entire package goes to the formatting department. All formatters (also called electronic composition artists) work in a state-of-the-art facility at individual workstations using Macintosh computers with large color screens. All workstations are networked to one of several color printers. It is interesting to note that the publisher produces all types of books using the capabilities of the centralized formatting group.

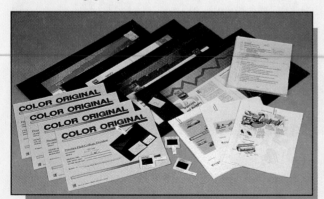

4 Before beginning work, the electronic specialists make sure all the pieces are in place. Meg Van Arsdale *(far left)*, electronic art manager, ensures that all art has been created to specification. Christy Mahon, formatter, lays out the project page by page. Grace Walkus, production director, is the liaison between formatting and the production editor and oversees the manufacturing of the book. Lorraine Patsco, manager of production services, manages the keyboarding of manuscript.

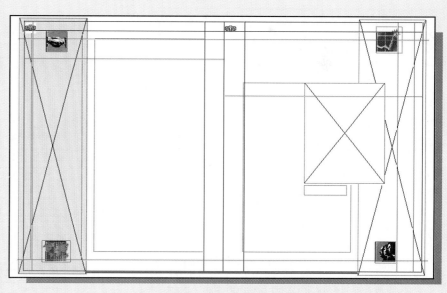

5 Once everything is ready, Christy uses a popular DTP package, QuarkXPress, to create a template following the designer's specifications. The template designates space for text, photos, captions, borders, boxes, and art. For example, the yellow block on the left page here is reserved for each chapter's table of contents.

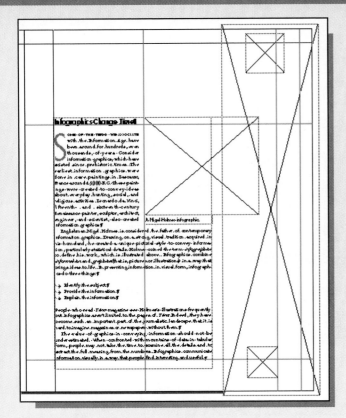

6 Next, the text—which has already been typed into a compatible word processing program (such as Microsoft Word)—is imported into the DTP file. Each text element is then fine tuned to meet the design specifications.

7 Third, the photos—which have been scanned and cleaned up in an image processing program like Adobe Photoshop—are inserted from a disk containing all the scanned images. Next, graphics (which can be created in a graphics program like Adobe Illustrator) are imported from a disk containing all the graphics files.

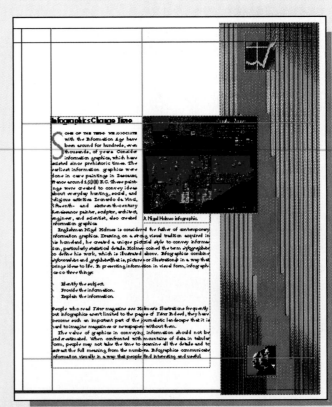

CHAPTER 2

A Tour of a Computer System

Learning Objectives

When you have completed this chapter, you should be able to:

1. Identify the five components of a computer system.
2. Explain the four categories of hardware and their functions, and discuss the relationship between hardware and software.
3. Differentiate between an operating system and an application program.
4. Identify eight types of software packages.
5. Explain the four components of information.
6. Distinguish between the users of information technology and IT professionals.
7. Describe the four types of procedures used in computer systems.
8. Explain the difference between single and multi-user systems.
9. List the thirteen information processing activities associated with the information handling functions of IT.

In Practice

After completing this chapter, you should be able to perform these activities:

1. Observe a business activity and discuss the process with the business managers or employees to learn how information technology influences their participation in the activity.
2. Examine a business or professional situation in which a software package is utilized and understand why the individual or organization has chosen to use that package.
3. Analyze a business or professional situation and identify the types of information that workers use in that situation.
4. Determine whether or not an information system application has any protection against intrusion or accidental loss of information.
5. Speak with IT professionals and determine whether their work deals primarily with hardware, software, or procedures.
6. Determine whether a particular business transaction that involves information technology makes use of a single or multi-user system.

Infographics Change Time

SOME OF THE THINGS WE ASSOCIATE with the Information Age have been around for hundreds, even thousands, of years. Consider information graphics, which have existed since prehistoric times. The earliest information graphics were done in cave paintings in Lascaux, France around 15,000 B.C. These paintings were created to convey ideas about everyday hunting, social, and religious activities. Leonardo da Vinci, fifteenth- and sixteenth-century Renaissance painter, sculptor, architect, engineer, and scientist, also created information graphics.

Englishman Nigel Holmes is considered the father of contemporary information graphics. Drawing on a strong visual tradition acquired in his homeland, he created a unique pictorial style to convey information, particularly statistical details. Holmes coined the term *infographics* to define his work, which is illustrated above. Infographics combine *information* and *graphics*—that is, pictures or illustrations in a way that brings ideas to life. In presenting information in visual form, infographics do three things:

- Identify the subject.
- Provide the information.
- Explain the information.

People who read *Time* magazine see Holmes's illustrations frequently, but infographics aren't limited to the pages of *Time*. Indeed, they have become such an important part of the journalistic landscape that it is hard to imagine magazines or newspapers without them.

The value of graphics in conveying information should not be underestimated. When confronted with mountains of data in tabular form, people may not take the time to examine all the details and to extract the full meaning from the numbers. Infographics communicate information visually in a way that people find interesting and useful.

A Nigel Holmes infographic.

---

8 After all the elements have been inserted, black-and-white proofs are submitted to the author and editors. Once final changes are made, the team sees and makes any necessary changes to a set of color proofs. The final DTP files and all of the support files are then forwarded to an output service bureau, which prepares the film from which the book is printed. To see how the two pages pictured here turned out, turn to pages 44-45.

9 As the last step before going to press, the output service bureau sends color proofs of the entire book for a final check by the production editor. These proofs are called ektaprints.

After the production editor gives final approval, the book goes on press. Four to six weeks later, the bound copies of the book are in Prentice Hall's warehouse and ready for shipment to your institution's bookstore.

CHAPTER 8

Developing Single-User Systems

Learning Objectives

When you have completed this chapter, you should be able to:

1 Describe the origin of single-user systems in business and understand why they have become so prominent and important.

2 Identify the distinguishing characteristics of a single-user system.

3 Explain the benefits of single-user systems in business.

4 Define the problem solving cycle and how it relates to the development of a single-user system.

5 Discuss the five steps involved in developing a single-user system.

6 Distinguish between choosing a single-user system and creating single-user applications.

7 Explain the importance of continuous evaluation and evolution in single-user systems development.

In Practice

After completing this chapter, you should be able to perform these activities:

1 Specify the questions you should ask a person who wants to develop a single-user system for financial analysis or desktop publishing.

2 Prepare a list of questions to ask an IT sales representative regarding the cost and performance characteristics of the computer and communications systems packages she offers.

3 Speak with the proprietor of a small business that uses information technology and determine whether he has a personal system that meets his operating requirements.

4 Contact a journalist at a local newspaper or at the campus newspaper, or a freelance writer, and discuss her use of information technology in her work.

5 Evaluate the role of a single-user system used by a salesperson who spends a great deal of time calling on customers in their homes or offices. Determine whether IT assists him in being more productive, effective, and competitive than he would be without IT.

6 Conduct a survey of computer dealers and determine whether they have a staff member who is experienced in helping *businesses* select the components they need for single-user systems.

Lights, Camera, Special Effects

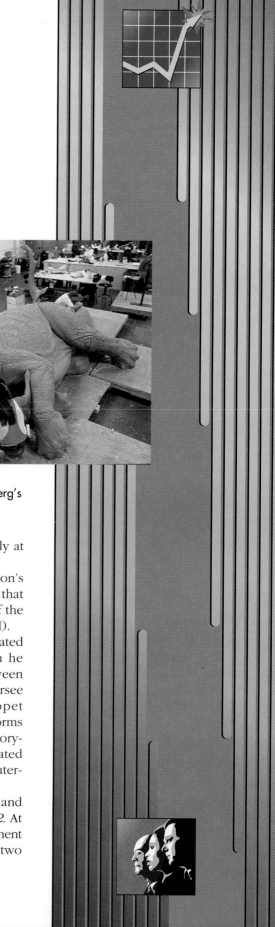

Model designers create a triceratops for Stephen Spielberg's *Jurassic Park*.

THE SETTING: THE PARTIALLY COMPLETed Jurassic Park, where eccentric billionaire John Hammond's team of genetic engineers has recovered and cloned dinosaur DNA, giving life to animals that have been extinct for millions of years. The time: the morning after the mighty tyrannosaurus rex has escaped, attacking two tour jeeps bearing VIPs. The action: paleontologist Alan Grant is trying to lead Hammond's grandchildren to safety. As they mount the crest of a hill, they see a herd of gallimimi running across the valley below them. Suddenly the herd wheels around and stampedes up the hill, directly at the terrified trio, as the T. Rex bursts out of the jungle in full pursuit.

This scene, from Steven Spielberg's hit movie of Michael Crichton's best-seller *Jurassic Park*, is even more amazing when you realize that the stampeding dinosaurs are the computer-generated handiwork of the visual effects team at George Lucas's Industrial Light and Magic (ILM).

In 1990, when Spielberg began preproduction, computer-generated imagery (CGI) wasn't advanced enough to simulate the realism he wanted. Initially, the bulk of the special effects were divided between Stan Winston Studio and Phil Tippett Studio. Winston would oversee the designing and engineering of full-size robotic and puppet dinosaurs, using everything from hydraulics to flight simulator platforms and specially written software. Tippett would create the animated storyboards used to plan action sequences, as well as the fully articulated miniatures his studio would shoot, frame-by-frame, using a computer-controlled camera.

By 1992, though, the ILM visual effects team led by Dennis Murren and Mark Dippe had created stunning CGI for *The Abyss* and *Terminator 2*. At Dippe's urging, animator Steve (Spaz) Williams retreated to his basement office. Working on one of ILM's supercomputers, he spent the next two weeks drawing the skeleton of a T. Rex, bone by bone. Then he put it all together, creating ten seconds of animation that showed the skeleton walking. Spielberg's team was impressed and gave ILM the go-ahead to create more test footage.

Working from a model created by Stan Winston Studio, computer graphics artist Eric Armstrong created a computerized skeleton of a gallimimus, animated it running, and duplicated the image from two angles to create the stampede effect. Next, lead animator Stephen Fangmeier used sophisticated rendering software to "paint" the skeletons, simulating the interplay of light and shadow across the skin of moving, three-dimensional animals.

Spielberg was so impressed that he expanded the role of computer-generated imagery, eventually dividing the work between ILM and Tippett Studio. (Tippett also acted as the film's dinosaur supervisor. A special broadcast system let the two teams confer without leaving their offices.) All of the dinosaurs in the finished film were either live-action (robots or full-size puppets), computer-generated, or a seamless combination of the two techniques. The finished film's 6-1/2 minutes of computer-generated images represented eighteen months of work by 50 CGI experts using about $15 million worth of computer equipment.   ■

THESE KINDS OF SPECIAL EFFECTS CAPTURE OUR IMAGINATION, BUT THEY AREN'T THE ONLY way the film industry uses computers. Screenwriters use specialized word processing packages that automatically format their scripts and monitor their length (no more than 120 pages). Assistant directors turn to computers to monitor everything from budgets and schedules to the number of extras needed on the set at any one time. Some directors even use their portable PCs to download weather information that helps them plan their shooting schedules. The one thing many of these systems have in common? They are single-user systems, designed to help people save time and money.

In this chapter, we discuss the development of single-user systems, exploring the capabilities of personal systems in general. (The terms "personal system" and "single-user system" are used interchangeably.) Because everyone has different needs, depending on his or her personal situation, this chapter will also help you identify your personal IT needs. In the first section, we describe the characteristics of single-user systems. Next, we look at the impact these systems can have on personal productivity, effectiveness, and creativity. In the last section, we examine the process of developing a single-user system. We discuss the process of developing multi-user systems in Chapter 11.

■ What Is a Single-User System?

single-user system or **personal system** An IT system used by only one person.

A **single-user system** is an IT system used by only one person. Usually composed of a PC or workstation, various input and output devices, and programs, it is tailored to the specific needs and wants of one person. Frequently called **personal systems**, single-user systems free their users from time-consuming routines or procedures and allow them to focus on the creative aspects of their work. Because personal systems are so cost-effective, they are now an important tool in both personal and business activities.

The Origin of Single-User Systems

In the early days of data processing—the 1950s, 60s, and 70s—when information technology was synonymous with large computers and vast communications networks, single-user systems were unheard of. At that time, computing meant spending large sums of money (often millions of dollars), hiring specialists to run the system, and keeping support personnel nearby (or at least on call) to clean, adjust, and repair the system's components. In acquiring an IT system, an organization knew it was making a substantial financial commitment.

Technological progress and innovation in the 1980s and 1990s changed many aspects of computing. Large computers are still in widespread use and will be for years to come. But personal computers, designed for individual users, are now the norm. PCs have powerful capabilities due to advances in electronics and engineering and, as a result of competition in the computer industry, are widely available at affordable prices. Today they are the dominant source of IT capability in many organizations. In fact, many universities, colleges, and training centers around the world now assume that students either own or have ready access to personal systems—that is, PCs and software.

Reality Check. Today there are millions and millions more personal computers installed worldwide than mainframe and midrange systems combined. The number of PCs in use (the *installed base*, see Figure 14.4) continues to grow annually.

Some organizations, like the publishing giant Simon & Schuster, have a goal of placing PCs on the desks of all their knowledge workers. The intention is often to interconnect these PCs with communications networks. But the main objective is to assist workers in being better at their job—to be more productive, effective, and creative.

Although some companies suggest a standard **configuration** (a specific combination of hardware and software in a system) for each type of worker in the firm, standards are very limiting. Most people will add their own software, adjust the system's features to suit themselves, and perhaps add hardware attachments that accommodate their needs. This is as it should be, for a single-user system is a personal tool, not a vehicle for making everyone alike.

> **configuration** The specific combination of hardware and software in a system.

The Characteristics of Single-User Systems

Three characteristics distinguish single-user systems (Figure 8.1). They are designed for hands-on usage, are tailored to an individual's requirements and preferences, and are used to improve personal performance.

Designed for Hands-on Usage. Single-user systems are **hands on**. This means that the user actually operates the system, entering data and information, directing the processing, and determining which types of output will be generated. Because the user directs the processing, he or she can watch, control, and adjust the activities as they occur, and can even stop processing if a change must be made. In contrast, large-scale shared systems are usually running at a remote location, often a great distance away from the individuals using the system.

The artist who uses a computer system to draw an illustration onscreen using a mouse or other pointing device is using the system hands-on. So is the writer who enters text using a keyboard and then prints the text on a laser printer. The trainer who creates a multimedia sequence of text, voice, sound, and animation on a PC by assembling a combination of keyboard entries, prestored music and art, and scanned images is also a hands-on user.

> **hands-on system** A system in which a user enters data and information, directs processing, and determines the types of output to be generated.

Tailored to personal preferences—To help synchronize the sound effects to the movie, Serafine has tailored his work studio to include not only keyboards and computers but also a large movie screen.

Used to improve personal performance—Serafine's personal system lets him quickly and easily alter sounds to achieve the desired effect. "Once the music is in the system," he says, "it's like Silly Putty. I can bend every sound."

Hands-on usage—Serafine operates the various components of the system himself.

FIGURE 8.1
The Characteristics of Single-User Systems
Frank Serafine of Serafine FX uses a single-user system to concoct sound effects for major motion pictures. To capture noises, Sarafine has jammed microphones in Jacuzzis, up air conditioners, and through sewer drains, then transferred the samples to a keyboard linked to a Macintosh II personal computer.

The information generated by a single-user system is usually stored within the system or on an attached secondary storage device. In larger multi-user systems, the information may reside at remote locations, not under direct user control.

Tailored to Personal Requirements and Preferences.   Single-user systems are tailored to the needs of their users.

- The hardware configuration chosen determines the system's speed, power, and capacity. For example, special effects designers may configure their personal systems to feature high-resolution color graphics, high-speed "flicker-free" animation, and stereo sound generation.
- The programs installed on the system create its "personality." Load one combination of programs and the system fulfills the requirements of a professional copywriter or novelist. Load a different set and it can assist a medical researcher.

Personal preference plays an important role in personal systems, too. Some people prefer to rely on a keyboard, while others prefer to use pointing devices for entering instructions and invoking processing activities. The choice of how to tailor a single-user system is, of course, personal.

Used to Improve Personal Performance.   Ultimately, the value of a personal system lies in making the person better at what he or she does. Whether that person works at home, in an office, or as part of a team, the purpose of the single-user system is the same: to assist that person in carrying out his or her activities. We'll be looking at many examples of how personal systems can improve performance in the pages ahead.

The Impact of Single-User Systems

When properly designed, single-user systems have three main effects: improved productivity, greater effectiveness, and increased creativity.

Improved Productivity.   We've spoken of productivity often in this book. As we saw in Chapter 1, productivity is a measure of accomplishment—the amount of work that can be accomplished with a given level of effort. Formally, if you want to get more accomplished in a period of time, or want to complete a task or project more quickly, you're concerned about productivity.

Formally defined, **productivity** is the relationship between the results (output) of an activity, work process, or an organization and the resources (inputs) used to create those results. Productivity can be measured by dividing the outputs by the inputs (Figure 8.2). A higher ratio means a higher level of productivity.

Productivity can be increased in three ways.

- Person A is more productive than Person B when A can complete a task in *less time* than B.
- Person X is more productive than Person Y if X can complete *more work* than Y in the same amount of time.
- Activities can be completed with fewer resources. For example, if an organization can conduct manufacturing, inventory management, or other business processes with fewer resources (people, space, financing, vehicles, and so forth), it increases its productivity.

Personal systems are designed to increase personal productivity. That is, they permit activities to be completed more quickly, allow more activities to be completed in a particular period of time, or allow a task to be completed with fewer resources. Single-user software packages for creating spreadsheets (Chapter 5), personal database systems (Chapter 6), and documents, manuscripts, and graphics (Chapter 7) are all designed to increase productivity. For this reason, they are often called **personal productivity software**. To aid the user, personal productivity software is making more and more use of artificial intelligence tools, as the Quality and Productivity box on page 301 discusses in detail.

Two warnings are in order here. First, productivity gains from working faster should not come at the expense of quality. Mistakes that come from working too fast will have to be corrected, perhaps eliminating the gains from working faster. And when quality suffers, one's reputation can be quickly damaged as well. Second, productivity gains should not come at personal expense to workers. If an organization chooses to use a PC to force more work out of its employees, any apparent gains are likely to be short-lived. People will tire of the emphasis on quantity of work and may seek ways to meet production goals while cutting corners. The result may be defects in products, shoddy service, careless mistakes, and lower quality.

The consulting firm Gestion y Control de Calidad (GCC) conducted a study of quality in Spain at the beginning of the 1990s. It found that the cost of defective products and services in the average Spanish company at that time was equivalent

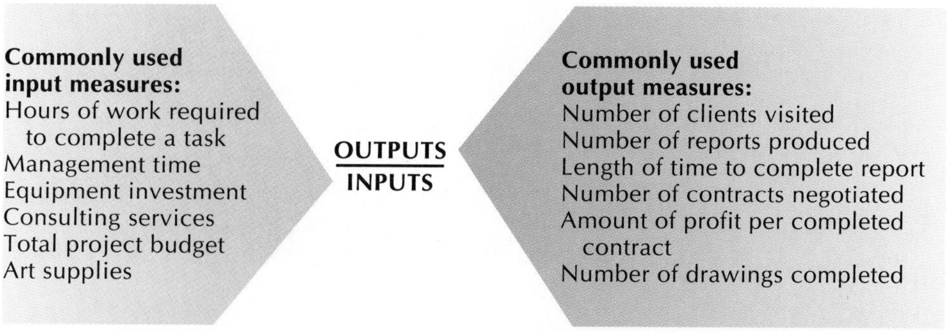

productivity   The relationship between the results of an activity and the resources used to create those results. Equal to outputs/inputs.

personal productivity software   Software packages that permit activities to be completed more quickly, allow more activities to be completed in a particular period of time, or allow a task to be completed with fewer resources.

FIGURE 8.2
Productivity: A Measure of Accomplishment

Commonly used input measures:
Hours of work required to complete a task
Management time
Equipment investment
Consulting services
Total project budget
Art supplies

$\dfrac{\text{OUTPUTS}}{\text{INPUTS}}$

Commonly used output measures:
Number of clients visited
Number of reports produced
Length of time to complete report
Number of contracts negotiated
Amount of profit per completed contract
Number of drawings completed

to 20% of sales.[1] This was four times higher than the level in Japan and West Germany, two countries known for high-quality products and services. The Spanish have invented the word *chapuza* to describe mistakes made through carelessness and neglect.

Proud of both their heritage and their country, the Spanish resolved to fix the quality problem. They set out to change things, beginning with their biggest national industry, tourism. For decades, Spain has been an international holiday playground for all of Europe, hosting visitors seeking to relax, play, and enjoy sports. Spain's chief tourism official, Ignacio Fuejo, examined the problem and decided how to proceed: "The main reason for the current crisis is the poor price-quality ratio." Recognizing that prices were not going to fall, Fuejo declared "The only solution is to improve quality." Quality programs, workshops, and training programs were launched with wide participation throughout the tourism industry.

It appears that Fuejo's initiatives are paying off. The world has witnessed Spain's efforts to improve quality. Barcelona hosted the Summer Olympics and Seville held the World Expo in 1992 (Figure 8.3). Visitors from around the world enjoyed the hospitality of these and other Spanish cities, while millions more learned about Spain through television programs and discussions with returning visitors. Spain's reputation as a place to visit is better than ever. And quality, not quantity, remains the watchword for the tourism industry; the Spanish know that if the quality is there, the quantity (of visitors) will be there, too. In addition, banks, auto manufacturers, and companies in many other industries have picked up the initiative, developing their own programs to enhance quality while maintaining productivity levels.

Greater Effectiveness.   Some people are described as effective workers, effective managers, or effective speakers. Some security procedures are considered "really effective." But what exactly is effectiveness?

effectiveness   The extent to which desired results are achieved.

Effectiveness, which we first defined in Chapter 1, entails doing the right things to accomplish a task. It is the extent to which desirable results are achieved.

[1]Specht, Marina and James McCarthy, "A Step in the Right Direction: Quality in Spain," *Financial Times* (October 29, 1990), p. 13.

FIGURE 8.3
Increasing Quality in Spain's Tourism Industry
Spain's quality initiative has made it an even more popular vacation spot than ever before.

QUALITY AND PRODUCTIVITY

Artificial Intelligence Moves into Personal Productivity Software

I F YOU USE TODAY'S POWERFUL PERSONAL PRODUCTIVITY SOFT-ware, you've probably encountered *artificial intelligence* (AI), a complex field with two main branches. The first branch continues the quest, begun in the late 1950s, to unravel the mysteries of human thought, speech, vision, and hearing. The second, sometimes called *applied intelligence*, looks for ways to build these human capabilities into computer programs, including some of the software that runs on today's personal computers. There are three AI tools:

- The *algorithm*, a collection of rules and step-by-step procedures used to identify patterns and perform tasks ranging from playing chess to spell checking and approving credit applications.
- The *neural network*, which tries to simulate the way the web of neurons in a living brain processes, learns, and remembers information. Instead of passively following rules and algorithms, neural networks can observe patterns, form associations, and learn by example and by trial-and-error. In one lab, for example, a robot taught itself to swing, arm over arm, from the ceiling like a gibbon—but only after it fell several times. In the business world corporations are now using neural networks to detect credit card fraud, predict the performance of stocks, and schedule airplane maintenance.
- *Fuzzy logic*, so called because it can solve problems involving ambiguous data and inexact instructions that don't fit the true–false patterns of traditional computer logic. So far, fuzzy logic is most often used in controllers embedded in computers, automobile components, consumer electronics, and home appliances, but it is also being used in decision-support systems in business, finance, and medicine (see Chapter 12).

Together, these tools promise to create an exciting new generation of silicon servants. They're already making computers easier to use. Here are just a few examples:

- *Handwriting recognition*. People who can't or don't want to use computer keyboards have been intrigued by the idea of pen-based computing. This is part of the appeal of the personal digital assistant (PDA), introduced in 1993. To make it work, designers had to develop handwriting recognition software, another type of pattern recognition. The first generation of this software used algorithms, with mixed success. The next generation will use neural networks.
- *Speech recognition*. Another type of pattern recognition, speech recognition can use algorithms, neural networks, fuzzy logic, or a combination of all three.
- *Expert or knowledge-base systems*. These systems use a large database of rules and algorithms to analyze problems and make decisions. Although expert systems are common in corporations and hospitals (see Chapter 12), they're also found in desktop software. One common example is the grammar checker. Another can be found in *Mavis Beacon Teaches Typing*, which covers both the conventional and Dvorak keyboards. The software uses an expert system to assess the user's skill level and progress. (If "Mavis" senses you're getting frustrated or tired, she'll even suggest a break or a typing-related game.)
- *Software agents*. A software agent goes beyond online help to offer interactive advice or instructions. Microsoft pioneered this technique, creating "Wizards" that lead users, step by step, through complex procedures, such as adding a chart to an Excel spreadsheet. A related Excel feature, "Tip Wizards," analyzes the way users work and suggests more efficient techniques. Agents are also available in such products as Quattro Pro (a spreadsheet), Microsoft PowerPoint (presentation graphics), Microsoft Word, and WordPerfect for Windows.

In the future, experts predict, software agents will play a bigger role in computing, anticipating their users' needs, sensing when they need help, and taking over routine or often-repeated tasks. As neural networks and fuzzy logic become more common, users may be able to tell their computers to "do what I mean" (DWIM) instead of "do what I say" (DWIS).

Already, General Magic in Mountain View, California, has created Telescript, a software language that can be used to create and dispatch software agents to the electronic marketplace of online information services and interactive television. Given relatively vague instructions ("Find the best price for a two-week cruise to Alaska, leaving the first week of June"), the agent will do your shopping and report back, letting you make the final decision.

People are effective when they take actions that produce desirable results. An effective speaker presents ideas, stories, and illustrations in a manner that not only gets and holds your attention, but also makes a point emphatically. The speaker seems to say the right things in just the right way.

Single-user systems help improve individual effectiveness when they help people do the right things. Perhaps a spreadsheet package can help an analyst perform a more extensive analysis of alternatives to produce a high-impact result. Or perhaps an artist can use a graphics package to create magazine illustrations that include more realistic characters and scenery. Both people have used their personal systems to increase their effectiveness.

Reality Check.   Productivity and effectiveness are both important in business, but the terms are not interchangeable. Productivity is concerned with quantity of work, the time or effort needed to produce a result, and the resources used in producing an output. Effectiveness, in contrast, is concerned with the *quality* of results.

Personal advantage emerges from a single-user system when you can use the system to your benefit. This idea draws on the principles of productivity and effectiveness. The key concept here is *leverage*, doing what you do best while using IT to compensate for your weaknesses.

For example, if you are a financial analyst, your single-user system should be configured to assist you in being the best possible analyst. Thus the primary goal of your analyst system should be to make you a better financial analyst. But if you are weak at writing reports, your system should also have the tools—that is, the software—to help you be a better writer. The prestored report formats, appendixes, and illustrations that can be used repeatedly, along with the other writing support features of a word processing program, can help you compensate for your weaknesses.

"Single-user system" is not just another name for "computer." Rather, it is a package of tools that should be designed to help you be the best at what you are or want to be.   ∎

Increased Creativity.   Creativity is hard to define, but most agree that it entails a high degree of artistic or intellectual inventiveness. Some people are born with creative ability; others have to work at it. Actually, everyone is creative in his or her own way. The challenge is identifying your creative areas and then finding a way to unlock the skills inside. Single-user systems can help here by providing tools that can do the work while you focus on the creative aspects of the activity. For example:

- A particular artist's strongest skills are design, layout, and use of color. Drawing images is not her strong point. A combination of clip art and scanned images can help her overcome this weakness so that she can focus her attention on deciding what to illustrate and how to create the desired image and message.
- A musician wants to focus on composing music by sitting down at his keyboard. He finds it distracting to write down the notes as he plays them. Using special software, he can compose music by playing it on an electronic instru-

ment. The software takes care of printing the notes or displaying them on a screen. While the composer writes, the PC captures the information and performs the appropriate processing.

- A journalist has more flair for describing natural disaster than she does for spelling and grammar. A personal system equipped with word processing software allows her to enter ideas and comments almost as quickly as she thinks of them and then to go back and make revisions, repeatedly if necessary. She can use automatic checking and correction software to ensure that her creative flair is correct to the word, letter, and period.

Often the creativity of financial analysts and other businesspeople is not viewed in the same way as the creativity of artists and writers. Yet financial analysts can be very creative in assembling investment packages, arranging financing for investments, and suggesting financial portfolios. While working on ideas for new products or packages, they don't want to be bothered with calculating returns on investment, payback periods, or payment and interest rates. So they use PC software to handle the calculations for them.

CRITICAL CONNECTION 1
Database Gives Composer More Time to Play Around*

Music Consultants Group

If you've ever watched any of a number of U.S. network TV shows, you have probably heard Jonathan Wolff's work. Wolff is a composer, and his company, Music Consultants Group, Inc. (MCG), of Burbank, California, provides the music that smooths a transition or sets a mood.

For years, Wolff kept his compositions on tape, relying on paper lists to help him find a suitable piece of music. Many times, it was faster to write something new than to hunt through the files. "It meant less time that I had to do music that absolutely had to be done," Wolff says.

In frustration, Wolff asked system developer Steven Lack to create a personal database for MCG. Lack created a menu-driven application that lets users cross-reference the database's five parts, browse easily, and create a sheet of music cues for each show. As an added bonus, Wolff has loaded the database on a notebook computer he carries to studio dubbing sessions. All of this means that Wolff can spend more time being creative and less time flipping through paper.

*Based on Christopher Lindquist, "Alpha Database is Music to Composer's Ears," *Computerworld*, November 9, 1992, p. 35.

Developing a Single-User System

Developing single-user systems is an exercise in problem solving. In this section, we briefly review the nature of problems and the problem solving process (which we first discussed in Chapter 1). We then apply this process to the development of a single-user system.

Problems and the Problem Solving Cycle

problem   A perceived difference between a particular condition and desired conditions.

A **problem** is a perceived difference between events and conditions as they are and as you would like them to be. Problems touch every aspect of our business and personal lives. For example:

- You find out that the cost of repairing your car is higher than its current value.
- The time of a business meeting is changed on short notice and now conflicts with another important meeting that you must attend. You cannot be in two places at once.
- You are offered a job at a rapidly growing company. The new job is riskier because the company is newer, but the salary is 50% higher than your current salary. You have also been offered a generous bonus plan that will make you part owner of the company in a few years. Yet you know that if you stay in your current position for two more years, you will exceed the new salary and face virtually no risk. You have to decide by tomorrow.
- The course you were planning to register for this term, your last before graduation, is closed and no additional registrations are allowed. The course is required for graduation.
- The stocks in which you invested have decreased in value by 25%, and their value is expected to go even lower in the next few months. However, one year from now the market price is expected to exceed your original purchase price by an attractive percentage. Selling the stock now provides tax advantages. Waiting will not produce any tax advantages this year, but may lead to long-term benefits.

You could undoubtedly add to this list. The point is clear, though: Problems are an everyday occurrence. They are not the exception, but the expectation. They remain problems only if you cannot solve them or turn them to your advantage.

Single-user systems are problem-solving tools when they make you more productive and more effective in recognizing problems, defining them, selecting strategies to deal with them, designing solutions, and implementing those solutions. These five activities comprise the **problem solving cycle** (Figure 8.4). The problem solving cycle is a structure that helps you address problems in a structured way. This approach is much more effective than lashing out at problems in an effort to eliminate them (or hoping that they will just go away). When problem solving is effective, each step in arriving at a solution narrows the distance between the perceived problem and the desired condition.

problem solving cycle
The five-step sequence of activities designed to address and solve problems in a structured way.

As we saw in Chapters 5 and 6, problem solving proceeds through five steps. It begins with recognizing the existence of a problem, defining the problem, and evaluating possible solutions from which a desired solution is selected. The solution is then designed and implemented. The entire problem solving process may take moments, hours, days, weeks, or longer, depending on the nature of the problem and the characteristics of the solution. Evaluation of the current understanding of the problem and the desired result is continual throughout the problem solving process.

In the pages that follow, we describe how one individual developed her own system—a single-user system—to aid her career. The process, outlined in Figure 8.5, begins with problem recognition and a preliminary investigation, and can serve as a model for developing many different types of single-user systems. The PC Buyer's Guide at the end of this chapter offers some simplified guidelines for first-time PC buyers.

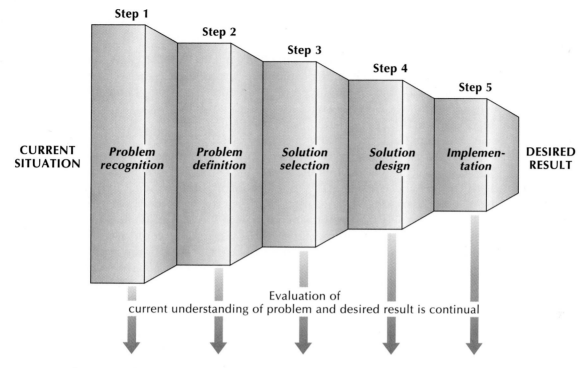

FIGURE 8.4   The Problem Solving Cycle
When problem solving is effective, each step narrows the distance between perceived problem and desired condition.

FIGURE 8.5
Developing a Single-User System

Step 1.   Problem Recognition: Conduct a Preliminary Investigation
Organize Preliminary Thoughts
Define the Problem
Assess Feasibility
    Cost Feasibility
    Operational Feasibility
    Technical Feasibility
Step 2.   Problem Definition: Determine the Requirements
Operational Requirements
Program Requirements
Storage Requirements
Step 3.   Solution Selection: Choose the New System
Choose the Computing Platform
Buy the System
Step 4.   Solution Design: Create the New Applications
Install Application Programs
Design Application Features
Test Applications
Document the System and Procedures
Step 5.   Implementation: Convert to the New System
Conversion
Training
Cutover
Evaluation and Evolution of the System

Step 1. Problem Recognition: Conduct a Preliminary Investigation

Throughout her days in college, at the Sorbonne in Paris, Monique had capitalized on her writing, research, and people skills by working as a freelance writer. She found this work exciting and rewarding. In addition to preparing and selling articles for publication in magazines, she also wrote sections of corporate annual reports and drafted portions of newsletters. After graduating, Monique decided that she could turn freelance writing into a successful career.

What led her to this decision? She had read about (and been part of) a 1990s business trend in which firms **outsource** many of their editorial activities to freelance writers and consultants. With outsourcing, firms contract out single jobs, or even a range of jobs, to specialists and experts, sometimes for years at a time. Outsourcing avoids the need for permanent in-house staff while allowing the firm to hire top-notch talent on a contract basis. (For more information on outsourcing and the opportunities it provides, see this chapter's Opportunities box.) Monique believed her track record as a professional writer, her recognized writing skills, and her ability to learn about new areas quickly would serve her well in this career.

Having made a decision to proceed, she realized that embarking on this career required her to invest in a personal system. She began by taking stock of her current tools and resources. With assistance from her family, Monique had acquired an Apple Macintosh computer when she first began her studies at the Sorbonne. She had spent many hours at the Macintosh in her apartment in the Latin Quarter (only a few minutes' walk from the university) and was well versed in its capabilities.

The Macintosh computer had served her well in college, but she knew that her needs required more capability than her current system was providing. It would be easy for her simply to buy a more powerful Macintosh and to transfer her word processing program to the new computer. But a great deal was at stake (her career!), so she organized her thoughts and decided to seek out new opportunities and study her options—even if that meant purchasing a different brand of computer and another word processing program.

Organize Preliminary Thoughts.   As the first part of her preliminary investigation, Monique needed to organize her thoughts. Before choosing the right IT combination, she felt she needed to:

- Determine her budget and visit computer stores to become acquainted with equipment and prices.
- Contact publishers and editors and ask what they require of their freelancers.
- Contact other freelance writers to see what IT they use and obtain their suggestions.

In addition to good technical information and advice, Monique wanted the system to fit her needs and desires. With this thought in mind, she began to clarify her needs and wants with respect to IT capabilities. To do so, she needed to define her problem more concretely.

Define the Problem.   To define her problem, Monique identified the three challenges she was facing:

CHALLENGE: Need to acquire the IT resources required to support a career as a freelance writer.

CHALLENGE: Current system does not have the necessary speed, capacity, or flexibility.

CHALLENGE: Need to increase both productivity and personal effectiveness ("I can't waste time preparing a unique invoice for each client; I need one that I can generate quickly and easily").

outsourcing   A business practice in which firms use freelancers and consultants, rather than in-house staff, for selected activities.

OPPORTUNITIES

PCs Help Consultants Seize Opportunities Created by Downsizing and Outsourcing

T HERE IS A DEFINITE DOWNSIDE TO *DOWNSIZING*, THE ELIMINATION of jobs, management layers, and functions to help corporations compete in the global economy. But downsizing is also creating a realm of new opportunities, as in-house staff outsources the workload to private contractors.

For example, Sears Roebuck and Company outsourced all of its transportation and shipping operations to Menlo Logistics, a subsidiary of Consolidated Freightways, Inc. Other tasks are assigned to temporary or contract workers from agencies such as Manpower, Kelly Services, or Olsten. (Of the estimated 7,000 temp agencies, Manpower is the largest, with about 600,000 employees, more than GM or IBM.) These agencies can supply everything from clerks to CEOs on a short-term or interim basis. But not all work goes to temp agencies; a significant part of the work is assigned to consultants and freelancers, most of them operating out of home offices.

The one thing most freelancers have in common? They all depend on information technology, especially the personal computer. Computers help them perform the services they get paid for, whether engineering, programming, interior design, or writing. But IT also helps them wear the many hats of the small business owner. Do you need to keep your books or do your taxes? Turn on the PC. Do you need to create a marketing presentation? Another job for the PC. Do you need to work onsite? Bundle up your laptop or notebook and head for the door. And if there's a blizzard, but you absolutely, positively have to deliver a job, just turn to your PC's fax modem. Programmer Michael Colucci even uses his PC to

Lawyer and mother Laura Masurovsky prefers freelancing from her Washington, DC home to working at her old firm. Her firm's willingness to outsource some of its work to freelancers has provided benefits to both parties: the firm saves on benefits costs, and Masurovsky spends more time with her family.

drum up business for his program, *The Invoice Store*. Instead of pounding the pavement, he turns to the small business forums found through such major online services as CompuServe, America Online, and Prodigy, as well as on local bulletin boards. Colucci estimates that 75% of his sales come from his online contacts.

Sources: Jaclyn Fierman, "The Contingency Work Force," *Fortune*, January 24, 1994, pp. 30–36; Julia King, "The New Spin-Offs," *Computerworld*, August 24, 1993, pp. 81–83; Rosalind Resnick, "The Electronic Schmooze," *Home Office Computing*, January 1994, pp. 86–88.

She also defined the constraints she faced:

> CONSTRAINT: A maximum of 50,000 French francs (FF) or $10,000 (from various sources) to invest on information technology.[2]
>
> CONSTRAINT: Regardless of personal preferences, the need to acquire a system compatible with those of editors and publishers.

Monique decided not to let her current hardware, software, and know-how—the Apple Macintosh she now uses—be a constraint. If she needed to learn the characteristics of new IT, she would do so because she wanted the best all-around system to support her career.

[2]Because of international currency fluctuations in which the value of different currencies change independent of one another, Monique wanted to price IT in both American dollars and French francs. She uses a conversion method of 5 FF per $1. Her method of paying for the new system would depend on the best currency value at the time. Considering dual currency prices is not unusual in international business transactions.

Assess Feasibility. After defining her IT needs, Monique needed to determine the feasibility of setting up a new system. Specifically, she had to consider three types of feasibility:

- *Cost feasibility:* "Can I pay the cost of a new system?"
- *Operational feasibility:* "Can I assemble and learn to use new hardware and software quickly?"
- *Technical feasibility:* "Is suitable hardware and packaged software generally available?"

If it turned out that her project was not feasible, she was going to have to think about a different path toward her career.

COST FEASIBILITY. "Can I get a complete system within my cost constraints?" Monique asked herself. Visiting several computer stores provided her with preliminary cost estimates for a range of different brands of computers and peripheral equipment. At the end of her preliminary survey, Monique listed the following estimates:

computer and monitor (including main memory, storage space, and disk drives)	FF 10,000 to FF 22,500	($2,000 to $4,500)
printer	FF 5,000 to FF 10,000	($1,000 to $2,000)
software	FF 10,000 to FF 20,000	($2,000 to $4,000)
scanner	FF 5,000 to FF 7,500	($1,000 to $1,500)
fax/data modem	FF 500 to FF 2500	($100 to $500)
Total	**FF 30,500 to FF 62,500**	**($6,100 to $12,500)**

Monique felt that her overall estimate of FF 30,500 to FF 62,500 ($6,100 to $12,500) indicated the feasibility of acquiring a powerful system with the necessary computer and communications capabilities while remaining within her financial constraint. She also reminded herself that supplies, such as additional disks and printer paper, would be paid for out of her normal operating/supplies budget. Hence she did not need to consider them as part of the system's acquisition cost.

OPERATIONAL FEASIBILITY. Could Monique set up and learn to use a new system? Monique's experience in using her Macintosh had given her a wealth of valuable know-how and experience. In fact, it was one reason that she was able to quickly assemble cost estimates on various equipment alternatives. She also believed this experience would serve her well in moving to new hardware and software, and had no doubt that she could learn the components of the new system quickly.

TECHNICAL FEASIBILITY. Was the technology that Monique needed available, and could it be acquired in a timely fashion? The information she received from computer retailers gave her confidence that she could meet her needs with brand-name computers, printers, and off-the-shelf (prepackaged) programs. Speaking to experienced users of those products also convinced her that the different components would work together to meet her needs effectively.

Now that Monique had completed her *general* preliminary investigation and determined that purchasing a new system was feasible, she needed to determine *precisely* what her new system needed to do.

Step 2. Problem Definition: Determine the Requirements

To think through her new system's requirements, Monique took a stroll down the Champs Elysées, making a mental note of the professional activities for which she was most often hired: drafting and editing text (magazine articles, newsletters, advertising brochures, and the like); designing document layouts and arranging text alongside photographs and clip art; and taking notes written by staff members and expanding those notes into a polished article.

She also took note of the business trends and IT advances influencing her work. First, she thought about the growing number of editors who were asking her to transmit manuscript copy electronically, over a telephone link, to the publisher's offices. Many were also requesting a follow-up disk copy and hard copy via courier or overnight mail. Monique was also receiving more requests to send documents by fax. "The publishing world revolves around facts and fax," she thought to herself. In the past she had used the communications capabilities of a friend's computer and had relied on the fax service at a local copy center. But she knew these options would be inconvenient for the volume of work she would be sending and receiving in the future.

Second, she had noticed, more and more publications were making back issues available on CD-ROM. Monique knew this trend could be an asset in conducting research for magazine articles and corporate annual reports. Maintaining CD-ROMs of important publications would reduce the space she needed to store copies of old articles while also decreasing the search time to retrieve information. In addition, developers of computer clip art were now distributing the art on optical disk.

Finally, she remembered the number of inquiries she had received over the last few months asking whether she was experienced in or willing to apply her journalistic skills to the production of multimedia presentations. She recalled the requests of certain clients, who wanted to develop multimedia training programs and sales information. Monique saw this as an opportunity in which she wanted to become involved. Unfortunately, her current system had neither an optical drive nor multimedia capabilities. And adding them to the current system would be both difficult and expensive, if possible at all.

Because of the many demands made on her time throughout college, she had been careful to keep a record of her editorial contacts: editors, marketing directors, graphic designers, and publishers. She recalled how often she had told herself: "All of my business world is contained in my card file." Her clients were scattered not only throughout her own country, but also throughout other nations and regions of the world. (Her knowledge of several languages and cultures, augmented by her study abroad experiences, had been an important factor in landing this international clientele.)

She also maintained a separate set of records for information sources—personal contacts, including executives, politicians, business staff members, and public relations directors. This file contained a separate card for each individual, nearly 500 entries in all. She wanted to put all these data and information into a database format that could be searched quickly and that could expand and evolve to meet her changing needs.

From this soul-searching session, Monique formulated three types of **requirements**, or features that must be included in her system. These were operational, program, and storage requirements.

requirements Features that must be included in an application or system.

Operational Requirements.   A system's *operational requirements* are those characteristics necessary to support a particular set of professional activities. Monique's list of operational requirements included:

- A set of IT tools for writing, editing, designing, and laying out documents
- The capability to send and receive documents electronically over telephone links
- The capability to send and receive documents by fax

- Ample storage capacity
- The capability to print black-and-white documents
- The capability to scan color documents
- The capability for color display of documents and information

FIGURE 8.6
Personal System Checklist

PERSONAL SYSTEM CHECKLIST

Computer:

Microprocessor	_____	(e.g., Intel "386," "486," or Pentium; Motorola 68030 or 68040)
Memory included	_____	RAM
Memory capacity	_____	RAM
Cache memory	_____	
Number of expansion slots	_____	
Other upgrade features	_____	
	_____	
Number of ports	_____	
Warranty	_____	Years

Additional for Laptop/Notebook Computers:

Battery type	_____	
Estimated use on full charge	_____	Hours
Computer weight	_____	With battery
Charger included?	_____	(yes/no)

Disk Storage:

Hard Disk Drives	_____	Manufacturer
	_____	Model
	_____	MB capacity
	_____	Data access speed
Warranty	_____	Months/years
Flexible Disk Drives	_____	Number included
	_____	Sizes (3-1/2",5-1/4")
	_____	Capacity (720K, 1.44MB, 2.88 MB; other)
Warranty	_____	Months/years
Optical Disk Drive	_____	(yes/no)
	_____	Manufacturer
	_____	Model
	_____	Data transfer rate
Warranty	_____	Months/years

Software Bundled with Computer:

Name	Type	Disk included?	Documentation included?	Software preloaded?
_____	_____	_____	_____	_____
_____	_____	_____	_____	_____
_____	_____	_____	_____	_____
_____	_____	_____	_____	_____
_____	_____	_____	_____	_____
_____	_____	_____	_____	_____

- The capability to run two to three applications at a time and to display multiple documents simultaneously

To guide her in appraising different solutions, Monique created the personal systems checklist in Figure 8.6.

FIGURE 8.6   *Continued*

Monitor:

Color	_____	(yes/no)
Capability	_____	(CGA, VGA, EGA, SVGA)
Size	_____	(13/14/15/17/20 inch; 330, 355, 381, 431, 508 mm)
Multisync	_____	(yes/no)
Warranty	_____	Years

Printer:

Manufacturer	_____	
Type	_____	Laser/dot matrix/other
Speed	_____	Pages per minute/lines per minute
Communication	_____	Serial/parallel
Port to be used	_____	
Warranty	_____	Years

Communication Modem:
(alternatively fax/modem)

Manufacturer	_____	
Modem speeds	_____	
Fax speeds	_____	
Fax resolution	_____	(100 DPI; 200 DPI; other)
Installation	_____	Internal board/external via communications port
Port to be used	_____	
Warranty	_____	Years
Software included?	_____	(yes/no)

Mouse:

Included	_____	(yes/no)
Type	_____	(serial/bus)
Software included?	_____	(yes/no)

Scanner:

Manufacturer	_____	
Resolution	_____	
Warranty	_____	Years
Software included?	_____	(yes/no)

Cables:

Printer	_____	Included/purchase _____ Length
Monitor	_____	Included/purchase _____ Length
Modem (fax/modem)*	_____	Included/purchase _____ Length

* Cable not needed for internal modem, fax, or fax/modem

Program Requirements.   Monique recognized that her computer hardware needs would be heavily influenced by her software requirements. Hence, she focused a great deal of attention on identifying the software packages she would need. She was certain that she could meet all of her program requirements with prepackaged software. Some adaptation of her working habits and tailoring of the software's setup might be necessary, but she did not foresee any serious difficulties in that area.

In many cases, the programs Monique examined were available for both Macintosh and IBM-compatible computers. In the instances when this was not the case, she found functionally comparable packages.

Program requirements influence both the amount of main memory needed and the amount of disk storage needed within a system. Monique's review of many different software packages (during her store visits and her discussions of program characteristics with friends and colleagues) provided her with ample information. Figure 8.7 shows her summary of internal program memory requirements and the price she could expect to pay for software.

Storage Requirements.   To estimate her secondary storage requirements, Monique identified the files and databases she intended to store on disk, calculating the space needed to store each one. Files and databases often grow with use, so she also estimated annual increases for each file. Her estimates are summarized in Figure 8.8.

After completing her estimates, Monique determined that she wanted a minimum of five times her current estimate. She decided to purchase 170 MB of disk space, a size that fit easily within the storage ranges supported on the systems she had examined. Expansion space for new programs and additional files also did not seem to be a constraint because of the excess capacity on systems she was evaluating and because additional storage capacity could be added later if needed.

FIGURE 8.7
Monique's Program Requirements (with Main Memory Requirements) and Approximate Cost of Software

Software Type	IBM Requirements	Approximate Cost	Macintosh Requirements	Approximate Cost
Word processing	4 MB memory 15 MB disk space	FF 1995/$399	4 MB memory 8 MB disk space	FF 1595/$319
Spreadsheet	2 MB memory 8 MB disk space	FF 1595/$319	2 MB memory 6 MB disk space	FF 1545/$309
Database	4 MB memory 6 MB disk space	FF 1995/$399	1 MB memory 4 MB disk space	FF 2145/$429
Drawing (includes clip art library)	8 MB memory 8 MB disk space	FF 1995/$399	5 MB memory 8 MB disk space	FF 2045/$409
Imaging	8 MB memory 6 MB disk space	FF 2995/$599	4 MB memory 6 MB disk space	FF 2995/$599
Desktop publishing	4 MB memory 6 MB disk space	FF 2895/$579	5 MB memory 6 MB disk space	FF 2995/$599
Data communications	1 MB memory 1 MB disk space	FF 445/$89	1 MB memory 1 MB disk space	FF 445/$89
Scanning	Included with scanner purchase		Included with scanner purchase	
Approximate Total Software Cost		**FF 13,915/$2,783**		**FF 13,765/$2,753**

Initial Data Storage Requirements
 Name and address file
  500 individuals @ 280 bytes each = 140,000 bytes (.14 MB of storage)
 Editorial development tools
  Dictionaries, thesaurus, and grammar tools @ .5 MB each: 1.5 MB
 Clip art (size requirements taken from documentation in package)
  Photo art   7 MB of storage
  Line art   3.5 MB of storage
 Active manuscript space
  5000 pages: 250 words per page @ 5 bytes per word   6.25 MB
 Total: 17.39 MB

Data expansion (update) requirements (annual)
 Name and address file expansion
  500 individuals @ 280 bytes each = .14 MB of storage
 Editorial development tools
  25% expansion   .375 MB
 Clip art
  25% expansion   2.6 MB
 Active manuscript space
 (presumes migration of older manuscripts to diskettes for off-line storage)
  7500 pages: 9.375 MB
 Total: 12.49 MB

 Grand total: **29.88 MB**

FIGURE 8.8
Monique's Data Storage
Requirements

Step 3. Solution Selection: Choose the New System

Everyone Monique spoke to had a favorite computer **platform**, the computer foundation on which applications are built. Many publishers, editors, and illustrators told her that they use Macintosh platforms in their business, while many people in other industries preferred an IBM-compatible platform. There were exceptions in both groups, however, and Monique had to make a final choice regarding the computer platform she'd prefer. She also needed to take the plunge and purchase the new system.

platform The computer foundation on which applications are built. The two most common platforms for PCs are IBM-compatibles and Apple Macintosh.

Choose the Computing Platform. In the end, Monique knew that whether she chose the Macintosh or IBM-compatible computing platform, she had to be able to communicate with and transfer data and information to the other platform.

 After much thought, Monique narrowed down her alternatives (Figure 8.9). She selected the software applications first, determining that they should drive her choice of computers, printers, and scanners. After considering price, performance, and the features she needed, she chose an IBM-compatible PC (but planned to keep her Apple Macintosh computer). The hardware cost slightly more than she had originally estimated, but she was pleased with her choice.

Buy the System. Monique purchased all of her hardware and software from a single dealer. Hence, she was able to pick up the computer, printer, scanner, and all the software in a single trip to the store. Prior to Monique's arrival, the computer dealer assembled and tested the computer and communications hardware. He also installed the fax/modem that Monique bought.

ALTERNATIVE 1

Software: Word processing (with dictionaries and related writing tools), electronic spreadsheet, desktop publishing, drawing, imaging, clip art, database management, and data communication programs

   System 7 operating system (current version)
   Software Cost: FF 13,765/$2,753

Hardware: 33 megahertz, Apple Macintosh (Motorola 68040 microprocessor) with 8 MB main memory, 230 MB hard disk, high-resolution color monitor, fax/data modem, keyboard and mouse; laser printer (adapter card included); high-resolution scanner (software and adapter card included)

   Hardware cost: FF 33,625/$6,725   **TOTAL COST:** FF 47,390/$9,478

ALTERNATIVE 2

Software: Word processing (with dictionaries and related writing tools), electronic spreadsheet, desktop publishing, drawing, imaging, clip art, database management, and data communication programs

   DOS operating system, Windows
   Software Cost: FF 13,915/$2,783

Hardware: 66 megahertz, IBM-compatible computer (Pentium microprocessor) with 8 MB main memory, 340 MB hard disk, SVGA display adapter and color monitor, internal fax/data modem, keyboard and mouse; laser printer (adapter card included); high-resolution scanner (software and adapter card included)

   Hardware Cost: FF 31,335/$6,267   **TOTAL COST:** FF 45,250/$9,050

FIGURE 8.9
Monique's Computing Platform Alternatives

Step 4. Solution Design: Create the New Applications

After bringing her new system home, Monique needed to create its new applications. For Monique, this process consisted of installing the application software, designing the application features, testing the applications' specific capabilities, and documenting the system.

Install Application Programs.   Both the operating system and Windows software were installed on the PC when Monique brought it home. All she had to do was unpack the printer and scanner, then plug them into the ports on the back of the computer. The computer dealer had included the cables needed to do this.

   Each of Monique's application programs was packed separately. As Monique opened each box, she did two things right away:

- Completed the registration card, which she would mail to the manufacturer on her next trip to the post office. When the manufacturer received the card, it would add her name to a mailing list for future announcements of enhancements and new versions.
- Made backup copies of each program disk to protect the master disks from accidental damage.

   She then installed each of the programs, using the backup copies, onto the computer's internal hard disk according to the manufacturer's step-by-step installation instructions. The install routine built into each software package prompted Monique with a few questions: On which disk drive do you want this system installed? What printer will be used with this program? To which port is the printer connected?

Had Monique run into any difficulty, she could have called the free technical support telephone numbers listed in the program manuals or used the softwares' help features. Fortunately, microcomputer software generally installs quickly and easily and usually does not require calls to technical support specialists. So even though Monique had the phone numbers handy during program installation, she did not need to use them.

Installing each program took from one to two hours, depending on the number of disks in the package. After she had installed each package, Monique started the program to ensure that it would run. Because she had decided to install all the programs at once, she used almost a full day to load all the programs.

CRITICAL CONNECTION 2
Dell Looks to Service and Support for Competitive Edge

It's four o'clock and you're racing to finish a proposal that's due at five o'clock sharp. Zap! Your computer dies. What do you do?

It's sad but true. Desktop computers sometimes fail. In fact, *PC World* has reported that a significant percentage of all PC buyers encounter some hardware failure, ranging from minor to serious, within two years of their purchase. It's no wonder, then, that many personal computer satisfaction surveys have found that service and support are customers' top concerns when purchasing personal systems.

It's also no surprise that direct marketer Dell Computer Corp. received consistently high marks for service and reliability, due in large part to the "Dell Vision" that holds that customers must be "pleased, not just satisfied." CEO Michael Dell sees support and service as one way to gain a competitive edge in the price wars sweeping the computer industry.

Design Application Features.   Before buying the system, Monique had determined that her needs for managing records would evolve. Hence, she had decided to use a database package rather than a prewritten name and address program that includes a predesigned database format. She knew from experience that many of the prewritten name-and-address programs presume a domestic address and telephone number—which was not appropriate for her purpose, because she worked with editors and publishers in many different countries. She also judged most name-and-address programs to be designed either for generating mailing lists and labels, or for use in sales management. Her needs were much broader, so she chose a powerful but easy-to-use database program.

Once she had loaded the database management software onto her computer, Monique had to define the features of her database application. She did so by entering the database descriptions shown in Figure 8.10 on the next page.

Test Applications.   Monique tested each personal productivity package—word processing, electronic spreadsheet, database management, drawing, and imaging—after installation. The testing process for each consisted of:

Data Item	Size	Type
Name	30	Alphanumeric
Building/floor	48	Alphanumeric
Street address	48	Alphanumeric
City	24	Alphanumeric
State	16	Alphanumeric
Country	16	Alphanumeric
Postal code	10	Alphanumeric
Telephone	16*	Numeric
Fax	16	Numeric
E-mail	24	Alphanumeric
Assistant	16	Alphanumeric
Assistant's telephone	16	Alphanumeric

*Provides space for international dialing codes

FIGURE 8.10
Designing the Database Application

- Creating a test document
- Storing the document
- Retrieving the document from storage
- Editing and storing the changed document
- Retrieving the edited document and inspecting the changes
- Printing the document

The test was as much an evaluation of Monique's understanding of the program's essential features as it was a test of the package. Of course, learning each program's advanced features required time, and Monique chose to learn these a little at a time by using the package in her work (rather than sitting down to master each feature described in the program manuals).

Because of writers', editors', and publishers' increased reliance on electronic transmission of manuscripts, Monique also conducted communications tests with several different publishers. Within a week, she found she could use two communications standards to communicate with everyone. Hence, she adjusted her communications software so that she could choose either standard at a click of the mouse. (We discuss communications in detail in Chapter 9.)

Monique also tested her PC's built-in fax by transmitting and receiving several documents. The tests went well, and within a single morning the fax was ready to use.

Document the System and Procedures.   After loading the software, entering the database specifications, and testing the applications, Monique gathered up all the documentation for the system. She placed the manuals accompanying the programs on her bookshelf for easy reference. In a clearly marked ring binder she placed a list of the serial numbers of all her equipment. She also recorded the serial number and version number of all her software and kept copies of every software licensing agreement and product warranty.

In a separate binder she placed the information describing her first database's definition. She also planned to use the same binder to keep copies of all her DTP layouts, worksheets created with spreadsheet software, and word processing formats. She also included procedures for using the different applications (including source documents, transmission of documents and output, and fax phone numbers) in a special procedure section of the binder.

Developing these procedures made Monique realize where she needed additional information (such as information regarding fax transmission and client telephone billing procedures) and that she needed to keep track of version numbers of manuscript drafts. She also established a schedule for making periodic backup copies of software, data, and documents. To keep her documents secure, she decided to store copies of important manuscripts in a safe deposit box at her bank.

Step 5. Implementation: Convert to the New System

Installing the prepackaged programs made them ready to use. Once all the software was loaded, Monique had to make a transition to the new system. Implementation of a single-user system involves conversion of existing records, training, and cutover. Here's what Monique did in these key areas.

Conversion.   After entering the database description into the database management software, Monique began converting her existing handwritten name and address lists into an electronic format. Entering and visually proofing each name and address took approximately 30 seconds. It took Monique half a day to enter the entire contents of her database. Once entered, the name and address file became a ready reference.

Training.   Each software package Monique purchased was accompanied by an onscreen tutorial designed to familiarize new users with the program. Monique had used these during the solution design phase to get acquainted with each program's basic characteristics. During the implementation phase, she used advanced tutorials to learn about the packages' special features and ways of adjusting the system's characteristics to suit her needs.

Because of its many powerful features, the desktop publishing software required a different approach. Although Monique had good knowledge of document design and layouts, she did not know how to prepare these with her new DTP software package. To overcome this weakness, she decided to attend a three-day workshop to learn the package's capabilities. She also subscribed to a user's magazine that includes instructions, tips, and case studies in every issue.

Monique's ongoing training included keeping abreast of developments in the IT and publishing industries. Periodicals, magazines, and industry newspapers are useful for doing so, both because of the articles they contain and the many advertisements in each issue. Figure 8.11 lists some of the most popular IT publications.

Cutover.   Because of her experience with similar packages running on her Macintosh, Monique was already familiar with the characteristics of the word processing and database systems. Thus she was able to put these to use right away. She began using the other applications more gradually. She did not discard her card file, choosing to hold onto it until she became comfortable with the new database software. She did not use her spreadsheet system until she had to prepare a project proposal for a major editorial project. After that, she used it constantly for many different aspects of projects, including the preparation of project proposals, budget creation, and cost management.

Evaluation and Evolution of the System

Monique's system is personal—it is a collection of carefully selected IT tools, adapted to her needs (both now and in the future) and designed to augment her

Magazines	Newspapers
Aldus	Computerworld Japan*
Business Week	Computer Shopper
Byte	InfoWorld
Compute	Le Monde Informatique
DBMS	Network World
Décision Micro	PC Week
Dr. Dobb's Journal	
Fortune	
Forbes	
Home Office Computing	
LAN Technology	
Macworld	
MacWeek	
MacUser	
Multimedia	
Multimedia Solutions	
01 Informatique	
PC Computing	
PC Magazine	
PC World	
Portable Office	
Presentation Products	
Publish	
Télécoms	
Windows	
WordPerfect	

Computerworld is published in a variety of national editions, including *Computerworld Argentina, Computerworld France, Computerwoche* (Germany), and *China Computerworld.*

FIGURE 8.11
A Sampling of Personal Systems-Oriented Periodicals and Magazines

know-how as a writer and journalist. As her career evolves, her IT needs will undoubtedly change. Hence, continuous evaluation of her system—which includes keeping up with new ideas and advances in software and hardware—is in her professional interest. Simple activities, such as subscribing to magazines and making contact with other people in your field, can be as important as IT in building careers.

Or, as Monique said, "Magnifique! Ce n'est que le début."[3]

[3]"Magnificent! This is only the beginning."

SUMMARY OF LEARNING OBJECTIVES

1 Describe the origin of single-user systems in business and why they have become so prominent and important. In the early days of data processing, large computers and vast communications networks were the norm. Although these large systems are still in widespread use, technological progress in the 1980s and 90s, coupled with increased affordability, has made personal systems the dominant source of IT capability in many organizations.

2 **Identify the distinguishing characteristics of a single-user system.** Single-user systems are designed for hands-on usage, are tailored to an individual's requirements and preferences, and are used to improve personal performance.

3 **Explain the benefits of single-user systems in business.** When properly designed, single-user systems have three main effects: improved productivity, greater effectiveness, and increased creativity.

4 **Define the problem solving cycle and how it relates to the development of a single-user system.** The problem solving cycle is composed of five activities: recognizing problems, defining them, selecting strategies to deal with them, designing solutions, and implementing those solutions. The process of developing a single-user system begins with problem recognition and is ongoing through system evaluation and evolution.

5 **Discuss the five steps involved in developing a single-user system.** The five steps involved in developing a single-user system are: (1) problem recognition—conduct a preliminary investigation; (2) problem definition—determine the system's requirements; (3) solution selection—choose the new system; (4) solution design—create the new applications; and (5) implementation—convert to the new system.

6 **Distinguish between choosing a single-user system and creating single-user applications.** Choosing a single-user system entails finding the right platform and tailoring it to personal requirements and preferences. Creating single-user applications involves installing the application programs, designing the application features, testing the applications' specific capabilities, and documenting the system and procedures.

7 **Explain the importance of continuous evaluation and evolution in single-user systems development.** Because an individual's needs change, a single-user system must evolve to meet those needs. To remain effective the user must be aware of the latest advances in hardware and software.

KEY TERMS

CRITICAL CONNECTIONS

Music Consultants Group

1. Database Gives Composer More Time to Play Around

Loading the database onto his notebook computer has been a real help to Jonathan Wolff at dubbing sessions. If a producer wants to make a last-minute change, Wolff can quickly search the database for a suitable replacement.

When he first started using the music database, Wolff's actual music was still stored on audio tape. This caused a slight delay while he searched for the right tape and loaded it onto a tape deck. Now, with the advent of multimedia, he is planning to build a link between the database and a Macintosh computer that will let him store, retrieve, and play his music through the computer itself.

Questions for Discussion

1. Describe how Wolff's personal system has increased his productivity and effectiveness.

2. How might Wolff's personal system give his company a competitive advantage?

3. What provisions has Wolff made for the continuing evaluation and evolution of his personal system?

2. Dell Looks to Service and Support for Competitive Edge

By the early 1990s, desktop computers were being sold by many companies in many ways. Packard Bell, for instance, began selling them through warehouse buying clubs. Today, name-brand companies like IBM,

Compaq, Dell, Gateway 2000, and AST Research each hold less than 25% of the PC market.

Compaq, hoping to fight this trend, recently announced a series of sharp price cuts. Consumers were delighted by the price war that followed. Soon industry observers were speculating that only the strongest companies would survive.

In addition to price cuts, Dell announced an expanded range of support and service options for its more expensive models. Along with its standard service plan—one year of onsite service and lifetime telephone support—Dell would offer the SelectCare plan to large corporate accounts. Under this new plan, customers could buy extended warranties that provided as much—or as little—service and support as they wanted. The options ranged from parts-only coverage for up to four years to onsite Critical Care Service and a Self-Maintainer Program designed to train the company's technical support staff. Within weeks, several other name-brand companies had followed Dell's lead, announcing their own extended support and service programs.

Questions for Discussion

1. Local computer dealers once justified slightly higher prices by offering more direct support, such as setting up and testing a desktop system prior to delivery. How do you think these dealers have been affected by recent developments in computer marketing?

2. By the early 1990s, many IT professionals who were used to dealing with mainframes and minicomputers found themselves linking PCs together in networks. How do you think this trend has affected the demand for support and service? Can you think of other trends that have affected the demand for support?

3. Some computer makers now offer three-year warranties with two years of onsite service. Why do you think onsite service is an important consideration in purchasing and setting up a personal system?

REVIEW QUESTIONS

1. What is a single-user system?

2. How did single-user systems originate? Why are large mainframe systems not considered single-user systems?

3. What are the three characteristics of single-user systems?

4. What is a "hands-on user"?

5. What is productivity? List three ways in which productivity can be increased.

6. How can single-user systems aid productivity?

7. What is personal productivity software?

8. Describe the importance of effectiveness and the role of single-user systems in improving effectiveness.

9. How are productivity and effectiveness different?

10. Define the concept of leverage.

11. What is a problem? What five activities comprise the problem solving cycle? How do these activities relate to the process of developing a single-user system?

12. What is outsourcing?

13. What three steps are involved in conducting a preliminary investigation into a problem?

14. What three types of feasibility must be considered in developing a single-user system? Describe each briefly.

15. Explain the three types of requirements that a single-user system must fulfill.

16. In choosing a new system, are needs or desires more important? Explain your answer.

17. What four activities are involved in the solution design phase of developing a single-user system?

18. Describe the three components of implementing a single-user system.

19. What role does evaluation play in the development of a single-user system?

DISCUSSION QUESTIONS

1. If Monique's budget for her single-user system is cut in half, how could she set priorities in deciding what hardware and software she should purchase? Can you identify an area in which she should *not* economize?

2. Corporate Fact Finders, DataSearch, and InfoQuest are all "information brokers," companies that do library and online database searches to meet their clients' research needs. For their services, information brokers are paid $40 to $300 an hour. If you were a freelance information broker, what requirements would your single-user system have to meet?

3. CompUSA and a number of other national computer chains offer regular training classes. Why are these training classes important to current and potential customers? Why might you take a training class *during* the preliminary investigation stage, rather than waiting until you actually buy and install a single-user system?

SUGGESTED READINGS

de Bono, Edward, (1970) *Lateral Thinking*. New York: Harper & Row. Describes a series of approaches to increasing creativity in identifying and solving problems. Can be applied to many aspects of IT use in business.

Edwards, Paul and Sarah Edwards, (1990) *Working from Home*. New York: Putnam. A practical discussion of the steps in setting up and marketing a personal business. Includes effective ways to analyze the characteristics of the personal support systems needed in the business.

Eyler, David R., (1990) *Starting a Home-Based Business*. New York: Wiley. Presents a complete "nuts and bolts" discussion of the requirements to start an independent business. Also describes the steps and considerations in selecting a cost-effective personal IT system.

Simon, Herbert A. (1957) *Administrative Behavior* (2d ed). Englewood Cliffs, NJ: The Free Press. A classic treatise on problem solving that examines the process and pitfalls of creating solutions to problems across a variety of business and personal settings.

CASE STUDY

User Groups Offer Support and Computing Tips

What's a workplace MUG? And what's it doing at Walt Disney Company, Domino's Pizza, Oakland (California) television station KTVU, and the Pentagon? MUG stands for Macintosh User Group, a place where employees can come together to share tips and exchange information about using their Macintosh PCs. MUGs are also one way that Apple Computer Co. builds loyalty among its customers.

User groups date back to the dawn of personal computing. In fact, the first "personal" computer, the Altair 8800, and the first user groups both appeared in 1975. In those days, personal computers didn't come preloaded with software. The Altair came in a kit, to be assembled at home by hobbyists who often wrote their own programs. It's no wonder that hundreds of these trailblazers flocked to user groups, where they could swap ideas, talk shop, and get help on their projects.

Today, there are more than 10,000 user groups in the United States alone. Although many members are IT professionals, the user groups are also a haven for novices who need help and basic training. Dues for local groups average about $30 a year and usually include monthly general meetings, special interest groups (SIGs), a monthly newsletter, a bulletin board service (BBS), training sessions, and discounts on group purchases of hardware and software. The general meetings, in particular, are a good place to socialize, gather tips, and watch vendors demonstrate hardware and software. They're also a good place for vendors to market their wares. A recent study of twelve user groups found that members approved IT purchases averaging $89,000 a year.

These statistics aren't lost on Apple. User groups had played an early and important role in its success. (In fact, Stephen Wozniak, co-founder of Apple Computer Co., had demonstrated the Apple I at meetings of the Homebrew Computer Club in Menlo Park, California, in the mid-1970s.) In 1985, Apple Computer created a separate division, the User Group Connection, to help user groups get started. In addition to a start-up kit for newly registered user groups, the division issues monthly mailings about Apple products and software. It also publishes *QuickConnect*, a newsletter filled with articles that can be reprinted in local user group newsletters.

Organizing the volunteers needed to start and operate a user group can be a challenge. That's why the User Group Connection operates a toll-free number that Macintosh users can call to find out whether a suitable user group or professional organization already exists. If not, users can follow the guidelines contained in the division's free, 96-page booklet, *Just Add Water, Workplace Edition*. (A separate edition is available for people who want to start a community-based MUG.) Some of the issues workplace MUG organizers need to consider include the following:

- Does your organization need a MUG? (It depends on whether the IT staff offers good support to Mac users.)
- What are the MUG's goals? Will the MUG focus on work tasks or on recreation a computing?
- Will the MUG meet during work hours?
- Where will the MUG meet?
- Will the MUG charge dues? (If so, the group has to appoint a treasurer and obey tax laws. If not, it needs to decide where it will get funding and support.)
- How will the MUG recruit and keep members?

By the end of 1993, workplace user groups—the kind appearing at companies, colleges, and government agencies—accounted for about 750 of the almost 2,000 MUGs registered with Apple. The chance to learn more about using the Mac at work is an obvious advantage. The MUG at Walt Disney Company, for example, was formed to help members keep up with the technology. But there are personal advantages, as well. Army Major Stephen Broughall, who helped establish the Pentagon MUG in 1985, says it has let him meet other, notable individuals throughout the Defense Department and helped him stay on top of industry news. Television station KTVU's consumer editor says, "I've talked to people now in this building that I normally wouldn't have much conversation with, because of the MUG."

Questions for Discussion:

1. Although Macintosh PCs have a strong and loyal following at some corporations, IBM and IBM-compatible machines are generally more common. How might the

Who Joins User Groups . . .

Professional/ staff specialist	33.7%
Chair/president/owner	28.3%
Department head or manager	12.1%
Technical/mechanical/production	7.7%
Supervisor	5.1%
Vice president/general manager	3.7%
Administrative assistant	1.8%
Secretary/clerical staff	1.8%
Other	6.1%

. . . and What They Like Best

Monthly newsletter	42.9%
Socializing with members	14.8%
Bulletin board services	12.4%
General meetings	12.2%
Special interest groups	9.5%
Training sessions	3.5%
Special events	2.6%
Shareware disks	1.3%
Group purchase	0.7%

Numbers may not total 100 due to rounding.
Source: California State University at San Bernardino, California, April 1992 user group demographic study.

workplace MUGs strengthen Apple's position among business users?

2. As a manager would you provide funding or other types of support for a MUG? As an employee, would you join a MUG?

3. MacIS, short for Managing Apple Computers in Information Systems, is an independent users group made up of about 400 IT professionals from Fortune 500 companies, such as Procter & Gamble. Members meet annually to vote on their top concerns and to appoint task forces to work directly with Apple to find solutions. What benefits does this user group offer to its members? To individual consumers? To Apple?

Sources: Deborah Branscum, "Workplace User Groups Offer Support," *Macworld*, November 1993, pp. 193–194; Sarah Klein, "User Groups Offer Something for Everyone," *PC World*, October 1993, pp. 37ff. Art used by permission of PC WORLD. Copyright © October 1993.

Over the past few years, buying a microcomputer system has emerged as the third most significant purchase most people will ever make—right behind buying a house or a car. Buying and setting up a single-user system should be a thrilling and fulfilling experience if you go about it systematically. The ten-step process that follows will help you bring a little method to the madness.

Step 1. Prepare yourself for the Information Age.

You wouldn't buy a car before you learn how to drive, and you shouldn't buy a PC before you understand its capabilities and what you can do with it. A course like the one you're taking now should help here, as would a general course or lab course geared toward microcomputer applications. If you're interested in a specific area, such as desktop publishing, look for a course that will give you a good overview.

Step 2. Determine your information and computing needs.

Take some time to think about both your current and future needs. If you think you might want to work with computer graphics or multimedia applications, check the minimum hardware requirements listed on various software packages and factor them into your research.

Think, too, about your work habits. Do you plan to work in one location or do you need the portability of a laptop or notebook computer? Will you be the only person using the computer or will you be sharing it with others? And will you want to exchange computer files with friends and colleagues? If so, you need to be sure your systems are compatible.

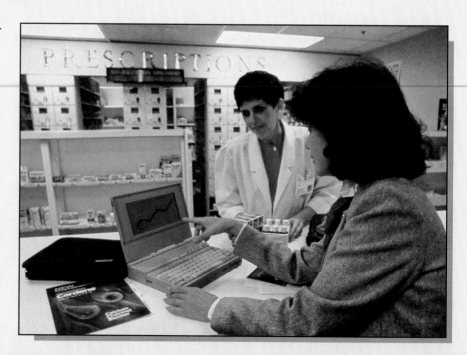

Step 3. Assess the availability and quality of software and IT services.

Determine what software and information services are available to meet your needs. Good sources of this type of information are periodicals, salespeople at computer stores, and acquaintances who have IT experience. Another good source of information is the IT courses you take and your instructors.

Step 4. Select a platform and investigate specific software packages for that platform.

Because most software is written to run on an IBM-compatible or Apple Macintosh platform, your choice of a platform will narrow down your software options.

Once you've chosen a platform, you're ready to take a closer look at specific software packages. Software packages with essentially the same capabilities may have price differences of several hundred dollars. Some graphics software creates displays of graphs in seconds, while others take minutes. Some software packages are easy to learn; others are more difficult. This and other software-rating information can be found in product reviews, IT journals, and via word-of-mouth. Considering the amount of time you will spend using software, any extra time you devote to evaluating your software options will be time well spent.

323

Step 5. Decide how much you are willing to spend.

Microcomputer systems can cost as little as a few hundred dollars or as much as $40,000. Assess your finances and decide how much you are willing to commit to the purchase of a personal system at this time.

Don't make the mistake of thinking, "I'll wait until the price goes down a little more." If you adopt this strategy, you may never buy a PC. If you wait, you may be able to buy a more powerful computer for less money. But what about your lost opportunity to increase productivity? Even a moderately priced system can make you more efficient and more effective.

Step 6. Choose a microprocessor.

One measure of state-of-the-art technology is the computer's processor. Most experts recommend a 20 MHz 386SX microprocessor at minimum. But if you want to explore more challenging applications, you may need a more powerful microprocessor, such as the Intel 486 or Pentium chip *(See Figure 3.9)*. Desktop publishing and other graphics-based applications function best with a powerful microprocessor, a large-capacity hard drive, and a high-resolution monitor.

Step 7. Compare micro configurations.

A keyboard and mouse are standard on most personal systems today. You will also want to scan advertisements and identify your needs with respect to memory capacity, secondary storage drives, monitor characteristics, and expansion slots.

Also important are warranty and service agreements. Many manufacturers offer a one-year warranty with free on-site service. *Technical support hotlines* are also common, but the service varies widely. Some companies provide users a toll-free 24-hour hotline; others charge as much as $50 per hour or limit the period of time support is available.

Retailers, too, usually service what they sell, sometimes on a carry-in basis. Another option is a maintenance contract. Many shoppers forego such contracts, though. They elect to treat their PCs like a television or car: One the repairs costs exceed a certain point, they simply shop for a replacement.

Step 8. Determine the additional peripheral devices, software, and accessories you need.

Your main consideration here will probably be selecting a printer, although you may also want to add other peripherals. You should also look at your software want-list and budget for furniture and other accessories. If you have a spending limit, the following cost ranges are useful for first-time buyers: a printer ($200-$1000); software ($100-$1500); maintenance ($0-$500 a year); diskettes and tape cassettes ($50-$200); furniture ($0-$350); insurance ($0-$40); and printer ribbons or cartridges, paper, and other supplies ($40-$400).

The main challenge here is setting your priorities. If you need a high-quality laser printer, for example, you may decide to delay the purchase of a fax-modem board.

Step 9. "Test drive" several alternatives.

Once you have selected several software and hardware alternatives, spend enough time to gain some familiarity with them. Does one keyboard have a better touch than others? Does one monitor seem sharper than others? Given the amount

of time you will spend at your computer, these are important considerations. If one system seems superior in all aspects *except* a keyboard or monitor, can you negotiate for a replacement?

Many software packages offer demonstration and/or tutorial disks, which walk you through a simulation of the key features. Salespeople at most retail stores are also happy to give you a "test drive"—just ask. Some stores will even let you bring in your own files and see how a system performs the applications that interest you.

This is a good time, too, to begin shopping for price. To get a good idea of the going prices for various hardware and software components, check the mail-order advertisements in computer magazines.

The worksheet in Figure 8.6 should help you compare configurations, prices, and your comments about the various systems you test.

Step 10. Select and purchase your system.

PCs and related hardware and software can be purchased through several channels. The most traditional are local retailers and outlets of nationwide chains, such as ComputerLand, ENTRE, and MicroAge. Another, newer channel is the computer superstore, which offers supermarket displays and steeply discounted prices. PCs are also sold in the electronics departments of most department stores and by electronics retailers.

Another alternative is the mail-order house. If you know what you want, you can call a toll-free number, give the operator a credit-card number, and your system will be delivered to your doorstep.

Another source is your employer. In cooperation with vendors, companies make volume purchases of PCs at discount rates, then offer them to employees at substantial savings. Many colleges sponsor similar programs to benefit students and professors.

Once you've made your purchase, the only tasks left are to open up the boxes, follow the instructions, and start enjoying your new system.

Personal Computing: The Good News...and the Challenges

I f YOU'RE A TYPICAL PC USER, AN HOUR IN FRONT OF YOUR computer can pass before you notice. That's good news if you're being productive, bad news if you're struggling to solve a mysterious hardware or software problem. Many people, interested mainly in what a personal computer can do for them, see red when they run into those rare but productivity-sapping delays and technical problems. You can understand their frustration—and minimize the amount you experience—if you understand a few of the forces working in the personal computer industry today.

An expanded market. As late as 1989, fewer than one in four homes contained a computer. This began changing in the 1990s when the computer industry began targeting the home market. Consider just a few of the factors that have convinced millions of consumers to bring a computer home:

- **Falling prices.** In a fierce struggle for market share, both computer makers and software publishers have been cutting prices. Often, "value-line" but powerful models with CD-ROM drives and sound boards are bundled with pre-installed, user-friendly software (such as Microsoft Works, which integrates a stream-lined word processor, spreadsheet, and database management system). Open the box, plug in a few cables, and you can start computing almost immediately.
- **New retail outlets.** At one time, hardware and software were sold almost exclusively in specialized computer stores staffed by and for "techies." Today, many of the same products are being sold by mail or in discount stores, where they are displayed alongside other consumer electronics.
- **Advertising and media coverage.** Exciting commercials, coupled with intriguing media coverage of the information superhighway (see Chapter 14), multimedia, virtual reality, and related topics, have raised consumer interest to a fever pitch. Even consumers who have never used a computer soon have begun to realize that they—and their children—need to learn more about computing.
- **Home-based workers.** Whether they are telecommuting or operating a home-based business, an increasing number of computer buyers are installing their systems in a home office. By the end of 1993, more than one in three homes contained a computer, and more than 60% of those computers were located in a home office.

Hidden costs. It's easy to focus on a low price and ignore some of the hidden costs of developing a single-user system. Does the price include the monitor? If you're interested in multimedia, do the sound board and CD-ROM drive meet the latest standards?

And then there is the issue of software. Most users want to add sophisticated, full-featured productivity programs, which cost $200 to $400 or more. Adding some fun software, like clip art, games, and a multimedia title or two, can easily double the price of your system. This assumes, though, that your new computer has enough RAM and hard-disk space to run all the software you want to install. (Many low-priced systems include small hard disks and the minimum amount of RAM needed to run the average program.) If you don't have the required amount of memory, you'll need to upgrade your new system (another $200 to $500).

Add in incidentals, such as a high-quality printer ($300 to $1,000 and up) and supplies, and you can see why the computer itself is a relatively small part of the total system cost. Add to this the sobering thought that last year's computer may not run this year's exciting new software at an acceptable speed, and you have some serious issues to consider.

Hidden complexities. Although PCs are being marketed alongside TVs and other consumer electronics, there is still a world of difference between a television and a PC. True, software publishers have done much to simplify computing. Graphical user interfaces (such as Microsoft Windows), batch installation routines, and online tutorials and help systems have all reduced the amount of time users spend poring over thick manuals filled with technical terms. In fact, many users never open these manuals.

Beneath these highly accessible interfaces, though, computers remain essentially "literal" devices that must follow complex programming instructions to perform increasingly complex marvels, ranging from graphics to multimedia and telecommunications. If a key command in a buried file is missing or wrong, or if you accidentally

Shopping for a computer has become a family affair as more and more couples are starting their own businesses or telecommuting to their jobs.

erase or damage one of these key files, the computer won't work. When that happens, you can try to troubleshoot the problem yourself or you can place a phone call to technical support.

Elusive support. At the same time they are cutting prices (and profit margins) to the bone, computer and software companies are facing a growing demand for fast, free, and friendly technical support. Providing these services is harder than it sounds. On the one hand, the computer industry has to satisfy the "time is money" business user who needs a reliable system that has been customized for maximum performance. On the other hand, it has to placate thousands of bewildered novices. (In 1992, Packard Bell fielded 20,000 calls the day after Christmas.) Together, these two types of users have jammed technical support lines, which in turn leads to long hold times and high levels of frustration. In response, companies are offering a wider variety of support options. Some offer an automated, phone-based troubleshooting session; others let you fax a description of your problem to the company. Still others offer support over online information services such as CompuServe. And still others offer fee-based support to demanding corporate users.

Discussion Questions

1. Is the need for support more important to business or home users? Explain your answer.

2. What do the dual forces of price cutting and increased demand for support mean for businesses within the computer industry? How might these competitive pressures affect consumers?

PART 4

Multi-User Systems

- Chapter 9: Multi-User and Network Computing
- Chapter 10: Shared and Distributed Data
- Chapter 11: Developing Shared IT Applications
- Chapter 12: Business Information Systems and IT in Industry

Talking With Bill Eaton
Senior Vice President and Chief Information Officer
Levi Strauss & Co.

Bavarian-born Levi Strauss stepped off a sailing ship in San Francisco in 1853. Not long after, he created the world's first jeans for miners in California's gold-rich hills. Today, Levi Strauss' ideals and vision live on, embodied in a corporation that flourishes—and in the millions of pants around that world that are guaranteed to shrink, wrinkle, and fade.

In this interview, Bill Eaton—Senior Vice President and CIO of Levi Strauss, where he's been a member of the IT team for more than 15 years—shares his experiences in the development of Levi Link, a world-class application of information technology that has changed the way Levi Strauss & Co. competes. I also asked Bill about his own secrets for career success and how others can be successful.

You're known world-wide for your accomplishments in deploying information technology, through such highly regarded systems as Levi Link, to enable Levi Strauss's success. Can you summarize your viewpoint on the value of information technology to business?

Although I'd describe myself as a heat-seeker,[1] when it comes to applying IT in business, it's more about what you can do with it. What is it enabling? What is it driving? The point is... we don't pursue it for technology's sake. We pursue it because it enables something or creates some opportunity or solves some problem. I've tried to take that approach. When my rate of change or pushing of the opportunity gets in front of the business's ownership, their readiness to take IT on, it will create some friction. There's an art form for CIOs to recognize when that's occurring. Sometimes, frankly, you have to slow and wait for things to get ripe enough so you can have a success.

[1]Individuals fascinated with the hardware and software details of information technology often refer to themselves by colorful names, such as "gearheads" and "heat-seekers."

"With Levi Link, we created the electronic linkages to our customers and suppliers. It was very, very successful. It showed very quickly what it was like to be able to move precise information about what was moving in the market place to this complex at the speed of light."

You're not talking about technology issues here, are you?

It's much broader than that. There are four things you have to do to get a successful enterprise today, especially a global enterprise:

(1) You've got to have the right business processes.
(2) You have to have the right enabling technology for those business processes.
(3) You have to have the right human skills, people skills; a trained and excellent work force that's flexible and knowledgeable, and has the right knowledge content.
(4) And you have to have a structure—an organizational structure—in which you can mix all of those ingredients in order to get a success.

How interdependent are these four things?

The way I see all those things, Jim, is that they're very interdependent. Whichever one of them is the weakest link is going to determine where your point of failure is. So, if you want to think about rolling out some enabling technology...it's not enough to think about just the technology. You have to ask yourself: "What do the business processes have to be to take advantage of this? Who has to own them? How does that ownership come about?"

You've got to think: What do people need to know about when you're ready to throw this over the transom? What special learning investment do we have to make?

What's the impact on the organization structure? Does this new information technology mean that we're not going to have the same people doing the same jobs and working in the same way?

What about the information technology?

Then you deliver the technology itself. You can talk about it from an information technology perspective. Where it fails is when we tend to think that all we have to do is deliver the system. If you don't deal with those other opportunities or points of failure, depending on how you want to define that, then the organization will, in the blink of an eye, absorb the new technology in a status quo way. You'll watch a $40 to $100,000 million investment in new technology create no business benefit.

If I want to do something, and it's of any sizable scope, I had better figure out who is the business owner. I had better team up with the organization design people. I had better figure out what people need to know. Then you can begin to think about deploying the technology.

Is Levi Link an example of that ?

Levi Link underscores some of the learning that is needed. With Levi Link, we created the electronic linkages to our customers and suppliers. It was very, very successful. It showed very quickly what it was like to be able to move precise information about what was moving in the marketplace to this complex at the speed of light.

The reason we wanted to do it was to align our manufacturing with what we were selling. What did it take? We had to figure out a standard identification to have the vendors mark our product. We had to convince the business units to spend money to put that on each garment when the retailers weren't asking to do it yet. We had to convince the retail industry to have the right standards to invest in bar coding. There had to be EDI [electronic data interchange] communication standards.

We teamed up with other companies—clearly taking the leadership role—to make it happen. All of that happened and we got the information here.

Then you had to look at the business processes to take advantage of the information. How did that come about?

I teamed up with our chief operating officer. Another art form for CIOs is to recognize what they can legitimately sponsor and what they can't. I started the momentum inside our company around the term "quick response," an important concept in the apparel industry, meaning "time-to-market." Then we leveraged that up after a couple of meetings to improved customer service. We saw it in a broader perspective. He and I became the executive sponsors to take on the customer service initiative.

We asked: So that we have the information here, what do we have to do to our people skills, and to the organization? What technology do we need to essentially smash all of the unnecessary time out of the supply chain? What do we have to do to achieve the customer service targets?

There were debates: What's it going to cost? What are the benefits?

As you think back on the folks who have started their career with Levi Strauss, or for that matter any company, do you see particular things the most successful people do to help their company and within that, help their career?

That's an interesting, complex question. You can answer it simply or you can answer it with a lot of context and complexity.

The simple answer is that [in the most successful cases] I see people that are in touch with what they stand for. You know, at a gut level, as individuals, and where their passion comes from. And if they are able—and this should be really simple for all of us, but I think it's extremely difficult— if you can be in touch with what turns you on about the work and what you choose to involve yourself in, you have the highest probability of success. I don't care whether it's information technology or another area of business, or whatever else.

At the college level and beyond into the workplace, we arrive with so many external forces, whether they be parents, friends, peers, or self-induced forces, about what success should look like. Therefore, it's almost impossible to find out what we enjoy. If I was giving

advice, I'd suggest forgetting what anybody else tells you and try to get in touch with what you get enjoyment out of. If you can match that enjoyment with the work opportunity, it'll carry you through for life and you'll get the most fun out of it.

It'll be fun for you. And if you don't, you'll not only be sort of miserable, you'll essentially search through career patterns until you are able to self-select the things you enjoy. The earlier you can figure it out, the better off you'll be.

CHAPTER 9

Multi-User and Network Computing

Learning Objectives

When you have completed this chapter, you should be able to:

1 Identify the reasons why multi-user systems are used in business.

2 Explain the three types of multi-user architectures and the advantages offered by each.

3 Discuss the three types of communications networks and the advantages offered by each.

4 Discuss the two types of communications channels used in networks and the ways that computers interconnect with them.

5 Explain the role of a network operating system.

6 Discuss the activities involved in network administration.

7 Describe eight network service applications used in business.

In Practice

After completing this chapter, you should be able to perform these activities:

1 Explain why an information technology infrastructure is important to business and society.

2 Visit a business that uses a local area network and determine how the network functions and the advantages it offers.

3 Evaluate the benefits of a wide area communications network to a company in the transportation, retailing, or manufacturing industry.

4 Discuss with the administrator of a local area network the types of applications running on the network and the functions performed by the network operating system.

5 Specify the components needed to create a communications network to link workstations, printers, and file servers in an office.

6 Speak with a network operations manager and discuss the steps she takes to ensure that the network capability is always available to those who need it and the actions she takes when communications problems arise.

7 Visit with a telephone company or PTT representative and discuss the company's position on developing additional communications capabilities as part of the nation's business and commerce infrastructure, as well as the ways in which both businesses and private citizens will benefit from these new capabilities.

Infostructure

IN THE INDUSTRIAL AGE, DESIGNERS included electrical and telephone outlets in homes and office buildings to meet the needs of residents and occupants. These capabilities became part of the *infrastructure*—the shared facilities that provide a foundation on which other activities can be built. No longer simple conveniences, the electrical and telephone systems have changed the way people work and live. The phone that you use to call family and friends is the same phone you use to place an order for delivery of food, to reserve concert tickets, or to arrange express delivery of a package.

The most important element of the infrastructure is its shared use. Shared use means that everyone benefits. When the same capabilities are made available to all, each individual can focus on using the infrastructure to meet his or her needs, without having to take the time to conceive,

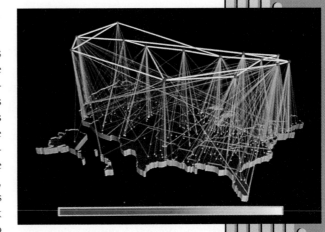

More than ten million people trade information via Internet, a network that connects businesses, research labs, libraries, and college campuses. The most used part of the system is the National Science Foundation's NSFNet. Pictured here is one month's traffic on NSFNet. The white lines are the roads most traveled, the purple lines the least traveled. Internet promises to be a major component of the world's developing infostructure.

develop, and maintain the system. Home builders, for example, know that most household utilities—a vital part of the infrastructure—will be available in a particular region. They can therefore focus on designing the right building, considering infrastructure only to make sure that the capability is available when they need it. Indeed, people have become so accustomed to having infrastructure at their disposal that they don't even think about using it. (How often do you think about *how* to plug a light into the electrical system in your home, apartment, or office?)

In the Information Age, electrical and telephone outlets are being supplemented by *information outlets* that provide instant access to information technology and data communications capabilities from a variety of sources. Millions of people will share the use of this *infostructure* to deliver business products and services. ▪

LTHOUGH THE INFORMATION INFRASTRUCTURE WILL UNDERGO CONTINUED EXPANSION, many of its components are already in place. This chapter examines these components, focusing on the creation of multi-user infostructures within organizations. Throughout the chapter, we will use many examples to demonstrate the ways businesses are creating and using their communications capabilities both to serve people and to be successful.

In the first part of this chapter, we consider the principles underlying multi-user systems and the role of communications networks. We then examine the architectures of multi-user infostructures. In the last part of the chapter, we examine eight multi-user applications that are part of the emerging business and social infostructure.

◼ Principles of Multi-User Systems

multi-user system A system in which more than one user share hardware, programs, information, people, and procedures.

We defined **multi-user systems** in Chapter 2 as systems in which more than one user share hardware, programs, information, people, and procedures. IT professionals often refer to using a network as *resource sharing*. Here we take a closer look at the purposes of multi-user systems and the role of communications networks.

The Purposes of Multi-User Systems

communication The process of sending data and information over a communications network.

A distinguishing characteristic of the Information Age is **communication**, which involves sending and receiving data and information over a communications network. (Communication is much more than telephone calls and letters.) At an increasing rate, business communication relies on multi-user systems. As Figure 9.1 shows, multi-user systems have three business purposes:

- To increase the productivity and effectiveness of the people using the system.
- To increase the productivity and effectiveness of the organizations in which the system is used.
- To improve the services provided to those who rely on others using multi-user systems.

FIGURE 9.1
The Purposes of Multi-User Systems in Business

Multi-user systems

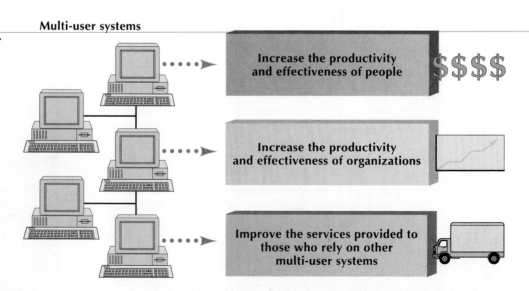

Increase the productivity and effectiveness of people

Increase the productivity and effectiveness of organizations

Improve the services provided to those who rely on other multi-user systems

Note that the emphasis here is on *people*. Solving problems or capitalizing on opportunities almost always involves other people. Perhaps they tackle a part of the problem, carrying out actions to overcome a challenge or remove an obstacle. Perhaps they have access to essential information or to someone else who can provide valuable insights or assistance. Or perhaps they work in the field or at home and need to stay in close contact with the home office (an important trend today that we discuss in detail in the People box entitled "The Joys of Telecommuting.") Business is a group or team activity—a system in which the different parts of the organization must coordinate their activities to be successful. This means that effective communication among people is an essential element of business success.

The Role of Telecommunications Networks

Communications networks are the key element in multi-user systems. A **communications network** is a set of locations, or **nodes**, consisting of hardware, programs, and information that are linked together as a system that transmits and receives data and information. When a computer is connected to another computer, both are part of a network. Networks may link users across relatively short distances or they may span wide areas. (We discuss the different types of networks in detail later in this chapter.)

It is becoming relatively easy to connect computers for multi-user activities. For this reason, networks are common in both large and small organizations. Once connected, these networks enable people and organizations to share and transmit important data and information while in the process overcoming the barriers created by geographic distances.

communications network
A set of locations consisting of hardware, programs, and information that are linked together as a system that transmits and receives data or information.

node A communication station within a network.

PEOPLE

The Joys of Telecommuting

TELECOMMUTING, THE GENERAL TERM FOR LETTING EMPLOYEES use telecommunications to work from a home office, is one of the fastest growing segments of the work-at-home trend. By the mid 1990s, experts predict, the number of U.S. telecommuters will grow from 5.5 million in 1991 to more than double that number.

For many employees, telecommuting offers a way to balance work and personal obligations. Denise Rixter, a regional marketing manager, appreciates the flexibility of telecommuting. "If my daughter gets sick or if there is a function at school, I will be there. I'll just work later that day on my promotion projects." Bill Grout, an editor, had a strong motivation for convincing his New York boss to let him telecommute from Burlington, Vermont: He wanted his son and daughter to grow up in a "more relaxed, friendly, and rural environment."

Telecommuting benefits employers as well as employees. Freed of the office's interruptions, many telecommuters' productivity increases by 15 to 25 per-

cent. Of course, telecommuting isn't for every employee in every job. That's why telecommuting arrangements are usually informal and available only to seasoned, valued knowledge workers with high levels of motivation and self-discipline.

Telecommuting may even benefit the economy. A recent study by the respected Arthur D. Little think tank concluded that increased telecommuting could save U.S. companies $27 billion per year by increasing productivity while reducing the amount of money spent on energy, maintaining the infrastructure, and controlling pollution. The state of California has been experiencing some of these benefits since 1984, when telecommuting and flexible hours were introduced to ease the traffic and pollution associated with hosting the Olympic games. Telecommuting is getting another boost from the U.S. government's Clean Air Act of 1990, which is encouraging employers to reduce the number of employees driving to and from the workplace.

✓ **Reality Check.**   Network computing is not a fad. Rather, it is a trend that has been evolving for many years—an evolution that involves computers of all sizes, from the smallest micro to the biggest supercomputer. There is a great deal of activity in this area as organizations interconnect office workers' desktop computers with those of workers in factories, at oil fields, and on construction sites. Increasingly, a microcomputer that is not connected to a network will be as useful as a telephone that is not connected to the international communications network.

Especially if you work with other people, it probably won't be long before you'll want to interconnect your desktop computer to other systems. Perhaps several people in your work group are working on a problem together. Or perhaps you are brainstorming independently and want to pool your ideas and information with your colleagues'. The information you need is on someone else's computer. There's no sense in photocopying a printout of that information when you can get a copy of it on diskette or—better yet—have it sent to you electronically. This is what networking is all about: using data communications capabilities to send, receive, and retrieve data and information from other nodes on the network. ■

■ Multi-User Architectures

architecture The structure of a communications network; it determines how the various components of the network are structured, how they interact, and when cooperation between the system's components is needed.

A communications **architecture** is the structure of a communications network; it determines how the various components of the communications network are structured, how they interact, and when cooperation between the system's components is needed. There are three types of multi-user system architectures: centralized architecture, distributed architecture, and architectures that combine elements of centralized and distributed systems.

Centralized Architecture

centralized architecture Communications architecture in which a computer at a central site hosts all of the network's hardware and software, performs all the processing, and manages the network.

host-based computing Centralized computing.

In a **centralized architecture**, all network hardware and software are found at a central site, usually in a computer center. Centralized computing is also called **host-based computing**. The central computer (or set of computers linked together at a single site) performs all processing and manages the network (that is, it *hosts* the network) (Figure 9.2). It may retrieve information from a database, store new information, or accept and transmit information from one individual to another. All security protection occurs through the host computer, which validates individual passwords and restricts the activities that individual users are allowed to perform. IT staff members make backup copies of information and programs from the original versions, which reside on the host computer.

Throughout the 1960s, 1970s, and most of the 1980s, information technology was largely centralized. Organizations ran their applications on centralized mainframe or minicomputers located in data centers. Initially, dumb terminals—a display and keyboard without a processor (see Chapter 4)—were connected to the mainframe by a cable. For this reason, the terminals could not be too far away from the computer center. Users had to come to the computer center to use the computer, hauling their work with them.

teleprocessing The processing capability allowed by connecting computers through telephone lines.

A major advance in network technology came in the late 1960s, when computer manufacturers developed ways for people to connect with the centralized computer through telephone lines. This **teleprocessing** capability was an important advance in IT because the central computer's processing power and storage capacity could

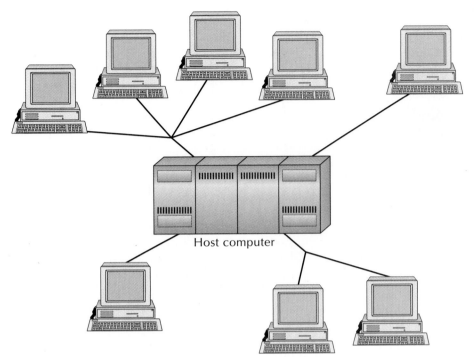

FIGURE 9.2
Centralized Architecture
In a centralized architecture, all network hardware and software are found at a central site, usually in a computer center. The central computer performs all the processing and hosts the network.

now be accessed and shared by many people from many locations simultaneously. People could remain at their work location and still use the host computer's processing capabilities. Figure 9.3 on the next page explains in detail how telephone communication works.

By the 1970s, minicomputers had enabled small and medium-size companies to establish computer networks without having to invest in expensive mainframe computers. Minicomputers could serve as hosts, providing that the volume of processing to be done was not so large as to overwhelm the processing and storage capabilities of the computer. Some companies also began using **front-end computers**, minicomputers loaded with special programs to handle all incoming and outgoing communications traffic in a host-based, centralized system (Figure 9.4 on page 339). With a front-end mini, the host computer is freed to carry out the processing, storage, and retrieval tasks for which it is best suited.

front-end computer In a centralized system, a minicomputer loaded with special programs to handle all incoming and outgoing communications traffic.

Distributed Architecture

The 1980s made it clear that people liked using microcomputers, which offered several advantages over mainframes. Using micros, people could sit at their desks, get quick access to data and information, and tailor the micro and software to their personal needs. Nonetheless, some managers (even some IT professionals) questioned the wisdom of heavy business investment in PCs. Microcomputers were underutilized, it was argued; either the PC emulated the dumb terminal it replaced (meaning that the built-in processing capabilities of the PC were largely unused) or the PC was used for a limited number of activities and for just a few minutes a day.

That was then. Today, as we approach the twenty-first century, microcomputers are used in ways undreamed of only ten years ago. Many people use them all day, every day. Each day, computers continue to increase in speed, storage capacity, and reliability while shrinking in size and cost. This "PC revolution" in business has been brought about in large part by several major trends in the business world, the most important of which are listed in Table 9.1.

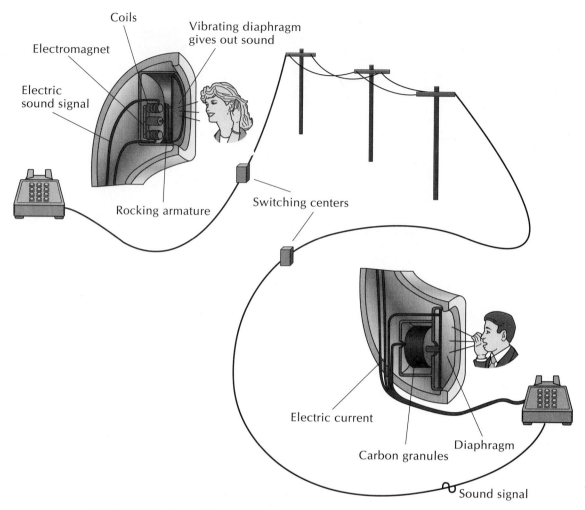

FIGURE 9.3   How Telephone Communication Works
When you speak into the telephone, a small microphone in the handset captures the sounds through a vibrating diaphragm, causing the electrical current flowing through the microphone to vary. From the handset, these electrical signals are sent over metal telephone wires. In the public telephone network, the electrical signals may be translated into light signals that may be beamed over fiber optic lines (see Figure 9.12). Alternatively, they may be converted into radio signals transmitted over radio networks or by microwave (see Figure 9.13).

How does a telephone call or data communication transmission get to the right place? How are so many conversations and messages sent over a communications network? Today's communications systems convert speech into digital form—the same digital codes used in computer systems. Using *multiplexing*, several messages can be packed together and sent simultaneously on the network. The messages are divided into blocks that are sent in very short intervals. Built into each block of data are identification and routing codes. When these are read by the digital switching components that are a part of the network, the message can be switched from one line to another, perhaps repeatedly, so that the message reaches its intended destination. Because data move at the speed of electricity or at the speed of light (186,000 miles per second), a message reaches its destination in a fraction of one second.

The identification codes make it possible to keep one message distinct from another and to ensure that the right data are sent to the proper destination. At the destination, a *demultiplexor* unpacks the various streams of data and routes the message blocks back to the correct telephone.

These same principles apply in computer communications (see Figure 9.18).

Source: From *The Way Things Work* by David Macaulay. Compilation copyright ©1988 by Dorling Kindersley, Ltd, London. Illustrations copyright ©1988 by David Macaulay. Reprinted by permission of Houghton Mifflin Company. All rights reserved.

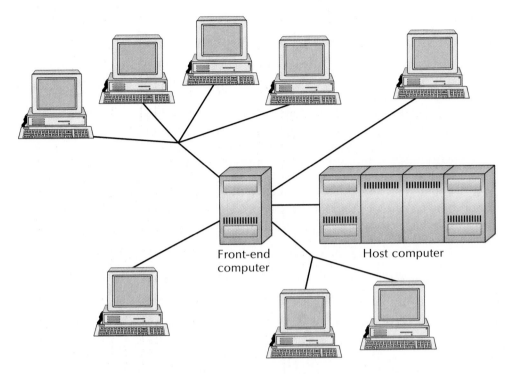

FIGURE 9.4
Centralized Architecture Using a Front-end Computer
A front-end minicomputer allows the host computer to carry out the processing, storage, and retrieval tasks for which it is best suited.

Front-end computer

Host computer

As a result of these trends, employees and executives have been dispersed throughout the world, at both company facilities and at customer locations. As these changes came about, business and government leaders began to challenge IT professionals: "Our people are distributed, so our information and our processing capabilities must be too." Driven by the need to compete effectively in a world market, businesspeople turned to IT professionals for help in answering the pressing questions:

- How can we get our products to market more quickly?
- How can we more effectively share information, both internally and with other companies?
- How can we get more value from our current IT capabilities?
- How can we interconnect different systems to achieve maximum efficiency?

TABLE 9.1   Trends Driving Business in the 1990s

- A growing awareness of the **international nature of business** and the emergence of global commerce.
- A heightened awareness of the **importance of speed** in responding to the needs and desires of consumers, customers, and suppliers regardless of their location, and the need to ensure that products and services are available when needed.
- A new awareness that **business alliances**—partnerships among businesses—can be created so that all parties to the alliance benefit from mutual cooperation.
- An awareness that people have to know what is happening in other areas of their firm, not just in their department (marketing, manufacturing, inventory management, and so forth). Instead of being concerned solely with their assigned departmental tasks, businesspeople are increasingly thinking about **cross-function business processes**. Entire business processes have been redesigned so that individuals focus on the complete set of tasks comprising the process from beginning to end rather than just activities within their work area.
- A new **emphasis on the roles of those companies with whom the firm interacts**, either as customers or suppliers. Suppliers have become recognized as an integral part of a company's success or failure and the satisfaction of its customers.

• How can we make different computer and communications systems work together?

distributed architecture A communications architecture in which the computers reside at different locations and are interconnected by a communications network.

The answers to these questions lie in distributed architecture. In a **distributed architecture**, computers—supercomputers, mainframes, midrange systems, and microcomputers—reside at different locations, rather than in a single data center, and are interconnected by a communications network. The computer at each location serves primarily the needs of that location. Through the network, the distributed systems can work together, retrieving information from some systems within the network and acting as a source of information supplied to other locations in the network.

distributed processing The running of an application on one or more network locations simultaneously.

A distributed architecture supports **distributed processing**, in which an application runs on one or more locations of the network simultaneously (Figure 9.5). In a distributed processing system, the hardware, software, or information needed

FIGURE 9.5
Distributed Architecture with Distributed Processing
In a distributed architecture, computers reside at different locations, rather than in a single data center, and are interconnected by a communications network.

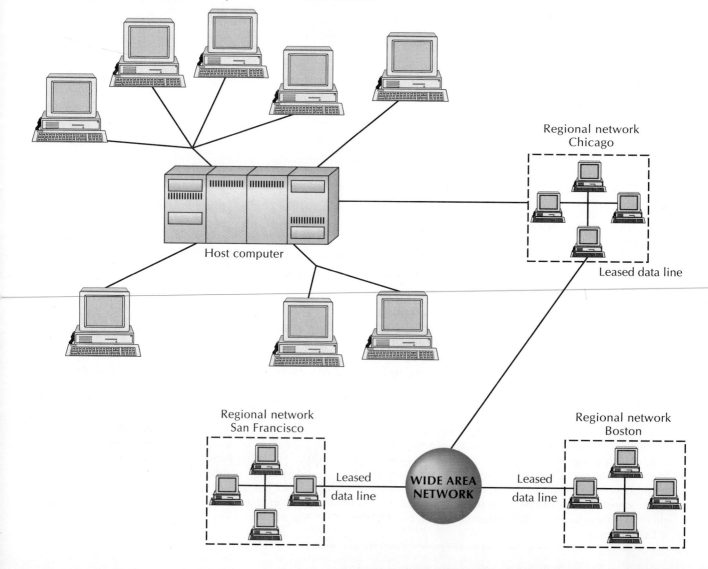

for the application may actually be physically located at a different location. **Distributed databases** (which we discuss in Chapter 10) are databases that reside on more than one computer system in a distributed network. Each component of the database can be retrieved, processed, or updated from any node in the network, rather than through a central host computer only.

Kmart, the large U.S. discount retailer with more than 2,300 stores nationwide, utilizes a very large distributed architecture (Figure 9.6). All of its stores use point-of-sale bar code scanning on all items going through the checkout counter. By means of a satellite link, this purchase information is transmitted immediately to merchandise buyers at the company's Troy, Michigan headquarters and to a large number of the company's suppliers. Credit authorization for those customers paying by credit card is also obtained through this communications link, thus speeding the checkout process while ensuring that the card is valid.

Each Kmart store is interconnected with one of the company's 12 distribution centers nationwide where inventory records are maintained. Sales information is transmitted continuously between the stores and the distribution centers' computers. In addition, Kmart's key suppliers, which have invested in their own computer systems that let them monitor inventories at the distribution centers electronically, automatically replenish the stock, with no approval from Kmart, when supplies run low.

Small suppliers can take advantage of these distributed capabilities as well. The hardware and software needed to set up this type of system costs under $15,000.

distributed database A database that resides on more than one system in a distributed network. Each component of the database can be retrieved from any node in the network.

FIGURE 9.6   Kmart's Distributed Architecture

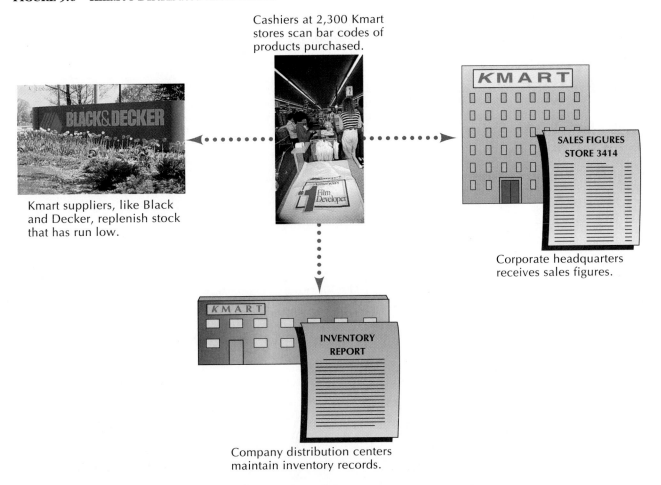

Cashiers at 2,300 Kmart stores scan bar codes of products purchased.

Kmart suppliers, like Black and Decker, replenish stock that has run low.

SALES FIGURES STORE 3414

Corporate headquarters receives sales figures.

INVENTORY REPORT

Company distribution centers maintain inventory records.

Combining Architectures

You should not conclude from the previous discussion that one type of architecture is always better than the other. Each has benefits and drawbacks. For example, centralized systems are easier to manage because of the central location. Distributed systems, though more difficult to manage, place information at the locations where it is used most often while ensuring that others in the system have access to it.

To take advantage of all the benefits of both configurations, companies can choose to combine architectures. In general, these **hybrid networks** combine centralized teleprocessing and distributed features. In hybrid networks, the computer at the top of the system (usually a mainframe) controls interaction with all the devices attached directly to it. The host does not, however, directly control those computers interconnected at lower levels of the network (Figure 9.7).

hybrid network   A communications architecture that combines centralized and distributed architectures to take advantage of the benefits of both.

Hybrid Networks in the Airline Industry.   Hybrid networks can take many forms. Some companies, for example, have combined networks that span vast geographic regions with others that link desktop computers within a single building. One such system now in widespread use in the airline industry evolved when many European airlines found themselves facing heightened competition from international airlines in the 1980s. To continue being successful, management decided, airlines would have to expand beyond their national borders. Doing so would not be an easy task, however, for two main reasons.

First, the travel agents—independent businesspeople who receive a commission when they sell a ticket for an airline—sell the majority of airline tickets. Travel agents can sell tickets for virtually all of the world's airlines and tend not to promote a single carrier. Second, no single European airline had the resources to

FIGURE 9.7   Hybrid Architecture
Hybrid architecture combines centralized and distributed features. The computer at the top of the network (here, the mainframe) controls interaction with all the devices attached directly to it. The host does not control the computers interconnected at lower levels of the network.

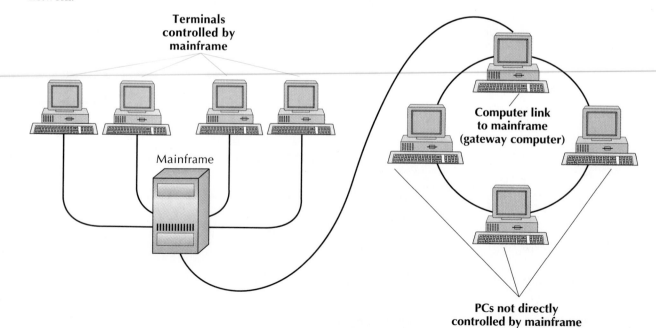

develop its own network to interconnect the travel agents in the many countries to which it flies. System development and operations costs were prohibitive. Nonetheless, each airline had to find a way to share information with travel agents about schedules, fares, and reservations.

Out of this necessity evolved an alliance among more than 20 airlines (including Air France, Iberia, Lufthansa, and SAS) and the network-based Amadeus system. Using the network, the airlines and a vast array of travel agents throughout the world can share flight information. Development of the Amadeus network also provided the foundation for other network-based travel services. For example, Amadeus is now used to book reservations for ferry and Hovercraft crossings, trains, and automobile rentals.

The strength of Amadeus lies in a hybrid network that links several computer networks. Each airline, hotel, or other business enterprise connected to Amadeus continues to operate its own computer network. Some of these individual networks are centralized and others are distributed; some span large areas and some span small areas; all use different combinations of computers, programs, and screen displays. Amadeus links these individual networks.

The combination of business alliances with a hybrid network architecture has changed the way international airlines compete and the markets they serve. But multi-user computing and communications networks are also of great interest to countries. In fact, an industry-sponsored study conducted by the Iacocca Institute at Lehigh University in the early 1990s recommended the creation of a nationwide communications network for linking factories across the United States. The goal: to boost the global competitiveness of U.S. manufacturers.

Under plans developed as part of the Iacocca study, the Factory America Net network will allow most companies to interconnect with the network. For example, a company developing a new product will be able to send a message across the network asking suppliers to provide information on their ability to develop and manufacture a component or to provide a service needed for the new product. The creation of **virtual companies**—business enterprises that come together operationally, but not physically, to design and manufacture a product is expected to be a result of this hybrid network.

virtual company A company that joins with another company operationally, but not physically, to design and manufacture a product.

The Factory America Net will undoubtedly grow and evolve as the concept advances from idea to reality. It is long-term in scope, designed to be an integral component of U.S. manufacturing strategies in the twenty-first century.

CRITICAL CONNECTION 1
Apple Computer Thinks Fast and Comes Out a Winner

Apple Computer had a problem. To hold its own against IBM computers and IBM clones in the lucrative corporate market, Apple needed a notebook computer—fast. But it was already clear that Apple's engineers couldn't develop a portable Macintosh on top of all the other products slated for 1991. Then it hit upon a solution. Would Sony Corp., one of Apple's suppliers, be interested in developing the PowerBook 100, the low-end model in Apple's new family of notebook computers? The answer was "Yes."

Apple's one-time partnership with Sony reflects several business trends of the 1990s; among them:

- *Pursuing short-term partnerships to seize market opportunities.* Using Apple's basic specifications, Sony engineers took the PowerBook 100 from drawing board to manufacture in less than thirteen months. In 1992, after 100,000 Sony-made models had flown off dealers' shelves, Sony and Apple ended their agreement.
- *Seeking alliances that take advantage of "core competencies."* Sony's core competency—the manufacture of miniature electronic components—was a natural complement to Apple's skill in designing "user-friendly" computers and software. Together, the two companies were able to accomplish more, faster than either could alone.
- *Extending mutually beneficial proposals to former or potential rivals.* To learn more about designing computers, Sony canceled other projects to free up staff and other resources that could be deployed for work with Apple. In return, Apple got a crash course in manufacturing miniature electronics from a world master.

Types of Networks

topology The configuration of a network.

Networks can interconnect devices and people across the hall or around the world. Networks come in three configurations, or **topologies**, as Figure 9.8 shows. The type of connection and the span of the network define the three types of networks: wide area, local area, and metropolitan area.

Wide Area Networks

wide area network (WAN) A network that interconnects sites dispersed across states, countries, or continents.

When companies and governments must interconnect sites dispersed across states, countries, or continents, they develop **wide area networks (WANs)**. These companies make use of wide area networks:

- London-based British Petroleum runs a worldwide wide area network linking its data centers, providing information about oil and exploration, energy distribution, chemical research and development to employees around the globe (Figure 9.9 on page 346). The network links hundreds of company sites in North and South America, Europe, and Asia. The company's main data center in Glasgow, Scotland is linked by communications channels to major business centers in Aberdeen, Glasgow, London, and Stavanger (Norway); U.S. hubs in Houston, Cleveland, and Anchorage; and South American hubs in Caracas (Venezuela) and Bogotá (Colombia). Business centers in Moscow and Jakarta (Indonesia) can also communicate with the main data center in Glasgow through the firm's wide area network. The network is designed to enable individuals at any location to operate as if they were at the host computer site.
- Toys 'Я' Us operates a wide area network that links more than 750 U.S. Toys 'Я' Us and Kids 'Я' Us retail stores, as well as 170 other locations in Europe and Asia. The system is designed to allow 30,000 employees to share inventory and sales information and to send messages to each other via electronic mail (dis-

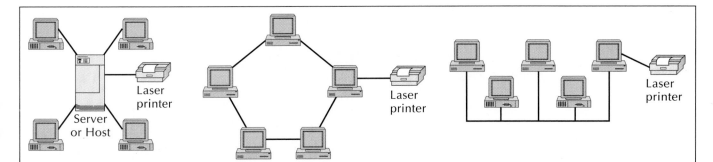

The *star topology* interconnects many different sites through a central computer system (a server). The central computer is typically a mainframe. Nodes may be other mainframes, midrange systems, or microcomputers. Sending a message from one node to another entails sending the message to the central server or host computer first, which receives and retransmits the message to the intended destination.

In the *ring topology,* each node is connected to an adjacent node. There is no central node. A message is sent from one node through the network. Each location examines the identification code in the message (which is inserted by network software) and accepts the message if it has the code. Otherwise, it transmits the message to the next node. The process continues until the message reaches its destination.

The *bus topology* is a linear network–a "data highway," so to speak. All nodes tap onto the bus. Data transmissions from one node are sent to every other node on the network. Each node examines the identification code, accepting those messages containing its code and ignoring the others.

FIGURE 9.8   The Topology of Networks
The topology of a network is its shape—the arrangement of the nodes or workstations of a network in relation to one another. In determining which structure to use, network designers consider the distance between nodes, the frequency and volume of transmissions, and processing capability at each node. There are three topologies.

cussed later in this chapter). This multi-level network interconnects each store to one of 19 regional centers located around the world. Information is then routed from the center to the company headquarters in Paramus, New Jersey. Toys 'Я' Us is also building a special network that will eventually allow direct broadcast of information to each store via satellite.

- Levi Strauss, the San Francisco-based clothing manufacturer and retailer, has a PC-based cash register in each of its stores. A network known as Levi-Link captures all sales transactions each day. At the end of the day, details of all sales are sent to a computer at headquarters. There the information is analyzed to determine what has been sold, which items must be shipped to replenish inventory at the store, and what goods need to be manufactured. Levi-Link helps to keep the stores fully stocked, thus allowing them to gain sales advantage over competitors who use manual inventory methods.

In all of these examples, information must travel over distances that are far too long to be spanned by a single cable linking one location to another. For this reason, teleprocessing is frequently used in wide area networks. The telephone lines used to link different sites to a central computer are generally not owned by the company but rather are leased from a telephone or communications company. In many other parts of the world, the telephone company is called the **Post, Telephone, and Telegraph,** or **PTT**. We discuss another type of transmission link for wide area networks in the section on communications channels later in this chapter.

Post, Telephone, and Telegraph (PTT) A general term used for the telephone company in countries other than the United States.

FIGURE 9.9 **British Petroleum's Global Wide Area Network**
London-based British Petroleum runs a worldwide WAN linking its data centers, providing information to employees around the globe. The network links hundreds of sites in North and South America, Europe, and Asia to the company's main data center in Glasgow, Scotland.

common carrier A company furnishing public communications facilities for voice and data transmission.

A company furnishing public communications facilities for voice and data transmission is called a **common carrier**. The most visible common carriers in the United States are AT&T (the largest common carrier), MCI, and U.S. Sprint. Common carriers in the United Kingdom include BT (British Telecom) and Mercury Communications. France has France Télécom, Germany has Bundespost, and Japan has Nippon Telephone and Telegraph.

Bandwidth.   The speed at which information is transmitted over a communications medium is determined by *bandwidth*. A greater bandwidth means that more information is sent through a medium in a given amount of time. The bandwidth of a network is measured (indirectly) by the bits of data transmitted per second:

- **Kilobits per second (Kbps)**—thousands of bits of information per second.
- **Megabits per second (Mbps)**—millions of bits per second.
- **Gigabits per second (Gbps)**—billions of bits per second.

Hence a transmission at 2,400 bits per second, a common speed for transmitting data from a terminal to a mainframe over a wide area network, is said to be at 2.4 kilobits per second.

Corporations often develop high-speed WANs that transmit over networks using **T-carriers**, very high-speed channels designed for use as backbones and for point-to-point connection of locations. A *backbone* is a high-speed transmission link designed to interconnect lower-speed networks or computers at different sites.

T-carrier A very high-speed channel designed for use as a backbone and for point-to-point connection of locations.

Transmission rates for U.S. T-carriers are: T-1 lines at 1.544 megabits per second, T-2 at 6.312 megabits per second, T-3 at 44.736 megabits per second, and T-4 lines at 274.176 megabits per second. Outside of the United States and Japan, T-carriers are known as *PCM carriers.*

Reality Check.   To put bandwidth in perspective, consider the following examples. A standard page of typed correspondence contains approximately 275 words—about 2,000 bytes or 16,000 bits (recall that a byte equals 8 bits) of information, including punctuation, spaces, and blank lines. Transmitting one page of correspondence over a standard modem will require approximately 6 seconds. Sending the page of correspondence at the faster voice transmission rate of 50 Kbps will take .28 seconds. Using a high-speed network, transmitting at, say 1.544 Mbps, it will take no more than 1/100 of a second to transmit the page of correspondence.

Suppose you wanted to transmit this entire book, of 600 pages, over a wide area network. Assuming that each page contains 3000 bytes (24,000 bits) of information, it would require:

- at 2400 Bps—7000 seconds (116 minutes, or approximately 2 hours).
- at 56,000 Bps—300 seconds (5 minutes).
- at 1.544 Mbps—10.8 seconds

Local Area Networks

Local area networks (LANs) interconnect computers and communications devices (printers, fax machines, and storage devices) within an office, series of offices in a building, or campus of buildings (Figure 9.10). They typically span a distance of a few hundred feet up to several miles. The network components (the nodes in a LAN), including the cable linking the devices, are generally owned by the company using the network.

You will typically not find mainframes on a LAN. LANs are usually comprised primarily of desktop computers and the printers designed to work with them. A desktop computer connected to a network is often called a **workstation**. (Alternatively, it may be called a node or a **client**.) The computer that hosts the network and provides the resources that are shared on the network is called the **server**. The server provides services to each of the workstations attached to it. When workstations access a server, they can use ("execute") the software residing on the server or process data in a file or database on the server.

The server typically has more primary memory and storage capacity and a higher processing speed than the other computers on the network. Some networks have multiple servers, either to provide a backup in case one is not working or to distribute databases more quickly for faster access to information.

A **file server** is a computer containing files available to all users connected to a LAN. In some LANs, a microcomputer is designated as the file server. In others, a computer with a large disk drive and specialized software acts as the file server. We will examine client/server computing in detail in Chapter 10.

local area network (LAN) A network that interconnects computers and communications devices within an office or series of offices; typically spans a distance of a few hundred feet to three miles.

workstation or **client** A desktop computer connected to a network.

server The computer that hosts a network and provides the resources that are shared on the network.

file server A computer containing files available to all users connected to a LAN.

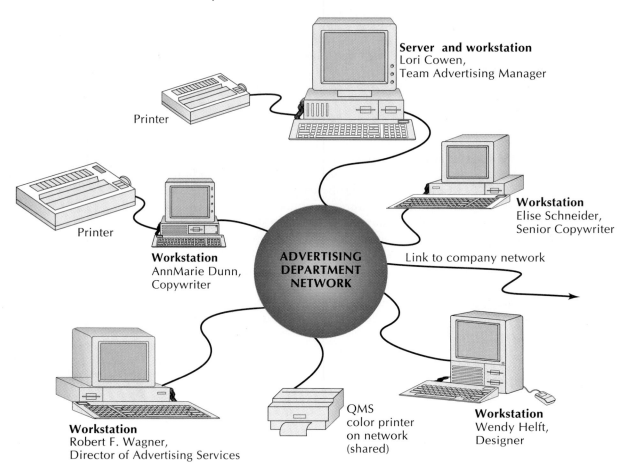

FIGURE 9.10   Local Area Network in an Advertising Department

LAN transmission speeds generally range from 1 to over 100 megabits per second. This speed will increase as new transmission technologies are developed.

Metropolitan Area Networks

metropolitan area network (MAN) A network that transmits data and information over citywide distances and at greater speeds than a LAN.

Metropolitan area networks (MANs), which have evolved from LAN designs, transmit data and information over longer distances than LANs (approximately 30 miles, or 50 kilometers) and may do so at greater speeds (up to 200 megabits per second). MANs also are often designed to carry more diverse forms of information than LANs are, including combinations of voice, data, image, and video. WANs are usually optimized for voice and data transmission. Western Union's MAN in Atlanta is shown in Figure 9.11 on pages 350–51.

MANs do not operate over telephone lines. Rather, to obtain the combination of high-speed and citywide transmission (hence the name *metropolitan area network*), fiber-optic cables are generally used as the transmission medium. SONET (synchronous optical networking standard) is a high-speed (45 megabits per second to 1.5 gigabits per second) network specification using fiber-optic channels. It is often used to obtain both the high-speed performance and the multimedia transmission capabilities that users want in metropolitan networks.

With research support from the University of Western Australia, Telecom Australia, headquartered in Sydney, has developed a metropolitan area network service that it is installing in selected cities in the South Pacific and Europe. Companies can subscribe to the service to augment their other networking capabilities. For example, Novo Dordisk AS, a multinational pharmaceutical supplier, uses Telecom Australia's MAN to provide high-speed interconnection of its existing scientific and administrative networks. The MAN provides faster performance times than the other alternatives available.

Reality Check. In recent years, the combination of faster computer processing and larger storage capabilities on smaller computers, coupled with high-speed computer networks, has led to a distinct trend toward computer *downsizing*. Applications that were previously run on shared mainframes are being moved to midranges; applications that were once run on midranges are now often run on powerful microcomputers. Yet all these different computers can be linked together by communications networks. Thus downsizing means more than just moving applications to smaller computers; it also means interconnecting different computers in a distributed environment.

The appeal of downsizing is very closely tied to costs. Midrange computers are cheaper than mainframes, and micros are cheaper than midranges. But there's more to downsizing than decreased costs. Companies can take advantage of the power now available in smaller computers while simultaneously standardizing applications across the organization.

As a result, application performance can improve. Often firms find that they can move an application to its own dedicated computer, which allows people to use it without having to wait for another application to finish running on a shared computer. Response time for data and information retrieval can be noticeably faster—an important benefit in a time when speed to market is a critical element of a firm's success.

Downsizing is not a fad, but a trend. It is fueled by the increased need for speed in business and commerce and enabled by the corresponding advances in information technology. ■

Multi-User Network Hardware

How are networks put together? In this section, we describe the hardware components of networks and the devices used to interconnect different networks.

Communications Channels: Physical and Cableless

A **communications channel**, also called a **communications medium**, links the different components of a network. There are two categories of communications channels: physical channels and cableless channels.

communications channel or **communications medium** The physical or cableless media that link the different components of a network.

Physical Channels. Physical channels use a wire or cable, along which data and information are transmitted. There are three types of physical channels: twisted pair, coaxial cable, and optical cable (Figure 9.12 on page 352).

- As we mentioned earlier, teleprocessing gave rise to the use of telephone wires as a popular medium for transmitting data and information between multiple user sites. They remain the most popular medium today, whether strung from

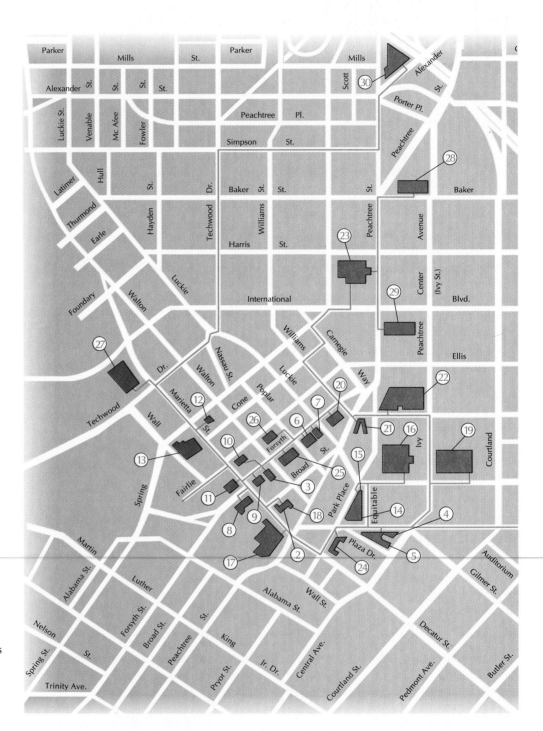

FIGURE 9.11
Western Union's Atlanta Metropolitan Area Network
Metropolitan area networks transmit data and information over longer distances than LANs and at greater speeds.

twisted pair A physical communications channel that uses strands of copper wire twisted together to form a telephone wire.

telephone poles, through underground conduits, or in the walls of buildings. Often referred to as **twisted pair**, this telephone wire medium consists of strands of copper wire that are twisted in pairs. Because twisted pair was developed for the transmission of voices and text, IT professionals refer to this medium as a *voice-grade channel*.

NETWORK LOCATIONS

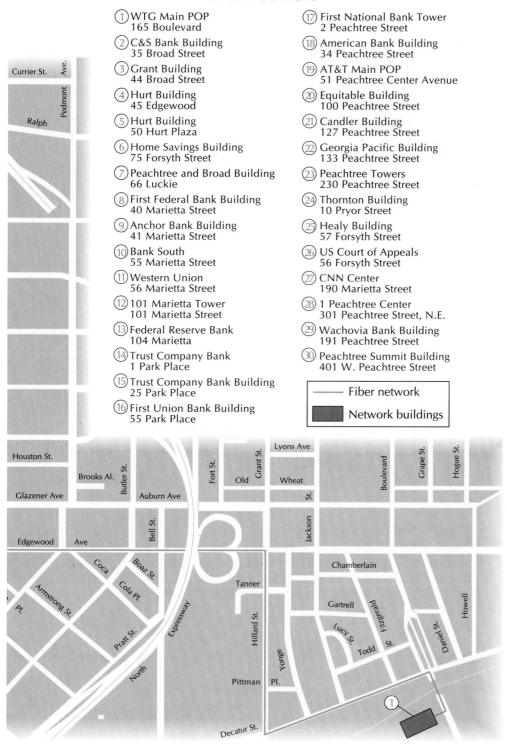

1. WTG Main POP
165 Boulevard

2. C&S Bank Building
35 Broad Street

3. Grant Building
44 Broad Street

4. Hurt Building
45 Edgewood

5. Hurt Building
50 Hurt Plaza

6. Home Savings Building
75 Forsyth Street

7. Peachtree and Broad Building
66 Luckie

8. First Federal Bank Building
40 Marietta Street

9. Anchor Bank Building
41 Marietta Street

10. Bank South
55 Marietta Street

11. Western Union
56 Marietta Street

12. 101 Marietta Tower
101 Marietta Street

13. Federal Reserve Bank
104 Marietta

14. Trust Company Bank
1 Park Place

15. Trust Company Bank Building
25 Park Place

16. First Union Bank Building
55 Park Place

17. First National Bank Tower
2 Peachtree Street

18. American Bank Building
34 Peachtree Street

19. AT&T Main POP
51 Peachtree Center Avenue

20. Equitable Building
100 Peachtree Street

21. Candler Building
127 Peachtree Street

22. Georgia Pacific Building
133 Peachtree Street

23. Peachtree Towers
230 Peachtree Street

24. Thornton Building
10 Pryor Street

25. Healy Building
57 Forsyth Street

26. US Court of Appeals
56 Forsyth Street

27. CNN Center
190 Marietta Street

28. 1 Peachtree Center
301 Peachtree Street, N.E.

29. Wachovia Bank Building
191 Peachtree Street

30. Peachtree Summit Building
401 W. Peachtree Street

———	Fiber network
▬	Network buildings

Twisted pair channels transmit at a variety of speeds, from as slow as 110 bits per second to as fast as 100 Mbps. The *feasible speed* of transmission is established by the carrier, independent of the data or information transported on the channel. The *actual speed* of transmission is determined by the hardware attached to the medium and the programs managing the communications process.

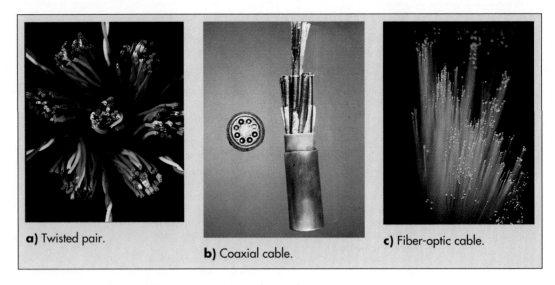

a) Twisted pair.

b) Coaxial cable.

c) Fiber-optic cable.

FIGURE 9.12   Physical Communications Channels
Physical communications channels transmit data and information along a wire or cable.

coaxial cable or **co-ax** A physical communications channel that uses one or more central wire conductors surrounded by an insulator and encased in either a wire mesh or metal sheathing.

- **Coaxial cable**, sometimes called just **co-ax**, consists of one or more central wire conductors surrounded by an insulator and encased in either a wire mesh or metal sheathing. Co-ax offers higher transmission speeds than voice-grade lines and a capability for transmitting all types of information effectively (not just voice and text). If you have cable television, you are using coaxial cable to receive the broadcast programs without interference.

  Coaxial cable comes in two types. *Baseband* cable, which carries a single communication or message at very high megabit speeds, is often used in local area networks. *Broadband* cable carries multiple signals simultaneously; each signal can be a different speed. Cable television uses broadband cable. Both types achieve bandwidths of more than 100 megabits speeds. These speeds will continue to increase through advances in networking technology.

fiber-optic cable A physical communications channel that uses light and glass fibers to transmit data and information.

- **Fiber-optic cable** is the newest type of physical communications channel. This high-bandwidth transmission medium uses light as a digital information carrier. Glass fibers, rather than wire, are the transmission medium. Because the glass fibers are much thinner than wire, many more fibers can be packed into a cable, with each transmitting at much higher speeds than twisted wire pairs or coaxial cable. And because laser (light) beams, rather than electricity, carry the data and information, fiber-optic cables are immune to electrical interference within buildings or when strung near electrical lines.

  The costs of manufacturing, installing, and maintaining fiber-optic cables are lower than those for wire channels. These advantages, combined with the benefits of high transmission speeds, make it easy to see why the use of fiber optics is growing at a rapid rate worldwide. Indeed, most telephone companies and PTTs are installing only fiber-optic cable when they lay new lines to expand their networks. Hence, if you make a telephone call or transmit data over a telephone line, there is a good chance they will be sent over fiber-optic cables, at least part of the way to their destination.

The term "line" is a carryover from the days when all data communications occurred over twisted pair lines. Today, IT professionals often use it to refer to all communications media, both physical and wireless.

✓ **Reality Check.**   Most office buildings have a communications network running through their offices. A **private branch exchange (PBX)** or **computer branch exchange (CBX)** is a private telephone system designed to handle the needs of the organization in which it is installed. Telephones—that is, *stations* or *extensions*—are interconnected with the network. Calls coming to the organization from outside lines are processed through the PBX, which switches the call to the appropriate internal extension. Calls originating inside the organization are routed by the PBX to an available outside line.

Most PBX systems today are computer based. Microprocessors manage the switching activities and keep track of the location of various extensions. Hence, PBX implicitly means CBX. ∎

private branch exchange (PBX) or **computer branch exchange (CBX)**   A private telephone system designed to handle the needs of the organization in which it is installed.

Cableless Channels.   The four most common types of cableless transmission media are microwave, satellite, infrared, and radio frequency. Depending on the needs of the company, these media may be used alone or in conjunction with each other and the three types of physical channels. Wireless channels will be the predominant network medium for pen-based computers and personal digital assistants, both still in their infancy (see Chapter 1). Experts predict that they will also be used more frequently for other types of computers as well.

MICROWAVE.   This form of cableless transmission uses high-frequency radio signals to send data and information through the air, without wire or cable connections between sites, all in a fraction of a second. **Microwave** signals can be transmitted using terrestrial stations or communications satellites. With terrestrial stations, relay towers stationed approximately 30 miles apart receive and retransmit communications to link source and destination sites. The path between each tower must be unobstructed, because the signals are sent in a straight line (Figure 9.13a). For this reason, microwave stations are often located on the tops of buildings in metropolitan areas or at the peaks of mountains and hills in remote regions.

SATELLITES.   The preferred method of transmission when information must be sent between sites where large distances must be spanned or obstructions are in the way

microwave   A cableless medium that uses high-frequency radio signals to send data or information through the air.

FIGURE 9.13   Terrestrial and Satellite Microwave Transmission

a) Terrestrial Transmission. In terrestrial microwave transmission, dish-shaped antennas placed approximately 30 miles apart relay signals from one to another. The path between each relay station must be unobstructed.

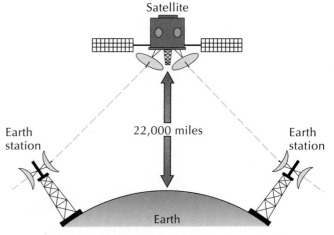

b) Satellite Transmission. In satellite microwave transmission, a satellite orbiting approximately 22,000 miles over the earth acts as a relay station that transmits a signal from one earth station to another.

FIGURE 9.14
Very Small Aperture Terminal Communication at Schneider National
A receiver mounted on top of Schneider National's truck cabs (left) allows drivers and headquarters to communicate anywhere and at any time. Schneider pays for access to an orbiting public communications satellite, from which its messages are beamed to its drivers' trucks (right).

satellite A cableless medium in which communications are beamed from a microwave station to a communications satellite in orbit above the earth and relayed to other earth stations.

very small aperture terminal (VSAT) A satellite earth station with an antenna diameter of under one meter.

is by **satellite**. With this type of cableless transmission, the significance of distance disappears. Each communication is beamed from a microwave station to a communications satellite in orbit 22,000 miles above the earth. Transmissions are relayed from one sending earth station to another or to multiple earth stations (Figure 9.13b).

Of growing importance are **very small aperture terminals (VSATs)**, which have been incorporated into corporate networking strategies at an increasing rate in recent years. A VSAT is a fairly inexpensive (only a few hundred dollars) satellite earth station with an antenna diameter of under one meter (40 inches). VSATs enable companies to use networks in creative and effective ways because the earth station can be installed just about anywhere and maintain contact with the orbiting satellite.

In the United States, Schneider National, a large long-haul trucking company based in Green Bay, Wisconsin, has equipped its trucks with VSATs (Figure 9.14). Mounted on top of the driver's cab, these receivers allow the company and driver to communicate anywhere, any place, anytime. The dispatcher at the company's office can determine the location of the trucks and send them messages instructing them to make additional pickups, to change their delivery schedule, or to perform any other task that would make the company more effective. Schneider pays for access to an orbiting public communications satellite. Its transmissions are sent to the satellite and in turn beamed to the truck, all in a matter of seconds.

cellular telephone A device used to send and receive voice conversations and computer and fax transmissions while allowing users freedom of movement.

Reality Check.   People's desire to have greater freedom of movement while staying in touch with the office, customers, or colleagues has created tremendous growth in **cellular telephone** use (Figure 9.15). Using cell stations located throughout a geographic region, cellular phones send and receive voice conversations (and can be used for computer and fax transmissions also). As long as the callers stay in the cell region, they can communicate over their mobile telephone. If a person travels beyond the cell region, a cross-region service provides the necessary service and billing authorization.

As businesses and people ask for extended calling capability, these cross-region services continue to expand. In Europe, for example, a Pan-European cellular communications network is emerging from the telecommunications company Groupe Spéciale Mobile (GSM). Using the GSM network, it will be possible to drive from Rome to Helsinki and use the same telephone along the way. The telephone will register on the cellular network of the country in which it is switched on; the GSM network will automatically update its location throughout the journey. Incoming calls will be automatically rerouted through the multi-country network. Similar capabilities will be available for fax and data transmission.

FIGURE 9.15
Cellular Telephone on the Job
Cellular telephones send and receive voice communications, and sometimes fax transmissions, via cell stations located throughout a geographic region. In terms of convenience alone, cellular telephones have increased productivity greatly. But because cellular conversations are easily eavesdropped upon, many companies prohibit their employees from discussing confidential business matters on cellular telephones.

INFRARED.   **Infrared** communications occur via a combined transmitter and receiver, or **transceiver**; data and information are transmitted in coded form by means of an infrared light beamed from one transceiver to another. Infrared systems are limited to a single area, such as an open retail store space or a large room, because the transmitter and receiver must be in sight of one another. Infrared communication between different areas or buildings can be achieved only if they are close to another (no more than 220 yards or 200 meters apart) and only if the transceivers are in windows of the buildings, visible to each other.

Kroger Co., a large supermarket chain based in Cincinnati, Ohio, has installed a series of infrared transceivers on the ceilings of its stores and equipped shopping carts with flat screen display terminals. As shoppers wheel their carts through the store, the transceiver senses their presence and transmits advertising and pricing information to the screen on the cart (Figure 9.16). In the produce department, the screen suggests innovative ways to cook seasonal fresh vegetables. As the consumer enters the frozen food section, the display shows information about special prices and this week's sales. In the snack food area, the consumer is reminded

infrared A cableless medium that transmits data and information in coded form by means of an infrared light beamed from one transceiver to another.

transceiver A combination transmitter and receiver that transmits and receives data or information.

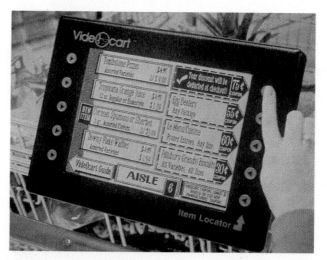

FIGURE 9.16
Infrared Marketing
VideOCart's supermarket system pioneered the use of infrared to sense the presence of shopping carts and transmit advertising and pricing information to a screen on the cart. The cart offers supermarkets the opportunity to call attention to new items, products on sale, and coupon specials. Shoppers can use the VideOCarts to locate hard-to-find items and favorite products.

about upcoming televised sporting events and the need to stock up on extra snacks for the family. The added expense of installing 30 to 40 transceivers in each store has been more than justified, Kroger managers say, by advertising revenues and the extra sales generated.

RADIO WAVES.   Sometimes called **radio frequency (RF) transmissions**, radio waves use transmission frequencies rented from public radio networks in a region. The company or individual user pays a monthly fee for air time and transmits information at the assigned frequency. A transmitter sends information to a receiver designed to accept the same frequency. Radio wave transmissions are not practical for transmitting large files or databases because of their relatively low transmission speeds (Table 9.2).

Governments in different countries regulate radio frequencies in different ways and assign the frequency ranges for varying purposes. In general, governments have not reserved any RF transmission frequency for local area network use.

There are two major players in the worldwide public radio network market. In the United States, Motorola and IBM have created as a joint venture the ARDIS company. In Europe, RAM Mobile Data Company uses a mobile data network system developed by the Swedish company Ericsson AB. Each of these companies provides a series of public radio channels in major metropolitan areas. These channels are available to users for a monthly fee that covers rental of air time and transmission equipment. The network companies run and maintain the network.

Otis Elevator uses a public radio network to transmit information to its field-service staff. Maintenance and service personnel can send and receive information about parts and procedures for servicing an elevator or diagnosing a problem. The company finds the network an effective way of routing personnel from one service call to the next (Figure 9.17).

In the United States, Otis's system has other benefits as well. Because the company can stay in touch with employees throughout the day, it does not have to assign the day's service calls in the morning or rely on telephone calls throughout the day. Instead, it is able to manage the entire service team in the most efficient and effective way possible, responding to customer emergencies that arise during the day or accommodating a service call that takes a little longer than expected. Both customer and company benefit from this wireless network.

Communications Channels for WANs and MANs

Three different communications channels are widely used by companies creating wide area or metropolitan area networks. These are public access networks, private networks, and value-added networks.

radio wave transmission or **radio frequency transmission** A cableless medium that uses frequencies rented from public radio networks to transmit data and information.

TABLE 9.2   Transmission Speeds of Communications Channels

Physical Channels	Transmission Speeds
Twisted pair	Over 100 Mbps
Coaxial cable	140 Mbps
Fiber-optic cable	Over 2 Gbps

Cableless Channels	Transmission Speeds
Microwave	275 Mbps
Satellite	2 Mbps
Infrared	275 Mbps
Radio waves (RF transmission)	275 Mbps

FIGURE 9.17
Otis Elevator's Service Network
Otis Elevator uses a public radio network to transmit information to its field-service staff. Maintenance personnel can send and receive information about parts and procedures via a portable handheld computer.

- **Public access networks**—The world's telephone companies and PTTs—that is, the common carriers—maintain certain networks for use by the general public, hence the term **public access networks**. Specialized carriers also operate other focused services, such as making satellite communications links available to the public. All carriers interconnect their networks with other networks to give their customers a seamless, integrated, single network. The complete set of public access networks is often called the **switched network**, so named because the telephone company operates and maintains the switching centers that make it possible to transmit a call or information from its origin through the nodes of the network to its destination. *Switched access* refers to communications access over a switched, nondedicated line. This means that the line is assigned to a different caller each time, and the completion of a call requires the carrier to switch between different lines to create a link between the caller and the desired destination of his or her call.

- **Private networks**—When organizations transmit large volumes of information regularly, it may be more economical and more effective for them to lease lines from a common carrier than to use a public access network. When an organization agrees to lease a line for a period of time, the carrier will *dedicate* the line to the company, or reserve that line for the exclusive use of that company. Hence **leased lines** are sometimes called **dedicated lines**. Networks comprised of dedicated lines are known as **private networks**.

- **Value-added networks**—A public data communications network that provides basic transmission facilities and additional enhancements (such as temporary data storage, error detection and correction, conversion of information from one form to another, and electronic mail service) is called a **value-added network (VAN)**. The VAN provider generally leases the transmission channels from a common carrier, providing the "value added" to its customer by investing in and operating the network so that the customer doesn't need to do so.

Communications Channels for LANs

Local area networks seldom use the public switched networks or satellite transmission channels because there is not much distance between the nodes on the network. Although wireless methods are increasing in popularity, fiber-optic, coaxial cable, and twisted pair lines remain the most common methods of connecting the nodes of a LAN. In most cases, the company simply has the cables installed on its premises by a wiring contractor. When companies and institutions expect a large

public access network A network maintained by common carriers for use by the general public.

switched network The complete set of public access networks, so named because the telephone company operates and maintains the switching centers that make it possible to transmit data or information.

leased line or **dedicated line** A communications line reserved by a company for its exclusive use.

private network A network made up of leased (dedicated) communications lines.

value-added network (VAN) A public data communications network that provides basic transmission facilities plus additional enhancements (such as temporary data storage and error detection).

number of people to use their LAN, they often build a high-speed transmission facility called a **backbone network** or an arrangement of such facilities. When developed as part of a wide area network, the channels are often T-carriers.

The Georgia Institute of Technology in Atlanta ("Georgia Tech") has developed a backbone network for its entire campus. Communications cable is buried in the ground, running near all campus buildings and laboratories. The backbone serves as a conduit that connects lower-speed communications lines or dispersed communications and computing devices. The lower speed components move data onto the backbone, where they are transported to the intended destination at high speed. At the destination, the data move off the backbone to the lower speed network and eventually to their intended recipient.

Connecting to the Channel

A communications medium provides only the capability to transmit and receive information. It is entirely separate from the other hardware components of the computer system: computers, printers, or other devices that determine *what* and *when* to communicate. Different devices are used to connect computers to WANs and LANs.

In WANs using the public telephone network, special devices called **modems** connect computers to the communications medium and translate the data or information from the computer into a form that can be transmitted over the channel. The term "modem," a contraction of the terms MOdulation-DEModulation, describes the device's operations. Computers generate digital signals (combinations of the binary zero and one), but voice-grade lines transmit analog signals. The modem on the transmitting end translates the digital signal into analog form so that it can be transmitted. On the receiving end, another modem transforms the analog signal into a digital form that the computer can process (Figure 9.18).

backbone network A high-speed transmission facility designed to move data and information faster than they otherwise would.

modem A device that connects a computer to a communications medium and translates the data or information from the computer into a form that can be transmitted over the channel. Used in WANs.

FIGURE 9.18　Converting Digital Signals to Analog Signals Using a Modem

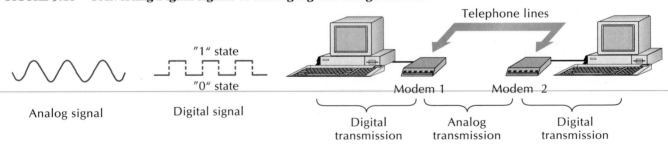

Analog signal　　　Digital signal　　　Digital transmission　　Analog transmission　　Digital transmission

The signals sent along a communications medium can be digital or analog. The phone system carries **analog signals**—continuous waves—over a frequency range.

Most types of computing equipment use **digital signals**, which code data into blocks of zeroes and ones.

When a computer sends data to a modem for transmission at a specified speed, it represents the digital blocks of zeroes and ones electrically as minus five and plus five volts, respectively. The modem changes, or **modulates**, the electrical signals into two analog frequency tones. It converts zeroes into a frequency of 2025 cycles per second (2025 hertz) and ones into a frequency of 2225 cycles (2225 hertz) per second.

This process is reversed at the receiving end of the transmission, where a second modem converts the analog signals back into digital signals.

Modems come in several different forms. *External modems* consist of circuit boards mounted inside a protective case and interconnected with the computer through a cable that plugs into a port on the computer (Figure 9.19a). *Card* or *internal modems* are circuit boards that can be pushed into a slot in the computer (Figure 9.19b). The communications line connects to both types through a plug on the modem. The speed of the modem determines how quickly data and information will be transmitted on the line.

Multiplexers that are used to connect terminals to an analog communication line also convert data from digital to analog signals and vice versa. These devices allow a single communications channel to carry simultaneous data transmissions from many terminals that are sharing the channel.

In the most commonly used LANs, both the devices and the network channels transmit digital information. Thus there is no need for a modem. A circuit board called a **network interface card** (Figure 9.20) plugs into the computer, printer, or other device, thus becoming part of the device itself. The network channel, in turn, connects to the interface card by way of a special plug spliced to the cable. If a wireless channel is used, the network interface card contains the transceiver for sending and receiving information.

The network card and the cable type used in the LAN must agree. Thus the choices for cable are affected by the network card (or vice versa). If an office area is wired for coaxial cable, the computer must be equipped with interface cards that will interconnect with coaxial cable.

CRITICAL CONNECTION 2
Peapod Makes Grocery Shopping Easy

If you don't like grocery shopping but have access to a computer with a modem, Andrew and Tom Parkinson would like to help you out. The Parkinson brothers are founders of Peapod Inc., an Evanston, Illinois–based company that combines online, 24-hour-a-day grocery selection at major grocery stores with Peapod's delivery service.

Peapod started small, in 1990, by signing an agreement to serve a single store for Jewel Food Stores Inc. A few years later, Peapod membership starter kits were being offered in Jewel Food Stores in thirteen Chicago suburbs and the north side of Chicago. In 1993, Peapod signed an agreement with Safeway, the giant supermarket chain, to launch a pilot program in the San Francisco area.

How does the system work? Peapod's communications software taps into the supermarket's database and presents a series of menus that let members browse the aisles, shop by item, brand name, and unit price, or even create personal shopping lists of family favorites. In addition to specifying special instructions ("Only buy green bananas"), members can indicate they have coupons and specify the day and time the groceries should be delivered. Peapod's trained shoppers fill the orders, pack the perishables in coolers, and whisk the completed orders to members, who hand over their coupons and pay Peapod. Many users say their savings more than offset the fees they pay to Peapod.

FIGURE 9.19   Modems

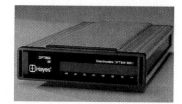

a) Hayes Optima 9600 external modem.

b) Hayes Smartmodem 9600B internal modem.

multiplexer A device that converts data from digital to analog form and vice versa and allows a single communications channel to carry simultaneous data transmissions from many terminals that are sharing the channel.

network interface card A printed circuit board used in LANs to transmit digital data or information.

**FIGURE 9.20
Network Interface Card**
The IBM Adapter II network interface card is used with the token ring network typology. Other types of interface cards are used for the star topology and the bus topology.

Interconnecting Networks

Because communications networks vary so widely in type and structure, it is not surprising that some companies operate many different networks. Distributed processing presumes multiple networks, and it is likely that people will want to interconnect networks to share information and other resources. We've discussed how computer and communications devices are interconnected, but how do networks themselves interconnect? It all depends on whether the networks are the same or different types and whether they are managed by the same or different software.

bridge and **router** Devices that interconnect compatible LANs.

Bridges and **routers** are devices that interconnect LANs, making it possible to send information from a device on one network to a device on another network. In essence, both take packets of information transmitted on one LAN and move them to another LAN. Hence, the two LANs can be treated essentially as one big LAN.

gateway A device that interconnects two otherwise incompatible networks, network nodes, or devices.

Gateways interconnect two otherwise different and incompatible networks, network nodes, or devices. The gateway performs conversion operations so that information transmitted in one form on the first network can be transformed into the form needed for transmission to its destination on the second network (Figure 9.21).

▪ Network Operating Systems

network operating system (NOS) A software program that runs in conjunction with the computer's operating system and application programs and manages the network.

Every computer that runs a network must have a **network operating system (NOS)**, a software program that runs in conjunction with the computer's operating system and application programs and manages the network. Like the operating system that controls the computer (the *computer* operating system), networks could not function without *their* operating system—the *network* operating system (Figure 9.22).

The NOS communicates with the LAN, WAN, or MAN hardware, accepting information transmitted from one device and directing it to another. It also manages the sharing of peripherals and storage devices, keeping track of the location of the devices and who is using them at a particular moment. Some widely used network operating systems are listed in Table 9.3.

Protocol and Communications Control

protocol The rules and conventions guiding data communications, embedded as coded instructions in the network software.

Every conversation, whether interpersonal or electronic, needs to proceed in an orderly fashion. How do computers know when and how to talk to one another? The rules and conventions guiding data communications are embedded as coded instructions in the network software. This **protocol** performs the following tasks:

TABLE 9.3   Widely Used Network Operating Systems

System Network Architecture (SNA)	The IBM network structure for linking applications on mainframes and midrange systems.
SNA Distribution Services (SNADS)	An IBM architecture for interchanging information through an SNA network. With SNADS, users can distribute information to other systems without worrying about the details of the other systems. SNADS can also link a variety of small processors into the network.
LAN Manager	Microsoft's operating system for local area networks running on IBM-compatible computers.
Apple Talk	Apple computer's network operating system for Apple computers, Macintosh computers, and the Apple Newton personal digital assistant.
Novell NetWare	The most widely used network operating system for microcomputers.
DECNET	The most widely used network operating system on Digital Equipment Corp. (DEC) computers.

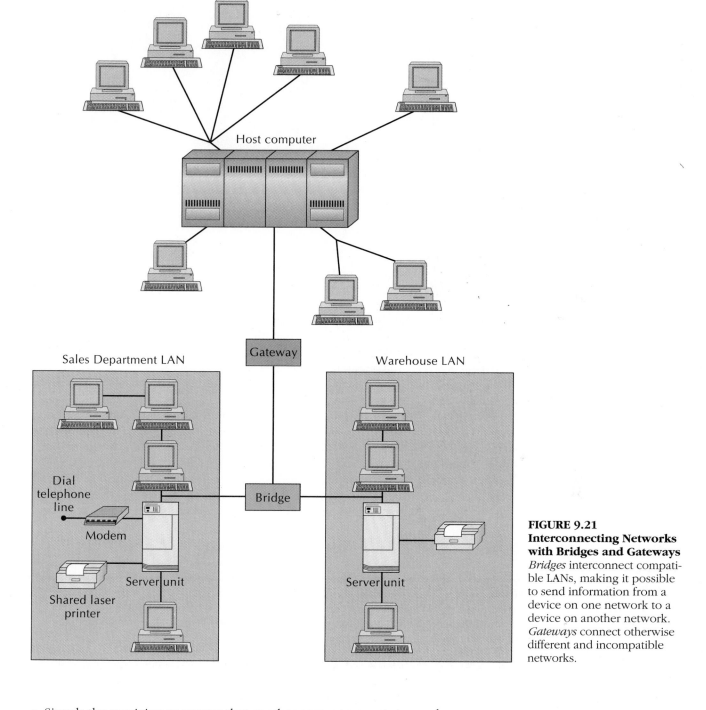

Host computer

Sales Department LAN

Gateway

Warehouse LAN

Dial
telephone
line

Modem

Shared laser
printer

Server unit

Bridge

Server unit

FIGURE 9.21
Interconnecting Networks
with Bridges and Gateways
Bridges interconnect compatible LANs, making it possible
to send information from a
device on one network to a
device on another network.
Gateways connect otherwise
different and incompatible
networks.

- Signals the receiving computer that another computer wants to send a message.
- Identifies the sender.
- Transmits messages in blocks, if it detects that each block is received as it is sent.
- Retransmits a message if it detects that the previous attempt was not successful.
- Determines when an error occurs and recovers from the error so that transmis-
  sion can continue.
- Signals the receiver at the end of the transmission that no more messages will
  follow.
- Terminates the connection.

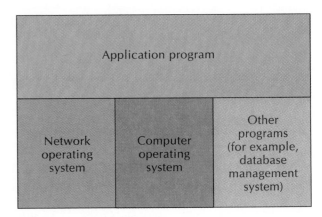

FIGURE 9.22
Network Operating System in Relation to Other Software
A network operating system runs in conjunction with a computer's operating system and applications programs and manages the network.

Many protocols have been established as standards in the use of information technology in wide area networks. The most common of these are Xmodem (developed for use between microcomputers), SNA (IBM's system network architecture), TCP/IP protocol suite (Transmission Control Protocol/Internet Protocol for large scale, high-speed backbone networks), X.25 (for public data networks), and x.400 (for electronic mail between different types of computers). In local area networks, two protocols are in widespread use: carrier sense multiple access (CSMA) and token ring. Table 9.4 summarizes the differences between these protocols. Table 9.5 explains some other terms used in communications control.

Protocol is needed between different components in communication. Hence, network designers develop communications using a seven-layer *open systems interconnection (OSI) model* (Figure 9.23). Computer application programs, network operating systems, and transmission protocol are defined within the OSI model, comprising what network professionals refer to as the system network architecture. (People using communication networks need not worry about these layers, as they are handled by the software and network personnel.)

TABLE 9.4   LAN Protocols

Carrier Sense Multiple Access (CSMA)	The CSMA protocol follows the rule, "Don't begin transmitting without first listening on the network to see if anyone else is using it. If not, send the message." A variation on CSMA called **carrier sense multiple access, with collision detection (CSMA/CD)** is designed to avoid the case where two microcomputers begin to transmit at the same time, each thinking it is the only network user. The CSMA/CD protocol says, in effect, "Listen before you transmit and *while* you transmit. If you detect someone else using the network (a *collision*), wait for the other transmission to stop and then start your message again." The CSMA and CSMA/CD protocols are built into the Ethernet network developed by Xerox corporation for LANs and into the LANs used by Apple Computer, Digital Equipment Corp., and some IBM systems.
Token Ring	The token ring protocol, so named because it is used with a ring topology, is based on a simple idea often used at large meetings: "Don't speak unless you have the microphone." When implemented as a LAN protocol, a *token* (string of bits) rather than a microphone is sent around the network. If no one is transmitting, the token is available for a member of the network to take and begin transmitting. When the transmission is completed, the token is sent back to the network so that another computer can retrieve it. Only one token means that there cannot be any collisions, because protocol allows transmission only when a computer is holding the token. The token ring protocol is used often in IBM and Novell LANs.

TABLE 9.5   Communications Control Terminology

Types of transmission lines		Types of transmission	
Simplex lines	Transmit data in one direction only (either send or receive)	*Asynchronous protocol*	Data are transmitted one character at a time. Transmission of data bits is preceded and followed by special start-stop sequences.
Half-duplex lines	Transmit data in either direction, but in only one direction at a time (alternate between send and receive)	*Synchronous protocol*	Transmission is continuous. The transmitting and receiving terminals must be synchronized—that is, in phase with one another. A clock (usually in the the modem) governs transmission by determining when each data bit is sent.
Full-duplex lines	Send and receive data simultaneously		

▨ Network Administration

The management of a network, usually called **network administration** or **network management**, consists of procedures and services that keep the network running properly. An important part of network management entails making sure that the network is available (or "up and running," as IT professionals say) when employees and managers need it. Other network administration activities include:

network administration or **network management**
The management of a network; the procedures and services that keep the network running properly.

• Monitoring the network's capacity to ensure that all transmission requirements can be met.

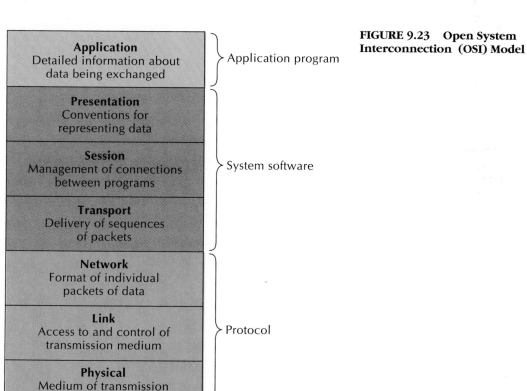

FIGURE 9.23   Open System Interconnection (OSI) Model

- Adding capacity to the network by increasing bandwidth, interconnecting additional nodes, or creating and interconnecting additional networks.
- Conducting training to assist individuals in using the network effectively.
- Assisting IT professionals in writing applications that will make good use of the network's capabilities.
- Backing up the network software and data regularly to protect against the failure of the network or any of its components.
- Putting security procedures in place to ensure that only authorized users have access to the network, and ensuring that all security procedures are followed.
- Ensuring that network personnel can respond quickly and effectively in the event of a network operational or security failure.
- Diagnosing and troubleshooting problems on the network when they occur and determining the best course of action to take.

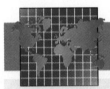

GLOBAL IT

The Challenge of Networking the European Community: A Test of Ingenuity

DRAWN BY THE PROMISE OF SELLING IN THE EUROPEAN Community (EC)—a European common market that encompasses more than 350 million consumers in Belgium, Denmark, France, Germany, Greece, Ireland, Italy, Luxembourg, the Netherlands, Portugal, Spain, and the United Kingdom—thousands of the world's companies have poured millions of dollars into European investments. Consider just a few of the challenges of designing and operating a WAN in Europe.

- *Varying levels of service and technical support.* The level and quality of service offered by public access networks varies from excellent (in London, Paris, and Frankfurt) to almost nonexistent (in Greece and Portugal).
- *Inconsistent standards.* Computing and communications standards backed by the EC still vary slightly from country to country, sometimes making it tricky to link countries electronically.
- *Laws and regulations.* Although many nations are deregulating their PTTs, the pace has not been consistent or predictable. Laws regarding privacy and the use of information are another challenge. Generally speaking, European laws are stricter than U.S. laws, although they vary from country to country. French law, for example, forbids the transfer of employee information across national borders. Faced with this barrier, Sonoco Products Co., a South Carolina recycling and packaging company, abandoned its plans for a network and decided to process payroll data locally.

- *High networking costs.* Due in part to the slow process of deregulation, communications costs in the United Kingdom are about four times higher than costs in the United States. For other European nations, experts suggest, multiply U.S. costs by eight to get a reasonable estimate. The good news is that this situation is changing.

Despite these challenges, a few brave souls are creating their own WANs. For example, Prudential Securities negotiated directly with Mercury and British Telecom, two of Britain's common carriers, to redesign a network linking its European offices to its headquarters in New York.

Most companies that want to do business in the EC, however, are turning to third-party vendors—either consultants or companies that specialize in creating international value-added networks. Gilette Co., for example, recently signed Syncordia, a subsidiary of a British common carrier, to handle its telecommunications in 180 countries. J.P. Morgan, in contrast, has turned to an AT&T subsidiary, AT&T Istel, for help in creating a 14-city network. "There is no way we could have installed the system in the same time frame [five months] with in-house sources," says the V.P. of global communications at J.P. Morgan. The vice president of MIS at Campbell Soup Co. agrees. "We're in the food business," he says. "I'm not interested in becoming an expert on pan-European telecommunications."

As in business in general, the success of a network is linked to the people who design and manage the network. Network specialists include *network designers*, who specify the necessary features of the network and oversee its construction and installation; *network administrators*, who manage the day-to-day operations of the network; and *network security personnel*, who develop and oversee the use of procedures designed to protect the integrity of the network and ensure that it is used in the intended manner by authorized persons. In large organizations, these roles may be filled by one or more different people. In smaller firms, one person may have multiple responsibilities.

The network professional's job is not always easy. Connecting wildly different systems to each other poses many challenges, as the Global IT box titled "The Challenge of Networking the European Community: A Test of Ingenuity" attests. The manner in which network professionals interact with the individual employees and managers of an organization—the users of the network—and with other IT professionals to accomplish their goals can have a dramatic effect on the perceived usefulness of the network and the extent to which it is used.

▖ Network Service Applications

The applications available on a communications network are called **network services**. In this section, we discuss the eight most frequently used network applications in business: electronic mail, voice mail, video conferencing, work group conferencing, bulletin boards, electronic funds transfer, electronic data interchange, and videotex.

network services The applications available on a communications network.

Electronic Mail

You probably know how frustrating telephone tag can be. You call someone only to find that he or she is not in. So you leave a message. The person returns your call at just the moment when you have stepped out to run an errand, attend a meeting, or get a cup of coffee. And so he or she leaves a message for you. When this sequence is repeated constantly, both parties can become very frustrated.

Electronic mail, sometimes called **e-mail**, and voice mail (which we discuss in the next section) are ways to avoid telephone tag and to overcome the communication barriers created by time and distance. E-mail is simply a service that transports text messages from a sender to one or more receivers. It ensures that your message is delivered, not lost in the mailroom or message center. When you send the message from your computer, the network transmits it to the proper destination and inserts it in the recipient's **electronic mailbox**, an area of space on magnetic disk in the server or host computer that is allocated for storing an individual's messages.

electronic mail (e-mail) A service that transports text messages from a sender to one or more receivers via computer.

Because messages are stored in a mailbox, the recipient need not be at the computer when messages arrive. When the recipient returns to the computer, he or she will be alerted, often by a flashing note, that a message has arrived, and can then display the message on the screen and decide to print the message, send a response, store the message for later review, or pass it along to another individual.

electronic mailbox An area of space on magnetic disk in the server or host computer that is allocated for storing an individual's messages.

E-mail messages can be stored on the network and replayed at a later date. They can also be *broadcast*—that is, sent to a number of individuals simultaneously. The sender need only type the message into the system, enter the identification names of the intended recipients, and instruct the network to send the information. The e-mail system does the rest (Figure 9.24).

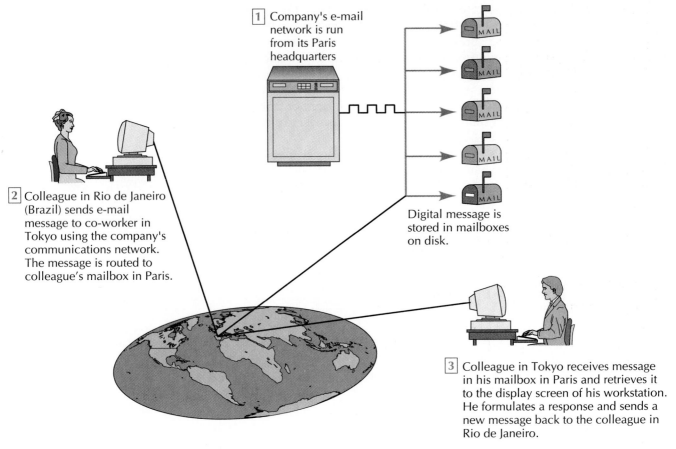

1 Company's e-mail network is run from its Paris headquarters

2 Colleague in Rio de Janeiro (Brazil) sends e-mail message to co-worker in Tokyo using the company's communications network. The message is routed to colleague's mailbox in Paris.

Digital message is stored in mailboxes on disk.

3 Colleague in Tokyo receives message in his mailbox in Paris and retrieves it to the display screen of his workstation. He formulates a response and sends a new message back to the colleague in Rio de Janeiro.

FIGURE 9.24   E-mail Network and Mailboxes
Electrical mail sent via a network can be stored, replayed, and broadcast to other nodes on the network.

✓ Reality Check.   The broadcast capability of e-mail is a feature included in the software that manages many networks. Broadcasting is not unique to communications networks, however. You are already familiar with this capability from other communications media—radio and television. The terms "radio broadcast" and "television broadcast" mean that the same transmission (music, news, or multimedia information) is sent to all receiving nodes that are turned on at the time. E-mail has an advantage over radio and television broadcasting, though. An e-mail transmission can be sent to many different nodes simultaneously, or it can be directed to a specific location. ■

People can acquire e-mail capabilities in three ways: by purchasing e-mail packages, by subscribing to public information services, or by using university networks.

• E-mail software packages can be purchased and loaded onto a network. Some of the packages available for the different types of networks are listed in Table 9.6. These software packages are purchased for a one-time fee. A copy is needed for each workstation that will send and receive messages.

TABLE 9.6   Widely Used E-mail Software Packages

PROFS	An acronym for PRofessional OFfice Systems, an IBM software package used with host-based networks. The White House staff members were among the first users of this package.
All-In-One	A system developed for Digital VAX computer systems.
VAX Notes	An alternate system developed for Digital VAX computer systems.
CC:Mail	A system designed to run on both Macintosh and IBM-compatible computer local area networks.
Mail	A system created by Microsoft that runs on both Macintosh and IBM-compatible computers.
Quick-Mail	A system created by the CE software company for Macintosh computers.

- E-mail capabilities are also available through commercial public data services. For a monthly subscriber fee, plus a variable charge based on usage, you can have a mailbox established on the network. Using your identification name, other users of the public network can send messages to you.

  The most widely used public data services offering e-mail are CompuServe, Prodigy, America Online, The Source, and MCI Mail. These services, sometimes called *information utilities*, are based in the United States but are accessible around the world.

- Finally, university faculty and students involved in faculty support can interconnect with the university's computer network, which, in turn, is connected to external communications networks such as Bitnet and Internet. From their desktop PCs, faculty members can exchange messages and documents with other faculty within the university and with faculty members at other institutions around the world. A growing number of businesses are also linking to Internet to send and receive messages.

E-mail at DEC.   Digital Equipment Corp.'s e-mail system is representative of the e-mail systems used in large companies across the globe. Nearly 30,000 nodes throughout Europe, Asia, the South Pacific, and North and South America are connected to DEC's e-mail system. When a staff member needs to get in touch with someone, he or she can send an e-mail message to the person simply by typing in the individual's name or computer address and the message. The network locates the individual and transmits the message to the recipient's mailbox, where it is held until the recipient is ready to read his or her mail.

DEC's e-mail system is used for much more than just electronic conversation, however; it also drives business opportunities and new product ideas. For example, when sales representatives, engineers, or members of the management team have questions about a problem they are wrestling with, they broadcast a message across the network: "An important Digital customer wishes to interconnect its home office in Framingham, Massachusetts with a manufacturing site in Jakarta, Indonesia, but has not worked with any communications carriers servicing that region. What experience have Digital staff members had with any carriers providing service in the area, good or bad? What advice do you have about approaching the carriers?" In a few hours, it is likely that the individual transmitting the message will have a wide variety of detailed responses to the inquiry—responses that help Digital's customers get accurate and timely advice and the company's assistance in capitalizing on an important business opportunity. In addition, the electronic conversation can continue between selected team members as additional questions are posed or more complex problems arise.

Voice Mail

voice mail A system that captures, stores, and transmits spoken messages using a telephone connected to a computer network.

Messages created in *text* form are sent through a network via e-mail. But businesses also use **voice mail** systems, which capture, store, and transmit *spoken* messages. Voice mail systems use an ordinary telephone connected to a computer network. A sender enters a message by speaking into the telephone. This message is transformed (digitized) from analog to digital form and then stored in the recipient's voice mailbox (Figure 9.25). Later, the recipient can use a phone to dial into the system and retrieve the stored messages, which are converted back to analog signals and played back over the telephone. As with e-mail, voice messages can be broadcast to others on the network, stored on the network, or replayed.

Many voice mail systems are available worldwide, some from computer vendors, others from providers of telephone equipment, and others from telephone companies or PTTs. In some cases, the voice mail system is run on a local or wide area network. In other cases, an organization may decide to keep voice mail separate from its computer networks.

While voice mail is becoming more popular every day, people are sometimes reluctant to use its capabilities because they do not like talking to a computer or a recording. Others think that the process of retrieving or replaying messages is too cumbersome. IT professionals will need to address these concerns if the use of voice mail is to continue growing.

Video Conferencing

video conferencing A type of conferencing in which video cameras and microphones capture sight and sound for transmission over networks.

Audio and visual communications come together in **video conferencing**, a type of conferencing in which video cameras and microphones capture sight and sound for transmission over networks (Figure 9.26). Video conferencing allows meetings to be conducted with the full participation of group members, who remain at their individual locations but are interconnected through a communications network. People can be brought together from far and wide this way. Large display screens show the other parties in the conference "live."

Video conferencing is more than just two-way audio and video. Because computers can be linked to the video conferencing network, documents and images stored on magnetic or optical devices are accessible to meeting participants.

FIGURE 9.25   **How Voice Mail Works**

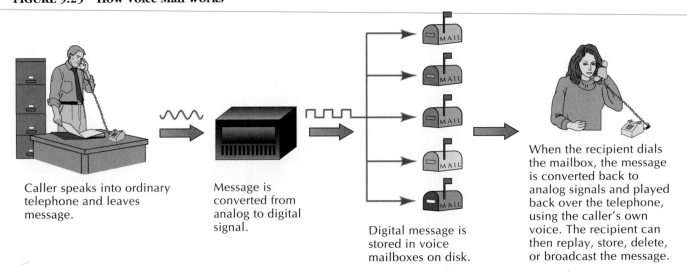

Caller speaks into ordinary telephone and leaves message.

Message is converted from analog to digital signal.

Digital message is stored in voice mailboxes on disk.

When the recipient dials the mailbox, the message is converted back to analog signals and played back over the telephone, using the caller's own voice. The recipient can then replay, store, delete, or broadcast the message.

FIGURE 9.26   Video Conferencing
Pediatric cardiologists at the University of Kansas Medical Center use video conferencing equipment to monitor the heartbeat of a patient 300 miles away. The screen on the left shows the patient's electrocardiogram.

Information retrieved from a central database or entered into a computer linked to the network can be transmitted to all conference locations simultaneously. But the individuals in the video conference do not have to use computers or terminals to participate. Rather, they can express their ideas verbally, with microphones capturing their comments and passing them to the network for transmission.

Air Products Europe, headquartered outside London, frequently conducts video conferences with its home office in Allentown, Pennsylvania. A video conference facility at each site uses satellite communications to put executives and managers in touch with each other, even though they are separated by the Atlantic Ocean. The facilities, which cost less then $100,000 each, have not only eliminated the need for many time-consuming cross-ocean trips but have also resulted in increased communication and information sharing between key executives. Air Products Europe's executives now say that they can't imagine running their business today without video conferencing.

Kmart also operates a video conferencing system linking its store managers. The company regularly broadcasts live satellite transmissions from its headquarters to all of its stores. Interactive presentations by senior executives enable store managers in the field to pose their questions by telephone and to hear immediate responses over the network.

CRITICAL CONNECTION 3
Video Conferencing: A New Way to Reach Out and Touch Someone

It isn't surprising that some of the pioneers of video conferencing are high-tech stars. Apple Computer, for instance, has ten video meeting rooms in the United States, three in Europe, and two in Tokyo, where local engineers use them to avoid the city's notorious traffic jams. Apple estimates that the $6 million investment has saved $28 million in travel costs, allowed more people to participate in key meetings, and improved decision making. Hewlett Packard, which began using video conferencing in 1983, now has 45 video rooms around the world. Video meetings have reduced the development time of some products by about a third.

And at United Technologies, engineers use video conferencing to participate in long-distance learning programs, such as accredited graduate-level engineering courses at various universities around the United States.

What *is* surprising is the way video conferencing is transforming less technical endeavors. At McCann-Erickson, for example, far-flung staffers use video conferencing to coordinate work on advertising campaigns. Video conferencing is also popular at the executive recruiting firm Korn/Ferry International, which recently used video conferences to find a public relations director for the Hong Kong and Tokyo offices of a U.S. corporation.

Work Group Conferencing

work group conferencing A type of conferencing that uses a software package called *groupware* to organize an electronic meeting in which participants' computers are interconnected from their various locations. Participants interact through a microcomputer directly linked to a server and their comments are broadcast to all others in the conference.

Work group conferencing uses a software package called *groupware* to organize an electronic meeting in which participants' computers are interconnected from their various locations. The participants may be in the same room, linked by a local area network, or geographically dispersed and interconnected over a wide area network. The electronic conference centers around the entry of ideas, comments, suggestions, and the retrieval and display of information. Typically, each participant interacts through a microcomputer directly linked to a server. Their typed comments are then broadcast to all others in the conference and stored for later analysis (Figure 9.27).

Work group systems are ideal for bringing far-flung individuals together via the network to tackle a problem. The group gets the benefit of shared thinking and distribution of information without the costs and time involved in travel.

It is likely that groupware and video conferencing capabilities will merge into a single service in the not-too-distant future. Experts expect this type of conferencing to retain the name *groupware* or *group support systems*. (We discuss group support systems in greater depth in Chapter 12 and the benefits of one specific groupware package, Lotus Notes, in the Photo Essay at the end of the chapter).

FIGURE 9.27
Work Group Conferencing
Team members and people from different functional areas of Seattle's Boeing Computer Services use groupware frequently to exchange ideas and discuss challenges. Meetings are generally conducted by a moderator, who stands at the front and center of the conference room.

Electronic Bulletin Boards

Electronic bulletin boards have come into widespread use along with desktop computers. The electronic version of a bulletin board is similar to the bulletin board at the supermarket where you post or read messages and announcements. With an electronic bulletin board, you dial into the board over a communications link and leave a message, a file, or a program. Others dialing into the bulletin board can retrieve the information and copy it into their system.

To create a bulletin board, you need only four things: a computer, a telephone line, a bulletin board program, and a telephone modem. Callers can dial the telephone number of the bulletin board and interconnect with it through the modem. The bulletin board program monitors who is calling, connects the caller, inserts or copies information, and disconnects the caller at the end of the session. Many bulletin board programs also provide password screening, ensuring that only individuals who provide the right password can gain access to the files and databases maintained within the system.

Electronic bulletin boards are often used to share information between members of clubs and organizations (Figure 9.28). However, many companies are finding them to be a good way of distributing product and service information to actual or potential customers. Best of all, the cost of creating a bulletin board is low. Good software is available at very low cost, usually well under $100.

electronic bulletin boards A network service application that allows messages and announcements to be posted and read. Accessed by dialing a telephone number and interconnecting with the bulletin board through a modem.

Electronic Funds Transfer

The world's banking community transfers information much more often than it transfers money. Seldom does money—actual coins and paper currency—move. *Information about money transfers* moves much more often.

Electronic funds transfer (EFT) is the movement of money over a network. In banking, a clearinghouse accepts transfer transactions and settles accounts for both the sending bank and the receiving bank. The automated teller machines we discussed in Chapter 4 also make use of EFT.

EFT is also used to settle credit card transactions by transferring funds between the seller and the bank issuing the credit card and to deposit payroll checks and government support checks directly into an individual's bank account. It is likely that in the future we will see even less actual movement of cash and even more information about funds transferred electronically.

electronic funds transfer (EFT) The movement of money over a network.

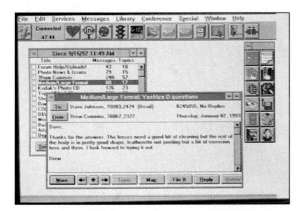

FIGURE 9.28
Electronic Bulletin Boards
Electronic bulletin boards are often used to share information among members of a community, club, or organization. Many companies also use them to facilitate communication among their employees and to distribute product and service information to their customers.

Electronic Data Interchange

electronic data interchange (EDI) A form of electronic communication that allows trading partners to exchange business transaction data in structured formats that can be processed by applications software.

E-mail is the transmission of text messages. **Electronic data interchange (EDI)**, in contrast, is a form of electronic communication that allows trading partners to exchange business transaction data in structured formats that can be processed by applications software. In industries from transportation (railroad and trucking) to automobile manufacturing to retailing, companies are using EDI to reduce the time needed to transfer business information and to obtain products and services. Approximately one-third of all business documents, including purchase orders, invoices, and payments, are moved by EDI (Figure 9.29).

EDI often uses value-added carriers that provide special communications services specifically for EDI. *Translation software* interacts with the computer to transform data from the format stored in a company's database into a form that can be transmitted. Translation software on the other end changes the received information into the form required by the receiving company.

FIGURE 9.29 Electronic Data Interchange (EDI)
EDI greatly simplifies business transactions by allowing trading partners to exchange data in structured formats.

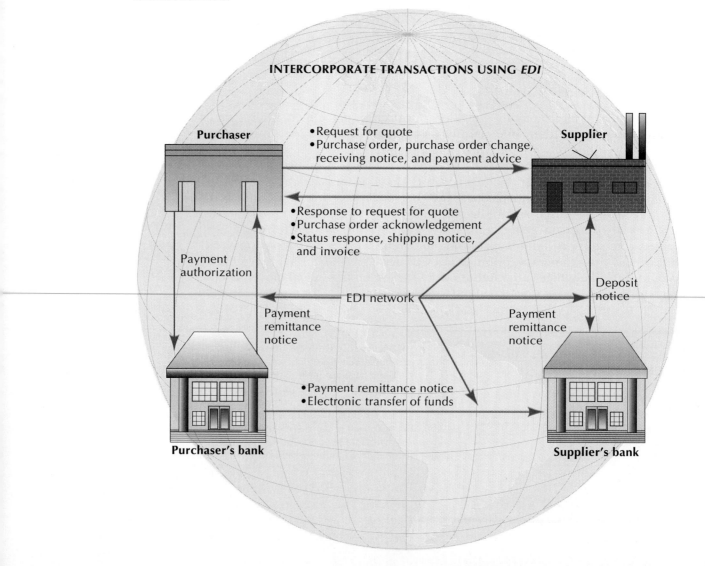

In the pharmaceutical industry, California-based Bergen Brunswig Corp. has launched its EDI-based Electronic Partnership Program to strengthen its links with its suppliers. The purchase orders and subsequent invoices and payments that Bergen Brunswig interchanges with its vendors account for nearly all of the merchandise distributed by the company. The company's business goal of dealing electronically with 100% of its suppliers is based on its desire to develop more accurate and timely ordering practices that will reduce inventory levels and improve cash management. In an industry in which the average after-tax profit is less than 1.5%, electronic opportunities can mean the difference between profit and loss. The time needed to process orders also diminishes when EDI is used. Drug wholesalers using EDI have reduced the order/delivery cycle by over 50 percent.

The role of EDI is rapidly increasing in international commerce. Two factors dramatically influence the more than $2 trillion of annual international trade: the flow of paperwork and delays in transit of goods and information. Entire staffs are devoted to tracking orders, payments, or shipping papers, working against diverse time zones and business customs. Some estimates suggest that the flow of paperwork in international trade creates costs equal to 7% of the value of the product traded. Here the benefits of EDI can be enormous. Shippers, transporters, customs agents, and customers send documents electronically, overcoming the barriers posed by geographic distance—barriers that cost valuable time. Because EDI makes such a difference in international trade, some companies have told their suppliers to "link up or lose out" (that is, implement EDI or lose them as a customer).

Videotex

British Telecom gave birth to **videotex** in the early 1970s when it developed a two-way, interactive, text-only service operating on mainframe computers. The system quickly evolved to include two essential features:

videotex A two-way, interactive, text-only service operating on mainframe computers that combines a video screen with easy-to-follow instructions.

- An easy-to-use interface that allows people to select options through successive menus providing choices and English-like commands.
- Medium-resolution graphics that present product and service information visually. On videotex, information is displayed one page at a time. People using videotex systems can both review and respond to information displayed on their computer or terminal.

Videotex systems are used in a variety of ways:

- SONY Corp. created a sales support videotex system that allows personnel to place orders, fill out expense accounts, and receive messages. Sales agents respond to information displayed on the screen by filling in an electronic form on the screen or answering inquiries with short statements.
- The Motor Vehicle Department of British Columbia (Canada) uses videotex to test driver's license applicants. Multiple-choice questions regarding driving laws and practices are presented on the videotex screen at the testing center. As applicants respond to each question, the system checks their responses against the correct answers stored on the host computer. Would-be drivers must pass the videotex portion of the exam before they can proceed with a road test.
- The Buick Motor Division of General Motors has created a database of more than 2,000 videotex pages describing automobile specification and design options. Interacting through a computer terminal, a salesperson and customer can together select different options and determine the price and availability

of the vehicle. The initial success of this Electronic Product Information Center (EPIC) led to an advanced version that allows people to see the automobile with chosen color, trim, and options displayed on the screen. When sales staff and customers are not using EPIC, the system automatically displays a series of videotex advertising pages.

Videotex is quickly growing into a data communications network for home shopping. Customers can peruse video display catalogs of merchandise, complete with price and product specifications. They can then enter their order and payment information directly into the videotex system. The payment funds will be transferred automatically from the customer's bank account to the vendor. Cable television companies are already providing videotex shopping services. It is likely that you will see even more of these services in airports, shopping malls, and sports arenas in the future.

▨ Networks and Business: A Final Word

As you leave this chapter, one thing should be clear: Communications networks are an essential component of IT. If you can't link up, you can't communicate, and you may lose out. That is the reality of business today.

SUMMARY OF LEARNING OBJECTIVES

1 Identify the reasons why multi-user systems are used in business. Multi-user systems are used in business (1) to increase the productivity and effectiveness of the people using the system; (2) to increase the productivity and effectiveness of the organizations in which the system is used; and (3) to improve the services provided to those who rely on others using multi-user systems.

2 Explain the three types of multi-user architectures and the advantages offered by each. In a *centralized architecture*, all network hardware and software are found at a central site where the central computer, or host, performs all of the processing and manages the network. Centralized systems are easy to manage. In a *distributed architecture*, computers reside at different locations and are interconnected by a communications network. Distributed architecture places information at the locations where it is used most often while ensuring that others in the system have access to it.

To take advantage of the benefits of both types of architecture, companies can choose to combine the two. In a *hybrid architecture*, a mainframe controls interaction with all the devices attached directly to it. The host does not, however, directly control

those computers interconnected at lower levels of the network.

3 Discuss the three types of multi-user and the advantages offered by each. The three types of networks are (1) *wide area networks* (WANs), designed to span large geographic regions; (2) *local area networks* (LANs), which interconnect desktop computers and communications devices within an office or series of offices; and (3) *metropolitan area networks* (MANs), which use fiber-optic cables to transmit various types of information around a city or metropolitan region.

4 Discuss the two types of communications channels used in networks and the ways that computers interconnect with them. There are two types of communications channels used in networks. The *physical channels* (twisted pair, coaxial cable, and optical cable) use a wire or cable along which data and information are transmitted. The *cableless channels* (microwave, satellite, infrared, and radio frequency transmission) are wireless transmission media.

In WANs, *modems* connect computers to the communications channel and translate the information from the computer into a form that can be transmitted over the channel. In LANs, a *network interface card* is used.

5 **Explain the role of a network operating system.** Every computer that runs a network must have a *network operating system (NOS)*, a software program that runs in conjunction with the computer's operating system and application programs and manages the network.

6 **Discuss the activities involved in network administration.** Network management consists of procedures and services that keep the network running properly. One important aspect of network administration entails making sure that the network is available when users need it. Other parts of the network administrator's job include: monitoring the network's capacity to ensure that all transmission requirements can be met; adding capacity to the network when necessary; conducting training to assist individuals in using the network; assisting IT professionals in writing applications; backing up the network software and data regularly; putting security procedures in place; ensuring that network personnel can respond quickly to an operational or security failure; and diagnosing and troubleshooting problems on the network when they occur.

7 **Describe eight network service applications used in business.** The eight network service applications most frequently used in business are: electronic mail, voice mail, video conferencing, workgroup conferencing, bulletin boards, electronic funds transfer, electronic data interchange, and videotex.

Electronic mail, or *e-mail*, is a service that transports text messages from a sender to one or more receivers via computer. *Voice mail* systems capture, store, and transmit spoken messages. Voice mail systems do not use computer keyboards, but rather a telephone connected to a computer network. *Video conferencing* is a type of conferencing in which video cameras and microphones capture sight and sound for transmission over networks. Large display screens show the other parties in the conference "live." *Workgroup conferencing* uses a software package called *groupware* to organize an electronic meeting in which participants' computers are interconnected from their various locations. Each participant interacts through a microcomputer directly linked to a main computer; these comments are broadcast to all participants in the conference. *Electronic bulletin boards* are similar to the bulletin boards at the supermarket where messages and announcements are posted or read. With an electronic bulletin board, users dial into the board over a communications link and leave a message, file, or program. Others dialing onto the bulletin board can retrieve the information and copy it to their system. *Electronic funds transfer* (EFT) is the movement of money over a network. *Electronic data interchange* (EDI) is a form of electronic communication that allows trading partners to exchange business transaction data in structured formats that can be processed by applications software. *Videotex* is a two-way, interactive, text-only service operating on mainframe computers that provides a video screen with easy-to-follow instructions.

KEY TERMS

CRITICAL CONNECTIONS

1.   Apple Computer Thinks Fast and Comes Out a Winner

The PowerBook, named by *Fortune* magazine as a "product of the year," is testament to the outstanding results that creative business problem solving can achieve in the marketplace. Another indication of success is a company's gross revenue per employee—an indicator of productivity and efficiency. Apple, with its newly adopted policy of pursuing strategic partnerships, earns $437,100 per employee—nearly four times that of rival Digital Equipment Corp. (DEC) and more than twice that of IBM.

Questions for Discussion

1. Delegating the creation of the low-end notebook model to Sony let Apple engineers concentrate on designing the SuperDrive, a disk drive that is compatible with both IBM and Macintosh software. Why might the SuperDrive have been an important part of Apple's strategy of appealing to corporate users?

2. Management experts claim that many corporations of the next century will have "no borders"—that the traditional boundaries between competitors, suppliers, and customers will melt away, making it hard to tell where one company ends and another begins. What might this mean for the global economy, for the United States, and the other nations of the world?

3. The "information infrastructure" we discussed at the beginning of this chapter is likely to be a computer network that will (a) act as an information clearinghouse for companies seeking virtual corporation partners; (b) speed the negotiation and signing of "electronic contracts"; and (c) let teams of workers from different companies work together. What might this vision mean for the managers of the twenty-first century?

2.   Peapod Makes Grocery Shopping Easy

The Parkinson brothers are hoping that key demographic trends will help Peapod grow. These trends include the increasing number of people who have access to modem-equipped computers, either at home or at work, and the growth of the time-poor "sandwich generation"—double-income families torn between caring for their children and their aging parents. Another boost may come from people with disabilities and the elderly, two groups with limited mobility. (Many adult children use Peapod to shop for their elderly parents.)

Although the Parkinsons initially targeted Chicago's more affluent suburbs, much of their business now comes from middle and lower income shoppers. "For people at the lower income levels," says Tom Parkinson, "it's sometimes cheaper to use the computer at work to order from us than to take a cab to and from the grocery store."

Questions for Discussion

1. Some experts estimate that half of all supermarket purchases are made on impulse. As a manager of a grocery store, would this make you more or less eager to enter into an alliance with Peapod? How could Peapod use your reaction to its advantage?

2. Some shoppers hesitate to let others pick out their produce. What other objections to Peapod's services can you think of? How could Peapod overcome these objections?

3. Peapod estimates that it has signed up about 1% of all shoppers in its service area, still short of the 4% to 5% it needs to prosper. What suggestions would you make to help Peapod increase its membership?

3. Video Conferencing: A New Way to Reach Out and Touch Someone

Private companies aren't the only ones to benefit from video conferencing. In Kentucky, for example, the Bureau of Prisons once spent over $200 each time it needed to send a federal prisoner and two guards to the Lexington, Kentucky, office of ophthalmologist John Garden. Today, a video conference system links Garden's office to an estimation room in the prison. The cost of the exam: a more reasonable $40.

Questions for Discussion

1. How do you think video conferencing will change job descriptions and business activities?

2. List some of the ways video conferencing can save money and time for both private companies and society as a whole.

3. In late 1992, AT&T introduced the VideoPhone 2500, a phone that can transmit the callers' faces as well as their conversation. The VideoPhone costs about $1,500 versus the $25,000 needed to equip a bare-bones video conference facility. As an investment manager, would the introduction of the VideoPhone make you more or less enthusiastic about investing in the companies making more traditional video conferencing equipment?

REVIEW QUESTIONS

1. Define a multi-user system and state the three business purposes of multi-user systems.

2. What is a communications network? What is a node?

3. Why do communications networks qualify as multi-user systems?

4. Discuss the nature of communications architecture and distinguish between the three types of communications architecture. What advantages and disadvantages does each type of architecture offer to business?

5. How do host computers and front-end computers differ? What purpose does each serve in a communications network? Is each a required component of a network?

6. Describe the distinguishing characteristics of a wide area network (WAN), local area network (LAN), and metropolitan area network (MAN). Under what circumstances do companies use each type of network?

7. What are the two types of communications channels?

8. Identify the three types of physical communication channels. Which has been in use for the longest period of time?

9. Describe the four types of cableless communications media.

10. Explain the differences among public access networks, private "leased line" networks, and value-added networks. What advantages does each offer to business?

11. Do LANs use the same types of communications channels as WANs? Explain.

12. What is the purpose of a modem? A network interface card?

13. Why do businesses sometimes want to interconnect communications networks? What are the two means for doing so? What determines which method of interconnection is used?

14. Describe the role of a network operating system in a communications network. How is it different from a computer operating system? Does using one eliminate the need for the other?

15. What responsibilities are entailed in network administration?

16. How are electronic mail and voice mail different? What advantages do e-mail and voice mail systems offer?

17. How are video conferencing and videotex different? What purpose does each serve?

18. Describe electronic data interchange.

DISCUSSION QUESTIONS

1. In the fall of 1991, the U.S. Congress enacted legislation aimed at building a nationwide, high-speed communications network of optical fibers. Should the federal government take an active role in creating this network? How would the network benefit a company that operates a WAN that spans 10 states?

2. Matson Navigation Co., a 110-year-old company that operates ships carrying cargo between the West Coast of the United States and Hawaii, uses electronic mail, fax, and local area networks linked to a mainframe to track containers on its ships and on the 600 trucks that pass through its terminal gates daily.

What type of network architecture is Matson using? What type of network is it using?

3. The Internet is a maze of nearly 10,000 networks worldwide that was originally created in the mid-1960s to facilitate the sharing of information between researchers at government agencies and universities. Even though thousands of company employees also exchange electronic mail on the Internet, company officials are often quick to stress that none of these messages involve confidential data. Why would officials stress this point?

4. Managers typically spend between 30% and 70% of their time in meetings. Why might this fact be inspiring companies to use workgroup conferencing?

SUGGESTED READINGS

Dertouzos, Michael L., "Communications, Computers, and Networks," *Scientific American*, 265, no. 3 (September 1992). This special issue contains 11 articles dealing with different aspects of multi-user computer systems and communications networks. Each article, written by an expert in the field, focuses on the implications of advances in IT for people, business organizations, and government.

Gilder, George, "Into the Telecosm," *Harvard Business Review*, 69, no. 2 (March–April 1992), pp. 150–161. Gilder presents a fascinating view of the future of multi-user computer networks. Taking a business perspective, he examines what companies and individuals can do with computer networks and what obstacles must be overcome. His global outlook argues that business leaders must develop national networks rather than "a tower of Babel" of private networks.

Horton, Patrick R., and Michael D. Morris, "A Shared Network Spreadsheet," *Byte*, 12, no. 8 (July 1987), pp. 185ff. Horton and Morris explore the many ways in which personal applications software can be shared in a multi-user local area network. Their article emphasizes such practical issues as maintaining application security and data integrity.

Kahn, Robert E., "Networks For Advanced Computing," *Scientific American*, 257, no. 4 (October 1987), pp. 136–143. Kahn describes how computers linked via networks can interact and share programs, information, and expensive hardware and explains why the physical link is not enough. One computer must be able to understand what a different computer is saying.

Stallings, William, *Local Networks* (3d ed.) New York: Macmillan, 1990. A standard textbook on the design, construction, and use of local area networks. Includes excellent comparative information regarding the tradeoffs that must be made in moving from mainframe-based wide area networks to local area networks.

Wright, Karen, "The Road to the Global Village," *Scientific American*, 262, no. 3 (March 1990), pp. 83–94. Wright's article explains why and how, after more than a century of electronic technology, society is extending itself globally, transcending both space and time barriers. Among the topics discussed are cooperative work, "infotainment," "knowbots," and virtual reality.

Satellites Help CNN Span the Globe

EXECUTIVES AT THE WORLD'S traditional television networks scoffed when Ted Turner announced plans for an all-news network in the late 1970s. What did Turner, head of an outdoor advertising business and small TV stations, know about journalism? At that time, Turner Broadcasting System (TBS) consisted of two independent television stations—one in Atlanta and one in Charlotte, North Carolina. Both aired a steady diet of old movies, sports, and reruns—usually opposite the U.S. television network news. Turner's Atlanta station broadcast just forty minutes of news—the minimum needed to meet U.S. licensing requirements—usually in the middle of the night.

But the doomsayers didn't count on Ted Turner's three most important qualities. One is his drive and determination. Dubbed "Captain Outrageous" for the "winner-take-all" daring that helped him win the America's Cup in 1977, Turner recalls, "I just love it when someone says I can't do something."

Turner's second strength is his vision, the ability to see the potential in a number of emerging trends:

- The emergence of cable television, an alternative to the established and powerful television networks.
- The popularity of all-news radio, a concept pioneered by WINS in New York during the 1960s. WINS' slogan, "Give us 22 minutes and we'll give you the world," became the model for the basic "news wheel"—the continuous repeating and updating of news stories interspersed with expensive advertising spots.
- The growing number of commercial communications satellites carrying transponders, devices that can be tuned to receive a signal from one satellite dish and relay it to another.

When Home Box Office, Time Inc.'s "premium" cable service, announced it would begin using satellite transmission, Turner decided to follow suit. Undeterred by the news that leasing a satellite transponder would cost $1 million a year, plus another $750,000 for the station's satellite dish, Turner plunged ahead. The decision converted his Atlanta station into, in his own words, a "superstation" whose signal blanketed the United States. If one transponder could blanket the nation, Turner thought, why not lease a second and a third, until he created a cable news network that covered the world?

Turner's third winning quality is his ability to create a team of people who share his vision and know how to turn it into reality. One of the most important members of Turner's team in the early days was Reese Schonfeld, a dedicated journalist who was struggling to create a video news service. When Turner asked him if an all-news network could be established, Schonfeld had visions of an all-electronic newsroom, linked by phone lines and satellite to newsrooms and reporters around the world. If Turner didn't have his own reporters on the scene, Schonfeld suggested, he could buy coverage of major events from independent journalists or local television stations.

The rest is history. Today, the network pioneered by Schonfeld lets Cable News Network (CNN) cover breaking news almost anywhere in the world. A good example is CNN's 1992 coverage of Operation Restore Hope in the African nation of Somalia, which has virtually no infrastructure. Reporters had to pack portable electricity generators, food, and water, in addition to the gear they needed to connect to CNN's news desk. This gear included laptop computers, collapsible satellite dishes that fit into oversize suitcases, and Inmarsats, portable telephones that incorporate tiny satellite dishes.

Following its debut in June 1980, CNN has garnered journalists' respect for its skill in using information technology to provide live, unedited coverage of historical events. CNN viewers watched firsthand the 1986 explosion of the space shuttle *Challenger*, the 1989 students' revolt in China's Tiananmen Square, and the 1991 Persian Gulf War. Today CNN airs in more than 130 million homes in 200 countries, where it is a fixture at airports and hotels catering to diplomats and the international community. Foreign ministries, including U.S. State Department consular offices, routinely monitor CNN around the clock. In 1991, CNN received the cable industry's highest award for its Persian Gulf coverage—which had been followed closely by both U.S. and Iraqi leaders. *Time* magazine named Ted Turner its "Man of the Year" for 1991. It was a heady triumph for a network that was started on a shoestring and a dream.

Along with his bold vision and his ability to see the "big picture," Turner is a manager with clear priorities for his

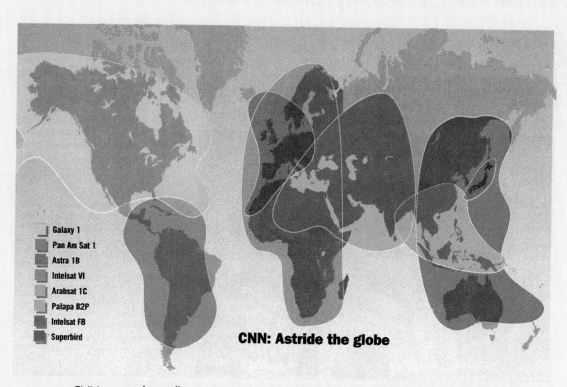

CNN: Astride the globe

Galaxy 1
Pan Am Sat 1
Astra 1B
Intelsat VI
Arabsat 1C
Palapa B2P
Intelsat F8
Superbird

CNN uses eight satellites to transmit news around the world. Its four most powerful satellites (named Astra, Palapa, Arabsat, and Superbird) circle almost the entire earth.

network and the people who work for him. The top priority for Turner's IT professionals is the creation of "flyaway phone systems"—portable satellite links—that will get CNN reporters access to whomever or whatever they need anywhere in the world. Turner's director of management information systems makes a guarantee to all end-users: "You need to talk to another department, another country even, and we'll get you there—without putting another box on your desk....My job is not to disrupt user comfort."

Questions for Discussion

1. Describe the different types of networks in use at CNN. How do these networks illustrate the principles of multi-user systems?

2. Turner is so committed to the concept of the global economy that he chides workers who use the term "foreign" instead of "international." How does CNN's success reflect the other business trends illustrated in Table 9.1?

Using Lotus Notes to Collaborate

Collaboration software (also called *groupware*), such as Lotus Notes, can be used as a conferencing system for group problem solving, as a tracking tool for project management, and as a library for policies, documentation, or news. Collaboration systems are much more convenient and powerful than e-mail, for they let people use their own personal productivity tools, including spreadsheets, presentation programs, and drawing packages, to share knowledge in the form of documents and responses to documents anytime, anywhere.

A Lotus Notes database is a collection of related documents stored under a single name. It can be small—for example, a phone directory used collectively by a project team—or it can be a large group of customer, supplier, or personnel records. Unlike structured relational databases, a Lotus Notes database contains *documents*. These documents can be as short or as long, and as structured or unstructured, as the person creating the document desires. In addition, Lotus Notes documents may contain graphics, tables, and a variety of type fonts, sizes, presentation styles, and attachments. Because all of a database's documents are stored on a server, all members of the collaborating team have shared access to the database.

Lotus Notes's principal work surface, or *desktop*, contains menus, tabbed pages, and database icons (which are stored on the tabbed pages). The program allows a network to include client systems that are either Apple Macintosh computers or IBM-compatible computers running Windows, OS/2, or UNIX. The menu bar across the top of the screen includes the familiar pull-down commands for opening, closing, and printing files (FILE), editing documents (EDIT), changing the view on the desktop (VIEW), and sending mail (MAIL). Six colored tabs at the top of the workspace represent pages. Clicking on the tabs allows the user to switch between pages.

Each icon in the workspace represents a different database. These databases may include a variety of different types of information, including discussions about customer projects, tracking of service requests, and address books. To use a particular database, you add its icon to a tabbed page by dragging the icon to the tab. Users usually leave open on the desktop the databases they need most often during the day. When they want to open a particular database, they need only double click on its identifying icon.

Here's how one company with offices in many different countries uses Lotus Notes to help manage projects.

The First Afternoon

1 Frank Bobson just received a request from an important customer who wishes to place a large order for a seemingly simple product, globes. However, because the world's regions have changed dramatically in recent years, the customer wants to be certain the globes reflect the latest changes in international political boundaries. Frank knows that getting the order depends on getting these globes to the customer fast. Realizing that accepting and delivering this order requires collaboration between team members, Frank wants to get a discussion going among all his team members, who work at various locations. For example, Thierry Bouchard is located in Neuilly, a city on the outskirts of Paris. Roberta Hughes is in San Francisco, and James Carlton and others are located in different parts of the building with Frank. Fortunately, all members of the team are interconnected through Lotus Notes.

To begin a discussion on this order, Frank clicks the Worldwide Discussion icon on his desktop. Once in Worldwide Discussion, he uses the word processing capabilities within Lotus Notes to pose a question to members of his team: "How fast can we turn the request around to save the sale to the customer, Education Resources, Inc.?" Frank needs this information in three days, but—being a good businessman—knows he has to convey a sense of urgency. He asks for a response by the same afternoon.

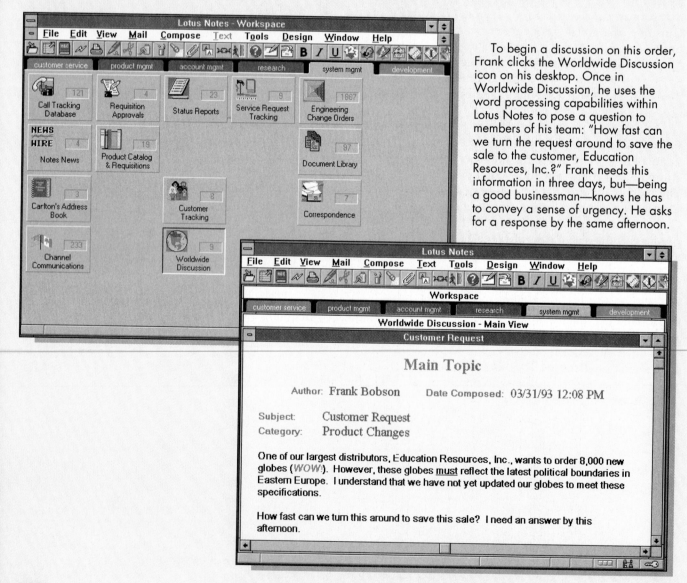

2 Frank decides to work through his lunch hour to assemble some background information on his request. He decides to check out the Customer Tracking database for any background information that might be useful to the group. After clicking on the Customer Tracking icon to open the database, he searches for the customer's name. Up comes the first document, a customer profile document created on January 21, 1993 by Hattie Henderson. The document provides the general information Frank's team needs to judge the importance of the customer and the necessity of carefully considering the request. The icon in the lower left corner of the screen indicates that more information is attached to the document. When Frank clicks on the icon, an additional window containing a table of sales data for 1991 and 1992 appears within the document.

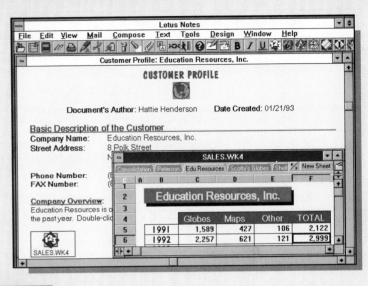

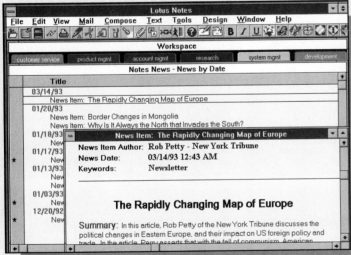

3 Frank also opens the News Wire database to get information on the political changes around the world affecting international boundaries. In News Wire, he finds a document titled *The Rapidly Changing Map of Europe*. By clicking on the document's title, he can instantly view the item's contents on his desktop. All of the information available to Frank on his Lotus Notes system is also available to other team members.

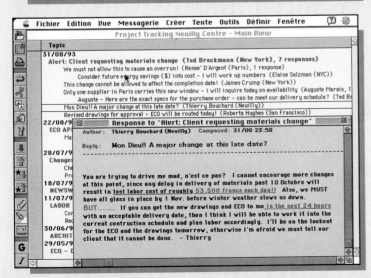

4 Thierry Bouchard, in the France office, receives Frank's message on his Apple Macintosh client system. His desktop contains the same features as other Notes users, except that he prefers to have the menu commands and other informative notes displayed in French. Upon receiving Frank's note, Bouchard immediately opens a set of documents from a recent rush job to review the handling of that order and whether that procedure might be useful now.

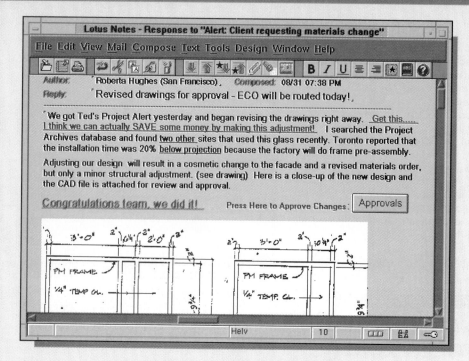

5 Roberta Hughes, in San Francisco, received Frank's document on her UNIX client system. Noting that Education Resources has requested a design change, she retrieves an electronic document prepared for an earlier project with a similar design change in the company's archives. The document includes a drawing of the design change. It also shows the button the document's author included at the time for approval of the drawing.[1]

---

[1] Lotus Notes facilitates committee approvals, without a face-to-face meeting, by making it possible for readers to signify their agreement by acting right on the document. Clicking the Approval button in this case signifies agreement. Notes transmits the concurrence to other team members.

The Next Morning

6 The next morning, Frank returns to his original message to find that two team members have submitted responses. He knows these documents have arrived because the comment "(2 Responses)" and a question mark icon have been added at the top of the document.

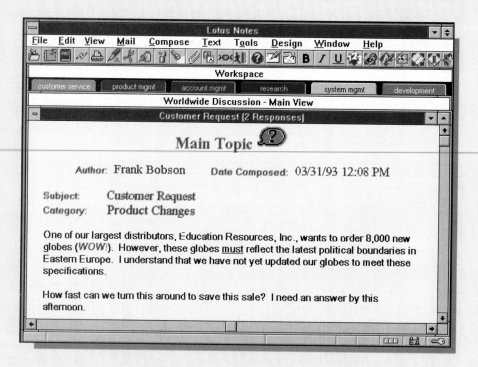

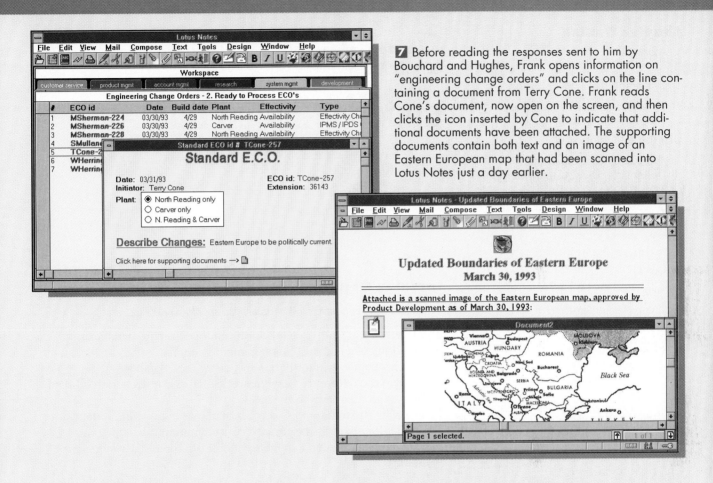

7 Before reading the responses sent to him by Bouchard and Hughes, Frank opens information on "engineering change orders" and clicks on the line containing a document from Terry Cone. Frank reads Cone's document, now open on the screen, and then clicks the icon inserted by Cone to indicate that additional documents have been attached. The supporting documents contain both text and an image of an Eastern European map that had been scanned into Lotus Notes just a day earlier.

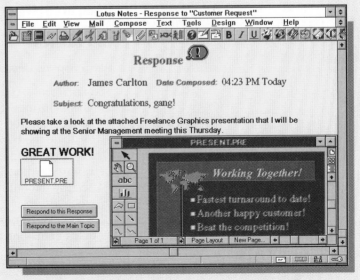

8 Even as Frank is reading Cone's document, James Carlton, another team member, is preparing to send Frank a message congratulating him on the order. Carlton's message will indicate that he sees no delay responding to the order because a new map of Eastern Europe's changed boundaries has already been prepared. To James's response is attached the new map that he prepared using Feelance Graphics (a presentation program running on his system) and copied into a Lotus Notes document. When Frank clicks on the icon labeled Present.Pre, the map is displayed on the screen. Carlton's document also includes buttons that readers can click either to comment on his response or to comment on the original topic created by Frank. When Carlton finished his response, Notes automatically forwarded it to everyone electronically linked into the discussion.

The team works back and forth throughout the morning to work out the details. By noon, Frank knows the job can be done. Lotus Notes allowed the group to collaborate electronically, sharing ideas, documents, and responses. No one was required to travel, send documents by courier, or even make lengthy telephone calls. In the end, the problem—and the opportunity—were managed quickly and with full participation.

CHAPTER 10

Shared and Distributed Data

Learning Objectives

When you have completed this chapter, you should be able to:

1 Identify the reasons organizations choose to share databases and the functions of a database management system.

2 Differentiate between shared and distributed databases.

3 Explain the difference between relational and object oriented databases and their uses in business.

4 Describe the differences between schemas, views, and indexes.

5 Discuss the benefits of client/server computing.

6 Distinguish between a database administrator and a systems programmer.

7 Discuss database administration procedures and concurrency procedures and why these are an essential part of a shared database system.

In Practice

After completing this chapter, you should be able to perform these activities:

1 Explain why organizations share data and information.

2 Visit a business that uses client/server computing and discuss the benefits it offers over the business's previous method of computing.

3 Evaluate the benefits of a distributed database to a company in the retailing, banking, transportation, or manufacturing industry.

4 Discuss with a database administrator the types of activities that occupy the bulk of his time and the decisions he finds most challenging.

5 Speak with a business's network manager and discuss the steps she takes in making distributed databases accessible to the people in her organization.

6 Visit with a database software salesperson and discuss the questions most frequently raised by companies deciding whether to purchase and install a database management system.

Banking on a Shared Database

FOR MANY YEARS, BANKS STRUCTURED their activities into departments specializing in particular products and services—savings, checking, consumer loans, commercial loans, and trust management, to mention just a few. Each department followed its own procedures and maintained its own records to ensure that the department operated as efficiently as possible. But what was most efficient for the bank was not always beneficial to customers, who often found that one department knew nothing about their relationship with other parts of the bank. For example, when you cashed a check, the teller would examine your checking account to determine your balance. If you were cashing a check drawn on a different bank, and the amount of the check was significantly more than the teller found in your personal checking account, you might have had to answer a host of questions from the teller. The questions, though easy enough to answer, are embarrassing and irritating—and a downright nuisance, especially when you have other accounts with the bank and the value of those accounts substantially exceeds the value of the check you wish to cash. They can also be embarrassing to the bank when it finds that you do a great deal of business with it.

Today, shared and distributed databases provide tellers with information on *all* accounts you have with the bank. When an account number or customer ID is entered into a banking system designed around shared databases, descriptions of all accounts and relationships are displayed for the bank employee's review.

People who waited on line for hours at banks just a few years ago are now doing much of their banking in a fraction of the time, thanks to ATMs and other IT breakthroughs. Databases shared by banks around the globe allow people access to their money and account information 24 hours a day.

A *MULTI-USER SYSTEM* IS A SYSTEM SHARED BY MORE THAN ONE USER. AS WE SAW IN Chapter 9, both hardware and programs can be shared. Multiple users in the same building can share computers, printers, and other hardware; people across the hall or in different cities, states, and countries can share a communications network. Different types of programs, including application programs, the network operating system, and the computer operating system oversee the activities of different components in the system.

In addition to sharing hardware and programs, people can also share data to make effective use of available resources and to become more productive. The set of data shared by a group of related businesses, for example, provides each business with a consistent view of a customer, supplier, resource level, or business transaction.

In this chapter, we examine the sharing and distributing of data among multiple persons. We begin by discussing the principles of data sharing and distribution and examining the structure of relational and object oriented databases. Throughout the chapter, we will see how data can be organized and stored to meet the needs of database users. We also will see the opportunities that client/server computing offers and the importance of good procedures. Finally, we will see that the sustained usefulness of shared databases is dependent on the people who manage them.

■ The Principles of Data Sharing

database A collection of data and information describing items of interest.

As we learned in Chapter 6, a **database** is a collection of data and information describing items of interest (sometimes called *entities*) to an organization. Data are collected on such entities as people, places, things, events, and conditions (Figure 10.1). Each *data item* in the database—whether numeric, text, image, graphic, or sound—describes an *attribute* of the entity.

Why Share Data?

Capturing, storing, and maintaining data in a database is an expensive process. In fact, managers who examine the human, physical, and financial resources they have invested in compiling their organization's data find that data collection and maintenance are very expensive indeed. Thus, it makes sense to use this important resource as often as possible and to manage it as effectively as possible. This entails making sure that all members of an organization who need the data will have access to them.

Sharing data means that all persons in the organization will work from the same set of data items for an entity. This consistency is important to the business's short- and long-term success. Imagine the problem on a university campus if the campus bookstore uses one enrollment figure from the registration database to order books for a course while the course instructor knows that a greater number of students were allowed to add the course.

When databases are shared, two facts quickly become evident: (1) People need different data from the database, and (2) People often need data organized in different ways. We'll see later in the chapter how these needs can be met even if people and databases are at different locations.

Database Management Systems

database management system (DBMS) A program that makes it possible for users to manage the data in a database and to increase productivity.

Databases are used by different applications and for multiple purposes. **Database management systems (DBMS)** are programs that make it possible for users to manage the data and to increase productivity. Through the DBMS, the data are accessed, maintained, and processed.

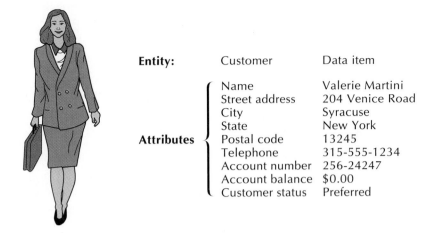

Instance of entity as database record

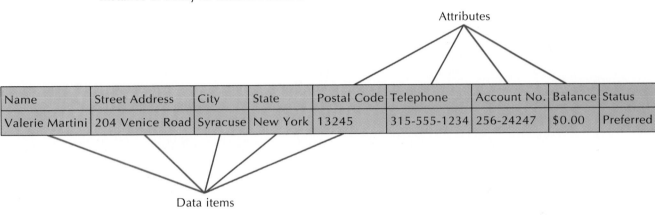

FIGURE 10.1   Entity Description in a Database System

The "customer" entity includes nine attributes and a data item for each attribute.

The database management system program operates in conjunction with the other programs running in a computer system, including the application program, operating system, and network operating system (Figure 10.2). It maintains the structure of the data and interacts with the other programs to locate and retrieve the data needed for processing. It also accepts data from the application program and writes it into the appropriate storage location.

The Functions of Database Management.   As we saw in Chapter 6, database management is meant to accomplish five objectives. A brief review is useful here:

- **Integrating databases**—Through database management, individual databases, created at various times or by different people, can be joined, in part or as a whole, to provide information needed to solve a problem or deal with a business issue.
- **Reducing redundancy**—Unnecessary or undesirable duplication of data across databases can be eliminated through database management. Some redundancy, however, can be desirable if it assists the people using the databases.
- **Sharing information**—People at remote locations can share stored data that are made accessible to them.

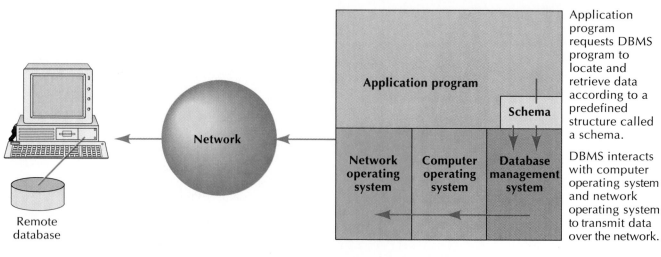

FIGURE 10.2   Relationship of DBMS to Other Programs in Computer Memory
A DBMS works in conjunction with the other programs running in a computer system.

- **Maintaining integrity**—Good database management ensures the integrity of the database by allowing controlled access to information, providing security measures, and ensuring that data are available when needed.
- **Enabling database evolution**—Database management systems help ensure that the database can evolve to meet the changing requirements of its users.

The database management system achieves these objectives through database creation, database inquiry, database updating, and database administration (see Chapter 6 if you need to review these terms).

CRITICAL CONNECTION 1
Database Eases California Identity Crisis

**Department of Motor Vehicles
State of California**

For many people, a driver's license is the key to freedom. But it's also an important piece of identification, vital to establishing legal identity and obtaining credit. In California, for example, law enforcement and government agencies bombard the Department of Motor Vehicles (DMV) with 1,000 to 1,500 requests to confirm license information every day. In the old days, each request would send a DMV employee off to hand-search millions of microfilm records. To boost efficiency, the DMV is creating an image database of all driver's license information.

The heart of the new system is a high-tech driver's license that contains images of the driver's color photograph, fingerprint, and legal signature, as well as a security hologram of the state emblem. On the back, a magnetic strip contains additional information, including the driver's date of birth, license plate number, and license expiration date.

The California system, the first of its kind in the nation, has easily boosted efficiency. Just doing away with fingerprinting has saved a great deal of time. In addition, the system's laser printer can create a crisp color image in less than a minute.

Distributed Databases

Databases are almost always shared among many users and applications. These **shared databases** can also be distributed. A **distributed database** is a database whose data reside on more than one system in a network. These data can be accessed, retrieved, or updated from any node in the network. Distributing data provides the needed data and information at a specific location, while allowing those same data to be used at other locations in the organization as well.

People using distributed databases need not be aware of the location of the database. The application programs, communications software, and database management systems interact with one another to identify, locate, and retrieve the data and information needed by the individual.

shared database A database shared among many users and applications.

distributed database A database whose data reside on more than one system in a network.

Partitioning and Replication

Databases may be distributed in two ways: partitioning and replication. With **partitioning**, different portions of the database reside at different nodes in the network. To partition effectively, the database designer divides the database into the logical or meaningful subsets needed to support a specific type of application or business usage. The actual storage location of each database partition is known to the database management system but is not something the database user need be concerned about.

When a database contains data that are included in another database, it is said to be **replicated**. Replicated databases are designed to speed the retrieval of data and, in turn, speed processing. Replication is particularly useful if certain parts of the database are required repeatedly for processing at different locations in a network. Avoiding the need for continual transmission of information requests and the subsequent transmission of the requested data means minimized delay and perhaps lower network or communications costs.

partitioning A method of database distribution in which different portions of the database reside at different nodes in the network.

replication A method of database distribution in which one database contains data that are included in another database.

Partitioning and Replication at Credit Lyonnais.   A good example of partitioning and replication in practice can be seen at Credit Lyonnais, one of the ten largest banks in the world. Headquartered in Paris, its more than 1,700 branch offices serve customers throughout France. The heart of the bank's operation is a multi-level distributed system that includes a distributed customer database, interconnected local area networks, and multiple mainframe data centers each running other banking databases.

Each of Credit Lyonnais's branch offices includes a LAN that links tellers, customer service representatives, loan officers, and the branch's managers. Each branch office is in turn linked to one of 18 regional centers, where midrange computers maintain a portion of a partitioned customer database (Figure 10.3). This relational database contains personal and financial profiles of the bank's customers in that region. Because the regional centers are linked to each other by multiple private digital communications lines, each center has access to database partitions at any of the other centers. (Prior to the creation of this system in 1992, each center maintained its own separate database. The databases were neither compatible with one another nor accessible to bank personnel outside of the region.)

In addition, each regional center is linked by communications lines to data centers running mainframe computers in the cities of Lyons, Tours, and Paris. These three centers have access to all the regional database partitions, store account balance information, and handle the processing of customer loan applications.

The combination of a multi-level distributed system and partitioned databases means that data and information are accessible to Credit Lyonnais personnel when

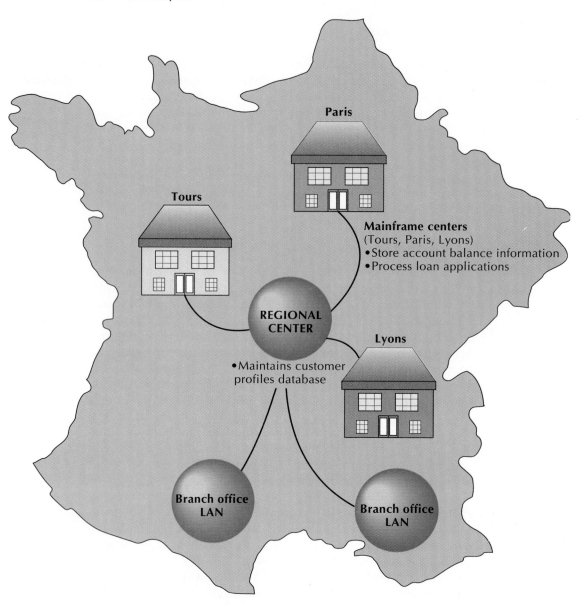

Paris

Tours

Mainframe centers
(Tours, Paris, Lyons)
•Store account balance information
•Process loan applications

**REGIONAL
CENTER**

Lyons

•Maintains customer
profiles database

**Branch office
LAN**

**Branch office
LAN**

FIGURE 10.3   Credit Lyonnais's Distributed Database System
Credit Lyonnais's distributed database system spans 1,700 branch offices, 18 regional centers, and 3 mainframe centers.

and where needed. This structure has an additional benefit: the potential to develop new business. For example, while tellers are assisting customers in depositing checks or making a withdrawal from a savings account, they can retrieve the customer's profile from the regional center. Should the customer have any questions about the transaction, the teller has the profile right there onscreen. This information enables the teller to determine whether the customer is a candidate for other bank services, which the teller can explain while serving the customer at the bank window. All parties benefit from the system: bank employees, managers, and customers. Employees make more efficient use of their time and spend less time shuffling papers and printed reports. Customers get better service, and managers spend more time on development of customer relations and new banking services, and less on handling special cases or managing cases of missing information.

Distribution Strategies.   Database designers decide to partition or replicate by choosing the strategy that best fits the manner in which an organization conducts its business. The two most common distribution strategies are geographic distribution and functional distribution.

In **geographic distribution strategy**, a database, or database partition, is located in a region where the data and information will be used most frequently. Credit Lyonnais, with its databases partitioned across 18 regions, uses a geographic distribution strategy. Each partition is accessible to bank employees in all the regions.

A **functional distribution strategy** stresses processing functions over physical location. For example, it is common for business units to distribute databases according to business functions. Figure 10.4 illustrates how a company might use a computer network to distribute the various components of its database. The sales database includes the names and addresses of current and potential customers, the manufacturing database holds the schedules for the production and assembly of finished goods, the inventory control database holds inventory records of materials, parts, and finished goods, and the accounting database holds records of revenues due the company and monies to be paid out.

Functional distribution strategies are effective only when communications networks interconnect each database or partition. If, for example, salespersons do not know what products are scheduled for manufacturing (information in the manufacturing database) or which customers' accounts are overdue (information in the accounting database), they will not be able to function effectively. Throughout the business world, executives, managers, and staff members are increasingly recognizing the interdependence between business functions. Multi-user networks make communication between the various business functions faster and easier than ever thought possible.

Designing a Distributed Database

In Chapter 1, we talked about the principle of high-tech–high-touch, which emphasizes the importance of considering the "people" side of information technology. In

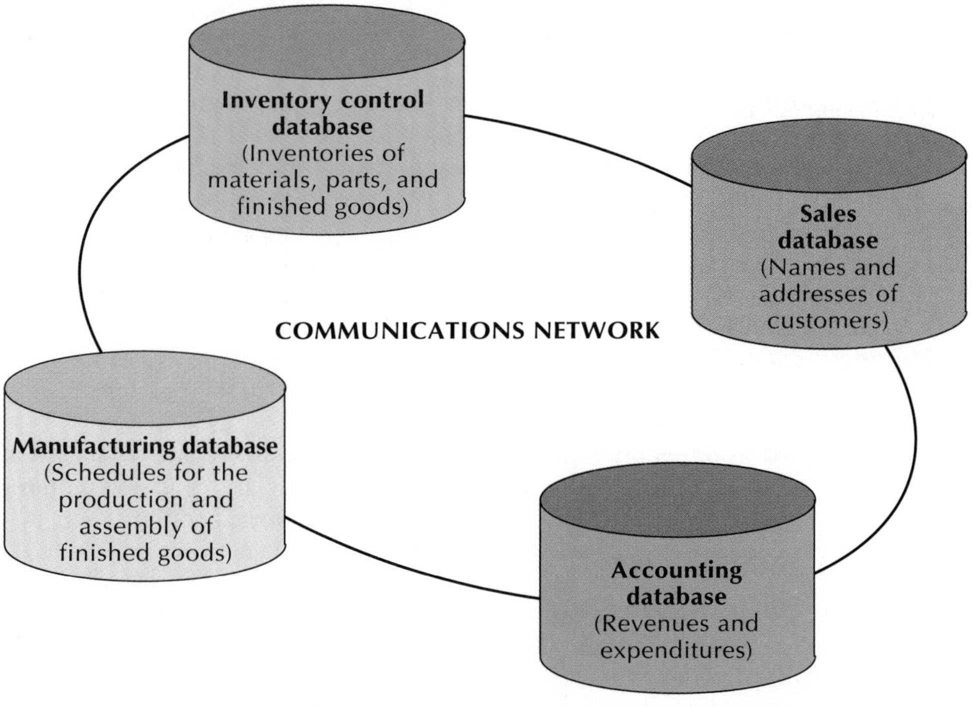

geographic distribution strategy A database distribution strategy in which the database is located in a region where the data and information are used most frequently.

functional distribution strategy A database distribution strategy in which the database is distributed according to business functions.

**FIGURE 10.4
Functional Distribution of a Database**
A functional distribution strategy stresses processing functions over physical location.

general, IT works best when it adjusts to people, not when people have to adjust to it. This simple principle of IT applies just as much to the design of distributed databases as it does to the design of software packages for individual users.

In general, the secret to making distributed databases effective is to keep their operational details invisible to their users. People using a database should be able to focus on the customer, supplier, or other business opportunity without having to worry about which database to use, how it is structured, or where it is located. The database management system should handle all the technical details behind the scenes. Users should not even be thinking about how the DBMS works. A **database directory**, a requirement for shared databases, keeps track of the location of data and information so that users do not have to. The database directory may be centralized, partitioned, or replicated.

Think, for example, about the vast public telephone network, which does an excellent job of applying the principle of high-tech–high-touch (see Chapter 1). To make a telephone call, all you need to do is pick up the receiver and dial a few numbers. The telephone network does the rest. It translates the number for processing by the network, retrieves routing information from the appropriate partition (the public phone system does not have a single centralized directory), uses the routing to connect you, and manages the entire process. The public phone system utilizes a distributed database in a way that makes everyone's life easier.

Other Design Factors.   In addition to the need for ease of use, distributed database designers are influenced by six factors:

- **Storage costs**—Duplicating data in multiple partitions increases storage costs. Hence designers must carefully monitor the volume of data in the distributed database and associated directories.
- **Processing costs**—Because the cost of processing data and information increases as the extent of database distribution increases, designers must ensure that the database is distributed only to those who will use it.
- **Communication costs**—The distribution of data increases the need for communication between nodes and, in turn, the costs of communication. The designer must ensure that these costs are justified by improvement in the business activities they support.
- **Retrieval and processing**—The location of data, coupled with the architecture of the communications network, determines response time (i.e., elapsed time due to retrieval and processing). Database designers must be aware that wider distribution may increase response time if data and information must be assembled from several remote locations. If the data needed most often are located at or near the node needing those data, retrieval and processing time may diminish substantially.
- **Reliability**—Designers must safeguard both the existence of and access to important databases. Higher levels of reliability often mean higher costs to duplicate database partitions, which allow retrieval of duplicated information maintained at another node if one node breaks down.
- **Frequency of updates and queries**—Designers generally locate databases at those locations that update the databases most frequently. If processing requires retrieval of data and information in response to queries, rather than just updates, local storage of a database or directory at a node may not be justified.

Although cost cutting is a fact of business life in the 1990s, merely minimizing costs is not enough to guarantee success. For a distributed database to be truly useful, the IT professional who designs it must weigh storage costs, processing speed, and relia-

database directory The component of a shared database that keeps track of data and information.

bility against the frequency of use for the database and the manner in which it is used (entering or changing data as opposed to retrieving data). The more frequently the database is used, the more important it is to evaluate these criteria properly.

Shared Database Structures

All databases, whether shared or not, must be defined. An important part of definition entails describing the data items and records comprising a database's structure.

Schema

The formal name for the definition of a database structure is its **schema**. The schema describes the names and attributes of each entity about which data are collected and stored. The schema provides a structure only and does not include data items (the customer's name or address, for example). You might think of the schema as a framework that outlines the structure of the database, showing the database's entities and the relations between them. Figure 10.2 shows the schema's relationship to other items in computer memory.

Each database has only one schema. Different databases use different schema.

schema The structure of a database.

Schema for Relational Databases.   As we discussed in Chapter 6, **relational databases** consist of data structured in a table format (a *relation*) consisting of rows and columns. The horizontal rows of the relation are called *records* or *tuples*. The vertical columns are called the *attributes*, or *fields*, and contain *data items* of a record. The term *record* can also refer to a grouping of data items that describes one specific *occurrence* of an entity. For example, a student database includes records of all relevant data for each student. Throughout this chapter, we'll use this second definition of record.

The schema for a relational database identifies the database by a unique name and describes the relations contained within the database. A relation in turn is defined by its data items, each of which is identified by a name, type (such as numeric or text), and length specification. In this manner, the schema gives a distinct structure to the relational database.

relational database A database in which the data are structured in a table format consisting of rows and columns.

Schema for Object Oriented Databases.   A newer type of database that is emerging alongside relational databases is the **object oriented database**. An **object** is a focal point about which data and information are collected. Hence, customers and orders—items we called "entities" when discussing rational databases—are also objects. Object oriented database systems store data and information about these objects.

Data and information can be stored about both entities and objects. However, unlike relational databases, object oriented databases store **actions**, instructions telling the database how to process the object to produce specific information.

The U.S. brokerage and investment firm Shearson Lehman Brothers has created an object oriented database as the basis for many of its business activities. In the database are account objects (customers); contract objects (management agreements between Shearson Lehman and firms that have signed investment contracts); and security objects (the descriptive details of stocks, bonds, and stock options). Each object contains the descriptive data you would expect (names, addresses, prices, and so on). Each also contains information describing when and how to purchase an investment instrument. Thus an individual account (the object) can buy a security, just as if a broker were initiating the action, but without human intervention.

object oriented database A database that stores data and information about objects.

object A focal point about which data and information are collected. Used in object oriented databases.

action An instruction that tells a database how to process an object to produce specific information.

Object oriented databases offer the capability to store more sophisticated types of data and information than relational databases do. For example, such complex information as three-dimensional diagrams, animated video clips, and photographs do not fit easily within the row and column structure of relational databases. However, because both data and processing instructions are part of object descriptions, such information can be handled in an object oriented database.

Both U.S.-based Boeing Aircraft Co. and England's British Aerospace Ltd. use object oriented databases to maintain data about the design, components, and maintenance of their multimillion dollar aircrafts. These object databases store detailed schematic drawings of the planes' interiors, exteriors, and electronic components, including their extensive cable and wiring systems. Manufacturing and cost information is also included in the databases.

Before moving to object oriented databases, the companies maintained their data on groups of separate databases. This system was costly and inefficient because it was difficult for designers and engineers to get a complete picture of the repercussions of a particular action. For example, if the cost of a component changed, a project engineer would first have to search the component database to see where and how many of that component was used. Then the engineer had to search the order database to see if the component were used in a specific aircraft configuration—and the manufacturing database to retrieve construction and assembly details related to the component. The process was time-consuming and prone to error. Today, drawings, cost, manufacturing, and assembly details regarding the component are all combined in the object database. Data and information are available much more quickly, and the cost of managing data and information is lower.

Other Database Schema.   Two other types of database schemas are worthy of mention here. *Hierarchical databases* store data in the form of a tree, where the relationship among data items is one-to-many (that is, one data item can be linked to several other data items). In *network databases*, the relationship among the data items can be either one-to-many or many-to-many (that is, several data items can be linked to several other data items). Detailed explanations of these types of databases are beyond the scope of this discussion; it is enough to say here that these databases store data in a way that makes access to them faster for certain types of queries and slower for others.

Reality Check.   Object oriented technology promises to be the basis for many types of applications in the future. The object oriented concept of combining data and processing instructions is now being embedded in programs (object oriented programs) and application development procedures (object oriented design), as well as in databases.

We can draw an analogy between objects and Lego blocks, the plastic building blocks that snap together. Each Lego can be attached to any other Lego to build any type of structure, whether a house, barn, skyscraper, motor vehicle, or medieval castle. If the builder, young or old, decides part way through the process to change the structure's design, he or she can either add more Lego blocks to the current design or reassemble the blocks in a different way. Objects can be used in a similar way. Although objects are different on the inside, they are like Legos on the outside in that an assortment of objects can be assembled in many different ways. Applications can be created by connecting individual objects to create a desirable result, quickly and efficiently.

Views

When a database is created, it is designed and stored according to a designer-determined structure of relations. As we noted earlier in this chapter, however, users of shared databases often want to organize the data differently from the way in which they are stored. Database management systems provide a way to address this need.

Users who want to organize data and information differently than they are stored in the database can use views. A **view** is a subset of one or more databases, created either by extracting copies of records from a database or by merging copies of records from multiple databases.[1] Like databases themselves, views have names and records comprised of data items. As Figure 10.5 shows, multiple views of data can be extracted from the database and used in any application, including calculation, sorting, and generation of reports and other output.

In one sense, a view is simply a logical grouping of data. It gives the appearance that data have been moved or combined to meet processing requirements, although the database's physical structure (schema) has not been altered. Savvy marketers have begun purchasing large databases and creating views to help them target advertising campaigns, as the Opportunities Box on page 400 titled "Database Marketing Opens New Doors" explores in detail.

view A subset of one or more databases, created either by extracting copies of records from a database or by merging copies of records from multiple databases.

[1]In some organizations, views are called subschemas—subsets of the schema. In effect, subschemas (views) partition the database among applications.

FIGURE 10.5 Views Extracted from Relational Database
Data from a relation can be extracted and used in many applications.

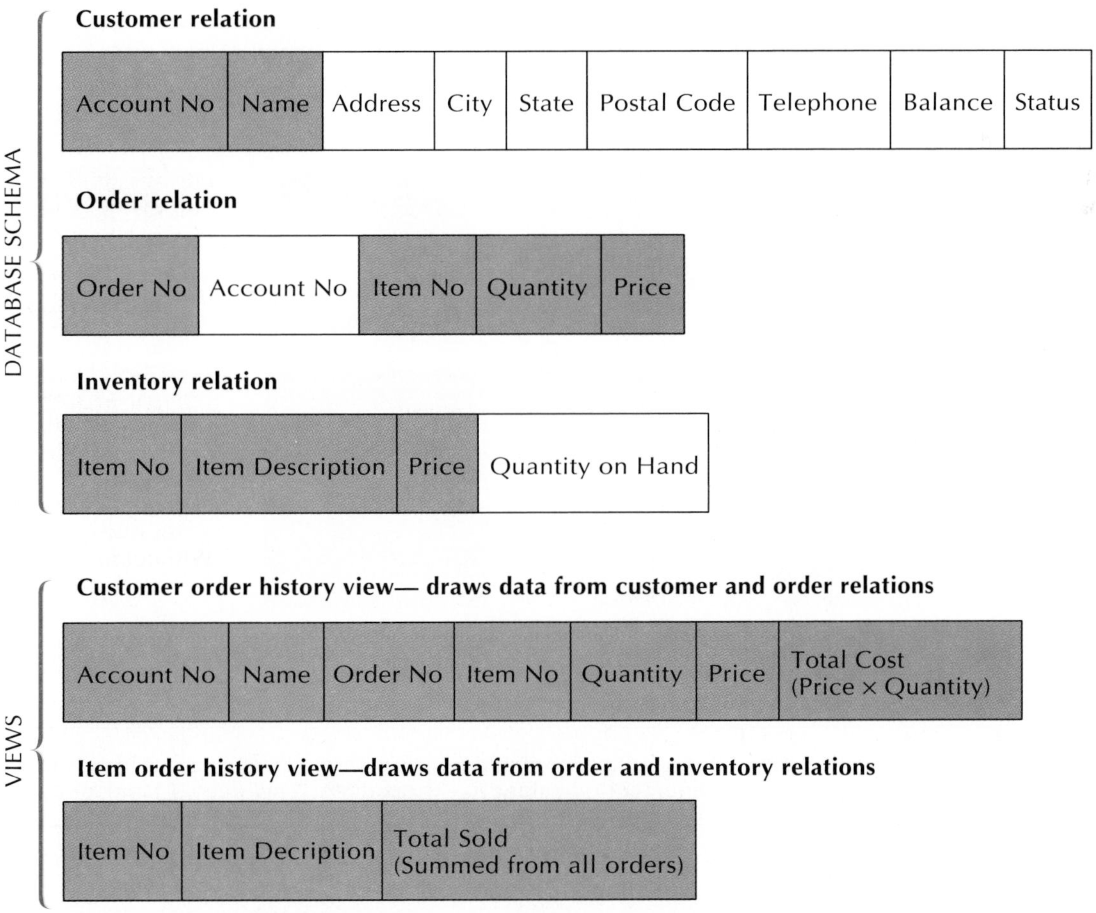

Viewing capabilities provide many benefits to business users. Among these:

- Views allow users to examine data in different ways without changing the physical structure of the database.
- Users can make changes in the data in a view while leaving the data in the database in its original form, unaltered.
- Database security is maintained because individuals and applications can be kept away from sensitive data, processing from the views rather than the database itself. Sensitive or protected data are not included in a view.
- Views shield users from changes in the physical database, such as when records are restructured to reside in a different location or in a different sequence.

Views from multiple databases can be combined to meet business requirements. The State of Georgia Department of Revenue, for example, has linked several different databases in an effort to collect the state sales and withholding taxes owed by businesses. During processing of income-tax refund checks, department staff members can use personal and business ID numbers to link the records for an individual's business income tax, the sales tax received from the business, and the withholding tax received from the company's employees, even though each database is maintained by a separate system and a different agency (Figure 10.6). When the Department of Revenue's computer determines that a refund is due to an individual, it can check with the other databases before cutting the check. If it finds a match with a record describing sales tax owed by the same person through his or her business, it can automatically apply the refund against the sales tax debt and at the same time send the individual a message saying, "We have determined that you still owe sales tax and have applied your income tax refund against that obligation." Without the ability to interrelate databases, many sales tax obligations would be more difficult to collect.

FIGURE 10.6
Using a View to Span Multiple Databases at the State of Georgia Department of Revenue
By linking several databases, the State of Georgia Department of Revenue can collect taxes owed before it issues refund checks.

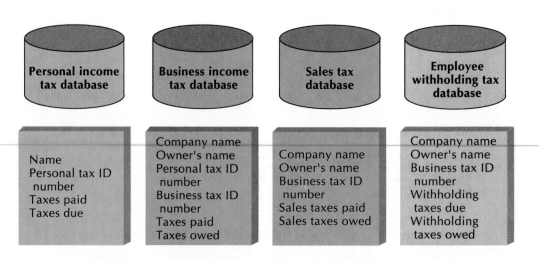

Department of Revenue cross–database view, created by using common data fields of personal tax ID number and business tax ID number

Name	Personal tax ID number	Business tax ID number	Amount of refund*	Business tax due*	Sales tax due*	Withholding tax due*

* Value determined by calculation

Indexes

An important advantage offered by databases and a DBMS is flexibility of retrieval. Views provide users with a way to assemble data from different databases. Indexes make possible the retrieval of data in different sequences and on the basis of different data items.

An **index** is a data file that contains identifying information about each record (the record key) and its location in storage. The **record key** is a designated field used to distinguish one record from another. For example, the record key by which university students are typically identified is a unique student ID number. Each number is unique in that it is assigned to only one student.

A DBMS is able to automatically build and use indexes according to specifications prepared by the database administrator, whose role we discuss later in this chapter. When an application, by providing the record key, requests the DBMS to retrieve a record, the DBMS quickly searches the index to find the right record key. It then accesses the database to locate and retrieve the record so that it can be processed by the application.

As Figure 10.7 shows, the index and search process take place "behind the scenes" as part of processing, so neither the index nor the search is visible to an individual user. Information about the student can be obtained by requesting the database to locate and retrieve the record for the person having a specific ID number. To speed retrieval, the database system searches an index containing all student ID numbers and location information for each record associated with the student's ID, subsequently retrieving data and information directly from the specified location. Indexes eliminate the need to search all records in a database to find the one needed.

The Fed Ex Index. Federal Express Corp., the Memphis, Tennessee–based overnight shipping company, uses an index to keep track of the location of each package shipped through its system. The company's central database at corporate headquarters in Memphis is accessible to all the company's drivers and telephone agents throughout the world. When a customer calls in to inquire about the location of a package, Fed Ex can provide a speedy response. Here's how they do it.

> **index** A data file that contains identifying information about each record and its location in storage.
>
> **record key** In a database, a designated field used to distinguish one record from another.

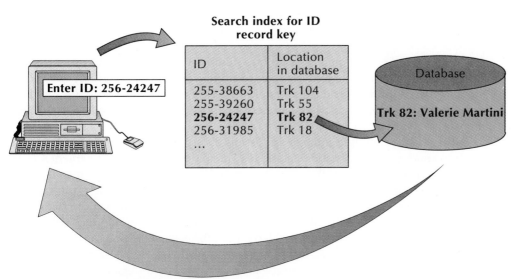

**FIGURE 10.7
Using an Index to Retrieve Data**
An index uses a record key—in this case, a student ID number—to locate and retrieve a record for processing.

Database Marketing Opens New Doors

IF YOU'RE A MARKETING WHIZ AND YOU CAN COMMUNICATE WITH database pros, you could have a very bright future in database marketing. Database marketing, also known as "target marketing" or "micro-marketing," uses views and indexes to manipulate existing databases and to find new customers and new selling opportunities.

Database marketing isn't a new phenomenon. American Express, Citibank NA, The Reader's Digest Association, and Spiegel are just a few of the pioneers who have been using the technique since the 1970s. What is new is the growing number of companies that are spending more on database marketing and less on traditional mass marketing.

This explosive growth can be traced to three trends that came together in the 1990s. The first is the splintering of the "mass market" into segments beyond the reach of a TV commercial. The second is the persistent low rate of economic growth, which has forced companies to take a hard look at the way they spend their marketing dollars. The third, and perhaps most important, trend is the increasing availability of databases containing consumer data and sophisticated new software that can extract marketing information for nontechnical users.

One of the biggest suppliers of consumer data is the U.S. Census Bureau. It is now selling sets of CD-ROM disks containing street maps showing economic and population data detailed down to city blocks. Marketers can feed these data into mapping software, which manipulates one or more databases to produce color-coded maps of the underlying data. Levi Strauss, for instance, is using mapping software to identify the best merchandise mix for each of its stores.

Another major source of consumer data is the point-of-sale scanner data collected in retail stores by A.C. Neilsen Corp. and Information Resources, two companies that specialize in collecting and organizing data. By analyzing scanner-based consumer data, a brand manager at Procter & Gamble realized that the most loyal customers of Oil of Olay products were older women. The result? An advertising campaign designed to attract new customers among teenagers and young women. In another division, P&G marketers correlated weather data with the sales of its cough and cold remedies; the resulting information helped them create special promotions and discounts that increased sales.

Of course, many companies already own a valuable database, created whenever they record a business transaction or record the customer information supplied on warranty cards. With the help of add-in database software, marketers can analyze these transaction databases to identify opportunities for reinforcing customer loyalty or increasing sales. Consider the strategy of Brady's, a San Diego–based chain of men's clothing stores, which asks customers to complete a card containing size and style preferences. Salespeople use the resulting database to identify customers who should be reminded about sales. The same database is used to be sure every shopper gets a birthday card containing a discount coupon worth $15. The result? Even though Brady's has cut its advertising budget by 60%, sales have increased by 10% and the chain grew from two to five stores in two years.

Source: Art based on figure in "Targeters Are Playing Consumer Match Game," by Nancy Ryan, *The Chicago Tribune,* December 22, 1991, Sect. 7, pp. 1, 5. Used by permission.

Each package is identified by a unique number (called an "airbill number"), by the name of the individual and company shipping the package, and by the recipient. Two million airbills enter the system every day. For this reason, a huge database (60 billion bytes) must be searched whenever a customer calls to ask, "Has my package been delivered?".

Fed Ex creates multiple indexes for its airbills database, one each for the airbill number, sender's name, sender's company, recipient's name, and recipient's company. When a customer calls with an inquiry, a customer service rep asks the caller for the airbill number. If the customer has this number handy, the rep can enter it into the computer and immediately display the shipment information on the video screen. If the caller does not have the airbill number, the rep will ask for shipper or recipient information and have the DBMS search through the appropriate index to obtain the desired information. The system also checks the name phonetically in case the correct spelling was not provided (Andersen, Anderson, and Andersson sound the same, for example). There is no question that DBMS capabilities help Federal Express give its customers the service they expect when, as the company's slogan says, "It's absolutely, positively gotta be there overnight."

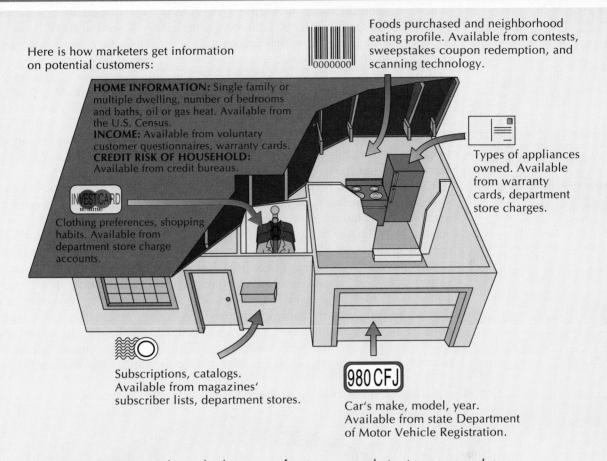

Here is how marketers get information on potential customers:

Foods purchased and neighborhood eating profile. Available from contests, sweepstakes coupon redemption, and scanning technology.

HOME INFORMATION: Single family or multiple dwelling, number of bedrooms and baths, oil or gas heat. Available from the U.S. Census.
INCOME: Available from voluntary customer questionnaires, warranty cards.
CREDIT RISK OF HOUSEHOLD: Available from credit bureaus.

Types of appliances owned. Available from warranty cards, department store charges.

Clothing preferences, shopping habits. Available from department store charge accounts.

Subscriptions, catalogs. Available from magazines' subscriber lists, department stores.

Car's make, model, year. Available from state Department of Motor Vehicle Registration.

Target marketing Modern technology is transforming mass marketing into target-marketing. By utilizing information from a variety of sources, companies can focus their sales efforts on specific consumer groups. Reprinted by permission: Tribune Media Services.

✔ Reality Check. Federal Express's tracking system uses neither an uncommon type of information technology nor custom-made hardware or software. Rather, the company is relying on the same information technology available to any business or organization. Nonetheless, Fed Ex is providing a combination of the good service and reliable information that its customers want.

The point to be taken from this example is one that you've seen before. The benefits of information technology do not come from IT itself. Instead, they come from the manner in which the technology is used. Federal Express's success comes from identifying its customers' needs and then using IT effectively to meet them. Computers, communications, and know-how are all equally important.

Of course, you have to keep moving ahead or competitors will catch up. Federal Express is receiving strong challenges from UPS and other competitors. In some areas, its competitors have taken the lead in use of IT. ■

Client/Server Computing

Businesses should avoid having separate databases, created and maintained by different application systems. *Islands of automation*, a term of the IT trade used to describe situations in which databases and applications cannot share related data, should also be avoided.

The sharing of data can be facilitated through file server computing (see Chapter 9). A **file server** is a computer containing files (including databases) that are available to all users interconnected on a local area network. Workstations connected to the LAN can request and receive data and information from the server. Figure 10.8 provides a review of how file server computing works. Success with file servers, coupled with advances in desktop computing capabilities, has led to client/server computing.

Client/server computing combines distributed processing and multi-user systems with database systems. All data and information retrieval requests and responses in client/server computing pass over the network. As Figure 10.9 shows, client/server computing can use a multi-level, distributed architecture to retrieve information from databases outside of the user's immediate network.

Client/server computing differs from host-based computing (see Chapter 9) in several ways. In a host-based architecture, data and information are stored, and applications run, on a central computer. People log on to the computer using a dumb terminal (or a microcomputer used as a dumb terminal) and run applications by a teleprocessing link. The terminal itself adds nothing to the processing.

In client/server computing, however, individual desktop computers play a significant role in processing. In essence, the application is running on the user's

file server A computer containing files that are available to all users interconnected on a local area network.

client/server computing A type of computing in which all data and information retrieval requests and responses pass over a network. Much of the processing is performed on the server, with the results of processing transmitted to the client.

FIGURE 10.8   **Data and Information Retrieval Using File Server Computing**

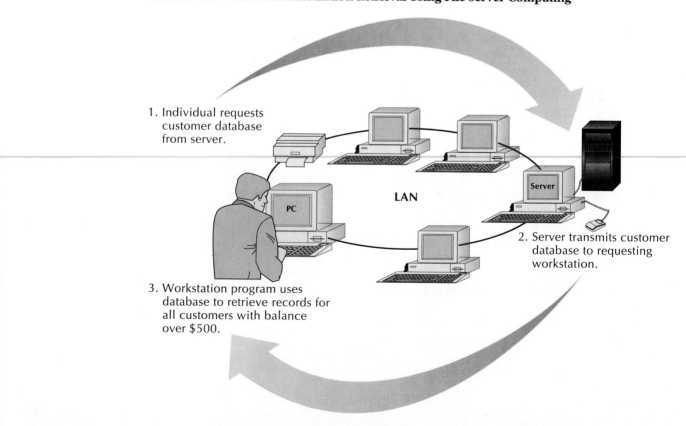

1. Individual requests customer database from server.

2. Server transmits customer database to requesting workstation.

3. Workstation program uses database to retrieve records for all customers with balance over $500.

LAN

PC

Server

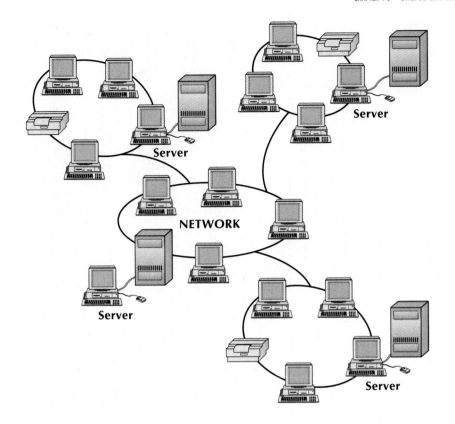

FIGURE 10.9
Multi-level Client/Server Architecture
Client/server company can use a multi-level, distributed architecture to retrieve information from databases outside of the user's immediate network.

desktop rather than on a remote computer. The **client**—that is, the desktop workstation—plays the lead role, initiating and driving the processing by requesting selected data and some processing from the main computer, or **server**. Once the server has performed the requested tasks, the requested data and information and the results of processing are transmitted back to the client.

client In client/server computing, a desktop workstation.

server In client/server computing, the main computer that performs procesing and transmits the results back to a client.

Client/Server Computing at Burlington.   Burlington Coat Factory, headquartered in Burlington, New Jersey, operates more than 200 retail outlets throughout the United States and Mexico. The company relies on a client/server computing architecture to link all its stores and distribution centers to headquarters. Point-of-sale cash registers are interconnected through a LAN to a powerful workstation that acts as a store processor (Figure 10.10). The store processor is a file server for the cash registers, providing product and pricing information while capturing each consumer's purchase for inventory information. Department managers needing inventory, sales, or other information interact with the system by means of PCs. Each store processor is also a communications gateway to the central host computer in New Jersey.

Burlington's headquarters system is comprised of a battery of processors that receive information from stores via a satellite-based communications network. The headquarters system processes incoming transaction data, updates company databases, redirects transactions—such as VISA/MasterCard authorization requests—to destinations outside the company, and accepts responses.

Burlington's client/server system provides rapid response to processing requests while linking different IT devices together, within individual stores and across the country. In addition, the system has an added benefit: it is extremely reliable because there are many different components and links in the network, making it unlikely that processing in the Burlington system as a whole will fail.

b) The host computer receives information from the individual stores and processes incoming data, updates company databases, and redirects transactions. The same information can then be used to automatically replenish stock at an individual store. The host computer even prints out the price tags and mailing labels.

FIGURE 10.10
Client/Server Computing at Burlington Coat Factory
Burlington Coat Factory relies on client/server computing to link more than 200 stores throughout the United States and Mexico.

a) Point-of-sale terminals at Burlington's stores are interconnected through a LAN to a workstation that acts as a store processor. Each store processor is also a gateway to the central host computer in New Jersey.

The Benefits of Client/Server Computing

Client/server computing offers several benefits to its users. Most important, the server processes database requests and the client takes the results and works with them. Thus, with client/server computing, as much of the processing as possible is performed on the server before the requested data and information are transmitted to the client. This means that specific information, *not* complete files or large sections of databases, are transmitted to the client.

Figure 10.11 shows how this process works. When a bank employee at a client computer wants to send a personalized letter to customers with balances over $500, the employee sends a request from the workstation program to the server asking the system to review the customer database. The server processes the database to identify those customers meeting the $500 criterion, then transmits only the records of those customers with balances over $500 to the client workstation. The employee's program extracts name, address, and balance information from the data and inserts them into a customized letter prepared through the word processing program on the client workstation. Without the shared processing between client and server, either entire databases would be copied from one system to another or repeated requests would be necessary to retrieve names and addresses.

In addition to saving time and money, client/server computing can make users more productive by ensuring their access to the information they need when they need it. Client/server computing allows many users to share common data resources, including files and databases as well as computer storage and printers. Sharing data and information eliminates the need for personal management of data and/or peripheral devices. Finally, client/server computing allows the integration of geographically distributed users and computing resources into a cohesive computer and communications environment. All of this means faster access to data and information, better service for customers, quicker responses to changes in the busi-

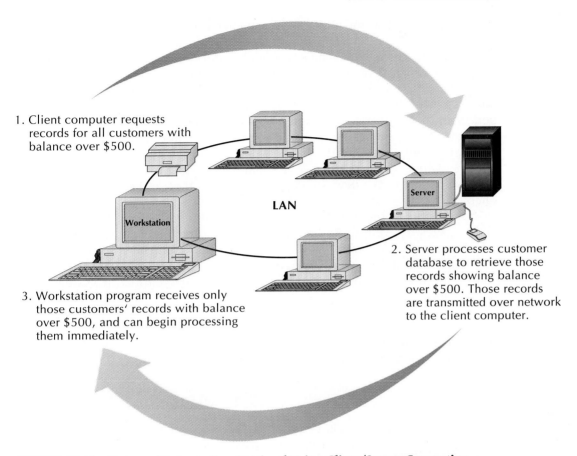

1. Client computer requests records for all customers with balance over $500.

LAN

Workstation

Server

2. Server processes customer database to retrieve those records showing balance over $500. Those records are transmitted over network to the client computer.

3. Workstation program receives only those customers' records with balance over $500, and can begin processing them immediately.

FIGURE 10.11   Data and Information Retrieval Using Client/Server Computing
In client/server computing, specific information—not complete files or large sections of databases—are transmitted from the server to the client.

ness environment, more efficient business processes, fewer errors, and in general, higher levels of productivity.

For more information on the best-known client/server system, the Internet, see the Photo Essay at the end of this chapter.

Client/Server Computing in Action: AMR Corp. and CSX Corp.   Frequently when companies turn cargo over to a shipper for transport to a customer, they lose contact with the goods. Unlike Federal Express, most shipping companies do not have a computerized tracking system that allows them to retrieve shipping and delivery information online and to know the exact location of the boat, plane, or railcar carrying their goods. AMR Corp.—the parent company of American Airlines—and CSX Corp., one of the largest land, ocean, and rail cargo shippers in the world, have teamed up to remedy this problem by developing the Encompass system for tracking the movement of freight worldwide. With the Encompass system, the status of any shipment can be determined from the time the goods leave the shipper's freight dock until they arrive at their final destination.

Putting the Encompass system in place meant linking manufacturers, shippers, and third parties worldwide, each of which had developed its own computing and communications systems and its own databases. To link all these different systems, the designers of Encompass turned to client/server computing

(Figure 10.12). AMR and CSX provide their customers (clients) with software that can be used on the clients' computers to request tracking information from servers in the Encompass network. Clients can book shipments, determine the route over which their freight will travel, manage their inventory in transit by determining its location and scheduled arrival dates, evaluate their own shipping activities through an operations analysis module, and even evaluate the performance of the transportation companies. They can also prepare essential shipping documents (air bills, shipment notices, purchase orders, shipping instructions, invoices, and the like). Online databases, high-speed communications networks, and powerful servers make it possible for all these activities to occur in real time. (Review the definitions of real time and batch processing in Chapter 2, if necessary.)

The benefits of the Encompass system to AMR and CSX are enormous. Like Fed Ex, they are offering a capability that is attracting new customers, thus increasing both companies' business. While other companies try to catch up, AMR and CSX will be staying several steps ahead by adding additional features and capabilities. People know-how leads to the creation of systems like Encompass.

CRITICAL CONNECTION 2
Client/Server System Speeds Information Flow at Pitney Bowes

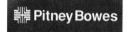

For Pitney Bowes, it was a common—but frustrating—problem. Under its old paper-based system, engineers in the Mail Systems unit spent too much time tracking down design engineers with their questions. (The engineers were scattered among five sites in Fairfield County, Connecticut.) Or the manufacturing department would find out—too late—that it was working with an outdated set of engineering drawings. The resulting delays cut deeply into the bottom line.

That's why Pitney Bowes is setting up a *concurrent engineering system* that will let all its engineers work simultaneously. The heart of the system is a shared database that contains a single consistent and current set of engineering drawings, specifications, and production schedule for each product. This database is maintained on "master servers" that are linked by fiber optics to "client" workstations on the engineers' desks. Now a design engineer can download preliminary specs directly to manufacturing and ask to have a prototype, or working model, created from the electronic specs. If a problem is found, the engineers can call up the same drawing on their respective screens and work out a solution over the phone. With this new system, the design cycle for some products has dropped from five or six weeks to just two or three days.

■ People

The people who work with databases are either applications programmers, who embed database interaction instructions in application programs, and end-users, who interact directly with the database using applications that they have created or that have been developed for them. Two types of IT professionals closely

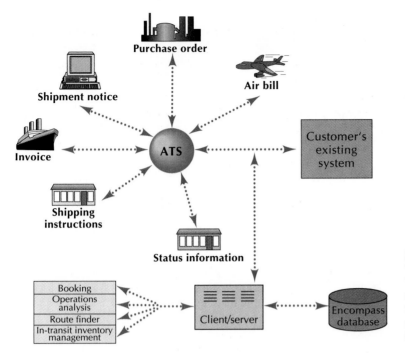

FIGURE 10.12
The Encompass System
With the Encompass system, shippers and carriers can determine the status of their shipments from the time the goods leave the dock until they arrive at their final destination.
Source: *Encompass*, AMR & CRX Corp.

connected to database development and management are database administrators and systems programmers.

Database Administrator

The IT professional with the most extensive database management responsibilities is the **database administrator (DBA)**, sometimes called the **data administrator**. The database administrator is responsible for managing all the activities and procedures (discussed later in this chapter) related to an organization's database. In some organizations, the database administrator is an individual. In others, a team of people fulfills this administration function. Each team member is responsible for some aspect of the data administration procedures. For more details on the DBA's daily activities, see the People box titled "Database Administrators: Unsung Heroes of the IT World."

database administrator (DBA) or **data administrator**
The IT professional responsible for managing all the activities and procedures related to an organization's database.

Systems Programmer

Organizations that use large, complex databases may work with a **systems programmer**, a software and hardware specialist who works with the physical details of the database and the computer's operating system. The systems programmer organizes the data on magnetic disk (or other storage medium) according to a structure determined by the database designer. The systems programmer also determines the optimal way of arranging records and objects in storage, and creates indexes and other devices for retrieval in conjunction with guidelines established by the database administrator.

systems programmer A software and hardware specialist who works with the physical details of a database and the computer's operating system.

Database administrators' primary responsibility is managing the database. This task occupies virtually all of their workday. Systems programmers spend only a portion of their time on database-related activities. The rest of the time they spend working with the operating system, managing the network, and handling other types of hardware and software matters.

PEOPLE

Database Administrators: Unsung Heroes of the IT World

"WE'RE SORT OF THE ENGINE THAT RUNS EVERYTHING," says Marilyn Cumberland, manager of the data administration/computer center at COMSAT Corp. in Washington, DC. Her comment underlines a basic reality of life on the DBA staff: Everyone takes her work for granted—until something goes wrong. And then they want it fixed—pronto.

This is especially true for the DBA staff charged with maintaining database security. "Data is a corporate asset," says Rod Horning, manager of information technology and security at Kelly-Springfield Tire Co. in Maryland, and its keepers need to be vigilant in protecting it from competitors, computer criminals, disgruntled employees, and even innocent bumblers.

That's why Horning and other database managers say they look for employees who have at least two to three years' experience as a systems programmer. "Programmers that come from the application side know what it is they're trying to secure, and they know how the operating systems work together," agrees Wendy Carr, IS manager of database security for Fresno County in Fresno, California. In addition, these seasoned professionals are able to handle the stress of troubleshooting end-user problems while keeping up with new technology.

But the DBA job isn't all hard work and no rewards. In fact, the salary range is one of the highest in the IT world. And, says Mike Ewanowski, a database administrator at Emory University, "It could be a springboard into upper management because you tend to see the big picture and deal with so many other users."

Sources: Leslie Goff, "Database Administrators: Super Stress Handlers," *Computerworld*, November 16, 1992, p. 179; and Kelly E. Sewell, "Administrators Protect Data from the Unauthorized," *Computerworld*, January 18, 1993, p. 71.

Marilyn Cumberland, data administrator at COMSAT Corporation, says about her job, "There's always something new and always a challenge. You have a new set of problems with every system you design, and you have to be able to anticipate them."

▪ Procedures

A *procedure* is a step-by-step process or set of instructions for accomplishing specific results. The procedures associated with databases are grouped under the general heading of **database administration procedures**.

database administration procedures The procedures associated with managing a database.

Database Administration Procedures

database administration The management of a database.

Database administration means managing the database. This entails doing what is necessary to develop and safeguard the database in the most beneficial way.

Procedures for data administration include six areas of responsibility:

- **Database planning.** Like any valuable resource, a database must be planned. Planning includes being aware of and understanding business needs and user requirements, selecting the DBMS, developing standards for usage, and outlining security strategies.
- **Database design.** To be as useful as possible, the database must be carefully designed. Designers define the records and objects—including the schema, data names, and length specifications—that comprise the database.
- **Database creation.** The database design is only a framework. The database becomes a reality when data are entered into the design and saved on a storage device.
- **Database maintenance.** As users' needs and demands change, the database may need adjustment. New records or objects may be added or changes may be made to the existing structures. Database maintenance pertains to the *structure* and *organization* of the database. Maintenance of the *contents* of individual records (the data items) is the responsibility of those using the database, not the database administrator.
- **Analysis of usage.** Managing a database means monitoring how and when it is used. If data and information retrieval patterns change, the database administrator may decide that maintenance is needed to restructure the database to meet new user requests.
- **Creation and monitoring of security procedures.** The existence and integrity of the database must be safeguarded at all times. Developing, implementing, and monitoring security procedures are all important parts of database administration.

Much of a database's value comes form the procedures the database administrator uses to develop and maintain the database. These responsibilities are quite different from those of individual users or systems programmers.

"Re-Engineering" Project to Rebuild Confidence in Blood Bank

Setting up a distributed database involves more than just collecting a pool of data. You may also need to "re-engineer" your procedures after they've been instituted to be sure they reflect current goals and information needs. Just ask the American Red Cross, which provides more than half the U.S. blood supply and is in the middle of a massive re-engineering project with a budget of $120 million. The need for the project came to light in 1990, when the Food and Drug Administration (FDA) shut down two regional blood centers and an investigation confirmed FDA charges that sloppy record keeping, computer errors, and poor communications were complicating the task of protecting blood recipients against disease.

In its defense, the Red Cross was quick to describe the new complexities of operating a blood bank. By 1990, for example, it was testing every unit of blood for ten different diseases. That meant that, between 1985 and 1990, Red Cross labs had had to conduct 100 million more tests than in the previous five years. To complicate the situation, 54 regional Red Cross centers weren't using the same procedures, the same blood-testing software application, or a network to facilitate communications. Clearly, changes were needed—fast.

Concurrency Procedures

Whenever more than one user has access to a database, there is a chance that several persons will want to access the database simultaneously. With **concurrent data sharing**, users are allowed to do exactly that. With **nonconcurrent data sharing**, individuals can use the data in a database only when no other person or application is processing the data. The database is shared, but not *simultaneously* by different people.

In developing a database or an application, a systems designer or database administrator must determine what type of sharing will be permitted. If two or more people want to retrieve and change existing records simultaneously, the result can be chaotic. To understand why this is so, consider the following example of concurrent data sharing:

1. Travel Agent A retrieves from the database a copy of the inventory record for seats available on Flight 10 to London on November 28. The record shows him that five coach seats remain available for sale.

2. At virtually the same instant, Travel Agent B retrieves a copy of the same record, wishing to book seats for her clients, who are traveling to London on November 28.

3. Both travel agents are proceeding based on the availability of five seats. Neither travel agent knows that another agent is using a copy of the record or preparing to books seats on the flight.

4. Travel Agent B's customers give the go-ahead for the reservation first, so B books seats for her four customers. The database system writes the change into the database, noting the names of the customers and adjusting seat inventory to show one remaining seat.

5. Travel Agent A's screen still shows that there are five seats available. A wishes to book a party of three for the flight to London. If the database allows him to do so, and then shows two remaining seats available (the original five minus the three sold by A), two passengers of the seven booked by A and B would be left without seats.

Systems developers can use several different strategies to avoid this type of situation. First, they can choose not to allow concurrent sharing. Second, they can decide to partition the database, with each partition assigned to one user or group of users. If different users access separate portions of the database independently, concurrent data sharing will be avoided. Third, systems developers can partition database processing. This strategy entails assigning the database to a particular user for a period of time (perhaps mornings rather than afternoons, or odd-numbered days rather than even-numbered days).

Travel agents need access to flight information 24 hours a day, so none of these strategies would be right for them. When concurrent data sharing is necessary, the proper procedures must be developed. The most common concurrency procedure involves sharing achieved through **record locking**. When a record is locked, another user cannot access or alter the record. The record is unlocked when the initial user finishes processing the record. Locking and unlocking occur automatically. Today's airline reservations systems use record locking to ensure that seats are not sold more than once. In the above example, Travel Agents A and B cannot sell the same seats on the same flight simultaneously. While one agent is assigning the seats, the other is locked from entering a sales transaction for the seats.

concurrent data sharing A database procedure that allows several users to access the database simultaneously.

nonconcurrent data sharing A database procedure that allows individuals to access a database only when no other person or application is processing the data.

record locking A concurrency procedure that prohibits another user from accessing or altering a record that is in use.

File-level sharing is also common in some systems that store unstructured information. For example, in a word processing or spreadsheet system, the principal document processed is a file. If file locking is specified by the designer, only one user or application will be able to use a specific document at a given moment.

Whenever record locking is used, there is a chance that two or more users will find themselves in a **deadlock**, a situation in which each user of the database is waiting for the others to free (unlock) the record. Although deadlocks are rare, the DBA must develop procedures for dealing with them should they occur. Typically, the solution is for the DBMS to detect the occurrence of the deadlock and issue a message to the users asking them to release the record or reenter the details of their transaction.

deadlock A situation in which each user of a database is waiting for the others to unlock a record.

A Final Word

Shared and distributed data create many opportunities for businesses to serve customers and conduct day-to-day activities. However, as in all other areas of information technology, computers and communications systems provide only potential capabilities. It is up to the firm's people to determine how and when IT can be used effectively and to achieve desired results.

SUMMARY OF LEARNING OBJECTIVES

1 Identify the reasons organizations choose to share databases and the functions of a database management system. Organizations choose to share databases because data collection and maintenance are very expensive. Managing these data effectively entails making sure all members of an organization who need them have access to a consistent set of data. The five functions of a database management system (DBMS) are: integrating databases, reducing redundancy, sharing information, maintaining integrity, and enabling database evolution.

2 Differentiate between shared and distributed databases. A *shared database* is a database shared among many users and applications. A *distributed database* is a shared database whose data reside on more than one system in a network. These data can be accessed, retrieved, or updated from any node in the network.

3 Explain the difference between relational and object oriented databases and their uses in business. *Relational databases* consist of data structured in a table format consisting of rows and columns. *Object oriented databases* store data and information about objects. Unlike relational databases, object oriented databases can store *actions*—

instructions telling the database how to process the object to produce specific information. Object oriented databases offer the capability to store more sophisticated types of data and information than relational databases do.

4 Describe the differences between schemas, views, and indexes. A *schema* is the structure of a database. A *view* is a subset of one or more databases, created either by extracting copies of records from a database or by merging copies of records from multiple databases. An *index* is a data file that contains identifying information about each record and its location in storage.

5 Discuss the benefits of client/server computing. Client/server computing combines distributed processing and multi-user systems with database systems. All data and information retrieval requests and responses in client/server computing pass over the network. This offers several benefits to users. Because much of the processing is performed on the server, specific information—rather than complete files—are transmitted to the client. In addition to saving time and money, client/server computing makes users more productive by ensuring their access to information when they need it.

6 **Distinguish between a database administrator and a systems programmer.** The IT professional with the most extensive database management responsibilities is the *database administrator (DBA)*, who is responsible for managing all of the activities and procedures related to an organization's database. A *systems programmer* is a software and hardware specialist who works with the physical details of the database.

7 **Discuss database administration procedures and concurrency procedures and why these are** an essential part of a shared database system. Database administration procedures include six areas of responsibility: database planning, database design, database creation, database maintenance, analysis of usage, and creation and monitoring of security procedures. In addition, concurrency procedures allow more than one user to access a database simultaneously. All these procedures are an essential part of a shared database system because they provide for an efficient, well-managed database and increased worker productivity.

KEY TERMS

CRITICAL CONNECTIONS

Department of Motor Vehicles State of California

1.   Database Eases California Identity Crisis

Initially, all requests for driver's license information in California are going to the DMV's central facility in Sacramento, the state capital. However, the ultimate goal is to let authorized law enforcement agencies access the DMV's image database directly via CLETS, the California Law Enforcement Telecommunications System. Already, highway patrol officers in Ventura County are testing a handheld computer terminal with a card reader that can pick up data from the license's magnetic strip and print out a citation. At the end of the shift, citation data will be downloaded directly into the traffic ticket system—eliminating the need for some paper records and making it harder for scofflaws to elude justice.

The new system may even help retailers who ask to see a driver's license before approving a customer's check. That's because the license's magnetic strip is compatible with the credit card readers found in most point-of-sale terminals.

Questions for Discussion

1. How does the DMV's new database illustrate the principles of data sharing discussed in the chapter?

2. Truck drivers who accumulate a number of traffic citations for unsafe driving or traffic accidents sometimes use illegal means to obtain a driver's license under a fictitious name. How would the California DMV system thwart them and protect innocent drivers?

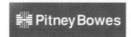

2.   Client/Server System Speeds Information Flow at Pitney Bowes

The concurrent engineering system under development at Pitney Bowes promises to do more than just boost engineering productivity. The real payoff will come down the road, once the company finishes a project that will integrate its concurrent engineering system with the databases used by the marketing, sales, and accounting applications. The result will be a paperless flow of information from the field sales force to the manufacturing execution systems and from marketing to engineering.

Salespeople will like the new system; they'll be using PCs to call up product prices, check inventory levels, and send orders directly to manufacturing—all without touching a single piece of paper. More importantly, the system will revolutionize the way Pitney Bowes creates and markets its products. In the old days, someone would decide what the market requirements are, then go to engineering, then manufacturing, and then ring up a person in sales and say, "Guess what—we have a product. Now sell it." Under the new system, every product will be assigned a core team with representatives from all departments—marketing, engineering, manufacturing, sales, and information systems. With the help of IT, the team will work together from Day 1, using marketing data on changing customer requirements to speed the development of competitive new products.

Questions for .Discussion

1. Engineers sometimes "reinvent the wheel," spending days and even weeks designing say a stamping mechanism, that may be similar to one on a product already in production. How might a concurrent engineering system change this?

2. How might its finished client/server system increase Pitney Bowes's ability to compete?

3. How does Pitney Bowes's system illustrate the principles of data sharing?

3. "Re-Engineering" Project to Rebuild Confidence in Blood Bank

Less than one year after the new Red Cross president announced the re-engineering project, IT staffers were admitting that the initial two-year timetable may have been too optimistic. A more realistic estimate, it seemed, was three years, due to the amount of time consultants from IBM, Andersen Consulting, and KPMG Peat Marwick were spending with representatives from the regional centers to analyze information needs.

A few moments' reflection can give you an idea of the challenges the experts face. On one level, the Red Cross faces a textbook inventory problem—how to match blood demand with blood supply at different locations, realizing that both tend to fluctuate throughout the year. Complicating the problem is the fact that blood has a "shelf life" of about forty days; after that it can't be used.

This leads to a set of basic requirements. First, a computer network linking the centers and national headquarters would speed the task of electronically checking "inventory" at other centers, as well as monitoring operating efficiency from national headquarters. Second, if the centers are going to exchange units of blood, the units need to be as interchangeable as possible. That means that each unit of blood should be tested and catalogued using the same procedures and software. (Right now, the 54 regional centers are using 20 different systems; under the new system, all testing will be consolidated at 10 labs using standardized procedures and custom-created software.) Third, the system needs to provide a way to identify and track the location of every unit of blood. If any tests come back positive, the computer system has to help the staff find the contaminated blood and make sure it is destroyed.

But setting up the distributed database system is just one part of the challenge facing the American Red Cross. The next challenge will come when it implements, or installs, the system. This process is expected to take about two years, as the regional centers are closed, one by one, to change equipment and train staff members.

Questions for Discussion

1. The Red Cross currently maintains a centralized Donor Deferral Registry at national headquarters in Washington, DC. This database of donors who should *not* be allowed to give blood has serious problems with data integrity, mainly because it relies on the manual entry of reports from the regional centers. How might this problem be avoided in the re-engineered system?

2. Use what you have learned about computer software and hardware to suggest ways the re-engineered system could help the Red Cross staff be sure contaminated blood is not released for use. (Hint: Consider the use of input devices such as bar codes and bar code readers.)

REVIEW QUESTIONS

1. What is a database? Why are databases shared?

2. What is the purpose of a database management system (DBMS)?

3. What is a distributed database? How is it related to or different from a shared database?

4. Define the two ways of distributing databases. How may a database be distributed between different locations?

5. What benefits do businesses gain from distributing databases?

6. Describe the difference between a functional distribution strategy and a geographic distribution strategy.

7. Discuss the factors that must be considered in designing a distributed database.

8. What is a database schema? How many schemas does each database have?

9. How are relational and object oriented databases different? What is an object? An action?

10. What is the purpose of a database view?

11. What is the difference between a database schema and a database view?

12. What is the function of an index?

13. What is client/server computing? What are its benefits?

14. Describe the relation between client/server computing, communications networks, and shared databases.

15. Describe the responsibilities of a database administrator and a systems programmer.

16. Describe the six areas of responsibility in data administration.

17. What is the difference between concurrent and nonconcurrent data sharing?

18. What is record locking and why is it used in shared database processing? What is a deadlock and how does it occur?

DISCUSSION QUESTIONS

1. Allegheny Ludlum Corp., a Philadelphia-based manufacturer of special steel and metals, is using IT to achieve above-average growth rates. A network that links the firm's plants in six states provides a steady flow of data and information from the shop floor to the marketing department.

   One of the company's recent strategies has been to move to systems using relational database management systems. Why might Allegheny Ludlum want to consider a move to object oriented databases? What management tool might help it evaluate the option of moving to an object oriented structure?

2. Texas-based retailer Neiman Marcus recently equipped its 27 stores and two warehouses with a set of client/server systems that will record point-of-sale data on a server within each store, as well as on a host at central headquarters. One goal is to automate the "client book" each sales associate keeps on the tastes and preferences of long-standing customers. What measures can the IT staff take to protect confidential client data from unscrupulous employees and still ensure that sales associates have the information they need to do their

jobs? What benefits would the client/server system offer the retailer's upper managers and how might they offset the need for security measures?

3. A team at Levi Strauss & Co. is overseeing a pilot project named Orion. Orion's goal is to determine whether client/server computing would offer significant advantages over the host-based computing the company now uses. What types of duties do you think this task force is performing? Why do you think there is no single person assigned to these duties?

4. Condé Nast Publications, Shearson Lehman Brothers, and Gruman Corp. are just a few of the companies that have instituted stringent portable computer protection policies designed to thwart industrial spies who steal portable computers for their hard disks full of sensitive company data, as well as modems set up to tap into the company's database. Should general managers or IT managers have primary responsibility for designing these security procedures? What does your answer indicate about the relationship between database administration professionals, IT professionals, and non-IT personnel in the age of distributed computing?

SUGGESTED READINGS

Bertino, Elisa, and Lorenzo Martino, "Object-Oriented Database Management Systems: Concepts and Issues," *Computer* (April 1991), pp. 33–47. In this article, Bertino and Martino explain how object oriented database technology combines the power of a computer programming language with effective data management techniques. The discussion includes careful explanations of terminology and explores the processing of applications developed using object structures.

Cattel, R. G. G., "Next Generation Database Systems," *Communications of the ACM*, 34, 10 (October 1991), pp. 30–120. This special issue contains eight comprehensive articles describing new developments and opportunities in shared database systems. All the articles presume a good understanding of the fundamentals of database management.

Martin, James, and James J. Odell, *Object-Oriented Analysis and Design.* Englewood Cliffs: Prentice Hall, 1992. An authoritative and in-depth examination of object oriented computing. The book introduces the basic terminology and concepts associated with objects, databases, and IT applications and offers suggestions for turning concepts into reality.

Ram, Sudha, "Heterogeneous Distributed Database Systems," *Computer*, 24, no. 1 (December 1991), pp. 7–9. This article is one of eight in-depth articles in a special issue devoted entirely to distributed databases. The piece examines a variety of issues, including development of schemas, security and recovery procedures in multidatabase environments, and obstacles to the management of distributed databases.

Sinha, Alok, "Client-Server Computing: Current Technology Review," *Communications of the ACM,* 35, no. 7 (July 1992), pp. 77-98. This informative article looks at the evolution of client/server computing, from its origin with the emergence of powerful PCs to its future with new network operating systems and powerful databases. It includes both a description of the uses of client/server methods in business and a detailed examination of the underlying technology.

Client/Server Systems Help Helene Curtis Ride Curl of Success

THE NEXT TIME YOU GO SHOPPING for toiletries, don't be surprised if you see a sales representative using a palmpad computer to take inventory of Degree deodorant, Suave body lotion, or the Suave, Finesse, Salon Selectives, and Vibrance hair care products. These sales reps are the foot soldiers in a drive that has made Helene Curtis Industries a major force in the fiercely competitive personal care industry. (In 1993 Helene Curtis was ranked number one in U.S. sales of hair conditioner and mousse/gel; number two, behind Procter & Gamble, in U.S. sales of shampoo; and number five in U.S. sales of deodorant. In addition, the company has been showing strong growth in Scandinavia, Japan, the United Kingdom, and Canada.) And the palmpad? It's part of a client/server system that is helping to reinforce Helene Curtis's already strong reputation for retail service.

The highly segmented $4 billion hair care market is especially challenging. First, there are the consumers, easily swayed by price, product image, and fads. (One industry report found that the typical U.S. household contains three to five different brands of shampoo at any one time.) To keep up, companies have to produce an ongoing stream of new products, all supported by eye-catching advertisements and promotions that reinforce market image and positioning. Helene Curits spends about 13 percent of its income—more than $160 million—on advertising every year.

And then there are the retailers, who need and expect certain kinds of service from manufacturers. Advertising and promotions directed at consumers, for example, are often coupled with manufacturers' discounts to retailers, allowing them to hold sales that pull price-conscious customers into their stores.

Pricing became an especially important concern in the tight economy of the late 1980s and 1990s. To keep overhead costs down, retailers at all levels began reducing their inventory levels. Wal-Mart, for example, warehouses only one to two weeks of merchandise. In toiletries, it turns its inventories twenty to fifty times a year—compared to the industry average of ten times a year. To make this kind of inventory system work, retailers need reliable feedback about their current sales and they need their orders filled promptly. Giant Wal-Mart has its own sophisticated information system for performing these tasks (see the Chapter 3 case). But smaller retailers are increasingly dependent on the sales reps from suppliers like Helene Curtis. That's why the sales reps from Helene Curtis are armed with pen-based palm computers.

The palmpads are part of a client/server system that was introduced in late 1993. With them the retail sales reps, who work directly with more than 40,000 store managers, can collect each store's sales data and tap into the national database for additional sales data. The result? The sales reps can act as consultants and account managers, giving store managers fact-based advice on their orders.

The palmpad system isn't the first client/server system created to help the Helene Curtis sales force. That honor goes to the system that appeared in the late 1980s, when the direct sales reps—the ones who work with corporate buyers for such large chains as Kmart—were given laptop computers. Instead of waiting weeks for updated product and customer information, reps can use their laptops to upload database queries in the morning and get reports later the same day.

Sales data from the two client/server systems, combined with syndicated market data from A.C. Nielsen Co., also help marketing executives at corporate headquarters. Consider what happened, for example, when Unilever introduced its Rave shampoo. At first, Helene Curtis market researchers assumed the new product was aimed at their Salon Selectives line. To compete, they thought, they might have to drop the price of the premium-priced Salon Selectives shampoos. Then they took a closer look at the sales data. The new shampoo, they realized, was actually aimed at Helene Curtis's bargain-priced Suave line. No action was needed. Thanks to the immediate market feedback provided by the client/server systems, the company avoided a rash—and potentially costly—reaction.

Using specially designed palmpads linked to a client/server system, Helene Curtis sales reps can tap into the company's national database and give individual store managers fact-based advice on their orders.

Questions for Discussion:

1. How do the client/server systems at Helene Curtis illustrate the benefits of client/server computing?

2. The palmpads let the field sales reps visit, on average, one more store a day. How might this be a competitive advantage for Helene Curtis?

3. Many stock analysts feel that Helene Curtis is well positioned for future growth. As evidence, they cite the company's ongoing introduction of new, higher-priced brands and its investment in the information systems needed to provide good retail service. What might these predictions mean for Helene Curtis's competitors?

Surfing on the Internet

The value of a network lies as much in *whom* it connects as *how* it connects. Internet is a vivid demonstration of the value of connectivity. A network of networks rather than one big network, Internet traces its origins to the 1960s. It was then that the U.S. Department of Defense established the network to provide researchers and government officials with access to such IT resources as radio telescopes, weather analysis programs, supercomputers, and specialized databases.

IT developments have been created as an outgrowth of the Internet. For example, electronic mail was born on Internet, and many believe that Internet will become the basis on which the U.S. Information Superhighway is built. In this photo essay, we explore the history and future of Internet, as well as what Internet can do today.

1 Vinton Cerf is known as the "Father of Internet" for his pioneering work in developing IT to support the network and for his unending efforts to help it grow. Cerf started with the principle that anyone should be able to talk to anyone else. Then he developed the TCP/IP protocol on which Internet is built. This protocol greatly facilitated the network's growth by making networks open and thus permitting interconnection between networks. Today, the ability to "surf on the Internet"— to go from network to network the way a surfer goes freely from wave to wave— gives Internet users an endless wave of connectivity.

2 Although originally started for the use of government and educational institutions, today over half of all U.S. Internet addresses belong to people who got them through a private employer or a firm providing commercial access to the network.

Any estimate of the number of people using Internet becomes quickly outdated because more than 150,000 new users join Internet each day. Host computers are added daily and the number of networks interconnected on Internet doubles every year. However, the rate of growth will likely peak at some time in the future. It has to, for at current growth rates everyone on planet Earth would be connected to the network by the year 2002.

The U.S. Government, through the National Science Foundation, pays a very small portion of the operating cost of Internet—less than 5 percent. The remainder is paid by the users. Universities and other institutions pay the cost of operating their host computers and interconnecting to the network. There is no charge for sending a message from one computer to another.

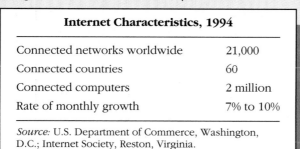

Internet Characteristics, 1994

Connected networks worldwide	21,000
Connected countries	60
Connected computers	2 million
Rate of monthly growth	7% to 10%

Source: U.S. Department of Commerce, Washington, D.C.; Internet Society, Reston, Virginia.

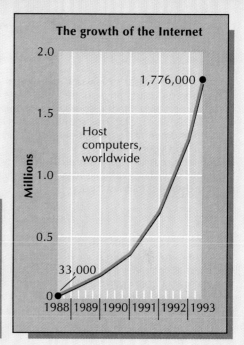

The growth of the Internet

Host computers, worldwide

1,776,000

33,000

1988 | 1989 | 1990 | 1991 | 1992 | 1993

Internet Address

3 Everyone on Internet has an address—an identification code that allows you to use Internet and permits other users to find and send messages to you. An Internet address consists of four components: (1) your personal identification, (2) the host computer, (3) the institution or organization, and (4) the domain name.

Your institution or organization manages the assignment of personal identification names. Often these are some combination of the individual's names and their location or work group within the organization. The institution also assigns one or more host computers to Internet, giving each host a unique identification code.

The Network Information Center is the central authority responsible for assigning a range of addresses to an institution or organization. The institution is responsible for assigning a specific host computer to one of the addresses within its range. Each organization also belongs to a domain that identifies the nature of its networks. Domain codes typically identify the type of organization or its location.

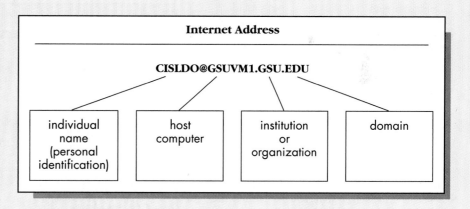

Internet Address

CISLDO@GSUVM1.GSU.EDU

individual name (personal identification)	host computer	institution or organization	domain

Domain

Name	Explanation
.AU	Country code for Australia
.COM	Commercial organization
.EDU	Educational institution
.GOV	Government organization

4 The following are some major features of Internet:

Usenet

Usenet, short for User's Network, is a system of worldwide discussion groups rather than an actual physical network. For example, there are Usenet discussion groups on physical fitness, computer technology, job listings, posting of personal résumés, diabetes, *Star Trek* shows and movies, The Beatles...virtually any topic you can imagine. If no discussion group exists for the topic you're interested in, you can start your own.

Usenet discussion groups are constantly being added and removed from Internet. The systems administrator at a particular host site determines whether to carry a Usenet discussion group.

Telnet

The essence of the "network of networks" concept, Telnet is the TCP/IP protocol that permits remote login from whatever computer you are currently using. Virtually any Internet computer can be accessed from your local system. This means that if you are away from your college or organization, you can use Telnet to access your system back at your main location. All you need do is use the Telnet protocol and provide it with your Internet address. Telnet takes care of finding and interconnecting to the system for you.

Gopher

Gophers[1] are computer systems that provide a series of menus that enable you to access virtually any type of textual information. They are the easiest to use of all Internet features because all you need to do is make selections from a menu. Whatever selection you make, the gopher will carry out the work, locating the file and displaying it for you.

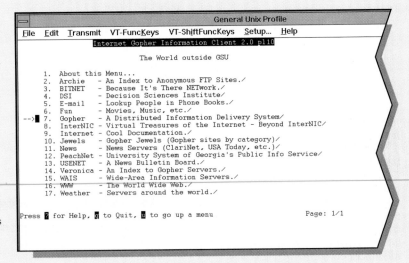

```
                                              General Unix Profile
  File   Edit   Transmit   VT-FuncKeys   VT-ShiftFuncKeys   Setup...   Help
        Internet Gopher Information Client 2.0 pl10

                          The World outside GSU

        1.  About this Menu...
        2.  Archie    - An Index to Anonymous FTP Sites./
        3.  BITNET    - Because It's There NETwork./
        4.  DSI       - Decision Sciences Institute/
        5.  E-mail    - Lookup People in Phone Books./
        6.  Fun       - Movies, Music, etc./
  -->▌  7.  Gopher    - A Distributed Information Delivery System/
        8.  InterNIC  - Virtual Treasures of the Internet - Beyond InterNIC/
        9.  Internet  - Cool Documentation./
       10.  Jewels    - Gopher Jewels (Gopher sites by category)/
       11.  News      - News Servers (ClariNet, USA Today, etc.)/
       12.  PeachNet  - University System of Georgia's Public Info Service/
       13.  USENET    - A News Bulletin Board./
       14.  Veronica  - An Index to Gopher Servers./
       15.  WAIS      - Wide-Area Information Servers./
       16.  WWW       - The World Wide Web./
       17.  Weather   - Servers around the world./


  Press ? for Help, ▌ to Quit, ▌ to go up a menu              Page: 1/1
```

---

[1] The name "gopher" was selected by the development team at the University of Minnesota that created this access system for Internet. The University of Minnesota's athletic teams are called the Golden Gophers.

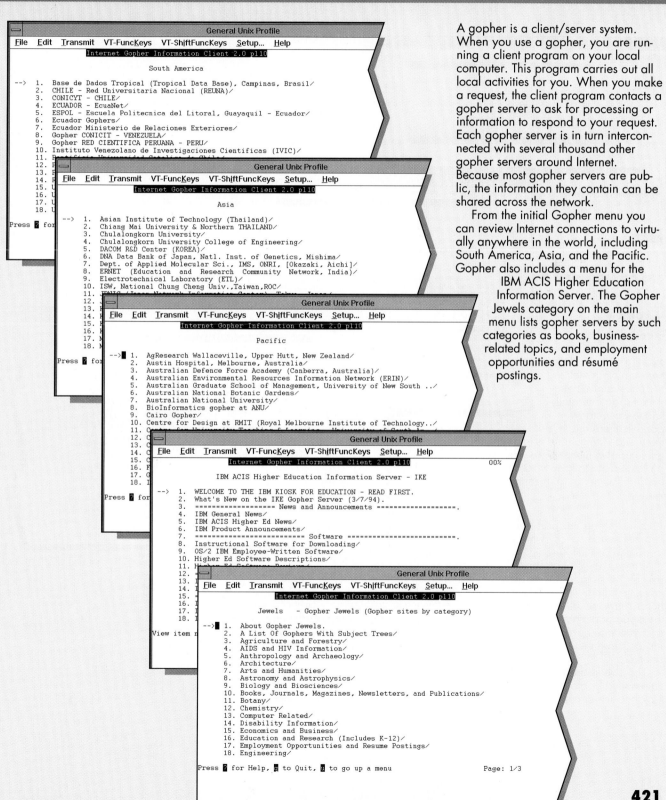

A gopher is a client/server system. When you use a gopher, you are running a client program on your local computer. This program carries out all local activities for you. When you make a request, the client program contacts a gopher server to ask for processing or information to respond to your request. Each gopher server is in turn interconnected with several thousand other gopher servers around Internet. Because most gopher servers are public, the information they contain can be shared across the network.

From the initial Gopher menu you can review Internet connections to virtually anywhere in the world, including South America, Asia, and the Pacific. Gopher also includes a menu for the IBM ACIS Higher Education Information Server. The Gopher Jewels category on the main menu lists gopher servers by such categories as books, business-related topics, and employment opportunities and résumé postings.

421

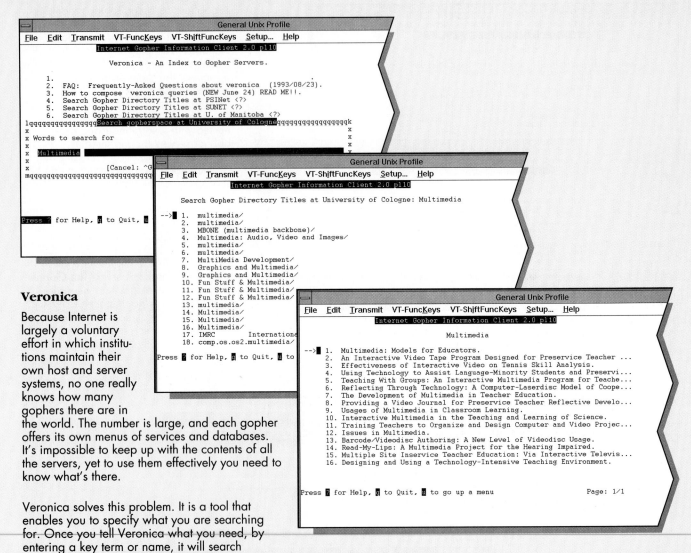

```
                          General Unix Profile
 File   Edit   Transmit   VT-FuncKeys   VT-ShiftFuncKeys   Setup...   Help
 Internet Gopher Information Client 2.0 p110

              Veronica - An Index to Gopher Servers.

    1.                                               .
    2.  FAQ: Frequently-Asked Questions about veronica  (1993/08/23).
    3.  How to compose  veronica queries (NEW June 24) READ ME!!.
    4.  Search Gopher Directory Titles at PSINet <?>
    5.  Search Gopher Directory Titles at SUNET <?>
    6.  Search Gopher Directory Titles at U. of Manitoba <?>
 lqqqqqqqqqqqqqqqqSearch gopherspace at University of Cologneqqqqqqqqqqqqqqqqqqk
 x                                                                            x
 x Words to search for                                                        x
 x                                                                            x
 x  Multimedia                                                                x
 x                                                                            x
 x                  [Cancel: ^G
 mqqqqqqqqqqqqqqqqqqqqqqqqqqqqqqq

 Press ? for Help, q to Quit, u
```

```
                                    General Unix Profile
     File    Edit   Transmit   VT-FuncKeys   VT-ShiftFuncKeys   Setup...   Help
     Internet Gopher Information Client 2.0 p110

       Search Gopher Directory Titles at University of Cologne: Multimedia

     -->  1.  multimedia/
          2.  multimedia/
          3.  MBONE (multimedia backbone)/
          4.  Multimedia: Audio, Video and Images/
          5.  multimedia/
          6.  multimedia/
          7.  MultiMedia Development/
          8.  Graphics and Multimedia/
          9.  Graphics and Multimedia/
         10.  Fun Stuff & Multimedia/
         11.  Fun Stuff & Multimedia/
         12.  Fun Stuff & Multimedia/
         13.  multimedia/
         14.  Multimedia/
         15.  Multimedia/
         16.  Multimedia/
         17.  IMRC          Internationa
         18.  comp.os.os2.multimedia/

     Press ? for Help, q to Quit, u to
```

```
                                         General Unix Profile
        File    Edit   Transmit   VT-FuncKeys   VT-ShiftFuncKeys   Setup...   Help
        Internet Gopher Information Client 2.0 p110
                                     Multimedia

       -->  1.  Multimedia: Models for Educators.
            2.  An Interactive Video Tape Program Designed for Preservice Teacher ...
            3.  Effectiveness of Interactive Video on Tennis Skill Analysis.
            4.  Using Technology to Assist Language-Minority Students and Preservi...
            5.  Teaching With Groups: An Interactive Multimedia Program for Teache...
            6.  Reflecting Through Technology: A Computer-Laserdisc Model of Coope...
            7.  The Development of Multimedia in Teacher Education.
            8.  Providing a Video Journal for Preservice Teacher Reflective Develo...
            9.  Usages of Multimedia in Classroom Learning.
           10.  Interactive Multimedia in the Teaching and Learning of Science.
           11.  Training Teachers to Organize and Design Computer and Video Projec...
           12.  Issues in Multimedia.
           13.  Barcode/Videodisc Authoring: A New Level of Videodisc Usage.
           14.  Read-My-Lips: A Multimedia Project for the Hearing Impaired.
           15.  Multiple Site Inservice Teacher Education: Via Interactive Televis...
           16.  Designing and Using a Technology-Intensive Teaching Environment.

       Press ? for Help, q to Quit, u to go up a menu                   Page: 1/1
```

Veronica

Because Internet is largely a voluntary effort in which institutions maintain their own host and server systems, no one really knows how many gophers there are in the world. The number is large, and each gopher offers its own menus of services and databases. It's impossible to keep up with the contents of all the servers, yet to use them effectively you need to know what's there.

Veronica solves this problem. It is a tool that enables you to specify what you are searching for. Once you tell Veronica what you need, by entering a key term or name, it will search Internet, looking for all the menu items that contain the key word or words you have specified. When it completes the search, it presents a custom menu of the items it has found. Selecting any item from this menu automatically connects you to the appropriate gopher, wherever in the world it may be located. And, unless you ask, you won't even know what server you are using or even the country in which it's located. In effect, Internet removes the boundaries separating one network from another.

The screens above show the steps you can follow to search a server at the University of Cologne to retrieve information on multimedia development. The Cologne server can be reached from anywhere in the world by way of Internet.

Archie

Archie is a worldwide database containing files that can be downloaded from systems around the world. The files may be software, documents, or data sets. Archie lets you perform direct database queries and searches, download data, or send messages to a distant server. Numerous Archie servers are running around the world, spanning five continents.

Suppose, for example, that you want to search for the *TV Guide to The Outer Limits*. After you enter the command **prog outerl**, Archie will search its database for the requested item, then display a status line with the number of entries found.

The marriage of computer networks and libraries is an outgrowth of Archie capability and a fast-growing area of Internet use. After many university, college, and school libraries networked themselves, the next logical step was to put their catalogs online and to make them reachable via Internet. When you can't find a book in your own library after an online search of its catalog, you can log onto Internet, surf over to the networks of other libraries, and search their online catalogs. Once you've located the book or document you want, you can request it through interlibrary loan. Approximately 300 libraries are online, nearly half of them outside of the United States. Hence, if you wish, you can search libraries in Australia, Germany, Mexico, New Zealand, Switzerland, and Sweden, to mention just a few.

Online libraries accessible under Archie are not limited to books. For example, the Research Libraries Information Network (RLIN) contains an online bibliographic database of over 40 million records representing catalogs of over 100 special collections, archives, and research libraries. In addition to books, it includes government records, maps, music scores, sound recordings, films, and photographs.

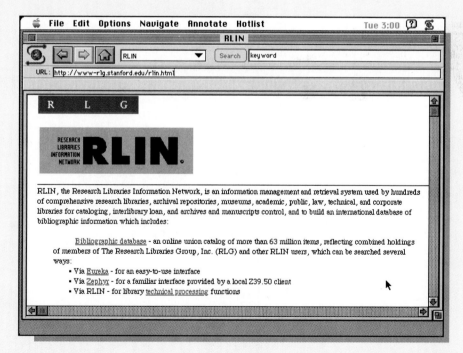

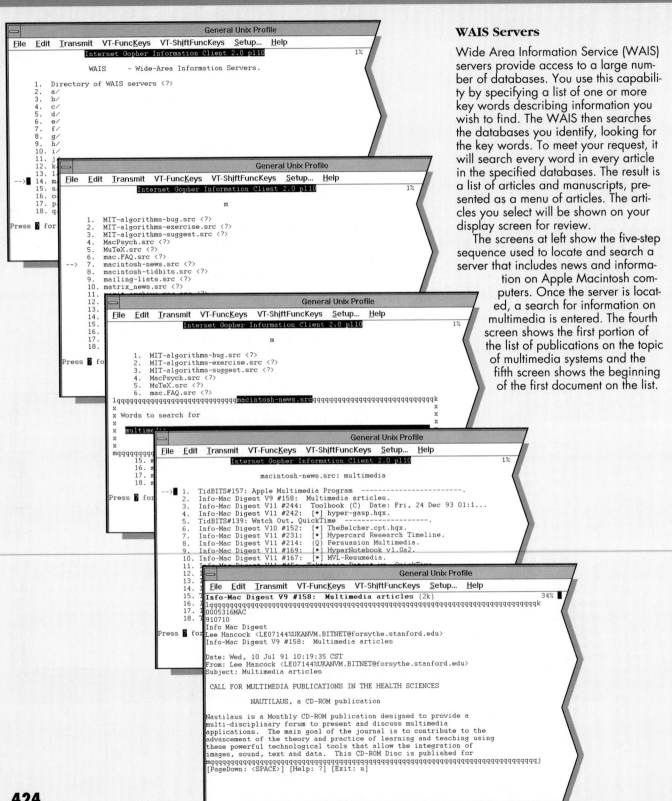

WAIS Servers

Wide Area Information Service (WAIS) servers provide access to a large number of databases. You use this capability by specifying a list of one or more key words describing information you wish to find. The WAIS then searches the databases you identify, looking for the key words. To meet your request, it will search every word in every article in the specified databases. The result is a list of articles and manuscripts, presented as a menu of articles. The articles you select will be shown on your display screen for review.

The screens at left show the five-step sequence used to locate and search a server that includes news and information on Apple Macintosh computers. Once the server is located, a search for information on multimedia is entered. The fourth screen shows the first portion of the list of publications on the topic of multimedia systems and the fifth screen shows the beginning of the first document on the list.

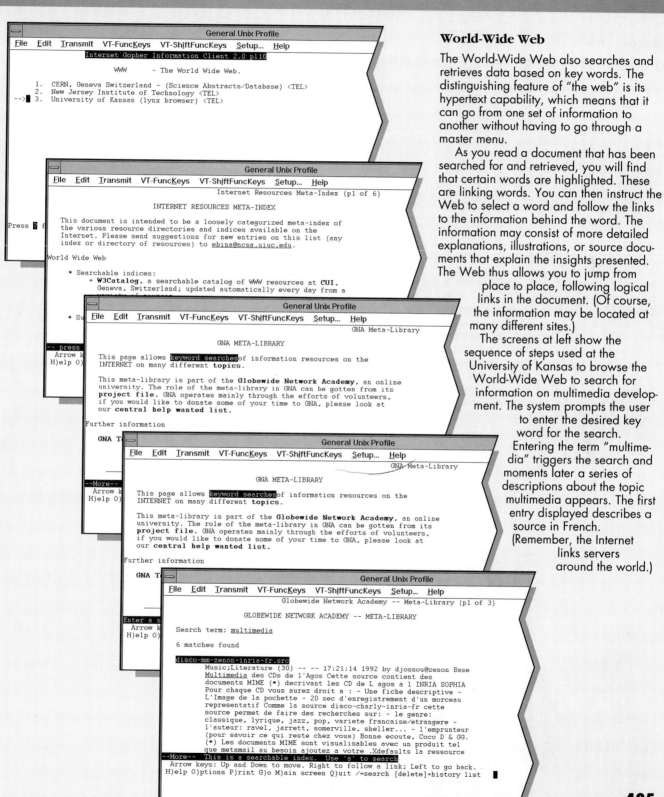

World-Wide Web

The World-Wide Web also searches and retrieves data based on key words. The distinguishing feature of "the web" is its hypertext capability, which means that it can go from one set of information to another without having to go through a master menu.

As you read a document that has been searched for and retrieved, you will find that certain words are highlighted. These are linking words. You can then instruct the Web to select a word and follow the links to the information behind the word. The information may consist of more detailed explanations, illustrations, or source documents that explain the insights presented. The Web thus allows you to jump from place to place, following logical links in the document. (Of course, the information may be located at many different sites.)

The screens at left show the sequence of steps used at the University of Kansas to browse the World-Wide Web to search for information on multimedia development. The system prompts the user to enter the desired key word for the search. Entering the term "multimedia" triggers the search and moments later a series of descriptions about the topic multimedia appears. The first entry displayed describes a source in French. (Remember, the Internet links servers around the world.)

Mailing Lists

Mailing lists interconnect people who choose to participate in an ongoing discussion on a particular topic. The messages might be comments and opinions; announcements; discussions of new products, tools, or services; book, article, theater, movie, or music reviews; or just about any other information that is of interest to a group of persons.

You join a mailing list by subscribing electronically. The information submitted by any group member is then automatically sent to you and appears in an electronic mailbox on the host computer to which you are attached. When you choose, you sign on to the system and read the information you have received.

Thousands of mailing lists exist on Internet, on virtually any topic you can imagine. You can choose to join as many as you want—and have time to read.

White Page Directory

Regular Internet users know that nothing is more important than the address of a person they wish to contact. Once you know someone's address, you can send him or her messages, transfer documents and programs, or initiate online conversations.

If you don't know a person's address, you can look it up on Internet in the same way you look up a telephone number in the white pages of a printed directory or on the electronic screen of a Minitel terminal. (Actually, the directory is a series of interconnected directories running on individual servers.)

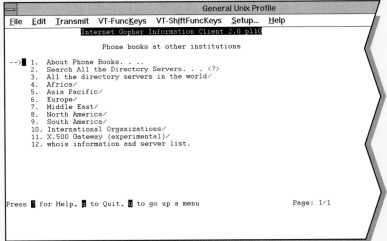

```
                                    General Unix Profile
 File   Edit   Transmit   VT-FuncKeys   VT-ShiftFuncKeys   Setup...   Help
              Internet Gopher Information Client 2.0 pl10

                    Phone books at other institutions

-->  1.  About Phone Books. . ..
     2.  Search All the Directory Servers. . . <?>
     3.  All the directory servers in the world/
     4.  Africa/
     5.  Asia Pacific/
     6.  Europe/
     7.  Middle East/
     8.  North America/
     9.  South America/
    10.  International Organizations/
    11.  X.500 Gateway (experimental)/
    12.  whois information and server list.




 Press ? for Help, q to Quit, u to go up a menu              Page: 1/1
```

Accessibility of the Internet

5 In San Francisco, 18 coffee houses have gone online to Internet, installing computer terminals that let customers interact with the network. Acting similar to jukeboxes for playing music, these Internet terminals accept quarters. Each quarter gives four minutes of use, during which time customers can send messages across the world or down the street to another coffee house, enter an online discussion on their favorite topic, or read through an electronic newsletter. Wayne Gregori, founder of SF Net, the firm that builds and programs the café terminals, says, "We specifically target cafés in low-income areas. We're trying to get the have-nots on the computer."

Electronic entrepreneurs are taking to the Internet like settlers in the United States and elsewhere took to free land during the early days of their countries. Carl Malamud, pictured below, created Internet Multicasting service. His weekly radio program is distributed over Internet Talk Radio, begun in 1993. Network users whose computers are equipped with speakers can download the program to their computers and listen to all or a portion of the program.

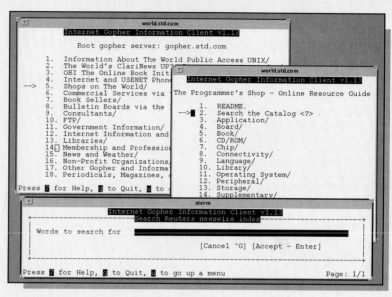

Internet for Business

6 As Internet has grown, business users have become accustomed to its capabilities and capitalized on them for commercial opportunities. The Commercial Internet Exchange is a public data internetwork that offers commercial, unrestricted connectivity while not violating the restrictions against commercial traffic on some portions of Internet.

Software Tool & Die (ST&D) is a Brookline, Massachusetts consulting firm that specializes in software development. The company links to Internet to provide consulting and programming services, sometimes without ever meeting its customer face-to-face. Through Internet, company officials converse using e-mail and transfer files easily and quickly. ST&D also runs a public access bulletin board system that makes software and services available.

Internet Information

7 Want more information on Internet? Check the local bookstore and you will find a wide variety of books on its features and capabilities. The *Internet Yellow Pages* lists the services and databases that are available. Directories are also available that describe the thousands of mailing lists on the network. Internet's popularity has also spawned newsletters and periodicals, including *The Internet Business Journal, The Internet Letter, and Internet World.*

CHAPTER 11

Developing Shared IT Applications

Learning Objectives

When you have completed this chapter, you should be able to:

1 Describe the principle functions and roles of a systems analyst.
2 Explain how a systems project begins and how its desirability is
determined.
3 Describe the six phases of the systems development life cycle.
4 Describe the tools and techniques available to systems analysts for
collecting data and developing IT applications.
5 Explain the roles of the four types of IT systems-development professionals.

In Practice

After completing this chapter, you should be able to perform these activities:

1 Explain why some systems projects succeed and others fail.
2 Discuss with a systems analyst the way he conducts a systems investigation.
3 Discuss with a chief information officer or IT director the way she
manages the development of new shared IT applications in her
firm.
4 Speak with a computer programmer or systems contractor and discuss the information he or she needs in a system specification to
create and deliver the right software and documentation.

A SABRE-Toothed Tiger

S OMETIMES A COMPANY'S COMPETITIVE advantage is tied into its ability to develop shared IT applications. Consider the experience of American Airlines of Dallas, Texas, which is recognized worldwide for its effective use of IT. The SABRE System developed by the airline has been a key ingredient in helping AA gain a competitive edge over other airlines.

SABRE was first conceived in 1959 as an internal system that would link the airline's offices and ticket counters. Sixteen years later, AA CEO Robert Crandall and Chief Information Officer Max Hopper determined they could use SABRE as more than a communications system within the airline and began marketing SABRE to travel agents, the people who sell the most tickets for the airline industry. AA expanded SABRE's capabilities to make it a convenient tool for booking reservations on *all* airlines, and quickly convinced a large portion of the country's travel agents to use the system. AA also successfully implemented a policy of charging other airlines a nominal "booking fee" if travel agents made reservations on their flights through the

Reservations specialists at American Airlines use state-of-the-art headphones and the SABRE shared information system to book both domestic and international flights. American receives millions of dollars of revenue annually because independent travel agents process flight reservations on other airlines through SABRE also.

SABRE system. This feature remains in effect today. American receives millions of dollars of revenue annually because independent travel agents process flight reservations on other airlines through SABRE.

In the 1980s, when deregulation increased competition in the industry and changed it almost overnight, Crandall stepped forward again. Recognizing SABRE's potential, he came up with the American Advantage Frequent Flier program, a marketing strategy that encourages travelers to fly with American by rewarding them with points redeemable for free travel. This program has resulted in a frequent flier membership of more than 11 million people and has created tremendous loyalty to American. In addition to locking travelers into flying with American Airlines to obtain the benefits of its computer-based frequent flier program, the SABRE system allows the airline's management to adjust its fares rapidly in response to competitors' ticket prices.

But the story does not end there. Seeking to capitalize further on SABRE's enormous capabilities, AMR Information Services (AMRIS—AMR Corp. is the parent of American Airlines) in 1988 announced plans to create a hotel, car rental, and travel reservation system to be called Confirm. A budget of $125 million was established for the project. Four companies agreed to participate as partners in developing and using Confirm: AMR, Marriott, Hilton Hotels, and Budget Rent A Car. The partners formed the International Reservations and Information Consortium (INTRICO) to oversee the development of Confirm and to market the system to the travel industry. The original plans for Confirm called for more than 3,000 programs running on two large mainframes at AMRIS's data center. The systems were to communicate with various hotel and rental-car airport reservations centers and to store data in a large, centralized database.

In October 1992, AMR announced that it was "suspending development" on Confirm. According to industry reports, the project was running well behind schedule and the partners disagreed about the system's features and functions—even though one partner had reportedly provided a set of specifications that stood literally six feet high. With the apparent failure of the project, the partners made many charges and countercharges about their original expectations, the development process, the feasibility of the system, and the capabilities of development personnel.

SABRE was a success while Confirm was a failure. Why? The Confirm concept was attractive and appeared to feature creative use of IT. Yet, in the end, the project's collapse was the result of the partners' failure to manage the development of a shared IT system. ■

I N YOUR CAREER, IT IS LIKELY THAT YOU WILL BE INVOLVED AT SOME POINT IN THE DEVELOPment of IT applications. If you are pursuing a career as an IT professional, you may be part of a development team or even the project leader. If you are an IT user, you will be consulted by IT professionals who want to involve you in the development activities for applications you will later use.

In this chapter, we look inside the process of developing shared IT applications. The first part of the chapter emphasizes the importance of good systems development management and describes the origin of systems projects and the systems development life cycle. The second half of the chapter discusses the tools available to systems analysts. Because just having the right tools is not enough, the chapter closes by discussing the skills that good systems analysts need to work effectively with businesspeople and to create effective applications.

The purpose of this chapter is not to teach you to be a systems analyst. Rather, it is designed to give you a good idea of what systems analysts do and how to work with them to develop effective shared IT applications.

■ Developing Shared Systems

shared system   A system in which two or more users share computers, communications technology, and applications.

Recall that a **shared system** is a system in which two or more users share computers, communications technology, and applications. The introduction of a shared system into a work group or organization affects everyone who interacts with the application or receives information generated by the system. For this reason, shared systems are usually developed by the organization's information technology group. This group goes by various names, including the information systems department, the management information systems (MIS) department, or the information resources group.

The development of shared systems is an important business activity because of the challenges it presents to the firm. As a firm embarks on a shared system development project, it must keep in mind several points:

1. A business is dependent on IT for its success.
2. Introducing a new system means introducing a change to the business.
3. Shared systems mean multiple viewpoints.
4. IT can create a competitive edge—or take it away.
5. Systems analysts (whose role we first discussed in Chapter 2) must understand the needs of business, but businesspeople must understand the needs of the analyst also.
6. Both systems analysts and users must anticipate problems that can arise with the new system.
7. Systems analysts must design the system to use the computer and communications capabilities available within (or that could be acquired by) the organization.

Every development project must be managed well to achieve the desired results. But even a company that does a good job of managing projects can still fail if it doesn't pay attention to the details of the specific project, as in the ill-fated Confirm project.

■ The Origin of a Systems Project

Systems development is the process of examining a business situation; designing a system solution to improve that situation; and acquiring the human, financial, and information technology resources needed to develop and implement the solution. **Project management** is the process of planning, organizing, integrating, and overseeing the development of an IT application to ensure that the project's objectives are achieved and the system is implemented according to expectations. Before development can begin, a project proposal is prepared by users or systems analysts and submitted to a steering committee.

Project Proposal

The **project proposal** is a result of problem or opportunity recognition and is a critical element in launching the systems study. Although the proposal's form varies from firm to firm, the proposal should always answer the following questions:

- What specifically is the problem?
- What details describe the problem?
- How significant is the problem?
- What is a possible solution to the problem?
- How will information technology help to solve the problem?
- Who else knows about this problem and who else should be contacted?

Whether the proposal has been triggered by a single event or by a recurring situation is also an important consideration. For example, AMR's managers and exec-

systems development The process of examining a business situation; designing a system solution to improve that situation; and acquiring the human, financial, and IT resources needed to develop and implement the solution.

project management The process of planning, organizing, integrating, and overseeing the development of an IT application to ensure that the project's objectives are achieved and the system is implemented according to expectations.

project proposal A proposal for a systems project prepared by users or systems analysts and submitted to a steering committee for approval.

utives saw that their major customers—business travelers and their travel agents—nearly always booked more than one type of reservation at a time. In addition to airline reservations, business travelers often require hotel and car-rental reservations. AMR saw a business opportunity in creating a shared system capable of handling all types of reservations simultaneously. A careful review of the resulting proposal led to a launching of the development project.

Steering Committee Review

steering committee A group of people from various functional areas of a business that determines whether a systems development project proposal is desirable and should be pursued.

Most companies do not want individuals to launch shared systems projects on their own. Rather, they direct that proposals be submitted to a **steering committee** that determines whether the project is desirable. The committee, usually made up of people from various functional areas of the business (for example, executives in marketing, accounting, purchasing, inventory control, manufacturing, sales, and information systems) determine if the project is desirable and should be pursued.

The Systems Analyst

systems analyst The individual responsible for working with users to determine a system's requirements and to describe the features needed in the system.

systems designer The individual responsible for doing the technical work of designing a system and its software.

programmer/analyst A person who has joint responsibility for determining system requirements and developing and implementing the systems.

Recall that the term **systems analyst** is used very broadly to refer to a person who develops all or a portion of an IT application. However, IT professionals distinguish among systems analysts, systems designers, and programmer/analysts, all of whom have different responsibilities. **Systems analysts** are responsible for working with users to determine a system's requirements and to describe the features needed in the system. **Systems designers** are responsible for doing the technical work of designing the system and its software. **Programmer/analysts** are responsible for determining system requirements *and* developing and implementing the systems. In essence, they act as programmer, systems analyst, and systems designer.

In business, it is very often the systems analyst who sees the development of a shared IT application through, from original conception to finished product. For this reason, we focus primarily on the systems analyst's activities in the pages that follow.

▮ The Systems Development Life Cycle

systems development life cycle (SDLC) The set of activities, in six phases, that brings about a new IT application.

The proposal submitted to the steering committee is the first step in systems development. The **systems development life cycle (SDLC)**, outlined in Figure 11.1, is the set of activities that brings about a new IT application. Like the process of developing a personal system (Chapter 8), the SDLC is a problem solving process. It consists of six phases:

- Problem recognition/preliminary investigation—Defining and investigating the problem.
- Requirements determination—Understanding the current system and the new system's requirements.
- Systems design—Planning the new system.
- Development and construction—Creating the new system.
- Implementation—Converting to the new system.
- Evaluation and continuing evolution—Monitoring and adding value to the new system.

Each of these stages is discussed in more detail in the sections that follow.

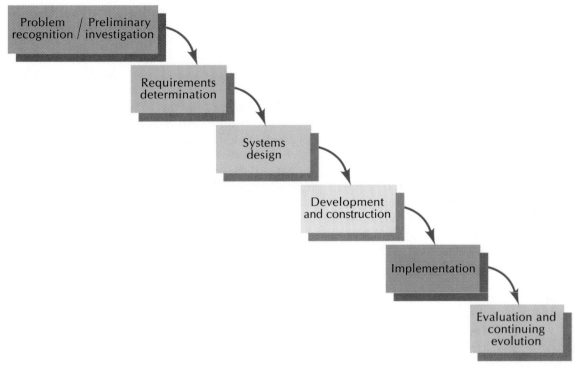

FIGURE 11.1   The Systems Development Life Cycle
The systems development life cycle begins with problem recognition but never really ends, for the new system must be continuously monitored and evaluated after it has been put in place.

Problem Recognition/Preliminary Investigation

Most businesses have more requests for systems development activities than they can possibly support. Hence, the first activity in the systems development life cycle—problem recognition/preliminary investigation—is conducted at the direction of the steering committee.

The purpose of the **preliminary investigation** is to examine the project proposal (1) to evaluate its merits and (2) to determine whether it is feasible to launch a project that will address the issues it raises. During the preliminary investigation, systems analysts work to clarify the proposal, determine the size and scope of the project, assess the costs and benefits of alternative approaches, and determine the project's general feasibility. They then report their findings to the steering committee along with a recommendation.

Systems analysts assess three types of feasibility: operational feasibility, financial/economic feasibility, and technical feasibility.

Operational Feasibility.   A project is *operationally feasible* if it meets the business's operating requirements and has a desirable effect on the company. If the project requires changes in current procedures, those changes must be acceptable for the project to be judged operationally feasible.

For example, United Parcel Service (UPS), the world's largest and most successful package delivery service, saw its business threatened by the growth of Federal Express's overnight service. UPS decided to examine the feasibility of expanding its business services to include both overnight package delivery and more effective use of its distribution and delivery capabilities. It conducted an investigation to determine if its operations, delivery procedures, and IT capabilities could be

preliminary investigation The first step in the SDLC. The activity in which the merits and feasibility of a project proposal are determined.

expanded to guarantee next-morning delivery. The company's executives and employees believed that developing the overnight business was desirable; they wanted to be sure it was feasible.

Financial and Economic Feasibility.   Even if the proposed system is technically feasible, it must be a good financial investment for the business to undertake the project. The project's benefits should exceed its costs. The benefits are judged on the basis of increased business, lower costs, or fewer errors as a result of the new system. The costs include the cost of conducting a full systems investigation; the cost of hardware, communications links, and software for the application being considered; and the cost if nothing changes—that is, if the proposed system is not developed.

The UPS vision depends on information technology not just for moving packages, but for moving information as well. Company executives recognized the importance of extending the company's ability to allow communication between the drivers of its 50,000 trucks and its distribution centers in improving the UPS delivery system. They also wanted to provide customers real-time information (see Chapter 2) about the location of their packages. A five-year, $1.6 billion effort was launched to accomplish these goals. Because UPS is a successful, well-managed, $16 billion company, an investment of this magnitude was financially feasible.

Technical Feasibility.   A project is *technically feasible* if the systems analyst can answer the following questions with "yes":

* Does the necessary computer and communications technology exist to do what the proposal suggests? Can the firm acquire this technology?
* Does the proposed hardware (whether currently installed or to be acquired) have the capacity to store or transmit the data and information required for the new system?
* Will the proposed system provide adequate responses to inquiries, regardless of the number of individuals who will use the system?
* Can the system be expanded at a later date?
* Does the proposed system guarantee accuracy, reliability, ease of access, and data security?

To determine the technical feasibility of linking its customers, drivers, and distribution centers, UPS contacted the operators of the largest cellular networks (see Chapter 9). After much discussion, UPS was convinced it could improve its distribution system with wireless communications. Working with four carriers—McCaw Cellular Communications, GTE Mobile Communications, PacTel Cellular, and Southwestern Bell Mobile Systems—the company established a custom-designed, nationwide network.

As part of the recently installed TotalTrack systems, UPS drivers are now connected to the cellular network through handheld computers attached to a combination cellular modem/telephone (Figure 11.2). The handheld computer automatically dials the closest carrier, which then interconnects to the UPS private network and the company's data center. Information about the pickup, delivery, or location of any package can be transmitted over the network.

UPS's cellular system was completed on time and within the $150 million budget allocation. Since implementing the system, UPS has transformed itself into a successful overnight package carrier while continuing to expand its highly efficient and profitable parcel service. It has duplicated virtually all of Federal Express's features and services in the overnight parcel business, including Saturday-morning delivery. (Until recently, UPS delivered only Monday through Friday.) IT was the

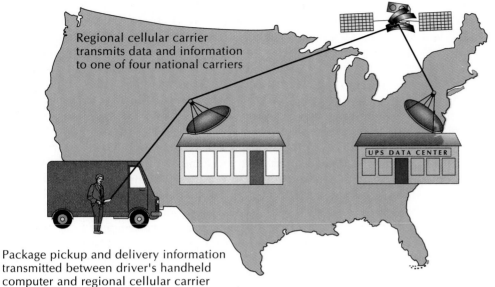

National cellular carrier transmits package information, via satellite, between the UPS data center, the regional cellular center, and UPS employees

Regional cellular carrier transmits data and information to one of four national carriers

UPS DATA CENTER

Package pickup and delivery information transmitted between driver's handheld computer and regional cellular carrier

FIGURE 11.2
United Parcel Service's Cellular Network for Package Tracking
UPS's new $150 million communications network has helped it compete with its major rival, Federal Express.

vehicle for turning the company's vision into reality. The UPS story will continue to evolve, making it an interesting one to watch for years to come.

Of course, not all proposals are feasible. This does not mean, however, that a development proposal judged infeasible is worthless. Sometimes proposals are sent back to the originator with a request for more information, then reexamined. Often, the preliminary investigation can reveal opportunities to change business processes and activities in a way that both improves the business and eliminates the need to invest in a new information system. In these cases, the proposal and the preliminary investigation both contribute to the business's ultimate goal: increased organization success.

Requirements Determination

A **requirement** is a feature that must be included in a system. It may be a way of capturing or processing information, a method of interacting with the system, a processing activity or result, a piece of information displayed or printed as a result of processing, or a function that can be performed to safeguard data and information. For UPS, the requirement was guaranteed overnight delivery and package tracking. For AMRIS, the requirement (never fulfilled) was the connection of business partners to allow them to share information and assist their customers.

During **requirements determination**, the systems analyst studies the current business situation, collecting and analyzing data and information to determine who is involved, what data and information are used, and how the current system can be improved. Requirements determination should address either or both types of improvement: process improvement and business improvement.

Process Improvement. A **process** is a structured activity that leads to a set of results (or, in systems terms, an *output*). The structure of the process specifies its

requirement A feature that must be included in a system.

requirements determination The second step in the SDLC. The study of the current business situation to determine who is involved, what data or information are needed, and how the current system can be improved.

process A structured activity that leads to a set of results (output).

sequence of activities and the flow of work from beginning to end. Processes cut across business functions, spanning the boundaries of departments and locations. A company's order-fulfillment process, for example, depends on the ability of the manufacturing, inventory, shipping, and accounting departments to work together to ship a customer's order and bill the account in a timely and accurate fashion.

process improvement An improvement in the way a business works.

Process improvement addresses the question, "Can we improve the way we work?" Before improvements to a system can be made, the systems analyst must know how activities are performed now, which procedures are effective, and which processes need improvement. Table 11.1 lists the questions that an analyst attempts to answer in evaluating a process. It is useful to think of the process as having a customer—an individual or group who receives the benefits or results of the process. Depending on how well the process is performed, the customer will be satisfied or dissatisfied.

The fast pace of business in the 1990s, coupled with competitive pressures and customer expectations of high-quality products and services, is causing managers and executives in many organizations to review *all* their business processes. Reshaping business processes, often called **reengineering**, simultaneously seeks to remove barriers that prohibit an organization from providing better products and services and to help the organization capitalize on its strengths.

reengineering The reshaping of business processes to remove barriers that prohibit an organization from providing better products and services and to help the organization capitalize on its strengths.

Reengineering is just one part of the "re- phenomenon." Businesses are redesigning, retooling, remaking, reshaping, restructuring, reorganizing, reestablishing, rebuilding, and repositioning to gain an advantage in the extremely competitive global marketplace. IT plays an important role in reengineering business processes. The five steps involved in the reengineering processes are outlined in Figure 11.3.

Business Improvement.   The capabilities of a business can be expanded through business improvement. **Business improvement** addresses the question, "Can we improve our business?" The UPS example above illustrates clearly how information technology can be used for business improvement.

business improvement An improvement in a business itself, usually in the form of increased sales or more satisfied customers.

There are four general ways in which IT plays a central role in business improvement: by helping firms offer new products and services, by speeding up business processes, by reducing the cost of products and services, and by helping firms enter new regions or markets.

OFFER NEW PRODUCTS AND SERVICES.   New products and services mean new ways to build a business. This type of business improvement arises when businesses identify and then meet the previously unrecognized wants and needs of their existing or potential customers.

TABLE 11.1   Evaluating a Business Process

- What is being done?
- How is it being done?
- How frequently does it occur?
- How great is the volume of transactions or decisions?
- How well is the task being performed?
- Does a problem exist?
- If a problem exists, how serious is it?
- If a problem exists, what is the underlying cause?
- Who is affected by the business process or work activity under consideration?

Step 1: Review	During the review of business processes, the systems analyst should document activities in the current process, determine what value or benefits are added by performing the process, and identify opportunities for improvement.
Step 2: Redesign	Reengineering is often most successful when company personnel are able to take a fresh look at how they carry out activities. Challenging traditional assumptions about the reasons to do things in a particular way often leads to process redesign. The result is often processes that are simpler, less time-consuming, and more effective than the processes they replaced.
Step 3: Reorchestrate	Redesign suggests new ways to do business. Reorchestration is the transition to those new ways. Realignment of responsibilities, adjustment of quality-control procedures, and implementation of new methods are essential. Reorchestration also means addressing the concerns of individuals who are directly affected by the changes. Failure to deal with human concerns may render reengineering efforts unsuccessful.
Step 4: Reassess	Measurement of results documents the impact of reengineering. Some changes may be better than expected and others may need rethinking. Only by evaluating the results can impact be determined.
Step 5: Recycle	Reengineering is not a one-time activity. Because opportunities and the competitive environment change constantly, rethinking business processes is always an agenda item for an organization's leaders.

FIGURE 11.3
The Reengineering Process
Reengineering means overhauling business processes and organization structures that limit the competitiveness, efficiency, and effectiveness of the organization.

The Regional Bell Operating Companies (RBOCs) in the United States (Ameritech, Bell Atlantic, BellSouth, NYNEX, Pacific Telesis, Southwestern Bell, and U.S. West) and PTTs in Europe and the Far East are using their IT capabilities to offer many new services to customers. Among these new services are call forwarding (in which calls are automatically rerouted to the recipient's actual destination rather than to the number dialed) and call waiting (in which a signal alerts a customer that a call is waiting to come over a link already in use). Weather and sports scores are also available, for a small fee, over the same lines.

Other new services in various stages of development by telephone companies include the delivery of movies, the monitoring of home security systems, and the reading of electric and gas meters. Customers benefit from the new, more convenient services, and the telephone companies earn higher revenue and develop a larger customer base.

SPEED UP BUSINESS PROCESSES.   Compressing the time it takes to do business can increase efficiency or produce a substantial competitive advantage. As both Federal Express and UPS know well, the ability to move information quickly and effectively can give companies an edge in taking business from their competitors.

The benefits of speeding up business processes are not limited to service industries, however. Manufacturing companies have found that responding more quickly offers them business advantages as well. As the time needed to complete a task is compressed, the risk of errors is reduced because decisions are made closer to the time when action is taken. Less risk usually means that businesses need to tie up fewer resources as a precaution against mistakes or poor estimates.

Toyota Motor Corp. of Toyota City, Japan competes worldwide on the basis of time. The company invented the Toyota production system, which aims at using the same manufacturing process to make many models of automobiles in small quantities. An essential component of this system is what has come to be known as *just-in-time production* (Figure 11.4). Toyota can now take orders for automobiles and deliver the custom-manufactured vehicle within the same week. Many of Toyota's competitors take four to six weeks to manufacture and deliver a custom-ordered vehicle.

Toyota takes time out of each step in manufacturing by making the processes simple and ensuring that the workers on the assembly line have all the information they need to assemble the car ordered by the customer. Doing things right means fewer delays and less time needed to rework improperly assembled vehicles.

At Toyota, compressing time also means more accurate scheduling and closer relations with suppliers. The company uses IT to receive and assemble all dealers' orders electronically. The parts and assembly lists needed to build each vehicle are prepared by computers that retrieve details from the company's databases. This information is then shared through Toyota's communications network with suppliers, who deliver the parts and assemblies, often several times daily, "just in time" for workers to install them in the vehicle. In addition to allowing the company to deliver the customer's choice of automobile much faster than competitors while maintaining high standards of quality, scheduling parts delivery closer to manufacturing time means less space and money tied up in inventory.

REDUCE THE COST OF PRODUCTS AND SERVICES.   Reduced costs give companies great flexibility in their pricing policies. If a competitor decides to compete by reducing the price of a product, the company can respond and still make a profit. *Price wars* occur when businesses can compete solely on the price they charge customers. In the end, the company that has the lowest costs is usually in the best position. (No business really wins in a price war—unless it is able to drive a competitor out of the industry—because reduced prices sometimes reduce profits, which are needed to finance future operations and expansion. Even the customer, who benefits from a price war in the short run, may lose out in the long run if companies drive each other out of business or if a survivor later raises prices.) IT, when used to help reduce costs of products or services, plays a central role in business improvement.

FIGURE 11.4
Just-in-Time Manufacturing at the Toyota Plant in Toyota City, Japan
Toyota's JIT system ensures that all assembly line workers have parts at hand when they need them. The parts and assembly lists for each vehicle are prepared by computers that retrieve information from the company's databases. This information is shared through the company's communications network with its suppliers, who deliver the parts "just in time" for workers to install them in the vehicle.

ENTER NEW REGIONS OR MARKETS. Companies can improve their businesses by using their IT capabilities to enter new geographic regions. For example, both Federal Express and UPS found that a growing number of their customers were expanding their businesses into new international regions. These customers had grown accustomed to overnight package delivery in the United States and expected the same capability abroad, whether in Canada and Mexico, Europe and the United Kingdom, or the Far East. They also wanted the same level of accountability, the same ability to find out the location of a package at any moment. After identifying this requirement, both companies expanded their delivery capabilities and the capabilities of their system to track packages shipped to international destinations. This chapter's Global IT box, "IT Comes to the Aid of Exporters," offers some advice for entrepreneurs interested in exporting their goods and services to international destinations.

Business improvement has its greatest impact when it enables a company to launch a new product or service that competitors cannot duplicate quickly or at all. Businesspeople call this type of improvement a *preemptive strike*. By launching a preemptive strike, the company captures the market for the product or service, satisfying customers' desires swiftly and to such an extent that they have no desire to switch to other products later.

American Airlines launched a preemptive strike when it implemented its computerized reservation system and related frequent flier program. Even though other airlines have tried to emulate this system, few have been successful. AMR retains approximately 50% of the U.S. market for travel-agent and fee-based reservation processing while the more than 50 remaining carriers fight it out for the rest.

Reality Check. Experience is an important factor in identifying systems requirements. Junior analysts tend to accept what they hear, see, or read about current business processes. But experience teaches them to recognize that processes change when an analyst becomes involved in a business situation. People tend to behave differently when under scrutiny and may change their actions to fall more in line with what is expected (a tendency called the *Hawthorne effect*). They may also make things look more difficult than they really are.

Experienced analysts use a variety of sources and methods to gather information. They compare the information obtained in one way or from one specific source with those obtained in other ways. They also seek to get inside the business or industry they are studying. Frequently, users will not inform an analyst of the details surrounding a business practice or an industry practice. Seldom is this an intentional withholding of information. Rather, this information is usually so integral to the process that the individual doesn't realize the systems analyst is not aware of it. Experienced analysts know how to get at this information.

Systems analysis entails more than simply gathering information and studying tools, techniques, and technologies. It means gaining knowledge and insight and using these to identify and solve problems. ∎

Systems Design

A system's *design* is the set of details that describe how the system will meet the requirements identified during requirements determination. The process of translating requirements into design specifications is **systems design**.

systems design The third step in the SDLC. The process of translating requirements into design specifications.

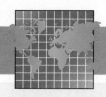
IT Comes to the Aid of Exporters

THOUSANDS OF SMALL AND MIDSIZE BUSINESSES ARE FINDING THAT exporting is a great way to increase sales. Consider, for example, the experiences of DMT Corp. and Interstate Engineering. DMT Corp., of Waukesha, Wisconsin, more than doubled sales by marketing its backup electrical generators to manufacturers in the Far East and Central and South America, where the electrical supply tends to be unreliable. At Interstate Engineering, exports to Germany, Italy, France, the United Kingdom, and Japan let the company cancel plans to lay off 10% to 15% of its 140 employees.

Unfortunately, too many companies hesitate to export, mystified by the requirements of international market research and bureaucracy. This situation may change soon, however, thanks to a growing collection of IT-based assistance from both government and private sources.

Demystifying International Market Research   One of the most detailed resources of international market research is the National Trade Data Bank (NTDB), a CD-ROM issued every month by the U.S. Commerce Department. Each disk compiles and indexes more than 100,000 export-related documents, detailed export and import statistics from the Census Bureau, national income and product accounts from the Bureau of Economic Analysis, and world production figures from the Department of Agriculture. Although many libraries, private firms, and marketing consultants subscribe to the NTDB, its biggest fans may be the trade specialists who work for the federal government. Their job is to work directly with local companies to help them build their exports.

Another source of market information is the Export Hotline, a free service cosponsored by AT&T, KPMG Peat Marwick, Delta Airlines, *Business Week, The Journal of Commerce,* the National Association of Manufacturers, the U.S. Council for International Business, and others. After callers use a voice-mail system to enter their selection from a menu of 78 countries and 50 industries, the system taps into a database to produce a customized marketing report that is faxed to the caller. The system can also generate a number of other documents, such as a country overview, an analysis of export, import, or investment issues, a list of key business contacts, direct marketing advice, shipping and transportation requirements, and tips on business travel, etiquette, and protocol.

Cutting Through the Red Tape   Of course, marketing is only half the battle. Exporters also have to meet the legal requirements of the countries in which they want to do business. This can lead to a bewildering flurry of forms, documents, and licenses. In an effort to simplify the process of getting an export license, the U.S. Commerce

Sales to foreign universities, research labs, and governments helped Linda and Robert Bernstein's SeaSpace Corp. grow from six to sixteen employees. The San Diego-based firm manufactures weather-satellite receiving systems. By 1992, 50% of the company's sales were coming from England, Germany, Italy, Japan, Korea, Portugal, Spain, and Taiwan.

Department has created a trio of computer systems that can be accessed by phone. To get general information, just call ELVIS—short for Export Licensing Voice Information System—a voice-mail system that offers information on licensing procedures, as well as ELAIN and STELA. ELAIN, the Export License Application and Information Network, lets callers apply for licenses electronically over the CompuServe network; STELA, the System for Tracking Export License Application, is an automated voice-response system that lets callers check the status of their application.

Meanwhile, a growing number of entrepreneurs are creating export-automation software, computer programs that can generate letter-perfect commercial invoices, country-of-origin certificates, packing slips, and export-declaration forms in various languages. The programs can also help exporters comply with domestic and international regulations, such as the U.S. table-of-denial screenings that restrict the types of technology that can be sold in certain countries.

Systems design takes place in three phases: preliminary (conceptual) design, prototyping, and detailed (physical) design.

Preliminary (Conceptual) Design. The preliminary design of a system specifies its distinguishing characteristics, conceptualizing the functions it will perform and how they will occur. Current systems capabilities will influence the design. The preliminary design typically specifies:

- Whether the system will be distributed or centralized.
- Whether the system will be developed by the company's staff members or by outside contractors or by purchasing a software package.
- Whether processing will use on-line or batch procedures.
- Whether data communications networks will be developed.
- Whether applications will run on microcomputers, midrange systems, mainframes, or a combination of these.
- The data and information that will be generated and the reports that must be produced.
- The files or databases needed for the system to function.
- The number of users and locations supported by the system.
- The capacity of storage devices.
- The number of printers and communications links between individuals, customers, suppliers, and others who will interact with the system.
- The personnel needed to operate the system.

After the preliminary design is prepared, it is presented to the users and to the steering committee for approval. Any changes needed in the conceptual design are made before the design moves into the prototype phase.

Diamond Star Motors Corp., located in Normal, Illinois, began as a joint venture between Chrysler Corp. of Detroit, Michigan, and Japan's Mitsubishi Motors Corp. in 1985. By 1991, Diamond Star had become a subsidiary of MMC. The company, which produces the Mitsubishi Eclipse and Galant, Eagle Talon, and Plymouth Laser, now has more than 3,200 employees.

Manufacturing activities at Diamond Star are patterned after Mitsubishi Motors' practices in Japan. Production associates begin their work day at 6:30 A.M. with stretching exercises (performed to the sound of music piped throughout the building). All employees, including managers and the 50-person Information Technology staff, wear the same uniform: gray pants and maroon shirts bearing the company logo over the left pocket and the employee's name over the right (Figure 11.5 on the next page).

Originally, Diamond Star intended to duplicate the manufacturing and business processes of the Mitsubishi plant in Okazaki, Japan. It quickly determined, however, that duplicating that plant's computer and communications systems was much easier than transplanting its business processes and related IT applications. Analysts discovered, for example, how dramatically Japanese finance and accounting practices differ from those in the United States. Japanese companies typically budget in six-month cycles, while U.S. companies usually create 12-month annual budgets. (The Japanese believe shorter budget periods give businesspeople better control over resources, enable them to forecast more accurately, and allow them to respond more rapidly to fluctuations in business.)

To launch the conceptual designs for the 30 new systems needed by the new company, Diamond Star's IT staff had to become familiar with the different cultures and business practices in the two countries. Some IT staff members spent time in Japan (from two to ten weeks) to become familiar with the Japanese sys-

FIGURE 11.5
Shared IT Applications at Diamond Star Motors
All Diamond Star employees, including managers and assembly line workers, wear the same uniform. This standard is part of the company's team-oriented approach to automobile design and assembly. Using sophisticated design programs linked to the company's network, engineers can communicate directly with the assembly line to create prototypes of the parts they've designed.

tems. In the end, not only did they design interfaces between each partner's computers to accommodate the different budgeting and reporting practices, they also developed IT applications to run one of the most sophisticated automated manufacturing lines in the world. This line includes an online vehicle tracking system that tells workers the location of every vehicle, an online vendor broadcasting system designed to ensure that parts arrive just in time for installation in a vehicle, and more than 100 assembly line robots (550 plant wide). Diamond Star's assembly line is 20% automated, compared to 10% automation in most automotive plants with the same capacity. A specially designed minicomputer helps to run and manage Diamond Star's assembly line. (We discuss these types of industrial applications in more detail in the next chapter.)

prototype A working model of an IT application.

Prototyping.   A **prototype** is a working model of an IT application that, compared to a complete system, is relatively inexpensive to build. Although it usually does not contain all the features or perform all the functions that will be included in the final system, the prototype includes elements that will allow an individual to use the system. By using the system, people can quickly determine what they like and dislike about it and what important features are missing from the design. If, for example, an individual using the prototype finds that the capabilities for certain types of processing or for handling exceptional situations are not built into the design, the system's requirements can be expanded.

Application prototyping has two primary uses. First, it is an effective method of clarifying the requirements that must be built into a system. Reviewing written specifications is not nearly as effective as working with the features firsthand. Second, prototypes are useful for evaluating a system's features. Users' reactions to methods of interacting with the system (through a keyboard or mouse, or by touching a menu option with a finger, for example) and the arrangement of information on a computer display can be gauged quickly and easily when the individual sits down at a workstation and actually uses the application (Figure 11.6).

As Figure 11.7 shows, the prototype is part of an *evolutionary system*. New information acquired from users during the prototype phase can be applied to modify the physical design early in the development process. Modified prototypes

FIGURE 11.6
Application Prototyping
IBM's Software Usability Laboratory allows systems design
and development personnel to monitor people's reactions to
a system prototype. Listening to future users' reactions to and
concerns about the new system is an important component
of the system development process.

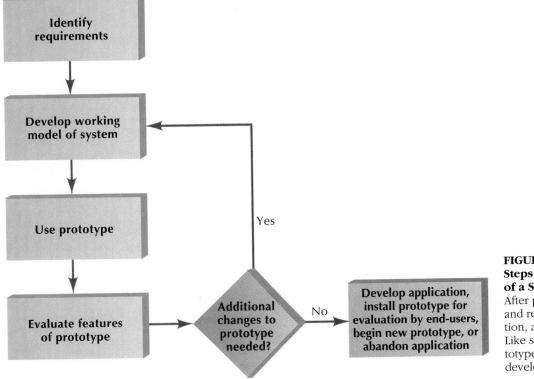

FIGURE 11.7
**Steps in the Development
of a System Prototype**
After preliminary investigation
and requirements determination, a prototype is created.
Like systems themselves, prototypes undergo evaluation,
development, and change.

can then be reevaluated. Making changes to a prototype is much less costly than
altering an application once it has been fully developed and implemented.

Detailed (Physical) Design.   The detailed, or physical, design of a system specifies its features. The accompanying documentation consists of definitions explaining the characteristics of the system, its processing activities, and the reports and
charts it can generate. Detailed design specifications usually are prepared in the
following sequence:

• **Output: Information and results.** Because output is the reason for developing a system in the first place, it is the starting point for detailed design. In the

layout description A chart that shows the exact location of data and information on a computer screen or in a printed report.

output design, the type, contents, and formats of reports and display screens are defined using **layout descriptions** that show the exact location of data and information on the screen and in a printed report (Figure 11.8).

- **Input: Data and information for processing.** Once they know requirements, designers work back to determine what processing activities are needed to produce the output and which data and information are to be provided as input by people using the system.
- **Stored data: Databases and files.** If data are not keyed, scanned, or otherwise entered as input by a system user, and are not transmitted to a computer by an electronic link, they may be retrieved from a stored database or file. Figure 11.9 shows the various input components of a sales system and their origins, all of which are specified in the detailed design.
- **Processing and procedures.** Methods are determined for achieving computing results and arranging data and information into a desired sequence. These methods are the *processing requirements*. Also important is the establishment of procedures for the people using the system. Table 11.2 shows some important systems procedures specified during detailed design. These include actions taken to back up files and maintain system security.

FIGURE 11.8   Layout Form for Printed System Output
Layout descriptions, sometimes drawn on paper and other times at the display screen, are used in physical design to show the exact location of data and information in a printed report and on screen. The layout form shown here was used to prepare the format of an inventory on hand report.

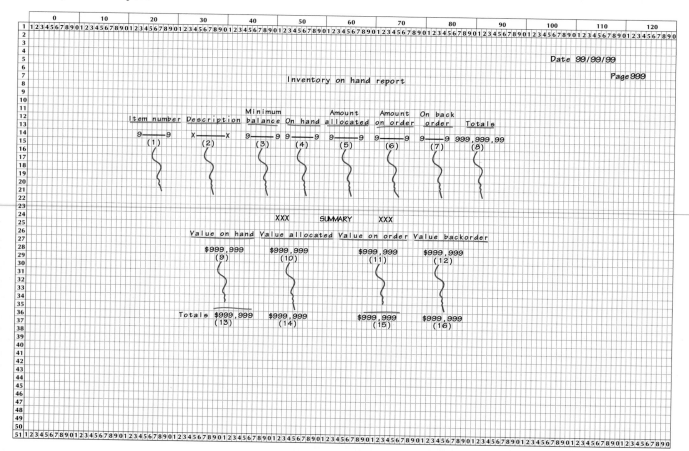

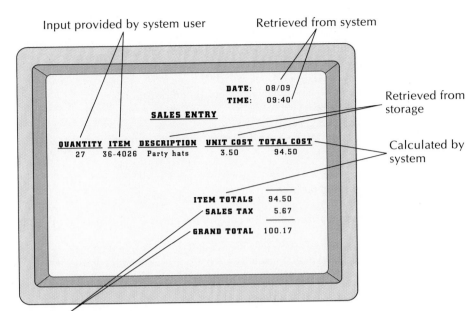

Input provided by system user

Retrieved from system

Retrieved from storage

Calculated by system

Tax rate retrieved from system; tax and grand total computed by system

FIGURE 11.9
Input Components of a Sales System and Their Origins
Data that are not entered by a user into the system may be automatically retrieved from a database or file stored in the system.

• **Controls.** In a shared system, individuals have responsibilities for activities and specific actions. Controls describe these responsibilities. For example, if transactions are accumulated into batches before processing, control information describes how the batches are identified, when they are processed, what files and databases they use, and how the computer operator determines that the batches have been properly processed. In the American Airlines system, controls describe how the weekly batches of ticket payments submitted by each agent will be audited for accuracy and processed within the system.

Confirm's design called for over 3,000 programs because of the many different activities necessary to manage cross-company business transactions. Some of Confirm's many design requirements are detailed in Figure 11.10.

TABLE 11.2   Design of Systems Procedures

Type	Definition
Data-entry procedures	Procedures for capturing data and entering them into the system. Identify which data originate with specific documents, input devices, or individuals.
Run-time procedures	The steps the system's user or operator takes to achieve the desired results. Identify the files and programs that must be included with the system.
Error-handling procedures	The actions a user or operator must take when unexpected or unacceptable results occur. Describe the steps to take when an error is detected or processing is disrupted for any reason.
Security and backup procedures	The actions taken to protect the system, data, information, or programs against accidental or intentional damage. Specify when and how to make duplicate copies of data and programs or actions to take to prevent sabotage.

Input
- Entry of reservation details for airlines, automobiles, or hotels.
- Entry of a wide variety of rates and charges for airline seats, automobiles, or hotel rooms.
- Entry of changes to previously entered data and information.
- Entry of inquiries to retrieve information about a specific transaction, individual, flight, vehicle, or hotel.
- Entry of requests to print reports, display information, or transmit details from one location to another.

Output/Reports
- Printed acknowledgments of reservations.
- Printed tickets or invoices.
- Printed reports summarizing the allocation of resources (airline seats, automobiles, or hotel rooms).
- Printed current status information or historical descriptions of the business activities of a customer, travel agent, or hotel.

Stored Data
- Transactions already entered into the system.
- Customer, travel agent, airline, automobile, or hotel characteristics.
- Descriptions of facilities, vehicles, or aircraft available to users of the system.

Processing/Procedures
- Descriptions of how transaction data are used to update files and databases or generate reports.
- Procedures for accepting, validating, and processing transactions.
- Procedures for backing up the system to safeguard sensitive data and information.
- Procedures for restarting an application that is interrupted for any reason.

Controls
- Methods for detecting invalid charges or credits.
- Steps for authorizing changes to charge rates and authorization codes in the system.

FIGURE 11.10
The Detailed Design of Confirm
The design of AMRIS's Confirm system called for more than 3,000 programs. Some elements of the design, based on requirements determination, are listed here.

Throughout the design process for any system, designers examine many alternatives to ensure that the desired features are included, to meet each business requirement, and to fit within the budgetary constraints of the project.

Reality Check. Have you ever noticed that good designs are hardly noticeable? When you get into an automobile, the car's physical features are pretty much the way you expect them to be. The speedometer, fuel gauge, and warning lights are in the same vicinity in most automobiles. So are the controls for the lights and windshield wipers. In each case, you reach for them without giving it a second thought. If the seat's position, steering wheel's tilt, or mirror's angle is not just right, you can make the necessary adjustments quickly and easily. These are all hallmarks of a good design.

In contrast, a bad design is noticed almost immediately. We can all think of instances when we had to fumble around to find the release for the hood, the gas tank cover, the ignition, or headlight control switch. When it's right, we don't give the design a second thought; when it's wrong, our lives are made more difficult. This is as true for computer and communications systems as it is for cars. ∎

Development and Construction

During development and **system construction**, the system is actually built. Physical design specifications are turned into a functioning system. The principle activities of development are the acquisition of software and services, computer programming, and testing (Figure 11.11).

Acquisition of Software and Services.   Increasingly, systems incorporate prepackaged software and services originating outside the company. During construction and development, systems designers may acquire software packages that perform specific functions (for example, data management, security, or backup) or special services (e-mail, electronic data interchange, voice mail, and so on) and incorporate them into the overall system design.

Communications software and network services are usually acquired rather than developed in-house. During design and construction, systems analysts work with communications carriers to design the network characteristics (such as the locations to be interconnected, transmission speeds, and management, backup, and error deduction procedures).

Programming.   After the company has acquired software and services, computer programmers turn processing specifications into software. The software created for the system will perform its capture, generation, processing, storage and retrieval, and transmission functions.

Programming may be done in-house or by outside contractors. The contractor receives the specifications and prepares the necessary software according to a development and delivery schedule set up by the client firm. Depending on the system, portions of the software may be delivered as they are completed or the entire set of programs may arrive in one package when the development process is complete.

Testing.   Once the system is constructed, it must be tested to determine if it (1) performs according to specifications, (2) performs as users expect it to perform,

system construction The fourth step in the SDLC. The process of turning physical design specifications into a functioning system.

FIGURE 11.11   Development and Construction of a System
Development and construction—the fourth stage in the SDLC—entails three activities: computer programming, acquisition of software and services, and testing.

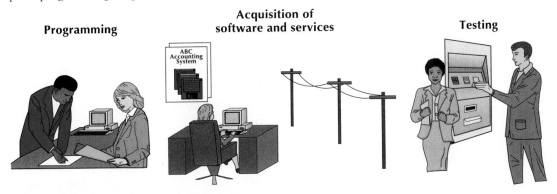

| Programming | Acquisition of software and services | | Testing |

Have computer programs written by company personnel or by outside contractors

Acquire and install prepackaged software purchased from outside sources

Acquire communications links and network services needed for new system

Test software, procedures, and features of new system

software testing The testing of software programs to ensure that the software does not fail.

test data Experimental files used to test software.

system testing The testing of a complete system—software, procedures, and guidelines.

and (3) detects errors that halt processing or produce erroneous results. During **software testing**, software programs are used with special experimental data files called **test data** to ensure that the software does not *fail*—that is, does not produce unexpected or incorrect results or interruptions in processing. The test data are created to determine whether the system will process them correctly. The systems analyst examines the processing results to see if they match expectations.

In **system testing**, the complete system—software, procedures, and guidelines—is tested. Also tested is the compatibility between different software modules used together in the system (for example, a data input module, a communications module, and a report writing module).

When UPS decided to develop its wireless network, it performed many different tests. It checked (1) the reliability of the handheld computer in extremely hot and extremely cold temperatures and in both high and low humidity, (2) the clarity of network transmissions under different weather conditions, (3) the speed at which drivers could enter data through the keyboard, (4) the system's response rate if a large number of drivers entered data simultaneously, and (5) the system's response if a driver entered an unauthorized transaction code or entered only a portion of the data needed to process a transaction. UPS worked with a small number of drivers to test the system before deciding to go ahead and equip all 50,000 drivers with wireless devices.

Reality Check. IT professionals, particularly systems analysts and computer programmers, use the word *bugs* to mean errors or unintended results. ("There's a bug in the software and it causes the program to fail if we report $0.00 sales for the day.") "How did they ever come up with that one?" you may wonder.

The term "bug" really came from a bug. Here's how it happened. Grace Murray Hopper, one of the pioneers of the computer field, was working in her laboratory one day, running a program she had developed. When the program produced an unexpected result, she tried to determine the cause. After rechecking the processing logic of the program and convincing herself it was correct, she began looking elsewhere.

In those early days of IT—the 1940s and 1950s—computers were quite different. They did not use transistors and chips, but rather mechanical relays that opened and closed. Hopper glanced at one of the relays and saw that it was not fully closed, even though the program logic dictated that it should be. Upon closer scrutiny, she found that a moth had become trapped in the relay, thus preventing completion of the circuit and correct execution of the program. She pulled it out and the program ran properly.

This is why programmers now talk about *debugging* their programs. ■

CRITICAL CONNECTION 1
Misadventures in Computing: U-Haul Plans to Try Again

U-Haul   Even a company that has successfully installed a new computer system needs to perform system testing. Take the experience of U-Haul International. Like many companies, U-Haul is hungry for the process and business improvements promised by client-server computing (see

Chapter 10). The company had already had a positive experience in the late 1980s, when it successfully created a computer network linking its 1,100 rental centers and 78 district offices. As a result of that massive project, paperwork and management reports that used to take two weeks to process were being handled in just hours and the clerical staff was trimmed from 250 to 50. Given this success, the next mandate from top management seemed both logical and reasonable: Let's downsize the computing at headquarters, moving from two mainframes to a client-server network.

Fortunately, a pilot project—whose goal was to move a human resource application from the mainframe to client-server computing—revealed a major flaw in the new system, which did not include many of the tools and utilities the company needed. The system's poor performance, coupled with inadequate development tools, forced U-Haul to declare the test a failure.

Implementation

During **implementation**, the new system is installed and put into use. New systems often bring many changes to a business, including new business procedures, different individual responsibilities, and adjustments in the flow of information. Three important aspects of implementation are training, site preparation, and conversion strategy.

> **implementation** The fifth step in the SDLC. The process of installing a new system and putting it to use.

Training.   Even experienced computer users need to become familiar with the features of a new system. During **training**, IT professionals show people how to use the system and how to keep the system running and reliable. Training covers all aspects of using the system, from routine procedures to periodic actions (for example, replacing printer cartridges) to emergency operations (for example, the steps to take in the event system security is breached).

We tend to think of "training" as the training of end-users who are part of a workgroup. But IT professionals also need training themselves when a new application is installed. IT professionals must often know both the user's procedures and the administrator's procedures to keep the network, server, or other components up and running.

> **training** The process by which people are taught how to use a system.

Site Preparation.   Sometimes new systems mean new equipment and furniture and the construction of additional facilities (for example, new electrical wiring, air conditioning systems, lighting systems, and security systems). These activities involved in preparing for the installing of a new system are called **site preparation**.

Site preparation can be minimal or extensive. If a new system requires the replacement of existing microcomputers with more powerful models, changes in the work site may not be needed. The old computers are simply unplugged and carried away and the new ones are installed in their place. If a local area network will be installed in an office for the first time, however, site preparation may entail running communications cables, building a cable connection room, and installing cable plugs in the wall.

When UPS decided to install handheld computers and modem/telephone links in its delivery trucks, it had to train drivers in their use. It also had to prepare the connections and mount the devices in the trucks while preparing communications facilities at its data center.

> **site preparation** The activities involved in preparing for the installation of a new system.

Conversion Strategies.   A **conversion plan** describes all the activities that must occur to change over to a new system. It identifies the persons responsible for

> **conversion plan** A description of all the activities that must occur to change over to a new system.

each activity and includes a timetable for the completion of each event. These activities include assigning responsibility for ensuring each activity is completed, assigning and verifying dates on the conversion schedule, listing all databases and files to be converted, identifying all the data and information required to build databases and files for the system, listing all new procedures that go into use during conversion, and outlining all the controls that will be used to ensure that each activity occurs properly.

Analysts choose from four conversion strategies in implementing the new system (Table 11.3). Each strategy has advantages and disadvantages.

direct cut over A conversion plan in which people stop using an old system and immediately begin using a new system.

- When time is tight or when dramatic changes will not be made in work processes or responsibilities, the analyst may decide to do a **direct cut over** to the new system. People stop using the old system and jump right into using the new system. This conversion method can be risky if any serious problems or misunderstandings about the new system exist. But it also offers a major benefit: If people are forced to use the system, they tend to work hard to ensure its success.

parallel systems A conversion plan in which both an old and a new system are used for a period of time, with the old system being gradually phased out.

- In a **parallel systems** strategy, both the old and new system are used together for a period of time. Parallel systems offers the greatest security if people are unsure of the usefulness or reliability of the new application. They know that they can always fall back on the old system. Yet this advantage can also be a disadvantage. If they feel they are giving up important responsibilities or personal prestige, people may not try as hard to make the new system work. They may even want the new system to fail.

pilot A conversion plan in which a working version of a new system is implemented in one group or department to test it before it is installed throughout the entire business.

- The **pilot** conversion method is often used when the new system involves new business methods or drastic changes in work processes. Under this method, a working version of the system is implemented in one group or department.

TABLE 11.3   Conversion Strategies

Method	Description	Advantages	Disadvantages
Direct cut over	The old system is replaced by the new one. The organization relies fully on the new system.	Forces users to make the new system work. There are immediate benefits from new methods and controls.	There is no other system to fall back on if difficulties arise with new system. Requires the most careful planning.
Parallel systems	The old system is operated along with the new system.	Offers greatest security. The old system can take over if errors are found in the new system or if usage problems occur.	Doubles operating costs. The new system may not get fair trial.
Pilot	Working version of system implemented in one part of the organization. Based on feedback, changes are made and the system is installed in the rest of the organization by one of the other methods.	Provides experience and testing before implementation.	May give the impression that the old system is unreliable and not error-free.
Phase-in	Gradually implement system across all users.	Allows some users to take advantage of the system early. Allows training and installation without unnecessary use of resources.	A long phase-in may cause user problems whether the project goes well (overenthusiasm) or not (resistance and lack of fair trial).

People know they are using a new system and that their experiences and suggestions may lead to changes in the system. When no additional changes are needed and the system is judged complete, it is installed throughout the entire business. This approach offers the ability to test the system before putting it into full use. Pilot programs avoid the risk of encountering a problem that affects a large number of people, but may give the impression that the old system is unreliable and not error-free.

- When it is not possible to install a new system throughout an entire organization or department at one time, the **phase-in** method is used. The conversion of databases, training of personnel, and installation of hardware and software are staged over a period of time ranging from weeks to months, depending on the system. Some people begin to use the new system before others. The phase-in method allows some users to take advantage of the system early, but long phase-ins can create user problems whether the project goes well or not.

phase-in A conversion plan in which a new system is gradually phased in over a period of time.

UPS did not acquire its wireless communications capabilities all at once. Rather, it pilot tested a few handheld computers and the cellular link to determine if they would work as expected. When evidence showed that they would, the company proceeded to roll out the system to all the drivers region by region. The pilot proved the concept and technology; a phase-in of the system followed.

Evaluation and Continuing Evolution

Once implemented, analysts perform **systems evaluation** to identify the strengths and weaknesses of the system. They want to determine if the system delivers the expected level of usability and usefulness and if it is providing the anticipated benefits.

systems evaluation The sixth step in the SDLC. The process of monitoring a new system to identify its strengths and weaknesses.

Systems are often used for many years. However, the organization, the people using the system, and the business environment will change. For this reason, all systems need to undergo continuing development, with features being added and capabilities augmented as new or improved technologies are introduced.

Given the complexity and time-intensiveness of the SDLC, there is much potential for error. The Quality and Productivity box on page 452 titled "The SDLC: Avoiding Problems Before They Occur" offers a list of the most common problems encountered in systems development. Forewarned is forearmed.

■ The Systems Analyst's Tools and Techniques

Systems analysts use a variety of techniques to collect data and tools to describe systems and document business processes. In addition to data collection techniques like interviews and sampling, analysts also use tools like system flowcharts, dataflow diagrams, data dictionaries, and computer-aided system engineering. All these tools help systems analysts to be productive and effective and to deliver a better final product.

Data Collection Techniques

Analysts determine system requirements by using any combination of five techniques: interviews, questionnaires, document examination, observation, and sampling.

- Analysts conduct interviews with a variety of persons (managers, staff members, employees, customers, and suppliers) to gather details about business processes. Interviews provide the opportunity to gather opinions about why

QUALITY AND PRODUCTIVITY

The SDLC: Avoiding Problems Before They Occur

THE U.S. GENERAL ACCOUNTING OFFICE (GAO) IS A FEDERAL government agency charged with monitoring the performance of other government agencies. Included in the agencies it monitors are the National Weather Service, Federal Aviation Administration, Patent and Trademark Office, Department of Justice, Department of Education, NASA, Internal Revenue Service, Department of Defense, and Department of Veterans Affairs. Because the government uses many IT applications and dedicates large amounts of financial and human resources to each application, the GAO frequently examines the development of the applications to determine whether the projects are developed on time, within budget, and with the intended results. Such information is useful for evaluating project managers and for developing future IT projects.

The GAO has identified 10 problems that occur repeatedly in the development and use of IT applications. These are, in order of frequency:

1. Inadequate management of the systems development life cycle
2. Ineffective management information as a result of poor systems procedures
3. Flaws in systems security, integrity, and reliability
4. Inability of multiple systems to work together
5. Inadequate resources to accomplish goals
6. Cost overruns
7. Schedule delays

Improper management of the systems development life cycle can turn a systems project into a money-devouring monster. The best defense against cost overruns is strong project management from start to finish.

8. Systems not performing in the intended manner
9. Inaccurate or incomplete data and information
10. Difficulty in accessing data and information

All of these problems point to the importance of effective project management.

---

structured interview An interview in which the questions are prepared in advance and each interviewee is asked the same set of questions.

unstructured interview An interview in which the questions may be prepared in advance, but follow-up questions may vary depending on the interviewees' background and answers.

questionnaire A sheet of questions used to collect facts and opinions from a group of people.

document examination/ record inspection The review of company documents about a system or opportunity under investigation.

current procedures are followed and to hear suggestions for improvement. In a **structured interview**, the analyst prepares the questions in advance and asks each interviewee the same set of questions. In an **unstructured interview**, the analyst may also prepare questions in advance but often varies the line of questioning depending on the participants' background and the answers they give to preceding questions. Unstructured interviews allow interviewees to bring up ideas or worries that do not fit into any structured area of questioning.

- When an analyst must contact a large group of people, **questionnaires** may be a useful way to collect factual information and opinions. Analyzing the responses provides important insights into the system or business process and often identifies individuals who should be interviewed.

- A great deal of important information already exists in company documents. **Document examination**, also called **record inspection**, is the review of manuals, reports, and correspondence about the system or opportunity under investigation. Inspecting samples of sales slips, order forms, and worksheets can also reveal a great deal about how work is done and how errors are made.

- If a systems analyst wants to know what steps an employee takes in performing a task, how long a task takes, or whether prescribed procedures are easy to use and work as expected, **observation**—actually watching the activities take place—may be the best way of collecting information. Observation provides information that cannot be obtained in any other way.

- With **sampling**, the analyst collects data and information at prescribed intervals, or may meet with some of the system's users to get a sense of the effectiveness of current procedures. For example, a sample of 10% of the staff who interact directly with customers may tell the analyst a great deal about the views held by the entire staff. Or the analyst could decide to examine one out of every ten orders to determine the typical number of items ordered.

observation The process of watching an activity take place.

sampling The process of collecting data and information at random at prescribed intervals.

All these techniques can yield valuable information about systems requirements. Most analysts use a combination of them to gain the best information possible.

If you were the analyst responsible for developing the UPS wireless system, what details would you have wanted and how would you have collected them? You probably would have used all the data collection techniques to gather the system information you needed. Perhaps you conducted structured interviews with drivers, distribution center employees, and managers to determine the biggest problems in tracking and delivering packages. You might also have conducted unstructured interviews to solicit personal observations, opinions, and suggestions for capitalizing on previously unrecognized opportunities or responding to challenging problems.

You also might have used questionnaires to survey a large number of people (including employees, customers, and suppliers) on very specific questions. Likes, dislikes, and the appropriateness of policies and procedures are among the issues you might have addressed through questionnaires.

Riding with drivers and working with distribution personnel would have given you firsthand information about the nature of their jobs and the situations they encounter daily. Observing the tasks they perform, the routines they follow, and the amount of time it takes them to complete specific planned and unplanned tasks would have yielded valuable insight into productivity.

Record inspection and sampling would have enabled you to examine shipping notices and airbills as well as customer account records. They would also have allowed you to see which types of customers ship packages most often and on what days activities are heaviest. Of course, your entire investigation probably began with review of UPS's written procedures and policies describing the handling of packages.

System Flowcharts

Of all the systems analyst's tools, system flowcharts are the easiest to use and understand. A **system flowchart** is a graphical description of a business process or procedure that uses standard symbols to show (1) the sequence of activities that take place in a process; (2) the data, information, or documents that are input to the process or generated (output) as a result of the process; and (3) the decisions that are made at each point in the process. Figure 11.12 on page 454 describes the most commonly used symbols in system flowcharts.

System flowcharts describe *logic*—the decisions made within a process that determine which course of action will be followed. A sample system flowchart for order processing is shown in Figure 11.13 on page 455. More complex processes will have several different process sequences.

system flowchart A graphical description of a business process or procedure using standard symbols to show decision logic.

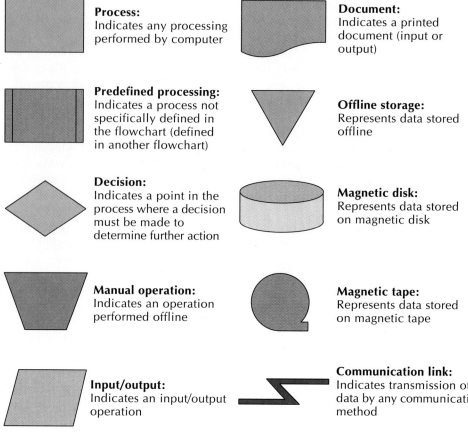

**FIGURE 11.12
Symbols Used in System
Flowcharts**

Dataflow Diagrams

dataflow diagram (DFD) A
chart showing the movement of
data through a system.

A **dataflow diagram (DFD)** shows the movement of data through a system, rather than decision logic. The primary emphasis of a DFD is the flow of data and information between people and processes and the changes that take place within a process. Like a system flowchart, a DFD shows data and information entering, leaving, or stored within the system. Different documents used within a system are represented in the DFD, but the conditions under which each is used are not (although they are in a system flowchart). The DFD does not include anything not directly related to the flow of data.

DFDs use four symbols: arrows, circles or rounded rectangles, squares, and open rectangles. The functions of each are explained in Figure 11.14 on page 456. The labels on each DFD symbol describe the system element.

Figure 11.15 on page 457 is a dataflow diagram illustrating the order and invoice-handling procedure at a well-known mail-order company. Note that it describes the processes but does not indicate when they are performed (for example, every Monday or on the 1st and 15th of each month). Dataflows or *vectors* (arrows) represent groups of data (order, payment, and shipment data), documents (orders, invoices, and other documents), or types of information (management approval/disapproval and so forth). Notice that the dataflows do not indicate how the information is carried; they do not tell us whether the information is communicated by telephone, e-mail, or personal messenger. This may seem surprising to you. However, remember that the purpose of a DFD is to describe the movement of data, not the devices causing the movement.

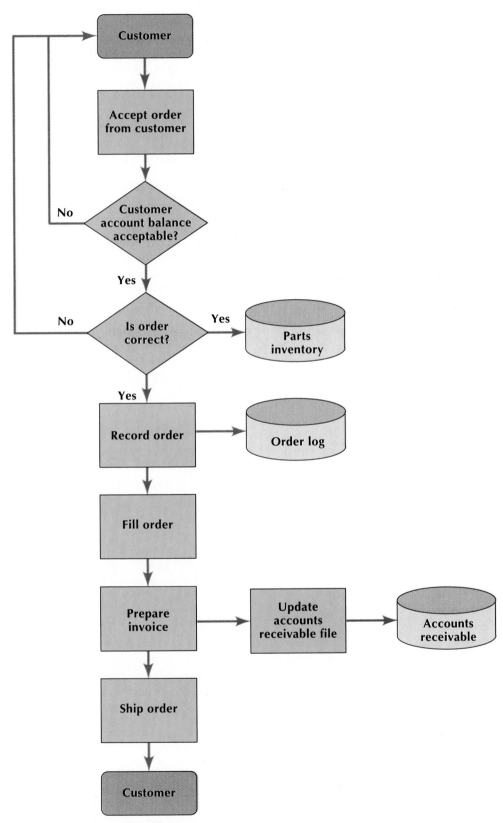

FIGURE 11.13   System Flowchart for Order Processing
The system flowchart pictured here is used by a retail firm for its catalog sales. The two
points in the process at which decisions must be made are indicated by diamond symbols.

SYMBOL

MEANING

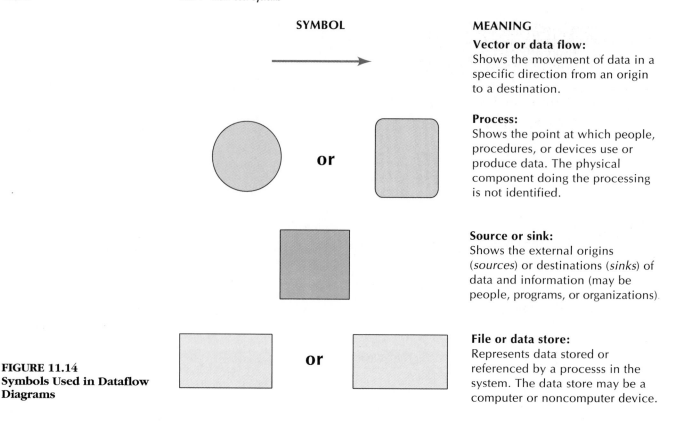

Vector or data flow:
Shows the movement of data in a specific direction from an origin to a destination.

Process:
Shows the point at which people, procedures, or devices use or produce data. The physical component doing the processing is not identified.

Source or sink:
Shows the external origins (*sources*) or destinations (*sinks*) of data and information (may be people, programs, or organizations).

File or data store:
Represents data stored or referenced by a processs in the system. The data store may be a computer or noncomputer device.

**FIGURE 11.14
Symbols Used in Dataflow
Diagrams**

Figure 11.15 shows that customers submit orders and payments ("settlement data") to the company. The principal information processes in this system, all identified by numbers, are entering orders (1.0), processing orders (2.0), producing invoices (3.0), posting payments (4.0), and maintaining accounts receivable (5.0). When orders are received from customers, they are approved or disapproved by management. Details of approved orders are then processed and recorded in an order log. The order is then prepared in production for shipment. An invoice is also prepared, with one copy serving as a packing slip accompanying the order. Another copy is used in preparing accounts receivable. Periodically, the records of accounts receivable are processed to adjust balances in accordance with payments and finance charges, and to provide management with an accounts receivable report.

Levels of DFDs.   There are different levels of DFD. A *system-level DFD* describes an entire system in summary form. Figure 11.15 is a system-level DFD. Additional DFDs "explode" processes to show more detail. Processes in a second-level DFD may in turn be exploded further to show more details and subprocesses. This process of exploding processes to show more detail is called **leveling**. Numbers on each DFD identify the diagram level. In Figure 11.16 on page 458, which shows three exploded processes from the DFD in Figure 11.15, DFD 2.1 describes order handling details, DFD 3.1 shows post-payment processing, and DFD 4.1 describes accounts receivable processing.

leveling The process of exploding processes in a dataflow diagram to show more detail.

Reality Check.   If you've ever watched an architect at work, you know that they work from *blueprints*, exact detailed plans for the building they are designing. (The name comes from the white lettering on blue

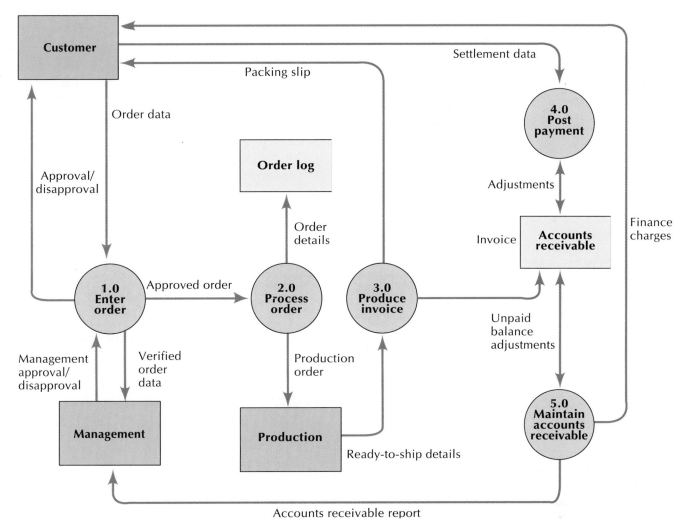

FIGURE 11.15 Dataflow Diagram for Order and Invoice Handling at a Mail-Order Company
This dataflow diagram includes five principal information processes: 1.0—order entry; 2.0—order process-ing; 3.0—invoice production; 4.0—posting of payments; and 5.0—maintenance of accounts receivable.

paper.) Every building's design consists of a series of blueprints, from the general to the very specific. Some show the shape of the building and its floor plan; others show locations of electrical outlets and ducts and pipes for heat and air flow.

A quick glance at a blueprint may leave someone outside the building profession overwhelmed by its symbols and technical terms. Yet, if you decide to build a house or create a layout for a new office under construction, you can very easily learn what key symbols and terms mean (the size of a door, the positioning of win-dows, and the location of closets and storage areas, for example). Think of system flowcharts and dataflow diagrams in the same way. They may appear quite abstract, yet they provide a great deal of information when you need to use them. ▪

Data Dictionaries

When system analysts develop dataflow diagrams, they also typically create a **data dictionary** (sometimes also called a **repository**), a catalog that lists and describes all the types of data flowing through a system. A data dictionary used in dataflow analysis

data dictionary or **repository**
A catalog that lists and describes all the types of data flowing through a system. Composed of data elements and a data structure.

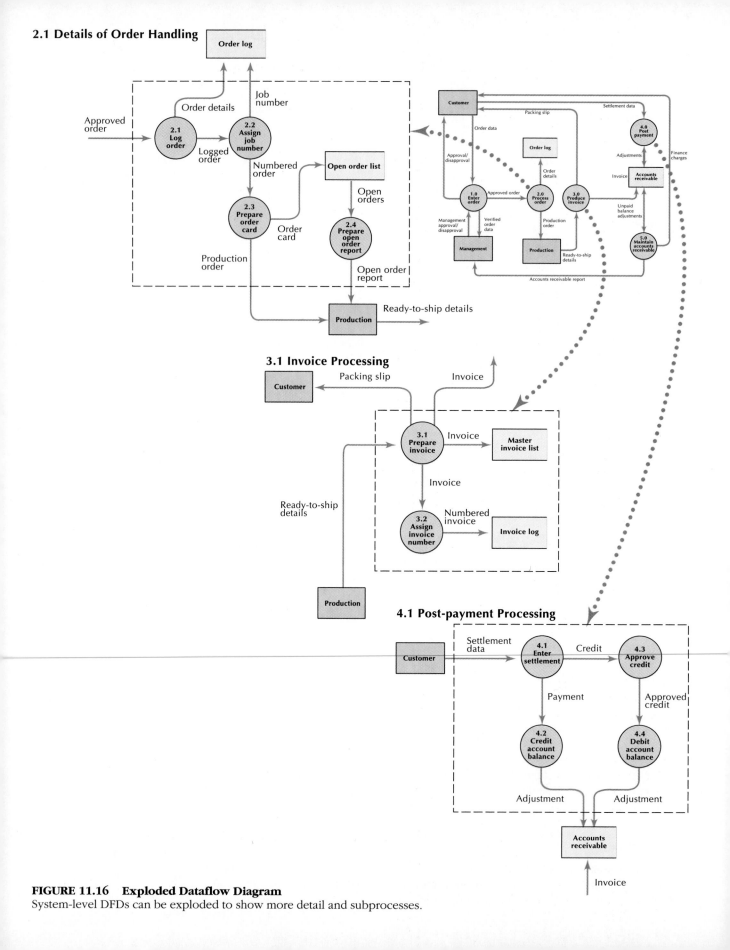

FIGURE 11.16   Exploded Dataflow Diagram
System-level DFDs can be exploded to show more detail and subprocesses.

contains two components: data elements and data structures. **Data elements** include data names, alternate names (aliases), and length allowances. The set of data elements used together and the name that collectively identifies the set is the **data structure**.

For example, the word "invoice" has a specific meaning in business, but the "invoice" data structure may be defined differently from one company to another. The system in use at a company has a data dictionary that defines the data elements that are included in that company's "invoice" data structure. (Whether invoice refers to a paper document or to an electronic format does not matter.) Figure 11.17 shows the data elements used by the Drazien Publishing Company's data dictionary to define invoice.

Analysts use data dictionaries for five reasons:

- To manage detail in large systems.
- To give a common meaning to all system elements.
- To document the features of a system.
- To facilitate evaluation of the system and determine where changes should be made.
- To locate errors and to find omissions.

Because they define the meaning of each data element in a system, data dictionaries are an important accompaniment to DFDs. They are also an integral component of CASE tools, which we discuss in the next section.

Computer-Aided Systems Engineering (CASE)

The newest and most powerful tool available to the systems analyst uses a computer's vast processing and storage capabilities. These **computer-aided systems engineering** or **computer-aided software engineering tools**, also known as **CASE tools**, are designed to improve the consistency and quality of systems while automating many of the most tedious and time-consuming systems tasks. CASE tools are used both to develop systems and to design the system's software.

The characteristics, capabilities, and components of CASE tools differ among the different brands available for purchase, some of which are listed in Table 11.4. However, most CASE tools contain the following features:

- **Charting and diagramming tools.** Because systems analysts spend a great deal of time analyzing data and processes, CASE tools typically include the capability to produce dataflow programs (both system-level and exploded views), data structure diagrams, and system flowcharts.
- **Centralized information repository.** A *centralized information repository* is a dictionary containing the details of all system components (data items, dataflows, and processes). The repository also includes information describing the frequency and volume of each activity. For example, if the analyst needs to know the high and low estimates of the number of invoices likely to be processed on a given day, he can retrieve the information from the central repository.

data element The component of a data dictionary that includes data names, alternate names, and length allowances.

data structure The set of data elements used together and the name that collectively identifies the set.

computer-aided systems engineering/computer-aided software engineering (CASE) tools A set of tools used in systems development to improve the consistency and quality of the system while automating many of the most tedious and time-consuming systems tasks.

TABLE 11.4
Leading CASE Tools

CASE Tool	Distributed by
Bachman Tools	Bachman and Associates
Easy CASE	European CASE Tools
IEF (Information Engineering Facility)	Texas Instruments
IEW (Information Engineering Workbench)	Knowledge-ware, Inc.
Intersolv	Intersolv
Method/ Foundation	Andersen Consulting
Oracle CASE	Oracle

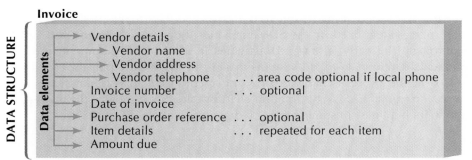

FIGURE 11.17
Data Structure for Invoice at the Drazien Publishing Company
Eight data elements in the Drazien Publishing Company's data dictionary define the term "invoice" as it is used at the company.

Invoice

DATA STRUCTURE

Data elements

Vendor details
→ Vendor name
→ Vendor address
→ Vendor telephone . . . area code optional if local phone
Invoice number . . . optional
Date of invoice
Purchase order reference . . . optional
Item details . . . repeated for each item
Amount due

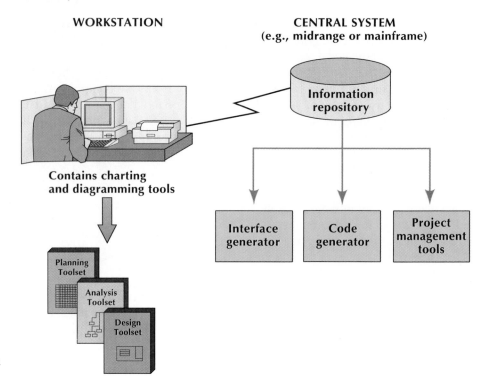

WORKSTATION

CENTRAL SYSTEM
(e.g., midrange or mainframe)

Information repository

Contains charting
and diagramming tools

Interface
generator

Code
generator

Project
management
tools

Planning
Toolset

Analysis
Toolset

Design
Toolset

FIGURE 11.18
CASE Tool Features
Although the capabilities of CASE tools differ among the packages available for purchase, most contain the features shown here.

interface generator A CASE tool that provides the capability to prepare sample user interfaces so that the creator can examine their features before preparing the final version.

- **Interface generators.** Recall that an *interface* is the means by which a person interacts with a computer. *Graphical interfaces*, such as those used by Microsoft Windows, OS/2, or the Apple Macintosh, use pictures and images. *Text interfaces*, such as those used by DOS, use key words and phrases to instruct the system in processing. Interface generators provide the capability to prepare sample user interfaces so that the creator can examine their features before preparing the final version. Interface generators allow analysts to present and evaluate many different interfaces and to make changes quickly and easily.

code generator A CASE tool that automates the preparation of computer software.

- **Code generators.** These tools automate the preparation of computer software. Although code generators are not yet perfected, many automate 75% to 80% of the computer programming needed to create a new system or application.

project management tools CASE tools that enable a project manager to schedule analysis and design activities, allocate people, monitor schedules and personnel, and print schedules and reports.

- **Project management tools.** As we've seen, development projects must be carefully managed to ensure that all tasks are completed properly and on time. Project management tools enable the project manager to schedule analysis and design activities, allocate people and other resources to each task, monitor schedules and personnel, and print schedules and reports summarizing the project's status.

Figure 11.18 summarizes the features of CASE tools.

front-end CASE CASE tools that automate the early (front-end) activities in systems development.

Front-end, Back-end, and Integrated CASE.   As Figure 11.19 shows, CASE tools are often categorized by the SDLC activities they support. **Front-end CASE** tools automate the early (front-end) activities in systems development, namely requirements determination and systems design. In these early phases, they help analysts describe process characteristics and record and analyze dataflows and processes. Front-end CASE tools' built-in charting capabilities relieve the analyst of the important but time-consuming tasks of drawing dataflow diagrams.

SEQUENCE OF SYSTEMS DEVELOPMENT ACTIVITIES

Front-end development   **Back-end development**

Analysis ——— Design ———	Development and Construction	——— Implementation ———	Evaluation and Continuing Evolution
(Preliminary investigation) (Requirements determination)			

Front-end CASE tools   **Back-end CASE tools**
Analysis tools   Code generator tools
Charting tools   Translation tools
Tools for logical design   Testing tools

Integrated CASE tools

FIGURE 11.19   Types of CASE Tools

Back-end CASE tools automate the later (back-end) activities in systems development, developing detailed information from general system descriptions. Some back-end CASE tools include code generators, translation tools, and testing tools.

Integrated CASE (I-CASE) tools span activities throughout the entire systems development life cycle. They incorporate analysis, logical design, code generation, and database generation capabilities while maintaining an automated data dictionary. I-CASE is actually a family of tools, all accessible from the same computer program and display screen. A sample I-CASE screen is shown in Figure 11.20.

Because of the complexity of integrating the entire SDLC's activities, only a few integrated CASE tools have been created. However, it is likely that more integrated tools will emerge as IT professionals continue to seek tools that link all the activities associated with systems development.

back-end CASE CASE tools that automate the later (back-end) activities in systems development.

integrated CASE (I-CASE) CASE tools that span activities throughout the entire systems development life cycle.

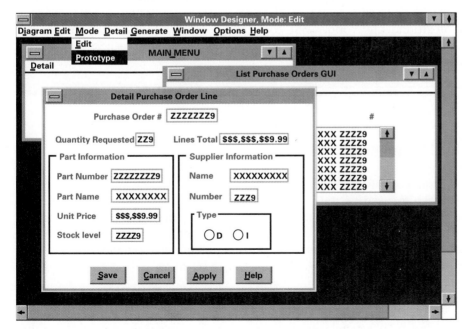

FIGURE 11.20
Display Screens of I-CASE Tool
Display contents are specified and arranged using the screen design tool. Data items are coded to show whether their contents will be numeric or character. Special codes that invoke specific actions are also shown on the display.

Reality Check.   Although CASE tools offer many valuable features and can assist the systems analyst in many ways, they are not a substitute for a good systems analyst. A great deal of the analyst's work is based on understanding what questions to ask, deciding when to probe more deeply into a business situation, and knowing which people to contact and how to get information. Systems design is also a creative activity, one in which insight and innovative ideas lead to well-designed applications. These skills cannot be automated. Automated tools will not replace good analysts, but they can make good analysts even better and more effective.   ■

CRITICAL CONNECTION 2
Levi Strauss & Company Learns the Value of Tailoring CASE Tools to Fit

Levi Strauss & Co. has a love-hate relationship with CASE tools. Although the company was one of the first and biggest customers for CASE tools, it found that its ambitions tended to exceed the still-evolving capabilities of the CASE tools. On one project, for example, the company set up teams of programmers, with the idea that the teams could work simultaneously to develop a local area network. The problem: The time gained by automating some of the early steps was lost during the programming stage, because the CASE tools were organized so that just one person could work on a section at a time. To counter this limitation, the IT staff at Levi Strauss combined a variety of CASE tools from several companies, creating, in effect, its own CASE tools. This led to another problem: Which glitches were caused by the ready-made CASE tools and which could be traced to the CASE tools developed in-house?

Nonetheless, Levi Strauss is committed to using CASE tools in its ongoing, massive effort to make both process and business improvements by reengineering its operations around the world. CASE tools, the company believes, are simply the best way of helping IT programmers develop the balance of business and technical skills they will need in the future.

■ IT Development Personnel

Because systems analysts play the central role in developing shared IT applications, we have focused on their activities throughout this chapter. In this section, we take a closer look at the job they do, the roles they play, and the skills that are critical to their success. We also discuss the other IT professionals with whom systems analysts work—chief information officers, computer programmers, and outside contractors.

The Systems Analyst—The Key Roles

Systems analysts play several roles in business. As we have seen, they play a major *development role* in analyzing business activities and formulating solutions. But they also play an important *facilitating role*. Good analysts recognize the value of eliciting information from people who will use IT to perform a job or manage a business process. These people are the best sources of information about problems, solutions, and obstacles to solutions. Part of the analyst's job, then, is to facilitate the exchange of this information.

Developing and implementing information technology means change. People need to learn new or altered work processes (and perhaps even new computer and communications systems) and take on different responsibilities. Although change can be exciting, people often resist change, particularly if they do not see a reason for doing so. Thus the systems analyst's third role is the vitally important one of **change agent**. In this role, the analyst acts as a catalyst for change and as a liaison between different parties involved in the creation and implementation of change.

change agent A person who acts as a catalyst for change.

The change agent's role is often depicted in the form of a three-step model (Figure 11.21). These three steps are (1) *unfreeze*—communicate with people about the reason for change to reduce potential resistance; (2) *change*—implement new activities, procedures, and applications; and (3) *refreeze*—ensure that people accept and use the new processes and procedures. In each of these roles, the systems analyst is directly involved in the business. Developing information systems means knowing about the business activities in which the applications will be used and how these systems can be changed to meet business's needs.

Consider professional sports. In the United States (and in the Far East) the national pastime is baseball. In Europe and South America, it's soccer. Throughout the world, professional sports have become big business. And many teams not only use IT to manage their business but also employ IT professionals—including systems analysts.

Systems analysts in the baseball business have to know about more than just computers, communications systems, and software if they are to contribute to the success of their organization. They also have to know the *business* of baseball and must be prepared to change the hardware and software they use to support the players, coaches, and managers of the team as the necessity arises.

Take the L.A. Dodgers of Los Angeles, California, for example. The team's information technology department (yes, the team has an IT department) is responsible for maintaining applications that keep track of more than 300 major- and minor-league players in the Dodger organization. Each player is accounted for as a company asset. When the team acquires a player, its accounting system is adjusted to add him to the organization's list of assets. When another is traded, a different transaction takes place. As the players' value to the organization changes, the records are adjusted to show this change in the asset value.

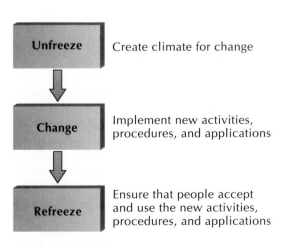

FIGURE 11.21
Model of Change Agent's Role
In addition to working as a change agent, systems analysts also play a development role and a facilitating role.

The Dodgers' systems analysts have also repeatedly modified the team's IT applications to handle new business practices: multi-year signing bonuses, salaries paid over many years (even after the player has retired or moved to another team), special injury clauses, and incentive bonuses paid if a player achieves a specified performance level.

Professional Skills.   The most successful systems analysts have five important professional skills: problem solving skills, the ability to focus on outcome, creativity, the ability to plan and run meetings, and excellent interpersonal communication skills.

- **Problem solving.** The problem solving process, which we first introduced in Chapter 1, seeks to identify differences between the current situation and what people want. Analysts play a key role in initiating the process by asking, "What is wrong?", "What is the cause of the problem?", and "What is the effect?"
- **Outcome thinking.** Good analysts complement their problem solving skills with an ability to focus on outcome. Analysts focus on outcome by asking, "What result is desired?", "Forgetting about constraints for a moment, what is the ideal result?", or "What is your vision of the way things should be?" This emphasis on outcome does more than stress the positive; it also unlocks thinking about possibilities rather than impossibilities. It recognizes the limitations of focusing solely on problems.
- **Creativity.** Creativity is the ability to look at the same thing as everyone else, but to see something different. Being creative means generating ideas. Doing so means forgetting about constraints (at least temporarily), relaxing rules, and letting alternatives rise to the surface. Some of us are not born innovators and don't ordinarily consider ourselves highly creative. Yet we know the power of good ideas and how quickly they can turn a difficult situation into an exciting opportunity.

  Good systems designs are often creative designs. UPS's decision to use wireless communications to link drivers to the company's data center was creative. It also made good business sense, because it allowed the company to offer new services that benefit customers and add to the company's business.
- **Meeting Skills.** Recall that one of a systems analyst's roles is that of facilitating information exchange. For this reason, planning and running meetings efficiently is a critical skill in the analyst's repertoire. Good meeting skills determine the value of the information analysts capture from people involved in the meeting. Good meetings begin with an agenda of the topics to be addressed and are structured in a way that allows all attendees to participate. Questions must be carefully crafted to elicit the desired information. Effective analysts also find ways to create enthusiasm among a meeting's participants, fostering an atmosphere in which people *want* to participate and share ideas.

  More and more meetings today are using electronic support tools. Group conferencing networks (discussed in Chapter 9) and group support systems (which we discuss in the next chapter) tend to foster more interaction among people. In a regular group discussion, only one person speaks at a time, but through a network many people can express their ideas. Electronic meeting tools also keep components anonymous so that people are free to speak without worrying about other participants' opinions. As the capabilities of these tools continue to evolve, electronic meeting systems are likely to become as important a tool in systems analysis and design as dataflow diagrams and flowcharts are today.
- **Communication Skills.** Good communication skills are essential for effective person-to-person discussions. Discussing ideas with users in their language (that

is, free of technical jargon), understanding what they are saying (and listening to what they are *not* saying), and knowing how to assemble all this information is invaluable and leads to better use of IT. Indeed, listening to people and trying to understand their ideas and opinions (and recognizing when you don't) is more than just politeness. Misunderstandings about business activities resulting in misstated systems requirements often account for more than 50% of the reasons that IT applications have to be changed after they've been implemented.

CRITICAL CONNECTION 3
Volunteer Systems Analyst Makes Orlando a "City of Light"

Profit-making businesses aren't the only organizations that can benefit from the process and business improvements spearheaded by a systems analyst. Just ask Ed Schrank. In 1991, he took a break from his job as a vice president at Welbro Constructors in Altamonte Springs, Florida, to become an "executive on loan" to the City of Light program in Orlando, Florida. An extension of President George Bush's Thousand Points of Light program, the local program was created to encourage communities to use volunteers and charitable donations to reduce the call for tax-supported aid to the needy.

Orlando's participation was sparked by its mayor, Bill Frederick, who realized that Orlando had many resources that were going to waste. A local business, say, might want to donate some used computers to a worthy charity. But who needs the computers? And who will pick up the machines and support their new users? There was simply no way to match the supply of volunteer help to those in need.

This was a problem for IT, thought Schrank. Orlando needed an "infostructure," an easy-to-use distributed computing system that would place basic PCs in churches, businesses, and schools, where volunteers could enter data about other volunteers and the skills and time they could offer. These data could then be transmitted to a database server, again managed by volunteers, where a special program could play matchmaker. And with that realization, Schrank became a change agent, dedicated to mustering the resources needed to carry out his vision.

The Chief Information Officer

In many businesses, one person is given the responsibility of managing and developing the firm's information technology capabilities. In large organizations, this person is often called the **chief information officer (CIO)**. (Some firms use instead the title IT director or director of information systems.) The position generally has a corporate rank of vice president (Figure 11.22 on the next page). (See the People box in Chapter 2 titled "CIO Becomes Key Advisor to CEO.") In smaller businesses the individual responsible for managing and developing the company's capabilities may also have additional responsibilities. Hence it is not uncommon to find IT management responsibilities assigned to the controller, finance director, administrative coordinator, or operations manager.

Systems analysts generally work for a CIO or for a director of development, who in turn reports to the person responsible for managing the firm's IT capabili-

chief information officer (CIO) The person given the responsibility of managing and developing the firm's information technology capabilities.

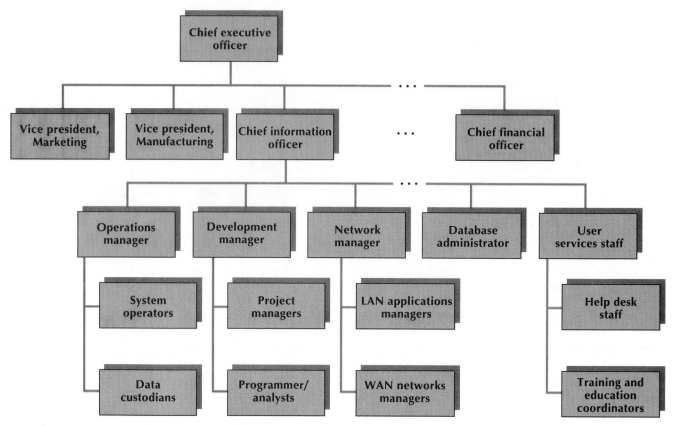

FIGURE 11.22   Organization Chart for Typical Information Systems Department
In large organizations, the chief information officer generally holds the rank of corporate
vice president.

ties. Communications about the firm's business plans flow to the analyst through
these people. The quality of communication can be an important determinant of
the firm's effective use of information technology for process or business
improvement.

Computer Programmers

As we noted earlier, *programmers* are responsible for turning detailed specifications into computer software that processes data and information effectively and
works with other computer programs (computer operating systems, network operating systems, database management systems, and so forth). They are also responsible for *documenting* the program, developing written explanations of how and
why certain procedures are coded in specific ways and how the system can be
used in the business. Analysts and programmers interact continually during the
development of a system, usually serving jointly on the project team.

Systems Contractors

Most large organizations have computer programmers (or programmer/analysts)
on permanent staff. Smaller firms often retain outside programming services on a
contractual basis.

   In some cases an organization may hire outside consultants to manage the
development of a system. This strategy is common when the organization chooses

not to assign any of its own personnel to the project or when it determines that it will be more expedient to have a third party handle the development. The term **systems contractor** is used to describe all types of outside personnel who contract with a company to develop IT applications. Some contractors are very small, even one-person shops. Others are worldwide, with offices in many cities.

Systems contractors often become experts by gaining years of experience with companies before starting their own consulting firms. Others use their experience as a basis for joining an established consulting firm. Yet many others go directly from college to the world of IT consulting.

Andersen Consulting, headquartered in Chicago, has its own way of educating its more than 21,000 employees about IT. New recruits hired into Andersen (at an average age of 25) spend their first three to four weeks training in the company's local office. Then they head off to one of four world training centers: St. Charles, Illinois; Manila, the Philippines; Singapore; or Veldhoven, the Netherlands. At the training center, they learn Andersen's methodologies for determining systems requirements, developing application specifications, and preparing computer programs. "Personal people," an Andersen objective, also means recognizing that people are as different as the countries, cultures, and corporations in which they work. Hence, Andersen seeks to draw out individual differences in its new hires and show people how to develop them as strengths in dealing with clients. Trainees also learn valuable business skills: how to interact with clients, how to work on a project team, and how to understand a business or industry. Not all the training is technical, however. You are likely to find new hires in the woods near the training center, climbing rope ladders or planning strategies to make their team a winner in a competitive outdoor game.

Visits to the four centers are not just for new recruits, however. Andersen sees education as a career-long activity. Depending on the area in which a person works, he or she can expect to spend from 300 to 750 hours at the education facility each year. Continual improvement is a critical ingredient in the makeup of Andersen consultants and the systems they develop, and it should be a career objective for you whether you work as a developer or user of information technology.

For more on Andersen Consulting, see the Photo Essay at the end of this chapter.

systems contractors Outside personnel who contract with a company to develop IT applications.

SUMMARY OF LEARNING OBJECTIVES

1 **Describe the principle functions and roles of a systems analyst.** Systems analysts are responsible for working with users to determine a system's requirements and to describe the features needed in the system. The systems analyst sees the development of a shared IT application through, from original concept to finished product.

2 **Explain how a systems project begins and how its desirability is determined.** A systems project begins with a *project proposal*. The proposal is a result of problem or opportunity recognition. The completed project proposal is submitted to a *steering committee*, usually made up of members from different functional areas of the business, which determines whether or not the project is desirable.

3 **Describe the six phases of the systems development life cycle.** There are six phases in the systems development life cycle: (1) problem recognition/preliminary investigation—the definition and investigation of the problem, (2) requirements determination—the process of understanding the current system and the new system's requirements, (3) systems design—planning the new system, (4) development and construction—creating the new system, (5) implementation—

converting to the new system, and (6) evaluation and continuing evolution—monitoring and adding value to the new system.

4 Describe the tools and techniques available to systems analysts for collecting data and developing IT applications. Systems analysts use a variety of techniques to collect data. The most common of these are *interviews* (both structured and unstructured), *questionnaires, document examination* (also called *record inspection*), *observation*, and *sampling*. The tools commonly used by systems analysts to design systems include *systems flowcharts* (graphical descriptions of a business process or procedure that describe decision logic), *dataflow diagrams (DFDs)* (graphs that show the movement of data through a system), *data dictionaries* (catalogs that list and describe all the types of data flowing through the system), and *computer-*

aided systems engineering (CASE) tools (which automate many of the most tedious and time-consuming systems tasks).

5 Explain the roles of the four types of IT systems-development professionals. In addition to their development and facilitating roles, *systems analysts* play the important role of change agent as they interact with the company's chief information officer, computer programmers, and systems contractors. The *chief information officer* (CIO) is the one person in an organization responsible for managing and developing the firm's information technology capabilities. *Computer programmers* are responsible for turning detailed specifications into computer software and for documenting the program. *Systems contractors* are outside personnel who contract with a company to develop IT applications.

KEY TERMS

CRITICAL CONNECTIONS

U-Haul

1.   Misadventures in Computing: U-Haul Plans to Try Again

Despite the pilot project's failure, U-Haul wasn't discouraged. The company now had a clearer idea of its hardware and software requirements and it was not locked into an agreement with vendors that couldn't meet those

requirements. It was free to explore at least three other options: (1) Buy more powerful computer workstations and equip them with software specially designed to simplify downsizing projects; (2) sign a contract with another company that would take over some of the mainframe operations while U-Haul explored various client-server options; and (3) reduce the scope of the project by keeping one of the two mainframes.

U-Haul admits that a document inquiry application that taps a huge customer history database may require the power of a mainframe. It is less certain that it will ever delegate computing tasks to another company, due to concerns about data security. Nevertheless, the company does plan to apply one lesson learned from earlier development projects. No matter how good a vendor's claims sound, U-Haul will never rely on a single vendor and it will always test each system before it makes a commitment.

Questions for Discussion

1. After the failure of the pilot project, U-Haul's director of systems development admitted the company had found itself on the "bleeding edge of technology." What considerations would you use to assess the risk of experimenting with new technology before proceeding?

2. What lessons does U-Haul's experience offer for other managers seeking the benefits of converting existing systems to client-server computing?

2. Levi Strauss & Company Learns the Value of Tailoring CASE Tools to Fit

Levi Strauss's success in customizing CASE tools hasn't gone unnoticed. Other companies such as The Gap have been visiting Levi Strauss to study its techniques and get the kind of nitty-gritty tips missing from most vendor demonstrations.

Like the IT staff at Levi Strauss, the visiting IT professionals don't expect CASE tools will ever completely automate the process of developing shared IT applications or eliminate the need for systems analysts. In fact, many are expanding their definition of CASE from a "set of tools" to a "way of thinking," a philosophy that forces IT professionals to model the business and take an enterprise-wide view of the company's functions and information needs.

Questions for Discussion

1. Many companies report that one of the biggest obstacles to revamping a computer system to achieve process or business improvements is the time needed to retrain IT professionals, who have sometimes been educated to take a narrow, technical approach to their work. Why, then, do you think many of these same companies are adopting CASE tools?

2. Use Levi's experience to explain why "go slow" is becoming a rule among many companies that are

adopting CASE tools. What other challenges might stand in the way of using CASE tools effectively, and what solutions can you offer to meet these challenges?

3. What should be an IT director's primary concerns in approving the adoption of CASE tools at his or her company?

3. Volunteer Systems Analyst Makes Orlando a "City of Light"

Ed Schrank also played the role of a developer and a facilitator for the city of Orlando when he solicited professional services, as well as hardware and software donations, from AT&T, IBM, the University of Central Florida, and other businesses. The director of IS at the Orange County Property Appraiser's Office volunteered to become the project's technical director, and members of local computer clubs helped to install the donated computer workstations. The resulting system, dubbed the Orlando Community Connection, entered the final testing phase early in 1993, about the same time the local public television station began broadcasting training sessions to volunteer coordinators. The complete system is designed to match 250,000 volunteers with the needs of 5,000 agencies at the rate of 25,000 matches per month.

Questions for Discussion

1. The donations from AT&T included Conversance, a sophisticated and expensive telephone system that calls volunteers and uses synthesized speech to tell them of volunteer opportunities that might interest them. Volunteers can also call the system, which uses voice recognition to accept changes to the volunteers' personal information. Do you think this "high-tech" feature was appropriate for the Orlando Community Connection? What generalizations can you draw from this example regarding the costs of developing a shared IT application?

2. What professional skills did Schrank need to carry out his vision? Which do you think were most important? Why?

3. Orlando established the Executive on Loan program in 1991 to allow business leaders to use their skills in developing service programs for the community. Would you support such programs? Why or why not?

REVIEW QUESTIONS

1. What is systems development? How are systems projects initiated?

2. Describe the purpose and contents of a systems development project proposal. Who initiates this proposal? Who reviews it?

3. Describe the purpose of a steering committee. Who serves on the committee? What role does the committee play in the development of an IT application?

4. What is the systems development life cycle?

5. Describe the purpose of problem recognition and preliminary investigation. Who performs this investigation?

6. What three types of feasibility are assessed during preliminary investigation?

7. What is a systems requirement? What is requirements determination?

8. What is the difference between process improvement and business improvement? What is their relation to requirements determination?

9. Identify and discuss four types of business improvement that can be created through effective use of IT.

10. What are the differences between preliminary design, prototyping, and detailed design?

11. What three activities are involved in systems development and construction?

12. Discuss the purpose of testing. What is the difference between software testing and system testing?

13. What is implementation? List and describe three important aspects of implementation.

14. What four conversion strategies are available to systems analysts?

15. What is systems evaluation?

16. Name the five data collection techniques used by systems analysts.

17. Distinguish between a system flowchart and a dataflow diagram.

18. What is leveling? Why is it useful in documenting dataflows?

19. What are the two components of data dictionaries?

20. Describe the features that most CASE tools have. What are the three kinds of CASE tools?

21. What five skills should a systems analyst possess?

22. With which other IT professionals are systems analysts likely to work?

DISCUSSION QUESTIONS

1. Although computer downsizing is proceeding smoothly at MCA Inc.—the $4 billion entertainment conglomerate based in Universal City, California—George A. Brenner, Director of Corporate Information Services, admits, "Our users need a lot [of] handholding and cuddling. We've had to put a lot of effort into employee training in order to teach people to be more attentive to the power on their desktops." What professional skills did Brenner need to identify this problem and to deal with the challenge it presented? Explain your answer.

2. Should companies be advised to select a mission-critical application as their first client-server appli-

cation, or should they select a small-scale test application first to gain needed experience? Explain your answer.

3. Holiday Inn is retooling its mainframe-based system after a client-server pilot project showed that the new system wasn't updating certain account information automatically. What information did Holiday Inn need to evaluate this shortcoming?

4. A growing number of companies have opened custom-designed laboratories for usability testing. At these labs, end-users can evaluate new IT systems and suggest improvements. Where and how do these usability tests fit into the system development life cycle?

SUGGESTED READINGS

Davenport, Thomas H., *Process Innovation: Reengineering Work Through Information Technology*. Boston: Harvard Business School Press, 1993. This timely book discusses the necessity and challenge of reexamining the processes underlying an organization's day-to-day activities, highlighting questions and issues while presenting a framework for addressing process redesign issues. Includes many examples of firms that have succeeded or failed in combining business change and IT initiatives.

Hammer, Michael, and James Champy, *Reengineering the Corporation: A Manifesto for Business Revolution*. New York: HarperBusiness, 1993. This book is based on the thesis that corporations must undertake a radical reinvention of the way they work. The authors provide clear guidelines on the redesign of business processes with special emphasis on the value of information technology in reengineering business.

Hammer, Michael, "Reengineering Work: Don't Automate, Obliterate," *Harvard Business Review*, 68, no. 4 (July–August 1990), pp. 104–112. The classic article that woke managers up to the need for rethinking the way they do business. It offers bold and challenging ideas that every executive and student of management must confront.

Hopper, Max, "Rattling SABRE—New Ways to Compete on Information," *Harvard Business Review*, 68, no. 3 (May–June 1990), pp. 118–125. A thought-provoking article on the changing role of IT in business. Written by American Airlines' chief information officer, who was the inspiration behind its SABRE computerized reservation system.

Porter, Michael E., *Competitive Advantage: Creating and Sustaining Superior Performance*. New York: Free Press, 1985. A definitive work for the manager trying to gain a competitive edge in the market. It shows how to choose a technological strategy that reflects both the company's capabilities and those of its competitors.

Stalk, George Jr., and Thomas M. Hout, *Competing Against Time: How Time-Based Competition Is Reshaping Global Markets*. New York: Free Press, 1990. This fascinating book shows how time constraints and the need for speed to market are reshaping business practices and restructuring industry. The authors document how time consumption, like cost expenditure, can be managed and how virtually all businesses can use time as a competitive weapon.

Strebel, Paul, *Breakpoints: How Managers Exploit Radical Business Change*. Boston: Harvard Business School Press, 1992. Dramatic changes in markets, technologies, and politics are changing the world, causing sudden shifts in business conditions. The discontinuities, or breakpoints, that result are an opportunity for those who recognize them. The book tells the story of several companies who recognized these opportunities and redeveloped their business systems to capitalize on change at the expense of those who did not.

Vitalari, Nicholas P., "Knowledge as a Basis for Expertise in Systems Analysis: An Empirical Study," *MIS Quarterly*, 9, no. 3 (September 1985), pp. 221–241. This important research-based article examines the differences between successful and unsuccessful systems analysts, integrating findings on the roles played by analysts and the skills that contribute most to success.

CASE STUDY

Shoot-Out Whets Sara Lee's Appetite for Client/Server Computing

SARA LEE CORPORATION

IF YOU ASSOCIATE THE NAME "SARA LEE" only with cheesecake, think again. Sara Lee Corp. also owns such familiar brand names as Hanes (knit wear), L'eggs (hosiery), Isotoner (slippers and gloves), Coach (leather accessories), Ball Park (hot dogs), Mr. Turkey (poultry products), and Kiwi (shoe polish and pharmaceuticals). Since the 1980s, the company has been buying a number of European brands, too. These include the Radox line of bath products favored in England since 1922; the Sanex bath products popular in Spain, Holland, Greece, and Portugal; Douwe Egbert's coffees, which are marketed under various brand names throughout Europe; Dim S.A., France's largest hosiery and underwear maker; and Vatter, Germany's largest hosiery maker.

Information technology plays an important part in improving efficiency, especially for a manufacturer like Sara Lee. That doesn't mean that Sara Lee's more than 100 divisions follow a single, corporatewide standard for information systems, though. As the company's vice president of corporate systems told a *PC Week* writer, "Sara Lee has too diversified an environment and too many types of operations to warrant [choosing] a single product or technology." Instead, Sara Lee's corporate IT staff acts as a team of consultants, taking the lead in evaluating new technology and compiling lists of suggested hardware and software options that divisions can use in developing their information systems.

Keeping on top of new technology is no small task. Over the space of eight months, for example, Sara Lee IT staff visited the top hardware and software makers, asking them about their future plans and trying to determine when the promise of client/server computing would be fulfilled.

Sara Lee is also a *PC Week* Lab Partner, one of a select group of corporations that work with *PC Week*'s technical experts and university researchers to test emerging technologies under real-world conditions. For example, Sara Lee teamed up with *PC Week* to sponsor an Industrial Automation Shoot-Out at North Carolina State University's College of Textiles. This two-week event followed months of preparation and involved hundreds of people, as well as contributions of time or equipment from dozens of companies. The goal: to test a new generation of supervisory control and data acquisition (SCADA) software for client/server computing.

SCADA software monitors, controls, and coordinates factory operations, providing feedback that minimizes the number of decisions that workers need to make. Typically, this software has been part of costly closed systems using mainframes or midrange computers. (In contrast, IBM and IBM-compatible PCs are open systems, which means that any number of companies can provide peripherals and software that can be interconnected to work with their systems.)

Closed systems have some drawbacks. First are their price and the fact that buyers can't mix and match competitively priced hardware from various companies. Second, closed systems tend to be inflexible, making it cumbersome to shift production in response to market conditions. Third, closed systems islands of automation, blocking the sharing of data and information needed in computer-integrated manufacturing (CIM). CIM, which we discuss in detail in the next chapter, is the use of computer systems to share information and integrate all business functions, from marketing to manufacturing. CIM can help companies become more nimble in responding to market opportunities and is a high priority for Sara Lee Corp.

Becoming more nimble was especially important to Sara Lee's textile divisions. As a whole, the U.S. textile industry was hit hard by global competition in the late 1980s and early 1990s and was forced to cut layers of management and retrain workers to keep them productively employed. It also invested heavily in total quality management (TQM) programs. The industry is now much stronger, but to remain competitive it needs the advantages of CIM and it needs to determine whether client/server computing can deliver them. That's why Sara Lee and *PC Week* designed the Shoot-Out to simulate the textile-dyeing operations of a Sara Lee Knit Products plant.

The Shoot-Out was designed to answer some key questions. Can the operation of a billion-dollar facility be entrusted to the new technology? (Factory-automation systems must collect, process, and present vast amounts of data in real time.) Is the user interface easy to use? (Workers faced with operational difficulties don't have time to decipher puzzling screen messages.) How well do

Sara Lee's U.S. brands...

...and its Eurobrands.

the systems communicate with the devices that actually operate factory equipment and processes? Together, the Shoot-Out team identified 200 judging criteria, which were then reviewed by IT professionals from more than 100 corporations.

Meanwhile, Shoot-Out team members were also working with Morton Machine Works Inc. to develop a simulation of the textile-dyeing process. With the help of ZD Labs in Foster City, California, other team members gathered the donated equipment needed to create a high-speed LAN for the simulated manufacturing system.

A month before the test, the team sent the seven participating software manufacturers a description of the simulation and the tasks their software would have to perform. The Shoot-Out itself had two phases: a series of timed tests to perform specific tasks, followed by two-and-one-half hour presentations to seven corporate judges representing a variety of industries. After all scoring was complete, Sara Lee executives identified three client/server packages they would suggest to the company's divisions.

Questions for Discussion

1. Why did Sara Lee go to the time, expense, and effort to co-sponsor the Shoot-Out? Why do you think the vendors choose to participate?

2. What does Sara Lee's participation in the Shoot-Out indicate about the relationship between corporate and divisional IT staff? How should the roles of these staff members differ?

3. After the Shoot-Out, the IT staff of the Knit Products Division used one of the three recommended SCADA products in a pilot project at a new state-of-the-art dyeing facility in Greenwood, North Carolina. If all goes well, the division will eventually expand the system, replacing six or seven existing systems. Does this plan represent product improvement, process improvement, or both? Explain your answer.

Andersen Consulting
Creates the Future Through Prototyping

Andersen Consulting was created in 1988 when Arthur Andersen & Co., the world's largest management consulting firm, divided itself into two firms: Arthur Andersen, specializing in accountancy, and Andersen Consulting, focusing on information technology and integration of systems into business. More than half of the Fortune 500 industrial firms are Andersen Consulting clients.

Andersen Consulting spends more than $300 million annually on research and development. Among its most important R&D facilities are seven "business integration showrooms" around the world: The Smart Store™, The Smart Store Europe™, The Hospital of the Future™ at The Health Strategy Center, The Retail Place, Logistics 2000, Process 2000, and The Oil Center. Each showroom is functional prototype of new systems of computers, communications, and Andersen's know-how in specialized practice areas: grocery retailing (U.S. and European), medical care, consumer goods retailing, supply chain integration, manufacturing, and petroleum. This photo essay examines two of these centers, Smart Store and The Health Strategy Center, and how businesses can use these centers' embedded IT capabilities for competitive advantage.

Smart Store™

1 Smart Store is Andersen Consulting's research and development center focusing on the consumer's supermarket shopping experience. Through a variety of prototype exhibits, the center provides insight into innovative ways to meet the overlapping needs of manufacturers, distributors, retailers, brokers, restaurateurs, and new entrants to the industry. New methods and techniques for integrating IT in the handling of food and packaged goods are showcased for both Andersen's current clients and its prospective clients. The store's "hands-on" approach enables visitors to test, rather than just analyze, the systems and facilities in action.

Smart Store looks at retailing from both the supply side (ensuring that adequate quantities of the right goods are on hand) and the demand side (meeting the needs and wants of customers purchasing goods). The supply side demonstrates how a product (for example, a bag of potato chips) flows to the consumer through a method called "seamless sales-based replenishment," which takes into account growers, distributors, and manufacturers. The goal is to remove costs and activities that do not add value for the consumer. On the demand side, IT is used to determine who the store's customers are, how those customers can best be reached, how to gain and sustain customer loyalty, and how to gain an edge over the competition.

2 Each "customer" at Smart Store has a frequent shopper card containing a unique bar code. When customers enter the store, they "swipe" the card across a scanner that identifies them to the store system. Using the system's individual personal profiles, store employees can then call up information on buying preferences to tell customers about special products and promotions in the store. The customer uses the frequent shopper card in other areas throughout the store, too.

The shopping carts in The Smart Store are video carts. The video screen on the cart can display information about special prices in the store's departments, but it can also do much more. If the customer needs assistance, pressing a button on the video screen will bring an attendant right over. A store manager may send an electronic message to shoppers asking them to participate in a special product evaluation, for which they will earn frequent shopper points. Or, if a shopper's profile indicates that she recently purchased a product that didn't satisfy her needs, the department manager (notified by the system that the shopper is in the store) may want to visit with her to ensure that the problem has been resolved. Far from acting as "Big Brother," this system is designed to delight the customer with the best possible service.

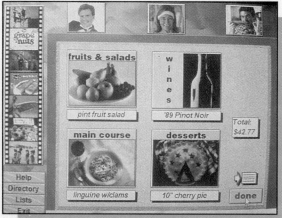

3 Shopper convenience is a major goal of The Smart Store. To expedite checkout, another version of the shopping cart contains a mini scanner. When shoppers select packages, they pass them across the mini scanner before dropping them into the cart. They can "unscan" an item any time if they change their minds elsewhere in the store. When they've completed shopping, they remove the scanner and download its contents at a monitor near the cashier. To protect the store, a security system automatically monitors items to ensure that they have been scanned into the system.

4 Some retailing firms want to automate the checkout process completely by eliminating cashiers. At the automated checkout demonstration, shoppers ring up their own purchases by running each package across a scanner in the counter. A laser beam scans the product identification code, which is then processed through the in-store computer where the item's price is retrieved and added to the cus-

tomer's purchase record. The system keeps track of special sale prices for the customer and quantities on hand for the store.

To pay the bill, shoppers swipe their buyer cards through the scanner and the amount of the purchase is automatically paid from their bank account: no need to mess with cash or checks unless the customer chooses to do so.

5 Some customers don't want to pick products from the shelf and push a cart around the store. Another area of Smart Store demonstrates a way to please this type of customer. To select an item for purchase, whether a box of breakfast cereal or a case of soft drinks, the customer locates the display of the desired item, lifts the cover containing the package facsimile, and waves a digital light pen over the optical shelf tag. The store's information system records the choice on the customer's purchasing list. When the shopper reaches the checkout area, the goods are already bagged. Alternatively, the shopper may have used the digital pen to tell the store to deliver the items to her home, in which case checkout is even more simple: she just pays her pre-calculated bill. Or shoppers may have not come to the store at all, instead using their television at home to do their grocery shopping.

The continuing evolution of The Smart Store involves more than just creating prototypes of new ways to use information technology. Rather, it aims to create loyal customers by testing new ways to provide effective customer service with good prices.

477

Health Strategy Center

6 Andersen's Hospital of the Future™ at the Health Strategy Center features forward thinking and the use of IT to demonstrate ways of reinventing health care services. Like all of Andersen's prototype centers, The Health Strategy Center emphasizes best practices, not just analysis of possibilities. The center consists of seven areas:

- *The focused care center*, almost a "mini-hospital," demonstrates the use of IT in "cluster care" for patients with similar medical conditions. Multiskilled care teams, cross-trained to treat patients from pre-admission to discharge, employ IT to simplify scheduling, improve resource management, facilitate communication, and enhance service quality. Communications systems are designed to interconnect the focused care center with other locations, including surgery scheduling, the physician's office, and other medical offices.
- *Centralized support services* consist of a medical center's operating rooms, materials management operations, and the activities of pharmacies, laboratories, and radiology. IT capabilities enable these service areas to communicate up-to-the minute information to other areas of the hospital (including medical staff), as well as to an entire health service network outside of the hospital.
- *Ambulatory care services* support the clinics, physicians' offices, and emergency care facilities that provide services to patients who are not admitted to the hospital at the time they need treatment. Information technology in the ambulatory care center gives medical staff access to patient data from other care providers. Multimedia teaching tools help patients understand their medical conditions and treatment alternatives, empowering them to make informed choices about the care they receive.

- *The home health demonstration room* demonstrates how physicians, nurses, and patient care agencies can provide and monitor the care received by patients at home. Portable computers ensure medical care providers full access to complete hospital medical records from the patient's home or any other location. This capability not only enables the hospital to reduce the cost of medical care, but also expands the boundaries of the "hospital without walls."
- *The intermediaries office* demonstrates the ways health insurance providers, managed care providers, and other intermediary organizations can use and distribute information to benefit all parties. IT enables participants to use automated member eligibility and benefit coverage inquiry tools for case management, cost containment, and utilization review.
- In the *employer's office*, a firm can use IT to enroll employees electronically in a medical plan and to review insurance and care plan usage as well as quality indicators. Being able to access and examine information effectively helps employers make the right decisions about health care coverage, balancing benefits that meet employees' needs with the need to control benefits costs.
- In the *supplier's office*, demonstrations show how IT makes possible efficient materials management, providing equipment and products at the right time, in the right amount, and at the right place. Because of the careful coordination possible with IT (including electronic data interchange), suppliers can ensure that supplies and materials are provided "just-in-time" to meet hospital and patient needs without holding excess inventory and tying up resources.

Andersen's Health Strategy Center in The Hospital of the Future, like all its prototype centers, is a continually evolving demonstration of business processes and technologies. Through the center, Andersen and its clients can conduct research, educate, and demonstrate the best practices in the hospital industry.

479

Chapter Outline

CHAPTER 12

Business Information Systems and IT in Industry

Learning Objectives

When you have completed this chapter, you should be able to:

1 Define and explain the purpose of information systems.

2 Describe the six types of business information systems and when each is used.

3 Summarize the purpose of computer-integrated manufacturing systems and manufacturing cells.

4 List and describe seven specialized types of CIM used in manufacturing.

In Practice

After completing this chapter, you should be able to perform these activities:

1 Explain why companies use different types of information systems.

2 Explain why transaction processing systems determine the success of all other business information systems.

3 Differentiate between the manner in which executives and other company personnel use business information systems.

4 Discuss with a manufacturing manager the manner in which IT is used today compared to a decade or two ago.

5 Discuss with a network manager the role communications networks play in linking manufacturing processes with other functions in the company, including inventory control, purchasing, and order processing.

6 Explain how a product designer or engineer uses CAD/CAM.

7 Specify the types of information needed to operate a flexible manufacturing system.

Rethinking Common Practices

TAKING THE TIME TO RETHINK COMMON practices can present tremendous business opportunity. In the 1920s, Henry Ford became a spectacular success by manufacturing automobiles in a completely new way. Ford ignored the rules of car manufacturing used by his competitors and started from scratch. Rather than use a system in which workers performed many different tasks as they moved around the vehicle (the system in use at other companies), Ford pioneered a new system—an assembly line on which the manufacturing work was broken into separate tasks, with each task being performed by people who specialized in the task. This new system used technology and time much more efficiently than the old system and gave Ford a major competitive advantage. The company was able to turn out vehicles in a shorter amount of time than its competitors who still followed the old system. In the assembly line method of building automobiles, the partially completed auto was transported by conveyor down an assembly line past the specialized workers, reducing the cost of manufacturing and improving the manufacturing management process.

In the 1920s, Henry Ford pioneered a new system of automobile manufacturing in which each job was broken into separate tasks, with each task being performed by people who specialized in the task. The new assembly line allowed Ford to turn out vehicles in a shorter time than his competitors. Today, in the 1990s, manufacturing firms that are rethinking common practices are also achieving a competitive advantage.

Today, in the Information Age, many companies that are rethinking the rules of business rather than relying on common practices are also achieving a competitive advantage. IT plays a major role in changing these rules by helping companies put processes together (rather than separating them, as the assembly lines of the Industrial Age had done). Few of today's companies can start from scratch, but the most effective ones are redeveloping their business and work processes, combining them in a way that makes the best use of today's advanced technology and know-how.

N THIS CHAPTER, WE EXAMINE THE ACTIVITIES OF MANY SUCCESSFUL COMPANIES THAT ARE using IT to run their business and to manage their manufacturing activities. We begin by looking at the various types of business information systems now in use throughout the business world. In the second part of the chapter, we focus on the applications of IT automation in manufacturing industries.

Business Information Systems

information system   A system in which data and information flow from one person or department to another.

business information system The family of IT applications that underlie the activities of running and managing a business.

Recall that an **information system** is a system in which data and information flow from one person or department to another. Frequently, the term **business information system** is used to refer to the family of IT applications that underlie the activities of running and managing a business (including the people and procedures associated with the applications). Six types of information systems are commonly used in business: transaction processing systems, management reporting systems, decision support systems, group support systems, executive support systems, and expert support systems.

Transaction Processing Systems

Businesses exist by managing *transactions*, events that involve or affect the enterprise. Transactions are at the heart of every company's business process (Figure 12.1).

transaction processing system (TPS) A shared business information system that uses a combination of information technology and manual procedures to process data and information and to manage transactions.

Processing transactions efficiently and accurately keeps a business running smoothly. If a company cannot accept or fulfill orders, record its sales, manage its inventory, bill for its products or services, collect money, meet payroll needs, or maintain income tax records, it will not stay in business very long. A **transaction processing system (TPS)** is a shared system that uses a combination of information technology and manual procedures to process data and information and to manage transactions. With a TPS, each transaction is handled according to standard company procedures. The characteristics of TPS are summarized in Table 12.1.

The TPS at Price Chopper Supermarkets.   In conjunction with its key suppliers, Price Chopper Supermarkets, a regional grocery chain in the northeastern United States, has developed an efficient TPS for processing delivery information. When deliveries arrive at a store, the driver connects a handheld computer to a communications cable on the loading dock outside the store. Invoices for the delivery are automatically transmitted to a store computer, which immediately checks the invoices for correct pricing and delivery authorization, using details downloaded daily from a purchasing and product authorization database at company headquarters.

Meanwhile, as the products are delivered into the store, the receiving manager counts the goods, entering the actual quantity delivered into another handheld computer connected to the store computer by FM radio signals (Figure 12.2). The com-

TABLE 12.1   Characteristics of a Transaction Processing System

- Processes a high volume of similar business transactions
- Supports multiple users in routine, everyday transactions
- Utilizes relatively simple procedures to control processing and ensure accuracy
- Produces documents and reports
- Updates files and databases

a) Stopping for fast food at a bodega in the "Little Havana" section of Miami.

b) Registering for the new semester's classes at the Registrar's office at Suffolk University.

c) Signing a lease at a Citroen dealership in Paris.

d) Purchasing tickets for a ride on a San Francisco cable car.

FIGURE 12.1
Business Transactions
Businesses exist by managing transactions, the events that involve or affect the enterprise. Transaction processing systems can help to manage a wide variety of transactions, from registration for a university course to lease signings at an auto dealership.

FIGURE 12.2
The Transaction Processing System at Price Chopper Supermarkets
When deliveries arrive at Price Chopper Supermarkets, drivers use handheld computers to transmit invoices and pricing information to both the store's computer and company headquarters. Meanwhile, as the products are delivered into the store, the receiving manager counts the goods, entering the actual quantity delivered into another handheld computer connected to the store computer by FM radio signals.

puter immediately compares the driver's counts to the receiving manager's counts. Any discrepancy can be adjusted while the supplier is still at the delivery dock.

Each day, the invoices from the many deliveries made to the store are uploaded from the store computer to an accounts payable system at headquarters. The system processes each invoice to detect errors or discrepancies and notifies the store manager of any problems. After verification, the invoices go into the company's accounts payable cycle.

The TPS Processing Sequence/Output and Reports.   A transaction processing system can process either online or in batches. (Review Chapter 2 if these terms are unclear to you.) Figure 12.3 summarizes the processing sequence and the five types of output produced during transaction processing: action documents, detail reports, summary reports, exception reports, and updated master data.

action document A document designed to trigger a specific action or to signify that a transaction has taken place.

- **Action documents** are documents designed to trigger a specific action or to signify that a transaction has taken place. At Price Chopper, for example, invoices are action documents intended to result in the payment of money. When a

FIGURE 12.3
The Transaction Processing Sequence and TPS Output

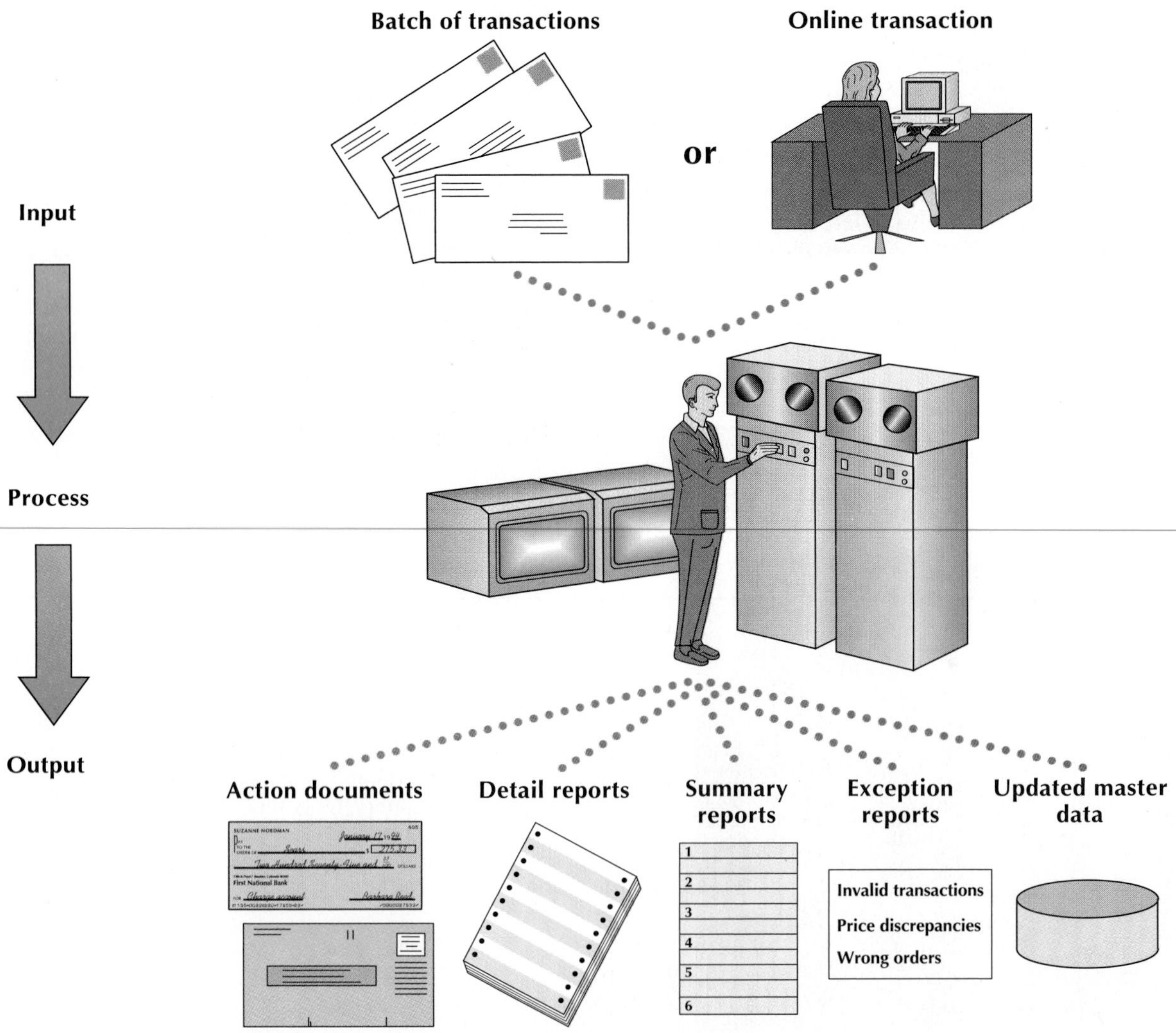

utility company produces a customer's monthly bill, it too is creating an action document designed to result in the payment of money. Similarly, state motor vehicle departments process their files regularly to determine who must renew their car registrations during a particular month, then send out an action document prepared by the system. Airlines' reservation transactions lead to action documents in the form of printed tickets and, in some cases, boarding passes with the individual's seat assignment.

- A **detail report**, sometimes called a **transaction log**, contains data describing each processed transaction. It includes enough details to identify the transaction and its most important characteristics. For example, if the transaction is the payment of an invoice, the detail report will list the transaction and indicate the amount of money paid, the check number or cash reference, the date of the transaction, and the individual or company making the payment. If any questions arise during or after processing, the transaction log serves as a ready reference.

- A **summary report** shows the overall results of processing for a period of time or for a batch of transactions and includes a grand total for all listed transactions and the average transaction amount. It lists in summary form the transactions that took place. Different versions of the report may be produced for various recipients. For example, a grocery store may produce one summary report for the bookkeeper, another for the receiving manager, and others for department managers. If they want additional data or information, they can request *detailed reports*, which also can be tailored to individuals.

- An **exception report** lists unusual, erroneous, or unacceptable transactions or results. An exception is any activity that falls outside normal guidelines or expected conditions. One Price Chopper exception report, for example, lists supplier prices that are different from those in the database, items delivered that the store does not carry, and items not ordered. The exception report is designed to call attention to the discrepancy and trigger an action to deal with it.

- Transaction processing systems also generate **updated master data**. When a transaction is processed, all records in the system must be adjusted. When a customer makes a payment, for example, the database must be adjusted to show a decrease in his or her account balance. When a supplier moves, the database must be updated to include the new address and telephone number. The people using the system should always be informed when master data change. In most cases, the detail report will include a summary of these changes.

Error-free transaction processing is essential. Because the data and information produced by transaction processing are used in the company's other business systems, a mistake in transaction processing can have a multiplier effect throughout the organization.

Management Reporting Systems

A **management reporting system** is designed to provide managers with information useful in decision making or problem solving. For example, the manager of a furniture store needs to make many decisions involving the purchase and replenishment of stock. These decisions include determining how much merchandise to order, whether a particular supplier is too expensive or carries low-quality products, and whether to continue offering certain products or services. The manager may also need to solve the problems of high labor costs or equipment repair costs. A management reporting system can help address these problems by retrieving and processing the data generated through transaction processing.

---

detail report or transaction log A report describing each processed transaction.

summary report A report that shows the overall results of processing for a period of time or for a batch of transactions and includes a grand total for all listed transactions and the average transaction amount.

exception report A report that lists unusual, erroneous, or unacceptable transactions or results.

updated master data An adjustment of all records in a system in response to a processed transaction.

management reporting system or **management information system (MIS)** A business information system designed to produce the information needed for successful management of a structured problem, process, department, or business.

The processing done by a management reporting system may use the actual "live" data in the system or a copy of the data. Working with a copy provides added security, protecting the master database from accidental or intentional damage or intrusion.

A person uses a management reporting system by requesting it to produce a certain report. Typically, the format and content of all reports are predetermined when the application is designed. The application simply retrieves the necessary data and information from a database or master file, processes them, and automatically presents the results in the specified format. For example, a Price Chopper district manager who wants to monitor the produce sales of all the stores in a district may have a report designed for that purpose and produced regularly. Each time it is prepared, the format will be the same, with the data and information reflecting recent business activity.

Management reporting systems are often called **management information systems (MIS)** because they are designed to produce information needed for successful management of a process, department, or business. They can help to support recurring decisions when information needs have been determined in advance. Table 12.2 summarizes the characteristics of management information systems.

MIS Reports at MCI.   Reports from management reporting systems are usually generated automatically at specified time intervals, whether hourly, daily, weekly, monthly, quarterly, or annually. However, virtually all systems of this type include the capability to produce reports on demand.

MCI Communications Corp., the public long-distance carrier headquartered in Washington, D.C., provides the customers of its "virtual network" service with three billing options. MCI will provide a record of all the customer's network transactions by (1) sending it electronically to the customer's designated computer center, where the details are printed out, (2) writing the data onto a magnetic tape or CD-ROM that is mailed to the customer, or (3) allowing the customer to download data from the MCI mainframe billing computer. MCI also provides its clients with management reporting software that allows them to process the data to produce over 20 standard reports. Divided into four categories, these reports enable managers to:

- Monitor network usage and list the longest calls, most expensive calls, and most frequently used identification codes or calling card numbers (Figure 12.4).
- Analyze calling history and patterns by identification code, calling card, and rate period (for example, full-price day rate or reduced evening rate).
- Report call frequencies, isolating the most frequently called numbers and area codes.
- Summarize calling traffic by city, state, and country.

TABLE 12.2   Characteristics of a Management Reporting System/Management Information System

- Uses data captured and stored as a result of transaction processing
- Reports data and information rather than details of transaction processing
- Assists managers in monitoring situations, evaluating conditions, and determining actions needed
- Supports recurring decisions
- Provides information in prespecified report formats, either in print or onscreen

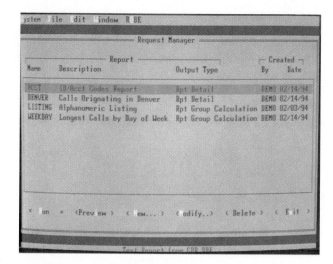

**FIGURE 12.4
MCI's Management
Reporting Software for
Clients**

When printed on paper, these reports for an average customer can fill 16 stan-dard-sized boxes! MCI enables its customers to obtain information in the form they desire while ensuring they have the information they need to manage tele-phone use.

Decision Support Systems

A **decision support system (DSS)** is a business information system designed to assist in decision making where the decision process is relatively unstruc-tured and only part of the information needed is structured in advance. The DSS helps the individual to structure the problem by providing the needed informa-tion. Typically, the uniqueness of the issues and the breadth of the problems will require the system to retrieve and process data from several files and data-bases and to use data provided online by individual decision makers simultane-ously.

Because information needs are not known at the beginning of a unique situa-tion, the reports and displays generated by a DSS are not designed in advance. Instead, the user will generally request the processing of data and the generation of information through inquiries such as "How many _____ have this characteris-tic?", "Under what circumstances did this occur?", or "What if _____ occurs?". Frequently, getting some information raises additional questions, which in turn creates the need for more information. For this reason, a DSS must have greater flexibility than a management reporting system. The characteristics of decision support systems are summarized in Table 12.3.

**decision support system
(DSS)** A business information system designed to assist in decision making where the decision process is relatively unstructured and only part of the information needed is structured in advance.

TABLE 12.3   Characteristics of a Decision Support System

- Assists people who make decisions where information requirements are not known in advance
- Supports problem solving and decision making where the situation is only partly structured
- Provides information needed to define and solve the problem
- Works both with files and databases *and* with people working online with the system
- Provides information in a format determined by the recipient at the time of need

There are several types of DSS:

- An *institutional DSS* is an application that allows the user to both retrieve and generate information needed to address a general problem area (for example, determining the viability of a merger or the price of a new product). The system contains a series of mathematical models that, when tailored to the characteristics of a specific problem, help in analyzing the situation. An institutional DSS is intended to be used on a continuing basis, even though the details of the situations in which it is used may vary.
- *DSS generators* are used to create applications quickly. They are not complete applications themselves. A DSS generator consists of a series of high-level commands that instruct the system to analyze data, simulate specific conditions, or produce reports quickly. A few commands can produce a great deal of valuable analysis and well-focused information.
- *DSS tools* are designed for very specific capabilities. For example, one DSS tool may produce graphic displays of information in bar-chart form. Another may analyze a file to determine categories of high and low business activity and variations in performance. Several DSS tools are usually used together, often with a DSS generator, to aid the problem solver in defining and then analyzing the problem.

DSS in the U.S. Congress.   Every time the U.S. Congress sets out to reevaluate revenue generation and the tax system, it faces a different situation. The economy is different, new legislation affecting revenues is in effect, and the spending needs of the government have changed. Before it can begin preparing a new tax package, it must first determine the intent of the new legislation (for example, raise more revenue, stimulate business spending on new plant and equipment, attract more investment to business research and development, or encourage more personal savings).

Analysts with the U.S. Congress can then use DSS generators to formulate models for evaluating a new tax or revenue proposal. For example, finding out that a change in investment tax credits will have an undesirable effect on the economy may cause them to adjust and then reevaluate a proposed tax credit. Alternatively, determining that a change in tax rates will affect middle-class savings negatively may cause them to readjust the proposed tax rates. Institutional DSS software makes it possible to change the components of the model easily, recalculating them to determine the likely effects of different proposals (Figure 12.5).

Keep in mind that every tax package is different. The creation of each new package involves determining what new information is needed. These characteristics suggest the need for a decision support system rather than an information or transaction processing system, in which reporting needs have been predetermined.

FIGURE 12.5
Decision Support Systems in the U.S. Congress
The decision making process in the U.S. Congress—which is sometimes considered agonizingly slow—has been helped along by a decision support system. Congressional analysts are now using DSS generators to evaluate the effects of new tax and revenue proposals on businesses, taxpayers, and the economy.

CRITICAL CONNECTION 1
DSS Takes the Guesswork Out of Building Energy-Efficient Homes*

For years, energy designers and researchers have been devising techniques for building comfortable homes that can slash heating and cooling bills by 30 to 50 percent. But the techniques aren't flooding the market, due in part to resistance by the construction industry. Many builders, used to building "to code" or minimum standards, find it hard to justify the extra cost of energy-efficient construction. Others simply lack the engineering skills needed to adopt the new techniques. This may change by the turn of the century, thanks to a number of programs designed to teach builders the new techniques and introduce them to a variety of new software tools.

Take, for example, the Energy Crafted Home Program, a trademarked program sponsored by several utilities and created with the help of a Harvard, Massachusetts, engineer. Most of the techniques taught at the seminars focus on ways to tighten the home's "envelope"—the boundary formed by the walls, ceilings, windows, and foundation. But make the envelope too tight, and you may let moisture or indoor pollutants build up. "Looking at a building as a total system is really too much for the human brain to encompass all at once," say some engineers. "But with the aid of computers we can do just that."

The two simplest decision support software tools designed for this purpose are BuilderGuide, from the Passive Solar Industries Council, and REM/Design, which was created by Architectural Energy Corporation of Boulder, Colorado. Both programs rely on a description of the home, climate data, and local utility rates to calculate the home's annual peak heating and cooling loads, energy costs, and so on. With the aid of the software, builders can compare the potential costs and savings associated with alternate construction techniques and floor plans.

Group Support Systems

A **group support system (GSS)** permits people to process and interpret information as a group, even if they are not working face to face. Like a DSS, a GSS supports people working in situations that are not fully structured. In these situations, an important part of problem solving involves conducting an analysis and determining what information is needed to make a decision.

Unlike DSS systems, however, in GSS systems information is generated by the system in response to questions posed by group members. Online interaction is an essential GSS feature. Individuals usually work on networked computer workstations, entering questions, ideas, suggestions, and comments that are shared electronically with other group members, sometimes anonymously. (We discussed an important part of group support systems, group software, in Chapter 9.)

Many companies have constructed specially designed group support rooms called *decision rooms* (Figure 12.6a). Similar in style to conference or board rooms,

group support system (GSS)
A business information system that permits people to process and interpret information as a group, even if they are not working face to face.

Based on: Charles Wardell, "The Science of Energy Efficient Homes," *Popular Science,* April 1993, pp. 96-99, 108.

(a) Decision room

(b) Remote decision network

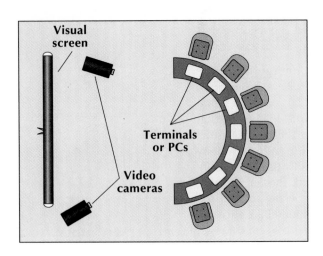

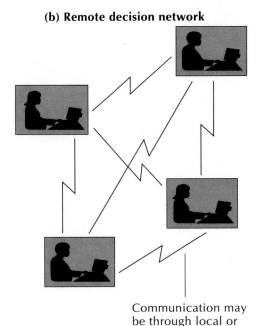

Communication may
be through local or
wide area network

FIGURE 12.6   Group Support Rooms
Users of a GSS can be linked together in a decision room or through a remote decision
network.

these facilities feature a large screen for display of information, individual workstations networked together, and a seating arrangement in which the group members
can see each other. Another type of group support room uses a *remote decision
network* (Figure 12.6b) format to link group members at remote locations by a
communications network that allows them to share databases, models, and GSS
software. Group members enter their questions, ideas, and comments through a
workstation; the network then displays these to other group members.

GSS sessions are typically managed by a facilitator who serves as an intermediary
between the system and the group and who is responsible for administering the
group's activities. The facilitator's job is to keep the group focused on the problem at
hand, to ensure that no individual dominates the discussion, and to draw out ideas.

Unlike the other business information systems discussed so far, a GSS does not
produce traditional printed reports. Rather, the questions, comments, and ideas of
each group session are captured in a database that can later be printed and
reviewed. Frequently, the most important result of a GSS session is a decision, or
series of decisions, about how to solve a problem or capitalize on an opportunity.
Table 12.4 summarizes the characteristics of group support systems.

TABLE 12.4   Characteristics of a Group Support System

- Supports situations that are not fully structured
- Assists in analyzing the problem under consideration
- Used by groups or teams, rather than individuals
- Emphasizes communication and generation of ideas and information
- Permits communication between team members at different locations, who participate through communications networks
- Involves a facilitator who keeps the group focused and draws ideas out of group members
- Generates a database of the group's questions, comments, and ideas rather than traditional reports

GSS at Marriott.   Business travelers are among Marriott Hotels' most important customers. One of the reasons Marriott is successful is because it meets the needs of these travelers, even though they change from year to year. Periodically, Marriott assembles hand-picked hotel managers, heads of housekeeping, front-desk personnel, catering managers, room-service coordinators, and bellmen to compare experiences regarding their guests. The meeting is conducted with a group support system, wherein hotel personnel enter their thoughts and criticisms regarding current capabilities and ideas for new services. For example, they may relate a guest encounter in which they provided, or could not provide, an important service the guest wanted.

Because the entries are made anonymously, Marriott finds that the rank or pay level of the employee is not a deterrent to sharing ideas. (Hourly desk attendants might otherwise feel intimidated by a hotel general manager.) When the ideas and comments are displayed visually, they are discussed openly without knowledge of their origin. In this way, the group can evaluate the comments honestly. You can probably see how such Marriott service features as guest voice mail, rentable portable computers, and cordless telephones might have originated through GSS sessions.

CRITICAL CONNECTION 2
Coopers & Lybrand Boosts Productivity with Lotus Notes

If you've ever played telephone tag, you can understand the frustration building up at Coopers & Lybrand. Too often, auditing teams at the accounting giant spent too much time trying to reach the few specialists needed to answer a client's complex financial and tax questions. That's why the company was willing to take a gamble, becoming in 1991 one of the first companies to adopt Lotus Notes.

Lotus Notes helped to advance the concept of *groupware*, software that turns a network into an electronic conference room with online access to company databases and outside information services. (You've already encountered this concept in Chapter 9.) By early 1993, 500 Coopers & Lybrand professionals were using Notes to organize and share financial and tax information, including advice and analysis from outside specialists. Professional services were being done faster and complex questions answered sooner. Within the year, Coopers & Lybrand was planning to install Notes for 2,000 client-service partners and staff.

Executive Support Systems

The activities of top-level executives in business and government are often quite different from those of middle managers and staff members. Rather than focusing on a single business process or an individual product or service line, as most middle managers do, executives spend most of their time meeting the challenges and opportunities that will affect the firm's future. When a serious problem arises—for example, an industrial accident or the potential loss of an important customer—they are also likely to be involved in determining the cause, dealing with the effect, and preventing its reoccurrence. Executives also spend a good deal of their time on activities external to the company. Uncovering new market opportunities, monitoring the activities of their competitors, and keeping an eye on impending legislation are among the executive's principle external concerns.

As you can probably guess, and as Figure 12.7 shows, executives spend much of their time in meetings. In fact, they spend very little time in their offices and have precious few moments of quiet time in which to contemplate the intricate plans and strategies they must put into effect. When they *are* in their offices, they need to be briefed on company developments quickly and in a way that provides them with useful and well-focused information. An **executive support system (ESS)**, sometimes called an **executive information system (EIS)**, is an interactive information system designed to fill exactly this need. An ESS encompasses a broad spectrum of company activities, presenting information on everything from entire business units to product and service lines to customers and suppliers.

Behind the scenes, the ESS software retrieves data and information from a variety of databases within or external to the company. The ESS usually displays information on the company's stock prices (if the stock is publicly traded), current orders booked, and market prices of important materials. (An airline executive will want to know the cost of fuel, for example, while an executive at an appliance manufacturer will undoubtedly monitor current steel prices.) The ESS also includes a communications link for retrieval of information from sources external to the company, such as *Dow Jones/News Retrieval* and similar services. Some systems also include DSS-like capabilities that let executives test "what-if" strategies and compare alternatives. Often companies will combine DSS, GSS, and ESS. A sample menu screen from an ESS appears in Figure 12.8.

ESS software includes powerful processing capabilities. These capabilities are necessarily to boil down large volumes of performance details to a few screens that will allow the executive to grasp the status of events and assess key business indicators quickly. These summaries are usually presented in a standard format and rely heavily on business graphics to display results and relationships between business variables.

Although an ESS generally displays feature summaries only, the data supporting these summaries are quickly accessible. The report on each display screen is usu-

executive support system (ESS) or **executive information system (EIS)** An interactive business information system, designed to support executives, which is capable of presenting summary information on company and industry activities.

FIGURE 12.7   How Executives Use Their Time
Executives spend, on average, about 70% of their time in meetings.
Source: Based on Henry Mintzberg, "The Manager's Job: Folklore or Fact." *Harvard Business Review* 53, 4 (July-August 1975) pp. 49-61.

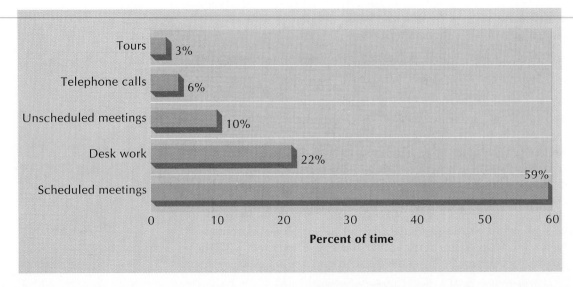

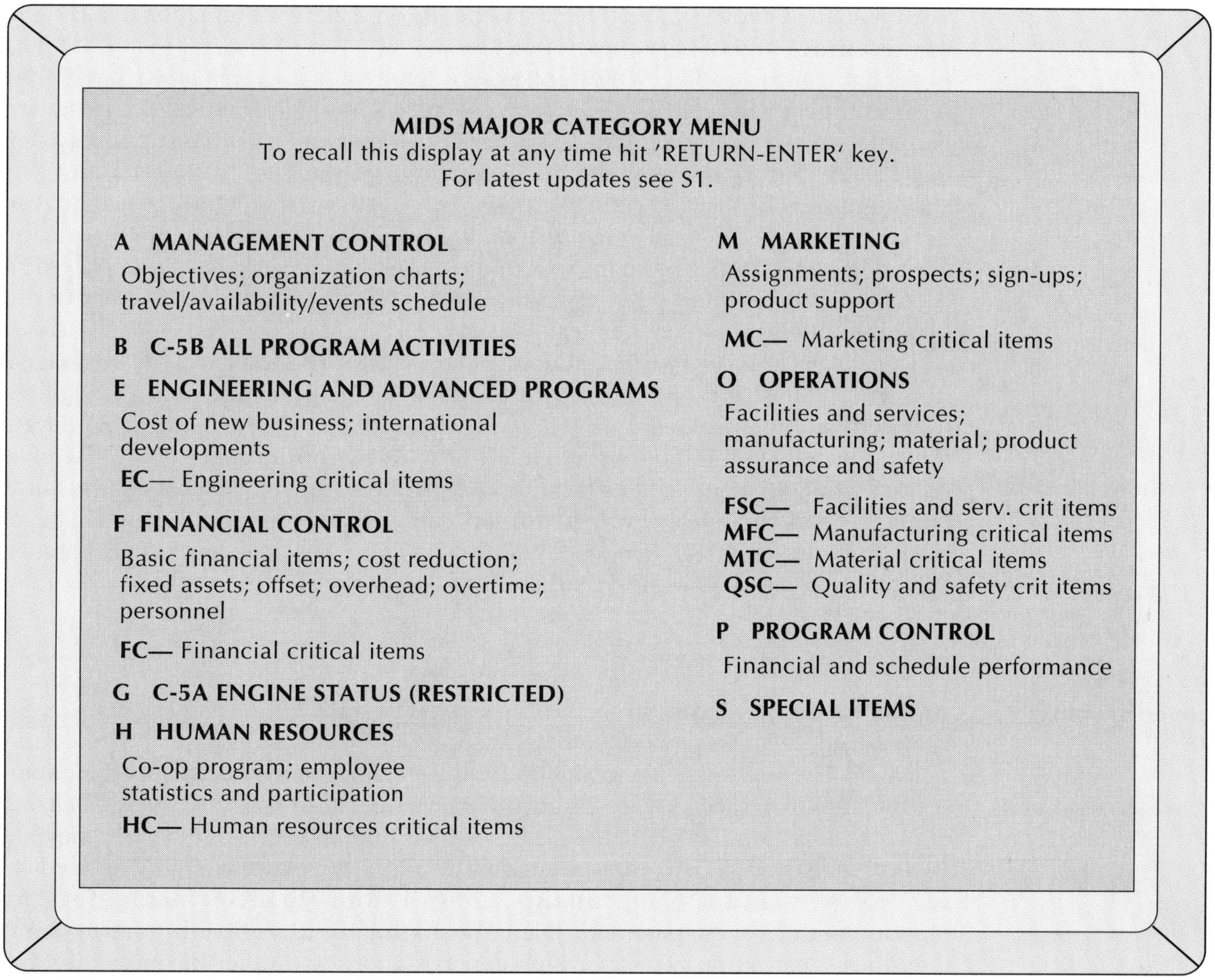

MIDS MAJOR CATEGORY MENU
To recall this display at any time hit 'RETURN-ENTER' key.
For latest updates see S1.

A MANAGEMENT CONTROL
Objectives; organization charts;
travel/availability/events schedule

B C-5B ALL PROGRAM ACTIVITIES

E ENGINEERING AND ADVANCED PROGRAMS
Cost of new business; international
developments
EC— Engineering critical items

F FINANCIAL CONTROL
Basic financial items; cost reduction;
fixed assets; offset; overhead; overtime;
personnel
FC— Financial critical items

G C-5A ENGINE STATUS (RESTRICTED)

H HUMAN RESOURCES
Co-op program; employee
statistics and participation
HC— Human resources critical items

M MARKETING
Assignments; prospects; sign-ups;
product support
MC— Marketing critical items

O OPERATIONS
Facilities and services;
manufacturing; material; product
assurance and safety
FSC— Facilities and serv. crit items
MFC— Manufacturing critical items
MTC— Material critical items
QSC— Quality and safety crit items

P PROGRAM CONTROL
Financial and schedule performance

S SPECIAL ITEMS

FIGURE 12.8
Main Menu of Executive Support System Showing Major Information Categories
From the main menu of an ESS, executives can call up summary information on most categories of information relevant to their business.

ally linked to detailed information that is available by clicking on an icon or entering a command. These supporting data can be presented in numeric or graphic form and displayed onscreen or printed. Table 12.5 summarizes the characteristics of an executive support system.

ESS at Whirlpool. With sales of approximately $7 billion annually, Whirlpool Corp. of Benton Harbor, Michigan, is the largest appliance manufacturer in the United States and Brazil and the second largest in Europe, Canada, and Mexico.

TABLE 12.5   Characteristics of an Executive Support System

- Offers quick, concise updates of business performance
- Permits scanning of data and information on both internal activities and the external business environment
- Highlights significant data and information in summary form
- Allows the user to access data supporting the summary information

The company believes that its success depends on making information available to its executives—and its customers—quickly.

Global companies like Whirlpool, where international events affect day-to-day business operations, rely on IT to keep executives in touch with each other and to help them make decisions. Whirlpool has developed an executive support system that lets executives retrieve data and information, regardless of their location, by clicking an icon to access data from commercial databases, Whirlpool databases, or the company's electronic mail system. If supply shipments to a particular region are unexpectedly disrupted, for example, an executive can use the system to determine the potential impact of the disruption and to devise alternatives to obtain supplies from other sources.

The system also includes a videoconferencing capability that allows managers from around the world to be brought together online. The system greatly reduces the need for travel while ensuring that decisions continue to be made, even during difficult times. During the Persian Gulf War in 1991, for example, Whirlpool used its videoconferencing facilities to arrange a partnership with a European business partner—even though the war had temporarily forced Whirlpool's top management to curtail their travel plans. Whirlpool's executive support system is much more than a convenience. It's a proven management tool.

Expert Support Systems

expert support system or **expert system** A business information system that uses business rules, regulations, and databases to evaluate a situation or determine an appropriate course of action.

An **expert support system**, or simply **expert system**, uses business rules, regulations, and databases to evaluate a situation or determine an appropriate course of action. These systems are designed to capture and apply consistently the expertise of a human specialist in a particular field. Because they are so specialized, expert systems are limited in the scope of their application. Nonetheless, they are extremely powerful. They are commonly used in such diverse areas as medical diagnosis, manufacturing quality control, and financial planning. The Opportunities box on page 496 titled "IT: Rx for the U.S. Health Care System?" describes some of the ways in which expert systems and other business information systems are being used to trim the costs of health care in the United States.

Expert systems usually process data provided by people interacting with the system through workstations. Alternatively, they may be part of a transaction processing system, analyzing data and information included in business transactions. When automobile makers assemble vehicle-order transactions, for example, they may use an expert system to review the orders' option packages to ensure they are appropriate. An expert system will know that if an automobile is built to include both air conditioning and a towing package that will allow it to pull a trailer, it must have an oversize radiator, heavy-duty alternator, and transmission cooler. The expert system will review the order details and report any discrepancy with the rules, thereby preventing costly mistakes. In essence, the system incorporates the specialized knowledge of an auto design engineer to produce the finished product (Figure 12.9).

rule base or **knowledge base** A database of rules in an expert system.

The heart of most expert systems is a database of rules called a **rule base** or **knowledge base**. The rule base is often expressed in the form of IF-THEN statements. The expert system at the auto plant described in the last paragraph, for example, might include a rule that says:

IF the vehicle requires a trailer package

And it will have air conditioning

THEN check to ensure it will have the following components: oversize radiator, heavy-duty alternator, and transmission cooler

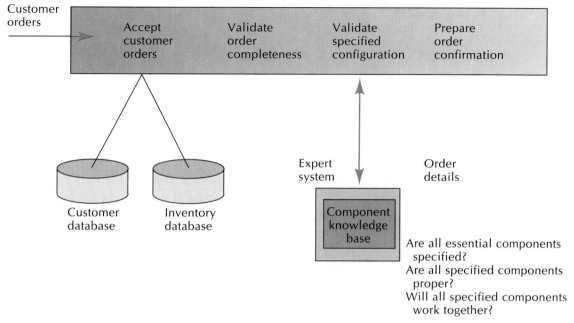

FIGURE 12.9
Expert System Embedded in Order-Entry Portion of an Auto Manufacturing System
An expert system embedded in an auto manufacturing system will review all order details
and report any discrepancy with the rules of manufacturing or good engineering.

   The ultimate result of using an expert system is the diagnosis of a problem or
determination of the cause of a problem. It may or may not include a recommendation for the appropriate action to take. Expert systems generally do not produce
formal detailed reports. (Table 12.6 summarizes the characteristics of an expert
system.) Mrs. Fields, the gourmet cookie franchiser, uses an expert system in its
retail operations. For more information, see the Case Study in Chapter 1.

Information Technology for Manufacturing Automation and Control

The challenge and opportunity of managing a business unit or company is removing the barriers that were erected when the Industrial Age brought about special-
ization. As we've seen throughout this book, information technology is helping
companies integrate their business processes and revolutionizing the way businesses operate.

TABLE 12.6   Characteristics of an Expert Support System

- Diagnoses situations and/or recommends a course of action
- Captures data and applies the expertise of a human specialist
- Limited scope of application
- Relies on rule base
- Processes data entered by people interacting with the system as well as details retrieved
  from other information systems

OPPORTUNITIES

IT: Rx for the U.S. Health Care System?

I N 1970, IT CONSUMED JUST $74 BILLION, OR 7.3% OF U.S. GNP (gross national product). By 1990, however, its appetite had grown to $667 billion, or 13.4% of GNP. Unchecked, experts predict, it will devour $1,616 billion, or 16.4% of GNP, by the year 2000. "It" is the U.S. health care system, and it's creating new opportunities for people who understand both health care and information technology. Consider some of the ways that IT is being used in the health-care industry:

- **Speeding the release of new drugs.** Seriously ill patients and pharmaceutical companies both charge that the Food and Drug Administration (FDA) is too slow to approve new drugs. (The agency usually needs about 30 months to review an application and its 10,000 to 1 million pages of supporting data.) Over the last ten years, though, a handful of pharmaceutical companies have shaved almost nine months off the approval process by filing applications electronically.
- **Cutting through the red tape.** Experts estimate that transaction processing systems using electronic data interchange (EDI) could save $4 to $10 billion a year in the processing of medical claims. The most ambitious effort to date may be the Healthcare Information Network, a nationwide network that uses toll-free telephone numbers to offer real-time processing of a variety of managed health care transactions.
- **Deciding which treatments really work.** Although patients tend to be impressed by expensive treat-

ments, many doctors (and insurers) aren't always sure they improve survival rates. This doubt led Dr. Paul Ellwood to create InterStudy, a Minneapolis research organization dedicated to "outcomes management," a scorekeeping system for treatment options. The system is based on a database that collects survey data from both doctors and patients during and after treatment of twenty-five major illnesses, including diabetes, cataracts, and hypertension.

Outcomes management is also being used by the U.S. Agency for Health Care Policy and Research. One of its research teams, for example, is evaluating the relative effectiveness of bypass surgery, balloon angioplasty, and medication in treating coronary heart disease. Another team is looking at the $24 billion annually spent on treating lower back pain in the United States.

- **Helping patients make better decisions.** Given a choice, informed patients may opt for less-expensive treatments that promise as much or more relief than more expensive or risky treatments. That's the reasoning at the Foundation for Informed Medical Decision Making, which is producing a series of interactive videodisks that can be offered to patients in doctor's offices, hospitals, and HMOs. The videodisks use plain English to explain the latest findings of outcomes management for such maladies as early-stage breast cancer, mild hypertension, and lower back pain.

Early results support the foundation's rationale. In the Denver region of the Kaiser Permanente HMO,

---

computer-integrated manufacturing (CIM) A manufacturing system that uses computers to link automated processes in a factory to reduce design time, increase machine utilization, shorten the manufacturing cycle, cut inventories, and increase product quality.

manufacturing cell A group of machines working together in computer-integrated manufacturing.

A similar revolution is taking place on the floor of manufacturing companies. Manufacturing systems have changed dramatically since Henry Ford redesigned his company's manufacturing processes. Today's factory finds people working in teams and relying heavily on computer and communications systems. **Computer-integrated manufacturing (CIM)** uses computers to link automated processes in a factory to reduce design time, increase machine utilization, shorten the manufacturing cycle, cut inventories, and increase product quality. In computer integrated manufacturing, machines work together in groups known as **manufacturing cells**. Parts and materials are moved between cells by automated guide vehicles, automated machines, and materials handling systems consisting of trolleys and carriers that move along guide wires or on conveyors. For most manufacturing companies today, the question is not *whether* to implement computers into their manufacturing processes, but *when*.

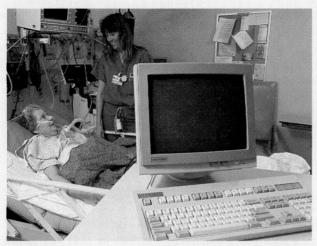

```
HELP DECISIONS
DATE TIME
06FEB 00:12   DRAW AN ABG 15 MINUTES AFTER MAKING VENTILATOR CHANGES.
              NO CHANGE TO TIDAL VOLUME SETTING.  SETTING REMAINS AT 500
              MILLILITERS.
              DECREASE VENTILATORY RATE SETTING BY 3, FROM 18 TO 15
              BREATHS/MIN.
              INCREASE FiO2 BY 10%, FROM 40% TO 50%.  DRAW AN ABG IN 15
              MINUTES.

06FEB 00:05   DRAW AN ABG 15 MINUTES AFTER MAKING VENTILATOR CHANGES.
              NO CHANGE TO TIDAL VOLUME SETTING.  SETTING REMAINS AT 500
              MILLILITERS.
              DECREASE VENTILATORY RATE SETTING BY 3, FROM 18 TO 15
              BREATHS/MIN.
              REDUCE FiO2 BY 10%, FROM 50% TO 40%.  DRAW AN ABG IN 15 MINUTES.


ENTER A COMMAND, TYPE ? FOR LIST OF COMMANDS OR
HIT (Return) TO EXIT--
```

a) This computer at an Intermountain Health Care hospital in Salt Lake City delivers instant medical advice to a team of intensive care specialists.

b) A close-up of a screen from Intermountain's health care information system.

where the foundation's videodisk on prostate enlargement has been used since 1989, surgery rates have dropped 45%, saving the HMO $170,000 to $200,000 a year.

- **Giving doctors a helping hand.** Some medical problems may be too complex for doctors, especially in the high-pressure world of intensive care. In treating adult respiratory distress syndrome, for example, doctors have to balance hundreds of variables from moment to moment. That's why a research team cre-ated an expert system, dubbed HELP, to support doctors at Salt Lake City's LDS Hospital. The system is helping to eliminate the 25% to 35% added to hospital bills when care givers have to correct such "mistakes" as post-operative infections. (Treating such an infection adds about $14,000 to a typical hospital bill.) After the HELP system was introduced, doctors were able to fine-tune the use of antibiotics, cutting the hospital's post-operative infection rate to less than half the national average.

✓ **Reality Check.** Companies in different parts of the world approach automation differently. Experts believe that U.S. and Japanese firms tend to address problems first at the level of the manufacturing floor. A full systems analysis and design effort follows. In contrast, most European companies examine the full system first, then break it down into individual processes and department functions. As a result, companies in different parts of the world have different priorities in using IT. Most Japanese firms implement CIM only when doing so is economically justifiable. Many U.S. companies follow a similar strategy, but emphasize short-term returns on their investment. European companies tend to focus on long-term manufacturing strategies, installing systems without as much emphasis on short-term gain. ◼

In essence, CIM fits the IT model we've used throughout this book. (Recall that information technology has three components: computers, communications, and know-how. See Figure 1.3.) Computers are at the heart of many manufacturing systems and are the source of intelligence embedded in lathes and machine tools. Computers control the actions and movements of arms, wheels, gears, and conveyors and examine process results. Database management systems store and retrieve manufacturing data and information, including product specifications, drawings, production procedures, set-up instructions, and multimedia training documents.

Communications also play a central role in manufacturing industries. Wide area networks link factories across the country and interconnect work areas within the same facility. In fact, a special protocol called the **manufacturing automation protocol (MAP)** has been devised to assist factory designers in interconnecting manufacturing tools, machines, and devices by providing a common language for the transmission of data.

The know-how needed for a successful CIM system is the same as it is in any other IT application. All the people involved with the system—analysts, communications specialists, database administrators, and IT managers—are responsible for developing the procedures that keep the systems in sync with business needs while safeguarding the firm against the loss of data, information, or processing capability. Using a CIM system properly means having the know-how to use the system to the firm's best advantage.

"Computer-integrated manufacturing" is a general, all-inclusive term used for computerized manufacturing systems. Five specialized types of CIM are material requirements planning and manufacturing resource planning, computer-aided design and manufacturing, robots, flexible manufacturing, and computer vision systems.

Material Requirements Planning (MRP) and Manufacturing Resource Planning (MRP II)

Manufacturing management is as important to a company's success as the quality of the products it manufactures and the manner in which it produces them. **Material requirements planning (MRP)** is the core of the entire production management process. Most manufactured products are made from a range of individual components. MRP systems keep track of the quantity of each part needed to manufacture a product. They also coordinate scheduled manufacturing dates with the lead time needed to have components delivered and assembled.

Manufacturing resource planning (MRP II) systems, which are essentially advanced versions of MRP systems that tie together all the parts of an organization into the company's production activities, include six essential subsystems (Figure 12.10):

- **Bill of materials management.** A *bill of materials* is the list of parts used in manufacturing an item. A sample bill of materials and an assembly order for a swimming pool filtration system are shown in Figure 12.11 on page 500. When a manufacturing company receives an order for a product, the system examines the bill of materials for the product and compares it to its current parts inventory. If needed, additional parts may be procured so that the ordered product can be manufactured.
- **Inventory management.** Inventory production schedulers keep track of what parts are on hand and on order. Using this information in conjunction with the bill of materials and the customer order, they determine which components must be ordered from suppliers. The manufacturing resource planning system helps inventory schedulers work with this information to determine the earliest date that manufacturing can begin.

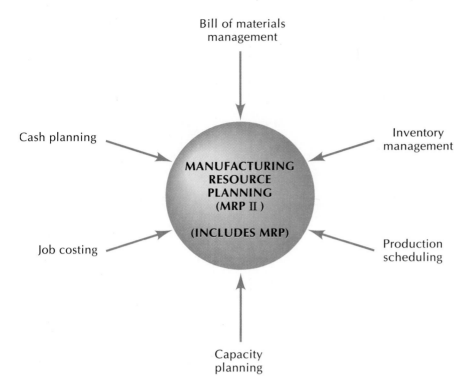

FIGURE 12.10
The Components of Manufacturing Resource Planning
Do not confuse manufacturing resource planning (MRP II) with material requirements planning (MRP). MRP is an important component of MRP II.

- **Production scheduling.** A company's *production schedule* specifies the planned use of its factory facilities and the quantity of items to be produced. Manufacturing resource planning allows production schedulers to examine the current schedule and to determine when additional activities can be added to the schedule without overloading plant capacity.
- **Capacity planning.** Each tool, machine, production line, and worker in a factory has a capacity, usually measured in output per hour. Manufacturing resource planning helps schedulers to incorporate manufacturing capacity into their schedules.
- **Job costing.** The level of costs and the sequence in which they will be incurred in manufacturing are extremely important to a business's bottom line. Manufacturing resource planning systems keep managers aware of both expected and unexpected costs throughout the production process.
- **Cash planning.** Business planning includes ensuring the company has sufficient cash flow to pay for materials and for workers. Manufacturing resource planning systems record the company's sources and uses of cash, both planned and actual.

Many types of report are produced by each component of the MRP II system. The systems are continually evolving to incorporate new features and additional capabilities. For this reason, they are often designated by generation name. For example, MRP II adds more capabilities for monitoring inventory of production resources.

Manufacturing Resource Planning at Raychem.   Raychem Corp.'s manufacturing facility outside of Vancouver, British Columbia, manufactures wiring systems for the aerospace industry. Wiring systems carry electrical power and control signals to various airplane devices. Because of the wide variety of aircraft designs in

Bill of Materials

Assembly number: 31436402
Assembly description: SWIMMING POOL FILTRATION SYSTEM
Drawing number:
Structure change: Drawing size:

Item number	Description	Type	Source	Unit of measure	Quantity/ assembly	Structure change	Dept. assembled in	Oper. assembled on

Assembly Order

Assembly number: 31436402
Assembly description: SWIMMING POOL FILTRATION SYSTEM
Order quantity: 50
                                                    Order number: 62566

Item number	Description	Unit of measure	Quantity per assembly	Expected quantity
531674	SCREW	01	6	300
531690	WASHER	01	5	250
728419	SCREW	01	5	250
1431478	SEAL	01	2	100
3519794	MOTOR	01	1	50
3572133	SPRING	01	2	100
31436130	PUMP SHAFT ASS'Y	01	1	50
31436301	SET COLLAR	01	1	50
31436315	CLAMP MOUNTING	01	1	50
31436338	SHIFTER COLLAR	01	1	50
31436345	SCREW	01	4	200

FIGURE 12.11
Bill of Materials and Assembly Order for a Swimming Pool Filtration System
A bill of materials is essentially a recipe for a product. It specifies the necessary ingredients,
the order in which they should be combined, and how many of each ingredient are needed
to make one batch of the product.

the industry, Raychem's manufacturing processes vary greatly. Planning production
and managing the details with paper forms—the way all companies managed the
production process in the past—is extremely time-consuming.

To cut down on the paper shuffling, Raychem has installed a paperless manufacturing system designed around client/server computing (review Chapter 10 if
necessary). In this manufacturing resource planning system, production data and
information are stored on servers that are accessible to a variety of workstations

and manufacturing tools. The system is interconnected with a computer-aided design/computer-aided manufacturing (CAD/CAM) system (discussed in the next section). Both planners and designers work online, retrieving information from the system's databases and devising production plans to meet the diverse needs of the company and its customers (Figure 12.12). Because so much of the work is done through networked workstations, paper reports are not generated very often. Also included in Raychem's system is a rule-based expert system used to create wiring design and manufacturing specifications and a design database that allows designers to draw on previous specifications.

As production occurs, the system captures data on the amount of time needed to set up machines and assembly lines and the amount of scrap materials produced. These data are fed back into the materials-planning and job-costing subsystems to improve subsequent jobs.

Computer-Aided Design and Computer-Aided Manufacturing (CAD/CAM)

For many years, automated manufacturing systems were synonymous with MRP. Today, computer-aided design and computer-aided manufacturing are also important components of most manufacturing systems. Product designers and engineers working on **computer-aided design (CAD)** systems use a powerful computer graphics workstation outfitted with programs that allow them to draw design specifications on the display screen. Working with a light pen, scanner, or mouse, they can specify the product's dimensions and show its lines, indentations, and other features with precision. Each element of the design appears on the screen as it is specified. Changes can be made quickly by adding, removing, or altering details on the drawing (Figure 12.13 on the next page).

CAD tools usually work in three dimensions, allowing the designer to specify and see the height, width, and depth of the product right on the screen. Designs can be rotated, tilted, and turned upside down so that every angle is visible for inspection. When a design is complete, it is stored on disk and ready for review, editing, or printing at any time.

CAD designs are frequently transmitted to **computer-aided manufacturing (CAM)** systems, which rely on IT to automate and manage the manufacturing process directly. Using the CAD database, CAM software controls tools and machines on the factory floor to actually manufacture the product designed on the CAD system.

computer-aided design (CAD) system A system that uses a powerful computer graphics workstation to enable product designers and engineers to draw design specifications on a display screen.

computer-aided manufacturing (CAM) system A system that relies on IT to automate and manage the manufacturing process directly.

FIGURE 12.12
Raychem's Manufacturing Resource Planning System
Planners and designers at Raychem work online, retrieving information from the company's manufacturing resource planning system to devise production plans. As production occurs, the system captures data that are then fed back into materials planning and job-costing subsystems to improve subsequent jobs.

FIGURE 12.13
CAD/CAM in Action at Litton Industries
Designers and engineers use computer-aided design and manufacturing programs to draw sophisticated design specifications onscreen. The photos shown here were prepared by Litton Industries as part of an investigation into improving its manufacturing systems.

a) To improve its material handling and control system, Litton studied the design, spacing, and layout of the machinery in use on the manufacturing floor.

b) Litton's designers then created a 3-D graphic simulation of the manufacturing floor using CAD/CAM software. By manipulating the simulation onscreen, they were able to experiment with new floor layouts and manufacturing techniques without building costly prototypes.

CAD/CAM systems require access to many computer and communications programs. For example, CAM systems obtain detailed product design information from the CAD databases and bills of materials from manufacturing resource planning systems. They communicate with the machines on the shop floors by way of high-speed, sophisticated communications networks.

CAD/CAM at Dayton-Walther Corp.   Dayton-Walther Corp., located in Dayton, Ohio, designs and manufactures truck, trailer, and automotive parts. It uses a CAD/CAM system equipped with graphics workstations to design these parts. Designers draw the points, lines, arcs, and other building blocks of each part on the computer screen using a digitizing tablet. Once drawn, these images can be rotated, zoomed in, or otherwise manipulated for close examination—all without use of paper, pencil, or drafting board.

To determine how well these designs will hold up under the stress of everyday use, engineers typically run the parts through a computer simulation. This process identifies weak points before the part is put into production and installed in Dayton-Walther's products. For manufacturing, the CAD designs are turned over to computer-aided manufacturing devices. For example, a die model for a part is cut with a numerically controlled machine tool using information transmitted from the CAD system.

CAD/CAM often pays for itself quickly. Dayton-Walther's management estimates that its system paid for itself in less than a year—and that's not counting the company's increased product quality and customer satisfaction.

Reality Check.   Product design itself usually accounts for 5% to 8% of a product's cost, but the decisions made by the designers typically account for 60% to 70% of the total costs. Discovering during production that a product is too difficult to build or that materials are too costly to use can mean serious problems. So can learning that the product contains features that make it difficult to sell after it has been manufactured.

Concurrent engineering can help to solve these problems before they happen. In a concurrently engineered project, teams of people from different departments take a "process view" of the product, focusing at the same time on parts, components, manufacturing, and testing. Design engineers, cost experts, manufacturing engineers, and marketing staff members work together to manage the design and development process. As each design detail is considered, so are its manufacturing, cost, and market characteristics. Ernst & Young, the U.S.-based international consulting firm, estimates that concurrent engineering typically shaves total product cost by 20 percent.

Concurrent engineering means the team members must work across their departmental functions to evaluate the activities of many departments. But this is just the beginning. Now emerging is the capability for companies to link their design teams, through communications networks and CAD systems, to machine tools located in a factory down the road or across the country. These factories can turn preliminary designs into prototypes that team members evaluate as part of the design process. ■

concurrent engineering A design and manufacturing method in which team members work across their departmental functions to evaluate the activities of many departments and manage the product development process.

CRITICAL CONNECTION 3
Boeing Takes Off with CAD Software

Quick! What has more than three million parts and flies? It's the Boeing 777, the world's largest twin-engine jetliner. It's also the first commercial airplane ever to be designed completely with CAD software. (Boeing's huge system included eight mainframe computers, 2,200 engineering workstations, and more than 5,400 engineering and technical employees during the peak design period.) In fact, because the plane was designed entirely on computer, engineers could "pre-assemble" the airplane digitally, skipping the expensive and time-consuming stage of building physical mock-ups.

With the help of CAD software and powerful workstations, engineers can factor stress, inertia, and weight analysis—represented as colored, shaded, three-dimensional solids on their screens—into designs. But the software is also an important communications tool. With it, everyone on the design team has access to the same, consistent set of engineering drawings and they can coordinate improvements and refinements as the design moves through the various stages. This capability is essential to Boeing's team-style approach to design.

Robots

A **robot** is a computer-controlled device that can physically manipulate its surroundings (Figure 12.14). On assembly lines, *pick-and-place robots* are usually programmed to carry out four functions: move to the location of a part, grasp the part, move to the location where the part will be used, and release its grip on the part. More sophisticated versions of robots, currently under development, will have the ability to *sense*—that is, to gather information about their immediate environment through a variety of sensing devices and to analyze this information and determine the proper course of action.

robot A computer-controlled device that can physically manipulate its surroundings.

Although the combination of increased computer power and decreased cost will undoubtedly lead to increased sophistication and capability in robots, don't expect robots to look like those you've seen in science-fiction movies. Industry has not yet given robots an "almost human" appearance, nor is it working terribly hard to do so. Most robots look exactly like what they are: a programmable machine. Some have manipulator arms and grippers ("arms and fingers") and others have computer vision systems ("eyes"), discussed below. But they remain machines with no personality or will of their own.

Flexible Manufacturing

CAM improves the efficiency of the entire manufacturing process by automatically setting up machines for the next job. This capability, known as **flexible manufactur-**

flexible manufacturing A manufacturing system that automatically sets up machines for the next job, thus reducing setup time and making smaller job runs feasible.

FIGURE 12.14
Robotics in Action
Don't let movies like *The Terminator* and *RoboCop* fool you. Although some robots have manipulator arms, grippers, and computer vision systems, they remain machines with no personality or will of their own. This constraint hasn't stopped them from being widely used, however.

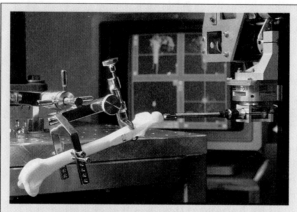

a) In veterinary medicine—Dr. Hap Paul developed a computer robot that drills a hole in a dog's femur so that a metal joint can be implanted to replace the natural joint.

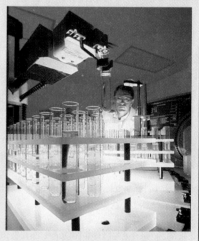

b) In laboratories—Robots are widely used to select and move test tubes so that lab technicians do not have to come in contact with the tubes' contents.

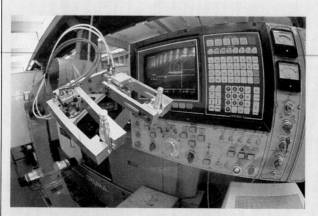

c) In manufacturing—Pick-and-place robots are frequently utilized to move parts into hard-to-reach areas.

d) In computer systems themselves—Mobile Robot Group's "Squirt" robot is used to repair the interior components of computers and other electronic systems.

ing, often reduces setup time by 75% while improving product quality 75 to 90 percent. Reduced setup time also makes smaller job runs feasible, providing more flexibility in scheduling while also reducing manufacturing lead times and the amount of inventory kept on hand. This chapter's Global IT box, "Flexible Manufacturing Challenges Traditional Assumptions," gives several additional examples of companies that have used flexible manufacturing for competitive advantage.

Flexible Manufacturing at Yamazaki Machinery.   Yamazaki Machinery of Oguchi, Japan, a manufacturer of machine tools, has been relying on flexible manufacturing systems since 1980. It built its first plant, consisting of two flexible manufacturing lines, at a cost of $18 million. When the company examined the impact of flexible manufacturing systems on profits, it determined that the return from such systems was overwhelming, as the following table shows:[1]

	Conventional Plant	Oguchi Flexible Manufacturing System Plant
Number of machines	68	18
Number of workers	215	12
Square feet occupied	103,000	30,000
Average days processing time per work piece		
Line A	35	1.5
Line B	60	3.0

The benefits from flexible systems accumulate year after year, not only saving the company money but also giving it an edge over its competitors who continue to use conventional manufacturing methods.

Computer Vision Systems

In manufacturing, product quality and consistency are essential for two reasons. First, customers will not accept poor-quality products. Nor do they have to, because competition in business ensures that most manufactured products will be available from more than one company. Second, poor quality costs the company money and decreases profitability.

Computer vision systems are rapidly becoming an important tool to improve quality and consistency. Often used for recognition of parts and automated assembly of finished goods, **computer vision systems** use computer sensors to detect shapes, images, and varying levels of detail that they compare with data stored in memory. Depending on the logic programmed into the system, they detect the presence or absence of a match and signal other devices in the manufacturing cell to take corrective action. Computer vision systems are also frequently used to scrutinize finished products and to detect imperfections and defects.

Vision capabilities are often embedded in robots. The integration of computer vision systems with robots increases the types of activities that robots can perform.

computer vision system
A system that uses computer sensors to detect shapes, images, and varying levels of detail.

Computer-Integrated Manufacturing at Saturn.   The Saturn automobile plant sits 35 miles south of Nashville, Tennessee. The 3,000-member Saturn team is living one of the greatest experiments in manufacturing. After an investment of eight

[1]Thomas G. Gunn, *Manufacturing for Competitive Advantage* (Cambridge: Ballinger, 1987), pp. 169-170. Copyright ©1987 by Ballinger Publishing Company. Reprinted by permission of HarperCollins Publishers, Inc.

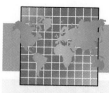

GLOBAL IT

Flexible Manufacturing Challenges Traditional Assumptions

FOR WENDY MORITA, THE PROCESS IS SIMPLE ENOUGH. SHE stops by the local Panasonic bicycle store and orders a custom-made bike from an attentive clerk. Two weeks later, she returns, happily paying anywhere from $545 to $3,200 for a bicycle that has been manufactured to her measurements, painted to her specifications, and embellished with her name. (By way of comparison, a standard model sells for between $210 and $510.) Little does she know that the bike was actually ready just three hours after her initial fitting, thanks to a fax machine that zapped her measurements to a small but high-tech factory. "We could have made the [delivery] time shorter," says Koji Nishikawa, head of sales, "but we want people to feel excited about waiting for something special."

Panasonic's secret—flexible manufacturing—is exciting more than a few bike owners. It's also inspiring manufacturing experts around the world, forcing them to rethink some basic assumptions.

Assumption: Each production line should produce a single, standardized product with limited variations. At Panasonic's bike factory, the single production line can produce eighteen models of racing, road, and mountain bikes in 199 color patterns and almost any size. That's a grand total of about 11 million variations. And at Toshiba, workers can assemble nine different word processors on the same line; on the next line, workers may be turning out twenty varieties of laptop computers. On a larger scale, Toyota uses "intelligent pallets," computer-controlled fixtures that work in rotation, picking up the parts for a specific model and holding them together

as they are tack-welded by robots. With these devices, Toyota routinely produces four body types or models on each line.

Assumption: Retooling the factory is an expensive and time-consuming task that always interrupts production.   In a traditional factory, retooling for a new model can take anywhere from three to twelve months. At Toyota and Nissan plants, however, robots can be reprogrammed while the line keeps running. The physical changeover can be made in a single shift at Toyota plants.

Assumption: To maximize efficiency and return on investment, produce on a large scale.   Traditional wisdom held that large production runs of standardized products would lower unit costs, which would, in turn, lower prices and pump up sales volume. Now flexible manufacturers are showing that *economies of scope*—the ability to spread costs across many different products—can be just as beneficial. The reason? Flexible factories that produce customized products to order can command high prices. (Witness the premium price Wendy Morita paid for her new bike.)

Assumption: Inventory can be used as a buffer between production and demand.   Driven by limited storage space, the Japanese pioneered the concept of just-in-time inventory, the delivery of parts and materials just as they are needed in manufacturing. (This frees up capital for other uses.) But flexible manufacturers are going beyond this: They are basing production on actual sales data and orders, rather than sales forecasts. The secret here, of course, is IT. Consider Kao Corp., Japan's largest soap and cosmetics company. Its information system lets

years and $3.5 billion, Saturn automobiles began rolling off the assembly line in 1991. The goal of General Motors (Saturn's parent company): to use an innovative manufacturing process to build world-class quality small cars priced below the cars sold by Japanese automakers.

To achieve this objective, GM's management was willing to break loose from its manufacturing traditions. They did so by combing the world for the best, most efficient manufacturing practices. (Seeking out the world's best practices in any area is known as *benchmarking.* The best practice becomes a benchmark against which a firm can compare its own performance.) In designing their new system, Saturn's designers, managers, and executives borrowed ideas from such well-known companies as Hewlett-Packard, Volvo, McDonald's, Nissan, and Kawasaki, along with 155 others.

The Saturn plant uses computer-integrated manufacturing and a hefty amount of automation. The typical Saturn has 10,000 parts or more. Hence, just keeping track

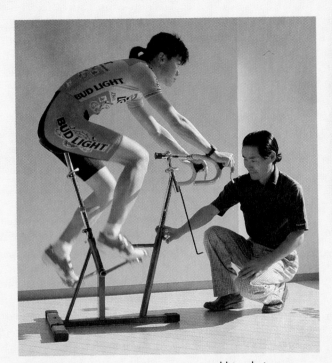

a) The first step in creating a customized bicycle is a customer fitting.

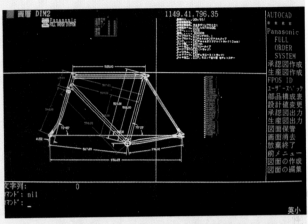

b) CAD software then produces a separate blueprint for each customized bicycle and transmits this to manufacturing.

it make products to order and then deliver them within twenty-four hours.

Assumption: Mass production can meet the needs of a mass market.   Henry Ford and hundreds of other industrialists made fortunes selling mass-produced goods to a mass market. Today's consumer is more demanding, though. Listen, for example, to Toshiba President Fumio Sato, who has been preaching the gospel of flexibility for over a decade: "Customers wanted choices. They wanted a washing machine or a TV set that was precisely right for their needs. We needed variety, not mass production." Wendy Morita—and millions of other consumers—would probably agree.

Sources: Susan Moffat, "Japan's New Personalized Production," *Fortune,* October 22, 1990, pp. 132-135; Thomas A. Stewart, "Brace for Japan's Hot New Strategy," *Fortune,* September 21, 1992, pp. 62-74. Copyright ©1990 and 1992. All rights reserved.

of the arrival of parts in time for use is a challenge. Saturn makes its own engines, transmissions, body stampings, seats, and instrument panels; in fact, 65% of its cars' parts are made right at the Saturn factory. Hence, communication within the manufacturing site is critical. All of these tasks are made possible by IT and good manufacturing management systems.

Saturn's manufacturing cells, complete with their robots (with computer vision systems) and automated guidance vehicles, can do only so much to make a quality automobile on time and within expected cost parameters, however. As in so many other companies, Saturn's success comes down to its people and their involvement in and commitment to the process. Management and assembly workers function as a team, sharing ideas and exchanging information. Information technology plays an important role by making the information accessible and interconnecting people and machines, but its role is secondary to that played by the people of Saturn.

The Saturn experiment seems to be working. Saturn automobiles are selling ahead of expectations. The company cannot make them fast enough, even after stepping up production as a result of huge demand from dealers and consumers. Several new Saturn models are on the drawing board. For a guided tour of how IT is being used at Saturn, see the Photo Essay at the end of this chapter.

A Final Word.   Information technology plays a pivotal role in the way companies develop or change their business practices. Whether in the office, on the manufacturing floor, or on the front line with customers and suppliers, information technology provides many potential advantages in capturing, processing, storing, and distributing information. Clearly, starting from scratch has its advantages. But, as always, the ability to capitalize on opportunity comes down to the people of the organization and the know-how they possess.

SUMMARY OF LEARNING OBJECTIVES

1 Define and explain the purpose of information systems. An *information system* is a system in which data and information flow from one person or department to another. *Business information systems* are the IT applications that underlie the activities of running and managing a business.

2 Describe the six types of business information systems and when each is used. There are six types of business information system. *Transaction processing systems (TPS)* are shared systems that use a combination of IT and manual procedures to process large volumes of data and information and to manage transactions. *Management reporting systems*, also called *management information systems (MIS)*, are designed to provide managers with information useful in structured decision making or problem solving. *Decision support systems (DSS)* are used to assist in making decisions where the decision process is relatively unstructured and only part of the information needed is structured in advance. *Group support systems (GSS)* permit people to process and interpret information as a group, even if they are not working face to face. *Executive support systems (ESS)*, also called *executive information systems (EIS)*, are interactive information systems designed to brief company executives on company and industry developments quickly. *Expert support systems*, or simply *expert systems*, use business rules, regulations, and databases to evaluate a situation or determine an appropriate course of action.

3 Summarize the purpose of computer-integrated manufacturing systems and manufacturing cells. *Computer-integrated manufacturing (CIM)* uses computers to link automated processes in a factory to reduce design time, increase machine utilization, shorten the manufacturing cycle, and increase product quality. In CIM, machines work together in groups called *manufacturing cells*. Parts and materials are moved between cells by automated guide vehicles, automated machines, and materials handling systems.

4 List and describe seven specialized types of CIM used in manufacturing. Seven types of CIM are used in manufacturing. *Material requirements planning (MRP)* systems keep track of the quantity of each part needed to manufacture a product. *Manufacturing resource planning (MRP II)* systems are advanced versions of MRP systems that tie together all the parts of an organization into the company's production activities. *Computer-aided design (CAD) systems* use computer graphics workstations outfitted with programs that allow designers and engineers to draw specifications on the display screen. *Computer-aided manufacturing (CAM) systems* rely on IT to automate and manage the manufacturing process directly. *Robots* are computer-controlled devices that can physically manipulate their surroundings. *Flexible manufacturing* improves the efficiency of the entire manufacturing process by automatically setting up machines for the next job. *Computer vision systems* use sensors to detect shapes, images, and varying levels of detail that they compare with data stored in memory.

KEY TERMS

action document 484
business information systems 482
computer-aided design (CAD) 501
computer-aided manufacturing (CAM) 501
computer-integrated manufacturing (CIM) 496
computer vision system 505
concurrent engineering 502
decision support system (DSS) 487
detail report/transaction log 485
exception report 485

executive support system (ESS) 492
executive information system (EIS) 442
expert support system or expert system 494
flexible manufacturing 504
group support system (GSS) 489
information system 482
management reporting system or management information system (MIS) 485
manufacturing automation protocol (MAP) 498

manufacturing cell 496
manufacturing resource planning (MRP II) system 498
material requirements planning (MRP) system 498
robot 503
rule base/knowledge base 494
summary report 485
transaction processing system 482
updated master data 485

CRITICAL CONNECTIONS

Architectural Energy Corporation

1. DSS Takes the Guesswork Out of Building Energy-Efficient Homes

Decision support software like BuilderGuide and REM/Design offers builders the advantage of helping them "sell" the techniques they sought (by showing the savings in energy costs). But it also helps potential home owners, who may need a larger mortgage to cover the higher costs of energy-efficient construction. Using the programs' output, consumers may qualify for an energy-efficient mortgage because the projected savings on utilities will leave them more money for a larger loan payment.

Questions for Discussion

1. Explain how BuilderGuide and REM/Design fit the definition of a decision support system.

2. The Energy Crafted Home Program is sponsored by a consortium of New England utility companies. Why do you think a utility company would sponsor a program designed to *reduce* energy consumption?

3. Output from software packages like BuilderGuide and REM/Design may eventually be used to create a national standard similar to the "energy guide" now found on all appliances. What might this mean for home builders as a professional group?

2. Coopers & Lybrand Boosts Productivity with Lotus Notes

Although Lotus Notes did boost productivity at Coopers & Lybrand, it took more than two years to install and build the largest and most complex Notes applications in use at Coopers and Lybrand and then train a critical mass of professionals and support personnel.

Part of the long lead time can be traced to technical issues such as increasing the capacity of the LAN or WAN used to run the software, deciding who controls key databases, constructing the Notes applications themselves, and so on. But technology isn't the only challenge. Managers also need time to rethink their group processes and work habits. Otherwise, users may stumble into such nasty pitfalls as information overload, electronic chitchat, and too many online meetings.

Questions for Discussion

1. Explain how Lotus Notes typifies the characteristics of a group support system.

2. Many experts believe that online meetings shouldn't replace all face-to-face meetings. Can you suggest some guidelines for deciding whether a meeting can go online?

3. How might you use groupware to be sure employees do not lose sight of strategic goals and deadlines?

3. Boeing Takes Off with CAD Software

Boeing's commitment to CAD software goes back to the mid-1980s, when it was limited mainly to use in design work. By 1989, though, Boeing's management decided the company needed to go a step further, to "digital preassembly," if it was going to make its billion-dollar investment in CAD pay off. In digital preassembly, parts that might be put together in an actual-size handmade mock-up are assembled, instead, on the computer screen. When Boeing did this, at the end of the third design stage in May 1991, it found 2,500 "interferences," places where parts didn't fit together or fit so closely that they couldn't be reached by maintenance workers. By fixing such glitches on the screen, Boeing hoped to minimize changes, errors, and the resulting rework by 5%—not bad on a multibillion-dollar project.

Questions for Discussion

1. How is Boeing's CAD-based engineering system similar to other business information systems? How is it different?

2. What would be your primary concern in installing a CAD system like Boeing's?

3. Why is engineering quality especially important to a company like Boeing?

REVIEW QUESTIONS

1. What is an information system?

2. What is a transaction? Why is transaction processing so important to successful business processes? Why do businesses have transaction processing systems?

3. Describe the five types of output produced during transaction processing.

4. Describe the characteristics of management reporting systems. What types of reports do they produce?

5. When do businesses use decision support systems? What are the three different types of decision support systems?

6. How do group support systems differ from decision support systems? When are group support systems used?

7. How do executive support systems help executives spend their time effectively? What types of information do executive support systems generate?

8. What is an expert system? Why are knowledge bases an essential component of expert systems?

9. Describe the purpose of computer-integrated manufacturing.

10. What is a manufacturing cell?

11. Why are manufacturing automation protocols (MAPs) important to the success of CIM?

12. Describe an MRP II system's capabilities and subsystems.

13. Explain the characteristics of CAD and CAM systems. Are CAD and CAM synonyms for one another?

14. What is concurrent engineering?

15. What are robots used for?

16. What competitive advantages does flexible manufacturing offer a company?

17. How are computer vision systems used to monitor and maintain quality?

DISCUSSION QUESTIONS

1. In 1993, Graceland began the process of replacing its hand-stamped, hand-sorted ticket system with a DBMS supporting a ticket reservation and fund accounting system. One goal was to eliminate long waits and lost reservations for the 700,000 fans who visit the Memphis estate of the late Elvis Presley each year. Another goal was to monitor the relative popularity of gift shop items and attractions like the Lisa Marie and Hound Dog II airplanes. Use what you have learned in this chapter to classify this business information system and explain your answer.

2. To help its marketing managers spot trends and identify opportunities for growth, Colgate-Palmolive Co. has installed Muse, a relational database system used to consolidate sales data electronically collected from subsidiaries in about 160 countries and to issue a summary report. What type of business information system is Muse? Explain your answer.

How could Colgate's Muse system be used to support its manufacturing divisions?

3. A survey of IT managers by The Yankee Group, a market research firm, found that managers' primary goal for the 1990s is the integration of manufacturing, engineering, and business groups. What business and IT trends do you think underlie this goal?

SUGGESTED READINGS

Clemons, Eric K., "Evaluation of Strategic Investments in Information Technology," *Communications of the ACM*, 34, no. 1 (January 1991), pp. 22-36. This article examines how information systems can make an enterprise more flexible, more responsive to customer needs, and more adaptable to rapidly changing conditions in competitive environments. Six lessons based on actual company experiences are presented as a guide to the successful use of information technology in business.

Earl, Michael J., "Experiences in Strategic Information Systems Planning," *MIS Quarterly*, 17, no. 1 (March 1993), pp. 1-24. Planning for information technology is a recurring theme in information systems literature. This article explores the IT planning experiences of 27 different firms and incorporates the results of extensive interviews with CEOs, senior user managers, CIOs, and information systems strategic planners.

Hammer, Michael, and James Champy, *Reengineering the Corporation*. New York: HarperBusiness, 1993. A widely read book that examines how businesses can rethink their most fundamental processes and the critical role IT plays in the reengineering process. The authors provide practical insight into ways of capitalizing on IT's capabilities to change business processes and create opportunity.

Tapscott, Don, and Art Caston, *Paradigm Shift: The New Promise of Information Technology*. New York: McGraw-Hill, 1993. A forward-looking book that explores how today's information technology can help an enterprise make the transition to higher quality products and service, creating business success. It explains how to take action to achieve the short-term benefits of IT while positioning the organization for long-term transformation.

CASE STUDY

At Corning, the Future Is Now

CORNING

THE FUTURE PRESENTED SOME challenges for Corning Inc. when James R. Houghton became chairman and CEO in 1983. Although the family-controlled business was best known for its consumer products—Corning Ware, Pyrex, and the like—it was also a major supplier of specialized ceramic and glass products to other manufacturers. Over the years, though, the company had become weighed down by low growth units that made everything from light bulbs to electronics. Almost 70% of Corning's revenues came from "low to middling" market shares in cyclical businesses. Profits had declined for three straight years. Meanwhile, the surrounding business world was marching faster and faster, trying to match the pace set by Japanese and European companies that had made major investments in computer-integrated manufacturing and total quality management. In market after market, it seemed, Corning faced a choice: Keep up or give up.

Houghton decided to fight back. Over the next six years, he sold marginal business units worth $500 million. He invested an equal amount in new businesses and joint ventures that would help Corning tap into lucrative new markets for such products as fiber optics and pollution-control devices. The company committed millions to research and development, too, looking for ways to adapt existing technology to new uses. Technology that Corning developed for use in sunglasses and headlights, for example, is now being used to improve the LCD screens used in portable computers.

To unify the company and give it direction, Houghton announced a commitment to total quality management (TQM). The basic premise of TQM is that a company is obligated to offer its customers "quality," a product or service that satisfies their requirements consistently and without fail. As one step in providing this quality, managers have to look at the production (or service) process as an integrated system and eliminate opportunities for failure and waste. And, because faulty supplies are a major source of waste, managers have to demand total quality from their suppliers. The latter imperative was especially important for Corning, a supplier *par excellence*. By the 1980s, for example, the U.S. television makers who had once bought Corning video glass had been replaced by Sony, Hitachi, and other Japanese companies, all of whom demanded total quality from their suppliers.

Houghton backed up his announcement by appointing a director of quality (the company's first), setting ambitious goals (to cut error rates by 90% by 1991), and sending every employee to a two-day quality seminar. He continues to visit 50 plants and joint ventures a year, holding open meetings in which he spreads the gospel of total quality, winning over cynics who are skeptical that TQM is "nothing more than the buzzword of the month." More importantly, he gave Corning employees some new tools.

Some of the tools involve the production process. Like many companies in the 1980s, Corning was marked by "islands of automation," isolated applications of CAD, MRP, robots, and so on, all lacking a central focus or tie to company strategy. To remedy this situation, the company spent millions on capital equipment, identified CIM as one of six key corporate strategies, and reorganized its engineering and manufacturing divisions to consolidate all CIM-related functions. A systems board of directors, with representatives from manufacturing, engineering, information services, and strategic planning, was formed to avoid turf battles and help the new departments focus on shared objectives.

CIM projects were then phased in at various plants, following a multistep process. First, a plan was devised to translate business goals into manufacturing goals. Then an audit was conducted to identify current practices and create a computer simulation to determine whether the process could be simplified. An audit at a distribution center in Greencastle, Pennsylvania, for example, showed that 40% of the 200 steps in one process could be eliminated. The simplified process became the basis of a second computer simulation of the new automation and information systems, so that bugs could be worked out onscreen. Only after the kinks were ironed out was the new CIM system actually installed on the plantfloor.

But CIM by itself wasn't enough. "We found that if you don't pay attention to the people aspects, such as empowering workers to make decisions, you could only get 50% of the potential benefit of restructuring," said Executive Vice President Norman E. Garrity. To emphasize the people side, Corning instituted a systematic effort to create a "partnership in the workplace" by bringing workers into the decision making process. Layers of management were eliminated in favor of self-managed work teams that had been trained to perform several jobs. This was a revolutionary change for Corning, a traditional organization where workers were more used to taking orders from supervisors than taking part in the decision-making process.

As part of its business restructuring, Corning brought workers into the decision making process. Pictured here is Corning's Erwin, NY factory, which workers redesigned according to their needs.

How well has this system worked? Corning recently let workers design a new plant that would produce molten-metal filters for catalytic converters. The workers chose an open space with high, sound-dampening ceilings, lots of windows, and a production line that clustered workers. Forty-seven job classifications were reduced to one; workers rotate through tasks on a weekly basis, earning more money as they complete training that qualifies them to handle additional tasks. Defects plummeted from 10,000 parts per million to just three.

In 1989, Corning became a finalist for the Malcolm Baldrige National Quality Award. That same year, Corning was one of twenty-six suppliers to receive a Performance Excellence Award from Hughes Aircraft. By 1990, the company was being held up as an example of how even a traditional industry can come shining through.

Questions for Discussion

1. In many companies, most training is given to middle- and upper-management. But, in 1983, Houghton set the goal that *all* workers would spend 5% of their work time in job-related training that encompasses both technical subjects and interpersonal skills. Why do you think he set this goal? What benefits would such training have for the workers and the organization?

2. Imagine that you are a consultant to manufacturers. What observations would you make to them about the relative importance of leadership, information technology, and worker training?

3. What lessons can be drawn from Corning's experience, for business leaders and managers in general?

Innovation and Saturn: Information Technology's Role in the Saturn Automobile

Computers themselves offer little competitive advantage to a company. But when combined with people's know-how, they can redefine the nature of a company's products and services and the way the company carries out its production activities. Together, computers and know-how can produce a substantial advantage in the marketplace.

A grand experiment in rethinking American auto manufacturing with IT has captured the world's attention. Spring Hill, Tennessee—a small town just south of the U.S. country music capital of Nashville, and hundreds of miles away from Detroit, the U.S. automotive capital city—is home to the Saturn automobile. A division of General Motors, Saturn has creatively combined its people's capabilities with other resources to deliver a high-quality, low-cost automobile. The company invested over $3.5 billion to create the concept and build the factory from scratch. Now, more than 300,000 automobiles roll off the Spring Hill assembly line annually. In this photo essay, we explore how Saturn is using IT to gain a competitive advantage in the cut-throat world of auto manufacturing and sales.

1 The know-how that comes from teamwork is a key element in Saturn's success. Throughout the eight-year process of developing the Saturn concept, designing the manufacturing facilities, and creating production processes, team meetings produced the most valuable and innovative ideas. Factory employees organized in teams of 8 to 10 members share in the making of wide-ranging decisions. These teams decide on and procure manufacturing equipment, hire co-workers, and establish assembly-line processes. They also have budget and supplier authority and can choose to reject parts from suppliers if they are too expensive or fail to meet worker-determined safety standards. More than 150 teams share ideas and power with top management.

2 The world's best practices are used throughout the Saturn facility. A team of Saturn workers, dubbed the "Group of 99," traveled the world, racking up more than 2 million miles to visit and benchmark some 160 world-class companies. The names of the companies they visited read like a Who's Who of business innovation and success: Nissan, Kawasaki, Volvo, Daimler Benz, McDonald's, Hewlett Packard, and many more.

3 Manufacturing sleek looking automobiles is one of the most challenging production efforts in the world. A typical automobile includes over 10,000 parts: the simplest nuts and bolts; molded sheet metal doors and fenders; complex engine and transmission assemblies; and precision sensors capable of detecting the most subtle changes in carburetion. IT components, in the form of microprocessors, circuit boards, and communication lines, perform the critical role of integrating the thousands of parts to provide the performance level demanded by buyers and technicians alike.

4 The mile-long Spring Hill plant is highly self reliant, building approximately two-thirds of its parts on site.

5 Lean production, a characteristic of Saturn manufacturing, was pioneered by Japan's Toyota Motor Corporation. Lean production uses "half the human effort in the factory, half the manufacturing pace, half the investment tools, half the engineering hours to develop a new product."[1] IT is integrated into the Saturn's entire engineering and manufacturing process. Robots and computer networks work side-by-side with people, each taking care of the activities they do best.

[1]Womack, James P., Daniel T. Jones, and Daniel Roos, *The Machine that Changed the World.* New York: Rawson Associates, 1990.

6 In traditional automobile manufacturing practices workers are virtually stationary, with individual task responsibilities. Saturn employees saw these practices as an obsolete "toil and shuffle" process, and rejected them in favor of teams of workers who ride along with the cars they are manufacturing as the vehicles move down the "skillet" (a wooden conveyor). All team members have the responsibility to shut down the line if they spot a problem. Pulling the nearest emergency handle will stop the line instantly. The problem must be corrected before the line can be restarted.

7 Driving the first completed Saturn off the innovative assembly line was exciting for management, union leaders, and employees. Its public unveiling was a celebration for all Saturn workers because it proved the importance of combining the capabilities of people, process, technology, and know-how—all essential ingredients in innovation and successful goal achievement.

8 Understanding the rules is important. But, as Saturn has demonstrated, knowing when to break them and create new ones is critical. Just how confident is the company in the quality of its product? Saturn offers 24-hour roadside assistance should a breakdown occur. And it gives all purchasers a 30-day, 1,500-mile money-back guarantee. If purchasers dislike the automobile for any reason, they get their money back.

9 The final—and perhaps most important—reviews for Saturn come from the experts, who praise Saturn for its solid workmanship, handsome interior and exterior design, and responsive handling.

The I-75 Corridor

At one time, all Japanese cars came from Japan, and people surmised that the quality of Japanese cars resulted from the commitment of Japan's manufacturing workers. Yet today, the leading Japanese automobile companies manufacture more automobiles in the Unites States than they do in Japan, and they do so with American workers.

Head south out of Detroit, along Interstate Highway 75, and you'll drive through a fertile countryside of green pastures and open farmland as you travel through Michigan, Ohio, along the Indiana border, through Kentucky, and into Tennessee. The fertile countryside has also nourished the growth of the American heartland's newest manufacturing corridor.

Along the drive you'll find Japanese-owned modern assembly plants that employ more than 30,000 U.S. automobile workers. The plants belong to Toyota, Nissan, Mazda, Suburu, and Isuzu. As you drive south past Nashville, you'll see the Nissan plant and then come to the home of Saturn—American owned, but using the best in world-class auto manufacturing technology.

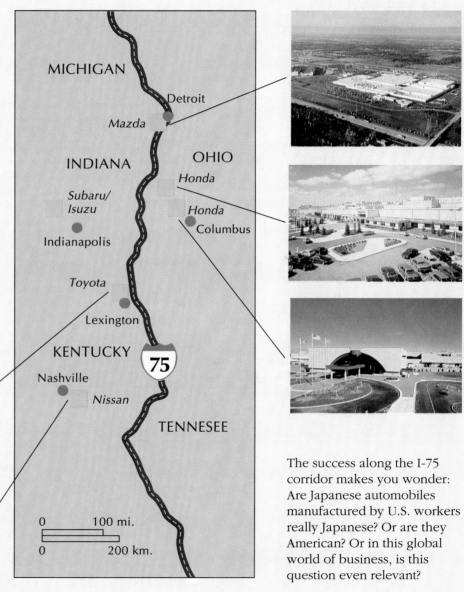

MICHIGAN

Detroit

Mazda

INDIANA

OHIO

Honda

Subaru/ Isuzu

Honda
Columbus

Indianapolis

Toyota

Lexington

KENTUCKY

75

Nashville

Nissan

TENNESEE

0   100 mi.

0   200 km.

The success along the I-75 corridor makes you wonder: Are Japanese automobiles manufactured by U.S. workers really Japanese? Or are they American? Or in this global world of business, is this question even relevant?

519

Telecommuting: Blazing a New Path to the Information Age

THE NODES ON A WIDE AREA NETWORK CAN BE ALMOST ANY-where—an office tower in Munich, an industrial park in Iowa, or the spare bedroom of a suburban split-level. These networks are at the heart of telecommuting, the general term for using telecommunications to work from a home office or a nearby telecenter, instead of traveling to and from work by car, bus, or train. Telecommuters make up the fastest growing segment of the work-at-home trend. Like many of the other changes brought by information technology, though, telecommuting offers both benefits and challenges.

Benefits for Society. Telecommuting found some of its earliest and strongest supporters in California, where long commutes over congested freeways frustrate commuters and natural disasters sometimes damage an already aging infrastructure. After a major earthquake buckled key Los Angeles freeways in January 1994, for example, Los Angeles County expanded its telecommuting pilot program, allowing one-third of its 45,000 employees to telecommute until the highways were repaired.

California isn't the only state with traffic and pollution problems, of course, and its state government is not the only one to encourage telecommuting. Urban areas around the world are grappling with "gridlock" on their streets, "winglock" at their airports, hazardous levels of air pollution, and mounting maintenance costs as both highways and airports struggle beneath the weight of millions of travelers. To force businesses to help solve some of these problems, the federal Clean Air Act of 1990 requires employers to slash the number of employees driving to work by 1996. Telecommuting is an obvious and cost-effective solution, says Jack Nilles, president of the Washington, D.C.-based Telecommuting Advisory Council. Compared to the cost of buying and operating a van pool, telecommuting can save employers as much as $8,000 per employee, Nilles estimates.

The concept of telecommuting got another boost in the early 1990s, when the respected research firm of Arthur D. Little published two reports. These reports, funded by six telephone companies and a manufacturer of telecommunications equipment, tried to quantify the potential savings of using telecommunications to reduce the *demand* for transportation, versus the potential savings of increasing the *supply* of transportation, either by building "smart" highways or high-speed trains linking major urban areas. The reports showed that substituting telecommunications for 10 to 20% of routine commuting, shopping, and business trips could save as much as $27 billion per year (Figure 1). These studies helped to boost interest in building an information superhighway of fiber optics that could handle the increased demand for telecommunications (see Chapter 14).

Strategic Advantages for Business. In addition to the benefits to society, working at home offers benefits to businesses as well.

FIGURE 1 How to Save $27 Billion a Year with Telecommuting
Potential savings if telecommuting, teleshopping, and teleconferencing replaced traditional transportation 10 to 20 percent of the time:

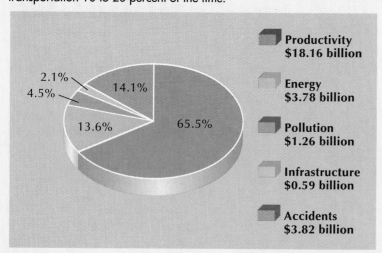

Productivity $18.16 billion

Energy $3.78 billion

Pollution $1.26 billion

Infrastructure $0.59 billion

Accidents $3.82 billion

Assumes use of telecommunications would:

- Allow six million automobile commuters to work at home.
- Replace almost three billion shopping trips annually.
- Eliminate almost thirteen billion business trips annually.
- Eliminate over six hundred million truck and airplane delivery miles annually through electronic transfer of documents.
- Eliminate 1.58 million traffic accidents and 1,137 fatalities annually.

Source: Courtesy Ashok B. Boghani and Arthur D. Little, Inc., 1991 and 1992.

- **More productive employees.** Freed of the stress of commuting and the distractions of the typical office for one or two days a week, many telecommuters are more satisfied and productive. In Los Angeles County, for example, telecommuters who participated in one pilot program were 12.5% more productive than their office-bound colleagues. According to the Arthur D. Little studies, increased productivity by telecommuters could be worth as much as $18 billion a year.
- **Lower overhead costs.** In the Pittsburgh area, IBM used a combination of staff cuts and telecommuting to vacate more than 80,000 square feet of expensive office space.
- **Access to a larger pool of talented workers.** When Lynn Stockstad's husband decided to return to school in Iowa, it looked as if Great Plains Software, in Fargo, ND, might lose one of its best market analysts. But company president Doug Burnum challenged her to do the job from Iowa. And she does—by telecommuting. According to a recent *Home Office Computing* survey of Fortune 1,000 companies, 72% feel that the desire to retain good employees will spur telecommuting in the next few years. Telecommuting can also help employers meet the requirements of the Americans with Disabilities Act, which requires employers to make "reasonable accommodations" for disabled employees.

Meeting the Challenges. To get all these benefits, though, businesses have to meet a number of challenges and answer a number of questions.

- **Who telecommutes?** Early experiments with telecommuting focused on workers with repetitive jobs (such as keypunch operators) and used stringent electronic monitoring, sometimes creating the electronic equivalent of a sweat shop. More recently, the focus has shifted to middle- and upper-level knowledge workers. Often, these telecommuters say they are more relaxed, have healthier diets, and exercise more often than they did before.

  Even so, telecommuting may not be right for every knowledge worker. If the job requires extensive face-to-face contact, telecommuting may not work. Also, is the worker known to be reliable and self-disciplined? Can he or she handle the isolation of working at home?
- **Who pays for the equipment, furniture, and support?** The answer is easy if you work in an office. But the answer isn't so clear for the telecommuter who works from home. At a recent telecommuting conference, some managers argued that telecommuters should buy their own equipment, claiming that the cost of buying and support-

ing duplicate equipment makes it difficult to cost-justify telecommuting. Other companies provide all equipment and pay for the extra phone lines required, arguing that doing so makes it easier to maintain standards and offer support. This is not a simple or inexpensive issue: Link Resources estimates that employers and employees spend $4.7 billion every year on telecommuter technology.
- **How do you manage a telecommuter?** At one time, managers assumed that if they saw employees working in their offices, they were being productive. This assumption breaks down for telecommuters, who must be trusted and judged on their ability to produce results. Some other knotty issues: If telecommuters are injured while working at home, are they covered by the company's insurance? What happens if the home is burgled? Because the employer-employee relationship is in many ways a legal one, most human resource specialists suggest that every company adopt a clear telecommuting policy that addresses such issues as: Under what circumstances can the telecommuting agreement be terminated? What performance standards is the employee expected to meet? What are the telecommuter's office hours? Who owns the equipment? Who pays for supplies and phone charges? Who is responsible for physical and electronic security? How often must telecommuters report to their supervisors? How will they obtain technical training and support? How often will telecommuters be evaluated? And will telecommuting affect eligibility for bonuses and salary increases?

Although many telecommuting agreements are informal and flexible, a recent survey by the Society for Human Resource Management found that 42% of its member companies with more than 5,000 employees had already implemented a written telecommuting policy.

Discussion Questions

1. Drew Deskur, director of telecommuting and manager of telecommunications for Shiva Corp. in Burlington, Massachusetts, has argued that telecommuting will not be broadly adopted unless employers pay for the telecommuter's equipment. Do you agree or disagree?
2. Some experts have said that if you can manage telecommuters effectively, you will become a better manager. What might this mean to you as a future employee? A future manager?
3. What are some additional pros and cons of telecommuting for society? For individuals?

PART 5

IT Issues and Opportunities

Talking with Al Gore
Vice President of the United States

Al Gore has a long record of interest and expertise in developing information technology to benefit the citizens of the United States. While a Senator in the U.S. Congress he introduced legislation aimed at creating a foundation for a national information superhighway. As Vice President, he has been very active in responding to questions and suggesting ways to bring about the creation of a national information infrastructure. Gore's views have generated considerable discussion around the world as other countries examine the future of IT as a part of their national infrastructure. Here, Gore speaks out on his views on the infrastructure as well as the role of the Internet.

How are we going to pay for the information superhighway?

When the Industrial Revolution began, for a century the greatest employment impact came from the retroactive application of new processes and technologies discovered and developed in the Industrial Age to agriculture.

In this country, over a 100-year timespan the employment in agriculture went from 50% of employment down to between 2% to 3% now, but the productivity is infinitely greater and the absolute production is greater. And many more jobs were created in industry than were lost in agriculture...

But in the same way the Industrial Revolution had an enormous impact on productivity and employment in agriculture, the information revolution is resulting in new processes, new techniques, and new inventions that when applied retroactively to industry result in the same hemorrhage of jobs that we saw a century earlier in agriculture. Automated factories, digital controls, new machinery—you can go right down the list.

And in 1950, 34% of our employment was in manufacturing. Today it's a little less than 17%. And yet again, productivity has jumped enormously, and if you look at manufacturing output as a percentage of gross domestic product, it's unchanged. It's the same today as it was in 1950, maybe slightly larger. And once again, new jobs are being created...

"A minimal first iteration of what the information superhighway needs to connect would, in my view, have to include every classroom, every library, every clinic and hospital. Universal service means universal service, including households. We have universal service for telephones to households now, but not to schools or classrooms. And that's absurd."

Of course now we are seeing information technologies and information systems result in enhanced productivity in services and in the information industry itself. So you have large layoff annoucements by telephone companies and this leads to the erroneous conclusion that there will be an overall net loss of jobs as a result of the information revolution. I don't believe that for a moment. I think especially if the United States continues to lead the world in the development and application of these new technologies and systems, we will have enormous gains in productivity and net wealth in our country, and in employment.

A year is not a long time to measure, but one year ago we were losing 10,000 jobs per month and now we're creating 150,000 jobs per month this year. The Counsel of Economic Advisors last week gave a report that included the following fact: Information processing equipment products accounted last year for three-quarters of the increase in industrial production.

Do you think the usefulness of the Information Superhighway has necessarily struck home with the traditional industries in the country, such as the manufacturing industries?

Well, I think it is striking home. I read somewhere recently about how the first computers to enter the workplace were used in much the same way typewriters were used, and the real gains in efficiency and productivity did not come until the re-engineering of the system —which was made possible by computers— took place. And I think in a similiar way, you are seeing a lot of manufacturers now cross the threshold and re-engineering their whole system of production to take maximum advantage of the new information technologies and the information superhighway in particular. And that's a development that going to pick up speed, where you'll see a lot more parts suppliers and subcontractors exchanging three-dimensional models over the network and using computational science to investigate new part combinations, and all kinds of things like that. It's already beginning to happen, and it's going to pick up speed.

Why should business care about your vision of the NII [National Information Infrastructure]? We have readers asking what this has to do with running a network for a business.

Any business that assumes the NII will not have a profound impact on its future is making a profound mistake. Just as the telephone system revolutionized how every business operates, just as the computer is even now revolutionizing the way businesses operate, the information superhighway will do the same. And new services we don't even dream of right now will be huge players in the economy of the next decade, and some existing businesses will be heavily impacted.

Could you define your view of universal service?

We called for a Joint Board to derive that definition out of real-world experience. It's not for us in the White House to create as an intellectual exercise what it looks like, but rather to catalyze a rich dialogue with the industry and the American people to define it very carefully.

In the telephone industry, around 94% is the definition of universal service.[1] As the cluster of services that come out of the information superhighway evolves, the definition of universal service will evolve. That, too, should be a dynamic, evolving definition just as the make-up of that services cluster should be dynamic and evolving as the industry develops.

---

[1] Providing basic telephone service to all households is termed "universal service." In the U.S., 94% of all homes have a telephone installed, a higher level than any other country in the world.

to households now, but not to schools or classrooms. And that's absurd.

There's a fear about intellectual property rights in publishing on the Internet. Can you talk about that?

It's a real challenge, but not an insurmountable problem at all. And what you will find is a demand-pull that creates the new mechanisms to solve these probelms. The new marketplace is going to be so attractive and so robust that it will evolve, just as the marketplace for music changed dramatically in the advent of radio. The enormous demand led to the evolution of broadcast blanket license mechanisms. Some permutation of blanket licensing might be adaptable to the information superhighway. I have to believe this enormous new market will hasten the evolution of new copyright structures that will lead to a rapid solution of that problem.

Should it be a digital line to every household as a baseline minimum?

Yes, I think so. But the baseline should include more than that.

Are you looking at universal service as Internet connectivity first by connecting every school and hospital, then every household?

Well, the Joint Board process will look at a number of things, including every household. A minimal first iteration of what the information superhighway needs to connect would, in my view, have to include every classroom, every library, every clinic and hospital. Universal service means universal service, including households. We have universal service for telephones

How will you as an elected offical use the information superhighway to stay in touch with your constituents?

I do hope to do it on a regular basis, but I don't know how regularly. I haven't decided that yet. Using the information superhighway in the White House is still complicated by some of the legal rules about what has to be made public.

Chapter Outline

CHAPTER 13

Issues in Information Technology

Learning Objectives

When you have completed this chapter, you should be able to:

1 Explain how the term "privacy" applies to information technology and why privacy is an important issue in the 1990s.

2 Describe the importance of ethics in the use of information technology and identify seven ethical issues associated with the use of IT in business.

3 Explain the IT professional's obligation to provide continued access to computers and networks and four methods used to ensure IT reliability.

4 Discuss the legal issues surrounding software piracy and three methods that have been used to prevent software piracy.

5 Distinguish among copyrighted software, public domain software, and shareware.

6 Describe ten ways to protect a system against intrusion.

7 Identify the three methods of virus detection used by virus detection software.

In Practice

After completing this chapter, you should be able to perform these activities:

1 Visit a government office and discuss with the staff its policies on copying computer software.

2 Specify the steps needed to detect the existence of a virus on your personal computer.

3 Speak with a network operations manager and discuss how she detects attempted intrusion and the steps she has taken to protect her system against intrusion.

4 Contact a local credit agency and request a copy of your credit report. Ask about your rights under current laws protecting personal privacy.

5 Evaluate an IT department's guidelines for protecting the company against a failure of system reliability.

6 Discuss with an IT professional the most challenging ethical issues he has encountered.

7 Conduct a telephone survey of information systems executives (IT director, chief information officer, or vice president for information systems) to find out whether they have an information technology or a business ethics policy at their company.

526

Fair Information Use

Lotus Development Corporation of
Cambridge, Massachusetts, is best
known for Lotus 1-2-3, its revolutionary spreadsheet program. In
April 1990, Lotus announced
plans to release Lotus Market-Place, a
computer processable database of the
names, addresses, demographic characteristics, and purchasing behavior of
more than 120 million Americans.
Equifax, Inc. (an Atlanta consumer-
information company) supplied the
data to Lotus from its massive databases.

The principal idea behind the
product was to provide the data in a
form suitable for processing by buyers' PC programs. From the database,
targeted mailings and advertising programs could be created. Users could
focus their sales efforts on those persons most likely to buy a particular
product or potential buyers at specific
income levels.

Nine months later, Lotus canceled
the product amid a public outcry
about the threat to consumer privacy.
After determining the additional costs
of meeting the public's concern for
privacy, Lotus did not believe the
database remained a viable product.

When you subscribe to a magazine or purchase merchandise
through mail order, your name
and address are sold to hundreds of organizations for use in
direct-mail marketing. Does this
constitute an invasion of your
privacy?

F EW PEOPLE WOULD DISAGREE THAT THE DEVELOPERS AND USERS OF IT SHOULD care about the effects of our tools on our colleagues and our global society. For this reason it is important to keep an eye attuned to the potential misuse of technology. In this chapter, we examine five areas of public and private concern—privacy, ethics, reliability, piracy, and computer crime—and their relationship to IT. Ever-increasing dependence on IT makes these issues more visible and more important than ever before.

■ Privacy

You've probably filled out countless forms and applications in your life: applications for college or university admission, magazine subscription cards, credit card applications, job applications…the list could go on and on. You've also provided information to local, state, and government bodies—the income and/or value-added tax agency, the motor vehicles registration bureau, the health insurance bureau, and the social insurance coverage bureau.

Where is that information now? Who has control of it? Who has access to it and for what purpose? Is there a chance the data are being used in ways you did not intend or have not authorized? Who knows about your personal history because they have access to data you have provided?

What Is Privacy?

privacy In IT, the term used to refer to how personal information is collected, used, and protected.

As it applies to information technology, **privacy** refers to how personal information is collected, used, and protected. The privacy issue has not arisen because of computers; at one time, the taking of photographs caused serious concern about invasion of personal privacy. However, the enormous capabilities of IT to store and retrieve data have amplified the need for the protection of personal privacy. Some consumer advocates have suggested that privacy protection is the leading consumer issue of the 1990s.

Some of the most heated privacy debates have been brought about by advances in telecommunications. Among these debates are these questions:

- Is the use of automated equipment to originate phone calls or collect caller information an invasion of privacy?
- Should telephone companies restrict the use of caller ID, which tells the person receiving the call the number of the calling party (Figure 13.1)?
- Is the telephone company's capability of knowing the location of an individual using a cellular phone an invasion of privacy?

FIGURE 13.1   Caller ID
AT&T's Caller ID unit, which displays the telephone number of incoming callers, has been the subject of intense debate. Some units also display the caller's name. Do you have the right to know who is calling your home or business, or does the caller have the right to his or her privacy?

Privacy Legislation

To protect individual privacy, national legislatures and parliaments have passed several important pieces of legislation. The principal legislation in the United States is summarized in Table 13.1. All of this legislation focuses on government records and has little influence over individual companies except as they do business with the federal government.

In 1973, the U.S. Department of Health, Education, and Welfare (now the Department of Health and Human Services) issued a publication titled *A Code of Fair Information Practices* as a set of rules for protecting personal privacy within government agencies. The guidelines contained in the code state that:

1. There must be no personal-data record keeping system whose very existence is a secret.
2. There must be a way for people to access the information about them in a record and find out how that information is used.
3. There must be a way for people to prevent information about themselves obtained for one purpose from being used or made available for other purposes without their consent.
4. There must be a way for people to correct or amend a record of information about them.
5. Any organization creating, maintaining, using, or disseminating records of identifiable personal data must ensure their reliability and must take reasonable precautions to prevent misuse of the data.

The Code of Fair Information Practices served as the basis of the Privacy Act of 1974, the principal law governing privacy-protection actions within the federal government.

TABLE 13.1   Major U.S. Privacy Legislation

Legislation	Description
Fair Credit Reporting Act (1970)	Allows individuals access to their credit records, to receive printed reports of the contents free of charge, and to challenge the contents in the event of errors.
Freedom of Information Act (1970)	Allows citizens access to data that have been gathered about them by federal agencies.
Privacy Act of 1974	Allows people to determine what information is collected about them, to prevent records obtained for one purpose from being used for another purpose, to have access to—and copies made of—information about them, to correct or amend records, and to file civil suits for damages that occur due to willful or intentional actions by individuals or organizations collecting the information.
Electronic Communications Privacy Act of 1986	Protects the privacy of electronic messages sent through public networks.

CRITICAL CONNECTION 1
The Dark Side of IT

"It was a story out of a Hitchcock film." That's the way Jeffrey Rothfeder describes Robert John Bardo's murder of Rebecca Schaeffer, a young television actress, in July 1989.[1] The LAPD later found that Bardo had been stalking Schaeffer for months, fantasizing that she returned the affections of her "biggest fan."

But Bardo's stalking had an eerie, high-tech twist: He had done it via computer. With the help of a private investigator, he had peered into online databases to find out where Schaeffer lived, what kind of car she drove, her phone number, the people she called, and how she spent her money. When a credit report showed she had charged a meal at a trendy Beverly Hills restaurant, Bardo imagined they had shared a romantic evening together. When he found that she drove a pick-up truck, he saw himself riding in the cab alongside her. When Bardo finally showed up at her door, however, Schaeffer didn't live up to Bardo's fantasies. Enraged by her "rejection," he returned and shot her in the chest.

This anecdote opens Rothfeder's book, *Privacy for Sale: How Computerization Has Made Everyone's Private Life an Open Secret,* an exposé of the ways that information technologies designed to help businesses and government agencies can be and are being used to compromise individual privacy and safety—not only in the United States, but throughout the industrialized countries of the world.

Ethics

The public's outcry over Lotus Market-Place was a result of its realizing for the first time that in the United States most records stored by companies and nongovernment organizations are not covered by existing privacy laws. Thus a company's policy on privacy matters is left primarily to its ethical policies.

ethics The standards of conduct and moral behavior that people are expected to follow.

Ethics are the standards of conduct and moral behavior that people are expected to follow. *Personal ethics* pertain to an individual's day-to-day activities; *business ethics* pertain to the actions of people in their various business activities, including the way in which they deal with colleagues, customers, and anyone else with whom the firm interacts. Some argue that it is difficult to determine where personal ethics end and business ethics begin, because one's personal ethics should always outweigh business ethics.

The distinction between ethical behavior and legal behavior is important. Ethics are the actions expected of people. In contrast, laws deal with required actions. An action may be legal but not ethical, or ethical but not legal.

Companies are challenged by many questions of ethics surrounding the widespread use of information technology. Not limited to IT professionals, these issues involve anyone in the company who provides data to or uses information from the company's systems.

[1]Rothfeder, Jeffrey, *Privacy for Sale: How Computerization Has Made Everyone's Private Life an Open Secret* (New York: Simon & Schuster, 1992), pp. 13–15.

Ethics and IT Usage In Business

Among the many ethical issues that business must confront are:

- **Electronic-mail privacy.** Do the contents of an e-mail system operated by a company, and intended for use by its employees, belong to the company? May the company do with the contents as it deems appropriate?
- **Software licenses.** What are the ethical requirements for acquiring and monitoring conformance to *software licenses,* which allow a company to use programs developed by another company? Are the ethical requirements here different from the legal requirements?
- **Software copyrights.** What are a company's obligations for determining who owns a software copyright? When is the company's obligation for enforcing software copyrights different from an individual's obligation to abide by a software copyright?
- **Hardware access.** Under what circumstances is access to a company's computer and communications hardware ethical? When is it unethical?
- **Intellectual property ownership.** When an information system contains the ideas, writings, expressions, and other items considered the intellectual property of an individual, what obligations does the operator of the system have to safeguard the property? What *is* intellectual property and how is ownership determined?
- **File access.** Under what circumstances is use of a file or database ethical or unethical?
- **Data ownership.** Who owns the data in a company's information system? The company, because it invested its resources to capture and store the data, or the individual or company described by the data?

Some IT directors and professionals believe the issue of ethics in information technology is not a major problem. Aside from some questions related to computer software—which is actually a legal issue—most cannot recall more than a handful of instances where ethical issues have surfaced.

In contrast, some researchers paint a different picture, one emphasizing the *threat* of ethics violations. They point out, for example, that company business codes seldom address computing and communications issues. They also suggest that IT professionals generally do not take an active enough role in defining ethics as a critical element of the Information Age, and that university and college faculty members need to do a better job of creating an awareness of ethical responsibilities in the use of computer and communication systems.

Reality Check.   There is a tendency among both users and developers of information technology to focus first on IT's capabilities for assisting them in a particular business situation. They are so caught up in the power of IT that their first inclination is to ask: "Can IT help solve this problem?" or "Can IT do this?". If the capabilities are affirmed, their position is implicitly, "If the system can do it, and the payoff is right, then let's do it."

From an ethical standpoint, a more appropriate question to ask before developing an IT system is "*Should* the system do this?" If the answer is yes, the system's capabilities can be determined. When ethics come first, implementing IT takes on a completely different perspective. ■

An Ethics Challenge

To understand the ethical challenges managers and employees face, consider how you would answer these 10 questions:

1. Is it right or wrong for managers to access the files or databases of people in their department or on their project team?

2. If data and information are stolen or illegally copied from a company's computer systems, should the IT director be held legally responsible for the loss?

3. If data and information are stolen or illegally copied by an outsider using the company's communications network, should the IT director be legally responsible for any damage done to the network as a result?

4. If a company has a policy stating that its e-mail system should be used only for company activities, does the company have the right to monitor its employees' e-mail messages?

5. Does a company have an obligation to inform employees that their e-mail could be monitored?

6. Should IT directors be held accountable for software licensing violations by members of their department or development teams? If the copyright holder of a program decides to press charges for damages, including lost revenue, resulting from illegal copying of the software, should the IT director be liable for payment of fines or serving time in prison if a court finds in favor of the software owner?

7. If an employee copies company software for personal use at home, should the company have the right to terminate the employee? If an employee copies company software for use at home to work on company business, but does not receive formal permission to do so, should the employee be terminated?

8. If an individual accidentally uses an illegal copy of copyrighted software, without realizing that it is either an unauthorized copy or copyrighted, should the individual be subject to legal action? Are people who find out they have used an illegal copy ethically bound to report their infringement to the copyright owner?

9. Should a company be obligated to notify its employees in advance when a check will be made to see what software is loaded on their system and whether the company owns the software?

10. Do personal ethics take precedence over business ethics? If a person decides that a company's ethical practices are wrong based on his or her personal ethics standards and is fired for failing to follow company guidelines, should the person be compensated for loss of his or her job?

FIGURE 13.2
Alana Shoars: Questioning the Rules
Shoars' 1991 suit against Epson America alleges that she was fired for challenging the company's practice of monitoring and printing its employees' e-mail messages. The suit poses both legal and ethical questions: Does a company have the right to monitor its employees' computer transactions?

This very short list could easily be expanded to include hundreds of similar questions. Users of information technology must answer these questions daily. The "wrong" answers can bring major consequences, as the experiences of Epson American show.

A Question of Ethics at Epson America.   Until 1991, Alana Shoars (Figure 13.2) was e-mail administrator at Epson America, a well-known manufacturer of computer hardware in Torrance, California. In March 1991, Shoars filed suit against Epson seeking $1 million in damages for wrongful termination, defamation, and invasion of privacy.[2] Then, in July 1991, Shoars filed a class-action suit against Epson, seeking $75 million for 700 company employees and approximately 1,800 outsiders whose e-mail had allegedly been monitored by Epson.

In both suits, Shoars contends that she was fired because she questioned and challenged the company's practice of monitoring and printing its employees' e-mail

[2]"Executive Report: IS Ethics," *Computerworld*, October 14, 1991, p. 84.

messages. According to news reports, the company took the position "This is our computer—we'll monitor if we want to."

The courts have accepted the suits as valid and important. It will take several years to settle them, but you can be sure the outcome will affect the activities of companies and individuals for years to come.

Developing a Code of Ethics.   Because it is impossible for anyone to list all the possible questions that could arise in a business situation, many companies have created a *code of ethics* to guide the behavior of their employees. Among the many IT professional groups that have established codes of ethics are the New York-based Association for Computing Machinery, part of whose code of ethics is reprinted in Figure 13.3, and the Association of the Institute for Certification of Computer Professionals in Des Plaines, Illinois.

Donn B. Parker, senior management consultant at SRI International in Menlo Park, California, and a leading expert in computer ethics, encourages IT professionals and users to use the following set of ethical guidelines:

FIGURE 13.3
Excerpt from the Association for Computing Machinery's Code of Ethics

---

Code of Ethics and Professional Conduct
Association for Computing Machinery

General Moral Imperatives:
- Contribute to society and human well-being.
- Avoid harm to others.
- Be honest and trustworthy.
- Be fair and take action not to discriminate.
- Honor property rights including copyrights and patents.
- Give proper credit for intellectual property.
- Respect the privacy of others.
- Honor confidentiality.

More Specific Professional Responsibilities:
- Strive to achieve the highest quality, effectiveness, and dignity in both the process and products of professional work.
- Acquire and maintain professional competence.
- Know and respect existing laws pertaining to professional work.
- Accept and provide appropriate professional review.
- Give comprehensive and thorough evaluations of computer systems and their impacts, including analysis of *possible* risks.
- Honor contracts, agreements, and assigned responsibilities.
- Improve public understanding of computing and its consequences.
- Access computing and communication resources only when authorized to do so.

Organizational Leadership Imperatives:
- Articulate social responsibilities of members of an organizational unit and encourage full acceptance of those responsibilities.
- Manage personnel and resources to design and build information systems that enhance the quality of working life.
- Acknowledge and support proper and authorized uses of an organization's computing and communications resources.
- Ensure that useres and those who will be affected by a system have their needs clearly articulated during the assessment and design of requirements. Later the system must be validated to meet requirements.
- Articulate and support policies that protect the dignity of users and others affected by a computing system.
- Create opportunities for members of the organization to learn the principles and limitations of computer systems.

Courtesy Association for Computing Machinery, inc.

- **Informed consent.** When in doubt about the ethics of a particular action, inform those whom your action will affect of your intentions and obtain their consent before proceeding.
- **The "higher ethic."** Take the action that achieves the greater good.
- **Most restrictive action.** Choose whether or not to take action (or avoid taking action) by assuming that the most severe loss that could happen will happen.
- **Kantian universality rule.** If an action (or a failure to act) is not right for everyone to commit, then it is not right for anyone to commit.
- **Descartes' "change in" rule.** A sufficient change in degree produces a change in kind. Although many small losses may be acceptable individually, taken as a whole they may result in unacceptable losses.
- **The owner's conservative rule.** Assume that others will treat your assets as belonging in the public domain. Explicitly declare the products of your efforts and your property as either private or public in reasonably visible ways.
- **The user's conservative rule.** Assume that any tangible or intangible item belongs to somebody else unless an explicit declaration or convention identifies it as in the public domain or authorized for your use.

Leaders in many companies and professional associations take the viewpoint that a code of ethics is a necessary component of a business's policies and practices. But they often emphasize that a special code of ethics *for information technology* is not needed. These people are not speaking against ethics in IT. Rather, they are pointing out that IT ethics must be part of the company's overall code of ethics because IT itself is so pervasive in business and industry and is a major part of a company's business practices.

In recent years, the concept of social responsibility has been frequently discussed as a counterpart to ethics. A company that exercises *social responsibility* attempts to balance its commitments—not only to its investors, but also to its employees, its customers, other businesses, and the community or communities in which it operates. McDonald's, for example, established Ronald McDonald houses several years ago to provide lodging for families of sick children hospitalized away from home. Sears and General Electric support artists and performers.

One area of social responsibility that has received a great deal of attention lately is responsibility toward the environment. Do companies have a social obligation to help the environment by purchasing computer equipment that uses less energy? Such equipment is now available, as the Quality and Productivity box titled "EPA Spurs the Push for Green PCs" discusses.

◼ Reliability

As companies become dependent on IT, they also become dependent on the continued availability of their computers and communication systems. With dependence comes the expectation that the service provider—whether an in-house IT professional or a hired IT service—will take the necessary precautions to ensure that service cannot be interrupted. **Reliability** is the assurance the system will do what it should when it should.

reliability The assurance that computers and communication systems will do what they should when they should.

There are currently no laws explicitly governing the need to ensure service reliability. However, because of the importance of IT to business operations, society generally treats service loss as a breach of trust.

Ensuring IT Service Reliability

Service reliability can be addressed at four levels: fault tolerant by using computers uninterruptable power supply systems, disaster recovery plans, or backup facilities.

QUALITY AND PRODUCTIVITY

EPA Spurs the Push for Green PCs

ALL AROUND THE WORLD, MILLIONS OF PCS GLOW AND WHIRR, left unattended while users answer the phone, go to meetings, or even leave for the day. This non-use costs U.S. consumers alone about $2 million a year, according to estimates from the U.S. Environmental Protection Agency. And then there are the indirect costs: To meet the electrical needs of PCs, power plants generate as much air pollution as 5 million cars. If the trend continues, PC use (and non-use) could add another 5% to the nation's demand for commercial electricity by the end of the decade.

To keep that from happening, the EPA has created the Energy Star program. The program, announced at a White House ceremony in June 1993, allows manufacturers to display a special Energy Star logo on PCs, monitors, or printers that fall into a "sleep" mode when not in use. To qualify, the machine's sleep mode has to use 30 watts of power or less; that's a 60% drop from standard machines, which draw 70 to 200 watts every moment they are on. To encourage participation, the EPA launched a major ad campaign in popular consumer magazines. To set an example, during his first year in office President Clinton issued an executive order mandating that the U.S. government—the world's largest buyer of computer equipment—purchase only Energy Star equipment from that year on.

By August 1993, seventy major computer manufacturers had signed up to take part in the program. For most, it was a fairly easy transition; they simply adapted techniques designed to conserve the battery life of portable computers. These techniques include power-management software, energy-conserving computer chips, energy-efficient power supplies, and screen-blanking software. (Ironically, "screen savers" that display flying toasters or Star Trek trivia do save screens, but use 20% more energy than blank screens.)

The EPA and manufacturers are both hoping the energy-conserving machines will appeal to consumers. Even if

AST's Bravo LP is an environmentally conscious microcomputer system made of recyclable metal. After a specified idle time, the electricity levels used by the CPU and monitor are cut in half. AST estimates this will trim about $50 off the user's annual electric bill.

they aren't concerned about the environment, they reason, users should like the idea of lower electric bills. IBM, for example, estimates that some of its new models can be operated for about $15 a year, versus the $150 to $250 electric bill required to run a conventional PC. The "green machines" should also appeal to computer buyers in Europe and Japan, where energy costs are high and climbing every year.

The most reliable system is one that never fails. **Fault tolerant computers** are designed with duplicate components. If one component fails (a *fault*), an identical component takes over, usually without the user's even reaalizing a fault has occurred. Many computers are not fault tolerant, nor do they need to be. However, when applications must run 24 hours a day nonstop, the extra cost of a fault tolerant computer is easily justified. many bank automated teller systems and air control systems rely on fault tolerant computers.

Because electrical power disruptions often underlie loss of computing capability, one of the most effective safeguards is the installation of **uninterruptable power supply (UPS) systems**. UPS systems ensure the continued flow of electricity, pro-

fault tolerant computer A computer designed with duplicate components to ensure reliability.

uninterruptable power supply (UPS) system A system that ensures the continued flow of electricity when the primary source of power fails.

duced by private generators or from storage batteries, when the primary source fails. A UPS helped the Miami data center of Comcast Corp. ride out Hurricane Andrew in 1992.

The second level of protection is the development of disaster recovery plans. Organizations should always assume that service will be lost at some point. When this occurs, the objective is to minimize the loss. **Disaster recovery plans** are procedures for restoring data lost when a system stops functioning. For computer networks, they include procedures for bypassing a failed segment of a network by using other communications lines.

The third level of protection against computer failure is the creation of an **off-site backup facility**. This is a computer center, often owned by the company, away from the company's main facility (Figure 13.4). **Hot sites** are fully equipped computer centers to which a company takes its backup copies of data and software and resumes processing. **Cold sites** are facilities outfitted with electrical power and environmental controls (heating and air conditioning), ready for the company to install a computer system (Figure 13.5). Often several different companies share hot and cold sites, each assuming there is little likelihood that they will ever need to use the site at the same time.

A common mistake in reliability planning is focusing on internal concerns and overlooking external causes. Because companies rely heavily on computer networks and outside software suppliers, the possibility of system failure coming from external sources must be considered. AT&T and Revlon found this out the hard way.

System Failure at AT&T.   In 1991, AT&T suddenly and without warning encountered a series of telephone system breakdowns around the United States. In

disaster recovery plan A procedure for restoring data lost when a system stops functioning.

off-site backup facility A backup computer center located away from a company's main facility.

hot site A fully-equipped backup computer center to which a company can take its backup copies of data and software and resume processing.

cold site A backup facility outfitted with electrical power and environmental controls, ready for a company to install a computer system.

FIGURE 13.4
Disaster Recovery Facility
Most disaster recovery facilities are created to ensure an uninterrupted flow of electricity in case of emergency. The buildings are usually nondescript from the outside; what's inside (see Figure 13.5) is much more important. The 151,000 square foot facility shown here houses multiple hot and cold sites.

FIGURE 13.5
Hot and Cold Sites
Given the need for computer reliability and the possibility of natural disasters, several companies have gone into the business of providing offsite backup facilities for companies that do not want to build their own. One of the most successful of these companies has been Comdisco, whose rentable hot and cold sites are pictured here.

a) Hot sites are fully-equipped computer centers to which companies take backup copies of their data and software to resume processing.

b) Cold sites are outfitted only with electrical power and environmental controls, and are ready for companies to install computer systems at a moment's notice.

a two-week period, telephone service to approximately 10 million customers was disrupted. This caused serious problems for the businesses who depend on telephone service as the lifeblood of their daily transactions.

AT&T sprung into action as soon as it detected trouble. The company assigned more than 200 technicians and engineers to work around the clock to identify and remedy the mysterious bugs causing the loss of service.

It turned out that the problem was not caused by AT&T but rather by a small supplier to the communications giant. The company's products had been incorporated into the AT&T network to control switching in the system. Many of these products were installed around the United States, so when they began failing the impact was felt nationwide. Neither AT&T nor its customers had ever experienced or planned for a failure of this type. AT&T's reputation for reliability was damaged in the short run, but its awareness of the impact of failure reached an all-time high.

Disruption at Revlon.   Ethical concerns and IT reliability issues come together quite often, as the experiences of Revlon (the internationally known maker of cosmetics headquartered in New York) have shown. Revlon signed a contract with software supplier Logisticon of Santa Clara, California to use Logisticon's inventory management software. Revlon complained that the software was not performing according to expectations and informed Logisticon that it would withhold a $180,000 scheduled payment for one portion of the contract and intended to cancel outright the other portion of the contract, valued at $600,000.

Logisticon allegedly decided to "repossess" the software because Revlon had not made the scheduled payments. To do so, Logisticon gained access to Revlon's computers over the telephone and activated commands that disabled the software. Revlon charged Logisticon with activating viruses (discussed in detail later in this chapter) that had been planted in the software, making the data incomprehensible. (Logisticon acknowledged disabling the software, but denied the use of viruses or destruction of Revlon's data.)

The disruption to Revlon's computers affected two main distribution centers in Phoenix, Arizona and Edison, New Jersey, halting approximately $20 million in scheduled product deliveries and idling several hundred workers. Revlon regarded Logisticon's actions as "commercial terrorism."[3]

Software Piracy

Ethical issues apply as much to the use of software as they do to the characteristics of software that companies deliver. Like data and information, software is a valuable component of a business system, because it is the element that oversees processing and transforms data into a useful form. Commercial software is often perceived as expensive and thus is subject to software piracy.

Piracy is the making of illegal copies of copyrighted information. **Software piracy** is the making of illegal copies of software. Software piracy is a serious issue because it is both illegal and widespread. Manufacturers and software industry groups estimate that as many as seven illegal copies are made for every legal copy sold by retailers.

software piracy The making of illegal copies of software.

Protecting Against Software Piracy

Although no software protection method is foolproof, three methods are widely used in the IT industry: copyright protection, copy protection, and site licensing.

---

[3]"Revlon Sues Supplier Over Software Disabling," *New York Times*, October 25, 1990, pp. C1 and C4.

copyright Legal protection of original works against unauthorized used, including duplication.

Software Copyright Protection.   A **copyright** protects original works against unauthorized use, including duplication, providing the owner visibly displays a notice of copyright on the product. The copyright notice is similar across many countries, although not all countries acknowledge the right of copyrighted ownership. Under the Universal Copyright Convention adopted by most countries, the copyright notice consists of three elements:

1. The symbol © (in the United States, the additional word *Copyright* or the abbreviation *Copr.* can also be used).
2. The year of first publication of the work.
3. The name of the copyright owner.

Copyright protection has been used for many years to protect books, magazines, music, and other original works (Figure 13.6). It also applies to computer software, databases, RAM, and ROM, and is the principal legal protection against duplication or outright theft of original ideas embodied in computer programs. Well-known programs such as Lotus 1-2-3, Word for Windows, WordPerfect, dBASE IV, Paradox, and CC:Mail are copyrighted and therefore protected by law from unauthorized copying or use.[4]

[4]Copyright owners can choose to allow others to use their copyrighted work. In such cases, a credit line indicating that use is authorized will be attached to each copy of the work. Copyright owners may require the payment of a royalty for use of the work.

FIGURE 13.6   Copyright Page
Copyright notices can range in length from a single symbol, date, and name to an entire page of information. Copyright pages in books often contain information in addition to the copyright line. Included on the page shown here are (top to bottom): library of Congress cataloging data; editorial staff credits; copyright information; printing information; the publication's international standard book number (ISBN), and international divisions of the publishing company.

Library of Congress Cataloging-in-Publication Data

Robbins, Stephen P.
    Essentials of organizational behavior/Stephen P. Robbins. —4th ed.
      p.   cm.
    Includes bibliographical references and index.
    ISBN 0-13-300096-6 (paper)
    1. Organizational behavior.   I. Title.
    HD58.7.R6   1994   93–26322
    658.3—dc20   CIP

Acquisitions Editor: *Natalie Anderson*
Assistant Editor: *Lisamarie Brassini*
Production Editor: *Edith Pullman*
Interior Design: *Rosemarie Paccione*
Cover Design: *Pencil Point Studio*
Cover Illustration: *Ken Coffelt*
Manufacturing Buyer: *Herb Klein*
Electronic Page Makeup: *Christy Mahon*

 © 1994, 1992, 1988, 1984 by Prentice-Hall, Inc.
A Paramount Communications Company
Englewood Cliffs, New Jersey 07632

All rights reserved. No part of this book may be reproduced, in any form or by any means, without permission in writing from the publisher.

Printed in the United States of America
10 9 8 7 6 5 4 3 2 1

ISBN 0-13-300096-6

Prentice-Hall International (UK) Limited, *London*
Prentice-Hall of Australia Pty. Limited, *Sydney*
Prentice-Hall Canada Inc., *Toronto*
Prentice-Hall Hispanoamericana, S.A., *Mexico*
Prentice-Hall of India Private Limited, *New Delhi*
Prentice-Hall of Japan, Inc., *Tokyo*
Simon & Schuster Asia Pte. Ltd., *Singapore*
Editora Prentice-Hall do Brasil, Ltda., *Rio de Janeiro*

When Microsoft Corp. recently released a new version of its DOS operating system, it worked with law enforcement officials to seize pirated versions of the software. Even before the program was widely distributed, law enforcement officials seized tens of thousands of illegally packaged copies. Diskettes, documentation, and the packaging itself were duplicated and wrapped in cellophane to look like the real thing.

Copy Protection.   Software developers and vendors have tried many schemes to make software copying impossible. **Copy protection** schemes involve hardware or software features that defeat attempts to copy a program or make the copied software unreliable.

No copy protection scheme developed so far has proven foolproof. Even worse, copy protection has hindered the copying of software by individuals who have legally purchased a program and want to make a backup copy to protect against damage to the original copy. Making a backup copy is usually allowed in most software license agreements (Figure 13.7).

To assist their users, most software vendors have dropped attempts at copy protection. However, they vigorously pursue legal action against software pirates under the copyright laws.

Software Site Licensing.   To assist large-volume users of programs and at the same time avoid software piracy, many software developers offer **site licenses**. Under these agreements, the purchaser (typically a company, university, or government agency) pays a fee to the manufacturer to make a specified number of copies of a particular program (and in some cases its documentation). In turn, the

copy protection A software protection scheme that defeats attempts to copy a program or makes the copied software unreliable.

site license An agreement under which a software purchaser pays a fee to the manufacturer to make a specified number of copies of a particular program.

This License Agreement is your proof of license.
Please treat it as valuable property.
Microsoft License Agreement

Proof of License

This is a legal agreement between you (either an individual or an entity), the end user, and Microsoft Corporation. If you do not agree to the terms of this Agreement, promptly return the disk package and accompanying items (including written materials and binders or other containers) to the place you obtained them for a full refund.

MICROSOFT SOFTWARE LICENSE

1. GRANT OF LICENSE. This Microsoft License Agreement ("License") permits you to use one copy of the specified version of the Microsoft software product identified above ("SOFTWARE") on any single computer, provided the SOFTWARE is in use on only one computer at any time. If you have multiple Licenses for the SOFTWARE, then at any time you may have as many copies of the SOFTWARE in use as you have Licenses. The SOFTWARE is "in use" on a computer when it is loaded into the temporary memory (i.e., RAM) or installed into the permanent memory (e.g., hard disk, CD-ROM, or other storage device) of that computer, except that a copy installed on a network server for the sole purpose of distribution to other computers is not "in use". If the anticipated number of users of the SOFTWARE will exceed the number of applicable Licenses, then you must have a reasonable mechanism or process in place to assure that the number of persons using the SOFTWARE concurrently does not exceed the number of Licenses. If the SOFTWARE is permanently installed on the hard disk or other storage device of a computer (other than a network server) and one person uses that computer more than 80% of the time it is in use, then that person may also use the SOFTWARE on a portable or home computer.

2. COPYRIGHT. The SOFTWARE is owned by Microsoft or its suppliers and is protected by United States copyright laws and international treaty provisions. Therefore, you must treat the SOFTWARE like any other copyrighted material (e.g., a book or musical recording) except that you may either (a) make one copy of the SOFTWARE solely for backup or archival purposes, or (b) transfer the SOFTWARE to a single hard disk provided you keep the original solely for backup or archival purposes. You may not copy the written materials accompanying the SOFTWARE.

3. OTHER RESTRICTIONS. This Microsoft License Agreement is your proof of license to exercise the rights granted herein and must be retained by you. You may not rent or lease the SOFTWARE, but you may transfer your rights under this Microsoft License Agreement on a permanent basis provided you transfer this License Agreement, the SOFTWARE, and all accompanying written materials and retain no copies, and the recipient agrees to the terms of this Agreement. You may not reverse engineer, decompile, or disassemble the SOFTWARE. Any transfer of the SOFTWARE must include the most recent update and all prior versions.

4. DUAL MEDIA SOFTWARE. If the SOFTWARE package contains both 3.5-inch and 5.25-inch disks, then you may use only the disks appropriate for your single designated computer or network server. You may not use the other disks on another computer or computer network, or loan, rent, lease, or transfer them to another user except as part of a transfer or other use as expressly permitted by this Microsoft License Agreement.

**FIGURE 13.7
Microsoft License Agreement for Computer Software**
Most software license agreements permit the purchaser to make one backup copy of the software, provided that the software is used on only one computer at a time.

Courtesy Microsoft Corp.

buyer agrees to keep an accurate record of who makes the copies and the computer or network on which they are installed.

Both parties benefit from site licenses. Purchasers have the convenience of making legal copies when necessary and for an average cost that is substantially (usually more than 50%) lower than the retail cost. Sellers gain large adoptions of software programs while avoiding pirated use of their software within an organization.

Public Domain Software

public domain software Any noncopyrighted software that can be used by the general public.

Not all software is copyrighted. **Public domain software** is any noncopyrighted software that can be used by the general public. The individuals or companies who wrote and therefore own the software have chosen to make the programs available to anyone who wants to use them.

shareware Software that is given away and freely distributed. The developer retains ownership, asks users to register with the owner, and requests a nominal fee for using the program.

Shareware combines the best features of copyrighted software and public domain software. Like public domain software, shareware is given away and freely distributed. However, the developer retains ownership and asks users to register with the owner and to pay a nominal fee for using the program. Registering allows users to receive notices of future updates to the programs and the nominal fee supports the continued development of the software.

Sometimes a company or individual offers software for a very small fee, often just $1. This small fee encourages people to use the software freely while simultaneously publicizing the issuer's claim of ownership. When you pay the $1, you are acknowledging the issuer's ownership.

CRITICAL CONNECTION 2
Software Police Out to Prove That Piracy Doesn't Pay

When you hear the term "police raid" anywhere in the world, you probably think of a crackdown on illegal gambling or drugs. But a few companies now associate the term with software piracy, thanks to the Software Publishers Association (SPA). Founded in 1984, the Washington, DC-based group has been trying to stamp out the illegal "softlifting" that costs its members an estimated $1 billion a year.

In most cases, the "software police" are tipped off when a current or ex-employee makes a call to the SPA's antipiracy hotline. (The hotline gets about 20 to 30 calls a day.) If the operator screening the call decides a problem may exist, the SPA will try to verify the tip through other sources. For example, it may ask the software publisher to count the number of registration records filed by a particular organization. If the tip indicates that many more copies of the software are actually in use at the company, the SPA will investigate further.

The next step is a letter to the company, asking it to cooperate in a voluntary audit of its software. Ninety-five percent of the companies cooperate fully, the SPA reports. But if the company refuses to cooperate or ignores the letter, the SPA will seek legal assistance. Soon after, the company may get a surprise visit from SPA, backed up by a federal marshall with a search warrant. So far, about 75 companies have been "raided."

■ Computer Crime and System Intrusion

The term **computer crime** encompasses any unauthorized use of a computer system (including software piracy) or theft of system resources for personal use (including computer processing time and network access time). It is also a crime to take any actions intended to alter data and programs or to damage or destroy data, software, or equipment. Table 13.2 lists the most common types of computer crime. All these are crimes committed through **intrusion**, forced and unauthorized entry into the system. Throughout this book we have discussed the importance of putting data and physical security measures in place. These methods discourage intrusion.

Computer crime through intrusion can occur in two ways. Hackers can break into a system, or software viruses can destroy programs and data.

computer crime The unauthorized use of a computer system or theft of system resources for personal use.

intrusion Forced and unauthorized entry into a system.

Hackers

A **hacker** is a person who gains access to a system illegally. Hackers usually gain access to a system through a network, but sometimes they will physically enter a computer or network facility.

Some people actually call themselves "hackers." In so doing, they are referring not to their ability to break into computers and networks, but rather to their technical skill for computer programming and making a system perform in innovative and productive ways. Hackers who break into systems also have good technical skills, but have chosen to apply them in undesirable (often illegal) ways. When

hacker A person who gains access to a system illegally.

TABLE 13.2   Types of Computer Crime

Data diddling	Changing data and information before they enter a system.
Data leakage	Erasing or removing databases and files from a system without indicating that they were removed or leaving any trace they ever existed.
Logic bomb	A program designed to execute when certain conditions occur. Designed to sabotage system data, programs, or processing (see also *time bomb*).
Piggybacking	Gaining access to a system or process by using the passwords or access codes of an authorized system user. Alternatively, taking over a terminal or workstation in use by an authorized user, perhaps while he or she has stepped away from the system momentarily.
Salami (data) slicing	Developing or modifying software to capture small amounts ("slices") of money in a transaction and redirecting them to a hidden account. The amounts are so small they go unnoticed, but accumulate to substantial amounts in large-volume transaction processing systems.
Scavenging	Searching trash cans, either figuratively through a computer system icon or literally in a computer center, to find discarded data and information or program details. Used to obtain confidential information or to learn the structure of a program.
Time bomb	A program designed to execute on a specific date. The program monitors the computer's internal clock/calendar. When the preset date arrives, the program comes to life, causing its damage.
Trapdoor	An illicit and unknown point of entry into a program or network that can be used to gain access to the system.
Trojan horse	A program that appears to do one thing, but actually does something very different. Named after the Trojan horse of ancient Greek lore because the program masquerades as a harmless application and then does its damage after it is loaded onto a disk or into computer memory.
Wiretapping	Using any device to capture data transmission electronically or to "listen" in on network conversations, especially those transmitted using wireless methods or over copper cables.
Zapping	Damaging or erasing data and information or programs. Usually possible because the criminal is able to bypass security systems.

"computer whizzes" turn their attention to good deeds, the results can be in the best interests of society, as the People box titled "Working Miracles with 'Outdated' Computers" discusses.

The number of hackers around the world has grown substantially over the past decade, primarily because of people's increased access to powerful desktop computers in schools, in offices, and at home. More computers, coupled with easily accessible network and communications capabilities, means more hackers of all ages. Consider these representative examples of hacking[5]:

- The United Press International (UPI) wire service reported that two Staten Island, New York youths were arrested on charges of invading and disrupting the com-

[5]*Software Engineering Notes*, 16, no. 1, January 1991, pp. 20–22.

PEOPLE

Working Miracles with "Outdated" Computers

IN A WORLD OF EVER MORE SOPHISTICATED TECHNOLOGY, IT'S easy to overlook the potential of older computers and their peripherals. In fact, the U.S. Environmental Protection Agency estimates that as many as 10 million outdated computers hit the dumpsters every year. But now the National Cristina Foundation is giving some of these "old" machines a new life. In the process, it's offering hope and new opportunities to the disabled and the disadvantaged.

The idea for the foundation dates back to the 1980s, when Bruce McMahan donated a used PC to a special education class attended by his daughter, Cristina. Dr. Yvette Marrin, the class's teacher, recalls, "When Bruce and I saw the miracles that happened in that class as people who couldn't hold a pencil were able to communicate for the first time in years, thanks to a couple of hundred dollars' worth of machine, we decided we had to share this miracle with others."

Today Marrin is president of the New York–based foundation, which actively campaigns for donations of used equipment that can be redirected to qualified schools and social service agencies. To make donating easy, the foundation maintains a toll-free number (1-800-274-7846), and it has nonprofit status, which means all donations are tax deductible. Donations have ranged from a single machine to the $104,000 worth of equipment pledged by Packard Bell. Metropolitan Life, donated 250 laptops when it bought new machines for its field agents. By 1993, the Cristina Foundation had "recycled" more than 100,000 used computers.

Like many organizations, the Cristina Foundation needs to maintain a high profile. An energetic presence, Dr.

Bruce McMahan with his daughter Cristina, who has cerebral palsy. The presence of computers in the classroom made such a difference for Cristina and her classmates that McMahan and Cristina's teacher, Yvette Marrin, decided they had to find a way to get similar technology to others in need.

Marrin makes sure the foundation has a booth at the major computer shows, where she and other "Cristinas" pass out pamphlets, answer questions, and take pledges. (People who visit the foundation's booth at the Las Vegas Comdex computer show might even meet Cristina McMahan, who now lives in California.)

Donations come in every day, but the Cristinas are always looking for more equipment and more volunteers. After all, there are still millions of old computers languishing in store rooms and clogging the nation's landfills. If you know of any—or you'd like to volunteer—why not give the foundation a call?

puterized voice mail system of a Massachusetts company. Their activities cost the firm $2.4 million. The youths used their home computer to dial into the system and obtain the system password. Then they changed the passwords for various units in the system, resulting in the loss of important messages and numerous business transactions. The youths allegedly focused on the Massachusetts firm when it failed to send them a poster that was supposed to accompany a paid subscription for a computer-game magazine published by the company.

- Australia's Compass Airline reported that its reservation system was being jammed. On one day alone, the new airline company received more than 25,000 calls. A computer had been used to dial the airline's reservation number repeatedly, then abort the call when the line was answered. The airline's CEO emphasized that Compass did not believe it was a rival airline.
- *The Independent* newspaper of London reported that at least five British banks were blackmailed by a group of hackers who had broken into the banks' central computer over a six-month period. This was the largest and most sophisticated breach of computer security ever experienced by British banks. The electronic break-ins, with their implicit threats of stealing information or sabotaging the systems by planting false data or damaging the banks' complex information systems, could have caused chaos for the banks. The hackers demanded substantial sums of money in return for showing the banks how their systems were penetrated.

The increased frequency of hacking, coupled with the newness of the problem as an issue of law, has led many governments to put legislation in place to deal with this form of computer crime. In the United States, Congress passed the *Computer Fraud and Abuse Act* in 1984. This federal legislation, which is supplemented by state statutes, appears to be a first step in positioning the judicial system to deal with the problem. The legal system is just starting to deal with the problem. Workshops and seminars are now offered to educate attorneys, judges, and other members of the judicial system in the challenges created by hackers and the problems their activities create. These workshops also explain proven strategies for prosecuting hackers.

Protecting Against Intrusion by Hackers. There is always the possibility that the individuals responsible for a computer crime are disgruntled former employees. Hence, good security means looking inside the company as well as outside.

Preventing unauthorized access to a system entails having good physical security. Hiring honest, reliable people is an obvious starting point. Figure 13.8 shows ten additional techniques helpful in deterring intrusion by hackers. These are:

- **Access passwords that are changed frequently.** Users should be required to enter personal identification codes and individually assigned code words to access the system. Passwords should be kept strictly confidential.
- **Restriction of system use.** Users should be given access to only the functions they need to use, rather than full-system access.
- **Limited access to data.** Users should be allowed to access only the data they need to perform processing within their area of responsibility.
- **Physical access controls.** Access cards and *biometric devices*, which recognize voice patterns, finger or palm prints, retinal eye patterns, and signatures, are among the most effective physical security systems (Figure 13.9 on page 545). It is difficult to fool these systems.
- **Partitioning of responsibilities.** Critical functions involving high risk or high value in the data being processed should be separated so that more than one

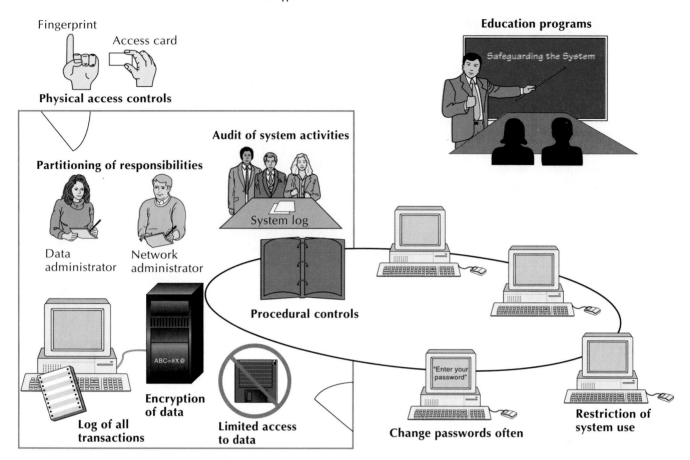

FIGURE 13.8   Ten Protection Schemes to Deter Computer Hackers

person must be involved to perform the processing. Database and network administrators should be given separate but important responsibilities for controlling access to the system.

- **Encryption of data.** Changing the appearance of data through scrambling and coding makes it more difficult to use information, even if a hacker is able to access it.
- **Procedural controls.** When clearly stated security procedures guide users and IT staff members, it is more difficult to breach security.
- **Education programs.** There is no substitute for well-informed staff members. Security education programs stress the threat of intrusion and hackers' methods and tactics, and provide guidelines on how to respond when intrusions are detected.
- **Audits of system activities.** In an *audit*, independent parties review transactions and computer processing to analyze their origin and their impact on the system, and to determine that these activities were authorized and performed by authorized individuals.
- **Log of all transactions and user activities.** Keep a record of each activity and the individual responsible for the activity.

Some companies use an additional method to supplement these techniques. When callers dial into the system, they provide the telephone numbers from which they are calling. The system may also sense the calling number automatically. The user then hangs up and the system, after verifying that the telephone number is valid and authorized, calls back the user. *Call back security* adds another layer of protection to the ten techniques discussed above.

a) Comdisco's security access cards are used widely throughout business and industry. Card keys are distributed to authorized individuals. The programming of the card key restricts the individual's access to only those areas he or she is authorized to enter.

b) Courtesy Recognition System's Handkey security system, used in many government buildings and prisons, reads palmprints.

FIGURE 13.9
Access Cards and Biometric Detection Devices
Access cards have been used as security devices for several years. Growing in popularity are biometric detection devices, which grant access to an area or system by recognizing physical characteristics.

Despite these precautionary measures, some hackers do manage to break into even the best-guarded systems. When a hacker has penetrated a system, it is important to determine whether any damage or theft has occurred and to know that there is a *trapdoor*—that is, an undetectable way of entering the system, bypassing the security system (see Table 13.2). Detecting even the smallest "loose end" can be helpful, as Clifford Stoll found out.

Clifford Stoll: Hunting Down a Hacker.   When Clifford Stoll (Figure 13.10), an astrophysicist, joined the Lawrence Berkeley Laboratory, a university research laboratory outside of San Francisco, he knew he would be responsible for managing a dozen mainframe computers (interconnected to thousands of other systems over more than a dozen networks) and over 1,000 user accounts. An additional computer was dedicated to gathering statistics and sending monthly bills to the laboratory departments using the machines.

Stoll began his second day at work by reviewing the computer usage records for the previous day. He quickly found that the books did not balance. Someone had used a few seconds of computing time without paying for it. There was a $.75 shortfall on a bill of several thousand dollars.

Puzzled by the imbalance, he dug into the scrambled code of the accounting software. When he could still not find an explanation for the discrepancy, Stoll became more puzzled. Several days later, Stoll found another accounting discrepancy of a few cents and a five-minute discrepancy between the amount of computer time logged and the amount actually charged to user accounts. Digging further, Stoll decided that someone—an intruder—had entered a lab computer from a network. He thought the intruder had found a loophole in the system's security that would allow him to enter the system and become a "privileged user." You become privileged by logging onto the computer with the system manager's password. Once inside, you can establish new passwords, open access paths, and generally roam through the system, changing records and databases at will.

Stoll was a fan of a popular movie of the time, *War Games*, in which a teenage hacker broke into a Pentagon computer and nearly started a global nuclear war. Even though Stoll wasn't worried about someone getting in to damage the lab's

FIGURE 13.10
Clifford Stoll: Spy Catcher
Stoll, an astrophysicist, noticed a 75¢ discrepancy in the computer access time billed to his lab. Stoll eventually traced the discrepancy to a mysterious secret agent in Pittsburgh, a spy ring in Germany, and the former Soviet Union's secret police.

computers, he wondered if he was living through a version of *War Games*. What did the hacker want and what were his intentions?

Stoll watched as the hacker came into the system repeatedly and erased his own tracks so that no one would know he had ever been there—unless a telltale accounting discrepancy remained. After monitoring the hacker's activities for several days, Stoll wrote a program that logged all the hacker's activities. Stoll let the intruder wander through the system while he carefully recorded every keystroke.

For over a year, Stoll stalked the elusive, methodical hacker as he prowled the Berkeley lab network and accessed the computer networks of more than a half-dozen national agencies, burrowing into sensitive information about military programs. Eventually, Stoll traced the hacker's origin to Hanover, Germany.

Next, Stoll set up a sting operation, tempting the intruder into accessing a set of data and then transmitting it to another location. The sting uncovered a spy ring in Germany linked to a mysterious agent in Pittsburgh. The spy ring was selling computer secrets to the former Soviet Union's secret police, the KGB, for cocaine and tens of thousands of dollars.

Stoll's experience, while extreme, points to the threat of criminal intrusion into computer systems. In his many television and newspaper interviews, Stoll always makes the point that computer espionage is the most important IT security issue of the 1990s.

CRITICAL CONNECTION 3
Standing Guard on the Electronic Frontier

ISS Security Certification Consortium

In recent years, U.S. government officials have made news when they arrested, indicted, and tried members of hacker groups bearing such exotic names as the Legion of Doom and Masters of Deception. But on a day-to-day basis, it's the company data security manager who patrols the electronic frontier, trying to ward off hackers and industrial spies. To do the job well, John A. Blackley says, you have to love change and you have to polish your sales skills. He should know. He's a certified information systems professional with more than ten years' experience.

The love of change comes in handy as he and other data guardians try to stay one step ahead of new technologies and the forces that threaten them. But Blackley also needs excellent sales skills to enlist the support of end-users who form the system's first line of defense. As Blackley describes it, "If we spend lots of money on access-control technology and do not educate our staff, we've wasted our money. And excellent negotiating skills are required because almost no one wants to set up another meeting just to hear about security." In fact, *Computerworld*, the leading newspaper of the computer industry, estimates that data security managers now spend over a third of their time "selling" data security programs and procedures.

Computer Viruses

virus A hidden program that alters, without the user's knowledge, the way a computer operates or modifies the data and programs stored on the computer.

Sometimes intrusion occurs by way of software. A computer **virus** is a hidden program that alters, without the user's knowledge, the way a computer operates or modifies the data and programs stored on the computer. The virus is written by individuals intent on causing damage or wreaking havoc in a system. It is called a "virus" because it reproduces itself, passing from computer to computer when disks are shuttled from one computer to another. A virus can also enter a computer when a file to which it has attached itself is downloaded from a remote computer over a communications network. An infected disk or diskette will continue to spread the virus each time it is used, as Figure 13.11 shows.

Each virus has its own characteristics—its own "signature," as computer experts say. Some destroy irreplaceable data by writing gibberish over the disks they infect. Others take control of the operating system and stop it from functioning. Still others embed commands into the operating system, causing it to display mes-

FIGURE 13.11   The Spread of a Computer Virus
Educational programs and the implementation of procedures are important steps in preventing the introduction and spread of viruses throughout a computer system.

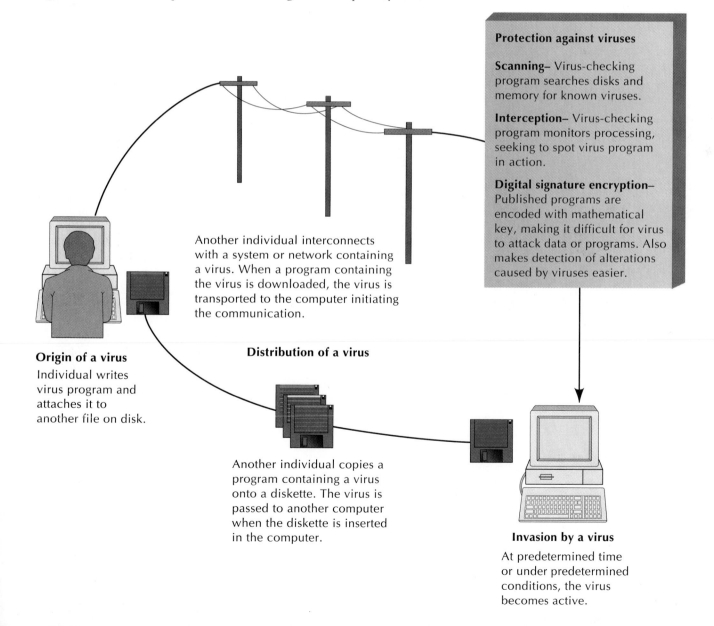

Protection against viruses

Scanning– Virus-checking program searches disks and memory for known viruses.

Interception– Virus-checking program monitors processing, seeking to spot virus program in action.

Digital signature encryption– Published programs are encoded with mathematical key, making it difficult for virus to attack data or programs. Also makes detection of alterations caused by viruses easier.

Another individual interconnects with a system or network containing a virus. When a program containing the virus is downloaded, the virus is transported to the computer initiating the communication.

Distribution of a virus

Origin of a virus
Individual writes virus program and attaches it to another file on disk.

Another individual copies a program containing a virus onto a diskette. The virus is passed to another computer when the diskette is inserted in the computer.

Invasion by a virus
At predetermined time or under predetermined conditions, the virus becomes active.

sages on the computer screen. The worst forms of virus are much more subtle, moving through data and changing small amounts of detail in selected files, so unnoticeable they are difficult to detect.

All types of computers are vulnerable to viruses. Microcomputers are particularly vulnerable because most were not designed with computer security in mind. The design of the next generation of PC is being developed with much greater concern for the detection of viruses and security in general.

Virus Protection.   Computer viruses are a fairly recent phenomenon. More than 1,200 computer viruses are now known, bearing such exotic names as the Michelangelo Virus and the Christmas Virus (Table 13.3).

To protect its systems against viruses, companies must buy *virus detection software*, programs that scan the computer's disks to detect the virus. There are three methods of virus detection: scanning, interception, and digital signature encryption.

Scanning programs search the computer and main memory to detect a virus. Most programs alert the user when a virus has been detected. The user can then signal the program to destroy the virus and, if possible, repair the data. *Detection programs* work behind the scenes, monitoring processing activities and signaling the user when a virus tries to infect the system. *Digital signature encryption*, an emerging technology, uses a mathematical coding scheme designed to foil a virus's attempt to attack programs and data. The Quality and Productivity box in Chapter 2 titled "Computer Viruses Spur the Push for Safe Computing" offers some additional procedural tips for protecting a system against viruses.

Stoned III at Novell.   Detecting and stopping viruses early is critical to maintaining data integrity. Novell—a Provo, Utah software publisher and the United States' largest supplier of office networks for personal computers—found this out the hard way. It recently sent a letter to approximately 4,000 of its customers warning them that it had shipped them copies of a disk to update their network software. The problem: The disk had been accidentally infected with a virus known as "Stoned III." This virus is known for disabling the computers it infects.

Novell traced the problem to a specific part of the manufacturing process but admitted that it was unable to determine how the virus infected its software in the first place. It later traced the origin of the virus to Europe just three months earlier. Somehow, the virus had traveled to the United States, on disk or via computer network, and eventually into the Novell manufacturing process. To prevent recurrence of similar problems, Novell has acquired special digital-signature software that makes it difficult for viruses to spread undetected on its future network software releases.

▆ A Final Word

The issues described in this chapter are real and may affect every individual directly or indirectly. The most important point to take from these discussions is simple: With the use of IT comes the need to (1) be aware of possible misuse and (2) take responsibility for safeguarding the resources under our control.

TABLE 13.3   Infamous Computer Viruses

Name	What Happens When Victim Uses an Infected Program or Disk
Stoned (aliases: Hawaii, New Zealand, Marijuana, Smithsonian, Hamo)	Possibly the most common virus in the United States. May display message, "Your PC is Stoned—LEGALIZE MARIJUANA." May damage disk directory and file allocation table (FAT—a disk directory the computer needs to retrieve files).
Michelangelo	A mutation of the Stoned virus, destroys contents of hard disk on March 6, the anniversary of the artist's birth in 1475. Gained national publicity in 1992; helped raise public awareness of computer viruses.
Christmas (aliases: XA1, XMAS)	On April 1, the virus destroys the file allocation table. Between December 24 and January 1 of any year, the screen is filled with a picture of a Christmas tree.
Friday the 13th (aliases: Jerusalem B, PLO Virus 1808, 1813, Israeli Virus, Pay Day, Anarkia, Arab Star, Black Friday, Hebrew University, Mendoza)	The first computer virus identified; caused widespread panic at Hebrew University of Jerusalem in July 1987. System slows dramatically. If virus is in memory on any Friday the 13th, it will delete every program executed. "Black Box" appears on the lower left side of the screen and scrolls up as the screen scrolls.
Whale (aliases: Mother Fish)	A "stealth virus" that uses layers of encryption and can infect files in 32 different ways. System slows down. Display flickers. Decreases available memory by 9,984 bytes. Using system command to fix disk errors will damage files.
Casino	On 15th of January, April, or August, screen displays a message that the FAT has been destroyed, even though the virus has saved a copy in memory. Offers user "a last chance to restore your precious data" by playing a slot machine game. If user loses, virus wipes out FAT. Casino-B variant destroys FAT whether user wins or loses game.
Falling Letters	Ten minutes after the virus is loaded into memory, all the characters on the screen fall to the bottom. Infects only floppy disks.
Disk Killer (alias: Ogre)	Damages disk; destroys files on floppy disks. May cause unexpected formatting of disk. Displays message, "Disk Killer…Warning! Don't turn off the power, or remove the diskette while disk killer is processing! PROCESSING! Now you can turn off the power." Once a certain number of disks have been infected, reformats hard drive, erasing all files.
MisSpeller (aliases: Typo Boot, Mistake)	Causes misspelled words in printed documents, even though the onscreen spellings are correct.
Zero Bug (alias: Palette)	Display shows a Smiley face character, which eats all the zeros.
Frere Jacques	Files increase in size. System plays tune "Frere Jacques" on Fridays.
Code 252	Flashes screen message, "You are infected with a virus. Ha, Ha, Ha. Now erasing all disks. Ha, Ha, Ha," although no files are actually erased.
T4-A, T4-B	Damages or deletes application and system files by trying to change the startup code or overwriting the file.

Sources: Based on Central Point Software, *Central Point Anti-Virus Users Manual*, Ch. 8, "Virus Dictionary," pp. 71, 77, 79–80, 81, 82, 83, 85, 92, 98, 107, 110; Michele Hasson, "Virus Alert," *MacUser*, November 1992, pp. 268–269; and Christopher O'Malley, "Stalking Stealth Viruses," *Popular Science*, January 1993, pp. 54–58, 92.

SUMMARY OF LEARNING OBJECTIVES

1 **Explain how the term "privacy" applies to information technology and why privacy is an important issue in the 1990s.** Privacy, as the term is used in information technology, refers to how personal information is collected, used, and protected. Although privacy has always been an important issue, the enormous capabilities of IT have amplified the need for protection of personal privacy.

2 **Describe the importance of ethics in the use of information technology and identify seven ethical issues associated with the use of IT in business.** In the United States, most records kept by companies and nongovernment organizations are not covered by existing privacy laws. Therefore, people must count on a company's ethical policies for protection of private information. Seven ethical issues that businesses must confront are electronic-mail privacy, software licenses, software copyrights, hardware access, intellectual property ownership, file access, and data ownership.

3 **Explain the IT professional's obligation to provide continued access to computer networks and the four methods used to ensure IT reliability.** As companies become dependent on IT, they become dependent on the availability of their computers and communications systems. With this dependence comes the expectation that the service provider—whether an IT professional or a hired IT service—will ensure that service cannot be interrupted.

Four methods are used to ensure IT reliability: *Fault tolerant computers* are designed with duplicate components. If one component fails, the duplicate automatically takes over. *Uninterruptable power supply systems* ensure the continued flow of electricity, produced from a backup source, when the primary source fails. *Disaster recovery plans* help to restore data lost when a system stops functioning. *Off-site backup facilities* provide a backup computer center away from the company's main facility.

4 **Discuss the legal issues surrounding software piracy and three methods that have been used to prevent software piracy.** *Software piracy* is the making of illegal copies of software.

Three methods are used to protect against software piracy. *Software copyright protection* protects original works against unauthorized use, including duplication, providing the owner visibly displays a notice of copyright on the product. *Copy protection* schemes defeat attempts to copy a program or make the copied software unreliable. *Software site licensing* can be used to assist large-volume users of programs and at the same time avoid piracy.

5 **Distinguish among copyrighted software, public domain software, and shareware.** Copyrighted software protects original works against unauthorized use. *Public domain software* is any noncopyrighted software that can be used by the general public. *Shareware* combines the best features of copyrighted software and public domain software. It is given away and freely distributed, but the developer retains ownership and asks users to register with the owner and pay a nominal fee for using the program.

6 **Describe ten ways to protect a system against intrusion.** Ten common ways to protect a system against intrusion are: change access passwords frequently, allow workers access to only the system functions they need to use, permit workers to access only the data that they need to use, establish physical security systems, separate critical processing functions so that more than one person must be involved, encrypt data by scrambling or coding information, adopt procedural controls, keep staff well informed through education programs, audit system activities, and keep a log of all transactions and user activities. Some systems also use call back security.

7 **Identify the three methods of virus detection used by virus detection software.** All types of computers are vulnerable to viruses. To protect against them, companies must buy and use virus detection software. There are three methods of virus detection. *Scanning programs* search the computer and main memory to detect a virus. *Detection programs* monitor processing activities and signal the user when a virus tries to infect the system. *Digital signature encryption* uses a mathematical coding scheme designed to foil a virus's attempt to attack programs and data.

KEY TERMS

cold site   528
computer crime   541
copy protection   539
copyright   538
disaster recovery plan   528
ethics   530
fault tolerant computer   535

hacker   541
hot site   528
intrusion   541
off-site backup facility   528
privacy   528
public domain software   540
reliability   534

shareware   540
site license   539
software piracy   537
uninterruptable power supply (UPS)
   system   535
virus   546

CRITICAL CONNECTIONS

1.   The Dark Side of IT

Rothfeder's 1992 book grew out of a 1989 cover story in *Business Week*, which won a number of awards.[6] Later, Rothfeder appeared on a program on privacy aired by WABC-TV in New York, where he demonstrated how his sources had taught him to use a personal computer and online databases to retrieve confidential information. In just a few minutes, he was able to construct a fairly detailed financial and personal profile of a producer and her husband, beginning with just their name and an approximate address.[7]

Questions for Discussion

1. Some of the privacy abuses Rothfeder describes can be traced to careless gatekeepers, like the investigator who approved Rothfeder's application for a "superbureau," a service that resells information from credit bureaus and other sources.[8] How can this type of abuse be prevented?

2. Many database records used to invade individual privacy are actually matters of public record. Many of these public records are now available online. (The sellers, buyers, and price of real estate is a good example of "public" information.) What might this mean to you as a marketing manager for a retail chain? As a private citizen?

3. Many European nations have data-protection agencies that oversee the creation and use of database systems containing confidential information. After years of resistance, there is growing support for

such an agency in other countries as well. What, in your opinion, would be the advantages and disadvantages of having such an agency for business? For private citizens?[9]

2.   Software Police Out to Prove That Piracy Doesn't Pay

One of the SPA's primary goals is to prove that piracy doesn't pay. If it finds illegal software during a voluntary audit, for example, it will assess a fine equal to the cost of the software. In 1991, SPA collected $3 million in fines. (The largest fine, $498,000, was paid by a company that had illegally copied 150 products published by 66 SPA members.) Then the "software police" will destroy every illegal copy. If the company wants to continue using the software (and the related data files), it has to buy legal copies.

The stakes are even higher if the company has refused to cooperate. Under U.S. copyright law, anyone who is convicted of willfully making an illegal copy of software can be fined up to $100,000. And commercial software piracy (the theft of at least 10 copies of a program, or more than $2,500 worth of software) is a felony that carries a prison term of up to five years and a fine of up to $250,000. At these rates, even the most expensive software is a bargain.

[6]Rothfeder, p. 5.
[7]*Ibid.*, pp. 107–111.
[8]*Ibid.*, pp. 18–20.
[9]*Ibid.*, pp. 147–152.

Questions for Discussion

1. Some individuals try to justify software piracy by claiming that software costs "too much" or that they can't understand the copyright notices. How do you think the SPA or the courts would react to this argument? What answers would you make to this argument?

2. In defending themselves in court, some companies claim that they have an antipiracy policy. As evidence, they provide a copy of a memo that was circulated to employees. Why do you think the courts have ruled that some of these companies' illegal activities were "willful"?

3. Boeing Co. in Seattle has a department of software accountability. This department maintains an inventory of all the company's software, including the hundreds of copies of CAD software used to design the company's products. Do you think Boeing's practice is a good model for business?

ISS Security Certification Consortium

3. Standing Guard on the Electronic Frontier

Security often appears to be an afterthought at companies setting up new systems. "After all," Blackley reports, "no one wants to hear that the new server can't be brought up on Monday because we don't know how to secure the data on it."

Often, IT professionals end up in the data security field, with little or no formal training. Some industry groups hope to change this in the near future, though. One of them is the International Information Systems Security Certification Consortium, formed in 1989 to identify people well qualified to resolve current and future security issues. To launch the program, the group began by certifying security experts on the basis of their work experience: a minimum of eight years in the data security area, with at least one year's experience in four of seventeen specialties, such as physical security, access control, and cryptography (the art of writing and deciphering code). In the future, though, professionals who want to be certified by the group will have to pass a two-part exam every three years.

Questions for Discussion

1. Why do you think security is such a "tough sell"? How could IT managers work with the IT staff to make the sell less tough?

2. Blackley says he spends a lot of time roaming the organization. What advantages does his "management by walking around" provide to the company?

3. Some IT professionals are skeptical of certification programs, arguing that test-taking skills are no substitute for real-world experience. What questions would you ask a person interviewing for the job of company data entry specialist? What skills would you seek in a person interviewing for a job as the head of a government agency charged with evaluating proposals for computer services by outside suppliers?

REVIEW QUESTIONS

1. What does the word "privacy" mean as it applies to information technology? Why is privacy a concern among those using IT and those affected by the use of IT?

2. Describe the five privacy provisions outlined in the Code of Fair Information Practices.

3. What are ethics? Can personal ethics be separated from business ethics?

4. Identify and explain seven ethical issues related to the use of IT in business.

5. Describe the ethical guidelines that Donn B. Parker of SRI International encourages IT professionals and users to adopt.

6. Why do companies have an obligation to ensure continued access to computer and communication systems once they have been made available to users?

7. Describe three methods of ensuring IT service reliability.

8. What is piracy? What is software piracy?

9. Describe three methods that companies can use to protect their software from piracy.

10. How are copy protection and copyright protection different?

11. Describe the differences between copyrighted software and public domain software.

12. What is shareware?

13. What are hackers and what is their role in system intrusion? Is system intrusion a crime?

14. Describe ten techniques for deterring computer intrusion by hackers.

15. What is a computer virus? How does a virus originate? How does it spread?

16. Name three techniques used to detect the presence of a computer virus.

DISCUSSION QUESTIONS

1. It is fairly easy to eavesdrop on cellular and cordless phone conversations because most of these messages are carried on analog radio waves that can be picked up by inexpensive radio frequency scanners. For this reason, Apple Computer has issued an instruction that employees should never discuss confidential matters over these devices. What might increased use of cellular phones mean to you as a private citizen? As a manager?

2. What ethical issues are raised by the existence of credit reporting agencies, such as TRW Information Services and Equifax Credit Information Services? Can you suggest any solutions for these issues?

3. In April 1992, a broken water pipe interrupted the electrical service at the Chicago Board of Trade Clearing Corp. In less than an hour, the company's manager of quality assurance had to put her disaster recovery plan in action. This involved shifting people and computer tapes to a backup site in a nearby suburb, where they spent four days coordinating recovery activities that kept all normal business activities operating. Why are such plans essential for businesses? Do different types of businesses need different types of recovery plans?

4. In a recent survey, *PC Computing* magazine found that 64% of respondents thought it permissible for company managers to search employees' hard disks for illegal copies of software. Do you agree that this activity is permissible or not? Explain your answer.

SUGGESTED READINGS

Loch, Karen D., Houston H. Carr, and Merrill E. Warkentin (1992). "Threats To Information Systems: Today's Reality, Yesterday's Understanding," *MIS Quarterly*, 16, no. 2 (June 1992), pp. 173–186. This article summarizes the results of a study investigating the concerns of information system executives about a variety of security threats. The results highlight a gap between the use of IT and the understanding of the security implications inherent in its use.

McLean, John. "The Specification and Modeling of Computer Security," *Computer* (January, 1990), pp. 9–16. A technical analysis of ways to limit potential damage caused by Trojan horse programs.

Stoll, Clifford. *The Cuckoo's Egg*. New York: Doubleday, 1989. A fascinating first-person account of Cliff Stoll's tracking of a spy through a maze of computer espionage. Provides insight into the operations of national networks as well as the strengths and weaknesses of computer security systems.

Straub, Detmar W., Jr. "Effective IS Security: An Empirical Study." *Information Systems Research*, 1, no. 3 (September, 1990), pp. 255–276. This article concludes that IT security has not been a high priority for most managers. Data gathered from over 1,200 organizations suggest that many permit their installations to be either lightly protected or wholly unprotected.

Wolinsky, Carol, and James Sylvester. "Privacy in the Telecommunications Age," *Communications of the ACM*, 35, no. 2 (February, 1992), pp. 23–25. Advances in telecommunications have brought about many new services while raising issues of personal privacy. The authors explore both sides of some of these debates.

CASE STUDY

Taking Aim at Telephone Toll Fraud

PUBLIC TELEPHONE COMPANIES AND PTTs HAVE LONG BEEN A favorite target of hackers. It all began decades ago when bright whiz kids found they could break into the U.S. telephone system and make long-distance calls without paying. But a lot has changed since then.

In the United States, AT&T, once a government-sanctioned monopoly, has been broken up, creating the "baby bells," like Pacific Bell and Ameritech. And AT&T is no longer the only U.S. long-distance telephone company; it now has to compete against MCI and Sprint. Even the technology has changed, as the telephone companies have installed complex digital switching systems controlled and monitored by sophisticated software.

Hacking activities have become more sophisticated too. Organized crime figures and drug dealers reportedly pay as much as $10,000 for the secrets that will let them make free, untraceable calls. Hackers may also set up a "call-sell" operation to sell stolen phone service to individuals and businesses.

To some extent, the target has changed too. Although hackers can invade the phone companies' new digital switching systems, many of today's phone hackers favor the switchboards maintained by large corporations and government agencies. To avoid the surcharges tacked onto phone credit card calls, for example, many companies purchase switchboards that incorporate a toll-free number. When employees call this number from a remote location and enter an access code, they get a dial tone that lets them make toll calls that are billed to the company. With enough patience (and an autodialer, which dials numbers automatically), the phone hackers can keep calling into the toll-free number until they stumble upon an authorized access code. Often, with the huge volume of calls made by a large organization, their unauthorized calls can go unnoticed for months. Some experts estimate that toll fraud may be costing U.S. businesses as much as $4 billion a year.

In theory, the company that owns the switchboard equipment is liable for its use and security, meaning it must pay for all calls, whether authorized or not. Some companies have challenged this theory. For example, Mitsubishi International Corp. sued American Telephone & Telegraph Co. over the security breach of an AT&T system installed in its New York office. Mitsubishi charged that AT&T had failed to provide a secure phone system, had not warned Mitsubishi about the potential for unauthorized use, and didn't respond quickly enough when Mitsubishi reported the unauthorized use. By the time Mitsubishi shut off the system's remote-access feature, hackers had made an estimated 30,000 unauthorized calls, costing Mitsubishi about $430,000. AT&T responded with a countersuit. Although the two companies finally settled out of court for undisclosed terms, the case raised new questions about who should pay for toll fraud.

To help their business customers protect themselves, the long-distance providers—such as AT&T, Sprint, and MCI in the United States—have developed seminars designed to show corporate customers how to improve security and detect and prevent fraud. Warning signs to look for: repeated busy signals, hundreds of very short calls (a sign that someone is using an autodialer to search for access codes), many calls at odd hours, and an unusual number of calls to faraway places where the company does little business. Using information obtained at a telephone company seminar, the communications coordinator at Empire Southwest Company in Phoenix, for example, realized the company was being billed for a startling number of calls to another state. The only problem: the heavy equipment dealer had few customers there. Before the company was able to tighten security, it had been billed for $150,000 in unauthorized calls.

Potential victims can also protect themselves with specialized information technology. Complementary Solutions, Inc., of Atlanta, for example, developed a program called Telemate FraudFighter, which uses artificial intelligence to "learn" a company's normal calling patterns. The program can be used to monitor specific extensions, calling regions, and access codes. If it detects unusual activity, it sounds the alarm. A new generation of equipment from AT&T uses a similar tactic; if it detects an inbound caller randomly searching for access codes, it calls the company's systems manager.

The major long-distance providers are also becoming increasingly vigilant in monitoring business toll calls and notifying their businesses' customers if they detect abnormal calling patterns that might suggest intrusion by hackers. In fact, a recent survey by consultants at Telecommunications Advisors, Inc. found that 23 percent of those surveyed first learned they were victims of toll fraud from their long-distance provider.

Questions for Discussion

1. Experts admit that no set of precautions will completely thwart a talented hacker. Why, then, is it important that companies institute as many security measures as practical?

2. AT&T, Sprint, and MCI have all shown a willingness to forgive some charges for unauthorized calls if the victimized company has taken reasonable security precautions. What types of precautions might the owners of a small business take to safeguard its phone system? What actions might the managers of a larger company take?

Sources: James Daly, "Toll Fraud Biting into Business," *Computerworld*, December 7, 1992, p. 71; William G. Flanagan and Brigid McMenamin, "For Whom the Bell Tolls," *Forbes*, August 3, 1992, pp. 60-64; Willie Schatz, "Pacific Bell Wants to Know Who's Calling, Please?" *Computerworld*, November 23, 1992, pp. 69, 73; James Daly, "Toll Fraud Threat Growing," *Computerworld*, March 22, 1993, pp. 47, 49.

Chapter Outline

CHAPTER 14

The Information Age: Next Steps

Learning Objectives

When you have completed this chapter, you should be able to:

1 Identify the "three Cs" of information technology and discuss how the definition of IT is changing in the Information Age.

2 Describe the importance of consumer electronics as an element of IT.

3 Explain the expanded definition of "communications carrier."

4 Discuss the change in the definition of "software" to incorporate content as well as programs.

5 Explain why TV is an important type of IT and how interactive TV works.

6 Discuss how the IT industry is changing.

7 Distinguish between a communications network and an information superhighway and give two reasons why world leaders are seeking to develop information superhighways.

8 Describe six issues involved in designing and developing an information superhighway.

In Practice

After completing this chapter, you should be able to perform these activities:

1 Contact a journalist or photojournalist and discuss the way she is capturing and reporting the news today compared to a decade ago, and seek her opinion on how the tools of journalism will change over the next decade.

2 Discuss with the manager of a computer store recent changes in the items he stocks, with particular emphasis on CD-ROM components and supplies.

3 Conduct a telephone survey of information systems executives (IT directors, chief information officers, or vice presidents of information systems) to determine whether they are monitoring the developments in consumer electronics and whether they are incorporating these developments into their long-range IT plans.

4 Visit a business and discuss the implications of the company's access to a national information superhighway.

5 Speak with a representative of a PTT or telephone company and determine her views on the roles of government, private enterprise, and communications carriers in developing a national information superhighway.

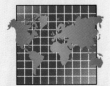

New News Tools

GOOD NEWS REPORTERS AND PHOTOGraphers are always prepared to cover breaking stories. And today's new news tools help reporters spend much more time in the field than they could a decade or two ago. A laptop computer and modem are now basic tools for many reporters. After they've written their stories on their PC, they connect the laptop to a telephone line and transmit the story back to an editor in the newsroom. Time and distance no longer get in the way.

The same is true for photojournalists. Chips that control focusing and light control have been around for more than a decade. But revolutionary advances have also occurred, changing the way photo stories are captured. Today's photojournalists have only to slip a diskette into their cameras and begin clicking. New photographic systems from Kodak of Rochester, New York, and Japan's Sony Corp. capture images electronically on disk instead of recording them on film. The systems also allow photographers to capture a few words identifying the time and location of the photo on disk. When the photo shoot is finished, the photojournalist does not need to develop the film. He or she can simply transmit the digital images back to the newsroom over a phone line.

Advances in information technology have transformed the way photojournalists work. New photographic systems allow photographers to capture images electronically on disk instead of recording them on film. These images can then be transmitted over ordinary phone lines to the newsroom.

Back at the office, the editor can insert the disk into a player and view the recorded images immediately on a high-resolution color television. Alternatively, the editor can slip the disk into a desktop computer and view the images on the computer's display screen. By pointing to an area of the photograph on the screen, the editor can capture the area and embed it in a word processing document, use it as part of the layout of a magazine cover, or create a color slide for a presentation. The same images can then be transferred to CD-ROM for permanent storage (and the disk in use can be erased and used to capture another breaking story). Entire libraries of photographic images can be created this way, all with full color and high resolution. (If you can't afford to send a photojournalist halfway around the world, never fear: For about $10–$30, you can purchase CDs full of the highest-quality images.) ∎

ARE TODAY'S PHOTOJOURNALISTS USING A CAMERA OR A COMPUTER? CAN ONE EVEN BE distinguished from the other? These kinds of questions are occurring with increasing frequency.

In this chapter, we discuss the next step in the Information Age, a step in which the very definition of IT is being rewritten. In the first part of the chapter, we explore the evolving definition of IT and its components. In the second part, we examine the steps that nations are taking to capitalize on the opportunities IT provides for the country and its people.

∎ New IT: The Convergence of Three Information Technologies

Throughout this book, we've examined the experiences of people, work groups, and companies using information technology. The examples we've used have emphasized the role of two technologies: computers and communications networks—"the 2 Cs of IT"—as well as the importance of know-how. But the definition of IT is changing through:

- The incorporation of consumer electronics.
- A broadened definition of "communications carriers."
- A broadened definition of "software."
- The arrival of interactive television.
- A redefinition of the IT industry.

The Incorporation of Consumer Electronics

As we move toward the twenty-first century, the definition of IT is being broadened through a convergence of three technologies. In addition to computers and communication systems, IT is evolving to encompass the "third C"—**consumer electronics**, electronic devices used to satisfy people's needs and wants, rather than to manufacture products or deliver services (Figure 14.1). You are already familiar with the products in this category: television, camcorders, VCRs, laser disc players, stereo and sound systems (Figure 14.2), and photographic systems that use CDs rather than film. To the list of well-known computer and communications companies like IBM, Apple, Digital, Group Bull, Toshiba, and Hitachi, we'll add a host of new names: Matsushita, Sony, Kodak, and Zenith, to mention just a few.

We've already seen how multimedia is changing the face of IT, paving the way for the incorporation of consumer electronics. Many people are coming to expect image, voice, and animation alongside data and text. As the multimedia phenomenon continues, it is likely that video records and CD players will become part of information technology also. As other types of consumer electronics are given processing power through chips and microprocessors, we'll see other changes as well.

consumer electronics
Electronic devices used to satisfy people's needs and wants rather than to manufacture products or deliver services.

FIGURE 14.1
The Converging Forces of Information Technology
As the year 2000 approaches, the definition of IT is broadening to include not only computers and communications, but also the "third C"—consumer electronics.

FIGURE 14.2
Consumer Electronics: The Fourth Component of Information Technology
Although consumer electronics are now used primarily to satisfy people's wants and needs rather than to manufacture products or deliver services, the definition of IT is evolving to include consumer electronics as well as computers, communications, and know-how.

a) Zenith's SL3283 television offers advanced video imaging capabilities for improved picture performance.

b) Sharp's VL-E30U videocamera fits in the palm of your hand and features a color screen.

c) Standard features in Zenith's VRL4210 VCR include onscreen programming, one-year eight-event recording, and 181-channel capability.

d) Pioneer's CLD-V2400 laser disc player includes remote control and bar coding capabilities.

e) RCA's tabletop stereo system consists of high-fidelity speakers, dual cassette deck, digital tuner with memory, control amplifier, multi-CD player with memory and oversampling features, and remote control.

CRITICAL CONNECTION 1
Philips Takes a Gamble on Multimedia

| Philips Electronics |

Multimedia got a boost in the early 1990s, when Philips Electronics announced CD-Interactive (CD-I), a technology designed to "teach your old television some new tricks." The heart of the system is the Imagination Machine, a device that looks like a VCR. Hooked to a stereo, it plays conventional 5-inch music CDs. Hook it to a television set, though, and it plays CD-I discs, compact discs containing interactive video. Children playing a *Sesame Street* disc, for example, can use the remote control to open an onscreen book and read with Ernie, or they can stage an interactive arithmetic lesson with the whole Sesame Street gang. CD-I titles, which cost $25 to $50 each, range from education to games and "infotainment," such as a self-guided tour of the Smithsonian.

For Philips, the Dutch electronics giant, it was a bold gamble with high stakes. In the past, Philips had developed the compact disc and the VCR with Japanese partners, who went on to dominate the market. To survive, Philips had to prove that it could both develop cutting-edge technology and market it well. By moving early and fast, Philips hoped to capture enough of the multimedia market to make CD-I an industry standard. When that happened, Philips could capitalize on the situation by licensing the technology to other manufacturers. But it would earn as much or more revenue selling CD-I discs produced by its subsidiary, Philips Interactive Media of America (PIMA).

Broadening the Definition of "Communications Carrier"

Today the word "communications" is often taken to mean telephone communications made possible by a communications carrier—the phone company or PTT. Yet the meaning of "carrier" extends beyond the telephone industry, as more people are realizing. Television networks and cable companies are increasingly becoming important parts of a nation's communications capacity. As we discussed in Chapter 9, communication cables can transport all types of digital and analog signals. Hence, computer data—as well as voice, video, and graphics signals—can be transported over the coaxial cables we associate with cable TV. Cable TV can carry much more than television programs.

In addition, the information technology underlying telephone transmission is growing more sophisticated. Telephone companies and PTTs have the capability to carry ordinary network TV programs over different types of communication links. Whether they will be allowed to do so depends on government policies. In most countries, federal or national governments as well as state public-service commissions regulate telephone companies and must grant the traditional voice carriers permission to transmit video. Several legal barriers have been removed recently; attempts to overcome more of them are likely to be vigorous over the next several years.

Broadening the Definition of "Software"

In the computer industry, the term "software" has frequently been used to mean "computer programs," the set of instructions that controls a computer or communications network. As the convergence of technologies continues, the definition of this term is being broadened to include *content*. Akio Morita, Chairman of Sony Corp., has viewed software for many years as any element that gives value to the hardware, a concept that extends the definition of software well beyond computer programs. Morita's views on software led Sony to purchase two U.S. entertainment companies: Columbia Pictures Entertainment, Inc. and CBS Records.

In describing Sony's decision to acquire CBS Records, Morita (Fig. 14.3) explained his innovative views on software as content:

FIGURE 14.3
Akio Morita: IT Visionary
Morita, chairman of Sony Corp., sees software as any element that gives value to hardware. His vision led Sony (once primarily a hardware company) to purchase two U.S. entertainment companies: Columbia Pictures and CBS Records.

> We have been engaged in a joint venture with CBS Records since 1968. If it had not been for this venture, the search for a record company to agree to record on our compact disc would have been a "mission impossible," when one considers how apprehensive established record factories would have been toward the emergence of new hardware. If we did not realize the benefit of software as early as we did, I wonder how long it would have taken for the CD technology to be as appreciated as it is now. Sony, by combining CBS Sony audio software to our CD hardware, created a new industry—the CD industry. The music industry, as a result, has grown with the transition from records to CDs.
>
> This success in hardware-software synergy illustrates that hardware alone, no matter how good, is not sufficient for either expediency or enrichment of human life. Moreover, it supports Sony's belief in how a good relationship between software and hardware can promote the further growth of both industries.

For Sony, the software—that is, the music (which is really recorded data and information)—gives value to the hardware.

Software also means images. Always on the cutting edge of IT, Microsoft is busy preparing CD libraries loaded with information, ranging from a *Musical Instruments* disc (an educational disc that recounts the history and sounds of musical instruments from all over the world) to a disc containing huge collections of photos of paintings by world-famous artists.

This broadening of the software concept marks a significant turning point for both Sony and Microsoft, and for IT in general. Now software will mean content—data and information—*as well as the means to manipulate it.* The world's art galleries, museums, filmmakers, recording companies, and television networks will be firmly tied to the IT industry. We've had examples of these industries' involvement in IT throughout this book, so it probably comes as no surprise that they have become an important part of the industry. What we don't know is whether they will continue to provide simply content—that is, software—for the industry, or will choose to become players in other ways too.

Interactive Television

Television is becoming an important type of IT for three reasons:

- First, although the number of microcomputers in the home in all industrialized countries is large—30 to 35 million in the United States and growing (Figure 14.4 on the next page)—the number of homes with television sets is typically 2 to 3 times larger. In addition, many homes have several TVs. In IT terms, the *installed base* of television sets is huge.
- Second, television technology is advancing rapidly, with new **high-definition television (HDTV)** emerging in Japan, Europe, and the United States (Figure 14.5). HDTV in the United States uses digital technologies to present sound and images over television screens that are much higher quality than those of regular TV. (In Japan, HDTV research has relied on older analog technology. We described analog systems in Chapter 9.) Television programs of all types, from

high-definition television (HDTV) A television system that uses digital technologies to present sound and images over high-quality television screens.

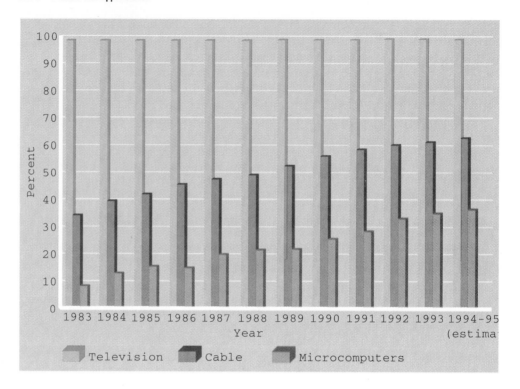

FIGURE 14.4
Percentage of U.S. Households with TVs, Cable Service, and Microcomputers, 1983–1993 and Projections
Although the percentage of U.S. households with televisions has held steady for the last decade, the percentage with microcomputers has increased 500%, from 7% in 1983 to 35% in 1993.

Sources: *Statistical Abstract of the United States, 1992;* Television Bureau of Advertising, Inc., Research Department; Electronic Industries Association, Marketing Services Research Center.

sports to opera to comedy to the nightly news, will be shown in vivid color with high-resolution images.
- Third, if HDTV uses digital technology, drawing a line between the TV and the PC will be difficult. HDTV also means more uses of IT components, since HDTV allows the incorporation of communications cables and wireless transmission methods into the TV set. Communications links in TV sets mean that vast amounts of data and information can be received and displayed. Digital data compression methods will make it possible for the home viewer to choose from hundreds of different TV channels being transmitted across a single fiber-optic cable running from the street into the home, apartment, or office. If TV has both computer and communications capabilities, its functions will change. Now a device for displaying broadcast programs, it will also become a device for transmitting information.

FIGURE 14.5
High-Definition TV
High-definition television images (right) show the fine picture detail achieved by quadrupling the video information transmitted on current TV broadcasts. The HDTV technology used to produce these high-quality images was developed by Zenith and AT&T, two members of the "Grand Alliance" developing the U.S. HDTV standard.

Interactive TV (ITV) will be a television with a keyboard, storage capability, and the capacity to transmit, as well as receive, vast amounts of information. ITV is creating many opportunities for forward-thinking entrepreneurs, as the Opportunities box titled "Looking for Gold on Interactive TV" details.

interactive TV (ITV) A television with a keyboard, storage capability, and the capacity to transmit and receive vast amounts of information.

OPPORTUNITIES

Looking for Gold on Interactive TV

INTERACTIVE TV IS GOOD NEWS FOR IT PROFESSIONALS, ESPECIALLY for the creative people who create entertaining multimedia and interactive television programs. In fact, *Morph's Outpost on the Digital Frontier*, a newsletter for multimedia professionals, estimates that as many as 100,000 people were working in multimedia by 1993. But there will be just as many opportunities for people who understand what the new IT means for traditional businesses.

Consider, for example, the viewer's challenge of navigating hundreds of channels. *TV Guide*, one of the United States's largest circulation magazines, is working on an onscreen guide to tell viewers what's on TV and how to find it. But it's not alone. Time Warner, Viacom, AT&T, Microsoft, Apple Computer, Ameritech, InSight, and Discovery Communications are all developing software for interactive TV systems. Bell Atlantic's entry, Stargazer, uses a graphic image of an electronic mall that viewers can roam via remote control. Here are a few other areas in which interactive TV is booming:

- *Retailing.* Spurred by the success of the Home Shopping Network and QVC Network, R.H. Macy, Nordstrom's, Toys 'Я' Us, and others are building experimental TV networks offering online, on-demand, interactive shopping. In time, some predict, your TV will be the gateway to an electronic mall with virtual mannequins created to match your measurements and coloring. By 2001, it is estimated, 17% of U.S. households will be spending almost $10 billion via interactive TV shopping. (By way of comparison, U.S. shoppers now spend $12 billion per year on catalog shopping, which is also expanding into interactive TV.)
- *Advertising and marketing.* The marketers who place commercials on the basis of television ratings, or estimated number of viewers, will be adrift in a world where viewers aren't tied to a specific schedule or list of options. (In fact, some viewers may pay extra, just so they can watch TV commercial free.) Instead, marketers might use demographic information to decide which household sees a commercial for an economy car and which household sees an ad for a luxury model.

Increasingly, advertising will compete with and even replace conventional programming. Case in point: the rise of the *infomercial*—the program-long commercial. Bell Atlantic Corp., for example, is producing a half-hour sitcom about the Ringer family to tout a number of Bell Atlantic services. In the future, viewers may use infomercials to comparison shop for cars and major appliances, instead of going from dealer to dealer.

- *Video rental and sales.* Many interactive TV experiments include some provision for video-on-demand. Instead of racing to the video store to find (or return) a copy of a new release, viewers use their remote controls to select a video title and a start time from an onscreen menu. Pay-per-view charges go directly to a credit card or cable TV bill. At issue here is the $12 billion U.S. consumers spend on video rentals and, in all likelihood, some of the $12 billion they spend on video games every year. In the future, some predict, feature films might go directly to interactive TV, or they might debut simultaneously in theaters and, at a slightly higher cost, on interactive TV.
- *Education.* Many school districts already operate a "homework hotline" so that parents and students can confirm assignments and due dates. So it is only natural to extend these programs to interactive TV. In New Jersey, for example, the Department of Education is creating an interactive TV system that lets students respond by remote control. The system then grades the papers, leaving the instructor more time to work with students. And at Northern Kentucky University, an experiment that compared an online course with a traditional program found that the online course cost 30% less and was rated more highly by students, who got better grades than their traditional counterparts.
- *Law.* Until the dust settles, look for some complex lawsuits over copyrights, program ownership, and distribution rights. Some companies are trying to jump the gun by actively buying digital or video rights. For example, Continuum Products, a Microsoft subsidiary, was created with one goal: to acquire nonexclusive digital rights to some of the world's most famous images.

Interactive Sports, Courtesy of Groupe Videoway.   Here's how *Fortune* magazine projected the future of interactive TV:

> While watching the San Francisco Giants, you'll be able to check the scores of other games under way, scan the lineups, or see a "baseball card" with the stats of any player. Switch to a…video on MTV [a cable television station featuring music videos]: You can send the artist fan mail, order the CD, or call up subtitles with the lyrics if you can't make out [the] words. Flip to *Beverly Hills 90210.* That cool blue blouse Brenda is wearing—you can order it for your teenager. Click. The latest stock quotes appear. Scrutinize a company's financials, then place a buy order directly with your broker.[1]

"Wishful thinking," you say. "Impossible," you think.

But not in Montréal, Canada, where Groupe Videoway is giving sports fans a glimpse of the future today. There, interactive television combines computing, communications, and consumer electronics all in a single system managed by a viewer through a simple converter box on top of the television set (Figure 14.6). Baseball fans can watch Montréal Expos games through the Groupe Videoway system. The converter is the interface to this system, which allows the viewer to

[1]Deutschman, Alan, "Bill Gates' Next Challenge," *Fortune.* December 28, 1992, p. 41.

FIGURE 14.6
The Groupe Videoway Multimedia System
The Videoway Multimedia System provides a wide range of services and applications, from interactive TV and home shopping to electronic mail services and database access.

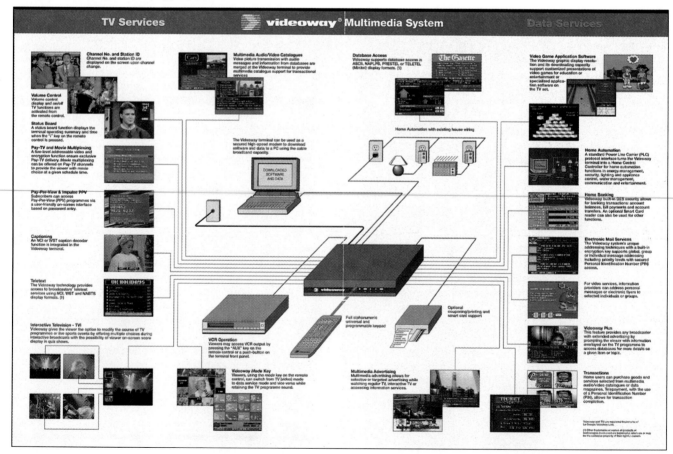

choose four different angles from which to watch the next pitch. A flick of a key on a handheld remote control device changes the view you see, even as the pitch is in the air.

Groupe Videoway's system also allows the viewer to watch more than one image on the television screen (Figure 14.7). For example, the main window might show the action of a hockey game full screen. Another window inserted below or to the right of the main screen displays information about the player, including statistics, career highlights, and perhaps current salary. Want to see the shot or save again? The Groupe Videoway system allows you to call up another window carrying instant replays, as well as a window showing the current score.

E•ON Corp. Puts You in Control.   Home shopping channels have enjoyed tremendous success in the last few years. Now E•ON Corp., a company started in Reston, Virginia as "TV Answer, Inc.," is using HDTV to take home shopping one step further. On the basis of work done by Fernando Morales, a Mexican engineer who created the technology on which the company is based, E•ON has developed an interactive television system based on digital transmission techniques.

With a small box attached to an ordinary television set, a viewer can transmit information from his or her TV to a base station operated by E•ON. The station in turn relays the signals, via satellite, to a broadcasting company, advertising agency, or home shopping firm. At the viewer's choice, the TV displays catalogs, travel guides, or virtually any type of information that can be transmitted, stored, or displayed (Figure 14.8).

The E•ON box, as you may have guessed, contains microcomputer, storage, and transmission components that send and receive the data and information dis-

FIGURE 14.7
Groupe Videoway Interactive Sports
Using the Videoway Interactive Sports System, viewers can use a main screen to watch the game and multiple windows (inserted to the right of or below the main screen) to see close-ups of the action, call up instant replays, and display players' and game statistics and scores.

FIGURE 14.8
E•ON Corp.'s Interactive TV System
Using a series of menus, subscribers to E•ON's interactive TV service can call up multimedia catalogs of their favorite stores' offerings. The system makes ordering as easy as clicking a button—viewers do not need to provide a name, address, or phone number, all of which are transmitted automatically by the system.

played on the screen. (Figure 14.9 shows the technology behind this process.) It also holds data on the location of both the viewer and the receiving sites. Hence, viewers need not enter their address or telephone number, nor are they required to dial a telephone number to reach the recipient at the destination with which they will interact.

E•ON's technology is currently able to process up to 600,000 viewer responses simultaneously in an area of 10,000 homes. These high-speed, high-volume capabilities mean the system is unlikely to become overloaded while transmitting multimedia information or accepting viewer responses.

Reality Check.   If you think all these advances in television, software, and consumer electronics mean more complexity, you're right. But more *complexity* is not the same as more *complication*. Many computer chips will be used to provide the services we've been discussing, manage the retrieval and storage of information, and carry out the processing needed for effective transmission of data and information. The chips—that is, the computers—will be

FIGURE 14.9   Interactive TV Transmission System
ITV uses a variety of transmission media, including modems, radio signals, and cable TV, to transmit information between the viewer and the central computer.

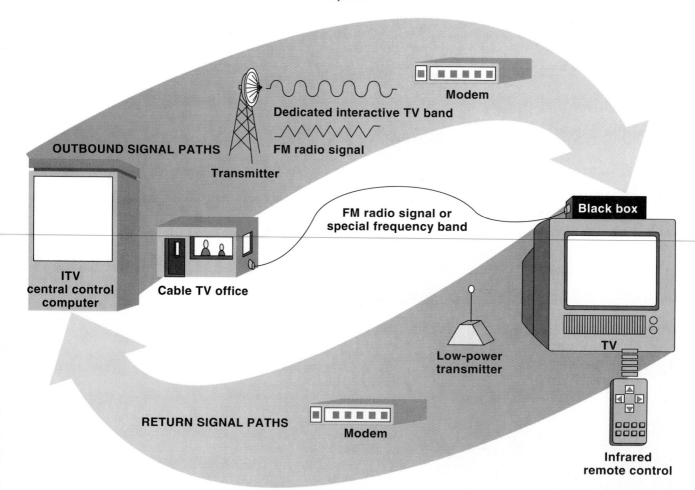

embedded in the system. The technology, not the individuals using the system, will handle the complex tasks.

Today's automobiles are more complicated too, because there are more processes taking place simultaneously in the electrical, engine, and drive-train systems. Yet because the typical automobile has more than 20 embedded computers handling the sending and processing of data, driving it is less complicated than ever before.

Have you noticed that when you get in an automobile, even one you've never driven before, you intuitively know where to place the key, how to start the engine, and where to find the gear shift? That's the way the new combined computer, communications, and consumer electronics systems will be too. People want to use them without having to think about how to use them. Hence, they must be intuitive. If they are not, they will fail. It's that simple…and that complex. ◼

Redefining the IT Industry

The convergence of the three Cs of IT will change both the meaning of IT and the capabilities we associate with it. But it will also change the IT industry as firms join forces to get the most value from their know-how.

Computer and chip vendors have already come together to form alliances, as evidenced by the partnership of IBM, Apple Computer, and Motorola in Talagent, a company whose goal is to develop a new generation of software for interacting with computers and multimedia systems. Microsoft, Intel, and General Instruments (a leading U.S. manufacturer of cable television decoder boxes) have combined forces to design a new control system for interactive television. Working together, they developed a system that makes it possible for viewers to select any of 500 television channels as they arrive via a single cable.

Nonetheless, cooperation may not be the trend in all parts of the IT industry. As we approach the year 2000, we can expect to see companies in the converging industries fighting it out. Public telephone companies and PTTs, cable television operators and television broadcast networks all want to participate in the IT industry traditionally viewed as the domain of computer hardware and software companies. Add the determination of the world's consumer electronics giants and the many newly emerging companies to innovate and capture market share, and you have the makings of rivalries as intense as that between Coke and Pepsi.

CRITICAL CONNECTION 2
COMPUTERTOTS Puts the Byte on Technophobia

A recent survey by Dell Computer Corp. confirmed what many have long suspected: 55% of Americans aren't comfortable using digital alarm clocks, VCRs, answering machines, computers, compact disc players, or car phones. In fact, 25% of all U.S. adults have never used a computer; 32% are actually afraid to use a PC. Although the scores for teens were much more encouraging, the survey shows how far many users have to go if they are to be comfortable living and working with new technology.

To a growing number of preschoolers, though, using a computer is child's play, thanks to an innovative franchise chain called COMPUTERTOTS. COMPUTERTOTS brings computers, printers, instructors, and fun software to preschools, day care centers, YMCAs, and other community centers. The service is free to the organizations; parents who want their children to participate pay $28 to $40 a month, depending on the child's age and the program length.

The program dates back to 1983, when two former special education teachers, Mary Rogers and Karen Marshall, founded Educational Computer Workshop (ECW) Corp. in a suburb of Washington, D.C. Their initial goal was to develop and market software that would carry out the principles of the Massachusetts Institute of Technology's computer projects for young children. From there, it was a relatively simple—and lucrative—step to sell their lessons to preschools and day care centers.

■ Toward an Information Superhighway

The Information Age has shown the world's leaders that a modern national telecommunications infrastructure is essential to maintaining and increasing personal, organizational, and national productivity. Increasingly, most leaders also believe that such an infrastructure is essential for participating in and competing successfully in global commerce.

The demand for this infrastructure points toward a growing need for an additional resource: a national information infrastructure. Analogous to a highway that carries vehicular traffic, an **information superhighway** is a communications network spanning a nation, carrying data and information traffic. From a technical viewpoint, it consists of fiber optics, satellites, and other communications links with huge amounts of transmission capacity. This superhighway will augment the quality of life by linking cities and people and serving as a gateway for the transfer of information for education, research, and commerce.

information superhighway A communications network spanning a nation, carrying data and information traffic.

Communications Highway Infrastructure

What precisely is a **communications infrastructure**? The U.S. Office of Technology Assessment is explicit in its definition: "The communications infrastructure is the underlying structure of technical facilities and institutional arrangements that supports communication via telecommunication, broadcasting, film, audio and video recording, cable, print, and mail."[2] This definition includes not only the hardware and program components of IT, but also the information, people, and procedures to develop, maintain, and apply the infrastructure for society's benefit.

communications infrastructure The underlying structure of technical facilities and institutional arrangements that supports communication via telecommunication, broadcasting, film, audio and video recording, cable, print, and mail.

A national information infrastructure can be "national" only if it does not exclude potential users by limiting physical access or imposing economic barriers (such as the cost of the service) on its use. In the Information Age, it is in the nation's best interests to ensure that all its industry and all its citizens have the access they need.

---

[2]U.S. Congress, Office of Technology Assessment. *Critical Connections: Communication for the Future.* OTA-CIT-407 (1990). Washington, D.C.: U.S. Government Printing Office.

Reality Check.   People frequently try to assess the benefits of investing in a service or building an element of infrastructure by measuring improvement monetarily or statistically. "How will we save by taking this step?" "To what extent will productivity improve?" "How will the costs of production be reduced?" Although these questions are important, focusing solely on financial questions ignores many equally important nonfinancial considerations.

A developed infrastructure is beneficial because it improves other services. New infrastructure can mean improved health care, better transportation, or higher achievements in education, for example. In many cases, it is impossible to quantify the benefits of investing in infrastructure fully, even though we know they're there. For instance, it is impossible to place a financial value on better health. We can describe the cost of poor health only in terms of increased medical costs, but this is only one very limited dimension of the health-care issue. Measuring medical costs alone says nothing about lower achievement levels, a lower standard of living, or even lost career opportunities.

The national highway infrastructure created in the United States produced completely new services and industries. It was not until the national highway system emerged that the interstate trucking system, United Parcel Service (UPS), Holiday Inns and the entire roadside motel industry, and interstate tourism grew. Clearly, building these highways did much more than help existing companies increase their revenues and productivity.

Building the right infrastructure builds future achievements and benefits for people. Infrastructure is a foundation whose value cannot be measured solely or accurately in dollars and cents.   ■

The Superhighway and National Competitive Advantage

In the Information Age, access to a global IT infrastructure, particularly through telecommunications, is at the heart of business and national competitiveness. In the 1990s business environment, it is not enough for many companies to seek a business edge only in their regional market, or even nationally. Companies must either compete internationally or at the very least keep an eye on global competitors, always prepared to develop a response to a rapidly surfacing challenge or opportunity.

For this reason, national leaders are seeking to connect IT sites within their countries to encourage the sharing of information in a way that makes each organization more competitive internationally. In the United States, Vice President Al Gore is promoting a national network of supercomputers located at major universities, research centers, and national laboratories. Gore's plan calls for interconnecting each node on the network by fiber optics, thus providing the capability for high-speed transfer of large quantities of data and information. The plan also calls for an evolutionary extension of current scientific networks in the United States.

Japan, Germany, and France are also developing plans and initiatives for national information highways. Japan intends to have its network completed between 2010 and 2015. Some U.S. experts say the United States is not moving quickly enough to do the same, estimating that at the current rate the United States will not have a national information highway until 2037. Nonetheless, the United States is much closer to a superhighway than are the nations of Latin America, many of which lack even basic phone service. (See the Global IT box on page 571 titled "Potholes on the Information Highway.") A national initiative is underway to push for more rapid development of a U.S. information superhighway.

Questions in the Development of the Superhighway

Questions, questions. When you're taking the first few steps along a path that will eventually turn into a cross-country superhighway system, plenty of questions are bound to emerge. As each of these questions is answered, the highway will move one step closer to completion.

Technical Questions.   The developers of the information highway face many technical questions: Will the highway be built from glass fiber or rely on wireless satellite links? What minimum bandwidth is needed? And on what underlying computer and communications technology will the highway be built? Many believe the Internet (see Chapter 9) will be the foundation on which the information highway will be built. The rate of IT change is rapid and accelerating. Today's ideal solution may change even as the highway is being built, and some features will be obsolete even before they are developed and implemented.

Reality Check.   Thoughts of developing a national information superhighway tend to turn naturally toward technical issues like communication lines, transmission speeds, and network reliability. Addressing these issues properly is, of course, essential.

Often overlooked, however, are the storage needs that a superhighway will create. Keep in mind that the network will be used more for transmitting than for processing data and information. The data will be stored in the network so they are accessible on demand. This means that huge servers will be needed to store the data. Imagine the complete video library of MGM, Columbia Pictures, and Paramount Pictures, plus every volume in the U.S. Library of Congress, all available online. All this information together is a drop in the bucket compared to the full scope of data and information that consumers and service providers alike will want to store. ■

Time and Cost of Development.   Every country knows that the costs of developing an information superhighway are high, although they are hard pressed to come up with an accurate figure when the project is likely to span decades. Many estimates of costs and development time for a U.S. information superhighway have been prepared, running as high as $140 billion and 25 years, but no one knows for sure.

The Role of Government.   What role will the government play in developing the information highway? In most countries, national highway systems were developed under government supervision and according to government specifications. Should this be government's role here too, or should IT industries make these decisions? Once the information highway is in place, should the government set standards and then enforce them? Should it regulate who can interconnect with the superhighway and for what purpose? Is the network more likely to be successful if it is managed by the government?

These issues are particularly tricky because there is no precedent for determining the respective roles of government and private enterprise. And, unfortunately, there may not be time to hear all of the arguments on both sides before a decision must be made.

Source of Funding.   Will companies and industries pay the cost of designing, developing, and running the national information highway? If not, is there any rea-

GLOBAL IT

Potholes on the Information Highway: A Challenge for Latin America

IMAGINE ORDERING PHONE SERVICE ONLY TO HEAR THAT YOU'LL have to pay a few thousand dollars and be patient. The phone company has about a million orders on backlog. If you can't wait one to five years for a legal installation, you may need to head for the black market or bribe a phone company employee. If you already have phone service, you can expect intermittent cross-talk, static, howls, incomplete calls, or no dial tone—in which case you have to decide whether the line is merely out of order or if it has been commandeered by a black market entrepreneur, who physically snips existing lines and runs them to new locations, leaving you stuck with the bill. Now try to imagine using such a phone system to compete in the global economy.

This quandary faced the "Big Three" economies of Latin America—Mexico, Argentina, and Brazil—for many years. After long debate, they announced in 1990 plans to privatize, or sell public shares in, a number of state-owned industries to private or foreign investors. To make the shares attractive to investors, they promised the new owners monopolies for four to ten years, as long as they met ambitious schedules for making major capital improvements. The companies for sale included telephone companies, banks, utilities, mines, airlines, mass-transit systems, and oil and steel companies. Venezuela and Chile soon instituted a similar program.

For the nations' leaders, the policy shift was a gamble with three goals. First, they wanted to reduce government payrolls and redirect the savings into economic growth programs. Second, they wanted to generate capital for launching social programs and reducing their foreign debt. Third, they wanted outside investment help to modernize and manage their infrastructures. Telecommunications capabilities were especially important here. Brazil's decaying phone system, for example, had led General Motors to move its Latin American headquarters from São Paulo, Brazil, to Miami, Florida.

By 1992, some of the world's leading telecommunications companies had bought major shares in the state-owned companies. Others, such as Motorola and AT&T, had signed contracts to build copper wire, fiber-optic, cellular, or two-way radio networks. (In many cases, cellular networks are the fastest way to provide basic phone service where none exists.) Financial institutions such as Citibank, Coopers & Lybrand, and Morgan Stanley provided financing, appraised assets, and negotiated terms.

In Mexico City, street vendor Pablo Sandoval shows his telephone equipment to a potential customer. Buying from a street vendor is one of the most efficient ways of purchasing a telephone in Mexico; getting basic phone service is much more of a challenge.

Still, the new owners faced some daunting technical challenges. In Mexico, nine of ten families lacked basic phone service. In Venezuela, more than a million phone lines had faulty connections. In Brazil, only 7% of the public network had been upgraded to digital technology. In Argentina, there had been no capital improvements over the previous decade; some switches dated back to 1913. Meanwhile, in Chile, most industry had no phone service at all.

The new owners and their managers also faced social and political challenges, including employees who feared massive layoffs. In Venezuela, a GTE-led consortium had to deal with a failed military coup and violent nationalistic street demonstrations.

Despite the risks and technical challenges, many investors have been delighted to find themselves in the middle of a telecommunications boom, fed by Latin America's high demand for modern phone service. Where else in the world could they find double- and triple-digit returns on their investments?

son that taxpayers should fund such an initiative? For that matter, *must* government fund an information superhighway if private industry cannot?

The huge cost of constructing a national information highway makes it unlikely that any single private source will undertake the project or investment. At best, this suggests that the highway will ultimately be comprised of a collection of interconnected networks—a network of networks, so to speak.

universal service The principle whereby it is assured that anyone who wants basic service can receive it at low cost.

Provision of Universal Service.   The principle of **universal service** in the telephone industry, whereby it is assured that anyone who wants low-cost, basic phone service can receive it, has been guiding government-regulated telecommunications companies since the 1930s. Will the same principle apply to the information highway? If so, will carriers be obliged to interconnect everyone in their region for the same basic service rate? Should businesses pay more for the interconnection than households do?

Many companies that provide communications service but are outside the regulated telephone industry, such as cable companies, are not bound by universal service rules. Will this situation change when an information superhighway is put in place?

Determining Success.   What determines the success of an information superhighway? If success depends on the revenues generated by the highway, what will people and companies be willing to pay for using the highway? Or should the success of the highway be evaluated on the basis of the new services and indirect benefits it stimulates?

Part of the problem of determining success stems from mixed thoughts on when the network should be constructed in the first place. Should an information highway be built to stimulate demand for consumer and business services? Or should it be developed only as a result of demand for those services?

CRITICAL CONNECTION 3
Bridging the Gaps in the Information Superhighway

Ameritech   Just one mile of fiber-optic cable. That's all Tom DeFanti wanted. DeFanti, codirector of an advanced virtual reality research center at the University of Illinois at Chicago, needed the one-mile cable to link his lab to AT&T's experimental fiber-optic network. The hook-up promised opportunities for both parties. For DeFanti's researchers, it presented the opportunity to send virtual reality and multimedia transmissions to other research centers. For AT&T, it provided a great way to test an upgraded fiber-optic technology and get practical answers to the technical challenges of high-speed data transmission. That's why DeFanti was so frustrated by the one-mile gap between his lab and the AT&T lines that lie about a mile away.

This gap illustrates some of the challenges facing the creators of the information superhighway. Ironically, though, the biggest challenge isn't a technical one. In fact, the fiber-optic technology AT&T was testing may become an economical and practical way of upgrading the speed and bandwidth of today's telephone system, paving the way for multimedia and other data-intensive transmissions. A shortage of optical fibers isn't a challenge either. In fact, many telecommunications experts say the nation already has an information superhighway made up of miles of "dark fiber," unused fiber-optic cables installed by the telephone companies, just in case they ever needed the extra capacity. Rather, the biggest challenge is deciding who controls the dark fiber and who has the right to use it: a question the government is attempting to answer.

A Final Word

The growth of the automobile industry in the 1920s, '30s, and '40s brought about the development of the interstate highway system in the 1950s and '60s. It took decades to built the network of highways that now crisscross the United States, and business has never been the same.

Air travel came a little later, bringing with it even greater opportunities. Yet it took many years to build the infrastructure supporting each development in the air-travel industry. Airport systems and air-traffic-control systems were developed relatively early in the era of flight. Yet only in recent years did travel agents and computerized reservation systems emerge. When they did, they played a principle role in restructuring the industry and the way people viewed the industry for both business and pleasure.

Business and society today are only a few years into the Information Age. The resources and infrastructure needed to keep up with the momentum of information technology are still being developed. Even though IT's impact has already been tremendous, we continue to look ahead, seeking to determine what *will be* and what *can be*.

In a few years, computers, communication systems, and consumer electronics will be one and the same. Computers will process all forms of data and information without distinction between numeric data or animated images. Telephones will handle images as easily as they do sound. Television and other consumer electronics devices will function as both computers and communication systems. No one has ever lived through such a convergence of technologies before, and it's clear that the real excitement of the Information Age will come first from asking the right questions, then using know-how to determine the right answers. Onward!

SUMMARY OF LEARNING OBJECTIVES

1 Identify the "three Cs" of information technology and discuss how the definition of IT is changing in the Information Age. The three Cs of information technology are computers, communications networks, and consumer electronics. The definition of IT is evolving through the incorporation of consumer electronics, a broadened definition of "communications carrier," a broadened definition of "software," the arrival of interactive television, and the redefinition of the IT industry.

2 Describe the importance of consumer electronics as an element of IT. Multimedia is paving the

way for the incorporation of consumer electronics—electronic devices used to satisfy people's needs and wants rather than to manufacture products or deliver services—into IT. Many people are coming to expect images, voice, and/or animation alongside data and text.

3 Explain the expanded definition of "communications carrier." With the advancement of technology, the term "communications carrier" has come to refer to more than just the telephone company or PTT. Television networks and cable companies are increasingly becoming important parts of a nation's communications capacity because communication cables can transport all types of signals.

4 Discuss the change in the definition of "software" to incorporate content as well as programs. In the computer industry, "software" has often been used to mean "computer programs." Recently, software has come to mean *content*—data and information—as well as the means to manipulate it. Software can also be seen as any element that gives value to hardware.

5 Explain why TV is an important type of IT and how interactive TV works. Television is becoming an important type of IT for three reasons: (1) While many homes have microcomputers, many more have television sets; (2) television technology is advancing rapidly; and (3) if *high definition TV (HDTV)* uses digital technology, drawing a distinction between TV and the PC will be difficult. If TV has both computer and communications capabilities, its functions will change. Interactive TV will be a television with a keyboard, storage capability, and the capacity to transmit and receive vast amounts of information.

6 Discuss how the IT industry is changing. The convergence of the three Cs of IT is changing the

IT industry as firms join forces to get the most from their know-how and the global economy becomes more competitive.

7 Distinguish between a communications network and an information superhighway and give two reasons why world leaders are seeking to develop information superhighways. An *information superhighway* is a communications network spanning a nation, carrying data and information traffic. It consists of fiber-optic networks with huge amounts of transmission capacity. Most world leaders believe that a modern national telecommunications infrastructure is essential to maintaining and increasing personal, organization, and national productivity. They also believe that it is essential for both participating and competing successfully in global commerce.

8 Describe six issues involved in designing and developing an information superhighway. There are six issues involved in developing an information superhighway: technical questions, time and cost, the role of the government, sources of funding, the provision of universal service, and the challenges of determining the success of the superhighway.

KEY TERMS

communications infrastructure   568
consumer electronics   558
high-definition television (HDTV)   561
information superhighway   568
interactive TV (ITV)   563
universal service   571

CRITICAL CONNECTIONS

Philips Electronics

1. Philips Takes a Gamble on Multimedia

Philips' Imagination Machine and the CD-I format offer some clear advantages. Chief among them are simplicity and familiarity; most consumers have television sets and they understand the concept of a VCR-like device that can play prerecorded titles. Another plus is the emphasis on education software.

But the Imagination Machine also faces a number of marketing challenges. True, consumers are excited about multimedia, but they are also confused by the options. Is the Imagination Machine just another game? (It can play many Nintendo titles.) Is it supposed to replace the trusty VCR? (Or are consumers supposed to fiddle with the connections every time they want to record a show or play a videotape?)

Price was another challenge. The Imagination Machine's original list price was around $1,000. Faced with high interest but sluggish sales, Philips dropped the price; by the summer of 1993, the list price was about $600. In the meantime, PC makers had launched their own price war. Multimedia PCs, once a high-priced rarity, were being sold at a discount, tempting consumers who might never have considered the purchase of a computer.

Despite the competition, Philips continued to make inroads into the consumer market. Within a year, it had demonstrated CD-I disks with full-screen, full-motion video, which could be used to show feature films. Soon, PolyGram Records, a Philips subsidiary, was releasing music videos on CD-I. By the summer of 1993, a number of electronics companies had announced they would support the Philips format for feature movies, and Philips had persuaded Paramount Communications to offer *Top Gun* and other popular titles in the CD-I format.

Questions for Discussion

1. Which elements of Philips' strategy seem most effective? Least effective? Explain your answers.

2. By mid-1992, Philips had supplemented its consumer model with an expandable, professional model geared to organizations that need to make interactive multimedia sales and training presentations. Many companies felt the Philips hardware and software, which included a portable unit with a color screen and cost about $3,000, was a cost-effective alternative to laser-disc-based systems costing about $13,000. What does this suggest to you about the marketplace for Philips CD-I products?

3. What does Philips' experience suggest about the near future of the Information Age for consumers? For manufacturers of consumer electronics and PCs? For the publishers of software?

2. COMPUTERTOTS Puts the Byte on Technophobia

By the end of 1993, COMPUTERTOTS had sold 130 franchises and was collecting revenues of more than $3 million, doubling both franchises and revenues over the previous year.

Many of the franchise owners are former corporate professionals, who appreciate the franchise's support and elastic schedules. Deborah Cole, for example, is a single mother who began her career as a salesperson for IBM and later became a regional sales manager at a major software company. Today she and her staff of fifteen have brought COMPUTERTOTS to more than 700 children in Chicago-area day care centers and schools. For the three- to five-year-olds, the half-hour sessions are filled with games, puzzles, graphics, and fun projects like using child-sized desktop publishing programs to create holiday greeting cards. Without knowing it, the children are learning a lot about technology and terminology—and having lots of fun in the process.

Questions for Discussion

1. Why do you think so many adults are uncomfortable using technology? What solutions can you suggest to remedy this situation?

2. What are the advantages of the COMPUTERTOTS program? The possible disadvantages?

3. Are private programs like COMPUTERTOTS enough to create the technological literacy needed for the future? If not, how might technological literacy be improved?

3. Bridging the Gaps in the Information Superhighway

Ameritech

The one-mile gap that stymied DeFanti represents a physical gap between AT&T's long-distance lines and the local lines controlled by Ameritech (formerly Illinois Bell). But it also represents a marketing and regulatory gap between Ameritech and its competitors. Ameritech had dark fiber in the one-mile gap that DeFanti could have used to link up to AT&T's lines, but Ameritech had a policy against leasing dark fiber to organizations that could install activating equipment and then bypass the telephone company, thus cutting into its profits.

The prohibition dates back to the mid-1980s, when other telephone companies began leasing dark fiber to a few select large customers. After smaller customers complained to the Federal Communications Commission—and won—the telephone companies labeled the practice an experiment and tried to drop it. The issue didn't go away, though. In the summer of 1993, while DeFanti was struggling to find his mile of dark fiber, the FCC and a federal court in Washington, D.C., were grappling with the question of whether the FCC could require the telephone companies to provide dark-fiber services to potential competitors. Many experts predicted that the telephone companies would fight the dark-fiber issue until government regulations were eased, giving the telephone companies the right to offer new and lucrative communications services.

Questions for Discussion

1. What does the dark-fiber issue indicate about the role of government in building the information superhighway?

2. Should Ameritech be required to lease dark fiber? Present an argument in favor of the telephone companies and an argument in favor of their potential competitors.

3. At present, government regulators base telephone rates on the initial cost of the system and the amount individual customers use it. What changes might be required in the future when high-speed, high-capacity data lines are able to transmit millions of bits per second? Can you suggest a fair basis for the telephone bill of tomorrow?

REVIEW QUESTIONS

1. In what ways is the definition of information technology (IT) changing?

2. What is the "third C" of information technology and what is its relationship to multimedia?

3. In what way is the definition of "communications carrier" changing? Why?

4. In what way is the definition of "software" changing? What does this change mean for IT in general?

5. Discuss three reasons why television is becoming an important type of IT.

6. What is high-definition television (HDTV)? How do United States developments in HDTV technology differ from those in Japan?

7. What is interactive TV?

8. How and why is the definition of the IT industry changing? What does this mean for consumers and businesses?

9. What is an information superhighway? Name two reasons why world leaders are seeking to develop an information superhighway.

10. What is a communications infrastructure?

11. Describe the relationship between an information superhighway and a nation's competitive advantage in global markets.

12. Give three examples of technical questions that the designers of an information superhighway must address.

13. Discuss the issues surrounding the role of government and the sources of funding in developing an information superhighway.

14. What is the principle of universal service and how does it relate to the information superhighway?

15. What criteria may be used to determine the success of an information superhighway?

DISCUSSION QUESTIONS

1. CUC, Inc., was losing money as a shop-by-PC service until it transformed itself into a buyers' club in which members shop by phone for discounts on travel, auto services, insurance, and more than 250,000 products. By 1993, CUC had 28 million members and was ready for a third transformation—into an interactive shopping network for the United States's 60 million cable subscribers. Why do you think CUC is more successful as a phone-based service than it was as a PC-based service? What are its chances as an interactive TV service?

2. What might the success of CUC and other interactive shopping services mean for retail-dependent businesses, like commercial real estate? For society?

3. Many interactive TV experiments are being sponsored by cable companies, like TCI, Inc., which already require a subscriber fee and may demand higher fees for the new interactive services. What are the pros and cons of such a fee-based service for cable and interactive TV?

4. AT&T recently cooperated with the telephone service provider in Mexico in building a digital network that would offer improved service for five major U.S.-Mexico border areas, including the free-trade zone containing many *maquiladoras* (United States-owned manufacturing plants located very close to border in Mexico). Why would AT&T enter into such an agreement?

SUGGESTED READINGS

Davis, Stan, and Bill Davidson, *2020 Vision: Transform Your Business Today to Succeed in Tomorrow's Economy*. New York: Simon & Schuster, 1991. An excellent discussion showing how computers and data communication networks are reshaping the structure of modern business, allowing firms to improve existing products and services and to create new ones.

Egan, B.L., *Information Superhighways: The Economics of Advanced Public Communication Networks*. Norwood, MA: Artech House, 1991. A comprehensive discussion of the issues, challenges, and opportunities surrounding the development of national communications networks.

Keen, Peter G.W., *Competing in Time: Using Telecommunications for Competitive Advantage*. Cambridge, MA: Ballinger, 1988. A balanced and practical analysis of the changing role of communications systems in business. Offers unique insight for both the IT professional and executive officers.

Malone, Thomas W., et. al, "Intelligent Information-Sharing Systems," *Communications of the ACM,* 30, no. 5 (May 1987) pp. 390–402. A thought-provoking discussion of a prototype information system designed to support problem-solving needs. The system can be tailored to personal needs and is useful for screening and filtering information transmitted through communication systems.

Toffler, Alvin, *Powershift*. New York: Bantam Books, 1990. A ground-breaking book in which Toffler, one of today's leading futurists, describes how knowledge is creating tremendous shifts in power at both the local and global levels.

Wriston, Walter B., *The Twilight of Sovereignty*. New York: Free Press, 1992. A discussion of the effects of the worldwide information revolution, with a look to the future.

CASE STUDY

R.R. Donnelley & Sons Co. Mixes Traditional Values with New IT

RR DONNELLEY & SONS COMPANY

IN BUSINESS, THE WINNERS ARE OFTEN the companies that can adapt traditional values to changing times. Take the case of Chicago-based R.R. Donnelley & Sons Co., the United States's largest commercial printer of books, catalogs, phone books, and magazines. Founded in 1864, the company has always seen itself as more than "just" a printer. In the words of Gaylord Donnelley, grandson of founder Richard Robert Donnelley, writing just after World War II: "We are very much a part of the knowledge industry. And at the same time…Donnelley is dynamically involved in news, merchandising, communication, and industry—in fact, in the breath and heartbeat of the national and worldwide human community." Today, Donnelley is using this vision to become a leader in the Information Age.

In the words of Donnelley CEO John R. Walter, "We want to be a supermarket for communications. We want to provide the greatest array of services for anyone who needs to disseminate information." To this end, the company has redefined its competition to include not just printers but any medium that distributes information, including television, radio, telephones, and computers. Under this new plan, the company has devoted itself to working with customers to meet their *future* needs. To do this, R.R. Donnelley has followed four basic strategies.

First, it streamlined its organization, creating a single division to oversee newer ventures in financial printing, computer-based mapping, electronic publishing, and computer documentation.

Second, it invested in new technology. In 1983, for example, the financial printing division began using a satellite network. With it, the company could print a securities prospectus simultaneously in the United States, Japan, and Europe. Furthermore, the prospectus could be delivered on paper, on disk, or both. Even the company's traditional but highly competitive businesses, like telephone directories, are getting a boost from high tech. Donnelley's FastAds system uses an Apple Macintosh, an electronic camera, a color printer, and a color TV to let salespeople create and proof ads on the spot. Once the client approves the ad, it can be sent over telephone lines to a Donnelley printing plant.

Third, Donnelley has formed strategic alliances. Perhaps its most important partner has been Compton's NewMedia, publisher of *Compton's Multimedia Encyclopedia,* which is bundled with many CD-ROM drives and multimedia computers. Under the terms of the 1992 agreement, Donnelley and NewMedia became a "publisher's publisher," a production and distribution service that can offer as much or as little help as a prospective CD-ROM publisher needs or wants. As part of the agreement, Donnelley got exclusive worldwide rights to use Compton's SmarTrieve Publishing Toolkit, which includes indexing and text search software needed to create interactive books and reference works. Some of the first titles the new partners handled included an interactive dictionary and thesaurus for Merriam-Webster, the *Billboard History of Rock 'n' Roll* (with music and video), and a multimedia golf guide to California and Hawaii.

Fourth, the company has positioned itself as a global printer, buying or building printing plants and related businesses in the United Kingdom, France, Spain, Scotland, Hong Kong, Mexico, and Barbados. One goal was simply to be close to international customers. Another was to use these new plants to offer better service. Consider the business of printing computer documentation and packaging diskettes, something Donnelley was doing for eight out of the top ten computer companies in late 1991. Because all the Donnelley plants use the same processes and equipment, as well as electronic mail, electronic data interchange, and CIM, the company can offer worldwide, real-time printing, inventory, and shipping of software products. As a result, new software releases can be launched on the same day, worldwide.

The new strategy racked up some impressive accomplishments. In just a few years, Donnelley…

- Worked with Intel Corp. to create a CD-ROM catalog. As the world's third largest maker of semiconductors, Intel needed to distribute 25,000 pages of technical data to 300,000 design engineers around the world, as well as add data on 50 new products a year. Donnelley rose to the challenge. In appreciation, Intel gave Donnelley an Outstanding Achievement award as a supplier with "unique and fresh solutions."
- Created a multimedia kiosk displaying a CD-ROM catalog of the 100,000 items sold through Tandy's Radio Shack electronics chain.

John Walter of R.R. Donnelly is using information technology to expand and customize his company's product and service line. Says Walter: "Probably about 50% of our revenues by [the year] 2000 will come from businesses that we weren't in ten years ago."

- Used a vast consumer database to help Nynex create a set of nine CD-ROM discs containing a national telephone directory of 77 million names and addresses.
- Provided the technology needed to transfer the complete text of *Fodor's '94 Travel Manager: Top U.S. Cities,* plus interactive maps, to a format compatible with Apple Computer's Newton, a personal digital assistant.

To some extent, of course, Donnelley had no choice but to go hi-tech. As security analysts were fond of pointing out, most of the company's strength was in mature, slow-growth, or even declining markets. Although these traditional ink-on-paper markets still produce the majority of the printer's income, the new ventures have the potential to bring in as much or more revenue in the long term.

As an example of the company's ongoing resilience, consider what happened when one of its biggest cus-tomers, Sears Roebuck & Co., announced it would stop printing its catalog—the "Big Book"—in 1993. The decision cost Donnelley $50 million in annual revenue. Nonetheless, within a few months, Donnelley was back at Sears, talking about ways it could help the retailer with database management, direct marketing, and logistics. The company is also exploring ways to offer material for interactive TV and looking into business opportunities in China.

Questions for Discussion

1. How do Donnelley's strategies reflect the changing nature of IT?
2. Which of Donnelley's strategies are most important? Most risky? Explain your answers.
3. How might the creation of the information superhighway affect Donnelley's business?

Looking for Directions on the Information Highway

WHILE THE VISION OF 500 CHANNELS WITH PAY-FOR-VIEW movies, interactive game shows, instant-replay sporting events, and teleshopping are thrilling, society faces a number of deeper questions about the new media and what they mean. Consider some of the issues:

Do people want to interact with their televisions? Although our television sets are on an average of seven hours a day, we seldom give them our full attention. Researchers who monitored TV viewers' brain waves have found that they quickly fall into patterns of relaxation and passivity. Other researchers have found that one-third to one-fourth of viewers are primarily involved in some other activity, such as household chores, talking, or even reading. Moreover, people give their highest attention to movies and their lowest to commercials and news broadcasts. Will these numbers change when viewers are given a chance to interact with their televisions? Trip Hawkins thinks so. He is president of 3DO Co., one of the many companies that is developing software for interactive TV. And he may be right, as a new generation of consumers bring new attitudes and expectations to the familiar activity of "watching" television.

What does "interactive" mean? At the simplest level, the answer is obvious. The viewers get to—have to—do more than select a channel and sit back. But will their interaction be limited to deciding *when* they will view programming offered by media giants—whether it is a news broadcast, a pay-for-view movie, or a videologue—or will their interaction determine the actual content? Will they have a chance to interact with other people or will they still be relatively isolated?

Compare, for example, the experience of playing along with a television game show with the experience of "talking" or playing the game with a live person at the other end of a modem. That is the experience millions of people now enjoy when they log onto computer bulletin boards and form electronic friendships with other bulletin board users. Howard Rheingold, a well-known writer on virtual reality and information technology, describes these electronic relationships as the basis of "virtual communities."[1] In writing about his experience with the WELL (short for the Whole Earth 'Lectronic Link), he describes the strong emotional bonds that lead electronic friends to bring their families and meet "in real life" at annual pot-luck picnics.

Will interactive TV mean the death of reading? Social critics complain that consumers' infatuation with television,

computer games, and videos is drastically cutting into the time they spend reading and thinking about great ideas and social issues. Media analyst Mark Landler, for example, notes that in 1993, Americans spent $340 billion on entertainment, versus just $270 billion in private and public funds for education.

Despite these gloomy predictions, book publishing is on the rise and newspaper revenues continue to increase. Due to time constraints, though, fewer people are reading daily newspapers. In response, many newspapers are going electronic. Consider the vision of Roger Fidler, founder of Knight-Ridder Tribune Graphics in Boulder, Colorado. Reasoning that the newspaper is already an interactive medium, he foresees the day when readers will use an electronic "newspanel" to call up summary headlines or more detailed, in-depth analyses and graphics, interspersed with discrete advertisements. Instead of being limited to publishing "all the news that fits," newspapers could combine the benefits of newspapers and magazines in a format that could be customized by the reader. As a bonus, newspaper and magazine publishers could reduce the amount of money they spend printing and delivering paper publications.

Readers of the *Chicago Tribune* can already sample Fidler's vision by logging onto Chicago Tribune Online, an electronic news service offered in conjunction with America Online/Chicago Online, and entering a "Chicago Online Newsextra" code. These codes, which appear at the end of traditional stories as filler items throughout the paper, allow readers to access additional information. In addition, America Online offers the text of several magazines.

How much are people willing to pay for the new services? Most people are forced to watch commercials as the price of "free" television. In addition, about 60% of U.S. households are now paying about $20 a month for basic cable services and perhaps $10 more for premium channels and the occasional pay-per-view special. But it is not clear how much more people will be willing to pay for the new range of interactive services. Rupert Murdoch, founder of Fox Broadcasting Co., thinks that people will balk if they have to pay $60 to $70 a month for interactive services. A Time Warner interactive TV experiment in Queens, New York, seems to reinforce Murdoch's view. Although Time Warner was pleased with the response, viewer resistance forced it to drop the pay-per-view price from $4.95 to $3.95 per movie.

If the new interactive services are too expensive, social critics worry, we may become a world of interactive haves

The future of interactive TV is bright, but some parents have expressed worries. Studies show that children who watch violence on television tend to engage in violent behavior themselves. Does this mean that violent interactive programs should be restricted to adults?

and have-nots, as the information highway bypasses poor or rural areas. This is one reason the U.S. Federal Communications Commission regulates the cost of basic cable, trying to ensure that it remains "affordable" to a majority of the nation's households.

Who will police the information technology?   Because electronic bandwith has been limited and because broadcast media are vital for dispensing the news and information needed by informed citizens, most nations regulate broadcasters. In the United States, for example, the Federal Communications Commission grants broadcast licenses that require the station to serve the public interest. In the early years, the FCC maintained strict standards, such as the Fairness Doctrine (stations must allow opposing viewpoints to be heard) and the Equal Time Rule (stations must provide equal coverage of opposing political candidates). To prevent the growth of media monopolies, companies could own only so many stations, and the amount of broadcast time devoted to commercials was strictly limited.

In the 1980s, though, the communications industry was one of many to be deregulated. Reasoning that competition in a free marketplace dominated by strong, commercial ventures would determine which broadcasters best served the public interest, the FCC began to liberalize some of its policies as it struggled with both technical and policy issues. Today, the FCC's policies and practices remain open to debate. If it is too slow to adapt to technical advances, some charge, the FCC will hurt the economy. If it gives up too much control to commercial ventures, others charge, it will let the quality of programming (which some already see as too violent and sexual) slip.

Finally, because we are so used to the idea of limited bandwith, no one knows what it will mean to have access to 500 channels. It may be that some of those channels will be used for "electronic democracy," letting citizens participate in government hearings from the comfort of their homes. Already, many local communities are televising town meetings and hearings over cable access channels. Citizens who don't have the time to attend can still watch and pick up their phone to air their opinions and get instant feedback from local officials—interactive democracy at its best.

Discussion Questions

1. Commercial television is often criticized for its commercialism, violence, and racial and gender stereotyping. How could these problems be controlled in the interactive future?

2. Why should business people be concerned about the way the media are used?

3. Some broadcast analysts are worried about the growth of "infomercials," which blur the distinction between talk shows and commercials. Is this a valid concern? Do consumers need to be protected against this sort of commercial appeal?

[1]See Howard Rheingold, *The Virtual Community* (Reading, Mass.: Addison-Wesley, 1993).

Numbers above the timeline at the center of the page correspond to the photos and caption numbers in red boxes.

5 Baron Gottfried Wilhelm von Leibniz designs calculation machine (working version produced in 1694 from earlier plans)

1 Lascaux cave paintings created

3 Johannes Gutenberg invents printing press

6 Charles Babbage devises "difference engine" to mechanize calculation of trigonometric and logarithmic tables

1
15,000 - 10,000 BC

2
3500 BC

3200 BC

Ts'ai invents paper
▲
AD 105

3
AD 1400

4
1642

5
1671

1729

6
1812

7
1831

▼
Egyptians first use ink

▼
Electronic pulses first sent over a wire

2 Sumerians develop a system of writing

7 Joseph Henry builds first electromagnetic telegraph

4 Blaise Pascal invents the Pascaline adding machine

8 Alexander Graham Bell patents first telephone

10 Howard H. Aiken, Ph.D. candidate at Harvard University, devises Mark I, the first large-scale automatic digital calculator

Charles Babbage designs "Analytical Engine"

Transatlantic telegraph cable is laid

Scottish inventor John Baird demonstrates his invention, the television

U.S. Congress passes the Communications Act of 1934, which creates the Federal Communications Commission (FCC), whose sole purpose is to regulate the U.S. telecommunications industry

| 1834 | 1838 | 1866 | 8 1876 | 9 1890s | 1921 | 1926 | 1928 | 1934 | 10 1937 | 11 1939 |

Samuel Morse develops Morse Code

U.S. Congress passes the Graham Act, which recognizes and legitimizes AT&T's monopoly for providing telecommunications services in the U.S.

First television programming begins in U.S.

9 Herman Hollerith, of the U.S. Bureau of the Census, devises punch card system and punch card machine

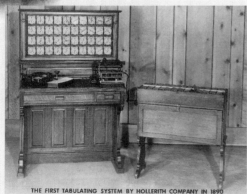

THE FIRST TABULATING SYSTEM BY HOLLERITH COMPANY IN 1890

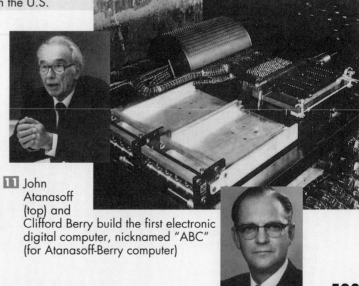

11 John Atanasoff (top) and Clifford Berry build the first electronic digital computer, nicknamed "ABC" (for Atanasoff-Berry computer)

14 UNIVAC I, the first commercially used computer, announced

12 U.S. FCC devises rules for commercial television broadcasting

William Shockley, Walter Brattain, and John Bardeen announce their invention of the transistor at AT&T Bell Laboratories

First packet radios are introduced to the U.S. market

12			13 ▲		14 & 15		16	▲	17	18	19
1940	1945	1946	1948	1951-1958	1951	1952	1953	1954	1959 - 1964	1959	1960	1963

John von Neumann, at Princeton University, develops concept of stored program computer

The vacuum tube (first) generation of computers

UNIVAC I used to tabulate the U.S. national election vote, declaring Dwight D. Eisenhower to be the elected president only 45 minutes after the polls closed

Digital Equipment Corporation builds the first successful minicomputer

13 J. Prosper Eckert, graduate student, and Dr. John W. Mauchly develop the Electronic Numerical Integrator and Calculator (ENIAC) at the Moore School of Engineering, University of Pennsylvania

15 First color television broadcast in the U.S.

16 IBM begins manufacture of line of business computers

584

17 Transistor generation (second generation) of computers

19 Theodore H. Maiman operates first laser

21 Bill Gates (right) and Paul Allen found Microsoft

IBM announces the System/360 line of computers—the first-ever family of compatible computers
▲
1964

20
1965-1970

Computer beats human opponent at chess for the first time
▲
1967

- Beginning of microminiaturized integrated circuit generation (fourth generation) of computers
- Robert Metcalf develops the first local area network (LAN) while at Xerox PARC
- U.S. FCC concludes a study known as Computer Inquiry I determining that, although the data processing and telecommunications industries are growing closer together, the data processing industry, which is unregulated, should not be subject to its control
▲
1969　　　　　**1971**　　　　　**1972**

Intel introduces the 8080 micro-processor
▲
1974

21
1975

Digital Research, Inc.'s Gary Kildall develops CP/M, first operating system for a microcomputer
▲
1976

22
1977

- Edgar F. Codd publishes the first in a series of papers defining relational databases
- Carterphone Decision by the FCC for the first time allows the attachment of non-telephone company devices to the telephone network
- Microwave Communications, Inc. (MCI) requires public telephone companies to interconnect the lines of private companies (like MCI) to the public telephone network, thereby giving their customers nationwide access

The first video game, Pong, becomes an overnight success

- Altair 8800, the world's first microcomputer system, is released as a kit to be assembled
- First user groups are formed
- Cray-1 supercomputer announced

- Commodore introduces PET microcomputer
- Tandy TRS-80 microcomputer introduced

18 COBOL specifications introduced; Grace Hopper, who coined the term "bug," is one member of the COBOL development team

20 Integrated circuit generation (third generation) of computers

22 Apple II microcomputer debuts (created by Steve Wozniak, bottom, and Steve Jobs, right)

23 5 1/4" floppy disk becomes the standard for microcomputers

24 CompuServe and The Source online services begin operation

27 First compact disc (CD) player sold

- Microsoft agrees to develop MS-DOS for IBM's forthcoming PC
- First relational database management system, Oracle, announced
- Pac-Man video game introduced
- Cable News Network (CNN) is launched

- Lotus announces Lotus 1-2-3
- WordPerfect Corp. introduces WordPerfect, an instantly popular word processing system running on many different microcomputers under DOS
- *Time* magazine names the computer "Man of the Year"
- The U.S. Federal Government releases its Modified Final Judgment, stating that the monopolistic nature of AT&T is now detrimental to the development of telecommunications. On January 1, 1984, At&T must divest itself of all 22 of its associated operating companies in the Bell System

- Apple introduces the Macintosh microcomputer and along with it releases the first windows-based interface
- The 3 1/2" diskette debuts
- IBM unveils the IBM PC Portable and the PC-AT
- AT&T divests itself of the 22 Bell operating companies; 6 regional Bell operating companies (NYNEX, Bell Atlantic, Bell South, Southwestern Bell, U.S. West, and Pacific Telesis) are created

23	24	▲	25	▲	26 & 27	▲		
1978	1979	1980	1981	1982	1983	1984	1985	1986

- VisiCorp introduces the VisiCalc spreadsheet package (created by Dan Bricklin and Bob Frankston) for the Apple II

- Nintendo introduces its first arcade videogame, Donkey Kong
- IBM introduces its first desktop computer, the Datamaster
- Adam Osborne introduces the first portable microcomputer, the Osborne 1
- Commercial mouse debuts with the Xerox Star office computer
- MicroPro, Inc. introduces WordStar, a word processing system running on many different microcomputers under DOS
  - FCC's Computer Inquiry II announces that computer companies can transmit data on the telephone network on an unregulated basis, that telephone companies can participate in data processing, and that basic telephone services will remain regulated but that enhanced services and equipment on the customer's premises will be deregulated

- Apple debuts its second family of computers, the Lisa
- IBM introduces the PC-XT, which uses the Intel 8086 chip, and the PC Jr.
- First inter-city fiber-optic phone system

- Intel debuts the 80386 chip
- Desktop publishing is born
- CD players sales surpass turntable sales

- IBM introduces the PC convertible microcomputer: part portable, part desktop PC
- Compaq unveils the first 32-bit PC, the Deskpro 386
- FCC's Computer Inquiry III allows the Bell operating companies and AT&T to offer enhanced services if they agree to a set of provisions, *open network architecture*, that entitle other companies to information about the network

25 IBM unveils the IBM PC

26 Compaq introduces the first PC clone, the Compaq Portable

28 Apple debuts the Macintosh II

29 IBM introduces the PS/2 series of microcomputers

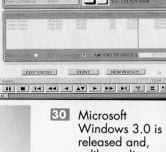

30 Microsoft Windows 3.0 is released and, unlike earlier versions, is a runaway success. Windows 3.0 quickly becomes the dominant interface for IBM-compatible computers

32 U.S. President Clinton and Vice-President Al Gore openly campaign for the development of a U.S. information super-highway

- Apple sues Microsoft and Hewlett Packard for copyright infringement over use of a windows interface
- Internet worm unleashed
- The Internet comprises 33,000 host computers

- Michael Hammer, in a landmark article in the *Harvard Business Review*, coins the term *re-engineering*, saying that IT should be used to rethink, rather than merely automate, business processes
- IBM debuts the PS/1 series
- U.S. Federal Trade Commission probes Microsoft for possible antitrust violations (but does not file a lawsuit)

- The University of Arizona (Jay Nunamaker and faculty colleagues) and Lotus both roll out software products inaugurating the era of groupware
- Pen computers introduced
- Object technology gains momentum and is critically examined for development in a wide variety of IT applications

- Viacom and Paramount agree to merge, a significant step along the path to the information super-highway
- Bell Atlantic and TCI call off their decision to merge, citing uncertainties in the regulatory environment surrounding cable TV and telecommunications

28 & 29 ▲						31 & 32	▲
1987	**1988**	**1989**	**1990**	**1991**	**1992**	**1993**	**1994**
▼	▼	30	▼		▼		33

- IBM and Microsoft announce joint development agreement for the OS/2 microcomputer operating system

- Adobe announces the Postscript standard for document and graphics printing

- Borland buys Ashton-Tate, creator of dBASE II-IV
- LAN software developer Novell and Digital Research, Inc. (DRI) merge

- IBM and Apple roll out highly successful notebook computers
- Intel announces the Pentium microprocessor
- Apple rolls out the Newton MessagePad, its highly anticipated personal digital assistant
- Internet comprises 1.8 million host computers
- U.S. cable giant Tele-Communications, Inc. (TCI) and Bell Atlantic announce a megamerger aimed at creating leadership in pursuit of the world of the information superhighway

31 Apple, IBM, and Motorola announce the Power PC RISC microprocessor

33 Apple rolls out the first PowerPC microcomputers

587

Concise Dictionary of IT Terminology

accelerator board   An add-in circuit board that increases a computer's processing speed.

accumulator   A register that holds the results of computation as each arithmetic operation occurs.

action   An instruction that tells a database how to process an object to produce specific information.

action document   A document designed to trigger a specific action or to signify that a transaction has taken place.

add-in board   A board that can be added to a computer to customize its features and capabilities.

address   An identifiable location in memory where data are kept.

address register   A register that contains the address of the data to be used in executing an instruction.

Agricultural Age   The period before the 1800s when the majority of workers were farmers whose lives revolved around agriculture.

animation   The process by which words and shapes move across a display screen.

animation program   A graphics program that makes it possible to add motion to images and drawings.

application generation   In a database system, the use of menus and simple commands to describe the application to a system program that creates the set of detailed commands.

application generation   In a database system, the use of menus and simple commands to describe the application to a system program that creates the set of detailed commands.

application program or **application** A type of software that consists of several programs working together.

architecture   The structure of a communications network; it determines how the various components of the network are structured, how they interact, and when cooperation between the system's components is needed.

area line chart   A type of business graphic included with electronic spreadsheet software. Shows the proportion in each category by combining lines or stacking lines on top of each other.

arithmetic/logic unit (ALU)   The part of the CPU that performs arithmetic and logical operations.

ASCII American Standard Code for Information Interchange.   A data representation system that uses seven-bit bytes to represent a character.

attribute   A category of data or information that describes an entity. Each attribute holds a fact about the entity.

audio response unit, speech synthesizer   An output device that transforms data or information into sound.

automated teller machine (ATM)   A limited-function terminal that usually contains a small video display, a keyboard consisting of only a few keys, and perhaps a sound speaker. They are most often associated with banks, where they are used to dispense cash, accept deposits, and transfer funds between accounts.

back-end CASE   CASE tools that automate the later (back-end) activities in systems development.

backbone network   A high-speed transmission facility designed to move data and information faster than they otherwise would.

backup copies   Extra copies of information or software made to protect against losses.

backup procedures   Procedures that describe how and when to make extra copies of information or software to protect against losses.

bar chart   A type of business graphic included with electronic spreadsheet software. Composed of a series of bars, each representing a particular element in the worksheet. The length of a bar represents the value of the data.

bar code A computer-readable code consisting of bars or lines of varying widths or lengths.

batch processing The grouping and processing of all transactions at one time.

binary system A system in which data are represented by 0s and 1s, which correspond to the electrical states of off and on.

bit A binary digit, 0 or 1.

bit mapping A feature of some monitors that allows each dot on the monitor to be addressed or controlled individually. Graphics created through bit mapping are sharp and crisp.

block The writing of one or more records onto a section of magnetic tape.

board A hardware device onto which chips and their related circuitry are placed.

bridge and **router** Devices that interconnect compatible LANs.

bus The path in a computer over which data are moved.

business graphics Visual presentations of information through charts, graphics, and symbols.

business improvement An improvement in a business itself, usually in the form of increased sales or more satisfied customers.

business information system The family of IT applications that underlie the activities of running and managing a business.

byte A storage location in memory; the amount of memory required to store one digit, letter, or character.

cache memory A form of high-speed memory that acts as a temporary holding/processing cell.

camera ready copy High-quality printouts that can be used as masters in printing.

camera ready copy High-quality printouts that can be used as masters in printing.

capture The process of compiling detailed records of activities.

CD-ROM disk Short for "compact disk–read only memory," an optical storage medium that permits storage of large amounts of information. CD-ROM disks can only be written to and cannot be erased.

cell In an electronic spreadsheet, the intersection of a row and a column.

cell address or **cell reference** The intersection of a particular row and column in an electronic spreadsheet.

cell pointer The cursor in an electronic spreadsheet.

cellular telephone A device used to send and receive voice conversations and computer and fax transmissions while allowing users freedom of movement.

central processing unit (CPU) or **processor** The computer hardware that executes program instructions and performs the computer's processing actions.

centralized architecture A communications architecture in which a computer at a central site hosts all of the network's hardware and software, performs all the processing, and manages the network.

change agent A person who acts as a catalyst for change.

character addressing The precursor to bit mapping that allowed only full characters to be sent to and displayed on a VDT.

character printer An impact printer that prints one character at a time.

chief information officer (CIO) The person given the responsibility of managing and developing the firm's information technology capabilities.

chip density The number of circuits on a single chip.

classifying The computer process of categorizing or grouping information according to a particular characteristic.

client In client/server computing, a desktop workstation.

client/server computing A type of computing in which all data and information retrieval requests and responses pass over a network. Much of the processing is performed on the server, with the results of processing transmitted to the client.

clip art Prestored files of graphic images.

coaxial cable or **co-ax** A physical communications channel that uses one or more central wire conductors surrounded by an insulator and encased in either a wire mesh or metal sheathing.

COBOL (COmmon Business-Oriented Language) The most commonly used business programming language.

code generator A CASE tool that automates the preparation of computer software.

cold site A backup facility outfitted with electrical power and environmental controls, ready for a company to install a computer system.

column The vertical elements in a spreadsheet.

common carrier A company furnishing public communications facilities for voice and data transmission.

communication The sending and receiving of data and information over a communications network.

communications channel or **communications medium** The physical or cableless media that link the different components of a network.

communications infrastructure The underlying structure of technical facilities and institutional arrangements that supports communication via telecommunication, broadcasting, film, audio and video recording, cable, print, and mail.

communications network A set of locations consisting of hardware, programs, and information that are linked together as a system that transmits and receives data or information.

communications program A program that manages the interaction between a computer system and a communications network and the transmission of data, programs, and information over the network.

complex instruction set computing (CISC) A computing instruction set that moves data to and from main memory so often that it limits the use of registers.

computer An electronic system that can be instructed to accept, process, store, and present data and information.

computer crime The unauthorized use of a computer system or theft of system resources for personal use.

computer engineers The IT professionals who design, develop, and oversee the manufacturing of computer equipment.

computer operators The IT professionals who oversee the operations of computers in data centers.

computer programming language A series of commands or codes that a computer can translate into the electronic pulses that underlie all computing activities.

computer vision system A system that uses computer sensors to detect shapes, images, and varying levels of detail.

computer-aided design (CAD) system A system that uses a powerful computer graphics workstation to enable product designers and engineers to draw design specifications on a display screen.

computer-aided manufacturing (CAM) system A system that relies on

IT to automate and manage the manufacturing process directly.

computer-aided systems engineering/computer-aided software engineering (CASE) tools   A set of tools used in systems development to improve the consistency and quality of the system while automating many of the most tedious and time-consuming systems tasks.

computer-integrated manufacturing (CIM)   A manufacturing system that uses computers to link automated processes in a factory to reduce design time, increase machine utilization, shorten the manufacturing cycle, cut inventories, and increase product quality.

computing   The computer process of calculating arithmetic results through addition, subtraction, and other arithmetic functions.

concurrent data sharing   A database procedure that allows several users to access the database simultaneously.

concurrent engineering   A design and manufacturing method in which team members work across their departmental functions to evaluate the activities of many departments and manage the product development process.

configuration   The specific combination of hardware and software in a system.

consumer electronics   Electronic devices used to satisfy people's needs and wants rather than to manufacture products or deliver services.

content line or **edit line**   The line of an electronic spreadsheet's control panel indicating the data or information being keyed into the spreadsheet.

contract programmer   An outside expert who is hired by a company to develop a certain program.

control unit   The part of the CPU that oversees and controls all computer activities according to the instructions it receives.

conversion plan   A description of all the activities that must occur to change over to a new system.

coprocessor chip   A special-purpose chip mounted on a processor board; it is designed to handle common functions quickly and efficiently.

copy protection   A software protection scheme that defeats attempts to copy a program or makes the copied software unreliable.

copyright   Legal protection of original works against unauthorized used, including duplication.

current cell or **active cell**   In an electronic spreadsheet, the cell in which the user is currently working.

cursor   A blinking box or line on a computer screen that indicates the point at which data or information will be input.

custom programming   In a database system, the writing of detailed procedures using the commands and functions built into the database management software.

custom software   The software written specially for a particular business.

data   Raw facts, figures, and details.

data bus   A bus that moves data between the central processor and memory.

data center or **computer center**   A facility at which large and midrange computer systems are located. These systems are shared by many users who are interconnected with the system through communications links.

data communication   The transmission of data and information over a communications medium.

data definition language (DDL)   A tool that allows users to define a database.

data dictionary or **repository**   A catalog that lists and describes all the types of data flowing through a system. Composed of data elements and a data structure.

data element   The component of a data dictionary that includes data names, alternate names, and length allowances.

data entry   The process of populating a database with data and information.

data item   The specific details of an individual entity stored in a database.

data manipulation language (DML)   A tool that allows users to store, retrieve, and edit data in a database.

data processing   The process of handling data and transforming them into information.

data structure   The set of data elements used together and the name that collectively identifies the set.

database   A collection of data and information describing items of interest.

database administration   The management of a database.

database administration procedures   The procedures associated with managing a database.

database administrator (DBA) or **data administrator**   The IT professional responsible for managing all the activities and procedures related to an organization's database.

database application   A computerized database routine for collecting, retrieving, or manipulating data to meet recurring needs.

database directory   The component of a shared database that keeps track of data and information.

database management program   A program that allows users to store information as interrelated records that can be retrieved quickly.

database management system (DBMS)   A program that makes it possible for users to manage the data in a database and to increase productivity.

dataflow diagram (DFD)   A chart showing the movement of data through a system.

deadlock   A situation in which each user of a database is waiting for the others to unlock a record.

decision support system (DSS)   A business information system designed to assist in decision making where the decision process is relatively unstructured and only part of the information needed is structured in advance.

decorative graphics   Graphics that are primarily ornamental.

default   The preset value that is assumed by a program, unless it is changed by the user.

design   The arrangement of a DTP document's information and a specification of its features.

desktop publishing (DTP)   The arrangement of textual information and images into a format that is easily understandable and visually appealing using a desktop publishing program.

desktop publishing (DTP) program   A program that combines text and image handling features with document design capabilities.

detail report or **transaction log**   A report describing each processed transaction.

development procedures   Procedures that explain how IT professionals should describe user needs and develop applications to meet those needs.

digitizer   An input device that translates measured distances into digital values that the computer can process.

direct cut over   A conversion plan in which people stop using an old system and immediately begin using a new system.

disaster recovery plan A procedure for restoring data lost when a system stops functioning.

disk caching A magnetic storage process by which a computer system stores information frequently read from a disk in RAM.

disk cartridge A magnetic storage system enclosed in a protective plastic cartridge that offers features similar to the hard disk, but is removable.

disk operating system (DOS) An operating system whose components reside on a disk and are brought into computer memory as needed.

disk pack A stack of disks, enclosed in a protective plastic cover, that can be lifted onto or off a disk drive.

diskette or magnetic disk A type of secondary storage in which data or information are stored magnetically onto flexible, flat, oxide-coated disks.

distributed architecture A communications architecture in which the computers reside at different locations and are interconnected by a communications network.

distributed database A database that resides on more than one system in a distributed network. Each component of the database can be retrieved from any node in the network.

distributed processing The running of an application on one or more network locations simultaneously.

document examination/ record inspection The review of company documents about a system or opportunity under investigation.

documentation An instruction manual that accompanies software. Also, a technical, detailed written description of the specific facts of a program.

dot matrix printer An impact printer that uses wire rods pushed against a ribbon and paper to form characters and images.

downloading The transfer of information from a central system to a desktop computer.

drawing program A program designed to create line drawings.

drive The device containing a secondary storage medium's read/write unit.

dumb terminal A terminal that sends whatever is entered through the keyboard to the main computer and displays whatever it receives from the main computer without doing any processing.

dynamic RAM (DRAM) RAM that holds data and information dynamically, not indefinitely. The computer must

continually refresh the RAM cell electronically.

EBCDIC Extended Binary Coded Decimal Interchange Code. A data representation system that uses eight-bit bytes to represent a character.

effectiveness The extent to which desirable results are achieved.

electrically erasable programmable read-only memory (EEPROM) chip A ROM chip that can be reprogrammed by electronically reversing the voltage used to create the idea or information.

electronic bulletin boards A network service application that allows messages and announcements to be posted and read. Accessed by dialing a telephone number and interconnecting with the bulletin board through a modem.

electronic data interchange (EDI) A form of electronic communication that allows trading partners to exchange business transaction data in structured formats that can be processed by applications software.

electronic funds transfer (EFT) The movement of money over a network.

electronic mail (e-mail) A service that transports text messages from a sender to one or more receivers via computer.

electronic mailbox An area of space on magnetic disk in the server or host computer that is allocated for storing an individual's messages.

electronic spreadsheet An automated version of the manual spreadsheet, created and maintained by a spreadsheet program.

entity A person, place, thing, event, or condition about which data and information are collected.

erasable optical storage (EOS) disk An optical storage disk that combines the erasability and editing options of magnetic storage devices with the performance, capacity, and reliability of optical storage.

erasable programmable read-only memory (EPROM) chip A ROM chip that can be erased by bathing it in ultraviolet light.

ethics The standards of conduct and moral behavior that people are expected to follow.

exception report A report that lists unusual, erroneous, or unacceptable transactions or results.

execution cycle (E-cycle) The last two steps of the machine cycle (execute

and store), which produce processing results.

executive support system (ESS) or **executive information system (EIS)** An interactive business information system, designed to support executives, which is capable of presenting summary information on company and industry activities.

expansion slot A slot inside a computer that allows a user to add an additional circuit board.

expert support system or **expert system** A business information system that uses business rules, regulations, and databases to evaluate a situation or determine an appropriate course of action.

exporting The process of writing a document to storage in a format needed by another application.

fault tolerant computer A computer designed with duplicate components to ensure reliability.

fiber-optic cable A physical communications channel that uses light and glass fibers to transmit data and information.

fields The columns of a relation. Also called attributes.

file server A computer containing files that are available to all users interconnected on a local area network.

film recorder An output device that transforms an electronic image on a computer screen into a film image.

flatbed scanner A large image scanner that works like office photocopiers.

flexible manufacturing A manufacturing system that automatically sets up machines for the next job, thus reducing setup time and making smaller job runs feasible.

floppy disk, flexible disk A type of magnetic disk made of flexible plastic.

font A complete set of characters in a particular typeface.

footer The descriptive text printed at the bottom of each page of a document.

format A document's physical appearance.

formatting Software capabilities that allow the user to change the appearance of characters both on the computer screen and when printed.

formula An electronic spreadsheet instruction describing how a specific computation should be performed.

front-end CASE CASE tools that automate the early (front-end) activities in systems development.

front-end computer In a centralized system, a minicomputer loaded with special programs to handle all incoming and outgoing communications traffic.

function A formula built into electronic spreadsheet software that will automatically perform certain types of calculation.

function key A key designed to assist the computer's user in entering data and information or to control processing.

functional distribution strategy A database distribution strategy in which the database is distributed according to business functions.

gap In magnetic storage, a space left before and after a block so that the tape drive can stop without skipping over any data.

gateway A device that interconnects two otherwise incompatible networks, network nodes, or devices.

general purpose register A register that holds data, addresses, or arithmetic results.

generation The process of organizing information into a useful form, whether as text, sound, or visual image.

geographic distribution strategy A database distribution strategy in which the database is located in a region where the data and information are used most frequently.

gigabyte, G-byte, GB, or gig One billion bytes.

grammar checker A word processing feature that scans the contents of a document to identify grammatical errors and poor phrasing.

graphic block A portion of a document containing any type of image information.

graphical user interface (GUI) A link to an operating system that allows users to use icons rather than command words to start processing.

graphics adapter card An interface board between a computer and monitor used to determine the monitor's resolution and use of color.

grid The guide used in DTP systems to aid in the structuring of information on a page.

group support system (GSS) A business information system that permits people to process and interpret information as a group, even if they are not working face to face.

hacker A person who gains access to a system illegally.

halftone A collection of minuscule dots that collectively portray a subject.

handheld scanner An inexpensive, handheld alternative to the flatbed image scanner.

hands-on system A system in which a user enters data and information, directs processing, and determines the types of output to be generated.

hard copy The paper output from a printer.

hard disk A type of secondary storage that uses non-flexible, non-removable magnetic disks mounted inside the computer to store data or information.

hardcard A magnetic disk attached to a circuit board that can be mounted in a microcomputer's expansion slot.

hardware The computer and its associated equipment.

head crash The situation that occurs when the read/write heads that normally float close to a magnetic disk's surface actually touch the surface.

header The descriptive text printed at the top of each page of a document.

hexadecimal system A data representation system that uses the digits 0 through 9 and the letters A through F.

high-definition television (HDTV) A television system that uses digital technologies to present sound and images over high-quality television screens.

host-based computing Centralized computing.

hot site A fully-equipped backup computer center to which a company can take its backup copies of data and software and resume processing.

hybrid network A communications architecture that combines centralized and distributed architectures to take advantage of the benefits of both.

icon A small picture that represents a command. Using icons to invoke commands is faster than invoking commands through the menu bar.

icon bar The line of an electronic spreadsheet's control panel that shows the icons used to invoke frequently used commands.

illustration graphics A collection of graphics tools used by professional illustrators to create three-dimensional drawings with depth, complex curves, shading effects, and thousands of different color combinations.

illustration program A program in which the computer screen becomes a drawing board on which artists translate ideas into visual form.

image Information in visual form.

image editing program A program that allows users to scan images into memory and retouch them.

image scanning The scanning process that translates images into a digital form.

impact printing A printing process in which the paper and the character being printed come in contact with one another.

implementation The fifth step in the SDLC. The process of installing a new system and putting it to use.

importing The ability to read text or numbers from one file into another, or the process of bringing an external file into a chosen format by converting its contents into the proper format.

in-house programmer A programmer who is employed by the company for which an application is developed.

index A data file that contains identifying information about each record and its location in storage.

index key or search key A data item used by database management software to locate a specific record.

indexing A database system's capability to find fields and records in the database.

information An organized, meaningful, and useful interpretation of data.

Industrial Age The period that began in the 1800s when work processes were simplified through mechanization and automation.

Information Age The period that began in 1960 in which the majority of workers are involved in the creation, distribution, and application of information.

information processing A general term for the computer activity that entails processing any type of information and transforming it into a different type of information.

information repository or **repository** A synonym for database.

information society A society in which more people work at handling information than at agriculture and manufacturing combined.

information superhighway A communications network spanning a nation, carrying data and information traffic.

information system A system in which data and information flow from one person or department to another.

information technology (IT) A term used to refer to a wide variety of items and abilities used in the creation, storage, and dispersal of information. Its three main components are computers, communications networks, and know-how.

information technology professionals   The people responsible for acquiring, developing, maintaining, or operating the hardware and software associated with computers and communications networks.

infrared   A cableless medium that transmits data and information in coded form by means of an infrared light beamed from one transceiver to another.

ink jet printer   A nonimpact printer that sprays tiny streams of ink from holes in the print mechanism onto the paper.

input   The data or information entered into a computer or the process of entering data or information into the computer for processing, storage and retrieval, or transmission.

input device   A device by which input is fed into a computer's central processor.

input/output (I/O) bus   A bus that moves data into and out of the processor.

input/output controller   A data controller with its own memory and processor that regulate the flow of data to and from peripheral devices.

inquiring   The computer process of satisfying a request for information through computation or retrieval of stored information.

installed memory   The amount of memory included by a computer's manufacturer on its memory board.

instruction cycle (I-cycle)   The first two steps of the machine cycle (fetch and decode), in which instructions are obtained and translated.

instructions   Detailed descriptions of the actions to be carried out during input, processing, output, storage, and transmission.

integrated CASE (I-CASE)   CASE tools that span activities throughout the entire systems development life cycle.

integrated circuit, chip, or microchip   A collection of thousands or millions of transistors placed on a small silicon chip.

integrating   The process of packing more transistors onto a single chip.

interactive TV (ITV)   A television with a keyboard, storage capability, and the capacity to transmit and receive vast amounts of information.

interface   The means by which a person interacts with a computer.

interface generator   A CASE tool that provides the capability to prepare sample user interfaces so that the creator can examine their features before preparing the final version.

intrusion   Forced and unauthorized entry into a system.

issuance   The computer process of producing and printing a document.

joystick   An input device used to control the actions in computer games or simulations. The joystick extends vertically from a control box.

justification   A word processing feature that allows the alignment of right and left margins.

kerning   The spacing between the characters in a word.

keyboard   The most common input device, usually consisting of letters of the alphabet, numbers, and frequently used symbols.

kilobyte, K-byte, KB, or k   One thousand bytes.

know-how   The capability to do something well.

knowledge   An awareness and understanding of a set of information and how that information can be put to best use.

knowledge workers   Workers involved in the creation, distribution, and application of information.

label   A piece of descriptive information pertaining to a row or column of an electronic spreadsheet.

laser printer   A nonimpact printer that uses laser beams to print an entire page at a time.

layout   The arrangement of the elements that comprise a DTP document.

layout description   A chart that shows the exact location of data and information on a computer screen or in a printed report.

leading   The vertical spacing between the lines of text on a page.

leased line or dedicated line   A communications line reserved by a company for its exclusive use.

leveling   The process of exploding processes in a dataflow diagram to show more detail.

light pen   An input device that uses a light-sensitive cell to draw images and to select options from a menu of choices displayed on a computer screen.

line drawing or **line art**   A graphic that consists of only simple lines and areas of black, white, or color.

line printer   An impact printer that prints one full line at a time on continuous form paper.

local area network (LAN)   A network that interconnects computers and communications devices within an office or series of offices; typically spans a distance of a few hundred feet to three miles.

machine cycle   The four processing steps performed by the control unit: fetch, decode, execute, and store.

macro   A time-saving mini-program, identified by a name and a series of keystrokes, which is used to perform commonly repeated actions.

magnetic disk   A general term referring to two types of disk: flexible/floppy disk and hard disks.

magnetic ink character recognition   A form of optical character reading in which preprinted information written in magnetic ink is read optically or sensed magnetically.

magnetic tape   A magnetic storage medium in which data are stored on large reels of tape.

mail merge   A word processing facility that allows the user to create and personalize multiple copies of a document.

mainframe   A larger, faster, and more expensive computer than a midrange computer, used for several purposes simultaneously.

management reporting system or **management information system (MIS)**   A business information system designed to produce the information needed for successful management of a structured problem, process, department, or business.

manufacturing automation protocol (MAP)   A protocol used by factory designers to provide a common language for the transmission of data.

manufacturing cell   A group of machines working together in computer-integrated manufacturing.

manufacturing resource planning (MRP II) system   An advanced MRP system that ties together all the parts of an organization into the company's production activities.

master page   In desktop publishing, a page containing the format and any information to be repeated on each page of the document.

material requirements planning (MRP) system   A system that tracks the quantity of each part needed to manufacture a product.

maximum memory   The most memory that a processor can hold.

megabyte, M-byte, MB, or meg   One million bytes.

megaflops   Millions of floating point operations per second; a measure of how many detailed arithmetic calculations the computer can perform per second.

megahertz (MHz)   Millions of electric pulses per second; a measure of a computer's speed.

memory, primary storage, or main memory   The section of a processor that holds data, information, and instructions before and after processing.

menu bar   The line of an electronic spreadsheet's control panel that contains the commands for working with worksheets, creating graphics, and invoking special data processing actions.

metropolitan area network (MAN)   A network that transmits data and information over citywide distances and at greater speeds than a LAN.

microcode   The instructions that coordinate the execution of the instructions to move data to and from memory.

microcomputer (personal computer or PC)   A computer that is relatively compact and usually found on a table or desktop.

microprocessor   The smallest type of processor, with all of the processing capabilities of the control unit and ALU located on a single chip.

microsecond   One millionth of a second.

microwave   A cableless medium that uses high-frequency radio signals to send data or information through the air.

midrange computer or minicomputer   A computer used to interconnect people and large sets of information, usually dedicated to performing specific functions. More powerful than a microcomputer.

millions of instructions per second (MIPS)   A measure of processor speed—the number of instructions the processor can execute per second.

millisecond   One thousandth of a second.

model   A plan that simulates the relationships between events or variables.

modem   A device that allows computer-to-computer dialogue. A modem connects a computer to a communications medium and translates the data or information from the computer into a

form that can be transmitted over the channel.

monochrome display   A video screen display that shows information using a single foreground color on a contrasting background color (for example, black on white).

mouse   An input device with a small ball underneath that rotates, causing a corresponding movement of a pointer on a display screen.

multi-user system   A system in which more than one user share hardware, programs, information, people, and procedures.

multimedia system   A computer system that can process multiple types of information simultaneously.

multiple instruction/multiple data (MIMD) method   A parallel-processing method that connects a number of processors that run different programs or parts of a program on different sets of data.

multiplexer   A device that converts data from digital to analog form and vice versa and allows a single communications channel to carry simultaneous data transmissions from many terminals that are sharing the channel.

multisync/multiscan monitors   Monitors designed to work with a variety of graphics standards.

nanosecond   One billionth of a second.

network administration or network management   The management of a network; the procedures and services that keep the network running properly.

network interface card   A printed circuit board used in LANs to transmit digital data or information.

network operating system (NOS)   A software program that runs in conjunction with the computer's operating system and application programs and manages the network.

network services   The applications available on a communications network.

network specialists   The IT professionals who design, operate, and manage computer communications networks.

node   A communication station within a network.

nonconcurrent data sharing   A database procedure that allows individuals to access a database only when no other person or application is processing the data.

nonimpact printing   A printing process in which the paper and the

print device do not come in contact with one another.

notebook computer, laptop computer   Smaller versions of microcomputers, designed for portability. All of their components, except a printer, are included in a single unit.

object   A focal point about which data and information are collected. Used in object oriented databases.

object oriented database   A database that stores data and information about objects.

observation   The process of watching an activity take place.

off-site backup facility   A backup computer center located away from a company's main facility.

operating system   A combination of programs that coordinates the actions of a computer, including its peripheral devices and memory.

operations procedures   Procedures that describe how a computer system or application is used, how often it can be used, who is autorized to use it and where the results of processing should go.

optical character reader   An OCR device that recognizes printed information rather than just dark marks.

optical character recognition (OCR)   A technology by which devices read information on paper and convert it into computer-processable form.

optical code reader   An OCR device used to read bar codes.

optical disk or CD-ROM   A storage medium, similar in design to the compact disks played on stereos, that can only be played and not written onto.

optical mark reader   An OCR device that recognizes the presence and location of dark marks on a special form as the form is scanned.

optical storage device   A device that uses a beam of light produced by a laser to read and write data and information.

orphan   The first line of a paragraph at the bottom of a page.

output   The results of inputting and processing data and information returned by the computer, either directly to a person using the system or to secondary storage.

output device   A device that makes the results of processing available outside of the computer.

outsourcing   A business practice in which firms use freelancers and consultants, rather than in-house staff, for selected activities.

page description language The language, embedded in a printer chip and integrated with software commands in a publishing program, that permits specification of the printed information's fonts, type sizes, and type styles.

paint program A program that allows the illustrator to control the color and density of individual dots that collectively create an image.

palmtop computer The smallest and most portable computer, typically used for a limited number of functions, such as maintaining a personal calendar or address file.

parallel processing Processing in which a computer handles different parts of a problem by executing instructions simultaneously.

parallel systems A conversion plan in which both an old and a new system are used for a period of time, with the old system being gradually phased out.

parity bit A bit used to detect errors in the transmission of data.

partitioning A method of database distribution in which different portions of the database reside at different nodes in the network.

pen-based computer A tablet-like computer controlled with a special pen.

peripheral equipment A general term used for any device that is attached to a computer system.

personal digital assistant (PDA) A portable computer generally used as a personal assistant.

personal productivity software Software packages that permit activities to be completed more quickly, allow more activities to be completed in a particular period of time, or allow a task to be completed with fewer resources.

phase-in A conversion plan in which a new system is gradually phased in over a period of time.

picosecond One trillionth of a second.

pictogram A type of business graphic included with electronic spreadsheet software. Depicts data by using an icon or symbol that represents the magnitude of the data values.

pie chart A type of business graphic included with electronic spreadsheet software. The proportions or percentage of the whole are shown as part of a circular graphic (a pie).

pilot A conversion plan in which a working version of a new system is implemented in one group or department to test it before it is installed throughout the entire business.

pixels The dots used to create an image. The higher the number of dots, the better the resolution of the image.

platform The computer foundation on which applications are built. The two most common platforms for PCs are IBM-compatibles and Apple Macintosh.

plotter An output device that draws image information (such as charts, graphs, and blueprints) stroke by stroke.

point size A measure of a character's height. One point equals 1/72 of an inch or .35 cm.

point-of-sale terminal A terminal that features special keys (such as sale, void, and credit) and a numeric keypad similar to that found on a calculator. Usually connected to a computer that processes data entered by an employee.

port A connector through which input/output devices can be plugged into the computer.

Post, Telephone, and Telegraph (PTT) A general term used for the telephone company in countries other than the United States.

preliminary investigation The first step in the SDLC. The activity in which the merits and feasibility of a project proposal are determined.

presentation graphics Graphics used as visual aids to support verbal presentations of comments and ideas.

primary storage, main memory, or **internal memory** Storage within the computer itself. Primary memory holds data only temporarily, as the computer executes instructions.

privacy In IT, the term used to refer to how personal information is collected, used, and protected.

private network A network made up of leased (dedicated) communications lines.

problem A perceived difference between a particular condition and desired conditions.

problem solving The process of recognizing a problem, identifying alternatives for solving the problem, and successfully implementing a solution.

problem solving cycle The five-step sequence of activities designed to address and solve problems in a structured way.

procedure A step-by-step process or a set of instructions for accomplishing specific results.

process A structured activity that leads to a set of results (output).

process improvement An improvement in the way a business works.

processing The process of converting, analyzing, computing, and synthesizing all forms of data or information.

processor or **central processing unit (CPU)** A set of electronic circuits that perform the computer's processing actions.

productivity The relationship between the results of an activity and the resources used to create those results. Equal to outputs/inputs.

program A set of instructions that directs a computer to perform certain tasks and produce certain results.

programmable read-only memory (PROM) chip A type of ROM memory chip that can be modified from its manufactured state only once. These modifications are not reversable.

programmer/analyst A person who has joint responsibility for determining system requirements and developing and implementing the systems.

programmers The IT professionals who use programming languages to create computer and communications network software.

project management The process of planning, organizing, integrating, and overseeing the development of an IT application to ensure that the project's objectives are achieved and the system is implemented according to expectations.

project management tools CASE tools that enable a project manager to schedule analysis and design activities, allocate people, monitor schedules and personnel, and print schedules and reports.

project managers The IT professionals who coordinate the development of a project and manager of the team of programmer/analysts.

project proposal A proposal for a systems project prepared by users or systems analysts and submitted to a steering committee for approval.

protocol The rules and conventions guiding data communications, embedded as coded instructions in the network software.

prototype A working model of an IT application.

public access network A network maintained by common carriers for use by the general public.

public domain software Any non-copyrighted software that can be used by the general public.

query   A question to be answered by accessing the data in a database.

query by example (QBE)   A query format in which the user fills in the blanks with simple commands or conditions.

query language   A computer language that forms database queries from a limited number of words.

questionnaire   A sheet of questions used to collect facts and opinions from a group of people.

radio wave transmission or **radio frequency transmission**   A cableless medium that uses frequencies rented from public radio networks to transmit data and information.

RAM disk   Disks created in primary memory that offer instant direct access to the data stored on them.

random access storage, direct access storage   The process of retrieving a particular record of information from any track directly.

random-access memory (RAM)   Memory that permits data or information to be written into or read from memory only as long as the computer is turned on.

range   A rectangular group of adjacent cells in an electronic spreadsheet. It may be composed of a row, a column, or several rows and columns.

read-only memory (ROM)   A type of storage that offers random access to memory and can hold data and information after the electric current to the computer has been turned off.

read/write head   A device that records data by magnetically aligning metallic particles on the medium. The write head records data and the read head retrieves them.

real-time processing   The processing of each transaction as it occurs.

record   A grouping of data items that consists of a set of data or information that describes an entity's specific occurrence.

record key   In a database, a designated field used to distinguish one record from another.

record locking   A concurrency procedure that prohibits another user from accessing or altering a record that is in use.

recording density   The number of characters per inch at which a drive writes data.

recovery procedures   Procedures that describe the actions to be taken when information or software must be recovered.

redlining   A word processing feature that makes editing changes visible in a document.

reduced instruction set computing (RISC)   A computing instruction set that takes data for the execution of an instruction only from registers.

reengineering   The reshaping of business processes to remove barriers that prohibit an organization from providing better products and services and to help the organization capitalize on its strengths.

register   A temporary storage area in the processor that can move data and instructions more quickly than main memory and momentarily hold the data or instructions used in processing and the results that are generated.

relation or **file**   The table in a database that describes an entity.

relational database   A database in which the data are structured in a table format consisting of rows and columns.

relational operator   A symbol that tells a database system to make a comparison to call up the requested data.

reliability   The assurance that computers and communication systems will do what they should when they should.

replication   A method of database distribution in which one database contains data that are included in another database.

requirement   A feature that must be included in a system.

requirements determination   The second step in the SDLC. The study of the current business situation to determine who is involved, what data or information are needed, and how the current system can be improved.

resolution   The clarity or sharpness of an image.

retrieval   The process by which a computer locates and copies stored data or information for further processing or for transmission to another user.

RGB display   A video screen display with the ability to create 256 colors and several thousand variations on them by blending shades of red, green, and blue.

robot   A computer-controlled device that can physically manipulate its surroundings.

row   The horizontal elements in a spreadsheet.

rule base or **knowledge base**   A database of rules in an expert system.

sampling   The process of collecting data and information at random at prescribed intervals.

satellite   A cableless medium in which communications are beamed from a microwave station to a communications satellite in orbit above the earth and relayed to other earth stations.

scanning   The process of transforming written or printed data or information into a digital form that is entered directly into the computer.

schema   The structure of a database.

scroll bar   A bar located at the right or bottom of the computer screen that allows the user to move around the screen—up, down, left, or right.

search and replace   A word processing feature that allows the user to scan a document for a particular word or phrase and replace it with a different word or phrase.

secondary storage, auxiliary storage   A storage medium that is external to the computer, but that can be read by the computer; a way of storing data and information outside the computer itself.

sector   A subdivision of a track on a magnetic disk, used to improve access to data or information.

security procedures   Procedures that are designed to safeguard data centers, communications networks, computers, and other IT components from accidental intrusion or intentional damage.

security software   Software that is designed to protect systems and data.

sensitivity analysis   The analytical process by which a computer determines what would happen if certain data change.

sequential processing   Processing in which the execution of one instruction is followed by the execution of another.

server   A computer that hosts a network and provides the resources that are shared on the network.

shared database   A database shared among many users and applications.

shared system   A system in which two or more users share computers, communications technology, and applications.

shareware   Software that is given away and freely distributed. The developer retains ownership, asks users to register with the owner, and requests a nominal fee for using the program.

single in-line memory module (SIMM)   A multiple-chip memory card inserted as a unit into a predesigned slot on a computer's system board.

single instruction/multiple data (SIMD) method   A parallel-processing method that executes the same instruction on many data values simultaneously.

single-user system or **personal system**   An IT system used by only one person. A system that stands alone and is not interconnected with other computers or shared by other people.

site license   An agreement under which a software purchaser pays a fee to the manufacturer to make a specified number of copies of a particular program.

site preparation   The activities involved in preparing for the installation of a new system.

software   The general term for a set of instructions that controls a computer or communications network.

software package   An application that focuses on a particular subject, such as word processing, and is sold to businesses and the general public.

software piracy   The making of illegal copies of software.

software testing   The testing of software programs to ensure that the software does not fail.

sorting   The computer process of arranging information into a useful sequence. Also word processing feature that allows the user to arrange lines and paragraphs of text alphabetically or numerically, or sets of information by date.

source data automation   A method of data entry in which details enter computers directly from their written or printed forms without the intermediate step of keying.

spell checker   A word processing feature that scans the contents of a document for misspelled words, the occurrence of two words in a row, and improper abbreviations.

spoken information   Information that is conveyed by sound.

spreadsheet or **worksheet**   A table of columns and rows used by people responsible for tracking revenues, expenses, profits, and losses.

spreadsheet program   A software package used to create electronic spreadsheets.

static RAM   RAM that retains its contents indefinitely, without constant electronic refreshment.

steering committee   A group of people from various functional areas of a business that determines whether a systems development project proposal is desirable and should be pursued.

storage   The computer process of retaining information for future use.

storage register   A register used to temporarily store data that have been moved from memory and are awaiting processing or are about to be sent to memory.

structured interview   An interview in which the questions are prepared in advance and each interviewee is asked the same set of questions.

structured query language (SQL)   The most widely used query language.

summarizing   The computer process of reducing a large volume of data into a more concise, easily used format.

summary report   A report that shows the overall results of processing for a period of time or for a batch of transactions and includes a grand total for all listed transactions and the average transaction amount.

supercomputer   The most powerful of computers, used to solve problems that require millions and millions of long and difficult calculations.

switched network   The complete set of public access networks, so named because the telephone company operates and maintains the switching centers that make it possible to transmit data or information.

system   A set of components that interact to accomplish a purpose.

system board or **mother board**   The system unit in a microcomputer, located on a board mounted on the bottom of a computer base.

system clock   A circuit that generates electronic impulses at a fixed rate to synchronize processing activities.

system flowchart   A graphical description of a business process or procedure using standard symbols to show decision logic.

system testing   The testing of a complete system—software, procedures, and guidelines.

system unit   The hardware unit that houses a computer's processor, memory chips, ports, and add-in boards.

systems analysts   The IT professionals who work with users to determine the requirements an application must meet.

systems contractors   Outside personnel who contract with a company to develop IT applications.

systems design   The third step in the SDLC. The process of translating requirements into design specifications.

systems designers   The IT professionals who formulate application specifications and design the features of custom software.

systems development   The process of examining a business situation; designing a system solution to improve that situation; and acquiring the human, financial, and IT resources needed to develop and implement the solution.

systems development life cycle (SDLC)   The set of activities, in six phases, that brings about a new IT application.

systems engineers   The IT professionals who install and maintain hardware.

systems evaluation   The sixth step in the SDLC. The process of monitoring a new system to identify its strengths and weaknesses.

systems programmer   A software and hardware specialist who works with the physical details of a database and the computer's operating system.

T-carrier   A very high-speed channel designed for use as a backbone and for point-to-point connection of locations.

teleprocessing   The processing capability allowed by connecting computers through telephone lines.

template   A worksheet containing row and column labels, and perhaps formulas, but not necessarily any values. It is distributed to people as a guide for analyzing problems or providing data.

terabyte, T-byte, or TB   One trillion bytes.

terminal   A combination keyboard and video display that accepts input, displays it on the video screen, and displays the output sent by the computer to which it is attached.

test data   Experimental files used to test software.

text   Written (narrative) information.

text block   A portion of a document that contains only text.

text document   Any document that can be created on a computer.

thermal printer   A nonimpact printer that heats wax-based colored ink and transfers it to a special paper.

thesaurus   A word processing feature that searches for and displays synonyms and antonyms for a particular word chosen by the user.

title bar   The line of an electronic spreadsheet's control panel that contains the program name and sometimes the name of the file in use.

topology   The configuration of a network.

track   The area in which data and information are stored on magnetic tape or disk.

trackball   An input device that is a ball mounted on rollers. As the user rotates the ball in any direction, the computer senses the movement and moves the cursor in the corresponding direction.

trainers   The IT professionals who work with end-users, helping them to become comfortable and skilled in using hardware or software.

training   The process by which people are taught how to use a system.

transaction processing system (TPS) A shared business information system that uses a combination of information technology and manual procedures to process data and information and to manage transactions.

transceiver   A combination transmitter and receiver that transmits and receives data or information.

transistor   An electrical switch that can be in one of two states, open or closed.

transmission   The computer process of distributing information over a communications network.

tuples   The rows of a relation. Also called records.

twisted pair   A physical communications channel that uses strands of copper wire twisted together to form a telephone wire.

typeface (type style)   A family of characters that have the same basic design.

uninterruptable power supply (UPS) system   A system that ensures the continued flow of electricity when the primary source of power fails.

universal product code (UPC)   A bar code that identifies a product by a series of vertical lines of varying widths representing a unique product number.

universal service   The principle whereby it is assured that anyone who wants basic service can receive it at low cost.

unstructured interview   An interview in which the questions may be prepared in advance, but follow-up questions may vary depending on the interviewees' background and answers.

updated master data   An adjustment of all records in a system in response to a processed transaction.

updating   The computer process of adding, deleting, or changing records in a database.

uploading   The process by which information is sent from a PC to a mainframe.

users or **end-users**   The people who use IT in their jobs or personal lives.

utility programs or **utilities**   Special programs used to perform tasks that occur repeatedly during processing.

value-added network (VAN)   A public data communications network that provides basic transmission facilities plus additional enhancements (such as temporary data storage and error detection).

value   A number that is entered into a cell of an electronic spreadsheet. It may be an integer, a decimal number, or a number in scientific format.

very small aperture terminal (VSAT) A satellite earth station with an antenna diameter of under one meter.

video conferencing   A type of conferencing in which video cameras and microphones capture sight and sound for transmission over networks.

video display terminal (VDT), monitor   A computer's visual display.

videotex   A two-way, interactive, text-only service operating on mainframe computers that combines a video screen with easy-to-follow instructions.

view   A grouping of the fields that a database will use to retrieve data.

virtual company   A company that joins with another company operationally, but not physically, to design and manufacture a product.

virus   A hidden program that alters, without the user's knowledge, the way a computer operates or modifies the data and programs stored on the computer.

voice input device   An input device that can be attached to a computer to capture the spoken word in digital form.

voice mail   A system that captures, stores, and transmits spoken messages using a telephone connected to a computer network.

voice-grade channel   A communications channel designed to transmit voices and text.

wand   An input device used to read a bar code and input this information directly into a computer.

wide area network (WAN)   A network that interconnects sites dispersed across states, countries, or continents.

widow   The last line of a paragraph at the top of a page.

Winchester disk drive   A disk drive that contains a read/write head, an access arm, and a disk in one sealed unit.

window   A section of the computer screen.

Windows   A single-user operating system that allows several programs to be operated simultaneously.

word   The number of bits a computer can process at one time.

word processing (WP)   The creation and management of text documents, and the tailoring of the physical presentation of those documents, using a word processing program.

word processing (WP) program   A program that allows the user to enter, change (edit), move, store, and print text information.

wordwrap   A word processing feature that allows the user to enter text in a continuous stream, without concern for the document's left or right margins.

work group conferencing   A type of conferencing that uses a software package called groupware to organize an electronic meeting in which participants' computers are interconnected from their various locations. Participants interact through a microcomputer directly linked to a server and their comments are broadcast to all others in the conference.

work processes   The combination of activities that workers perform, the way workers perform these activities, and the tools that workers use.

worksheet area   In an electronic spreadsheet, the rectangular grid of rows and columns that comprise the worksheet.

workstation or **client**   A desktop computer connected to a network.

write once, read many (WORM) optical disk   An optical storage medium that allows users to write information to a disk only once, but to read it many times.

Photo Credits

■ **Part 1**   Interview with Akio Morita: speech to the Japan-America Society. Photos: **3** Carlo Carino/Contrasto/Reo/SABA; **4** Photoquest.
■ **Chapter 1**   **5** Superstock; **7** courtesy Toyota Motor Sales; **11** logo courtesy of Claire Adami/Fidelity Investments; **13** <u>clockwise from top left</u>: courtesy of Toshiba; Superstock; FPG International, courtesy Grid Systems Corp.; FPG International; **14** L. Felzmann, Odyssey/Matrix International, Inc.; **16** Hewlett Packard; IBM; John Greenleigh/Apple Computer, Inc.; Hewlett Packard; courtesy Grid Systems Corp.; Frank Pryor/Apple Computer; **17** IBM; **18** Digital Equipment Corp.; courtesy Craig Computer Corporation; **22** <u>clockwise from top</u>: courtesy United Technologies-Otis Elevator; Honeywell; Brian Smith/Stock, Boston; 3M; John Nollendorfts/Picture Group; **27** Steve Jennings; **29** John Sturrock/Tony Stone Images; Tom Sheppard/Tony Stone Images; Pete Saloutos/Stock Market; IBM; **31** logo courtesy McDonald's Corporation; **38** logo courtesy Mrs. Fields; **39** Arizona Daily Star; **40-43** IBM.
■ **Chapter 2**   **45** courtesy Nigel Holmes; **48** IBM; Apple Computer, Inc.; IBM; Bob Daemmrich/Stock Boston; **49** Microsoft; Logitech, Inc.; Hewlett Packard; Logitech, Inc.; **50** Intermech; FPG International; Harris Corporation; **51** IBM; **52** courtesy Intel Corporation; **53** NEC; Hewlett Packard; Radio Schack; **55** . BASF Corporation; Conner-Pancho; Optimum; 3M; BASF Corporation; logo courtesy Price Waterhouse; **58** courtesy the HyperGlot Software Company; **61** courtesy Adobe Systems; **66** IBM; IBM; Bob Daemmrich/Stock Boston; Superstar; **71** logo courtesy Rainbow Technologies; **74** logo courtesy McKeeson; **84** David Brownell; **86-89** courtesy NIgel Holmes; **91** Home Shopping Network.

■ **Part 2**   Interview with Juan Rada: by the author. Photos: **93** courtesy of Juan Rada and the author; **94** Photoquest; **95** Photoquest.
■ **Chapter 3**   **97** UPI/Bettmann; **99** logo courtesy Children's Hospital, British Columbia; **105** IBM; Amdahl; **106** IBM; **107** *both*: Intel Corporation; **109** *both*: High Techsplanations; **110** logo courtesy BSW International; **112** Gamona Liaison; **116** logo courtesy Chemical Bank; **123** logo courtesy WalMart; Andy Freeberg; **125** Ted Horowitz/Stock Market; courtesy Intel Corp.; **126** IBM; Chuck O'Rear/courtesy Intel Corp.; courtesy Intel Corp.; **127** National Semiconductor; IBM; National Semiconductor; **128** *both*: courtesy Motorola; **129** courtesy Motorola; SCI Systems, Inc.; courtesy Motorola; **130** SCI Systems, Inc.; courtesy Intel Corp.; IBM; **131** <u>both</u>: Intel Photography.
■ **Chapter 4**   **133** courtesy News Electronic Data; Torin Boyd; **137** IBM; **138** Maxell Corporation of America; BASF Systems Corp.; **139** courtesy Iomega; **140** courtesy Quantum Corporation; **142** courtesy Compton's News Media Jazz; **143** courtesy Panasonic; IBM; **144** IBM; **145** American Express; **147** IBM; Bill Pappas/Diebold, Inc.; IBM; **150** courtesy McKesson Corporation; **154** courtesy MicroTouch Systems, Inc.; courtesy Logitech, Inc.; **155** courtesy Logitech, Inc.; Joseph Nettig/Stock Boston; **157** courtesy Truevision, Inc.; courtesy Sony; **158** courtesy Tulare County Dept. of Public Social Services; **159** Apple Computer, Inc.; IBM; **163** courtesy Epson; IBM; courtesy Data Products Corp.; **164** courtesy Tektronix, Inc.; Hewlett Packard; courtesy Eltron International, Inc.; **166** Hewlett Packard; **167** courtesy Mirus Industries Corp.; **172** Frito-Lay; **173** Frito-Lay; **174** Gamma-Liaison; Seth Resnick/Gamma-Liaison.

■ **Part 3** Interview with Cloene Goldsborough: by the author. Photos: **178** courtesy of Sprint; **179** Sprint.

■ **Chapter 5** **181** Bettmann; Telegraph Colour Library/FPG International; **186** logo courtesy Donald H. Kraft & Associates; **194** Hewlett Packard Company; **204** Teri Stratford; **219** Jim Egan/ColorLab.

■ **Chapter 6** **221** Teri Stratford; **224** Brian Wood; **225** logo courtesy Farmland Industries, Inc., Inc.; **248** logos courtesy Haven Corporation; photos *clockwise from top left*: Gregory D. Baker; *rest*: courtesy Firefighters Bookstore

■ **Chapter 7** **251** Elaine A. Cardella; **257** Teri Stratford; **258** *both*: courtesy World Perfect Corp.; **273** courtesy Paper Direct, Lyndhurst, NJ; **279** courtesy Claris; **280** Schell/Mullaney; **281** courtesy Time Arts; logo courtesy Dun & Bradstreet; **287-91** Frank La Bua.

■ **Chapter 8** **293** Louis Psihoyos/Matrix; **296** Fredrich Cantor/Onyx; **298** Teri Stratford; **305** Ed Kashi; **313** logo courtesy Dell Computers; **320** logo courtesy Apple Computer Co.; **322** Stock Boston; Compaq; **323** Teri Stratford; IBM; John Greenleigh/Apple Computer; **324** Michael A. Keller/Uniphoto; C&I Photography; courtesy *Computer Express*; **325** Teri Stratford; Superstock; Peter Poulides; **327** Wynn Miller/Tony Stone Images.

■ **Part 4** Interview with Bill Eaton: by the author. Photos: **329** courtesy Bill Eaton and the author; **331** Photoquest.

■ **Chapter 9** **332** Donna Cox, Robert Patterson, NCSA, University of Illinois; **341** *left to right:* courtesy Black & Decker; John Giordano/SABA; **343** logo courtesy Apple Computers; **352** courtesy AT&T Archives; AT&T Bell Laboratories; Sperry Corporatio; **354** *both*: courtesy Hayes Microcomputer Products, Inc.; logo courtesy Peapod; IBM; **369** Eli Reichman; logo courtesy Hewlett Packard; **370** logos courtesy United Technologies, McCann-Erickson; Phil Schofield Photography; **371** courtesy CompuServe, Inc.; **379** logo courtesy CNN; **380** Forbes; **382-85** courtesy Lotus Corp.

■ **Chapter 10** **387** IBM; **404** *both*: Dave Male Photography; **406** logo courtesy Pitney Bowes; **408** courtesy Marilyn Cumberland, COMSAT Corporation; **409** logo courtesy American Red Cross; **416** logo courtesy Helene Curtis; **417** Andy Goodwin, AST Research; **418** Martin Simon/SABA; **423** Research Libraries Information Network; **426** Tom Wolff; **427** courtesy *Internet Business Journal, Internet Letter,* and *Internet World.*

■ **Chapter 11** **429** courtesy American Airlines; **438** Tom Wagner/SABA; **440** Christopher Covatta/Gamma-Liaison; **442** courtesy Diamond Star Motors; **443** IBM; **452** Michael Witte; **461** Bob Michaels, Texas Instruments; **462** logo courtesy Levi Strauss; **465** logo courtesy Welbro Constructors, Inc.; **472** logo courtesy Sara Lee Corporation; **473** *both*: courtesy Sara Lee Corporation; **474-76** Arthur Andersen & Co.; **477** John Abbott; Arthur Andersen & Co.; John Abbott; John Abbott; **478** *both*: Arthur Andersen Consulting.

■ **Chapter 12** **481** Bettmann; **483** Donald Dietz/Stock Boston; Richard Pasley/Stock Boston; Greg Meadows/Stock Boston; Mike Mazzaschi/Stock Boston; **483** Bill Houlton, Intermec; **487** courtesy MCI; **488** Mark Reinstein/FPG International; **489** logo courtesy Architectural Energy Corporation; **491** logo courtesy Coopers & Lybrand; **497** Tim Kelly, Fortune; Tim Kelly, Time Life Photo Lab; **501** courtesy Raychem; **502** *both*: Lon Harding, courtesy Litton Industries; **503** logo courtesy Boeing; **504** Ken Kobre/Picture Group; Ted Horowitz/Stock Market; Richard Nowitz/Stock Market; Louis Psihoyos/Matrix International, Inc.; **507** *both*: Louis Psihoyos/Matrix International, Inc.; **512** logo courtesy Corning; **513** Mike Greenlar/Duggal; **514** *both*: courtesy Saturn Media Center; **515** Andy Sacks/Tony Stone Images; *rest*: courtesy Saturn Media Center; **516** AP/Wide World Photos; Kevin Horan; courtesy Saturn Media Center; **517** courtesy Saturn Media Center; AP/Wide World Photos; Time; **518** *both*: courtesy Saturn Media Center; **519** courtesy Auto Alliance; courtesy Honda of America Mfg., Inc.; courtesy Honda of America Mfg., Inc.; courtesy Toyota; courtesy Nissan Corp.; **521** Teri Stratford.

■ **Part 5** Interview with Al Gore: Open interview with journalists. Photos: **523** Teri Asche; **525** Doug Armand.

■ **Chapter 13** **527** Teri Stratford; **528** AT&T; **532** Bob Riha/Gamma-Liaison; **535** courtesy AST Research, Inc.; **536** *all*: courtesy Condisco Disaster Recovery Services; **540** logo courtesy Software Publishers Association; **542** courtesy National Cristina Foundation; **545** courtesy Condisco Disaster Recovery Services; courtesy Recognition Systems, Inc.; Gamma-Liaison.

■ **Chapter 14** **557** Corinne Dufka Reuter/Bettmann; **559** courtesy Zenith Electronics Corp.; courtesy Sharp Electronics Corp.; courtesy Zenith Electronics Corp.; courtesy Pioneer; Samara Photography, Inc./Thompson Electronics; **561** Carlo Carino/ SABA; **562** courtesy Zenith Electronics Corp.; **564** courtesy Groupe Videoway; **565** courtesy Le Groupe Videotron Lte., Montreal; courtesy E.ON Corporation; **567** logo courtesy Computertots; **571** Larry Luxner; **578** logo courtesy R.R. Donnelley & Sons; **579** Michael L. Abramson; **581** Teri Stratford.

■ **Appendix** **582** D. Mazonowicz/Art Resource; Erich Lessing/Art Resource; Ewing Galloway; courtesy IBM; *rest*: Bettmann; **583** AT&T Co., Photo Center; Bell System; courtesy IBM; Teri Stratford; IBM; *rest*: Teri Stratford; **584** Neal Peters/Lester Glassner Collection; Neal Peters Collection; Neal Peters Collection; Teri Stratford; Teri Stratford; AP/World Wide Photos; Teri Stratford; **585** courtesy IBM; James S. Davis/Dava Still Media Depository; UPI/Bettmann; Melgar Photography, Inc.; *rest*: AP/Wide World Photos; **586** courtesy IBM; courtesy CompuServe; The Source Information Network; courtesy IBM; Compaq Computer Corporation; Ted Morrison/Still Life Stock; Apple Computer, Inc.; **587** courtesy IBM; Microsoft; Microsoft; courtesy IBM; courtesy IBM.

Indexes

Name, Company, and Product Index

 TRAVEL
RELATED
SERVICES
An American Express company

 **Architectural Energy Corporation**

 **Levi's**

 **CHEMICAL**

 Coopers
&Lybrand

Donald H.Kraft & Associates

 Farmland

MᶜKesson

 CNN

 **COMPUTERTOTS**
Computer Fun . . . for little ones

 **DELL**

 McDonald's

HELENE
CURTIS

Price Waterhouse

 **HAVEN**
CORPORATION

 British Columbia's
Children's Hospital

 **BOEING**

RR DONNELLEY
& SONS COMPANY

 **SPA**

 Pitney Bowes

McCANN-ERICKSON

 **Frito Lay**

 **WELBRO**
CONSTRUCTORS, INC.

WAL★MART

 *Mrs. Fields*
COOKIES

The
Mail Order
Wizard

 HEWLETT
PACKARD

CORNING

 Paramount
Paramount Publishing

 **Fidelity**
Investments

Peapod

RAINBOW
TECHNOLOGIES